Global Financial Reporting

JOHN FLOWER

with Gabi Ebbers

palgrave

Published by
PALGRAVE MACMILLAN
Houndmills, Basingstoke, Hampshire RG21 6XS and
175 Fifth Avenue, New York, N. Y. 10010
Companies and representatives throughout the world

PALGRAVE MACMILLAN is the global academic imprint of the Palgrave
Macmillan division of St. Martin's Press, LLC and of Palgrave Macmillan Ltd.
Macmillan® is a registered trademark in the United States, United Kingdom
and other countries. Palgrave is a registered trademark in the European
Union and other countries.

ISBN 0–333–97696–7 hardback
ISBN 0–333–79477–X paperback

This book is printed on paper suitable for recycling and
made from fully managed and sustained forest sources.

A catalogue record for this book is available from the British Library.

10   9   8   7   6   5   4   3   2
11   10   09   08   07   06   05   04   03

Printed and bound in Great Britain by
Creative Print and Design (Wales), Ebbw Vale

Global Financial Reporting

Contents

part three
THE INTERNATIONAL ACCOUNTING STANDARDS BOARD   215

List of Exhibits

LIVERPOOL JOHN MOORES UNIVERSITY
LEARNING & INFORMATION SERVICES

Preface

The subject matter of this book is financial reporting at the global level, with particular emphasis on the larger multinational enterprises, such as the USA's General Electric, Japan's Toyota, Germany's DaimlerChrysler, France's Vivendi and Britain's BP Amoco. There are two commonly-accepted approaches to the study of financial reporting at the global level: the 'country approach' and the 'issues approach'. With the country approach the basic unit of study is the individual country. Through an examination of financial reporting as practised in various countries, the student gains an understanding not only of the accounts of enterprises from these countries but also of the richness and diversity of accounting throughout the world. The arguments in favour of the country approach may be summarised as follows:

Financial reporting is still basically regulated at the country level. Even the largest and most globally oriented of the 'global players' is obliged to follow national rules and standards when drawing up its financial statements. Among the advocates of the country approach are Walton, Haller and Raffournier who, in the preface to their textbook *International Accounting* (International Thompson Business Press, London, 1998), justify their position in the following terms:

> We take the view that accounting in any one country at any one time represents the result of an evolution over many years. This evolution has taken place against a cultural backcloth which imbues each country's rules with many particularities, and institutions have been created which are unique in each country. We think therefore a holistic approach offers a more profound way of addressing international accounting differences.

The authors of the present book are basically in agreement with the position set out in this quotation. In particular, they consider that the present practice of financial reporting can only be fully understood with reference to its historical development and that the greater part of this historical development has taken place at the level of the individual country. In order to understand how financial reporting has reached its present position, then, an examination of the development at the country level is essential.

The first part of this book adopts the 'country approach'. Part One sets the scene with an analysis of the factors that cause national differences in financial reporting rules and practice; in Part Two the rules and practices of a number of countries are analysed, using a country-by-country approach, with one chapter per country.

However the greater part of the book does not adopt the country approach. In Part Two, only five countries are examined in detail. In most textbooks that adopt the country approach, many more countries are covered; for example Walton, Haller and Raffournier cover no less than twenty-two countries. The authors of the present book limit themselves to five countries for the following reasons:

(i) The five countries (USA, Japan, Germany, France and Britain) are the most important for the study of global financial reporting, as measured by most criteria: GNP, share of world trade, number of multinational enterprises and, most significantly, influence on the development of global financial reporting rules and practice.

(ii) The authors' aim is not to provide a treatise of financial reporting as practised in a large number of countries, but rather to analyse and explain financial reporting as practised at the global level. This can be done quite adequately through an examination of the five most important countries.

(iii) The authors believe that five is about the maximum number of countries that a student can study without becoming bored by the inevitable repetition and losing interest in the whole process.

In April 2001, an event occurred which is certain to have far-reaching consequences on the future development of financial reporting at the global level. The International Accounting Standards Board (IASB) took over from its predecessor, the IASC, the task of setting standards for the world. Undoubtedly the IASB will be an important new force in global financial reporting. Thus the whole of Part Three is given over to an exposition and analysis of this body, in effect adopting the 'country approach' to the examination of an international institution.

The alternative way to study financial reporting at the global level is to adopt the 'issues approach'; the breakdown of the subject is by topics and not by countries, the more important topics and issues being analysed globally. The authors believe that the 'issues approach' has certain advantages in presenting the complex and diverse material of global financial reporting. In particular there is less chance of the student losing interest through the repetition that inevitably accompanies the country approach. Furthermore the IASB's standards provide a very convenient framework for the exposition and analysis of the major issues on a global basis. In effect the increasing globalization of financial reporting (as evidenced in the enhanced role of the IASB) has reached the stage where the country approach is no longer sufficient. Hence the greater part of the book adopts the issues approach: Part Four considers the various elements of the financial statements and Part Five certain other issues, selected for their topical interest.

TARGET READERSHIP

The book is designed for final-year undergraduate and postgraduate courses in accounting and finance. The emphasis is on the 'why' and not the 'how' of accounting – to analyse and explain the practice of financial reporting at the global level, with particular reference to the financial statements of the larger multinational enterprises and to the standards of the International Accounting Standards Board.

Acknowledgements

The authors would like to express their thanks to Professor Makoto Nakano of Hiitotsubashi University and Professor C. Richard Baker of the University of Massachusetts for guidance on the financial reporting of Japan and the United States, respectively. They also acknowledge the help given by Andrew Lymer of the University of Birmingham on matters relating to the Internet.

They also express their appreciation to the following enterprises which agreed that extracts from their financial statements should be included in the book:

Alcatel, Aventis, BASF, Bayer, BP Amoco, Cadbury Schweppes, Daimler-Chrysler, FIAT Group, Ford Motor Company, Fujitsu, General Electric Company, General Motors, Henkel, News Corporation Ltd, Peninsular and Oriental Steam Navigation Company, Nissan, Peugeot, Roche, Royal Dutch/Shell Group, SAP, Skandia, Sony, TotalFinaElf, Tottenham Hotspur PLC, Toyota, VIAG, Vivendi, Volkswagen AG.

The authors and publishers would like to thank the following for permission to reproduce copyright material.

International Journal of Accounting, for Exhibits 2.9 and 2.10, from Doupnik and Salter, 'External environment, culture and accounting practice' 30(3). © 1995 Elsevier Science.

International Accounting Standards, Exposure Drafts, and other IASB publications are copyright of the International Accounting Standards Committee Foundation, including its International Accounting Standards Board. Please address copyright enquiries to: IASB Publications Department, 7th Floor, 166 Fleet Street, London EC4A 2DY, United Kingdom. Telephone: +44 (020) 7427-5927, Fax: +44 (020) 7353-0562, E-mail: iasb@iasb.org.uk, Internet: www.iasb.org.uk. All rights reserved. No part of IASB's publications may be translated, reprinted or reproduced or utilized in any form either in whole or in part or by any electronic, mechanical or other means, now known or hereafter invented, including photocopying

List of Abbreviations

AAA	American Accounting Association, USA
AARF	Australian Accounting Research Foundation
AG	Aktiengesellschaft, Germany
AICPA	American Institute of Certified Public Accountants
ASB	Accounting Standards Board, UK
ASC	Accounting Standards Committee, UK
ASSC	Accounting Standards Steering Committee, UK
BADC	Business Accounting Deliberations Council, Japan
CICA	Canadian Institute of Chartered Accountants
CNC	Conseil National de la Comptabilité, France
CNNC	Compagnie Nationale des Commissaires aux Comptes, France
COB	Commission des Opérations de Bourse, France
CPA	Certified Public Accountant, USA
CRC	Comité de Réglementation Comptable, France
DRS	Deutscher Rechnungslegungs Standard (German accounting standard)
DSOP	Draft statement of principles
DSR	Deutsche Standardisierungsrat (German Standardization Council)
ED	Exposure draft
EITF	Emerging Issues Task Force, USA
EU	European Union
FASB	Financial Accounting Standards Board, USA
FAS	Financial Accounting Standard, USA
FDI	Foreign direct investment
FRS	Financial Reporting Standard, UK
GAAP	Generally accepted accounting principles
GoB	Gründsätze ordnungmässiger Buchführung (Principles of orderly book-keeping)
HGB	Handelsgesetzbuch (Commercial Code, Germany)
IASB	International Accounting Standards Board
IASC	International Accounting Standards Committee
IAS	International Accounting Standard
ICAEW	Institute of Chartered Accountants in England and Wales
IdW	Institut der Wirtschaftsprüfer, Germany

IFAC	International Federation of Accountants
IOSCO	International Organization of Securities Commissions
JICPA	Japanese Institute of Certified Public Accountants
KK	Kabushiki kaisha
MNE	Multinational enterprise
NYSE	New York Stock Exchange
OECD	Organization for Economic Cooperation and Development
OEC	Ordre des Experts Comptables, France
PCG	Plan Comptable Général, France
PLC	Public limited company, UK
R&D	Research and development
SA	Société anonyme, France
SEC	Securities and Exchange Commission, USA
SEL	Securities and Exchange Law, Japan
SSAP	Statement of standard accounting practice, UK
STRGL	Statement of total recognised gains and losses
UNCTAD	United Nations Conference on Trade and Development
UN	United Nations
US GAAP	US generally accepted accounting principles

part one

Background

The foundation for the analysis of global financial reporting is established during the three chapters that are included in Part One. These lead to a more detailed analysis in subsequent chapters.

In Chapter 1, global financial reporting is defined as financial reporting considered globally and not from the viewpoint of any specific country. The importance for the accounting student of an understanding of global financial reporting is explained. The globalization of the world's economy is analysed with reference to both developments in international trade and cross-border investment and the growth of multinational enterprises. The countries of the Pentad (USA, Japan, Germany, France and Britain) are introduced and it is explained why the book's emphasis is on these countries, and particularly on their multinational enterprises. The diversity of financial reporting practice between countries is identified as the major factor that makes the study of global financial reporting so difficult and yet so interesting.

Chapter 2 analyses the causes of this diversity and explains it in terms of differences between countries in the factors that shape the financial reporting of enterprises. This chapter serves as an introduction to the detailed study in Part Two of the financial reporting of the five countries of the Pentad.

Chapter 3 is an introduction to the rules of financial reporting and the bodies that set these rules (the rule-makers), which form the principal subjects for the rest of the book.

chapter one

Globalization

Chapter objectives

- To explain the value to the accounting student of a study of global financial reporting
- To examine the globalization of the world's economy with reference to the growth in both international trade and cross border investment (both foreign direct investment and portfolio investment) and to the globalization of finance
- To examine the role of the multinational enterprises in the globalization process and to present the characteristics of the 50 largest
- To introduce the countries of the Pentad (USA, Japan, Germany, France and Britain) and to explain why this book concentrates on the financial reporting of these five countries

1.1 WHY STUDY GLOBAL FINANCIAL REPORTING?

The subject of this book is global financial reporting; it deals with the financial reporting of business enterprises throughout the world as a whole with no undue emphasis on any particular country. It is aimed at students of accounting, most of whom study financial reporting from the viewpoint of practice in their own country. Why study financial reporting from a global viewpoint? There are two very good but rather different reasons:

- It enables students to gain a better understanding of financial reporting in their own country
- For very many accountants a knowledge of global financial reporting is essential

3

The study of financial reporting as practised in other countries enables students to put into perspective practice in their own country. If, in the course of their studies, students never come in contact with any other approach to financial reporting but that which is practised in their own country, there is a danger that they will accept these practices uncritically as the best (and possibly the only) way. By studying the particular rules, conventions and methods employed in other countries, students are better able to appreciate the strengths and the weaknesses of those of their own country. There is considerable evidence that the practice of financial reporting throughout the world is converging; that practice in most countries is slowly developing towards a common model. The progress is slow but seemingly inexorable. This means that, even if students are only interested in financial reporting as practised in their own country, the study of financial reporting at the global level will provide insights as to how the subject may develop at the national level.

Very many accountants fulfil functions which require a good knowledge of financial reporting as practised in other countries and at the global level. The proportion of accountants in this position will undoubtedly increase in the future, and it is likely that the accountants of the twenty-first century will be considered to be uneducated and incapable of operating effectively if their knowledge is limited to financial reporting as practised in their own country. This development is linked to the globalization of the world economy which is the main subject of this chapter.

1.2 THE GLOBALIZATION OF THE WORLD ECONOMY

The term 'globalization' refers to the process whereby the economies of the world's countries are becoming ever more closely interconnected and integrated. It is a process that has been going on for at least the last five hundred years but which has reached a crescendo in the last three decades. Four aspects of globalization have a particular impact on financial reporting:

■ International trade
■ Cross border investment
■ The multinational enterprises
■ Global finance

Exhibit 1.1 *Global merchandise exports and imports*

	1970	1980	1990	1999
Merchandise Exports				
USA	43	226	394	695
Japan	19	130	288	419
Germany	85	193	410	540
France	18	116	217	299
UK	19	110	185	268
Rest of world	131	1199	1832	3361
Total global exports	315	1974	3326	5582
Merchandise Imports				
USA	43	226	517	1059
Japan	19	141	235	311
Germany	30	188	346	473
France	19	135	234	287
Britain	22	116	223	318
Rest of world	96	1095	1866	3377
Total global imports	229	1901	3421	5825

Note: Total exports do not equal total imports because of data collection problems

Source: IMF, *International Financial Statistics*

1.3 INTERNATIONAL TRADE

In the past 30 years there has been a remarkable increase in world trade, as evidenced by the statistics for exports and imports presented in Exhibit 1.1.

Between 1970 and 1999 global exports and imports increased more than fifteen times, at an annual rate of over 10 per cent. There are a number of reasons for this extraordinary increase:

The macroeconomic reason

In accordance with the economic law of comparative advantage, two countries can increase the total quantity of goods consumed by their citizens (and therefore their standard of living) by each specializing in the production of those goods that it makes more efficiently and exchanging their surpluses. This law seems obvious in the case where each country is absolutely more efficient than the other country in the production of particular goods. Adam Smith, the eighteenth-century Scottish philosopher who is regarded as the founder of the modern science of economics, demonstrated it with the example of trade between Britain and Portugal. Britain could produce textiles more efficiently than Portugal, whereas the reverse was true with wine. Both countries benefited by exchanging British textiles for Portuguese wine. However the law also applies when one country is more efficient than the other in producing both goods; both countries would benefit by specialization and exchange, when, as is normally the case, the degree to which the first country is more efficient is not the same for all goods. This is known as the law of comparative advantage. It has been described as the one law of economics that is not intuitively obvious but is certainly correct.[1] A pertinent demonstration of the force of this law is the observed increase over the last thirty years in the standard of living in those countries where the increase in trade has been greatest: notably the five countries listed separately in Exhibit 1.1 – USA, Japan, Germany, France and Britain.

The microeconomic reason

The global figures presented in Exhibit 1.1 are the result of the actions of countless enterprises increasing their exports and imports. Enterprises engage in trade for a number of reasons. They import materials and products that are cheaper abroad than in their own country; they export to foreign countries as a means of expanding their sales more quickly than the growth in their home market and of using up spare productive capacity. The great improvement in transport and communications, particularly telecommunications, in recent decades has undoubtedly increased the ability and willingness of enterprises to export and import.

The political reason

At the end of the Second World War, the United Nations set up the General Agreement on Tariffs and Trade (GATT) with the aim of promoting international trade, particularly through removing barriers to trade. At that time the principal barriers were high tariffs which added greatly to the cost of imports. In a series of negotiating rounds, the principal trading nations agreed to very substantial reductions in these import tariffs. The GATT agreements which covered the whole world have been backed up by regional pacts which provided for even freer trade between the countries in specific regions: for example the European Union, the North American Free Trade Area and Mercosur. It would seem that the politicians of these countries became convinced of the economists' arguments that free trade would benefit their citizens. In 1997, GATT was replaced by the World Trade Organisation (WTO) with slightly enlarged aims. The WTO is now seeking to liberalize international trade in services and to reduce non-tariff barriers. Non-tariff barriers are measures,

such as import quotas and complex technical and administrative requirements, that foreigners find more difficult to comply with than do local
producers. Governments often introduce non-tariff barriers in response
to pressure from local producers who are losing customers to foreign
importers. Although the population as a whole benefit from freer trade,
certain sections of society (notably the less efficient local producers) are
made worse off and are motivated to take political action to protect
their interests, for example to lobby the government to introduce tariffs
and non-tariff barriers.

Exhibit 1.1 refers only to exports and imports of goods. However international trade in services is also important and has been growing even
more quickly than trade in goods. The growth in international trade has
consequently meant that an increasing number of accountants are confronted with the need to understand the financial statements of foreign
enterprises, notably those of their suppliers and customers.

1.4 CROSS BORDER INVESTMENT

A further aspect of globalization is the great increase in investment that
crosses international borders. An enterprise or an individual can invest
in a foreign country in two rather different ways:

- Foreign direct investment
- Portfolio investment

The difference between the two is that, with foreign direct investment, the investor is involved in the management of the foreign enterprise,
generally because the amount invested is substantial in relation to the
foreign enterprise's capital, whereas with portfolio investment the investor plays a more passive role.

Both forms of cross border investment have grown very substantially
in recent years.

1.4.1 Foreign direct investment

Many enterprises do not limit themselves to exporting and importing
goods and services. They find it expedient to set up permanent estab-
lishments in foreign countries. For example, an enterprise that imports
materials and products may set up a permanent purchasing office in the
forcign country. However, in a second stage, it may decide to set up its
own facility in the foreign country (factory, mine or plantation) to produce the goods that it needs. There may be several motives for such an
action: it may be to assure security of supplies; it may be more profitable

for the enterprise to produce the goods itself rather than buy them from local producers; or it may be 'empire-building' on the part of the enterprise's management. The equivalent stages for an exporting enterprise are first a distribution and service network, with a production facility in the second stage. There are several advantages of producing in the foreign country: it saves transport costs, it may be more profitable because of the availability of cheaper factors of production (especially labour) and it may be easier to tailor the product to the needs of the local market. In the second stage, local production replaces exports, but there is often a third stage in which the goods produced in the foreign facility are exported to other countries in the region and even back to the enterprise's home country.

The growth in the foreign operations of enterprises is demonstrated by the statistics on foreign direct investment (FDI). FDI is defined by the United Nations as an investment by an enterprise in an entity located in a foreign country that involves both a long-term relationship and an element of control. With FDI, a parent enterprise makes an investment in a foreign affiliate; the foreign affiliate may be under the sole control of the parent enterprise (as with a subsidiary) or control may be shared with other partners (as with associates and joint ventures). Exhibits 1.2 and 1.3 presents FDI statistics taken from the United Nations World Investment Report.

Exhibit 1.2 *Flows of foreign direct investment, 1999*

	Investor countries Outflows			Host countries Inflows		
	$mn	%	$ per head	$mn	%	$ per head
USA	150 901	18.86	565	275 533	31.84	1032
Japan	22 743	2.84	182	12 741	1.47	102
Germany	50 596	6.33	620	26 822	3.10	329
France	107 952	13.50	1858	39 101	4.52	673
UK	199 289	24.91	3431	82 182	9.50	1415
Benelux	70 786	8.85	2721	49 647	5.74	1908
Other EU	81 201	10.15	545	107 306	12.40	721
Total EU	509 824	63.73	1368	305 058	35.25	819
Other developed countries	48 297	6.04	887	43 117	4.98	792
China and Hong Kong	22 395	2.80	18	63 468	7.33	52
Rest of world	45 768	5.72		165 570	19.13	
Global total	799 928	100.00		865 487	100.00	

Note: Total outflows do not equal total inflows because of data collection problems

Source: United Nations, *World Investment Report 2000*

Exhibit 1.3 *Stock of foreign direct investment, 1999*

	Investor countries Outward stock			Host countries Inward stock		
	$mn	%	$ per head	$mn	%	$ per head
USA	1 131 466	23.77	4236	1 087 289	22.78	4070
Japan	22 743	0.48	182	38 806	0.81	310
Germany	420 908	8.84	5159	225 595	4.73	2765
France	298 012	6.26	5129	181 974	3.81	3132
UK	664 103	13.95	11 434	394 560	8.27	6794
Benelux	465 857	9.79	17 907	396 418	8.31	15 237
Other EU	487 751	10.25	3277	453 775	9.51	3048
Total EU	2 336 631	49.10	6270	1 652 322	34.63	4434
Other developed countries	786 121	16.52	14 442	452 383	9.48	8311
China and Hong Kong	198 575	4.17	162	438 405	9.19	357
Rest of world	283 797	5.96		1 102 776	23.11	
Global total	4 759 333	100.00		4 771 981	100.00	

Note: Total outward stock does not equal total inward stock because of data collection problems

Source: United Nations, *World Investment Report 2000*

Exhibit 1.2 refers to investment flows in the year 1999. They are analysed by investor country (the country in which the parent enterprise is located) and by host country (the country in which the foreign affiliate is located). As might be expected, most of the investment funds are provided by the developed countries, (principally the USA, Japan and the member states of the European Union) which account for more than 90 per cent of the FDI outflow. However the developed countries are also the principal recipients of these investments; they account for over 70 per cent of the FDI inflow. The principal source and recipient of FDI funds is the European Union (EU). The figures are enormous; for the UK the outflow of FDI in 1999 was over $3000 per man, woman and child of the population, whereas the inflow was also very substantial (over $1000 per head). However in certain developed countries the inflows were relatively much lower, particularly in Japan and Germany.

Exhibit 1.3 refers to the FDI stock at the end of 1999, that is, the accumulated past investments, including retained profits (which are treated as an inflow for the year in which the profits are earned and retained). Exhibit 1.3 gives figures for both outward stock (analysed by investor country) and inward stock (analysed by host country). The pattern is very similar to that of Exhibit 1.2. Almost 90 per cent of the world's stock of FDI is held by the developed countries, of which 49 per cent is held by the EU. Again the figures are enormous; for example, in the EU as a whole the total stock of outward investment is over $6000 per head and inward investment over $4000 per head.

A common feature of Exhibits 1.2 and 1.3 is that FDI consists principally of developed countries investing in other developed countries. There are a number of reasons why enterprises in the developed countries prefer to invest in other developed countries rather than in the developing countries:

■ The population of the developed countries is richer and provides a readier market for the enterprise's products

■ Certain factors of production, notably skilled labour, specialized services and reliable infrastructure, are more readily available in the developed countries

■ Enterprises are wary of the political risks associated with certain developing countries (for example, expropriation of their assets)

The United Nations estimates that the total assets held by foreign affiliates at the end of 1999 was $17 680 000mn ($17 trillion (tn)). This is over three times higher than the stock of FDI at that date. The extra assets are financed by local borrowings and shareholdings. The total sales of foreign affiliates in 1999 is estimated to be $13.5tn, which is almost twice the figure for the worldwide export of goods and services in that year, and this ratio has been increasing in recent years. This indicates that firms have reached the second stage outlined in the previous section and use foreign affiliates more than they use exports to service foreign markets. The total value added by foreign affiliates (wages, taxes and profits) is estimated to be $2.1tn. These figures are vast. To put them into perspective, they should be compared with the total of the world's GDP, estimated to be £30tn. All the statistics confirm that foreign affiliates are a very significant element of the global economy. The impact of FDI on financial reporting is considered later in section 1.7.

1.4.2 Portfolio investment

Portfolio investment is investment by enterprises and individuals in other enterprises that does not involve any element of control. There is not a clear-cut distinction between portfolio investment and FDI in an associate. The United Nations uses a cut-off point of 10 per cent: where an enterprise owns more than 10 per cent of another enterprise, the second enterprise is considered to be an associate and the first enterprise's investment is treated as FDI; where the ownership proportion is less than 10 per cent, it is considered to be portfolio investment. Portfolio investment is a major source of investment funds for many countries. However with portfolio investment, the investors have no control over the management of the foreign enterprise; hence they will in general only buy its shares if they are able to sell them again without great difficulty should problems arise. For this reason portfolio investment is most important in countries that have a well-developed stock exchange. In recent years many developing countries have built up their capital markets and for them portfolio investment has become a significant source of investment inflows. The United Nations estimates that for the developing countries as a whole portfolio investment inflows in 1997 were about $100bn having grown from less than $10bn in 1990; these figures should be compared with $172bn for FDI inflows to developing countries in 1997. It gives no estimate for portfolio investment inflows for developed countries, but it is generally agreed that they are much higher.

The growth in portfolio investment has considerable implications for financial reporting, notably the need of investors to understand the accounts of foreign enterprises and of enterprises to make their accounts comprehensible to foreign investors.

1.5   THE MULTINATIONAL ENTERPRISES

The global statistics presented in the previous two sections are certainly impressive but rather dry. To put some life into them, it is necessary to look at the enterprises behind the statistics. The United Nations estimates that, throughout the world, there are over 60 000 multinational groups, each consisting of a parent corporation together with its affiliates (subsidiaries, joint ventures and associates). On average each parent has ten foreign affiliates; hence the total number of enterprises in the multinational groups exceeds 600 000. The economic importance of these multinational groups can be gauged by the United Nations' estimate that they account for about a quarter of the total world output. Although a multinational group generally consists of very many separate entities, it is common to refer to it as a multinational *enterprise* or MNE for short, and this designation will be used from now on.

Each year, as part of the World Investment Report, the United Nations publishes a survey of the world's 100 largest MNEs. Exhibit 1.4 presents information about the world's 50 largest MNEs, taken from the UN's analysis of their 1998 accounts. The authors have adjusted the UN's figures to take into account certain mergers among the top 50 enterprises which occurred in 1999, so that the exhibit did not include enterprises that no longer exist as separate entities. The exhibit ranks the leading MNEs by the size of their foreign assets; that is, assets located in countries other than that of the parent corporation, being figures for the group as a whole (parent corporation, plus all affiliates both domestic and foreign).

Most of the MNEs listed in Exhibit 1.4 are household names; there are 12 automobile manufactures (General Motors, Ford, Toyota, Daimler-Chrysler, Volkswagen, Honda, Renault, BMW, Mitsubishi, Nissan, Peugeot and Fiat) and five oil companies (ExxonMobil, BP Amoco, Royal Dutch/Shell, TotalFinaElf and ENI) which together make up over a third of the 50 MNEs listed. There are no banks, insurance companies and other financial institutions; they have been excluded from the analysis, because the United Nations found it impossible to measure their assets in a way that facilitated a meaningful comparison with those of the industrial enterprises listed in Exhibit 1.4. There are only three enterprises from the service sector: News Corporation, Nortel Networks and Telefónica. This is because, in general, service enterprises tend to be smaller than industrial enterprises on the measure of size used by the United Nations (book value of foreign assets). Various aspects of this table will now be considered in more detail.

The parent enterprise

The third and fourth columns of Exhibit 1.4 give certain information about the enterprise at the head of the group, notably its corporate form and the country in which it is registered. All the parent enterprises listed in Exhibit 1.4 are corporations. A corporation is governed by the law of the country in which it is registered and hence the particular legal characteristics of corporations differ somewhat from country to country. However there is one fundamental characteristic that is common to all countries: a corporation is a legal entity that is separate from the shareholders, managers and other persons connected with the corporation. As a separate entity, a corporation can enter into contracts and own property in its own name; it continues in existence even if all the shareholders and managers were to die. This characteristic of a corporation is known as 'corporate personality'; in law a corporation is a 'person', to distinguish it from human beings it is termed a 'legal person' whereas people are 'natural persons'. Corporate personality is at the heart of the second general characteristic of corporations: limited liability. The liability of the individuals who provide the corporation's capital (the shareholders) is limited to the amount of their shares. They are not generally liable for the corporation's debts. This is the natural consequence of 'corporate personality'. The shareholders are liable to pay to the corporation the amount stated in their contract with the corporation, which will generally be the amount payable on their shares. However they have no contract with and hence no liability towards the corporation's creditors. These debts are owed by the corporation, which is a separate person from the shareholders.

In order to warn creditors that they are dealing with a corporation whose liability is limited, there is a rule in many countries that corporations must add certain distinguishing letters to their name. For example, in the UK, corporations must add the letters PLC, which stands for 'public limited company'. These letters are presented in the third column of Exhibit 1.4 to give an indication of the corporate form of the parent enterprise. The key to these letters is presented in Exhibit 1.5, which shows that, in many countries, there are two different corporate forms: thus in the UK there are both public limited companies and private limited companies, the latter being distinguished by the letters 'Ltd'. The different legal characteristics of the two corporate forms vary considerably from country to country. In general the basic corporate form is more suitable for large enterprises and the alternative corporate form for small enterprises; thus it is common for the law to prohibit corporations of the alternative form from raising capital by an offer to the general public. However not all countries have such a rule; for example, there is no prohibition on a German GmbH offering its shares publicly. In certain countries there is only one corporate form; this is the case in the USA. Almost all of the largest multinational groups are headed by a corporation of the basic corporate form; however there are exceptions, notably the German Bosch Group (number 60 in the UN's list) headed by Robert Bosch GmbH.

The country of the parent enterprise

The country of registration of the parent corporation is given in the fourth column of Exhibit 1.4. The significance of this information for financial reporting is that corporations are obliged to follow the law of the country in which they are registered in drawing up their annual accounts (both those of the individual corporation and the consolidated accounts). The implications of this rule are examined later in section 1.7.

The world's largest MNE according to the criterion used in Exhibit 1.4 (foreign assets) is General Electric whose parent, the General Electric Company Inc, is registered in the state of New York in the USA. No less than five of the top eight MNEs are American. However this pattern is not repeated for the MNEs that occupy the next 20 places where there is only one more American-based MNE. In fact most of the MNEs in the top 50 (listed in Exhibit 1.4) are based in Europe. The best overall picture is given by an analysis of the top 100 MNEs, as given in Exhibit 1.6.

This analysis shows that the greater part (50.5 per cent) of the larger MNEs are based in Europe, with 26 per cent based in the USA and

Exhibit 1.4 The world's top 50 multinational enterprises

Rank	Name of Group	Parent corporation Corporate form	Country of registration	Group assets Foreign ($bn)	Total ($bn)	Trans-nationality index (%)	Website
1	General Electric	Inc	USA	128.6	355.9	36.30	www.ge.com
2	ExxonMobil*	Inc	USA	78.8	112.8	69.34	www.exxonmobil.com
3	BP Amoco*	PLC	UK	75.9	91.4	45.80	www.bpamoco.com
4	General Motors	Inc	USA	73.1	246.7	30.90	www.gm.com
5	Royal Dutch/Shell	NV/PLC	NL/UK	67.0	110.0	58.00	www.shell.com
6	Ford Motor Co	Inc	USA	62.3	237.5	35.40	www.ford.com
7	Toyota	KK	Japan	44.9	131.5	50.10	www.global.toyota.com
8	IBM	Inc	USA	43.6	86.1	53.00	www.ibm.com
9	Aventis*	SA	France	41.0	61.9	70.45	www.aventis.com
10	TotalFinaElf*	SA	France	40.4	70.2	58.29	www.totalfinaelf.com
11	DaimlerChrysler	AG	Germany	36.7	159.7	50.40	www.DaimlerChrysler.com
12	Nestlé	SA/AG	Switzerland	35.6	41.1	94.20	www.nestle.com
13	Volkswagen	AG	Germany	33.9	70.1	53.80	www.volkswagen-ir.de
14	Unilever	NV/PLC	NL/UK	32.9	35.8	90.10	www.unilever.com
15	Suez Lyonnaise des Eaux	SA	France	31.1	84.6	45.60	www.suez-lyonnaise-eaux.fr
16	Wal-Mart Stores	Inc	USA	30.2	50.0	37.20	www.wal-mart.com
17	ABB	SA/AG	Switzerland	29.3	32.9	89.10	www.abb.com
18	Diageo	PLC	UK	27.9	46.3	76.70	www.diageo.com
19	Honda	KK	Japan	26.3	41.8	60.20	www.honda.co.jp
20	Siemens	AG	Germany	25.5	66.8	53.60	www.siemens.com
21	Renault	SA	France	23.6	43.2	61.80	www.renault.com
22	BMW	AG	Germany	22.9	35.7	59.90	www.bmw.com
23	News Corporation	Ltd	Australia	22.9	33.6	78.70	www.newscorp.com
24	Mitsubishi	KK	Japan	21.7	74.9	32.70	www.mitsubishi.co.jp
25	Sony	KK	Japan	21.6	52.5	59.30	www.world.sony.co.jp

26	Nissan	KK	Japan	21.6	57.2	42.60	global.nissan.co.jp
27	Bayer	AG	Germany	21.4	34.3	62.80	www.bayer.com
28	Roche	SA/AG	Switzerland	21.2	33.5	71.60	www.roche.com
29	VIAG	AG	Germany	20.4	34.8	55.30	www.viag.com
30	Philips	NV	NL	19.0	32.8	77.80	www.philips.com
31	Seagram	Ltd	Canada	18.8	22.2	94.80	www.seagram.com
32	Cable & Wireless	PLC	UK	17.7	28.5	67.50	www.cwplc.com
33	Hewlett Packard	Inc	USA	17.6	33.7	53.20	www.hp.com
34	Mitsui	KK	Japan	17.3	56.5	34.90	www.mitsui.co.jp
35	ENI	SpA	Italy	16.9	48.4	34.10	www.eni.it
36	Alcatel	SA	France	16.7	34.6	59.10	www.alcatel.com
37	DuPont	Inc	USA	16.7	38.5	41.70	www.dupont.com
38	BASF	AG	Germany	16.7	30.4	57.90	www.basf.com
39	Peugeot	SA	France	15.9	39.8	44.20	www.psa.fr
40	Texas Utilities	Inc	USA	15.8	39.5	35.00	www.txu.com
41	Itochu	KK	Japan	15.1	55.9	21.50	www.nisshoiwai.co.jp
42	Sumitomo	KK	Japan	15.0	45.0	26.30	www.sumitomocorp.co.jp
43	Coca-Cola	Inc	USA	14.9	19.2	70.60	www.coca-cola.com
44	Nortel Networks	Ltd	Canada	14.3	19.7	70.80	www.nortel.com
45	Nissho Iwai	KK	Japan	14.2	38.5	24.90	www.itochu.co.jp
46	Fiat	SpA	Italy	14.2	76.1	32.10	www.fiatgroup.com
47	Vivendi	SA	France	14.1	57.1	31.50	www.vivendi.com
48	Motorola	Inc	USA	14.0	31.0	45.80	www.motorola.com
49	Telefónica	Sa	Spain	13.8	42.3	29.90	www.telefonica.es
50	Rio Tinto	PLC/Ltd	UK/Aust.	12.4	16.1	80.40	www.riotinto.com

Notes: *The figures are taken from the World Investment Report 2000 (United Nations, 2000), adjusted by the authors for the following mergers that occurred in 1999:

(1) Exxon and Mobil to form ExxonMobil
(2) BP Amoco and Chevron
(3) Hoechst and Rhone-Poulenc to form Aventis
(4) TotalFina and Elf Aquitaine to form TotalFinaElf

Exhibit 1.5   *Forms of corporations*

	Basic corporate form		Alternative corporate form	
	Legal name	*Initial*	*Legal name*	*Initial*
France	Société Anonyme	SA	Société à responsibilité limitée	SARL
Germany	Aktiengesellschaft	AG	Gesellschaft mit beschränkter Haftung	GmbH
Italy	Società per Azioni	SpA	Società a responsabilità limitata	Srl
Netherlands	Naamloze Vennotschap	NV	Besloten vennotschap met beperkte aansprakelijheid	BV
Sweden	Aktiebolag	AB	(no alternative corporate form)	
Switzerland	Aktiengesellschaft	AG	Gesellschaft mit beschränkter Haftung	GmbH
UK	Public limited company	PLC	Private limited company	Ltd
USA	Corporation	Inc	(no alternative corporate form)	
Japan	Kabushiki kaisha	KK	Yugen kaisha	YK
Australia	Public company	Ltd	Proprietary company	Pty
Canada	Public corporation	Ltd	Private corporation	Ltd

Exhibit 1.6   *The top hundred MNEs: analysis of the country of the parent corporation*

USA	26
Japan	17
Europe	50.5
Other countries (Australia, Canada and Venezuela)	6.5
Total	100

Source: United Nations, *World Investment Report 2000*

17 per cent in Japan. Less than 7 per cent are based in other countries: Canada, Australia and Venezuela. Certain groups are headed by two parent corporations; an example is the Royal Dutch/Shell Group which has two parent corporations: Koninklijke Nederlandsche Petroleum Maatschappij NV (Royal Dutch), a Dutch corporation, and Shell Transport and Trading Company PLC, a British public limited company, which are linked by a cooperation agreement. In allocating MNEs to countries, these groups have been split between the countries of the parent corporation, which accounts for the fractions in Exhibits 1.6 and 1.7.

The analysis by country of the European-based MNEs is presented in Exhibit 1.7. The three largest economies (Germany, France and the UK)

Exhibit 1.7   *Analysis of the European MNEs in the top one hundred*

	Number
France	12
Germany	12
UK	8.5
Switzerland	4
Netherlands	4
Sweden	4
Italy	4
Finland	1
Spain	1
Total	50.5

Source: United Nations, *World Investment Report 2000*

account for two thirds, but a significant number of large MNEs are based in the smaller European countries, notably Switzerland, Sweden and the Netherlands.

The transnationality index

The penultimate column of Exhibit 1.4 gives an indication of the extent to which each group's assets, sales and employment are located in or related to foreign countries as opposed to the country of the parent enterprise. The transnationality index is calculated as the average of three ratios: foreign assets/total assets; foreign sales/total sales; and foreign employment/total employment. A high value of the transnationality index suggests that a group is more oriented towards foreign countries than to the country of the parent enterprise. General Electric, the top group in Exhibit 1.4, has a transnationality index of only 36.3 per cent, which is far lower than that of the second in the list: ExxonMobil with 69.3 per cent. This shows that General Electric is less oriented towards foreign activities, compared with ExxonMobil. It is ranked as the largest multi-national largely because overall it is so much larger; its total assets are much larger than ExxonMobil's, with the result that, even though only 36 per cent of its assets are located abroad (compared with 69 per cent for ExxonMobil), nevertheless its foreign assets are larger.

1.6   THE GLOBALIZATION OF FINANCE

The multinational enterprises are the driving force behind a further aspect of globalization: the globalization of finance. A hundred years ago, almost all enterprises, even the very largest, obtained the finance that they required for their operations in their own country, for example through their local stock exchange or bank. However with the growth of their international operations, the larger enterprises began to look to foreign countries for some part of their capital requirements. In effect, as the multinational enterprises grew ever larger, they found that their local sources of finance were unable to meet all their demands. It became increasingly common for the larger MNEs to have their shares listed on a foreign stock exchange in addition to the listing in their home country.

The recent growth in cross-border finance transactions is brought out by the statistics in Exhibit 1.8. In the countries that are there listed, the value of such transactions has increased remarkably in recent years, so that one may now consider that, for many investors and enterprises, the global capital market is more important than the national one.

The New York Stock Exchange ('Wall Street') is the world's largest and the natural source of finance for the MNEs; by offering its shares for sale on Wall Street, an MNE is able to draw on the financial resources, not only of the American economy (by far the largest in the world), but also of savers from many other countries who are attracted to the American capital market by its greater liquidity and its reputation for being efficient and well regulated. In December 2000, there were over 400 foreign companies listed on the New York Stock Exchange, comprising 22 of the 39 non-US MNEs listed in Exhibit 1.4. They include enterprises from all the major countries: Toyota, Sony and Honda from Japan, DaimlerChrysler from Germany, Aventis and TotalFinaElf from France, and BP Amoco from Britain. Also the holding companies of two Anglo-Dutch groups are listed in New York; Shell Transport and Trading Company PLC and Unilever PLC from Britain, and Koninklijke Nederlandsche Petroleum Maatschappij NV and Unilever NV from the Netherlands. For these MNEs, the American capital market is a major source of finance and the fact

Exhibit 1.8 *Cross-border transactions in bonds and shares as a percentage of GDP*

	1980 (%)	1990 (%)	1998 (%)
USA	9	89	230
Japan	8	119	91
Germany	7	57	334
France	5	54	415

Source: Bank for International Settlements

that they are listed in New York exercises a major influence over their financial reporting, for reasons that are analysed later.

The route commonly followed by a multinational enterprise is that it starts life as a business whose activities are almost entirely limited to its home country. In a first phase, it builds up its imports and exports. In a second phase it expands its operations in foreign countries by setting up permanent marketing and production facilities, involving increasing amounts of investment. The logical third phase is for the multinational to obtain its finance abroad. Gradually the enterprise transforms itself from a narrowly-based national enterprise into a truly world-wide business – a 'global player'. This transformation may be illustrated with the example of Aventis. In formal legal terms Aventis is a French société anonyme which was created in December 1999 through the merger of Hoechst (a German AG) and Rhône-Poulenc (a French SA). However in reality Aventis is much more than a French enterprise – it is a world wide corporation. This fact is demonstrated by the analysis of its shareholders which is presented in Exhibit 1.9. Only 10 per cent of Aventis's shareholders are identified as being French, a proportion lower than that of the USA, Germany and even Kuwait.

1.7 THE FINANCIAL REPORTING OF THE MULTINATIONAL ENTERPRISES

As the previous sections have demonstrated the multinational enterprises are the principal actors in the globalization of the world economy and the emphasis in this book is on the MNEs. The principal problems faced by the MNEs in the area of financial reporting stem from the diversity of law and practice throughout the world. The financial reporting of an

Exhibit 1.9 *Analysis of the shareholders of Aventis SA*

Country of shareholder	% of total shareholders
USA	22.0
Germany	15.1
France	10.7
Britain and Ireland	10.2
Rest of Europe	5.0
Kuwait	13.9
Employees	3.5
Rest of World	0.3
Unidentified	19.3

Source: Aventis annual report 1999

enterprise is governed by the law and practice of the country in which it is registered. In preparing its accounts, the enterprise observes a complex set of detailed rules and prescriptions that govern the form and content of financial statements of corporations registered in that country. These rules cover a wide spectrum, ranging from, at one extreme, laws and government regulations (which the accountant is legally obliged to obey) to, at the other extreme, accounting conventions (which the accountant follows through habits inculcated during training for the profession). In between these two extremes are various forms of rules which typically have less authority than law but more authority than conventions, of which the most important are accounting standards. Each country has its own unique set of laws, standards and conventions that govern its financial reporting. Furthermore each country is different in the extent to which these rules are obeyed or, more subtly, which rules are obeyed and which are ignored. The totality of the rules and practice that govern financial reporting in a country is known as the 'national accounting system'. The diversity in national accounting systems is the source of most of the problems in global financial reporting, but is also the reason why it makes such a fascinating field of study.

1.8 THE PENTAD

In its World Investment Report the United Nations refers to the 'Triad' of the USA, Japan and the European Union. However in the field of financial reporting a more useful grouping is the 'Pentad' of the USA, Japan, Germany, France and Britain. The reason is that, in financial reporting, the European Union is not yet a single homogeneous unit. The separate European countries still retain their individual identities. As will be shown in later chapters there are substantial and significant differences in the national accounting systems of Germany, France and Britain, with the consequence that it is not yet possible to refer to an EU accounting system. The emphasis in this book is on the countries of the Pentad, for the following reasons:

(a) They are by far the most important actors in the globalization of the world economy; together they account for almost half of world trade (imports and exports), 60 per cent of outward FDI and 50 per cent of inward FDI (both flows and stocks).

(b) Most of the world's largest MNEs are based in one of these five countries. Of the top hundred MNEs, over 75 per cent have their parent registered in the Pentad. This means that most of the foreign enterprises with which accountants are likely to have dealings will come from one of the countries of the Pentad.

(c) Most major developments in the theory and practice of financial reporting stem from the countries of the Pentad. In these countries may be found examples of all the different forms of financial reporting that are of any significance from an economic or theoretical viewpoint. A decade ago this was not the case, because socialist accounting, as practised in the Soviet Union and its satellites, represented a valid alternative. However, with the collapse of communism, there is now no serious rival to financial reporting as practised in the countries of the Pentad.

1.9 THE REST OF THE BOOK

The monumental subject of global financial reporting is dealt with in the rest of the book in the following fashion:

(a) **The remaining chapters in Part One** complete the presentation of the background to the subject by setting out, in Chapter 2, an analysis of the causes of the diversity in national accounting systems which makes the study of global financial reporting so complicated and yet so fascinating and then presenting in Chapter 3 an exposition of the nature of the rules that govern financial reporting.

(b) **Part Two** examines the national accounting systems of each of the five countries of the Pentad, seeking to explain the differences between them in terms of the historical development and of each country's unique national characteristics. This part includes an analysis of the EU's role in financial reporting.

(c) **Part Three** discusses the need for a single set of rules to govern financial reporting at the global level and identifies the International Accounting Standards Board as the body most likely to provide such rules. It explains this body's structure, its function and the nature of the standards that it issues.

(d) **Part Four** deals with the form and content of the financial statements. Whereas the emphasis in Part Two was on the differences between countries, the approach here is to analyse each issue from a theoretical and practical viewpoint leading to an exposition of the IASB's rules and of the practice in the Pentad.

(e) **Part Five** covers certain issues in financial reporting, which have been chosen because of their importance and interest. As in Part Four the analysis is based on an examination of the IASB's rules and of practice in the Pentad.

At the end of each chapter, there is a set of review questions that are designed to test the reader's understanding of the material covered. Also advice is given on further reading that may be undertaken with a view to deepening the reader's knowledge of particular subjects.

1.10 THE USE OF THE INTERNET

The Internet is having a considerable impact on the teaching of accounting. Some pioneering universities have reorganized whole courses around the Internet, dispensing with books altogether. Whilst admiring the enterprise of such bodies, the authors consider that the printed page still has considerable advantages over the monitor screen, and they believe that most students prefer the convenience and readability of a book, which they can consult anywhere at any time, to the cost and hassle of finding a computer, logging in, waiting for a response and finally getting a headache from the flickering screen! However this does not mean that the authors disregard the Internet – quite the contrary. They regard it as a most useful teaching resource, which used in conjunction with this book can greatly enrich the learning experience of the reader. In particular they advise the reader to use the Internet in the following ways:

(a) **To access journal articles.** Many journals have a website, where the text of past issues may be accessed and, if necessary, downloaded. Generally there is a charge for this service which makes it uneconomic for the individual reader. However many university libraries have taken out a subscription with the journal publisher which permits registered students to use the service free of charge. Hence readers should consult their local librarian. Generally the Internet is the most convenient way of obtaining the articles and papers referred to in this book.

(b) **To visit the websites** of bodies and organizations that are involved in the development of financial reporting, such as standard setting bodies, professional accountancy associations and regulatory bodies. Almost all the more important bodies maintain a website which often contains material of interest to the student of financial reporting, for example an explanation of the body's aims and functions, a review of its current activities, details of its regulations/standards and information about its publications. A list of useful website addresses is given in the annex to this chapter.

(c) **To obtain examples of financial statements.** Financial statements are the raw material of financial reporting. In the following chapters, there will be many examples of financial statements of major multinational enterprises that serve to illustrate particular points made in the text. However the reader can easily find further examples through the Internet. Almost all the major multinational enterprises have their own website, which, in the great majority of cases, include information about the financial statements. Generally this is either a facsimile of the printed annual report (including graphs and pictures) or a version of the financial statements specially adapted for the Internet. In most cases, the information may be either accessed online or downloaded for subsequent examination. The more advanced sites also have facilities for users to process the information, for example to develop their own forecasts. The website addresses of the 50 largest MNEs are given in Exhibit 1.4.

SUMMARY

The importance for the accounting student of global financial reporting was analysed. The globalization of the world's economy was described, with particular reference to the growth both in international trade and cross border investment (both foreign direct investment (FDI) and portfolio investment) and to the creation of a global capital market. The role of the multinational enterprises (MNEs) in the globalization process was examined; the fifty largest MNEs were identified and described. The countries of the Pentad (the USA, Japan, Germany, France and Britain) were introduced.

Review questions

1. What are the two reasons for studying global financial reporting?

2. By how much has international trade grown in (a) the last 30 years? (b) the last decade?

3. What is meant by the terms 'foreign direct investment' (FDI) and 'portfolio investment'?

4. What countries are (a) the major sources of FDI? (b) the major recipients?

5. Why are all the major multinational enterprises corporations? What are the advantages of this legal form?

6. What proportion of the world's one hundred largest MNEs are European corporations?

Review questions (cont'd)

7. What is the significance of the country of incorporation of an MNE for its financial reporting?

8. What proportion of the global total is accounted for by the countries of the Pentad in the following areas: (a) world trade (b) foreign direct investment (c) the larger MNEs?

Note

1. For a fuller explanation of the law of comparative advantage, see any good introductory text on economics, for example Mankiw (1998), Chapter 3.

References

Lymer, A, Debreceny, R, Gray, G and Rahman, A *Business Reporting on the Internet*, IASC, London (1999).

Mankiw, NG *Principles of Economics*, Dryden, Forth Worth (1998).

Micklethwait, J and Wooldridge, A *A Future Perfect: The Essentials of Globalization*, Crown Publishers, New York (2000).

United Nations *World Investment Report 2000*, United Nations Conference on Trade and Development, New York (2000).

Further reading

The World Investment Report which is published by the United Nations (United Nations, 2000) contains a wealth of information on the multinational enterprises and foreign investment. More information about the use of the Internet in financial reporting is to be found in 'Business reporting on the Internet' (Lymer and others, 1999). For an in-depth analysis of the benefits of globalization, see Micklethwait and Wooldridge (2000).

Useful Internet addresses

The more useful Internet sites for the student of global financial reporting are listed below. The addresses are correct at 30 June 2001. However it is not uncommon for addresses to be changed. In that event, the reader should use the computer's browser to locate the desired site.

Standard setting bodies

IASB: www.iasb.org.uk
FASB: www.rutgers.edu/accounting/raw/fasb
ASB: www.asb.org.uk
DSR: www.drsc.de

Professional accountancy associations

IFAC: www.ifac.org
AICPA: www.aicpa.org
ICAEW: www.icaew.co.uk
JICPA: www.jicpa.or.jp
CICA: www.cica.ca
ICAS: www.icas.org.uk

Regulatory bodies and stock exchanges

SEC: www.sec.gov
IOSCO: www.iosco.org
FIBV: www.fibv.com
New York Stock Exchange: www.nyse.com
London Stock Exchange: www.londonstockexchange.com
Deutsche Börse: www.exchange.de
Tokyo Stock Exchange: www.tse.or.jp

Other international bodies

UNCTAD: www.unctad.org
OECD: www.oecd.org
Bank for International Settlements: www.bis.org

Academic bodies

EAA: www.eiasm.be/EAA
AAA: www.rutgers.edu/accounting/raw/aaa

Other useful sites

www.accountingeducation.com. This is a most useful site in that it provides a host of links to other sites and also opportunities for interaction with other students and teachers.

chapter two

The Causes of Diversity

Chapter objectives

- To explain the diversity of financial reporting practice with reference to the factors that influence and shape financial reporting practice in each country
- To describe and analyse the more influential factors; notably three institutional factors (the state, the corporate financing system and the accountancy profession), a number of environmental factors and culture
- To examine empirical research that confirms the importance of these factors

2.1 THE CONTINGENT THEORY OF ACCOUNTING

As was explained in Chapter 1, each country has its own unique set of rules that govern the financial reporting of the enterprises located in that country. This leads to a remarkable diversity in the financial statements prepared by enterprises from different countries. This diversity covers all aspects of financial reporting, including the types of statements, the amount of disclosure in these statements and the methods used to measure the items contained in these statements. This chapter analyses the causes of this diversity.

A generation ago it was widely believed that accounting was essentially a technical subject with fixed principles and rules that applied universally throughout time and space, that these principles and rules were to be established by careful study and that they were to be passed on from one generation of accountants to the next by proper training. This belief was widely held by British accountants, who considered that the principal reason why another country's accounting system differed from that of Britain was simply that its accountants were less enlightened.

This theory is now completely discredited. It is widely accepted that accounting has been created by society as a means of gathering and communicating information. The financial statements serve as a bridge between the enterprise and those who have a need for information about the enterprise, between those who prepare the accounts (known as 'the preparers') and those who refer to the accounts as a means of satisfying their information needs (known as 'the users'). A country's accounting system is the product of a complex process during which accounting rules and practice are developed largely through the interaction of preparers and users. Each country's financial reporting has been shaped by its environment, that is by the economy and the society in which it developed. Since each country's environment is different, so is its accounting system. This is known as the 'contingent' theory of accounting[1] – accounting is fashioned by the factors that surround it, that are contingent to it. The current wisdom is summarized by Hopwood (1991) in the following terms, 'rather than being a . . . technical phenomenon, accounting is now recognized as being something shaped by culture, institutional configurations and the socio-historical context of the specific societies in which it emerged.'

2.2 THE FACTORS THAT SHAPE FINANCIAL REPORTING

An impression of the complexity of the process that leads to the creation of a country's accounting system is given in Exhibit 2.1, which is adapted from a similar figure in Gray (1988). The financial reporting of enterprises is determined by a country's accounting rules and by the practice of accountants in applying, interpreting and, sometimes, ignoring these rules. The rules are set by institutions such as the political system, the legal system and the accountancy profession, with some influence from accounting practice. In their turn, the institutions are influenced by the national 'culture' and the environment. Accounting practice is influenced by accounting rules (note that the influence of accounting rules and accounting practice is mutual) and by the accounting 'subculture', the latter being influenced by the national 'culture'.

The factors presented in Exhibit 2.1 may be divided into the three categories recognized by Hopwood in the passage quoted above:

(a) **Environmental factors**, which may be further divided into external (to the country) and internal. Examples of external factors are colonization, trade and inward foreign investment. Examples of internal factors are technology and the level of education. Some environmental factors are persistent (for example the effects of technology); some may be more in the nature of a shock, as for example a war or a

Exhibit 2.1 *The interplay of the environment, institutions and culture*

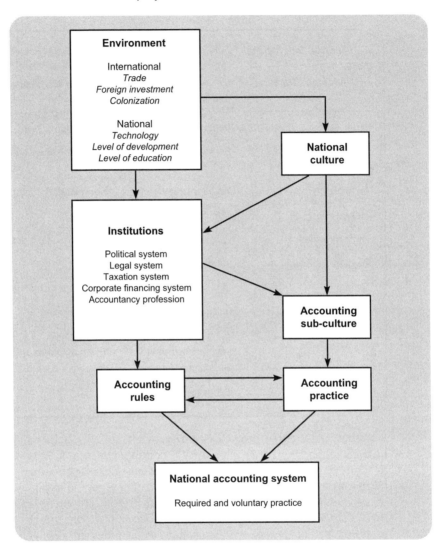

surge of inflation. Hopwood refers to these environmental factors as the 'socio-historical context'.

(b) **Institutions**, such as the political system and the legal system.

(c) **Culture,** The term 'culture' as used here refers to the set of common values, ideas and beliefs that are shared by most of the inhabitants of the country (the national culture) or by a subgroup (the accounting subculture).

Exhibit 2.2 *The factors that influence financial reporting according to three leading textbooks*

Comparative International Accounting by Nobes and Parker	International Accounting by Choi, Frost and Meek	International Financial Accounting by Roberts, Weetman and Gordon
Legal systems	Legal systems	The legal system
Providers of finance	Sources of finance	The corporate financing system
Taxation	Taxation	The taxation system
Culture	Culture	Culture
The profession		The accounting profession
Inflation	Inflation	
Accidents		Accidents of history
	Political and economic ties	The exporting and importing of accounting
	Level of economic development	The political and economic system
	Education level	

Within these three broad categories, what are the factors that shape financial reporting in each country? A number of scholars have sought to identify them; the lists of factors that are presented in three leading textbooks are summarized in Exhibit 2.2. There is a remarkable degree of agreement among these authors; four factors are mentioned in all three books and a further five factors in two books. The present authors' preferred list of factors is given below. It includes all the factors mentioned in two or more of the cited textbooks plus one or two new factors. Note that most of the factors listed are institutional factors, being the first three major headings.

(a) **The state**, which may be considered under four aspects:
  (i) The political system;
  (ii) Law;
  (iii) Taxation; and
  (iv) The regulation of dividends.

(b) **The corporate financing system**, which may be subdivided into:
  (i) The capital market; and
  (ii) Direct provision.

(c) **The accountancy profession.**

(d) **Environmental factors**, including:
  (i) Other interested parties
  (ii) Accounting theorists
  (iii) Inflation
  (iv) Colonialism
  (v) Accidents of history.

(e) **Culture.**

2.3 THE STATE

In most countries, the state is the strongest influence on the national accounting system. This influence will be considered under four aspects.

2.3.1 The political system

The influence of the political system on financial reporting is well illustrated by the role that accounting plays in a totalitarian state, of which a good example is provided by the Nazi regime which ruled Germany from 1933 to 1945. The government sought to control every aspect of the economy with the specific aim of increasing the country's ability to wage war. The financial reporting of enterprises was subordinated to this end. In 1937, the German government issued a decree imposing a uniform accounting system on all enterprises. The decree's preamble gives a very clear indication of the government's aims:

> The new aims of the German economy call for increased output and efficiency from business enterprises. The fulfilment of this great task requires a thorough knowledge and close control of all business transactions. Thus a well-developed accounting system is a primary factor in the reorganization of industries. The public interest, and in particular the aims of the four-year plan, demand that the accounting system of all enterprises should be arranged on uniform principles. (Quoted in Choi and Mueller (1992) p. 47)

After the defeat of the Nazi regime and its replacement in Germany by a democratically elected government, this decree was repealed and the present German government no longer seeks to impose a uniform financial reporting system on enterprises.

All the countries considered in this book are liberal democracies to a greater or lesser degree. The state does not seek to impose its will on the financial reporting of enterprises to the extent that the Nazis did. However this does not mean that the state has no interest in the matter. Even in a democracy, the state is interested in the financial reporting of enterprises for two reasons:

(a) The state may own a certain number of enterprises. In many countries, most utilities (such as water supply and public transport) are owned and managed by the state. The financial reporting of these state-owned enterprises is subject to the direct control of the government. Where it does not own these utilities, the state generally seeks to control their profits and prices. The state needs to be assured that these are calculated in an appropriate way, which inevitably involves considering the financial reporting of the regulated enterprise.

(b) But, in most democratic countries, state-owned and regulated enterprises represent only a small proportion of the economy; most enterprises are privately owned. However it is generally accepted that the state is responsible for the smooth running of the economy; the state may intervene in the functioning of the economy in order to achieve certain generally accepted objectives, such as full employment, economic growth and the avoidance of cyclical fluctuations. Hence governments take measures that directly affect enterprises in the private sector of the economy; these measures range from taxation which affects all enterprises generally to measures targeted at specific enterprises, such as aids to investment or employment in specific regions or sectors. In carrying through its policies, the government needs accurate and timely information from enterprises, both to find out whether intervention is necessary and subsequently to check that its intervention has had the desired effect. In effect, the government is one of the most important users of the financial statements of enterprises. It has both the motivation and the power to ensure that these financial statements provide it with the information that it needs.

The attitude of the state towards the financial reporting of enterprises varies considerably throughout the world. This matter is considered in more detail in the following chapters; in general, the governments of France and Japan are more inclined to intervene in the financial reporting of enterprises than are those of the USA and Britain. Germany is rather a special case. Because the present German government aims to distance itself from the former Nazi regime, its policy is less interventionist than that of Japan and France, but rather more than that of the USA and Britain.

The taxation of enterprises by the state has particularly important effects on financial reporting. However it is more convenient to deal with this after having considered the influence of law in general.

2.3.2 Law

All countries in theory irrespective of their political systems, have the fundamental principles of financial reporting laid down in the law. An important factor is that the great majority of the larger enterprises are corporations, which are artificial 'legal persons'; they do not exist naturally but are created by a legal process. It is therefore almost inevitable that the law should lay down rules that govern the activities of the 'persons' that it has created, including their financial reporting. However, even in respect of enterprises consisting of natural persons (individuals and partnerships), the state considers that it is appropriate to regulate their activities, including financial reporting, but generally to a lesser degree.

It is often claimed that a country's legal system influences the nature of financial reporting in that country. In the USA, in Britain (except Scotland) and in most of the countries of the former British Empire, the legal system is based on Common Law. The statute law (that is the law enacted by the legislator) lays down the general principles which are interpreted and developed by the judges in specific legal cases. In effect, there is built up a body of case law (consisting of judgements in particular cases) which supplements the statute law. In other countries, notably those of Continental Europe and Japan, the legal system is based on Roman Law, which in principle is a written code that sets out in detail the rules to be followed. The code is enacted and periodically amended by the legislator; the judges consider that their task is to apply this code not to develop it.

With respect to financial reporting, throughout the world in both Common Law countries and Roman Law countries, the basic rules are set out in the statute law enacted by the legislator. Generally, in Common Law countries, the statute law is less detailed. However, in contrast to the general position outlined in the previous paragraph, in the area of financial reporting the courts of law have not supplemented the statute law with a body of case law. The reason appears to be that judges have been reluctant to become involved in a such a complex and technically difficult field. Hence it might be felt that, given the paucity of court judgements, the differences in the legal system are not a major cause of diversity in financial reporting. However research by Doupnik and Salter (1995), which is explained in detail in section 2.7, shows that the legal system (Common Law or Roman Law) is a major factor in explaining differences in national accounting systems.

2.3.3 Taxation

In all countries, enterprises pay taxes to the state. Some of these taxes are identical to those levied on individuals: for example, taxes on the assessed value of buildings and registration taxes on motor vehicles. The levying of these taxes on enterprises raises no particular problems. However other taxes are specific to enterprises, particularly to corporations. In all countries, there is a tax levied on the profits of corporations and, everywhere, it is a significant source of government revenue. Exhibit 2.3 indicates, for the major countries, the rate of tax on corporation profits; that is the proportion of the profits taken by the state. It is clear that throughout the world the state is a major partner in all corporations – it takes for itself about a third of their profits.

This interest of the state has profound implications for financial reporting. Clearly the state cannot allow the corporation to choose the methods by which the taxable profit is computed. In order to protect its tax revenues and to assure that the tax burden is shared equitably between corporations, the state has to prescribe uniform rules for the computation of taxable profits. These rules generally cover those areas where the calculation of the amount involves judgement on the part of the accountant, for example, in assessing the annual depreciation on a machine or the level of the provision for doubtful debts. It is precisely these areas where the tax authorities are determined that tax-payers should not be permitted to exercise discretion, because they are concerned that they will use it to reduce their tax charge to an unwarranted degree. However it is probable that the corporation's shareholders will not consider that the profits computed in accordance with these tax rules are the most appropriate measure of the corporation's performance from their point of view. There are two basic reasons for this:

Exhibit 2.3 *Rates of tax on a corporation's profits*

Country	Rate of tax (%)
USA	35%
Japan	41%
Germany	25%
France	34%
United Kingdom	30%

(a) The state's interest is principally in devising rules that will enable it to collect an amount of tax with reasonable certainty, with the minimum of administrative cost and with the least opportunities of evasion on the part of the taxpayer. The state is not primarily interested in an accurate measure of the corporation's profits (which is the principal interest of the shareholders), but rather in one that facilitates the collection of the most revenue.

(b) On occasions, the state adapts the tax rules with the specific aim not of raising revenue but of achieving other socially-desirable objectives. For example, the state may seek to achieve a higher level of capital investment in a particular region, and, with this aim in view, it may permit corporations that set up a factory in the region to charge the full cost of the plant as a tax deductible expense in the first year. The state is prepared to accept the reduced tax revenue because it gives greater priority to the promotion of investment. However, for shareholders who want to assess the corporation's performance, the appropriate level of expense to be taken into account is the regular depreciation of the asset, both in its first year and in subsequent years. Charging the full cost of the plant in the first year leads to an overstatement of expenses in the first year and to an understatement in later years.

In certain countries, corporations commonly follow the tax rules in preparing their financial statements. In these countries, there is generally a basic rule that the tax payable by a corporation is based on the figures reported in its accounts. There is often a rule that an expense may only be charged against taxable profit, if it has been recorded in the books of account and in the financial statements. In this way, the state is able to secure the willing compliance of the tax-payers in using the tax rules for the accounts. Even in those areas where the tax law permits some discretion, for example in allowing the corporation to choose whether or not to include overheads in the valuation of work-in-progress, the corporation will make the choice with a view to gaining the maximum tax advantage.

There are three major advantages in making reporting to shareholders (in the financial statements) identical with reporting to the tax authorities:

(a) **Administrative convenience:** The corporation benefits from having only one accounting system and one calculation of profits for both financial reporting and for tax. The tax authorities benefit because the tax return is simpler, being essentially the financial statements with a few adjustments.

(b) **Prevention of tax fraud:** The rule that the expenses claimed in the tax return should be identical with those recorded in the books of account greatly facilitates the tax authorities' control.

(c) **Equity between stakeholders:** The state may be considered to be a partner alongside the shareholders, a partner which in most countries is entitled to about a third of the profits. It is logical and reasonable that each partner's share of the profits should be calculated on a consistent basis. A related point may be illustrated with the help of the previous example. Where a corporation has received a tax benefit because it built a factory in a disadvantaged region, this benefit should not be spent in paying higher dividends to shareholders; this can be prevented by expensing the cost of the plant in the first year, which reduces the profits available for shareholders' dividends. The burden of helping the disadvantaged region is shared between the shareholders and the government.

However there are also disadvantages which stem from the fact that the interests of the tax authorities are not identical with those of other users of the accounts. As already mentioned the computation of profit that best serves the needs of the tax authorities will generally not be the most appropriate for investors.

In no country are a corporation's financial statements identical with its tax computation. However, in certain countries, the influence of tax is very marked; many of the rules that govern the content of the financial statements of corporations are laid down by the taxation authorities. The financial statements are said to be 'tax-driven'. It is generally agreed that this is the case in Japan, Germany and France. However, in these countries (as is generally the case throughout the world), tax is levied on individual corporations and not on groups of corporations. For this reason, taxation tends to exert greater influence over the accounts of the individual corporation than it does over the consolidated accounts.

In the USA and Britain, there is no general legal rule that the financial statements must follow the tax rules. Hence accounts in these countries are considered not to be tax-driven. However this does not mean that tax has no influence on financial reporting for two reasons:

- Many smaller enterprises find it convenient and economical to use the tax rules in drawing up their financial statements, as this saves them the bother and expense of making a second set of calculations for tax purposes
- For certain items in the financial statements, there may be a specific legal obligation to follow the tax rule; this is the case with the LIFO valuation of inventory in the USA

Whereas the first factor is more relevant for the financial reporting of smaller enterprises, the second applies to all enterprises, including the larger MNEs.

2.3.4 The regulation of dividends and the maintenance of the corporation's capital

In the previous section, it was suggested that the tax on a corporation's profits may be regarded as that part of the profits to which the state is entitled as a partner in the corporation. Hence the state sets the rules of financial reporting in order to regulate the distribution of profit between the government and the shareholders. However the state has a further interest in distributions made by corporations. The shareholders of a corporation enjoy limited liability; the amount that they are obliged to pay to the corporation is limited to the value of their shares. Once the shareholders have paid the corporation for their shares, the corporation cannot demand any further payment. This means that often the only funds that the corporation has available to pay its creditors are those represented by the initial capital paid in by shareholders. In effect the corporation's initial capital represents a minimum reserve fund which persons who extend credit to the corporation can treat as a guarantee that they will be repaid. It is essential that this fund should not be reduced by payments to the shareholders. Hence, in most countries, there is a legal principle that dividends may only be paid out of profits, that is out of increases in the value of the corporation's capital. This serves not only to protect creditors but also prevents the shareholders from being deceived into believing that the corporation (and the managers) are doing well, when they receive dividends which in fact have been paid out of capital. Therefore financial reporting also serves to determine the maximum amount that the corporation may distribute to its shareholders.

However countries differ in the importance placed on ensuring that the corporation's capital is not depleted by unwarranted dividends. In certain countries, of which Germany is the most important, corporations are obliged to use prudence in valuing assets and liabilities, that is to use methods that ensure that assets are not overvalued and liabilities not undervalued. The same emphasis is not placed on preventing the undervaluation of assets or the overvaluation of liabilities. In fact these are preferred since this gives even greater assurance that the corporation's initial capital is maintained and hence that creditors are adequately protected. In fact prudent valuation methods, which have the effect of limiting dividends, generally enhance the value of the fund available for the payment of creditors – that is the real value of this fund will generally be higher than the value reported in the balance sheet. However, in other countries, such as the USA and Britain, it is considered preferable to report an unbiassed figure for assets (not overvalued and not undervalued), because this information is more appropriate for shareholders.

As with taxation, the influence of prudence is most marked in the individual accounts; the considerations that lead to a prudent valuation of assets do not apply to the consolidated accounts. The creditors must look for repayment to the individual corporation with which they have a contract and not to the group. Dividends are paid by individual corporations, not by groups. It is the capital fund of the individual corporation that must be protected.

2.3.5 Conclusion: the dominating influence of the state

The above analysis demonstrates that the state is a most important influence on financial reporting. The state lays down the rules that govern the financial reporting of enterprises with the aim of achieving a number of objectives of which the most important are the regulation of the economy, the collection of taxes and the protection of creditors. However the importance that the state attaches to these objectives and the degree to which it intervenes in financial reporting varies considerably from country to country. In certain countries, the prescriptive nature of a legal system based on Roman Law combined with the need of the state to safeguard its tax revenues and to protect the position of creditors makes the state the predominant influence in financial reporting. This is notably the case with the three major countries, Japan, Germany and France.

Moreover in all countries, the state is the principal means by which the other factors (to be analysed in the rest of this chapter) influence financial reporting, in that the state enacts laws in response to the pressures and demands of the interested parties.

2.4   THE CORPORATE FINANCING SYSTEM

The way in which enterprises are financed has a profound influence on their financial reporting. Financing involves the supplier of finance (for example, a wealthy individual or a bank) transferring resources to an enterprise for a certain period; the enterprise invests these resources with the aim of making a return that will enable it to make repayments to the financier; these repayments should be sufficient to compensate the financier for being deprived of her resources, that is the financier makes an initial payment to the enterprise in the expectation of receiving future benefits.

The financier needs information about the enterprise's financial position and performance both prior to the decision to grant finance (in order to gain assurance that the enterprise will be able to make the necessary future repayments) and thereafter during the period of financing (in order to decide whether to continue the financing or whether to intervene in order to protect her interests). Hence the enterprise's financial reporting is crucial to the financing process.

The connection between the financier (whether individual or institution) can be made either directly or through the capital market. Which method is used (through the market or directly) has a great influence over the nature of the enterprises's financial reporting.

2.4.1 The capital market

History

In most developed countries, the market for the provision of finance for enterprises is centred on the stock exchange. The first commercial stock exchange is claimed to be the Amsterdamse Effectenbeurs (Amsterdam Stock Exchange) where the shares of the Verenigde Oost-Indische Compagnie were traded as early as 1602. Over the next two centuries, this body and the stock exchanges of Paris and London developed into important financial institutions. However these stock exchanges were almost exclusively engaged in the buying and selling of government stocks, with occasional trades in the shares of the great commercial corporations such as the Compagnie des Indes Orientales in Paris and the East India Company in London. It was only in the later nineteenth century, with the growth of the larger industrial and commercial corporations, that trading in shares, as opposed to government stock, became a significant proportion of the business of these exchanges. Now there are stock exchanges in almost all developed countries and very many developing countries; in many countries they are an important source of finance for industry and commerce.

The world's stock exchanges

The world's principal stock exchanges are listed in Exhibit 2.4 which gives figures for the twelve largest countries and for a sample of developing countries, being totals for all stock exchanges located in each country. In order to give an indication of the importance of these stock exchanges as a source of capital for enterprises in each country, this exhibit shows the amount of the market capitalization of listed domestic enterprises, calculated as the total number of shares of national (as opposed to foreign) corporations that are listed on that country's exchanges, multiplied by the market price per share.[2] As with many tables in this book, the monetary amounts are expressed in Euros, the common currency of the European Union.

Exhibit 2.4 *The stock exchanges of the world*

Rank	Country	Domestic corporations Market capitalization at 31 December 1999 (€ mn)	% of GDP
1	USA	16 604 185	224
2	Japan	4 544 410	88
3	United Kingdom	2 848 784	248
4	France	1 499 495	98
5	Germany	1 428 873	61
6	Canada	799 520	141
7	Italy	726 565	64
8	Netherlands	693 597	173
9	Switzerland	691 539	221
10	Hong Kong	607 689	397
11	Spain	430 656	77
12	Australia	426 672	116
Selected developing countries			
	Brazil	227 438	32
	India	111 989	31
	Mexico	91 535	27

Source: Fédération Internationale des Bourses de Valeur

The most striking feature of Exhibit 2.4 is the dominance of the stock exchange as a source of finance for American enterprises. The total market capitalization of American enterprises is greater than the aggregate of all the other countries shown. As a means of assessing the importance of the stock exchange within a particular country, Exhibit 2.4 presents figures for market capitalization as a percentage of Gross Domestic Product. It confirms the importance of the stock exchanges in the American economy. In most other countries, the stock exchanges are in relative terms less important compared with the USA, even when the size of the country's economy is taken into account. With respect to the importance of the capital market, there is a clear distinction between the developed countries and the developing countries; the stock markets of the developing countries are much smaller both in absolute size and relative to GDP than those of the developed countries. Hong Kong is in a category of its own; formally it is part of China, a developing country, but it has its own separate economic system which provides its population with a standard of living comparable to that of a developed country. Within the ranks of the developed countries included in Exhibit 2.4, one can draw a distinction between

- those countries where the capital market is large relative to the size of the economy: USA, Britain, Switzerland and the Netherlands
- those developed countries where the capital market is (relative to the size of the economy) significantly smaller: Japan, Germany, France, Italy and Spain. Canada and Australia are marginal cases.

One may conclude that the stock exchange is a significantly less important source of finance for enterprises located in the second group of countries.

2.4.2 Direct provision of finance

The stock exchange is an effectual source of finance only for large enterprises. For enterprises below a certain size, it is not economic to undergo the trouble and expense involved in obtaining a stock exchange quotation.[3] Hence, even in those countries which Exhibit 2.4 shows as having the most developed capital market (USA, Britain, Switzerland, and the Netherlands), all except the largest enterprises have to rely on other sources of finance. In the other developed countries (which include such major economies as Japan, Germany and France), these other sources of finance are significant even for the larger enterprises. Three sources are particularly important:

- Banks and financial institutions
- Family members, friends and close business associates
- The state

Banks and financial institutions

In all countries, banks provide short-term funds for businesses, for example to finance fluctuations in inventory over the business cycle. In Japan and Germany, it is common for banks to provide finance on a long-term basis; this is particularly the case in Germany, where banks often make long-term loans to corporations and even acquire large blocks of shares.

Family and friends

In all countries, family members and friends are the most important source of finance for small businesses. However, in France and Germany, small and medium-sized businesses have a greater relative importance in the economy, compared with the situation in the USA and Britain.

The state

In all countries, the state provides financial assistance to business in the form of subsidies for operations that are considered to be socially desirable, for example to stimulate capital investment in disadvantaged regions or to provide jobs for the unemployed. The state is the major source of finance for business in the Eastern regions of Germany (the former German Democratic Republic) and for similarly backward regions in other countries. In Japan and France, the state is a major source of funds for research.

These three sources have the common characteristic that the suppliers of finance contract directly with the enterprise and not through the market. They are able to obtain the information that they need about the business's affairs through their direct contacts with the management. This is self-evident in the case of family members and business associates. Banks will insist on being provided with regular information about the business's financial position, revenues and costs, as a condition for providing finance. The same will be true of the government, when it makes special grants. Hence, for these suppliers of finance, the regular financial statements (the balance sheet and the income statement) are not the most important source of information about the business, in sharp contrast to the role that they play in relation to outside shareholders.

2.4.3 The form of financing: equity versus debt

The way in which an enterprise is financed may have a significant influence on its financial reporting; the distinction between equity and debt is especially important. Persons who provide funds to an enterprise in the form of loans (debt) are not particularly interested in the level of future profits above the level that enables the enterprise to make future payments of capital and interest; their main interest is in the security of their loan, which can be better assured by the enterprise using prudential methods for the valuation of assets and assessment of profits. On the other hand, the principal interest of those who provide finance to the enterprise in the form of equity (ordinary shares) is in the future surplus after the claims of debt-holders have been met; in fact their information needs are far wider than those of debt-holders and they will press for greater disclosure by enterprises. The figures of market capitalization given in Exhibit 2.4 relate to equity and not debt. As a general rule, it can be stated that, in those countries which are highly ranked by the statistic 'Market capitalization as % of GDP' (notably the USA and Britain), equity is a significantly more important source of finance for enterprises compared with those countries that are lower ranked (notably Japan and Germany).

2.4.4   The influence of finance on financial reporting

The capital market

The fact that a corporation's shares are listed on a stock exchange has a profound influence on the nature of its accounting. Listed corporations generally have hundreds, even thousands, of shareholders. The annual accounts become the principal way in which the corporation communicates with its shareholders. Enterprises present their balance sheets and income statements in a way that makes them more easily understood by shareholders and supplement them with other reports, such as cash flow statements, that provide additional information helpful to the readers. The enterprise has an incentive to be as informative as possible about its affairs in order to encourage investors to buy its shares, thus keeping the share market price at a high level, which lowers the cost of capital, but more importantly, deters take-over bids.

Over the last thirty years take-over bids have become an increasingly important feature of the stock exchanges in certain countries, notably in the USA and Britain. In a take-over bid, an enterprise (the bidder) seeks to take over control of another enterprise by buying its shares. In order to persuade the existing shareholders to sell their shares, the offer price has to be significantly higher than the market price before the bid. However the bidder anticipates making a profit from the transaction by selling certain of the enterprise's assets and by operating the remainder more efficiently, possibly in conjunction with the bidder's existing assets. In general a take-over bid will be profitable only if an enterprise's shares are undervalued on the stock exchange, in relation to the value of the enterprise's assets if either sold or operated more efficiently.

Following a successful take-over bid, control of the enterprise passes from the former shareholders to the new shareholder, the bidder. What is at stake in a take-over bid is the future control of the enterprise; hence the term applied to take-overs in general: 'the market for corporate control'. In recent years, in both London and New York, the stock exchange's function as a provider of capital for enterprises has been largely superseded by its role as the venue for the market for corporate control. The situation in the other stock exchanges is rather different. In the past, take-over bids were almost impossible because of legal, institutional and cultural obstacles, but in recent years the situation has changed markedly. In 1999 there were a number of highly publicized take-over bids on the Paris and Frankfurt stock exchanges. The most striking evidence of the change was provided early in 2000 by the hostile bid by the British company, Vodafone, for the major German enterprise, Mannesmann, which was ultimately successful despite the determined opposition of the German enterprise's management and the strong misgivings of the German political and economic establishment.

One of the main preoccupations of the managers of a listed enterprise is to prevent a take-over bid, which, if successful, would result in them losing their jobs. The surest way of deterring a take-over bid is to keep the market price of the enterprise's shares at a high level. Financial reporting can make a major contribution to achieving this aim.

Direct sources of finance

Where the principal source of finance for business is not the capital market, the financial reporting of enterprises has to be motivated and directed towards satisfying other needs than those of shareholders for information. Typically this is provided by the demands of the government, both for information to assist its economic planning and to raise taxation. Nobes (2000) sums up the position very well: 'In most continental European countries and in Japan, the traditional paucity of "outsider" shareholders has meant that external financial reporting has been largely invented for the purposes of protecting creditors and for governments, as tax collectors or controllers of the economy.' Enterprises tend to place more emphasis on drawing up their accounts to satisfy the demands of the tax authorities, particularly with the view to minimizing the tax charge, and to give less emphasis to meeting the information needs of investors. In this situation the accounts are said to be 'tax-driven'. Where the accounts are drawn up on a tax basis, the shareholders have to make a supplementary calculation of profit from their point of view; this is relatively easy for shareholders with close links with the management but much more problematic for outside shareholders.

2.5 THE ACCOUNTANCY PROFESSION

The third institutional factor to be considered is the accountancy profession.

The distinction between accountants and auditors

The accountancy profession may be expected to exercise a considerable influence over financial reporting. In this connection, it is important to distinguish between:

(a) **The accountant**, whose function is to prepare the financial statements. Normally this will be an employee of the enterprise, but, in certain European countries, it may be an outside professional, particularly with small enterprises.

(b) **The auditor**, whose function is to audit the financial statements. The audit of an enterprise generally consists of an examination of the enterprise's operations and financial position, with a view to reporting whether these are properly represented in the financial statements.

In some countries, there is a clear distinction between accountants and auditors; in effect they are separate professions. However, in this chapter, to simplify matters the term 'accountancy profession' is used generally to describe the two professions together.

The history of the profession

The origins of the world's accountancy profession go back to nineteenth-century Britain. At that time, the growth of the British economy and, in particular, the increase in the number of large enterprises organized in the form of limited companies, created a demand for a body of professional men[4] to undertake certain tasks in connection with this new form of business organization. Initially the principal function of these professionals, who were known as accountants, was to administer the bankruptcy of failed companies; they were the grave-diggers of business. However it soon became clear that the personal qualities of independence, integrity and competence in financial matters that qualified the professional accountants for the task of winding up a company, were also highly relevant for its audit. Thus it became the practice for the shareholders of larger companies to appoint professional accountants to audit the accounts that had been prepared by the companies' managers.

The professional accountants soon began to organize themselves into professional associations, with a view to enhancing their status by enforcing standards of training, competence and integrity. The first body to be set up was located in Scotland: the Society of Accountants of Edinburgh founded in 1853. It was quickly followed by similar bodies in Glasgow and Aberdeen. Almost a century later, in 1951, these societies merged to form the Institute of Chartered Accountants of Scotland, which by tracing its origins back to the Edinburgh Society, claims to be the oldest professional body of accountants in the world.[5] England lagged somewhat behind Scotland in that the Institute of Chartered Accountants in England and Wales was not founded until 1880.

Shortly after the formation of the British bodies, the first professional societies of accountants were set up in Canada (1880), Australia (1885) and the USA (1887). In all cases, accountants from Britain played a major role in their foundation. On the continent of Europe, except in the Netherlands, the development of the audit and accountancy professions lagged behind Britain, in that the first societies were not founded until the next century: in Italy in 1906 (see note 5), in Germany in 1932 and in France in 1935. The earliest Japanese society was formed in 1927 but was completely reorganized in its present form in 1949.

Initially the principal function of the members of these professional associations was to act as auditors. The demand for an audit grew out of the separation of ownership from control in corporations, which first became significant with the growth of large enterprises in the later nineteenth century. In principle the auditor stands between the preparer of the financial statements (the enterprise's management) and their principal users (the corporation's owners, that is the shareholders) and reports on the accounts that are prepared by the former for the benefit of the latter. In many countries, auditors were a strong influence on the financial reporting practice of corporations; the management turned to them for advice on how to draw up the corporation's accounts and generally followed the advice given, as to do otherwise would run the risk of a qualified audit report, with its attendant dangers.

The present position

Information about the professional accountancy bodies in selected countries is presented in Exhibit 2.5. In order to develop statistics covering a number of countries, it is necessary to have a uniform definition of 'accountant'. The definition used in Exhibit 2.5 is that an accountant is a member of a professional association that belongs to the International Federation of Accountants (IFAC), which is the body that brings together the accountancy and audit professions at the world level. Exhibit 2.5 gives the following information for each country:

■ The number of the professional bodies in that country that belong to IFAC. In most countries there is more than one body; the record is held by Britain with no less than seven bodies

■ The date of the foundation of the oldest body or of its earliest forerunner

■ The number of qualified accountants and auditors, both in absolute terms and relative to the population

There is an important qualification to be made regarding Exhibit 2.5, which should be kept in mind in interpreting the data. For certain countries, notably Britain, the USA, Canada and Australia, the membership figures refer to both auditors and accountants: less than 20 per cent of the qualified accountants in these countries are engaged in audit: the great majority are employed as accountants in business and administration. In the other countries, that is Japan and the continental European countries, there are either no professional associations of accountants, that is the associations represent only auditors (this is the case in Germany) or,

Exhibit 2.5 *The world's accountancy and audit profession*

Professional associations (members of IFAC)	Number	Date of foundation*	Qualified accountants Total number	Qualified accountants Per million inhabitants
USA	2	1887	403 000	1496
UK and Ireland	7	1853	218 400	3540
Japan	1	1927	12 320	98
Germany	1	1932	7600	93
France	2	1935	13 700	235
Italy	2	1906	64 500	1128
Netherlands	1	1895	8700	558
Canada	3	1880	185 000	6229
Australia	2	1885	113 000	6243
India	2	1949	101 789	108
China	1	1988	127 000	103

* Date of foundation of the oldest professional body or its predecessor

where they do exist, they represent only those accountants who work as independent professionals (as in France).

Probably the most interesting information in Exhibit 2.5 is set out in the final column, which gives, for each country, the number of accountants per million inhabitants. The variation between countries is remarkable, ranging from over three thousand accountants per million inhabitants in Canada, Australia and Britain to about one hundred (one thirtieth of the British figure) in Germany and Japan. It is very clear that in the USA, Britain and the countries of the former British Empire, the accountancy profession is much stronger than in Japan and in Continental Europe, where only the Italian and Dutch professions match those of the 'Anglo-Saxons'.

The influence of the accountancy profession on financial reporting

There are three basic reasons why a country's accountancy profession may be expected to influence its financial reporting:

(a) The legislators in framing the laws may seek advice from the experts in accounting, that is the accountancy profession.

(b) Since it is impossible for the laws to cover every aspect of financial reporting, there is considerable room for additional rules that supplement the law, notably accounting standards. It seems probable that the accountancy profession would have considerable influence in the standard-setting process.

(c) However even standards cannot cover every eventuality. Hence much has to be left to the skill and judgement of the accountant who prepares the accounts and the auditor who audits them.

Whether, in fact, in a particular country, the accountancy profession is a major influence on financial reporting depends essentially on two factors:

- The extent to which the rules of financial reporting are laid down in the law
- The strength and prestige of the profession

In fact, both factors combined make the accountancy profession a major influence on financial reporting in the 'Anglo Saxon' countries: USA, Britain and certain countries of the former British Empire, such as Canada and Australia.

In other countries, the profession has not had the same degree of influence, reflecting its comparatively recent formation and its lack of numbers. In Japan, both factors combine to weaken the profession's influence. It is a similar situation in Continental Europe, with the exception of the Netherlands, where members of the Dutch institute have considerable prestige principally because they are considered to be exceptionally well trained. Curiously, Italy is not an exception to the general rule. Although it has the second largest profession in Europe (after that of Britain) and a number of accountants per million inhabitants comparable to that of the USA, it is generally considered that the Italian profession has relatively little influence over the Italian accounting system.

2.6 ENVIRONMENTAL FACTORS

So far, three major institutional factors have been discussed: the state, the corporate finance system and the accountancy profession. Undoubtedly, in all countries, they are the major factors that influence financial reporting, although the weight of each of the three varies considerably from country to country. This section considers the principal environmental factors – the elements of the international and national environment that are not part of a country's institutional structure. They are a rather diverse group.

2.6.1 Other interested parties

In addition to the state and the providers of finance, there are other parties interested in the financial statements of enterprises, including employees and the public in general.

Employees

The enterprise's employees clearly have a major interest in its financial position and performance; the financial statements provide information that is helpful in making decisions such as whether to demand higher wages (if necessary backed up by strike action) or whether it would be better to seek another job. The state, in enacting laws, should have a particular interest in meeting the needs of this group, which is numerically larger than any other category of users. In certain European countries, such as France and Belgium, the law obliges enterprises to prepare special financial statements for the benefit of employees.[6] However, in general, the influence of employees and of their representatives, the trade unions, over financial reporting seems to be rather less than might be expected from the size of this user group.

The general public

In recent years the public has become increasingly aware that the activities of businesses have an impact not only on those directly involved in the business (shareholders, employees, suppliers and customers) but also on the whole of society, in such matters as: pollution of the environment (for example, discharge of toxic effluents into rivers); depletion of the world's scarce resources (for example, use of fossil fuels); harmful products (for example, cigarettes); dangerous processes (for example, nuclear electricity); antisocial employment practices (for example, racial discrimination) and so on. The list of the business activities on which the general public has a real need for information is endless. Therefore groups, such as Friends of the Earth, have put pressure on enterprises to publish more information on these activities. This pressure is already having an influence on the financial reporting of enterprises, which may be expected to increase in the future.

2.6.2 Accounting theorists

Accounting is both a practical and a theoretical subject, and it is to be expected that the theory of accounting would have some influence over the practice of financial reporting. Several outstanding individuals have contributed to the development of the theory of accounting. Undoubtedly the most influential has been Luca Pacioli, an Italian friar, who in 1494 wrote the first book on double-entry book-keeping 'Tractatus particularis de computis et scripturis' (treatise on the details of accounts and records) which was in fact only an annex to a much larger scholarly work on mathematics 'Summa de Arithmetica, Geometria, Proportioni et Proportionalita'. Pacioli did not invent double-entry book-keeping, which appears to have developed spontaneously in the city-states of Northern Italy around two hundred years earlier. His importance is the impetus that his book gave to the dissemination of the technique, not only within Italy but further afield. Within fifty years of its publication, it had been translated into Dutch, French and English, and was widely copied. By the end of the sixteenth century, double-entry book-keeping, known after its inventors as the 'Italian method', was widely established throughout Western Europe as the most modern method of accounting for both business and government.

No other individual comes close to matching the influence of Pacioli over financial reporting. However in almost every country one finds a national 'accounting hero' whose work had a significant impact on financial reporting: persons such as Eugen Schmalenbach in Germany, Gino Zappa in Italy and Theodore Limperg in the Netherlands. Each made his own personal contribution to the development of accounting theory, as one of the authors has analysed elsewhere (Flower, 1996). In Britain, the cradle of the accounting profession, the 'accounting heroes' have tended to be outstanding professional accountants, whose strength lay in practice rather than theory; men like Lawrence Dicksee and Frederic de Paula.[7] On the other hand, in the USA, academics have been much more influential; for example William Paton of the University of Michigan and Henry Rand Hatfield of the University of California, who developed alternative theories of the accounting entity in the earlier years of the twentieth century. However it would seem that only rarely does the influence of the individual extend very widely either in space (outside his native country) or in time (for many years after his death). In this respect, Pacioli is very much the exception.

2.6.3 Inflation

The influence of inflation on financial reporting is most apparent in the countries of Latin America. Several of these countries, such as Brazil, Chile and Mexico, have suffered high rates of inflation in recent years, often exceeding 100 per cent per year. Not surprisingly this experience has left its mark on financial reporting practices of these countries, in that price-level adjustments are a common feature of the financial statements of enterprises. Curiously, the impact on financial reporting in Germany of the catastrophic inflation of the early 1920s, when during 1923 prices increased on average by over 500 per cent per month, has been quite the opposite. The German government refuses to allow any form of inflation-adjusted accounting on the grounds that, by recognizing inflation in this way, society's will to resist inflation is weakened. The principles of inflation-adjusted accounting were first developed by the German academics, Eugen Schmalenbach and Fritz Schmidt; however they have not found favour in their own country. Although other developed countries, such as the USA and Britain, have also experienced quite high rates of inflation as recently as the 1970s, this has left no permanent impact on financial reporting practice.

2.6.4 Colonialism

The influence of colonialism is clearly demonstrated by the financial reporting systems of countries which are now independent but which formerly were part of the British or French empires. With very few exceptions, these countries adopt the rules and practices of their former colonial masters. Thus in West Africa the two neighbouring countries of Gambia and Senegal have quite different financial reporting systems: that of the Gambia based on British practice and that of Senegal on French practice. This is an example of what Parker (1994) terms the importing and exporting of accounting.

The close similarity between financial reporting practice in Britain and that in Canada, Australia, South Africa and New Zealand can be attributed to the latter four countries having been members of the former British Empire. However this reason cannot be advanced in the case of the USA, since financial reporting in both Britain and the USA developed in their present forms after the USA gained its independence in 1783. The similarity between British and American accounting must be attributable to the close economic ties between the two countries and particularly to the close relationship between the accounting professions which is further analysed in Chapter 5.

2.6.5 Accidents of history

One aspect of the influence of history has already been mentioned: the legacy of colonialism whereby countries tend to follow the law and practice of their former colonial masters. A more recent example of 'colonialism' is the introduction of the Plan Comptable (national chart of accounts) in France in 1943 (Standish, 1990). At that time, France was under German occupation, which clearly was a major factor in the French adopting what was essentially a German idea.

Another example of the accidents of history is the impact of the depression of 1929–33 on financial reporting in the USA. It was widely believed that a major cause of this depression was the misleading accounts published by American corporations in the boom years of the 1920s which tended to present an excessively optimistic picture of the enterprises' profits and prospects. In reaction, the American authorities introduced regulations aimed at preventing these practices, notably by refusing to permit revaluation of assets above historical cost. The similar rule in Germany can be traced to the financial crisis of 1873. In 1870 the law had been changed to make the formation of corporations (AGs) much easier. Between 1871 and 1873 the number of AGs increased fivefold. However many were formed by unscrupulous company promoters, who made themselves rich by issuing shares at inflated prices based on misleading accounts. Very many of these newly formed corporations failed, causing great financial loss to investors and creditors. As a reaction, the government introduced strict accounting rules based, as in the USA, on historical cost.

2.6.6 Other environmental factors

Other environmental factors that are mentioned by some authors are:

- The level of economic development
- The general level of education
- The state of technology

Although all are clearly relevant, it is rather difficult to assess their impact on a country's accounting system.

2.7 CULTURE

The consideration of culture has been left to last for two reasons: firstly culture is rather different from the other factors so far considered and secondly the analysis of culture has so far not led to any very clear conclusions.

Much of the recent study of the influence of culture on financial reporting is based on the work on Hofstede (1980) and accepts his definition of 'culture' as being the shared set of values and beliefs that distinguishes one human group from another. Hofstede defined four dimensions of culture which are widely accepted by researchers:

Individualism versus collectivism

Individualism stands for a preference for a loosely-knit social framework in society wherein individuals are supposed to take care of themselves and their immediate families only. Its opposite, collectivism, stands for a tightly-knit social framework in which individuals can expect their relatives, clan or other in-group to look after them in exchange for unquestioning loyalty.

Large versus small power distance

Power distance is the extent to which the members of a society accept that power in institutions is distributed unequally. People in large power distance societies accept a hierarchical order in which everybody has a place which needs no further justification. People in small power distance societies strive for power equalization and demand justification for power inequalities.

Strong versus weak uncertainty avoidance

Uncertainty avoidance is the degree to which members of a society feel uncomfortable with uncertainty and ambiguity. When this feeling is strong, it leads to beliefs promising certainty and to maintaining institutions protecting conformity. Strong uncertainty avoidance societies maintain rigid codes of belief and are intolerant towards deviant persons and ideas. Weak uncertainty avoidance societies maintain a more relaxed atmosphere in which practice counts more than principles and deviance is easily tolerated.

Masculinity versus femininity

Masculinity stands for a preference in society for achievement, heroism, assertiveness and material success. Its opposite, femininity, stands for a preference for relationships, modesty, caring for the weak and the quality of life.

It is important to understand that Hofstede was not making any value judgements as to whether any particular form of society was 'better' than another. He was simply observing. This is the reason for his using awkward terms like 'large power distance' rather than emotive terms like 'authoritarian'. However his use of the term 'masculinity' (which he thought to be value-neutral) infuriates modern feminists, which is an interesting example of changing social attitudes.

On the basis of a study of over 100 000 employees in some 40 countries of the large American multinational, IBM, Hofstede scored the countries according to these four dimensions. His scores and rankings for the more important countries are given in Exhibit 2.6. Note that in this exhibit, a high score refers to a high value for the first named characteristic. For example, the USA has the highest score in the row headed 'Individualism versus collectivism'; this means that this country is more individualistic than the others.

Exhibit 2.6 *Hofstede's scores and rankings for selected countries*

	France	Germany	Japan	Britain	USA
Individualism versus collectivism					
Score	71	67	46	89	91
Rank	10	15	22	3	1
Large power distance versus small power distance					
Score	68	35	54	35	40
Rank	15	43	33	43	38
Strong uncertainty avoidance versus weak uncertainty avoidance					
Score	86	65	92	35	46
Rank	12	29	7	47	43
Masculinity versus femininity					
Score	43	66	95	66	62
Rank	35	9	1	9	15

Source: Adapted from Hofstede (1980)

What has all this to do with accounting? Hofstede was not an accountant and his interest was in business organization in general. The application of his ideas to accounting was provided by Gray (1988). He proposed that national accounting systems could be characterized by their position in relation to four 'accounting values', which are the principal values of the accounting subculture:

■ professionalism versus statutory control
■ uniformity versus flexibility
■ conservatism versus optimism
■ secrecy versus transparency

The first two relate to the nature of the regulatory system; the third to measurement; and the fourth to disclosure. He proposed that each of these 'accounting values' were associated with three or four of Hofstede's cultural dimensions; his proposed relationships are presented in Exhibit 2.7.

Exhibit 2.7 *The relationship between Gray's 'accounting values'*
and Hofstede's cultural dimensions

	Professionalism	Uniformity	Conservatism	Secrecy
Individualism	+ +	− −	−	− −
Strong uncertainty avoidance	− −	+ +	+ +	+ +
Large power distance	−	+	none	+ +
Masculinity	none	none	−	+

The explanation of Exhibit 2.7 is as follows:

Professionalism versus statutory control

Financial reporting may be regulated in one of two contrasting ways which lie at opposite ends of a spectrum; at one extreme, practice is governed by a strong and independent accountancy profession which sets the standards for its members; at the other extreme, there is tight control by the government. Gray suggests that professionalism is strongly associated with individualism (hence the '+ +' in Exhibit 2.7) and with weak uncertainty avoidance (Exhibit 2.7 has '− −' because professionalism is negatively related with strong uncertainty avoidance). He further suggests that there is a weak relationship between professionalism and small power distance.

Uniformity versus flexibility

The two ends of the spectrum in this case are, at one extreme, all enterprises using the same rules for their accounts and, at the other extreme, the rules being adapted and modified to suit the circumstances of each individual enterprise. Gray suggested that uniformity would be strongly related to collectivism (the other extreme to individualism) and to uncertainty avoidance, with a weaker relationship with power distance.

Conservatism versus optimism

Conservatism is a well known characteristic of those accounting systems that strongly emphasise a prudent valuation of assets. Gray uses the term 'optimism' for the opposite of conservatism. This term is not ideal, for optimism is not a characteristic of any national accounting system; rather certain systems place less emphasis on conservatism than do others. Gray suggests that there is a strong association of conservatism with uncertainty avoidance; a conservative measure of assets provides some protection against the uncertainty of future events. He suggests that there are weaker relationships with collectivism and femininity.

Secrecy versus transparency

National accounting systems vary considerably with regard to the amount of information disclosed by enterprises. Gray suggests that secrecy is strongly associated with power distance (to preserve the position of those in power), with uncertainty avoidance (to restrict information disclosures so as to avoid conflict and to preserve security), and with collectivism (to keep information within the clan); but only weakly related with masculinity.[8]

Gray did not attempt to verify his theory by an empirical study. This has been subsequently attempted by a number of academics; their conclusions are examined in the next section.

2.8 SYNTHESIS: THE ANGLO SAXONS VERSUS THE REST OF THE WORLD

Exhibit 2.8 brings together certain salient facts relating to the more important factors that have been discussed in the previous sections for the selected five countries. On the basis of these data, it would seem that the five countries can be divided into two groups:

(a) **The Anglo-Saxon countries:**[9] This term is commonly applied to the USA, Britain and other developed English-speaking countries (notably Canada and Australia). These countries are characterized by a legal system based on Common Law, a modest influence of taxation on financial reporting, the stock market being an important element of the corporate financing system and a strong accountancy profession.

(b) **The Rest**, that is Japan, France and Germany, which are characterized as having a legal system based on Roman Law, a strong influence of taxation on financial reporting, a less important capital market and a weak accountancy profession.

Is there a similar division in relation to the accounting systems of the countries in the two groups? If so, this would provide persuasive evidence that the factors mentioned in Exhibit 2.8 have a significant influence on financial reporting. This question was researched by Doupnik and Salter (1995). They collected information on a hundred accountancy practices (45 relating to measurement and 55 relating to disclosure) in the form of the percentage of enterprises in each country that followed a particular practice. In all they covered 50 countries including the five

Exhibit 2.8 *Synthesis of the major influences on financial reporting*

	USA	Britain	Japan	Germany	France
Legal system	Common Law	Common Law	Roman Law	Roman Law	Roman Law
Influence of tax	Relatively weak	Weak	Relatively strong	Relatively strong	Relatively strong
Stock market capitalization[a]	224%	248%	88%	61%	98%
Size of accountancy profession[b]	1496	3540	98	93	235

Notes

[a] As a percentage of GDP
[b] Accountants per million population

countries of the Pentad. They then divided the 50 countries into two groups on the basis of their data on accounting practices, using the statistical technique of cluster analysis, which creates groups of objects that have similar characteristics according to the input data. It is important to appreciate that this was a purely mathematical operation involving no judgement on the part of the researchers. The two groups that came out of this analysis were:

(a) **Group A1.** This is an Anglo-Saxon group of 26 countries including the USA, Britain, 16 countries of the former British Empire, the Netherlands and five countries that all have more or less close connections with the three aforementioned countries. This may reasonably be termed an 'Anglo-Saxon' group although the Netherlands would probably be surprised to find itself so described.

(b) **Group A2**, being the rest of the world, including Japan and all the major countries of Continental Europe.

Hence the division of the world into two groups according to the influential factors is mirrored by this statistical analysis of financial reporting practice. This is strong evidence that the factors listed in Exhibit 2.8 do, in fact, influence financial reporting.

Doupnik and Salter then, using cluster analysis, further divided the 50 countries into more than two groups. They found that divisions into six groups and subsequently into nine groups were statistically significant. Exhibit 2.9 presents in diagrammatic form the groups that emerged from the cluster analysis. The composition of these groups is largely consistent with common sense, in that most groups have an internal cohesion; they are made up mostly of countries with similar characteristics.

Exhibit 2.9 may be analysed as follows (the identifying letters and numbers are those used by Doupnik and Salter; the group titles are the invention of the authors):

(a) Subdivisions of the Anglo-Saxon group:

    C1: USA subgroup consisting of the USA, Canada, Bermuda and Israel

    C2: British subgroup consisting of Britain, 16 countries of the former British Empire, the Netherlands and four other countries

(b) Subdivisions of the Rest of the World:

    B2: Latin America: Argentina, Brazil. Chile and Mexico with Costa Rica split off at the nine cluster level

    C5: 'Mainstream Europe': France, Italy, Spain, Portugal, Denmark and Norway, plus Korea and Columbia

    C6: 'Rag bag': A very diverse group made up of Belgium, Panama, two African and three Asian countries

    B4: Finland and Sweden

    B5: Germany

    B6: Japan

To gain an idea of the qualitative characteristics of the financial reporting practice of the countries in these groups, Doupnik and Salter calculated average scores for disclosure and measurement for each group: a high score for disclosure meant a high level of disclosure and a high score for measurement indicated relatively complex, less conservative measurement practices. The position of the various groups according to their disclosure and measurement scores are presented in Exhibit 2.10.

The significance of their research may be summarized as follows:

(a) It provides objective evidence to support the supposition of many academics that, with regard to financial reporting, the world may be divided into two groups: the Anglo-Saxons and the Rest.

(b) Financial reporting in the Anglo-Saxon countries may be characterized as providing greater disclosure and using less conservative measurement methods, compared with the Rest. This is demonstrated in Exhibit 2.10 by the point for group A1 (the Anglo-Saxons) being significantly above and to the right of point A2.

(c) Within the Anglo-Saxons, there is a significant difference between the USA and Britain, with the USA having significantly more disclosure and being significantly less conservative than Britain. This is demonstrated by the point for group C1 (the USA subgroup) being above and to the right of point C2 (the British subgroup)

(d) Within the Rest of the World group, financial reporting practice in two of the selected countries (Germany and Japan) is significantly

Exhibit 2.9 *Doupnik and Salter's classification of national accounting systems*

Two cluster level

Six cluster level

Nine cluster level

A1 Anglo-Saxons

A2 Rest of the World

| **C1**
USA group

USA
Canada
Bermuda
Israel | **C2**
British group

Australia
New Zealand
14 members of the
former British Empire
Netherlands
NL Antilles
Luxembourg
Philippines
Taiwan |

B2
Latin
America

B4
Finland
Sweden

B5
Germany

B6
Japan

B3
Rest

C3
Costa Rica

C4
Mainstream
Latin
America
Argentina
Brazil
Chile
Mexico

C5
Mainstream
Europe
France
Italy
Spain
Portugal
Denmark
Norway
Korea
Columbia

C6
'Rag bag'
Belgium
Egypt
Liberia
UAE
Saudi Arabia
Thailand
Panama

60

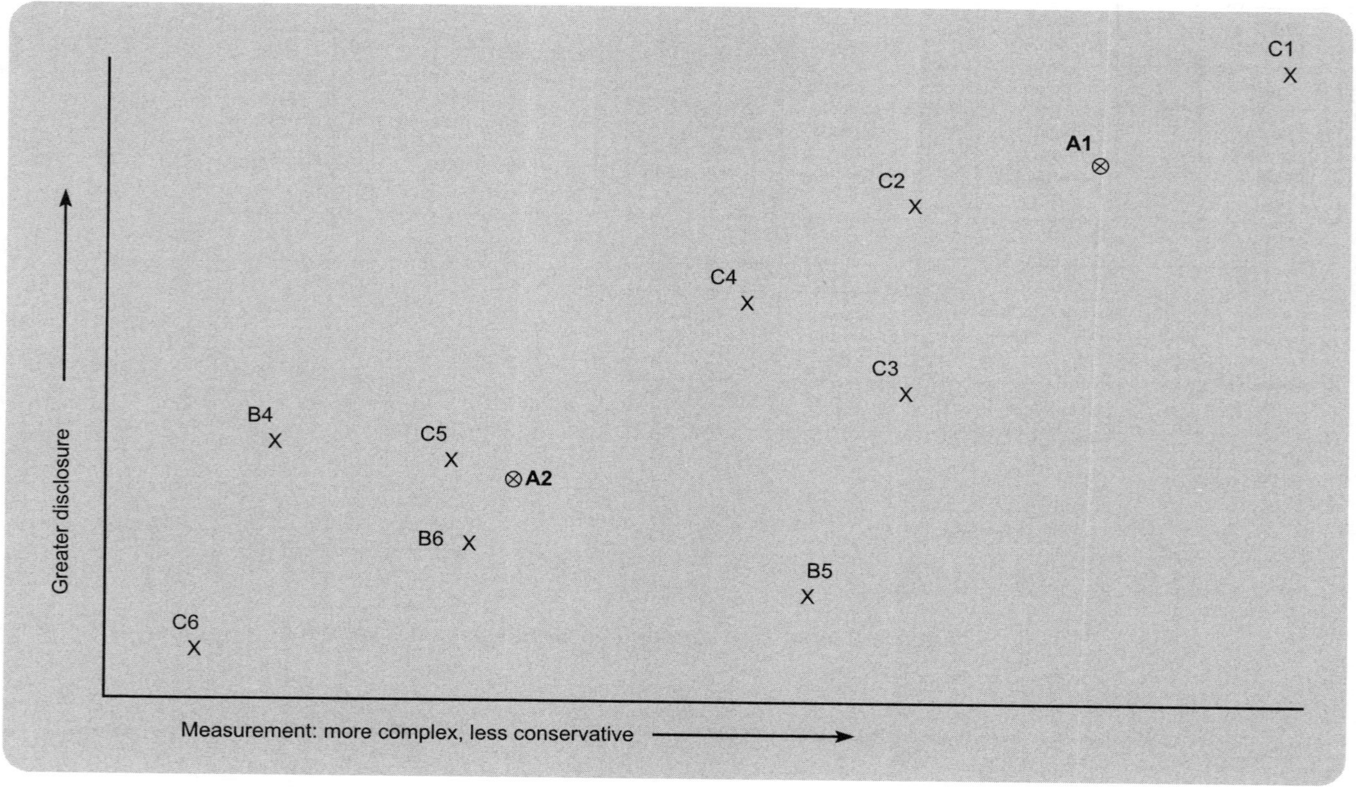

Exhibit 2.10   The position of the clusters with regard to disclosure and measurement

different from that of the other countries in the group. The statistical analysis separates both countries from the other countries and from each other. Exhibit 2.10 demonstrates that practice in Germany (point B5) is significantly different from that in the group as a whole (particularly in relation to measurement), whereas practice in Japan (point B6) and in France (part of group C5) is close to the average of the group.

Doupnik and Salter then went on to consider to what extent the division of the world into these groups could be explained by the various institutional, environmental and cultural factors discussed earlier in this chapter. They considered all four of Hofstede's cultural dimensions, three institutional factors (legal system, corporate financing system and taxation, but not the accountancy profession) and three environmental factors (level of economic development, educational level and inflation). Their findings were:

(a) **The two-group division.** This division could be largely explained, in order of significance, by:

   (i) The legal system. Most countries in the Anglo-Saxon group had a Common Law system and most countries in the other group had a code system. However the correlation was not 100 per cent; for example the Netherlands (a member of the Anglo-Saxon group) has a codified legal system.

   (ii) The importance of the stock market. Market capitalization as a percentage of GDP is significantly higher in the Anglo-Saxon group.

   (iii) The cultural trait of uncertainty avoidance as measured by Hofstede. The members of the Anglo-Saxon group have lower scores for this cultural dimension.

(b) **The more detailed divisions.** The three factors that explained the two-group division were also the most significant. Other factors explained the separation of particular countries. Hence the separation of Japan from the rest of group A2 is largely explained by its relatively more important capital market and its high score for the cultural dimension of masculinity. The separation of the Latin American countries (group C4) is largely explained by their higher levels of inflation. However the analysis was not helpful in explaining some of the groups, notably that of Germany.

Doupnik and Salter conclude that institutional factors, notably the legal system and the corporate finance system, are the principal explanation for differences in national accounting systems. However cultural factors, notably uncertainty avoidance and, to a lesser extent, masculinity are also important. They admit that their analysis did not satisfactorily explain the complete range of international accounting diversity. The authors are in general agreement with the analysis of Doupnik and Salter. They would however give greater weight to the accountancy profession (which was not included in the analysis) and to taxation.[10]

2.9 CONCLUSIONS

The analysis in this chapter demonstrates clearly that a country's accounting system is a product of its institutional framework, its social and economic environment and its culture. Since the mix of these factors differs from country to country, each country's accounting system is different. In the following chapters these differences are analysed in detail for the five countries of the Pentad.

SUMMARY

The factors that shape a country's financial reporting were analysed and classified in three broad categories; institutions, the environment and culture. The most important institutional factor is the state; the state has both a strong interest in financial reporting (for reasons that were explained) and the capability (through laws) of ensuring that its demands are met. The influence of the corporate financing system on financial reporting was analysed, distinguishing between financing through the capital market and the direct provision of finance. The extent to which enterprises in different countries relied on these two sources of finance was considered. It was concluded that, where an enterprise's shares were listed on a stock exchange, this had a major impact on its financial reporting. The accountancy profession was considered with reference to the differences between countries in the size and influence of the accountancy profession. A number of environmental factors were examined: the enterprise's employees, the general public, accounting theorists, colonialism and accidents of history. The influence of culture was examined, with reference to Gray's application to accounting of Hofstede's general theories. Finally the empirical research of Doupnik and Salter was examined and it was concluded that it confirmed the importance of many of the factors considered in this chapter.

Review questions

1. What are the three broad categories of factors that shape a country's financial reporting?

2. For what reasons does the state have a considerable interest in the financial reporting of enterprises even in democratic countries?

3. What are the principal differences between Roman Law and Common Law? What are the principal Common Law countries?

4. What are the advantages of having the calculation of profit for tax purposes the same as that for financial reporting purposes? What are the disadvantages?

5. What countries have the highest value for the market capitalization of domestic enterprises in absolute and relative terms?

6. In what ways does the fact that a corporation's shares are listed on a stock exchange influence its financial reporting?

7. Why is it considered likely that an enterprise's financial statements are a more important source of information for a minority shareholder than they are to a bank that lent the enterprise money?

8. Which countries have the largest accountancy profession in absolute and relative terms?

9. In which countries does the accountancy profession have the greatest influence on financial reporting and for what reasons?

10. Why may the employees of an enterprise be expected to be interested in its financial statements?

11. For what reasons may persons who have no business connection with an enterprise (as shareholder, lender, supplier, employee or customer) still demand information about the enterprise's activities?

12. Give examples of countries that have imported their financial reporting rules from another country.

13. What is the meaning of the term 'culture' as used in this chapter?

14. Explain the relationship between Hofstede's four cultural dimensions and Gray's accounting values.

Review questions (cont'd)

15. In what way did the research of Doupnik and Salter confirm that the major countries may be classified into two broad groups (the 'Anglo-Saxons' and the 'Rest') according to their financial reporting practice?

16. To what extent did Doupnik and Salter confirm the relevance of Hofstede's analysis of culture?

Notes

1. See Schweikart (1985).
2. The shares of foreign enterprises have been excluded because Exhibit 2.4 seeks to demonstrate the importance of the stock exchange as a source of finance in the local economy. Furthermore, since foreign enterprises are almost invariably also listed in their home country, to include them would involve double counting.
3. It is generally considered that the stock exchange is not an economic source of finance for corporations with a capital of less than about €10mn.
4. The term 'men' is completely correct for nineteenth-century Britain. The principal British accountancy body, the ICAEW, did not admit its first woman member until 1919. However times are changing and, in 1999, this body for the first time elected a woman as president.
5. The world's first professional accountancy association was probably the Collegio dei Rasonati which was founded in Venice in 1581. However this body disappeared with the dissolution of the Venetian Republic in 1797. Hence the Scots claim that theirs is the most senior association that is still in existence. However Zambon (2001) claims that the present Italian professional body, the Collegio dei Ragionieri (listed in Exhibit 2.5 as having been founded in 1906), can trace its origins to at least 1805. Perhaps the dispute between the Scots and the Italians on this matter is not yet definitively settled.
6. For an explanation of the position in Belgium, see Chapter 8 of Lefebvre and Flower (1994).
7. For an appreciation of the contribution of Dicksee and de Paula, see Kitchen and Parker (1980).
8. The text of Gray's article in *Abacus* (1988) states that secrecy is negatively related to masculinity. However this is clearly a printing mistake.
9. The words 'Anglo' and 'Saxon' are derived from the names of two Germanic tribes, the Angles and the Saxons, who in the Fifth Century invaded the British Isles, driving out the previous inhabitants, the Britons, who fled to the 'Celtic fringes' (Wales, Scotland and Ireland). The Angles brought with them their own language which became known as English and changed the name of the country to England. Over a thousand years later a further wave of migration,

this time from the British Isles, spread the English language and English culture all around the globe, but particularly to North America. Hence the term 'Anglo-Saxon' as used today refers, not to Germany (where the Angles and Saxons have left their traces in the two place names: Angeln, a district in southern Schleswig Holstein, and Saxony, a federal state in the eastern part of the country), but to England (and the other countries with which England is united in the United Kingdom: Scotland, Wales and Northern Ireland) and those other countries that have adopted the English language and to a greater or lesser extent English culture. Of these, by far the most important is the USA; but other important countries of the 'Anglo-Saxon' group are Canada, Australia and New Zealand.

10. In the authors' opinion the reason why the Doupnik and Salter analysis did not show taxation to be a significant explanatory factor was that they input the wrong data. They used the marginal rate of tax, whereas they should have input a variable that indicated the extent to which a country's financial reporting was tax-driven, for example the proportion of the items in the financial statements that are based on the tax computation.

References

Choi, F and Mueller, G *International Accounting*, Prentice-Hall, Englewood Cliffs (1992).

Doupnik, T and Salter S 'External environment, culture and accounting practice', *International Journal of Accounting*, **30**(3) (1995), pp. 189–207.

Flower, J 'Three "Accounting Heroes" of Continental Europe', *Essays in Accounting Thought*, I Lapsley (ed.), ICAS, Edinburgh (1996), p. 201.

Gray, SJ 'Towards a theory of cultural influence on the development of accounting systems internationally', *Abacus* (March 1988), pp. 1–15.

Hofstede, G *Culture's Consequences: international differences in work-related values*, Sage, London (1980).

Hopwood, A 'The future of harmonization in the Community', *European Accounting* (1991), pp. 12–21.

Kitchen, J and Parker, RH *Accounting Thought and Education: six English pioneers*, ICAEW, London (1980).

Lefebvre, C and Flower, J *European Financial Reporting: Belgium*, Routledge, London (1994).

Nobes, C 'Causes of international differences', *Comparative International Accounting*, C Nobes and R Parker (eds), Prentice Hall, London (2000), Ch. 2.

Parker, RH 'Importing and exporting accounting: the British experience', *Accounting History: some British contributions*, RH Parker and BS Yamey (eds), Clarendon Press, Oxford (1994).

Standish, P 'Origins of the Plan Comptable Général: a study in cultural intrusion and reaction', *Accounting and Business Research*, **20**(4) (1990), pp. 337–51.

Schweikart, J 'Contingency theory as a framework for research in international accounting', *International Journal of Accounting* (1985).

Zambon, S 'Italy', *European Accounting Guide*, D Alexander and S Archer (eds), Aspen, Gaithersburg (2001).

Further reading

For a discussion on the influence of culture on financial reporting see Gray (1988).

Regulation

In Chapter 1 the concept of a country's accounting system was introduced, being defined as the set of rules that governs the practice of financial reporting in that country. In financial reporting there are many different types of rules and they cover a very wide spectrum, ranging from, at one extreme, laws which must be obeyed under sanction of penalties imposed by the state, through accounting standards, which, according to the country, may or may not possess the authority of law, to, at the other extreme, accounting conventions which have no legal standing but which, nevertheless, accountants generally follow. However all these rules, irrespective of their authority, are significant for an understanding of financial reporting practice in a country, that is for the analysis of the behaviour of accountants when they prepare financial statements. Much of this book is given over to an analysis of these rules, with this chapter serving as a general introduction. However, before commencing this task it is appropriate to ask the fundamental question: 'why, in financial reporting, are rules necessary?'

3.1 WHY ARE RULES NECESSARY?

3.1.1 Preparers versus users

In financial reporting, the need for rules arises from a fundamental conflict between preparers and users, between the accountants who prepare the financial statements and the users who refer to these statements in order to obtain information about the enterprise. This opposition between preparers and users can be traced to the separation of ownership from control which is a characteristic of larger enterprises that require more capital than can be provided by the owner-manager. These enterprises are generally organized in the form of corporations which draw their capital from a large number of shareholders. It is impractical for all these providers of finance to be involved in the management of the corporation, hence the shareholders are obliged to delegate the running of the enterprise to one or more managers, whose stake in the capital of the corporation may be relatively small. Commonly, as part of the arrangement, the managers are required to report periodically to the providers of finance on how they have fulfilled their delegated task; the principal means of reporting are the financial statements. As a result of this development, the major industrial and commercial corporations are now controlled by professional managers over whom the shareholders, the formal owners of the corporation, have only tenuous and, at best, sporadic control.

3.1.2 The reluctance of preparers

With the separation of control from ownership, there is a danger that the managers will take decisions that are not in the best interests of the shareholders, such as to pay themselves excessive salaries or, more subtly, to invest in projects that increase their power and status ('empire building') but which yield little in the way of profit for the shareholders. More significantly, the managers, who control the form and content of the financial statements issued by the corporation, will make sure that these portray a picture that is favourable to themselves; for example, they will not provide full and frank information on investment projects that have failed – this is 'bad news' which must be kept from the shareholders. In fact there is no incentive for managers to give any meaningful information at all in the financial statements. This is because 'knowledge is power'; a person who possesses information has a certain power which is greatly diminished if the information is shared with other people. In particular managers will be most reluctant to disclose voluntarily any information that may be used by the shareholders and other providers of finance to monitor and assess the managers' performance. The managers will make sure that the financial statements are bland and uninformative, although no doubt with the aid of much creative and artistic skill, they will succeed in painting a very rosy picture of the corporation. They will certainly not make a serious effort to meet the needs of the users.

3.1.3 The information needs of users

What are the needs of the users of financial statements? Although it is not impossible that certain people may value financial statements for their intrinsic qualities, such as their effectiveness as a fly swotter, it is generally agreed that users read financial statements to obtain information and that they need this information not because it is valuable in itself but because it helps them make better decisions. Thus the principal objective of financial reporting is to provide information that is valuable to users. So in deciding what the financial statements should contain, the information needs of the users of financial statements must be considered. These needs may

Exhibit 3.1 *The users of financial statements*

User group	Reason for needing information	Possible decisions
Shareholders		
Stewardship function	Monitor performance of managers	Dismiss managers
Investment function	Valuation of shares	Sell/buy/hold
Providers of finance (banks etc.)	Assess enterprise's financial strength and stability	Extend or refuse credit
Workers		
Short term	Assess the enterprise's ability to pay wages	Strike for higher wages
Long term	Assess future employment prospects	Seek another job
Customers	Assess the enterprise's future stability	Agree long-term contract
Suppliers	Assess the enterprise's financial strength	Extend credit
Government		
Taxation	Compute taxable income	Demand payment of taxes
Management of the economy	Assess economic performance	Make new laws
The general public	Assess the corporation's contribution to the general welfare	Lobby the corporation or the government
The enterprise itself (the preparer)		
Distribution	Calculate distributable income	Recommend dividend
Taxation	Calculate taxable income	Pay taxes

be assessed by analysing the decisions that users have to make for which the information contained in financial statements may prove helpful.

The information needs of the users of financial statements are summarized in Exhibit 3.1, which distinguishes between the following broad user groups:

The shareholders

These are formally the owners of the enterprise and, in all countries, the enterprise is legally obliged to report to them. Shareholders require information about the enterprise for two rather different reasons:

(a) **To monitor the performance of the enterprise's management with a view to intervening if this performance is not satisfactory.** This relates to the stewardship function of accounts; the enterprise's management has to report to the shareholders on its stewardship of the resources with which it has been entrusted. It is important to note that, even with stewardship, the individual shareholder needs information in order to assist her in making decisions; in this case the decision on whether or not to vote for dismissal of the manager. Information is not an end in itself but a means to an end. Of course the shareholder may decide to take no action and to leave the present management in place; but a decision to do nothing is nonetheless a decision.

(b) **To make investment decisions – whether to sell their shares or alternatively buy more shares.** Again the shareholder's decision may be to do nothing: to maintain her existing holding. However ideally a decision to hold on to the shares should be a deliberate decision taken after comparing alternative investment opportunities. The persons interested in assessing the value of the enterprise's shares as an investment include not only the enterprise's shareholders but also those who are considering becoming shareholders, that is potential investors. The principle that the user group should be extended to cover possible future members of the group also applies to the other categories of users which will now be considered.

Other providers of finance

In addition to the shareholders, there are other providers of finance to the enterprise, such as banks. In contrast to shareholders they are not the owners of enterprise, but rather 'outsiders' whose rights are determined not by the enterprise's constitution but by their contract with the enterprise. However, their information needs are similar to those of shareholders. They need to assess the ability of the enterprise to meet its commitments under the loan contract – to make periodic interest payments and to repay the loan at the due date. They need to make this assessment both before making the loan (at the stage that they are only a potential provider of finance) and during the currency of the loan. It is common for the loan contract to provide that the lender has the right to intervene (for example, to appoint a receiver to manage the enterprise), if the financial statements indicate that the lender's investment is at risk (for example, that the enterprise's debt/equity ratio has risen to dangerous levels).

Workers

The enterprise's employees are an important and numerous user group. They need information on a number of matters relating to their employment relationship with the enterprise, for example on the enterprise's ability to pay higher wages. Before deciding on whether to press their case for a wage increase, say by going on strike, the workers should consider whether the enterprise has the capacity to pay higher wages; the financial statements should provide useful information on this matter. In practice, the analysis of the financial statements is generally made not by the workers themselves but by their representatives, the trade unions. Hence the user group needs to be extended to include all those who represent and advise the persons who are directly interested in the enterprise. This principle applies generally to all categories of users: hence the shareholder group should be extended to include stockbrokers and financial journalists, who advise shareholders and potential shareholders on their investments.

The individual worker should, in principle, examine the financial statements so as to assess the enterprise's capability to offer secure and rewarding employment over the longer term. He should make this analysis both before accepting employment and afterwards (to assess whether it is advisable to seek a better job elsewhere). However in practice only a few employees look at the financial statements as a means of assessing their employment prospects. Generally these are persons whose career prospects are closely tied to the enterprise's fortunes, such as managers and highly specialized employees.

Customers

In most cases the enterprise's customers are not particularly concerned about its financial strength and stability as, if the enterprise were to fail, they could go elsewhere. However there are exceptions. For example a customer may be considering concluding a long-term contract which would make it dependent on the enterprise for the supply of essential materials and components.

Suppliers

It is common for suppliers not to demand immediate payment for goods and services supplied to the enterprise. In that case, the suppliers are in effect making short-term loans to the enterprise and they need information about the enterprise's ability to repay the loan. They need this information both before extending credit and in deciding whether to cut off future supplies when the enterprise is slow in paying its debts. Where the supplying enterprise is considering entering into a long-term contract, which could involve it in significant capital expenditure, it is in the same position as customers and has the same need for information about its counterpart's long-term financial strength and stability.

The government

The government needs information about the enterprise to assist it in two important areas.

(a) **Taxation.** Most governments levy a number of taxes on the enterprise: on its activities (sales taxes), on its wealth (property taxes) and on its income (profit taxes). The financial statements provide the information that the government requires in order to compute how much the enterprise should pay. The function of the financial statements in providing the basis for taxation is of vital importance for both the government and the enterprise: for the government to facilitate the collection of its revenues, and, for the enterprise, because it has an immediate and concrete impact on its cash outflows.

(b) **Management of the economy.** Governments need to monitor the performance of enterprises as part of their general function of managing the economy. For example, if the economy is 'overheating' with a consequent danger of inflation, the government can seek to remove the excess demand by taking countermeasures such as increasing taxes or raising interest rates. The financial statements of enterprises in general provide information on the state of the economy. The following items in the accounts are of particular interest to government economists: profits (if too high or increasing rapidly, this may be evidence of 'overheating'), inventories (if too low or decreasing, this is further evidence of excess demand), and capital expenditure (if too low, insufficient is being set aside for the future and it may be advisable for the government to take measures to stimulate investment, for example by increasing fiscal incentives).

The general public

The general public has an interest in the performance of enterprises. It wants information on such matters as their impact on the environment (air and water pollution), the dangers associated with their products (for example, cigarettes) or processes (nuclear power stations), and their business practices (for example, if they discriminate against certain social groups). The people who are affected by the enterprise's activities can range from the local community (for example, in the case of noise pollution) to the whole world (where the enterprise's factory is emitting large quantities of carbon dioxide and other gases that lead to global warming). As with all users, they need information in order to decide whether or not to take some action – in this case the action could be to put pressure on the enterprise with the aim of persuading it to change its policy or to lobby the government to change the law.

The enterprise itself

The enterprise itself may be considered to be a user of the financial statements that it prepares and makes available to the other users. The amount of profit that the enterprise reports may have a direct impact on the amount of taxes that it will pay to the government and on the amount of dividend that it will pay to its shareholders: in effect the enterprise's decision on these two important matters is largely conditioned by the figures contained in its financial statements. It should be noted that this use by the enterprise's management of the published financial statements is quite different from its use of the management accounts.

3.1.4 The use of accounting numbers in contracts

It is common in certain countries for numbers or ratios that are derived from the financial statements to be included in the terms of contracts made by the enterprise. Examples are:

(a) **Debt covenants:** Bodies such as banks that lend money to the enterprise often seek to protect their investment by including in the loan contract terms (known as covenants) that limit the enterprise's freedom of action in the event of a deterioration in its financial position. For example, the lender may be given the right to appoint a receiver to manage the enterprise or the enterprise may be required to repay the loan immediately. In order to ensure legal certainty, the contract specifies when these clauses should come into effect; typically the event is defined in terms of numbers contained in the enterprise's financial statements, for example when the enterprise's liabilities exceed its equity or when the debt/equity ratio exceeds a specified value.

(b) **The employment contracts of managers:** Frequently the employment contracts of the enterprise's managers and senior staff include
   a provision that the employee is entitled to a bonus calculated as a
   specified function of the enterprise's profit as reported in its income
   statement.

In such cases, it is theoretically possible for the contract to include
details of how the accounting numbers are to be calculated. However
this is rarely done, given the complexity of the problem. The common
position is that reference is made to the enterprise's financial statements.
However it is very clear that, in these circumstances, enterprise's management should not be allowed complete freedom in deciding on the
principles to be used in the preparation of these financial statements.

3.1.5 The need for rules

There is general agreement that the managers of enterprises need to be
induced by outside forces to produce financial statements that provide
the information demanded by users and that provide an objective basis
for contracts with the enterprise. There is a school of thought which
holds that preparers will be motivated by market forces to provide voluntarily all the information that users demand, for otherwise the users
would withhold the resources that the enterprise needs to prosper, notably
funds provided by shareholders and other suppliers of finance. However
most commentators do not believe that this in fact happens. This view
is well expressed by Solomons (1983, p. 107):

> The market cannot be depended upon to discipline promptly enter-
> prises that are left free to choose what to report and how to report to
> their investors and creditors. Even if good accounting can be relied
> upon to drive out bad in the long run, too much damage may be
> inflicted in the short run to make freedom from regulation in this
> field an acceptable policy.

Given this failure of the market, there is no force that inhibits corporate management from providing only that information which it considers
in its interest to supply. In this situation enterprises must be compelled
to provide appropriate information by the imposition of rules by outsiders.
The position has been well captured by Burggraaff who, in a very readable paper (Burggraaff, 1983), states that the major function of rules is
'to reduce the freedom of preparers, in order to satisfy some of the demands of the users'.

However, although most commentators accept that rules are necessary,
they also regret this necessity. They recognize the following limitations
of any system of imposed rules:

(a) **The imposed rules should be the minimum that are required to counteract the alleged imperfections of the market.** There are strong reasons for believing that the allocation of resources achieved through market forces is the best for society as a whole and that there is a danger that any interference with the market may lead to a reduction in the general welfare. Hence any imposed rules must be clearly directed towards and limited to the correction of proved market failures.

(b) **The costs of regulation should always be borne in mind.** Regulation, like any other economic activity, is only worthwhile if its benefits exceed its costs. Some of the costs are obvious, such as those incurred by enterprises in maintaining appropriate accounting systems. However the less obvious, indirect costs are probably much more significant. One such indirect cost has already been mentioned: the danger of misallocation of resources through interference with the market.

(c) **Even if the market is not completely effective** as a means of disciplining enterprises, this does not mean that the alternative, say government regulation, will be any more efficient. Against 'market failure', there should always be set the possibility of 'government failure'.

(d) **Any system of imposed rules leads to the danger that innovation and progress will be stifled.** Enterprises will be restrained from experimenting in new forms and methods of financial reporting. One may legitimately doubt that the rules imposed by authority are the very best conceivable. The dangers have been well expressed by Baxter, who in a cogent article (Baxter 1981) sets out the arguments for and against rules, coming out finally strongly against. He is highly sceptical of man-made rules: 'Only god-like creatures know where the truth lies. It follows that ex cathedra pronouncements by human authority are tendentious and inevitably will sometimes be wrong. The most eminent authorities erred persistently on, for instance, the shape of the earth, the origins of life, and the circulation of the blood . . . We cannot with complete confidence expect infallibility in the future.' He cites two famous historical figures in support: Sir Francis Bacon, the philosopher statesman of Elizabethan England, 'Truth is the daughter, not of Authority, but of Time' and Isambard Kingdom Brunel, the nineteenth-century engineer and entrepreneur, 'rules will embarrass and shackle the progress of improvement tomorrow by recording and registering as law the prejudices and errors of today'. Accountants should never accept that their principal function is to apply the rules set by authority; they should always treat these rules with scepticism and be prepared to exercise their own intelligence and judgement. Above all they should not be beguiled by an apparently comprehensive and formidable structure of laws and rules into giving up exercising their intelligence and judgement.

The dangers and drawbacks of rules should always be kept in mind. However, for the reasons given earlier, it is generally accepted that in financial reporting some imposed rules are a regrettable necessity.

3.2 THE ROLE OF THE GOVERNMENT

Since the market cannot assure the provision of the information, both in quantity and in quality, that is demanded of enterprises by important groups in society, the government, at the instigation of these groups, is obliged to intervene. This result is made all the more inevitable in that the government itself is an important user of information. Hence governments enact laws that regulate financial reporting. At the heart of every regulatory system will be found laws.

3.2.1 The politics of law-making

The making of financial reporting law by the legislature is essentially a political process, for two reasons:

(a) The actual rules that are laid down will influence the distribution of wealth between social groups. For example, the rules may be changed to allow enterprises to capitalize research and development expenditure; this change in the rules would probably lead to enterprises reporting higher profits, at least initially, which would benefit shareholders (who may expect higher dividends), managers (who may receive larger bonuses based on reported profits) and the state, as tax collector (which may expect to receive more taxes computed on the basis of reported profits). Also manufacturers of research equipment and research departments of universities may be expected to benefit, as enterprises are no longer deterred from undertaking research by its effect on reported profits. But the change is very likely to be to the detriment of other groups, such as lenders, creditors and workers, who would all suffer in that cash would have left the company (in the payment of dividends, bonuses and tax) thus diminishing the resources at the company's disposal and rendering its financial and economic future somewhat less secure. This subject is dealt with in the literature on 'the economic consequences of financial reporting', which is well summarized in Blake (1992).

(b) The balancing of the interests of the different social groups in setting the rules involves the normal political processes of consultation, lobbying, debate, bargaining and, in the end, voting. The enactment of laws by the legislature after the customary political process, is the normal way in which a democratic society settles questions involving the distribution of wealth among its members.

3.2.2 The advantages of law

The setting of the rules of financial reporting by law has a number of advantages which have been well analyzed by Bromwich (1992, pp. 256–7), who sets out two incontrovertible advantages:

■ The legitimacy and social acceptance of the rules are assured, at least when they have been set by a democratically-elected legislature

■ Compliance with the rules may be enforced through society's usual procedures, the ultimate sanction being penalties imposed by the courts

Bromwich also claims that governments, by using their taxation and subsidy powers, may be able to mitigate the undesirable side effects of an accounting rule that, in other respects, is socially desirable. However this seems rather improbable, as it presupposes a fundamental change in government behaviour. Normally governments set the rules of financial reporting to achieve tax objectives, not vice versa.

3.2.3 The need for additional rules

The advantages of law are clear cut. However, generally the legislator prefers to limit the role of law to the laying down of the objectives and the more important principles of financial reporting and to leave the development of the detailed rules to other bodies. There are a number of good reasons for such behaviour which have been analysed exhaustively by Baldwin and McCrudden (1987). They may be summarized as follows:

(a) **Detail:** Financial reporting is simply too detailed for every aspect of it to be covered in the law.

(b) **Priorities:** Compared with all the other matters that compete for the legislature's time and attention, financial reporting is rarely the most important or the most urgent. Hence there is a danger that the legislature will neglect the subject and that the necessary laws will be enacted only after considerable delays, so that, by the time they come into force, they are already out of date. Law is rarely an effective way of dealing with urgent problems or with new developments in financial reporting. Hence it is reasonable for the legislator to leave these tasks to other bodies, which may be expected to act with greater expedition and efficiency.

(c) **Technical complexity:** Much of financial reporting concerns highly technical matters. It is likely that the typical member of the legislature will not be well informed on these matters and will not be unhappy to pass the responsibility to another body, which, possessing the necessary technical competence, is likely to do a far better job. The legislator is probably glad to be relieved of an uncongenial and boring task.

(d) **Cost:** Given the low priority that it gives to financial reporting, the state may decide that it is not economic to allocate resources to the development of detailed rules, particularly as it would be costly to acquire or hire the necessary technical expertise.

(e) **More democratic:** Given the typical legislator's lack of interest and expertise in financial reporting, there is a danger that, if the law purports to regulate financial reporting in detail, the source of its provisions will be some anonymous civil servant and not the democratically-elected representatives of the people. Therefore it may be more democratic to leave the setting of the detailed rules to a body that either better represents the people concerned or has the time and resources to consult them fully. This may lead to more open and better informed rule-making.

(f) **Political considerations:** The decision not to legislate may be influenced by political considerations. The government may decide that a particular issue is so controversial and divisive that whatever decision it takes it will be criticized. It prefers not to be involved and is very happy to 'pass the buck' to some other body. This has three advantages: it relieves the government of the problem, it gives the impression that the problem is being tackled and it furnishes a perfect scapegoat when the problem is not solved. It also deflects the activities of lobbyists and pressure groups which the government may find embarrassing.

(g) **Continuity:** Since the political composition of the legislature may change quite frequently and since it only legislates on financial reporting sporadically, there is a danger that the laws that it enacts will be inconsistent and lack any basic principles. It is possible that the rules developed by other bodies may be more consistent, since their composition may be more stable and they will give sustained attention to their task.

3.3 THE HIERARCHY OF RULES

For all the reasons given in the previous section, it is very common that the laws enacted by the legislator tend to be limited to laying down the objectives and the more important principles of financial reporting. The legislature provides the framework and leaves it to other bodies to fill in the detail. Hence, in the regulatory system, the law is supplemented by

Exhibit 3.2 *The hierarchy of rules*

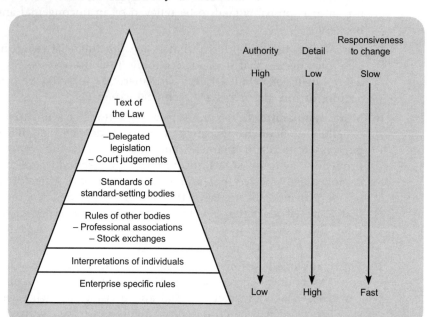

a whole range of additional rules, set by other bodies. The set of rules may be considered as a hierarchy. The principal elements of this hierarchy are presented in Exhibit 3.2, which, following Ordelheide (1999), shows the hierarchy in the form of a pyramid.

Ordelheide makes three general remarks about the hierarchy of rules. They are illustrated by the vertical lines in Exhibit 3.2.

(a) **Authority:** The authority attached to a rule decreases as one descends through the levels of the hierarchy, that is the further the rule is removed from law.

(b) **Detail:** The rules become more detailed and more concrete as one descends through the levels of the hierarchy, with incomplete and un-clear rules established at one level being further elaborated at a lower level. There is a development from general principles to particular rules.

(c) **Responsiveness to change:** The responsiveness to change increases as one descends through the levels of the hierarchy. When a new accounting issue arises (for example, how to report a newly-invented financial instrument), the accountant who prepares the accounts has to find a solution immediately. She can seek advice from individuals, who will generally be able to respond more quickly than the bodies higher up the hierarchy, whose rule-making procedures are generally more formal and therefore slower.

Each level of the hierarchy will now be considered.

3.3.1 Law

Law is at the top of the hierarchy; it is the dominant element for two reasons:

(a) The other rules must be consistent with the law, both with its general principles and its specific provisions. In virtue of the authority given by society to the legislature, any conflict between the law and a rule lower down in the hierarchy must be resolved in favour of law.

(b) Law provides the criteria by which it can be judged whether the other rules are to be accepted as valid and authoritative, that is whether they may be included as proper elements in the hierarchy of rules.

3.3.2 The second level: delegated legislation and court judgements

Delegated legislation

In many countries, it is common for the legislature to enact laws that delegate to named bodies (generally government ministries and state agencies) the authority to issue rules in defined areas. These rules are designated by a number of different terms: decrees, orders, regulations, instruments, and so on. Since these rules are issued under the authority of law, they have the force of law. They are particularly common in France and Japan, where most of the detailed rules of financial reporting are laid down in government decrees.

Court judgements

The courts of law have a major role to play in the functioning of the system of rules. They issue judgements on the acceptability of the rules. The courts may be asked to rule on the constitutionality of a law en-acted by the legislature, but their more common task is to decide on the legality of the rules lower down in the hierarchy. Thus the courts may declare that a particular rule is invalid because it is not in conformity with the law. In principle this rule should no longer be considered to be part of the system of rules. Alternatively, the courts may decide that the rule does conform with the law and thus enhance its authority, as when, for example, it confirms the interpretation of the law given by a particular individual. In fact, in certain circumstances, the courts by endorsing a particular rule may thereby incorporate it into the body of the law. However, in the field of financial reporting, it is relatively rare for the courts to rule on the acceptability or otherwise of a rule lower down in the hierarchy and then generally only after a considerable delay; the great majority of these rules have not received the endorsement of the courts.

3.3.3 The lower levels of the hierarchy

The rules of the remaining levels of the hierarchy (standards, recommendations and interpretations) do not form part of the law; they are included in the system of rules because, to varying degrees, they are complied with by the preparers of accounts, essentially because of the prestige and expertise of the bodies and individuals involved.

Standards

Accounting standards are a feature of the regulatory system in most developed countries. They fulfil three functions:

- They provide authoritative interpretations of the law, where this is ambiguous or unclear
- They expand the legal rules where these do not cover a point in sufficient detail
- They supplement the law by providing authoritative rules on matters not covered by the law

In effect, the gap left by the inability or unwillingness of the legislature to lay down detailed rules has, in many countries, been filled by standards issued by standard-setting bodies. These bodies exist in all the major Common Law countries and their standards are an important supplement to the law; examples are the USA's Financial Accounting Standards Board and the Accounting Standards Boards of the UK, Canada and Australia. In Roman Law countries, the statute law tends to be more detailed. However, in general, it is impracticable for statute law to cover in detail every aspect of financial reporting. Hence many Roman Law countries have also found it expedient to develop institutions whose function is to fill out the detail of the law. Examples are Japan's Business Accounting Deliberation Council, France's Conseil National de la Comptabilité and the Netherlands's Raad voor de Jaarverslaggeving. Until recently there was no equivalent body in Germany; however in 1998, this gap was filled with the foundation of the Deutsche Standardisierungsrat. These bodies fulfill much the same function as the standard setting bodies in the Common Law countries.

However countries differ considerably in the degree of authority attached to standards, as is explained when the national accounting systems of the Pentad countries are analyzed in later chapters.

Recommendations of professional associations

It is common for professional accountancy associations to issue recommendations to their members on matters related to financial reporting. As the term 'recommendation' implies, these rules are not binding on the members, but may nevertheless be widely followed for two reasons: out of loyalty to the association and as a safeguard in the event of a dispute arising in relation to accounts that the member has prepared or audited. Given the central role that professional accountants play in the preparation and audit of financial statements, the rules of professional associations may be very influential, particularly in areas not covered by other rules.

Stock exchange listing rules

All stock exchanges have rules relating to the financial reporting of corporations whose shares are listed on the exchange, with the aim of ensuring that the public receives all the information that it needs in making investment decisions. These rules typically specify the form and content of the reports that corporations should publish both initially (when their shares are first listed) and subsequently. The stock exchanges have a very effective way of ensuring that corporations respect these rules: they can refuse to list the shares of the erring corporation. In the past, the stock exchanges in the countries with the most developed capital markets (the USA and Britain) were a major force in improving the financial reporting of listed corporations; however, as the other rules in the hierarchy (especially standards) have become more detailed, their importance has become more marginal.

Interpretations of individuals

In all countries, individuals, such as leading lawyers, accountants and professors, publish their personal interpretations of the rules of financial reporting in the form of books and articles. The fact that these personal writings are considered to be part of the hierarchy of rules is an indication of the broad meaning given to the term 'rule'. These interpretations may be considered to be 'rules' to the extent that they are widely followed by the preparers of financial statements, which in turn depends very much on the status and prestige of the writer. In fact in only one country of the Pentad, Germany, are the writings of individuals an important element of the regulatory system.

Enterprise specific rules

The lowest level of the hierarchy is termed 'enterprise specific rules'. The concept is that, if the accountant in the course of preparing the enterprise's accounts comes across a matter that is not regulated by a rule higher up the hierarchy, then she is forced to devise her own rule. As shown in Exhibit 3.2, these rules have the least authority but are very adaptable to new situations.

3.4 THE NATIONAL REGULATORY SYSTEM

The hierarchy of rules presented in Exhibit 3.2 applies to all countries. However individual countries vary considerably in the importance given to particular categories of rules, both in the amount of detail set out in the law and in the nature, scope and authority of the rules lower down in the hierarchy. Each country has its own unique system for setting the rules of financial reporting; the components of this system are the rule-makers of financial reporting: the legislature, government agencies, the courts of law, the standard setting bodies, the stock exchange authorities, the professional accountancy associations and so on. The different weights given to the various categories of rules in each country can be attributed to differences in the authority and power of these rule makers. Exhibit 3.3 gives an indication of the different characteristics of the national regulatory systems of the five countries of the Pentad in that it presents an estimate of how much each category of rule contributes to the detailed regulation of financial reporting. The table gives only a very broad indication of the quantitative importance of the various rules; for each country the totality of final reporting rules is divided between the various categories in a rough and ready way. In interpreting this table, it should be born in mind that, in all countries, law provides the authority for the other rules. However in certain countries, most notably the USA, the law on financial reporting is very brief; the detail is provided by other rules, notably accounting standards. In the other countries, the law is more detailed. In Japan and France much of the detail is set out in delegated legislation; in Germany and Britain in the text of the statute. Accounting standards are an important source of rules in all countries except Germany, where the standard-setting body was founded only in 1998.

In Part II, the national regulatory systems of the five countries in the Pentad are examined in more detail.

Exhibit 3.3 *The quantitative importance of the various categories of rules*

	USA	Japan	Germany	France	Britain
Law	X	XX	XXX	XX	XXX
Delegated legislation		XXX	X	XXX	X
Accounting standards	XXXXX	XX	X	XXX	XXX
Professional recommendations	XX	X	XX	X	X
Stock exchange rules	XX	X	X	X	XX
Writings of individuals			XX		

In Chapter 2 the diversity in financial reporting practice throughout the world was explained in terms of the different environment in each country, including different institutions and culture. To these factors should be added the nature of the national regulatory system. The environment is the underlying cause for the differences between national accounting systems; the regulatory system is the medium through which these underlying differences express themselves in financial reporting rules and practice.

SUMMARY

The subject of the chapter is the rules of financial reporting. The question was asked 'why are rules necessary?' and the answer was that they are necessary because otherwise preparers are unlikely to provide the information demanded by users, notwithstanding the dangers attached to any system of imposed rules. The information needs of users were analysed. The essential role of government and of law in the system of rules was emphasized, and also the need to supplement law by additional rules. The hierarchy of rules was described, consisting of law at the top, with delegated legislation, court judgements, accounting standards, recommendations of professional accountancy bodies, stock exchange regulations, and firm specific rules in the lower levels. The broad characteristics of the national regulatory systems of the countries of the Pentad were sketched.

Review questions

1. What is the fundamental conflict between the preparers and the users of financial statements?

2. Outline the various categories of users. What information needs may they reasonably expect to be met by the enterprise's financial statements?

3. What are the disadvantages of imposing a set of rules on the preparers of financial statements?

4. What is the essential function of law in the hierarchy of financial reporting rules?

5. Why is it generally necessary to supplement the law with additional rules? In what ways do these additional rules differ from law?

6. Why is law-making generally a political process?

7. What are the three functions of accounting standards?

References

Baldwin, R and McCrudden, C *Regulation and Public Law*, Weidenfeld & Nicolson, London, (1987).

Baxter, W 'Accounting Standards – Boon or Curse?' *Accounting and Business Research*, **12**(1) (1981), pp. 3–10.

Blake, J 'A Classification System for Economic Consequences: Issues in Accounting Regulation', *Accounting and Business Research*, **22**(4) (1992), p. 305ff.

Bromwich, M *Financial Reporting, Information and Capital Markets* Pitman, London (1992).

Burggraaff, J 'The political dimensions of accounting standard setting in Europe', *Accounting Standard Setting: an international perspective*, M Bromwich and A Hopwood, (eds), Pitman, London (1983), p. 184.

Ordelheide, D 'Germany', *Accounting Regulation in Europe*, S McLeay (ed.), Macmillan – now Palgrave, Basingstoke (1999).

Solomons, D 'The Political Implications of Accounting and Accounting Standard Setting', *Accounting and Business Research*, **13**(2) (1983), pp. 107–18.

Further reading

If they look at nothing else, students are urged to read Baxter (1981) which is an excellent analysis of the arguments for and against rules, giving much food for thought for those who consider rules to be essential. Solomons (1983) provides some good counter arguments. Chapter 11 of Bromwich (1992) covers much the same ground as this chapter but in a rather more theoretical and rigorous fashion. For the economic consequences of accounting rules, see Blake (1992).

part two

Country Studies

In Part One the diversity of financial reporting around the world was discussed and illustrated in general terms. In this part, this diversity is considered in greater detail through an examination of financial reporting in the five countries of the Pentad: Britain, USA, France, Germany and Japan. For each country, there is a description and analysis of financial reporting rules and practice, covering the following points, in so far as they are relevant for an understanding of the financial reporting of that country's enterprises:

- the historical development
- the institutional framework, including consideration of all the elements that were found in Chapter 2 to be influential: the state, the corporate financing system and the accountancy profession
- the regulatory system, including a review both of the principal rules and of the bodies that make these rules, covering the whole hierarchy of rules which was introduced in Chapter 3 and illustrated in Exhibit 3.2: laws, regulations, standards, and firm specific rules

One objective of this analysis is to demonstrate the essential characteristics of each country's financial reporting and to bring out the differences between countries, whilst noting any similarities. Certainly, by the end of this part, the reader should have a far clearer and more informed view of the diversity within the Pentad.

The final chapter in this part presents an analysis of the European Union's activities relating to financial reporting.

chapter four

Britain

Chapter objectives

- To set out the principal features of the British accounting system, with particular emphasis on the following matters:
  - the historical development of British financial reporting, beginning with the growth of limited companies in the nineteenth century
  - the institutional factors that have been and still are the predominant influences, notably the law (the Companies Acts), the accountancy profession and the stock exchange
  - the role of accounting standards and of the Accounting Standards Board
- To outline the major features of British generally-accepted accounting principles (UK GAAP) including the significance of the 'true and fair view' rule

4.1 WHY BRITAIN IS IMPORTANT FOR THE STUDENT OF FINANCIAL REPORTING

Britain is particularly important for the student of global financial reporting for two reasons:

(a) **Britain is a major actor in the global economy.** As is demonstrated by the statistics given in Chapter 1, Britain stands alongside the USA as being the leading source of funds for foreign direct investment and ranks second to that country as a recipient (see Exhibits 1.2 and 1.3). More significantly, given the subject matter of the present book, it ranks fifth in terms of the number of major MNEs that come under its jurisdiction (Exhibits 1.6 and 1.7). However, these statistics do not fully explain the importance of Britain for a study of global financial reporting; for this we have to consider the historical development.

(b) **A century-and-a-half ago, in the middle of the nineteenth-century, Great Britain was the world's leading industrial power.**[1] The Industrial Revolution started there in the eighteenth century and within a century Britain had grown from essentially a commercial and maritime power to become the most powerful industrial nation that the world had witnessed up to that time. The importance of this fact for this book is that it was just in this period that the foundations of the present system of financial reporting were being laid. For this reason, this analysis of the present system of financial reporting in Britain starts with a study of its historical development.

4.2 THE ORIGINS OF BRITISH FINANCIAL REPORTING

The origins of financial reporting as currently practised around the world can be traced to mid-nineteenth-century Britain. At that time, the phenomenal growth in industry that had marked the previous hundred years was in danger of being checked by a shortage of capital. The process of industrialization had led to a significant growth in the number of large enterprises: examples were the cotton mills of Lancashire, the iron works of central Scotland and, above all, the first railway companies. These new enterprises all made use of recently invented machines, which required large amounts of capital, larger than could be provided by the persons who owned and managed the business. It was necessary to draw on the wealth of persons who were not closely involved in the enterprise. However this was not practicable in a partnership, which was the predominant form of business organization at that time. Since each partner was personally liable for the debts of the entire partnership, few were prepared to invest in a partnership unless they had complete confidence in the ability and honesty of their fellow partners, which implied not only that partners could be drawn from a very limited group (persons who knew each other well) but also that each partner had to involve himself closely in the affairs of the partnership on a continuing basis, simply in order to ensure that his private fortune was not put at risk through the incompetence or dishonesty of his fellow partners.

What was needed to overcome this problem was to allow enterprises to become corporations. As already explained in Chapter 1, the corporation[2] is the ideal form of business organization for large enterprises; it has the two principal advantages of corporate personality and limited liability for its shareholders.

There had been corporations in Britain before the Industrial Revolution, for example the Hudson Bay Company, founded in London in 1670, whose shares are still traded on the London Stock Exchange. However, in the past, such corporations were not common, principally because the government sought to limit their numbers. The main reason for this reluctance was that corporations were often used as vehicles for fraud. A well-known example is the wave of speculation known as the 'South Sea Bubble' which occurred in London in 1720. Many unscrupulous promoters took advantage of an atmosphere of frenzied speculation, created by rumours of the great profits to be won by trading with South America, to set up corporations, whose shares they sold at great profit, but which subsequently were found to have no substance. The authorities responded by placing severe restrictions on the formation of new corporations; corporations could be formed only by Royal Charter or by special Act of Parliament.

However by the middle of the nineteenth century it had become evident that Britain's future economic development depended crucially on the ability of the growing industrial enterprises to organize themselves as corporations. The necessary legal framework was provided by a series of laws between 1844 and 1862 which greatly simplified the process of forming a corporation; henceforth a Royal Charter or special Act of Parliament was no longer necessary; the principal formality was that the corporation's constitution (which had to meet certain conditions) had to be registered with a government office known as the Companies Registry. The principal laws were the Joint Stock Companies Act of 1844 and the Limited Liability Act of 1855. Contrary to the general rule with corporations, the 1844 Act did not confer the privilege of limited liability on shareholders and for this reason was little used. When limited liability was granted by the 1855 Act, the corporation was required to advertise the fact that its shareholders' liability was limited by adding the word 'limited' at the end of its name. In 1862 these laws were consolidated in the Companies Act.

These acts led to a considerable increase in the number of corporations; within a generation, almost all large enterprises were organized as corporations. Britain was the first European country to make the corporate form of organization generally available to business enterprises. However the other major European countries soon followed Britain's example: notably France in 1867 and Germany in 1870. As is explained in Chapter 5, the USA was a generation ahead of Britain, the first American law dating from 1811.

4.3 THE SEPARATION OF CONTROL FROM OWNERSHIP

The change from the partnership to the corporation as the common form of organization for large enterprises had a profound impact on financial reporting. This stems from the separation of control from ownership in a corporation, which in principle does not exist in a partnership.

Since the shareholders in a corporation are not personally liable for the corporation's debts, they do not have to concern themselves closely with its management. In fact this would be impracticable in most large corporations which, on account of their substantial capital requirements, often have thousands of shareholders. British company law provides that the management of the corporation is the responsibility of the directors, who are officers of the corporation, elected periodically by the shareholders. In fact the power to elect (and to dismiss) the directors is the principal right possessed by the shareholders in relation to the management of the corporation. In general, they do not have the right to interfere in its management; that is the prerogative of the directors. In effect, with corporations, there is a clear distinction between control (in the hands of the directors) and ownership (lying with the shareholders). It is common for the directors to own some shares but generally the total number of shares owned by the directors amounts to only a tiny fraction of the corporation's capital. The majority of the shareholders play no part in the corporation's management. This was true with the first British corporations formed after the corporate form of business organization became generally available in the mid nineteenth century; it is even more true today.

With the separation of control from ownership, the financial statements take on the important role of transmitting information about the corporation's financial position and performance from the directors to the shareholders. Initially British law required that each year the directors present a 'full and fair' balance sheet to the shareholders. However this legal requirement was soon repealed and was not reinstated until 1900, with the consequence that, throughout the second half of the nineteenth century, there was no legal obligation on companies to present accounts to their shareholders. Nevertheless, most companies did in fact issue such accounts. Some present-day commentators attribute this behaviour to the response of companies to market pressure, that the directors were induced to render accounts as a means of attracting investors and of retaining their support. However convincing evidence on this point is lacking. Three factors are mentioned in the contemporary literature:

(a) **The law:** The Companies Act of 1862 included a suggested model constitution for a company, which included rules governing the preparation of the annual financial statements that were to be presented to the shareholders and for the appointment of auditors, who were to report on whether the balance sheet was 'a full and fair balance sheet, containing the particulars required, and properly drawn up so as to exhibit a true and correct view of the state of the company's affairs'. Many companies adopted this model constitution although they were not legally obliged to do so.

(b) **The accountancy profession:** In the second half of the nineteenth century, the British accountancy profession, starting from small beginnings, became increasingly influential (see section 4.4.4). Its members provided the auditors for most of the larger limited companies. Since the law was completely silent on the principles to be followed in drawing up their accounts, companies tended to rely on their auditors for guidance.

(c) **The stock exchange:** Many of the newly incorporated companies had their shares quoted on a stock exchange. The London Stock Exchange had a rule that required a listed company to deposit its annual balance sheet with the exchange.

As will be demonstrated in the following section, these three factors have continued to dominate financial reporting in Britain ever since.

4.4 BRITAIN'S INSTITUTIONAL FRAMEWORK

This section examines the principal institutional factors that influence the present practice of financial reporting in Britain. Each of the factors that were identified as important in the Chapter 2 will be considered.

4.4.1 The state

In nineteenth-century Britain, the predominant political philosophy was 'laissez-faire'. The state intervened very little in economic affairs on the grounds that, if left to themselves, individuals, guided by Adam Smith's 'invisible hand', would act in the best interests of society as a whole. Hence, initially, the state played a very minor role in the development of financial reporting. The Companies Act of 1862 set out model rules concerning accounts which a company could adopt if it so wished but there was no compulsion. This act remained in force for the rest of the century. In the twentieth century, the practice developed of amending the Companies Act at fairly frequent but irregular intervals. Thus there were substantially revised Companies Acts in 1900, 1907, 1928, 1947, 1967, 1981 and 1989. Each revision extended in a significant fashion the law's domain in the field of financial reporting. The principal additional requirements imposed by each successive law are summarized in Exhibit 4.1.

As can be seen from this exhibit, it was not until 1900 that companies were legally obliged to present a balance sheet (the most rudimentary form of financial statement) to shareholders and it was not until 1928 that the content of the balance sheet was defined in any way. Before 1928, there was no requirement for an income statement (known in Britain as a profit and loss account) and it was not until 1947 that its

Exhibit 4.1 *The relentless growth of British Company Law*

Date of Companies Act	Principal additional requirements
1900	Balance sheet to be presented to shareholders
	Balance sheet to be audited by an auditor
1907	Public companies to file balance sheets with Company Registry
1928	Limited specification of the content of the balance sheet
	Profit and loss account to be presented to shareholders
1947	Consolidated balance sheet and profit and loss account (limited specification of contents)
	Accounts must give 'a true and fair view'
	Auditor must be a qualified professional
1967	All companies to file accounts with the Companies Registry
1981	Individual accounts: prescribed formats and valuation rules
1989	Consolidated accounts: prescribed formats and valuation rules

contents were specified in even a limited way. Consolidated accounts were not required by law until 1947. The publication of accounts was not compulsory until 1907 and at first applied only to public companies (larger companies in which the general public held shares). By the Companies Act of 1900 companies were required to appoint an auditor but it was not until 1947 that the auditor had to possess a professional qualification. The 1980s witnessed a significant advance in the detail of regulation. Detailed formats for the balance sheet and the profit and loss account were prescribed for the company's individual accounts (1981) and for the consolidated accounts (1989); these acts also laid down for the first time general rules for the valuation of the items in the accounts. The reason for this burst of legislative activity is that the British government was required as a condition of its membership of the European Union to incorporate into its law that body's rules relating to company accounts. This matter is explained in more detail when the European Union is dealt with in Chapter 9. By the end of the twentieth century, Company Law regulated financial reporting in considerable detail.

4.4.2 Taxation

In Chapter 2 taxation was identified as a major influence on financial reporting. However its influence in Britain is much less than in certain other countries covered in this book, notably Japan, Germany and France. In Britain, there has never been a formal legal rule that the calculation of the amount of tax to be paid by an enterprise should be based on the figures reported in the accounts. A major reason for this is that, in Britain, the imposition of a tax on income predated the establishment of generally accepted accounting principles for financial reporting. Income tax was introduced in 1799; at that time there were no generally accepted principles for the calculation of the income of an enterprise so the tax authorities had in many areas to develop their own rules. When accountants started to develop general principles for financial reporting during the second half of the nineteenth century, they did not follow the tax rules.

The separation of tax and financial reporting is best illustrated with reference to depreciation. The tax authorities do not recognize the depreciation charge in the profit and loss account as a tax-deductible expense. Instead, in respect of certain defined categories of fixed assets, they allow a percentage of the asset's capital cost to be deducted from taxable income each year. The asset categories and the percentages are defined by law. Not all asset categories are covered; for example, no deductions are allowed for buildings used for commercial purposes. Furthermore the annual percentages defined in the tax law are generally quite different from the rates that accountants consider appropriate for the calculation of depreciation in the income statement; for example in the past the tax authorities have allowed a very large proportion of an asset's capital cost to be charged against taxable income in the year of acquisition. The net effect is that an enterprise's income for tax purposes will generally be different (and often substantially so) from its income as reported in the profit and loss account.

There are other areas where specific tax rules require that income and expenses be calculated in a way different from that reported in the accounts. But depreciation is certainly the most important in quantitative terms. However, it is impossible for the tax rules to cover every eventuality and, when there is no specific tax rule, the law lays down that profits for tax purposes are calculated according to the ordinary principles of commercial accountancy. Hence it is not correct to assert that tax has no influence on financial reporting. There are two rather different situations in which tax has a most marked effect:

(a) Where the financial reporting rules offer some choice, the accountant in preparing the financial statements will often opt for the rule that minimizes the tax burden. A good example of this effect is given in a recent law case.[3] The judge allowed as a deduction from taxable income the charge for a provision for the future repair of aero engines, even though the costs had still to be incurred and the time for the overhaul had not yet arrived. The grounds for his decision were that there was no specific tax rule in this area and that commercial accounting as reflected in the company's audited accounts accepted the charge as an expense. If the company had not reported the charge in its accounts, it would have lost the case. Hence any company that wishes to justify its claim to use a method of calculating taxable income and expenses on the grounds of normal commercial practice must use this method in its financial reporting.

(b) Many enterprises find it convenient to use the tax rules for their financial statements, as this saves them the trouble and expense of preparing two statements, one for tax purposes and one for financial reporting purposes. This is only possible in those cases where the financial reporting rules are not so specific that they forbid the use of the tax rules. However this leaves a wide area in which the tax rules are acceptable for financial reporting purposes and many enterprises take advantage of this fact. This is particularly the case with smaller enterprises, where financial reporting is often of secondary importance as they can communicate with their shareholders directly.

Notwithstanding these reservations, it is undoubtedly correct that the financial reporting of British enterprises is less influenced by tax than is the case in other countries. As regards the larger British multinationals, the argument set out in paragraph (b) carries no weight; for them financial reporting to shareholders is too important to be compromised by the need to save money by combining the tax and financial statements. However, for these enterprises, the argument set out in paragraph (a) is certainly relevant with the inference that, in certain fairly limited areas of the financial statements, taxation does exercise some influence.

4.4.3　The corporate financing system

In Chapter 2, the United Kingdom was identified as having a highly developed capital market. As shown by the statistics presented in Exhibit 2.4, the market capitalization of domestic corporations on British stock exchanges is, in absolute terms, larger than that of any country other than the USA and Japan, and, in relative terms (that is in relation to the size of the local economy), is larger than either of these two countries, substantially so in the case of Japan. In the nineteenth century there were stock exchanges in all the principal British cities. However the London Stock Exchange has always been the most important and over time has absorbed the other exchanges.

Apart from its size, the London Stock Exchange differs from the exchanges in most other countries in the relative importance of foreign listings. The number of foreign enterprises listed in London (448) exceeds that of any other exchange, including New York (406), NASDAQ (429) and Tokyo (43). The importance of foreign companies for the London Stock Exchange is brought out more clearly by the statistics for turnover. In fact, in recent years, the value of dealings on the London Stock Exchange in the shares of foreign enterprises has exceeded that of British companies.

No other exchange comes close to this figure; generally the value of foreign dealings is less than 10 per cent of the total – for New York the figure is 8 per cent and for Tokyo less than 1 per cent.[4]

The shares of all the large British MNEs are quoted on the London Stock Exchange. The financial reporting of these companies is directed to satisfying the needs of the capital market, for the reasons given in Chapter 2: to facilitate the raising of new capital, to keep the cost of capital low and to prevent take-over bids. Take-over bids have been an important feature of the London Stock Exchange for at least the last thirty years. The threat of a take-over bid is the principal reason why the directors of listed companies give so much attention to providing shareholders with full and timely information about the company's position and prospects, for otherwise there is a danger that the share price may fall to a low level attracting a hostile bid.

4.4.4 The accountancy profession

There is general agreement that, in Britain, the accountancy profession is an important actor in financial reporting. The British profession possesses a number of special characteristics which differentiate it from those of other countries.

Seniority

Compared with those of other countries, the British accountancy profession has a relatively long history. The more influential professional associations trace their origins to the nineteenth century and are significantly older than their counterparts in other developed countries. The first professional association to be formed was the Society of Accountants of Edinburgh in 1853. Within a few years similar bodies were formed in Glasgow and Aberdeen. In 1951 these three bodies merged to form the Institute of Chartered Accountants in Scotland, which by tracing its origins back to the Edinburgh Society claims to be the world's oldest accountancy association.[5] The Institute of Chartered Accountants in England and Wales was founded in 1880 by the merger of a number of societies which had been formed some ten years earlier. The Institute of Chartered Accountants in Ireland was founded in 1888; at that time the whole of Ireland was under British rule and, to this day, this institute covers both Northern Ireland and the Republic of Ireland.

Size

The British accountancy profession is enormous. In Britain, there are more than 200 000 qualified accountants (members of professional associations that belong to IFAC) which is more than any other country in the world except the USA, which has some 400 000 members. There are more accountants in Britain than in all the other European countries combined. In relative terms, Britain, with some 3500 accountants per million inhabitants, has more accountants than the USA (circa 1500 per million) and is only exceeded by two other Anglo-Saxon countries, Canada and Australia.

Fragmented nature

An important feature of the British profession is its fragmented nature, which is exemplified in the data presented in Exhibit 4.2. There are no less than seven British accountancy associations that are members of IFAC (plus a few that are not members). Connected with the fragmentation of the profession is the fact that only a minority of British qualified accountants work in professional firms that provide accountancy and audit services. The majority work as employees in industry, commerce and administration. Two bodies cater almost exclusively for such accountants: the Chartered Institute of Management Accountants and the Chartered Institute of Public Finance and Accountancy. In addition a majority of the members of the other institutes are similarly employed;

Exhibit 4.2 *The British accountancy profession*

	Date of foundation*	Number of members	Proportion in public practice (%)
Institute of Chartered Accountants in England and Wales	1870	105 500	29
Institute of Chartered Accountants of Scotland	1853	13 500	39
Institute of Chartered Accountants in Ireland	1888	8 205	44
Association of Chartered Certified Accountants	1891	42 000	32
Chartered Institute of Public Finance and Accountancy	1885	11 600	0
Chartered Institute of Management Accountants	1919	35 800	4
Institute of Certified Public Accountants in Ireland	1943	1 000	10
Total		217 605	25

Note: * date of foundation of earliest predecessor body

only a minority work as independent professionals or as employees in a professional firm.

Private status

One reason for this multitude of bodies is that they were all founded as private associations, frequently in competition with each other. The British accountancy associations are not state bodies, but rather private bodies which carry out certain public tasks allocated to them by the state, which in its turn exercises a very limited degree of supervision. The profession is largely self-regulating. When, in 1989, the British government was obliged under the terms of the EU's Eighth Directive to introduce a system of state licencing of auditors, it delegated the responsibility to the professional institutes after it had satisfied itself that they had an adequate system for assuring the competence and integrity of their members.

The factors sketched in the above paragraphs account for the special position that the accountancy profession occupies in British society. However there have been significant changes in the profession's standing over the last 150 years. In the nineteenth century, British Company Law did not seek to regulate financial reporting in any way (see section 4.4.1); there was no obligation on companies to issue accounts or to appoint an auditor. Nevertheless most larger companies did prepare financial statements for the their shareholders, accompanied by an auditor's report. The reason was probably that this made it easier for them to raise capital and to retain the support of the shareholders. The auditors were generally 'Chartered Accountants' (that is members of one of the newly founded institutes), who had established a reputation for competence and integrity. Chandler and Edwards (2000) estimate that over 98 per cent of the 1100 companies listed on British stock exchanges in 1886 subjected their accounts to an external audit, although there was no legal obligation to do so, and that over three-quarters of the audits were performed by professional accountants. Given the lack of guidance in the law, these accountants exercised very considerable influence over the form and contents of the accounts that they audited. In effect they were virtually the sole arbiters of the rules of financial accounting.

The high point of the British profession's prestige came in the early years of the twentieth century. From 1900 onwards, British Company Law began to lay down the rules of financial reporting. At first this had little impact on the profession's dominant position, as generally the legislators followed the advice of the profession, which was the acknowledged expert in the field. However in 1931 an event occurred which was to have a major impact on the profession. In what became known as 'The

Royal Mail case', the auditor of a major British company, the Royal Mail Steam Packet Company, was charged with the criminal offence of fraud because he had reported favourably on a set of accounts in which the company had reported a profit; in fact it had made a large loss which it had offset by drawing on secret reserves. Leading members of the accountancy profession gave evidence in support of the auditor to the effect that the manipulation of the accounts in this way was acceptable accountancy practice and the auditor was in fact acquitted.[6] However the general public were scandalized that the auditor had failed to warn the shareholders of the misleading nature of the accounts. It became clear that the public's confidence in the accountancy profession had been badly shaken. In response accountants changed their practice with regard to secret reserves, but the damage had been done. It became generally accepted that the profession should not be the sole arbiter of the rules of financial reporting and that increased intervention on the part of the law was necessary. A thorough reform of the financial reporting provisions of the Companies Act was made in 1947 (having been held up by the Second World War). Over the next fifty years, as detailed in Exhibit 4.1, the law's provisions became increasingly detailed, entailing a progressive decline in the profession's influence over the determination of the rules of financial reporting.

The same development occurred with regard to accounting standards. When the first standard-setting bodies were set up in the 1970s, they were composed entirely of accountants. However, over time, the accountants found themselves obliged to share the process of setting standards with other actors in the financial reporting field. Thus, progressively during the twentieth century, there was a decline in the British accountancy profession's influence over financial reporting, so that now it is but one among several instead of being the overwhelmingly dominant influence that it was at the start of the century. Undoubtedly the fragmentation of the profession was a factor in the decline of its influence as it was never able to present a united front to its rivals.

Curiously, as its influence over financial reporting declined, in other respects the profession grew. Its numbers increased from about 7000 at the start of the century to over 200 000 at the end. Moreover over the century, British accountants came to occupy a remarkably important position in the management of industrial and commercial companies, not only as financial directors but in general management. Very many British enterprises have professional accountants as their chief executive; in this respect, other professions, such as engineering and the law lag far behind. The accountants have established themselves in such a strong position in the British economy that they have been described as the 'priesthood of industry' (Mathews, Anderson and Edwards, 1998).

4.5 THE BRITISH REGULATORY SYSTEM

4.5.1 A model of the British regulatory system

Exhibit 4.3 presents a model of the UK's system for the regulation of financial reporting. It shows both the principal financial reporting rules and the bodies that make these rules, being:

- The Companies Act enacted by Parliament
- Accounting Standards issued by the Accounting Standards Board
- Listing rules made by the Stock Exchange
- Professional rules made by the accountancy profession

These four categories of rules are now considered in more detail.

4.5.2 The Companies Act

Law lies at the centre of the British system. The basic rules are laid down in the Companies Act. Although these rules apply only to limited companies (corporations), all except the smallest British enterprises take this legal form and are therefore subject to this law.[7] The present Companies Act dates from 1981, but it was substantially revised in 1989. The law sets out the rules relating to the financial reporting of companies in considerable detail covering such matters as:

(a) **The form and content of the financial statements to be prepared by limited companies;** these are the balance sheet, the profit and loss account and the notes to the accounts. There is no legal obligation to prepare any other statements, such as a cash flow statement.

(b) **The valuation rules to be used in the financial statements;** historical cost is stated to be the basic principle, but preparers are permitted to use a number of alternative valuation rules.

(c) **The publication of the accounts:** they are to be sent to the shareholders and filed with the Companies Registry.

(d) **The auditors:** their function, duties, powers and qualifications.

The Companies Act prescribes in considerable detail the format to be used for the financial statements, but is far less prescriptive as to the accounting principles to be followed in determining the numbers to be reported in the accounts. The principal reason for this differential treatment is that the UK, as a member of the European Union, is obliged to incorporate into its law that body's directives, which are more detailed and prescriptive on formats than they are on other aspects of accounting.

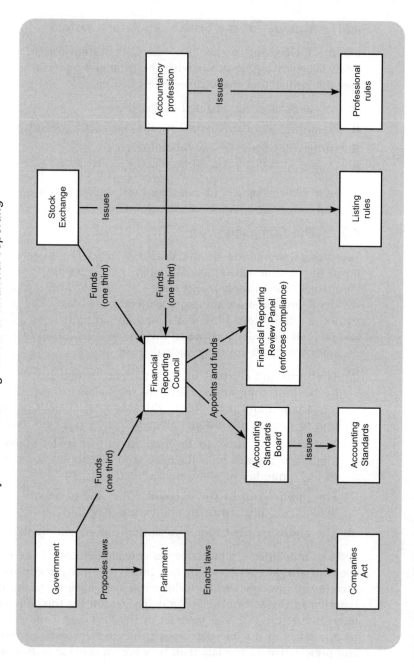

102

Exhibit 4.3   *The British system for the regulation of financial reporting*

4.5.3 Accounting standards

The Accounting Standards Board (ASB) is the UK's official standards setter. The Companies Act lays down that large companies are obliged to report whether their financial statements have been prepared in accordance with the ASB's standards and to give particulars of any material departure with the reason for it. Although the degree of authority conferred in this way is rather limited (it is lawful for a company to ignore the ASB's standards if it gives the reason), in fact, for reasons that are explained later, the level of compliance by large enterprises is very high. Hence the ASB is a very important element in the UK's rule-making system.

The way in which standard setting is organized in the UK is set out in Exhibit 4.3. There are three principal bodies.

The Financial Reporting Council (FRC)

This is the umbrella organization. It has three functions:

- To provide the funds for the other two bodies; in fact one third of the funds comes from the government, one third from the accountancy profession and one third from the London Stock Exchange and other financial institutions
- To appoint the members of the other two bodies: the ASB and the Financial Reporting Review Panel (FRRP)
- To exercise overall supervision over the activities of the other two bodies

In practice the FRC has not interfered in the operations of the other bodies, for example the ASB issues its standards on its own authority without consulting the FRC. The FRC is not formally a public body; however its chairmen and three deputy chairmen are appointed by the government, which also nominates two further members. The chairman and deputy chairmen nominate the remaining twenty or so members, most of whom are prominent in the business world. Although the FRC is not a very active body (it meets only twice a year), it fulfils the very important function of guaranteeing the independence and integrity of the standard-setting process, for instance by acting as a buffer between the ASB and potential pressures, say from the government or other providers of funds. In many ways the FRC is a typical British compromise. Clearly in principle the state is in a position to exercise great influence both through its power of appointment and through its funding. In practice the government does not interfere; the FRC itself claims that it is 'not government-controlled but part of the private sector process of self-regulation' (FRC, March 1998).

The Accounting Standards Board (ASB)

The ASB consists of two full-time members, the Chairman and the Technical Director and eight part-time paid members, who are supported by a staff of about ten professionals. Its task is to issue accounting standards. Since its formation in 1990, it has issued some fifteen Financial Reporting Standards. For the issue of a standard, it follows a set procedure, known as 'due process', the principal element of which is extensive consultation, which generally includes the issue of a discussion paper to interested parties and subsequently the publication of an exposure draft with an invitation to the public at large to send in comments. Although, through this process of consultation, the ASB seeks to reach a consensus with other interested parties, it considers that a consensus is desirable but not essential, as is shown by the following quotation from its official literature:

> Although the Board weighs carefully the views of interested parties, the ultimate content of an FRS must be determined by the Board's own judgement based on research, public consultation and careful consideration about the benefits and costs of providing the resulting information. (ASB, 1993)

This principle applies even to the ASB's inner workings: to issue a standard, a majority of only seven of its ten members is required, which means that a minority of three can be overridden. In fact most standards have received the approval of the entire board: to date only three standards have been accompanied by a statement of dissent by a member who voted against it.

In addition to Financial Reporting Standards, the ASB has endorsed twenty-seven Statements of Standard Accounting Practice that were issued by its predecessor body, the Accounting Standards Committee (ASC); it has also issued over twenty abstracts of the Urgent Issues Task Force, which as its name implies deals with relatively minor matters of interpretation and application of standards that need to be dealt with urgently.

The totality of the rules issued by the ASB covers a very wide field. They include an obligation on enterprises to prepare and issue two financial statements that are not mentioned in the Companies Act: the cash flow statement and the statement of total recognized gains and losses. This is a remarkable indication of the power of the ASB (which is not formally a state body) to place additional obligations on companies. Other standards deal with matters that are either not covered in the Companies Act or dealt with only in general terms, such as foreign currency translation, leasing, and derivatives. Much of the ASB's output is concerned with laying down the detailed rules for the preparation of consolidated accounts, which are described in only the most general terms in the Companies Act.

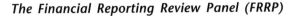

The Financial Reporting Review Panel (FRRP)

The FRRP's function is to enforce compliance with the accounting provisions of the Companies Act and the ASB's standards. When it considers that the financial statements of a company do not comply with the law or these standards, it has the power to apply to the court of law for an order that the company must modify its accounts. Furthermore, the court has the power to order that the company's directors must pay personally for the cost of any modifications. Before applying to the court, the FRRP always seeks to persuade the company to modify its accounts voluntarily. It deals with about thirty cases a year and, so far in every case, the company has agreed to modify its accounts or, very occasionally, has succeeded in persuading the FRRP that it was right. The FRRP, during the ten years of its existence, has never had to resort to the ultimate deterrent of a court order. Undoubtedly it has been very successful in raising the level of compliance with the ASB's standards. It would seem that company directors are very reluctant to run the risk of being obliged to pay personally for any corrections to the accounts necessitated by a failure to respect the ASB's standards.

4.5.4 Stock exchange listing rules

The London Stock Exchange has issued a number of rules that companies whose shares are listed on the exchange must follow in the preparation of their financial statements. In the nineteenth century, these rules were a major influence over the financial reporting of listed companies but, in recent years, as the other rules (notably the Companies Act and the ASB's standards) have become more detailed and prescriptive, the London Stock Exchange's own rules have become relatively less important. However there are still a few obligations that the London Stock Exchange imposes on listed companies that are additional to those imposed by the law and by standards; for example it requires listed companies to publish a summary of the profit and loss account covering the previous ten years whereas the law requires only the figures for the previous year. However the stock exchange is still a major force in UK financial reporting for two reasons:

(a) **It insists that the financial statements of listed companies comply with the ASB's standards.** This backing by the London Stock Exchange is the principal reason why British listed companies invariably follow the ASB's standards – if they did not they would be in breach of the stock exchange's regulations. The stock exchange has a very effective way of ensuring that companies obey its rules: it can suspend the quotation of the erring company's shares; generally merely the threat of this sanction is sufficient to bring it into line. It should be noted that the London Stock Exchange does not require non-British companies that are listed on it to follow the ASB's standards; they are required to present their accounts in accordance with their local law or with internationally accepted standards, notably US GAAP or the IASC's standards.

(b) **The stock exchange is the venue for the capital market and for the market for corporate control**. Through the simple fact of their shares being listed on the stock exchange, large British companies are motivated to adopt a very open and informative approach to their financial reporting.

4.5.5 Professional rules

The British professional accountancy associations issue recommendations to their members on matters not covered by the law and standards: for example, in 1996 the Institute of Chartered Accountants in England and Wales issued a recommendation on materiality, a subject that is mentioned but not defined in law or in standards. However few of these recommendations cover matters of significance. At one time these were an important source of rules. The first British standard-setting body, the Accounting Standards Steering Committee which was set up in 1970, was an organ of the accountancy profession. However over time the profession had to share the standard-setting process with other parties. The accountancy profession now channels its rule-making activities through the ASB. It provides one third of that body's funds and always comments in a thorough fashion on its proposed standards. Furthermore eight of the ASB's members are qualified accountants. Although the ASB's members must pledge themselves not to take instructions from any other body, that does not mean that they do not tend unconsciously to adopt the approach of the professional accountancy associations as they have been conditioned by their training and many years of working as professional accountants.

4.5.6 Accepted practice: 'true and fair view'

The lowest level in the hierarchy of rules depicted in Exhibit 3.2 is termed 'firm specific rules'. The concept is that, if the accountant of an enterprise in the course of preparing the accounts, comes across a matter that is not regulated by a higher rule, she is forced to make up her own rule, possibly with the help of the auditor. The Companies Act provides some guidance since it lays down some general rules that accountants should follow in preparing financial statements. The most important of these general rules is set out in the very first article of the 1981 Companies Act, which states:

Every balance sheet of a company . . . shall give a true and fair view of the state of affairs of the company as at the end of its financial year and every profit and loss account . . . shall give a true and fair view of the profit or loss of the company for the financial year.

Furthermore, the Companies Act states that the requirement to give 'a true and fair view' overrides all its other provisions. Where a company's accounts that have been drawn up according to the detailed provisions of the Companies Act do not give 'a true and fair view' then additional information must be given. If, notwithstanding this additional information, the accounts still do not give 'a true and fair view', because of the impact of a particular rule in the Companies Act, then the company should not follow this rule – the general requirement to give 'a true and fair view' overrides the particular rule.

There has been much discussion of the meaning of the term 'a true and fair view'. The term is not defined in the Companies Act and has not been further clarified in any court judgement. In 1983, the British accountancy profession published the opinion of two leading lawyers on its meaning (Hoffman, 1983). This opinion was updated ten years later (Arden, 1993). Given the eminence of the lawyers (both later became judges), these opinions must be regarded as the most authoritative statement on the subject. They make a number of important points:

(a) 'A true and fair view' is a legal term whose meaning is to be established ultimately by the courts of law; the ordinary meaning of the words is irrelevant; what is important is their legal meaning.

(b) In deciding on this matter the judges would look for guidance to the practice of professional accountants. In the words of the opinion, 'the courts will treat compliance with accepted accounting principles as prima facie evidence that the accounts are true and fair'. Note the term 'accepted accounting principles'; in effect the lawyers were saying that 'true and fair' means what in fact accountants do, provided that it is 'accepted'.

(c) However the courts would give great weight to the ASB's standards in deciding whether a particular accounting principle is consistent with a true and fair view. This is because the Companies Act gives particular recognition to the ASB's standards.

The ASB has used point (c) to claim greater authority for its standards, even to the extent of issuing standards that conflict with specific provisions of the Companies Act. An example is SSAP 19 (a standard of the ASC that has been endorsed by the ASB) which states that investment properties should not be subject to annual depreciation charges but should rather be revalued each year. This is contrary to the Companies Act which states that depreciation must be charged on all assets with a finite life. The ASB insists that its standard must be followed and not the specific provision of the Companies Act, basing its case on the overriding requirement (contained in the Companies Act) to give 'a true and fair view' and on the ASB's acknowledged position as the interpreter of the meaning of this term.

The 'true and fair view' rule in the Companies Act and the use made by the ASB of this rule has given a certain eclectic character to British financial reporting. This is illustrated by the standard on investment properties referred to in the previous paragraph which is based not so much on the application of consistent principles as on the needs of the property companies, a particularly influential and insistent group of preparers. A more general example is the widespread use of 'modified historical cost' under which most fixed assets are reported at historical cost less depreciation but certain selected assets are reported at their market value. Many enterprises make use of the ASB's lax standards in this matter to report selected assets with long lives, such as land and buildings, at market value. This increases their asset base and their equity value with little or no increase in the depreciation charge. This mixture of valuation bases for fixed assets (historical cost and market value) is not logical and not consistent; its principal justifications are that it is popular with preparers and that it provides additional information for users.

It is rare for individual accountants to seek to depart from specific provisions of the Companies Act or of the ASB's standards on the grounds of the need to give 'a true and fair view'. When they do they are invariably called to order by the FRRP. Hence for the individual accountant, the significance of the 'true and fair view' rule is that it provides the justification for following accepted accounting practice in areas not covered by the law or by standards.

4.5.7 Synthesis: UK GAAP

The corpus of rules followed by British accountants for the preparation of accounts make up generally accepted accounting principles or GAAP for short. The components of UK GAAP have been outlined in the previous section, being:

■ The provisions of the Companies Act
■ The accounting standards issued by the ASB
■ Stock exchange listing rules
■ Professional recommendations
■ For matters not covered by the other rules, the practice of leading accountants and companies that are widely accepted as possessing authority

The five components form a hierarchy. Law is at the top of the hierarchy. Its rules have the greatest authority; where the other rules conflict with the law, they are have no authority. It is the law that gives authority to the other rules. This is very clear in the case of the ASB's standards which are expressly recognized in the Companies Act. Even the ASB's claim that a standard may override a specific provision in the Companies Act is consistent with the supremacy of the law, as it is based on Section 1 of the same Companies Act which establishes the overriding character of the 'true and fair' rule. The last element in the hierarchy, accepted practice, is the least well defined. It is important, because of the inability of law and standards to cover every aspect of financial reporting. However, in present-day Britain, it is the least important element. This was not the case at the start of the twentieth century, when standards did not exist and the Companies Act contained only a few, vague provisions as to financial reporting. At that time, financial reporting was governed by the practice of leading accountants. However the role of accepted practice in determining GAAP has declined over the century with growth in the importance of law and standards.

4.6 THE PRINCIPAL CHARACTERISTICS OF BRITISH FINANCIAL REPORTING

The principal characteristics of financial reporting in Britain may be summarized as follows:

- A strong emphasis on the role of financial statements in providing information for the capital market, particularly as concerns the larger listed companies
- A far weaker emphasis on the taxation function of the financial statements which is important mainly for smaller enterprises
- A strong accountancy profession which at the start of the twentieth century dominated the practice of financial reporting. Although, over the next hundred years, there has been a significant decline in the profession's role, it is still an important influence
- A growing importance of the law as a source of rules. Throughout the twentieth century, the role of the state in financial reporting grew as that of the accountancy profession declined, which can be attributed to two factors: public dissatisfaction with the performance of the accountancy profession and the need to incorporate the European Union's directives into British law
- An important role for the Accounting Standards Board, whose standards expand and supplement the law

■ A rather eclectic approach which is based on the 'true and fair view' rule and is best illustrated by the widespread use of 'modified historical cost'

SUMMARY

The historical development of financial reporting in Britain was described with particular reference to the growth of limited companies in the nineteenth century. Three important influences over financial reporting were identified and analysed in detail: the law, notably the Companies Acts, the accountancy profession and the stock exchange. The UK's regulatory system was described and the important role of the Accounting Standards Board emphasized. The 'true and fair view' rule was explained. Finally a synthesis was presented of the principal characteristics of British financial reporting.

Review questions

1. Why is Britain important for the study of global financial reporting?

2. What were the three dominant influences over the financial reporting of British companies in the nineteenth-century? How has the relative importance of these three factors changed over the past century?

3. How did the role played by the Companies Acts develop over the past one hundred and fifty years?

4. What are the principal characteristics of the British accountancy profession?

5. What is the role played by the Accounting Standards Board in setting the rules for financial reporting?

6. What is the meaning and significance of the legal requirement that the accounts must give 'a true and fair view'?

7. What is meant by the term 'modified historical cost'?

Notes

1. Kennedy (1988) has calculated that Great Britain's predominance as the world's leading industrial power lasted from circa 1800, when it overtook France, to circa 1900, when it was overtaken by the USA.
2. The British commonly use the term 'company' for what in this book is termed a 'corporation'. However the authors prefer the term 'corporation' for two reasons: (a) The term 'company' is imprecise; for example it is often used to denote a partnership, as in Arthur Andersen & Company, whereas 'corporation' is a clearly defined legal term; (b) The term 'corporation' has wider international acceptance and is not associated with any particular country.
3. Further details of the case, Johnson *v.* Britannia Airways Ltd., are given in Lamb *et al.* (1998).
4. All statistics in this paragraph relate to 1999 and were retrieved from the website of Federation Internationale des Bourses de Valeurs (www.fibv.com).
5. The Scots' claim is disputed by the Italians; see note 5 of Chapter 2.
6. For more information on the Royal Mail case, see Napier (1995).
7. The principal exception are enterprises in the public sector which are outside the scope of this book.

References

Arden, M 'The true and fair view requirement', *Accountancy*, **112**(July 1993), p. 125.

ASB 'Forward to Accounting Standards', *Accountancy*, **112**(July 1993), p. 120.

Chandler, R and Edwards, JR 'Creating Accountability', *Accountancy*, **125**(1280) (2000), pp. 152–3.

Cook, A 'Requirement for a true and fair view – a UK standard-setter's perspective', *European Accounting Review*, **6**(4) (1997), pp. 693–704.

Cooke, T 'United Kingdom – Individual Accounts', *Transacc: Transnational Accounting* 2nd edn, D Ordelheide (ed.), Palgrave, Basingstoke (2001).

FRC 'A brief outline', FRC, March 1998.

Freedman, J 'Defining taxable profit in a changing accounting environment', *British Tax Review* (special issue) (1995), pp. 434–44.

Gordon, PD and Gray, SJ *European Financial Reporting: United Kingdom*, Routledge, London (1994).

Hoffmann, L 'Counsel's opinion on true and fair', *Accountancy*, **107**(November 1983).

Kennedy, P *The Rise and Fall of the Great Powers*, Random House, New York (1988).

Lamb, M, Nobes, C and Roberts, A 'International variations in the connection between tax and financial reporting', *Accounting and Business Research*, **28**(3) (1998), pp. 173–88.

Mathews, D, Anderson, M and Edwards, J *The Priesthood of Industry: the rise of the professional accountant in British management*, Oxford University Press, Oxford (1998).

Napier, C 'The history of financial reporting in the United Kingdom', *European Financial Reporting: a history*, P Walton (ed.), Academic Press, London (1995).

Parker, RH 'Regulating British corporate financial reporting in the late nineteenth century', *Accounting Business and Financial History*, **1**(1) (1990), pp. 51–71.

Stacy, G 'True and fair view: a UK auditor's perspective', *European Accounting Review*, **6**(4) (1997), pp. 705–9.

Taylor, P 'United Kingdom – Group Accounts', *Transacc: Transnational Accounting*, 2nd edn., D Ordelheide (ed.), Palgrave, Basingstoke (2001).

Walton, P 'The true and fair view in British accounting', *European Accounting Review*, **2**(1) (1993), pp. 49–58.

Further reading

The most comprehensive analysis of British financial reporting is to be found in Gordon and Gray (1994), in which Chapter 5 is to be particularly recommended. For the historical development, see Napier (1995), for the 'true and fair view' rule, see Walton (1993), Cook (1997) and Stacy (1997), and, for the role of standards and the Accounting Standards Board, see the Financial Reporting Council's annual report (which also covers the FRRP) and the ASB's web-site (www.asb.org.uk). For a detailed presentation of the rules, see Cooke (2001) and Taylor (2001). For a more detailed analysis of particular points, see Parker (1990) for the development of company law in the nineteenth century and Freedman (1995) for the relationship between accounting and tax.

chapter five

The USA

Chapter objectives

- To explain the importance of the US GAAP (United States Generally Accepted Accounting Principles) for global financial reporting

- To sketch the origins of American financial reporting with particular reference to the close ties between the USA and Britain in the nineteenth century and to the impact of the 1929 'Wall Street crash'

- To analyse the institutional factors that influence American financial reporting, notably the state (including taxation), the stock exchange, the accountancy profession and the universities

- To set out the elements of the American regulatory system (Congress, the SEC and the FASB) and to assess the role and relative importance of each

- To set out the components of US GAAP and to assess the significance of the 'present fairly' rule

5.1 THE IMPORTANCE OF THE USA

The importance of the USA for the study of global financial reporting derives principally from that country's economic strength. The USA is by far the world's largest economy. The five countries of the Pentad are in fact the world's five largest economies, and together account for more than half of the world's output, as measured by gross domestic product (GDP). The USA's economy is by far the largest of the five, being some 50 per cent larger that of Japan, some three times larger than that of Germany, some five times larger than that of France and over six times larger than Britain's. The USA is the principal driving force behind the globalization process that was described in Chapter 1. Its imports and exports are larger than those of any other country. It is a principal source of foreign direct investment (FDI) and also receives more FDI than any other country (see Exhibits 1.2 and 1.3). There are more American multinational enterprises (MNEs) in the top 100 than those of any other country (see Exhibit 1.4). These very numerous and powerful American MNEs are legally obliged to draw up their accounts according to United States Generally Accepted Accounting Principles (US GAAP). The term US GAAP stands for the totality of the rules that govern financial reporting in the USA. However the influence of US GAAP extends beyond the USA. Very many non-American MNEs also prepare accounts that are in conformity with US GAAP, for reasons that will be explained later; examples are the British PLC, BP Amoco, the German AG, DaimlerChrysler, and the Japanese KK, Toyota. Furthermore US GAAP has had and still has a very strong influence over the rules in other countries, where the rule-makers often adopt rules that are very similar to, and are clearly derived from, those of US GAAP. A similar influence is equally apparent over the International Accounting Standards Board's standards, which, given their importance for global financial reporting, are covered in detail in Parts Four and Five. Hence a broad understanding of US GAAP is essential for the student of global financial reporting. With this aim, this chapter covers certain general aspects of US GAAP: its historical development, the factors that have moulded it and how its rules are set.

5.2 THE ORIGINS OF AMERICAN FINANCIAL REPORTING

The USA goes back to 1776, when thirteen British colonies revolted against rule from London. With some help from France and Spain, they succeeded in asserting their independence, establishing the United States of America, whose constitution was ratified in 1787. However, despite the break of the political link, economic and social ties with Britain remained strong. For the first hundred years of the new country's existence, Britain was its principal trading partner and the principal source of its immigrants. An important factor was that during this period, Britain was the more powerful country. It was not until late in the nineteenth century that the USA overtook Britain in terms of both population and of economic strength and that immigration from other European countries (notably Germany, Scandinavia and Eastern Europe) exceeded that from Britain. However, by that time, certain abiding characteristics of the new country had become established, of which the most striking is the prevalence of the English language.

These factors explain why in the nineteenth century, developments in financial reporting in the USA closely mirrored those in Britain. In some fields, the USA was ahead of Britain. Thus the corporation became established as the predominant form of business organization for larger enterprises rather earlier in the USA than in Britain. The state of New York enacted a law which made limited liability generally available to manufacturing enterprises in 1811, which was some 44 years before the equivalent legislation in Britain (see Chapter 4, section 4.2). On the other hand, in the development of the accountancy profession, the USA lagged behind Britain. The Institute of Accounts of New York, characterized by the historians of American accountancy (Previts and Merino, 1998) as 'the earliest professional accounting organization in the United States', was not founded until 1882, almost 30 years after the foundation of the first British body, the Society of Accountants of Edinburgh in 1853. As is explained in more detail later, British chartered accountants played a major role in setting up the American profession.

In the nineteenth century, accountants in Britain and the USA faced the similar problem that the law gave virtually no guidance as to the form and content of financial statements. In both countries, enterprises had to develop for themselves the procedures to be followed for the preparation of the accounts, and accountants were the principal source of advice to enterprises on this matter.

At least in the nineteenth century, there were no great differences between British and American accountants in the accounting principles that they applied. This can be attributed to the close links between the two professions, as exemplified in the textbooks used in accountancy training: for example, Thomas Jones, identified by Previts and Merino (1998) as the most important American textbook writer of the mid nineteenth century, was born in England. However the traffic was not all one way: Benjamin Booth, whose 'Complete System of Book-keeping' (praised by a contemporary as the first English work illustrative of the modern Italian method) was published in London in 1789, was an American who was forced to flee the country because he had supported the losing side in the American War of Independence.

The reference in the above quotation to the *modern* Italian method is to the use of specialized journals, such as sales and purchases day books, which are a more efficient way of processing large numbers of transactions compared with the procedure recommended by Pacioli of recording each transaction separately first in a waste book and then in a journal. In devising ways of dealing with large quantities of accounting data, the USA has always been in advance of Britain. Thus the punched card machine was invented by an American, Hermann Hollerith, and its first application was to tabulate the results of the US census of 1890. To exploit his invention, Hollerith formed the Tabulating Machine Company, which in 1924 merged with two other enterprises to form International Business

Machines Inc. It was this company, better known by its initials IBM, which in the 1950s, virtually on its own, developed the business applications of the electronic digital computer, a machine which had been developed for military purposes during the Second World War. In the application of computers to accounting, the USA leads the world.

However in other areas, British and American accounting practice throughout the nineteenth century developed largely along parallel lines. In certain fields, American practice developed more quickly; this was particularly the case with the financial reporting of corporations, which can be attributed to the longer experience of American accountants with this legal form. The most striking example of American leadership is in the development of consolidated accounts. Many American groups prepared consolidated accounts before the turn of the century, for example the American Cotton Trust in 1886, whereas the earliest British consolidated accounts date from 1910 (Edwards and Webb, 1984). Previts and Merino (1998, p. 128) comment, 'American accountants were able to benefit from the expertise of the British professionals and at the same time to innovate, adapt and progressively determine new and different schemes of disclosure in light of the different environment of the American capital market'. The very considerable influence that the capital market, particularly the New York Stock Exchange ('Wall Street') had and still has on American financial reporting is analyzed in section 5.3.3. The particular aspect of the American environment that gave rise to consolidated accounts was the development of holding companies, generally in the form of trusts, in the later decades of the nineteenth century, the most notorious example being the Standard Oil Company of John D. Rockefeller, which in 1880 controlled 80 per cent of the country's oil refining capacity. The American accountancy profession displayed considerable flexibility and imagination in developing an accounting technique that provided useful information to investors in the changed environment.

The 'Wall Street crash' of 1929 had a profound impact on American financial reporting. During the 1920s the American economy boomed. Corporations reported record profits and the market price of their shares on the New York Stock Exchange rose higher and higher. To many people investing in shares seemed an infallible way of making money. New investors attracted by the profits being made drove prices up even higher. However prices rose only because everyone expected them to rise. In October 1929 the bubble burst. In one month the stock market index fell by a third, causing the ruin of many investors, particularly those who had purchased shares on borrowed money. The financial chaos and the loss in business confidence lead to the great depression which reached its lowest point in 1932 with the stock market index at only 15 per cent of its pre-crash level and with over 25 per cent of the American working population unemployed. There was a reaction against business and inevitably the accountancy profession came in for criticism. There was a general suspicion that, in the years before the crash, many major corporations had issued misleading accounts in which both assets and profits had been significantly overstated. There were two major problems: the inflation of asset values (often achieved by valuing assets on the basis of future profits and including lavish amounts for goodwill) and the lack of detailed figures in the income statement which prevented investors from discovering that much of the reported profits stemmed from unrealized increases in asset values. In the 1920s the prevailing political philosophy was 'laissez-faire'; the government refused to intervene to regulate financial reporting on the grounds that the best result for society as a whole would be achieved through letting such matters be decided by market forces, that is through Adam Smith's 'invisible hand'. Not surprisingly, after the crash there was an insistent public demand that this 'invisible hand' be replaced by the 'visible hand' of government regulation.

The long-term impact of the great crash on American financial reporting was twofold:

(a) The government, concluding that accounting was too important to be left to the accountants, decided that it must act to regulate the financial reporting of the major corporations. It did this by setting up the Securities and Exchange Commission, which is covered in detail in section 5.4.2.

(b) Historical cost became accepted as the maximum value at which assets might be reported. It was felt generally by accountants and non-accountants alike, that most of the serious abuses of financial reporting of the 1920s which, rightly or wrongly, were considered to have been a major cause of the crash, stemmed from reporting assets at above historical cost.

5.3 THE INSTITUTIONAL FRAMEWORK

5.3.1 The state

The USA is a federation. The powers of government are divided between the Federal government, based in Washington, and the governments of the fifty separate states. For non-Americans the Federal government is the more relevant; it consists of three branches: the executive headed by the President, the legislature (Congress) and the judiciary (the Supreme Court). The American constitution provides that the Federal government has the right to regulate commerce between the states but it also provides that all powers not specifically reserved for the Federal government reside with the states. Hence the Federal government has the power to regulate the financial reporting of enterprises whose activities extend over more than one state, which covers most large enterprises and certainly all the larger American MNEs.

In fact the Federal government has made great use of its power to regulate the activities of larger enterprises, for the United States is a highly regulated country. This was not the case in the nineteenth century when the prevailing philosophy was that government should not interfere in economic matters but the failings of private enterprise, particularly as evidenced in the great depression of the early 1930s, convinced the American people that government intervention was necessary to ensure the economy was managed in the public interest at both the macro and the micro level. For the regulation of business enterprises, the Federal government has not used the instrument of law, which has been the chosen method of the governments in Britain and other European countries. There is no equivalent in the USA of the British Companies Act.[1] Instead the Federal government has set up state agencies whose function is to oversee and regulate specific areas of the economy; examples include the Federal Trade Commission, the Federal Power Commission and the Federal Communications Commission. In the field of financial reporting, the responsible state agency is the Securities and Exchange Commission, which is covered in section 5.4.2.

5.3.2 Taxation

American enterprises pay taxes to both Federal and state governments. The principal state taxes are on sales and property, and rarely cause any problems for financial reporting. The principal Federal tax is on the enterprises' profits and is a major source of government revenue. As in Britain, financial accounting and reporting is, in principle, distinct from tax accounting. The rules for the determination of taxable income are laid down in the Internal Revenue Code which is administered by the Internal Revenue Service. There is no general rule that income and expenses for tax purposes have to be the same as those for financial reporting purposes or vice versa. However, many of the rules are the same and in practice the taxable income is computed as the financial accounting income adjusted for those items where the rules are different. Nevertheless, for most enterprises, taxable income differs substantially from financial accounting income, principally because of differences in the deduction for depreciation. This gives rise to the need to provide for deferred taxation in the financial accounts, which is one of the most controversial subjects in American accounting.

There is one major exception to the general rule of the separation of financial accounting and tax accounting. The Internal Revenue Code gives enterprises the option of using the LIFO method of inventory valuation

Exhibit 5.1   *Inventory valuations in published accounts*

	LIFO (balance sheet) $mn	FIFO (notes) $mn	Increase: FIFO over LIFO $mn	%
General Motors	10 638	12 528	1890	17.8
Ford	1800	3000	1200	66.6
General Electric	5305	6316	1011	19.1

Note: the figures for General Motors and General Electric refer to their world-wide inventories. Hence the increase from LIFO to FIFO is proportionally smaller than for Ford, whose figures refer only to its American inventories

for the computation of taxable income, but only on the condition that it is also used in the enterprise's financial accounts. The reason for this restriction is that, when some thirty years ago Congress modified the tax law to permit the use of LIFO, it considered that it would be inequitable for the enterprise's shareholders to benefit from a change that resulted in lower tax revenues for the government. In effect Congress insisted that in this matter the enterprise's income from the government's viewpoint and from the shareholders' viewpoint be measured according to the same principles.

This tax rule has had a considerable impact in two areas:

(a) LIFO is far more common as an inventory valuation method in the USA than it is in other countries, particularly in comparison with Britain where it has been virtually outlawed, as the ASB's standard states that normally LIFO will not give a true and fair view of closing inventory.

(b) The financial statements of the many enterprises that use LIFO are affected, notably in the amounts reported for inventory and costs of production. Since, over the last thirty years, the general tendency has been for prices to rise, the use of LIFO normally results in enterprises reporting lower inventory values and higher costs compared with other methods. The differences can be considerable, as is evidenced by the figures given in Exhibit 5.1.

5.3.3 The corporate financing system

The most striking feature of the American corporate financing system is the importance of the stock exchange. In the USA, many more corporations have their shares listed on a stock exchange compared with other countries. For them, the capital market is a most important source of finance. The larger corporations go to the market to raise additional capital;

smaller enterprises seek to have their shares listed once they have reached a certain critical size, both to facilitate the raising of further finance and to enable the founders to realize some of the capital gains on their investment. However even more important is the stock exchange as the venue for the market for corporate control. Take-over bids are very common in the USA and, in such an environment, corporate management takes great care to ensure that the investing public receives full information about the enterprise's position and performance so as to ensure that the market price of its shares reflects their full value. The principal function of financial statements from the viewpoint of corporate management (that is the preparers) is to keep the market value of the corporation's shares at a high level.

The dominance of the stock market explains why it is generally agreed in the USA that the principal function of financial statements is to provide information for investors. An important factor here is that a high proportion of the American population own shares in listed corporations; in 1990 it was estimated that 51mn Americans owned shares, that is one in five of the population. In the USA share ownership is not limited to wealthy individuals as in many other countries. Hence there is general public support for government action to improve the financial reporting of the larger listed corporations. The widespread pattern of share-ownership explains why so much emphasis is placed in the USA on disclosure: on the dissemination by the enterprise of information about its activities to the public at large.

The influence that the capital market has on the financial reporting of American corporations is well summed up in the following excerpt from a paper by a leading government official:

> Financial accounting and reporting in the USA has developed into a system where public companies present the facts surrounding their business and operations with great transparency . . . In this system information is king and also queen. Our public companies lay out the facts and let the market participants decide on how the facts should affect security prices and how capital should be allocated . . . Keeping information private has a cost. That cost is reflected in reduced security prices . . . an issuer's securities may not be fully priced by participants in the . . . market place if disclosures . . . are opaque. If investors have a choice as to whether to buy the securities of two issuers – one whose disclosures are great and transparent and one whose disclosures are minimal and opaque – the investor will select the securities of the issuer whose disclosures are great and transparent. (Schuetze, 1994)

5.3.4 The accountancy profession

The American accountancy profession is the world's largest as is apparent from the figures given in Exhibit 2.5. There are two American professional bodies that are members of IFAC: the American Institute of Certified Public Accountants (AICPA) with 328 000 members and the Institute of Management Accountants with some 75 000 members. The AICPA is the more important body in the field of financial reporting. Its members are all Certified Public Accountants (CPAs), but not all CPAs are members of the AICPA. The CPA qualification is granted by the states and it is not legally required for a CPA to become a member of the AICPA in order to exercise the profession. However the AICPA estimates that three out of four CPAs are members. The AICPA's membership is split roughly equally between accountants who work in the public accountancy profession and those who work in industry (about 40 per cent in each: the remainder work in government, in education or are retired).

The USA's earliest professional accounting association was the Institute of Accounts of New York founded in 1882. It organized meetings for its members at which technical and professional papers were discussed. At one such meeting, in 1886, a member gave a paper on 'French and American Account Keeping Contrasted' which according to Previts and Merino (1998) was 'the first known professional address on international accounting matters in America'. However this meeting was even more significant as it was attended by a visiting British Chartered Accountant, Edwin Guthrie, who by request gave a description of the Institute of Chartered Accountants in England and Wales which had been founded some six years previously. Almost certainly this was the impulse that in the following year led a group of members of the Institute of Accounts to cooperate with a number of British Chartered Accountants resident in New York to set up the American Association of Public Accountants, AAPA, the forerunner of the present day AICPA. Both the first president and the first secretary of the AAPA were British; the vice president and treasurer were American. The AAPA's first task was to lobby the legislature of the State of New York to enact a law protecting the title of 'Certified Public Accountant'; it was finally successful in 1896 when the Certified Public Accountants Law of New York came into effect. This law provided that the CPA examination should be administered, on behalf of the state government, by the University of the State of New York and not by the AAPA. Thus from its very beginning the American accountancy profession was marked by two characteristics which are still very important:

- The universities were closely associated with the accountancy profession; this is covered in more detail in the next section
- Entry to the profession was controlled by the state authorities and not by the professional associations (as was the case in Britain)[2]

Initially expatriate British accountants dominated the AAPA. As a reaction, native-born CPAs set up their own societies in New York, Pennsylvania and Illinois. When these societies merged with the AAPA in 1905, there was a contest for the post of president between Lowes Dickinson, a leading expatriate British Chartered Accountant, and Elijah Sells, an American CPA and co-founder of the firm of Haskins and Sells. The election of Elijah Sells marked the end of any significant British influence over the American profession. After a number of name changes, the present title of the American Institute of Certified Public Accountants (AICPA) was adopted in 1957.

During the twentieth century the American profession witnessed very much the same growth in numbers as that of Britain. The membership of the AAPA (later the AICPA) rose from 9500 in 1945 to 95 000 in 1973 and to over 300 000 20 years later. The reasons for this growth were (in chronological order):

(a) A greater demand for audit services as the public and the government demanded more thorough and effective audits in the wake of the Wall Street crash of 1929.

(b) A growth in the number of accountants employed by both enterprises and public administrations on internal control and internal audit work as organizations became bigger and more complex.

(c) A considerable growth in demand for taxation advice as the Federal income tax became ever more complicated and was extended to an ever greater part of the population. Prior to 1941 fewer than five million Americans paid income tax; in 1996 over 115 million were filing income tax returns.

(d) A remarkable development in the consultancy activities of the major firms.

About half of the AICPA's membership is employed in industry and government; the parallel growth in their numbers reflected the increasing demand in large organizations for all forms of internal audit and control services. However, unlike their British counterparts, few CPAs make it to the upper reaches of management.

Over the twentieth century there was significant merger activity among accountancy firms which resulted in the larger firms becoming ever larger. By 2000, the market for public accountancy services was dominated by just five firms, 'The Big Five' – their names and other details are given in Exhibit 5.2.

Exhibit 5.2 *'The Big Five'*

	National origin of main component firms	Number of employees*	Annual fee income ($mn)
Arthur Andersen	USA	82 000	8400
PricewaterhouseCoopers	USA and UK	52 000	21 500
Ernst & Young	USA and UK	63 000	9200
KPMG	USA, UK, Netherlands, Germany	66 000	13 500
Deloitte Touche Tohmatsu	USA, UK, Japan	58 000	11 200

Note: * Partners plus professional staff (worldwide)

Source: *Accountancy*, **128** (August 2001), (1296), p. 20

There are three main points to be made about the 'Big Five':

(a) **All of the 'Big Five' are combinations of national firms.** The extent to which they are managed as a single enterprise varies considerably: for example, Arthur Andersen is much more centralized than KPMG which is more like a loose confederation.

(b) **All are very large enterprises.** In terms of number of employees, they rank with the world's largest MNEs.[3] They are truly multinational enterprises with offices in most of the larger countries.

(c) **Although all of the 'Big Five' are made up of firms from many countries, in all cases the American firm is the biggest and the most influential.** Arthur Andersen has the strongest American character. It was founded in Chicago in 1913 by Arthur Andersen, an American whose parents came from Scandinavia. The firm grew rapidly, almost entirely by organic growth and not through mergers, which explains why it has a stronger central management than any of the others and also a more pronounced American character. In each of the other four of the 'Big Five', British firms played a leading role in setting up its precursors but, over time, the American side of the firm became increasingly important so that now it predominates. Given the dominant role of the Americans and the British, the 'Big Five' are rightly considered to be Anglo-Saxon firms, notwithstanding a significant presence of other countries, notably in KPMG (Germany and the Netherlands) and Deloitte Touche Tohmatsu (Japan).

5.3.5 The universities

The universities are an important feature of the institutional framework of financial reporting in the USA, to a far greater extent than in any other country. As already mentioned, right at the beginning, their principal contribution was to administer the CPA examinations. However they soon took on the task of educating entrants to the profession. The first university course in accounting is believed to be a series of lectures on 'the theory and practice of accounting' given at the Wharton School of the University of Pennsylvania in 1883. By 1930, more than three hundred universities and colleges were offering a BA in accounting and over a third of American practitioners had college degrees. Thirty years later all new entrants were required to have a BA degree and at present the proposal that an MA degree in accounting should be required is under active discussion.

However the most important contribution of American universities to financial reporting has been in the development of accounting theory. In the USA, the theories developed by academics have had a considerable influence on the rules and practice of financial reporting. Of particular importance in this respect has been the work of the American Accounting Association (AAA), which is the association that represents the university teachers of accounting. The all-embracing title, adopted in 1935 to replace the more modest but more accurate title of American Association of University Instructors in Accounting, gives an indication of the association's ambitions and scope. Throughout the twentieth century, the AAA has taken as a principal objective the improvement of financial reporting practice.

In the earlier years of the twentieth century, the most influential academic was William Paton, Professor of Accounting at the University of Michigan from 1917 to 1959. His long life (he died in 1991 at the age of 101) spanned the whole formative period of American financial reporting. During his most active period, in the 1920s and 1930s, he was the author of numerous books and articles on the theoretical aspects of accounting, of which two were of particular significance:

(a) In 'Accounting Theory, with special reference to the corporate enterprise' (published in 1922), he developed the enterprise theory, in opposition to the prevailing proprietary theory. Although the enterprise theory never became fully accepted and present practice is still based on the proprietary theory, this book made Paton's reputation as America's leading accounting theorist. The relative merits of the two theories are discussed further in Chapter 16.

(b) In 'An introduction to corporate accounting standards', which was written jointly with A.C. Littleton and published by the AAA in 1940, Paton set out a completely logical and practical method of applying historical cost accounting to the measurement of the income of the corporation. The approach was known as 'matching and attaching'; costs were carried forward as assets in the balance sheet until they could be matched against realized revenues. With this approach the income statement dominated, as the primary function of financial statements was to measure the enterprise's income; the balance sheet became little more than a link between successive income statements, a depositary for items of revenue and expense that were waiting to be reported in the income statement. The 'matching and attaching approach' was considered by most practitioners to be a convincing answer to the criticisms levied against accounting in the wake of the 1929 Wall Street crash. It provided the theoretical basis for financial reporting practice for the next thirty years. Only in recent years has its predominance been questioned with the development of the balance sheet approach to income determination.

One of the AAA's most significant contributions to the development of financial reporting has been to promote the idea of a conceptual framework, which is covered in more detail in Chapter 13.

5.4 THE AMERICAN REGULATORY SYSTEM

The principal elements of the American system for the regulation of financial reporting are set out in Exhibit 5.3, which presents the three main actors: the government, the SEC and the FASB, whose respective roles will now be examined.

5.4.1 The government

In the hierarchy of rules presented in Exhibit 3.2, law is at the top. The USA is no exception to this general rule. In the USA the legislative power is exercised by the Congress (which has two houses, the House of Representatives and the Senate), subject to a limited power of veto by the President. The American legislature has enacted very few laws that deal with the detailed rules of financial reporting. Instead it has set up a government agency, the Securities and Exchange Commission (SEC), and given it the authority to formulate these rules. However, since the SEC was set up by a law, the primacy of law was maintained. Moreover, on a few occasions, the Congress has enacted laws containing detailed financial reporting rules, in this way emphasizing where the ultimate authority lies. Given the significance of these rare assertions of the power of Congress, they are analysed in detail in section 5.4.4.

5.4.2 The SEC: the Securities and Exchange Commission

The SEC was set up by the Securities Exchange Act of 1934, as part of a series of laws passed in the wake of the 1929 Wall Street crash. The

Exhibit 5.3 *The US system for the regulation of financial reporting*

```
        US
    Government                                    8 Sponsoring
     President                                    Organizations
   and Congress

                    Appoints                          Appoint
                    and funds
                                                         │
         Lobbies                                         ▼
                                                       FAF
                        SEC                          15 Trustees
                         5
                    Commissioners
                     plus staff                      Appoints
                                    Delegates        and funds
    Enacts

                                    Lobbies            FASB
                                                     7 full-time
                                                      members
                     Issues

                                                      Issues

                        FRR                            FAS
                     Financial                       Financial
       Laws          Reporting                      Accounting
                     Releases                       Standards

    Key:
    SEC    Securities and Exchange Commission
    FAF    Financial Accounting Foundation
    FASB   Financial Accounting Standards Board
```

Commission consists of five Commissioners appointed by the President, with the advice and consent of the Senate, for a term of five years; they are assisted by a large staff of some 2000 professionals and administrators.

The SEC's principal function is to regulate the stock exchanges. Clearly financial reporting has an important impact on the functioning of the capital market and the SEC gives great attention to this matter. However the SEC's authority extends only to corporations whose shares are listed on an American stock exchange, plus a handful of very large unlisted enterprises. It is estimated that the SEC's writ covers only some 12 000 corporations out of the total of three million. The SEC requires all corporations under its jurisdiction to make periodic returns, consisting of a full return once a year, which includes a full set of financial statements, plus less detailed returns at quarterly intervals. Its staff checks these returns to ensure, inter alia, that the financial statements comply with US GAAP; in cases of non-compliance, the SEC can impose penalties that include fines and suspension of the erring corporation's shares.

The SEC has been granted the power by Congress to define US GAAP. However, shortly after its foundation, the SEC decided to delegate this function to a standard-setting body in the private sector – currently the FASB (described in the next section). In 1973, it confirmed this delegation in the following terms: 'principles, standards and practice promulgated by the FASB will be considered by the Commission as having substantial authoritative support, and those contrary to such FASB promulgations will be considered to have no such support' (SEC, 1973). The reasons why a body with the power to set rules may decide to delegate it to another body have already been discussed in Chapter 3.

However the SEC is still responsible to the American government for the proper operation of the capital market and therefore has to assure itself that the rules promulgated by the FASB are appropriate. It achieves this in two ways:

(a) By keeping in close contact with the FASB and making sure that this body is fully aware of its views; the relationship between the SEC and the FASB has been described as one where each side seeks to achieve 'mutual nonsurprise', in that the SEC makes sure that the FASB is aware of its thinking on important issues and the FASB keeps the SEC informed on the progress of its proposals.

(b) By issuing its own rules when it considers that the FASB's rules are wrong. The SEC's rules are contained in documents known as 'Releases', they are binding on listed corporations and override the FASB's standards. However the SEC has generally been satisfied with the rules promulgated by the FASB and only occasionally has had to go to the length of issuing its own rule, essentially as a means of reminding the FASB who is the boss.

5.4.3 The FASB: the Financial Accounting Standards Board

The FASB is the USA's principal financing reporting rule-making body. It is the latest in a line of standard-setting bodies, its predecessors being the Committee on Accounting Procedure, (CAP 1938–59) and the Accounting Principles Board, (APB 1959–73). Both previous bodies issued statements about the contents of US GAAP. Those of the CAP were termed 'Accounting Research Bulletins' (ARBs) and those of the APB, 'Opinions'. Although these bodies no longer exist, their pronouncements are considered to be authoritative statements of US GAAP unless they have been overruled by a subsequent FASB standard or SEC release.

The FASB is a private body. The seven members of the Board are appointed by the Financial Accounting Foundation (FAF), which is also a private body. The FAF provides all the funds, but does not interfere in the operations of the FASB, which issues standards on its own authority. This arrangement was chosen in order to ensure that the FASB could arrive at its decisions free of outside financial pressures. The relationship between the FAF and the FASB is essentially the same as that between the UK's FRC and ASB. In fact, as the FASB was founded some seventeen years before the ASB, one suspects that the British copied the Americans.

The FAF is appointed and funded by eight sponsoring organizations: AICPA (financial accountants and auditors), AAA (academics), AIMR (users), FEI (preparers), IMA (preparers), GFOA (public sector), NSA (state accountants) and SIA (users).[4] An important point to note is that the sponsoring organizations cover a wide spectrum of society, embracing all groups with an interest in financial reporting. It was widely felt that the FASB's two predecessors, the CAP and the APB, failed because they were too narrowly based, as they were dominated by financial accountants.

The seven members of the FASB are well-paid, full-time experts, appointed for a period of five years, with the possibility of reappointment for one additional five-year term. In order to assure their independence, they are obliged to sever all connections with their previous employer. For example, one of the recent members, Gerhart Mueller, not only had to resign his position as Professor of Accounting at the University of Washington but also was obliged to give up his activity as a writer of textbooks. Given that the board members are chosen for their expert knowledge of financial reporting, all but one are CPAs and five of the current seven members were practising accountants at some time in their previous career. Although the FASB is more widely based than its two predecessors, it would seem that, at the level of the body that actually makes the standards, it is still dominated by accountants.

The board is supported by a large staff of some fifty well-qualified professionals. Its budget, largely spent on salaries, exceeds $15mn per year. It is generally agreed that these resources make the FASB the world's best-equipped standard-setting body, far surpassing all the others. By way of comparison, the 2000 budget of Britain's ASB was about $4mn and that of the IASC about $3mn.

The FASB's most important function is to issue statements that define US GAAP; these statements fall into three categories:

(a) **Financial Accounting Standards (FAS).** Since its formation in 1973, the FASB has issued over 130 FASs. Given the relative lack of laws enacted by Congress or of releases from the SEC, the FASs form by far the largest corpus of rules relating to financial reporting.

(b) **Concept statements.** Between 1978 and 1985, the FASB issued six statements of financial accounting concepts which, together with a seventh statement issued in 2000, make up the FASB's conceptual framework. A conceptual framework aims to set out the objectives and general principles of financial reporting, but contains no detailed rules. Its function is to provide guidance to the FASB in formulating these detailed rules and to the public in interpreting and implementing them. The role of a conceptual framework in the rule-making process is considered in more detail in Chapter 13 in relation to the IASC's framework.

(c) **Other statements:** These include FASB Interpretations and Implementation Guides and Consensus Positions of the Urgent Issues Task Force. This latter body (which is part of the FASB 'family') consists of about twenty members from public accounting and industry, whose function is to deal rapidly with urgent matters, such as perverse interpretations of FASs or newly-invented accounting techniques.

In developing its statements, the FASB follows a set of procedures known as 'due process'. The principal features of 'due process' are:

(a) **Formality:** The FASB's decisions are not arbitrary; they are always the outcome of a formal procedure laid down in the FASB's constitution. For example, to issue a standard, five members of the Board must vote in favour.

(b) **Consultation:** The FASB is obliged to consult widely before issuing a standard. It does this by:

(i) Consulting the Financial Accounting Standards Advisory Council (FASAC) on all matters relating to its activities, including adding a project to the agenda. The FASAC consists of more than thirty members who are broadly representative of preparers, auditors and users of financial information

(ii) Setting up a task force of outside experts to assist it in the preparation of a standard

(iii) Issuing a discussion document which sets out the problem and presents alternative solutions; this document is distributed widely with an invitation to submit written comments

(iv) Holding a public hearing at which anybody may comment on the matter

(v) Issuing an exposure draft that sets out the proposed text of the standard, again with an invitation to submit written comments

The FASB is obliged to consider carefully the views of all constituents before reaching a decision. However it has stated that 'the ultimate determinant of concepts and standards must be the Board's judgement, based on research, public input, and careful deliberation, about the usefulness of the resulting information'.

(c) **Publicity**: All important decisions are taken in a meeting to which the public is admitted; all relevant documents are made publicly available. A major aim of this policy is to avoid any impression that the FASB's decisions are influenced by covert pressure from powerful lobbies. Lobbying certainly takes place but it must be open.

5.4.4 Congress v. the SEC v. the FASB

The role of the three rule-makers (Congress, the SEC and the FASB) and their interrelationships may be made clearer by an analysis of three incidents in recent history.

The Investment Tax Credit

The first incident involved the FASB's predecessor, the Accounting Principles Board (APB). In 1962, the American government introduced a new tax incentive, the investment tax credit. The taxpayer was to be permitted to deduct a substantial part of the cost of newly-acquired assets (other than land and buildings) from his tax liability for the year in which the asset was placed in service. At that time there were two acceptable methods of accounting for the investment tax credit:

(a) **Flow-through**: The full amount of the tax benefit was credited to the income statement in the first year. This approach was favoured by the preparers (as it enabled them to report higher initial profits) and the government (which had introduced the credit as a means of stimulating physical investment and was concerned that its incentive effect would be weakened if it did not lead to an immediate increase in reported profits).

(b) **Deferral**: The tax benefit was to be spread over the life of the asset. This approach was favoured by many leading members of the accountancy profession who considered that the flow-through approach conflicted with the matching principle.

The APB favoured the deferral approach and issued Opinion No. 2 which stated that this was the only acceptable approach. However the APB's Opinion was contested by a powerful coalition of preparers and certain major accountancy firms which lobbied the SEC. The SEC came to the conclusion that 'substantial authoritative support' existed for both methods and in 1963 issued Accounting Series Release No. 96 which permitted the use of either method. The APB was obliged to issue Opinion No. 4, which also permitted both methods. Commenting on the incident, Miller, Redding and Bahnson (1998) remark: 'The APB attempted to deal with the investment tax credit in 1962 as an accounting issue instead of as a political issue.'

In 1967, the APB again attempted to outlaw the flow-through method but was obliged to back down in the face of opposition from the government and a clear signal from the SEC that it would not support the APB.

In 1971, the APB made a last effort. This time, mindful of its defeats in 1962 and 1967, it prepared the ground carefully by gaining the prior support of both the government and the SEC for its proposals. However the APB's proposals ran into considerable opposition in the Congress, no doubt influenced by the lobbying of preparers. A Senate Committee reported that it was 'concerned that the investment credit ... should have as great a stimulative effect on the economy as possible. Therefore ... it would appear undesirable to preclude the use of "flow through" in the financial reporting of net income'. This led to Congress including a clause in the 1971 Revenue Act to the effect that the tax payer was not bound by anyone's rules as to how to report the tax savings from the investment tax credit in the financial statements. The APB withdrew its proposal and issued a statement deploring Congressional involvement in the establishment of accounting principles.

It is generally agreed that the long-running saga of the investment tax credit in which the APB over a decade suffered three humiliating defeats, was a major cause in the loss of this body's prestige and authority, which led ultimately to its replacement by the FASB.

Accounting for oil exploration costs

In 1978, the FASB issued FAS 19 'Financial Accounting and Reporting for Oil and Gas Producing Companies' which inter alia required these companies to use the 'successful efforts' method of accounting for exploration costs; only exploration costs that resulted in commercially exploitable oil and gas fields should be capitalized. Many oil companies preferred the 'full cost' method (under which all exploration costs were capitalized) and accordingly lobbied the SEC. In response the SEC issued Accounting Series Release No. 252 which allowed a choice between the two methods. The FASB was obliged to back down and issued FAS 25, which rescinded the offending parts of FAS 19. Subsequently the FASB worked with the SEC to develop a method of reporting exploration costs that was generally acceptable to all parties. The approach, which involved reporting in the notes details of proven reserves, was set out in FAS 69 (issued in 1982), which received the SEC's approval.

Accounting for share options

In recent years, share options have become a significant part of the total emoluments of the senior staff of American corporations. Under the current rules, the granting of an option is only reported as an expense to the extent that the strike price is less than the market price at the time of issue. In fact, for virtually all options, the strike price is fixed as equal to or greater than the current market price, leading to a reported expense of zero. This treatment results in a substantial understatement of the cost of the option when subsequently the market price goes up; in fact such an increase is normally expected and explains why the option is generally regarded as a valuable element of a remuneration package.

In 1993, the FASB sought to change current practice and issued an exposure draft which proposed that the granting of an option should be reported as an expense equal to its fair value at that date. This proposal led to a storm of protest which is graphically described by Zeff (1997). The opponents of the measure succeeded in portraying it as a threat to the whole practice of granting share options which were a major element of the remuneration of thousands of people. There were public demonstrations which were reported in the press and on television. Many Americans learned for the first time about the FASB which was represented as a sinister organization intent on depriving true-blooded Americans of their fundamental liberties. They lobbied Congress; Congress lobbied the SEC; the SEC lobbied the FASB; in additional both Congress and the SEC threatened to intervene more directly. The result was predictable; the FASB withdrew its proposal that the cost of share options should be reported as an expense in the income statement.

These three incidents demonstrate clearly two important characteristics of the American system for the regulation of financial reporting:

(a) **It is fundamentally political.** The FASB claims that standard-setting is a technical activity carried out by experts who are guided by research and basic principles. It developed its conceptual framework to back up this claim. However these experts are only permitted to set the rules within the limits set by the politicians. Where a subject is of little political interest, the FASB is left to develop its standards following its 'due process'. But in matters that society considers to be important, the FASB has to give way. The USA is a democracy not a technocracy. Miller, Redding and Bahnson, whose book *The FASB: the people, the process and the politics* (1998) is by far the best exposition of this body, ask the question 'Is the FASB a political institution?' and give the unequivocal answer 'a clear yes'.

(b) **Ultimate authority lies with the legislative power (Congress), subject to the veto of the President.** The SEC has to consider the views of

Congress in carrying out its regulatory function and the FASB has to acknowledge the superior authority of the SEC, a body granted this authority by a law. However the SEC was created by a law and can be abolished by a law

5.5   US GAAP

The hierarchy of US GAAP

The expression US GAAP (US Generally Accepted Accounting Principles) refers to the totality of rules relating to financial reporting that are recognized as acceptable by the SEC. A more accurate title would be US SECAAP (SEC Accepted Accounting Principles). Apart from the relatively few specific laws enacted by Congress and releases issued by the SEC, the principal component of US GAAP is the body of Financial Accounting Standards issued by the FASB – over 130 FASs at the last count and rising. However even this enormous mountain of paper is insufficient for the definition of US GAAP. Other statements are recognized as part of GAAP. The authoritative definition of what is included in GAAP is set out in the AICPA's Statement of Auditing Standard No. 69, which has been accepted by the SEC. This statement sets out GAAP in the form of a hierarchy with four levels:

(a) Financial Accounting Standards, Interpretations issued by the FASB and statements of the FASB's predecessors (the CAP and the APB) in so far as they have not been overruled by an FAS.
(b) Statements of position of the AICPA.
(c) Consensus positions of the Emerging Issues Task Force.
(d) Interpretations of the AICPA and staff papers of the SEC and the FASB.

What is interesting about the above hierarchy is the continuing strong position of the AICPA. Not only are the rules of the CAP and the APB (both in their day dominated by the AICPA) still recognized, but the AICPA's Statements of Position occupy a high place in the hierarchy. Coupled with the fact that six of the current seven members of the FASB are CPAs, this would seem to suggest that professional accountants are still a strong force in the regulatory system.

The 'present fairly' rule

American auditors are required by their professional rules to report that the financial statements that they have audited 'present fairly, in all material respects, the financial position of the XYZ Corporation . . . in conformity with generally accepted accounting principles' (AICPA, Statement of Auditing Standards, No. 69). The question arises as to the meaning of 'present fairly'. Does this phrase have the same impact as 'true and fair view' in Britain, where it is used as a justification for not following specific rules, even those laid down in the Companies Act? The answer is an emphatic 'no'. The American phrase is 'present fairly... in conformity with GAAP'. It is not permitted to depart from a rule in GAAP on the pretext that this is necessary to 'present fairly'. This is made clear in the AICPA's Code of Professional Conduct. It is a disciplinary offence for a CPA to issue an unqualified audit report on accounts that do not conform with GAAP.[5] To make the matter completely clear the AICPA has defined GAAP as being the elements of the hierarchy presented in the previous section.

5.6 THE ESSENTIAL CHARACTERISTICS OF AMERICAN FINANCIAL REPORTING

The essential characteristics of the financial reporting of American corporations may be summarized as follows:

(a) **Highly regulated.** Financial reporting is highly regulated. Foreigners may think of the Americans as a freedom-loving people who resist being told what to do by the government. This is certainly not the case with financial reporting. American corporations are obliged to apply the rules of US GAAP, which are laid down in quite extraordinary detail, in the very voluminous documents listed in section 5.5.

(b) **Information for the capital market.** It is widely accepted that the primary function of financial statements is to provide information for the capital market.

(c) **High level of disclosure.** The influence of the capital market is most obvious in the very high level of disclosure required by US GAAP. American corporations provide more information about themselves than do those of any other country – as demonstrated by the research of Doupnik and Salter, which was presented in Chapter 2 (see Exhibit 2.10).

(d) **Measurement of assets and profits.** Whereas the position with respect to disclosure is clear, that with respect to the measurement of assets and profits is much more complex. The Wall Street crash of 1929 had a very strong impact on financial reporting which is still apparent today, over 70 years later. Thus the SEC is a strong champion of historical cost and has generally resisted any proposal that assets might be reported at above historical cost. Thus, for example, the British concept of 'modified historical cost' is anathema to the Americans; it is strictly forbidden to report fixed assets at market value when this is above historical cost. However this prohibition is clearly inconsistent with the provision of full information to the capital market. To a certain extent, the conflict has been resolved by providing full information in the notes whilst maintaining historical cost as the valuation basis in the balance sheet. However, in recent years, the voices of those who demand that market values should also be reported in the balance sheet and income statement have become louder and are beginning to be heard. An important factor is the strong influence of the American universities (see section 5.3.5). By and large academics are in favour of greater use of market values in the financial statements and they appear to be winning the argument. For example even the SEC is in favour of reporting certain financial instruments at market value. Doupnik and Salter found that, with regard to measurement, the USA was less conservative than all other countries and used more complex measurement practices (see Exhibit 2.10). The authors contest the finding on conservatism, since, with respect to 'modified historical cost', Britain is certainly less conservative than the USA. However they accept that, in many fields, US GAAP demands complex and sophisticated measurements. Hence, with regard to asset and profit measurement, the American position is both complex and currently rather fluid, which renders problematic a definitive judgement on the matter.

SUMMARY

The origins of American financial reporting in the nineteenth century were examined and the importance of the British connection in these formative years was demonstrated. The impact of the 'Wall Street crash' was analysed, as leading to greater government regulation and the setting of historical cost as the upper limit to the reported values of assets. The institutional factors that influence financial reporting in the USA were identified as the state, taxation (notably in relation to LIFO), the stock exchange, the accountancy profession and the universities. The American regulatory system was examined, including an analysis of the respective roles of the state (the government and the Congress), the SEC and the FASB. Finally the components of US GAAP were listed and the significance of the 'present fairly' rule discussed.

Review questions

1. Analyse the relationship between British and American financial reporting in the nineteenth century. In what areas was Britain ahead of the USA and in what areas was the reverse the case?

2. What was the impact of the 1929 'Wall Street crash' on American financial reporting?

3. How does the American government seek to regulate financial reporting?

4. In what area does taxation have a strong impact on the accounts of American corporations?

5. What are the respective roles of the SEC and the FASB?

6. What is meant by 'due process'?

7. What are the components of US GAAP?

8. What is the significance of the 'present fairly' rule?

Notes

1. The individual states and not the federal government are responsible for the incorporation of companies. Hence each state has its own law that regulates the financial reporting of enterprises registered in that state. However in general these laws are far less detailed than the British Companies Act and, for the larger enterprises, the regulations of the Federal Government (as described later in this chapter) are far more significant.

2. The examination that candidate CPAs have to pass in order to qualify for the profession is now set and administered by the AICPA. However the actual decision to admit someone to the profession is the prerogative of the state boards of public accountancy.

3. For example, Pharmacia and Upjohn Inc, which is the world's 100th largest MNE according to a United Nations report (United Nations, 1999) has 30 000 employees and total sales of $10.4bn.

4. The full titles are: AICPA – American Institute of Certified Public Accountants; AAA – American Accounting Association; AIMR – Association for Investment Management and Research; IMA – Institute of Management Accountants; GFOA – Government Finance Officers Association; NSA – National Association of State Auditors, Comptrollers and Treasurers; SEI – Securities Industry Association.

5. The AICPA rule 203 allows an exception in circumstances in which compliance with GAAP would produce misleading information if the exception is clearly and completely described in the audit opinion. However this exception has no operational effect as it is virtually never invoked. On this matter Professor Zeff has commented: 'While it is true that rule 203 of the AICPA Code of Professional Conduct provides that there may be circumstances in which the auditor could believe that adherence to promulgated GAAP could make the financial statement misleading, experienced US auditors tell me that they cannot recall ever seeing "rule 203 exceptions", especially in the financial statements of companies subject to the Securities and Exchange Commission, which would comprehend almost all publicly trade companies' (quoted in Alexander and Archer, 2000).

References

Alexander, D and Archer, S 'On the myth of "Anglo-Saxon" financial accounting', *The International Journal of Accounting*, **5**(4) (2000), pp. 539–57.

American Institute of Certified Public Accountants *Statement of Auditing Standards No. 69*, AICPA, New York.

Edwards, JR and Webb, KM 'The development of group accounting in the United Kingdom', *Accounting Historians Journal* (Spring 1984), pp. 31–61.

Fischer, N, Iannaconi, T and Lechner, H 'United States – Group Accounts', *Transacc: Transnational Accounting*, 2nd edn, D Ordelheide (ed.), Palgrave, Basingstoke (2001), pp. 2987–3054.

Fischer, N, Iannaconi, T and Lechner, H 'United States – Individual Accounts', *Transacc: Transnational Accounting*, 2nd edn, D Ordelheide (ed.), Palgrave, Basingstoke (2001), pp. 2851–986.

Miller, P, Redding, R and Bahnson, P (ed.), *The FASB: the people, the process and the politics*, Irwin, Homewood (1998).

Previts, GJ and Merino, BD *A History of Accountancy in the United States*, Ohio State University Press, Ohio (1998).

Schuetze, WP 'What is the future of mutual recognition of financial statements and is comparability really necessary?', *European Accounting Review*, **3**(2) (1994), pp. 330–4.

Securities and Exchange Commission *Accounting Series Release No. 150*, SEC, Washington (1973).

United Nations *World Investment Report 1999*, United Nations, New York and Geneva (1999).

Zeff, S *Forging Accounting Principles in Five Countries* (eds), Stipes Publishing Company, Illinois (1972).

Zeff, S 'Playing the Congressional card on employee stock options', *The Development of Accounting in an International Context*, T Cooke and C Nobes (eds), Routledge, London (1997).

Further reading

For the historical development, see Previts and Merino (1998), particularly Chapter 8 which deals with the period since 1973 and therefore covers the present situation. For more information about the regulatory process, see Miller, Redding and Bahnson (1998), notably Chapter 2 (structure), Chapter 3 (due process) and Chapter 5 (political conflicts). For the respective roles of the SEC and the FASB, see Zeff (1972) and (1997) and also visit these organizations' web sites: www.sec.gov and www.rutgers.edu/accounting/raw/fasb. For a detailed analysis of the rules of financial reporting see the two cited references to Fischer *et al.* (2001).

chapter six

France

Chapter objectives

- To trace the historical development of financial reporting in France
- To analyse the principal influences over the financial reporting of French enterprises, emphasizing the dominant role of the state and the secondary roles played by the capital market and the accountancy profession
- To set out the principal features of the French regulatory system, with special reference to the Plan Comptable Général
- To outline recent developments concerning the consolidated accounts of French multinational enterprises

6.1 THE IMPORTANCE OF FRANCE FOR THE STUDENT OF FINANCIAL REPORTING

The study of financial reporting in France is important for three principal reasons:

(a) France is a major economic power. It is the world's fourth largest trading nation as measured by exports (see Exhibit 1.1); as regards foreign direct investment, it is third in the world for outflows and inflows (see Exhibit 1.2). There are seven French enterprises in the top 50 MNEs: Aventis, TotalFinaElf, Suez Lyonnaise des Eaux, Renault, Alcatel, Peugeot and Vivendi.

(b) France has had a significant influence over the development of financial reporting in other countries, notably those of Southern Europe, such as Spain and Italy, and former French colonies, such as Algeria and Senegal.

139

(c) France has a distinctive approach to financial reporting, in which the state plays a major role and which is fundamentally different from that of the other four countries studied here, particularly the Anglo-Saxon ones. The French financial reporting system has a very long and distinguished pedigree dating back more than three centuries.

French scholars complain bitterly that foreigners are totally ignorant of the French contribution to the science of accountancy. Hopefully this ignorance will be somewhat reduced by the following analysis of the French financial reporting, which starts with an account of its origins.

6.2 THE ORIGINS OF FRENCH FINANCIAL REPORTING

The history of formal accounting in France goes back to 1673, which means that France can trace the origins of its present system back to a date that is earlier by over a century than almost all other countries. In 1673, Jean-Baptiste Colbert, who was the Contrôleur Général (in effect the Minister of Finance) of the French king Louis XIV, issued a decree that marked the start of a long-running interest of the French state in accountancy. The decree required all merchants to maintain accounting records; it required them to 'have a book which contains all their trans-actions, their bills of exchange, their debtors and creditors and the money expended to support their business'.[1] The directive did not indicate how the books of account were to be kept.[2] However, in 1675, Jacques Savary, a colleague of Colbert, published an accounting textbook, Le parfait négociant (the perfect merchant) with the aim of explaining to merchants how to meet the decree's requirements. It should be noted that the 1673 decree was concerned solely with the internal records of merchants; it made no mention of the financial statements. Over a century was to pass before the French state began to show an interest in this subject.

The reason for Colbert's interest in accountancy is evident from his other achievements. As Louis XIV's principal economic adviser for around twenty years, he was instrumental in turning France into the foremost economic power of Europe. He reorganized the administration, balanced the budget, encouraged exports, developed the merchant navy, improved communications and promoted the growth of industry. He created or encouraged both public and private businesses, of which some still exist (for example Saint Gobain). Mikol (1995) defines Colbert's ideology in the following terms: '"Colbertism" was a set of economic practices rather than a theoretical stance: it asserted the state's role as entrepreneur as reinforcing from an economic perspective the political centralization which started with Philippe August in the thirteenth century'. Essentially Colbert's aim was the greater glory of France. Even the humble accountant sitting in his office dutifully recording entries in the books of account in obedience to the 1673 decree contributed to this great end by ensuring that business was conducted in a more orderly fashion, thus reducing bankruptcies and improving business confidence. But Colbert was but the first of a long line of public servants, which stretches to the present day, who considered that a strong centralized interventionist state was essential for the promotion and defence of France's interest. Since Colbert's day, the French state has found many further ways in which it can make use of the accountant's skills.

The next date of importance is 1807 when the Code de Commerce (Commercial Code) was enacted. This was part of the Code Napoléon, which was one of the lasting achievements of the French Revolution: the setting down of the entire law in the form of a written code. The Code de Commerce incorporated Colbert's decree and also included, for the first time in French law, references to a statement of assets and liabilities and to a statement of profits and losses. However these statements were only required in the case of bankruptcy. The principal innovation of the Code de Commerce was the creation of the société anonyme, which still exists today. The société anonyme is a corporation whose capital was provided by shareholders who enjoyed limited liability. The curious word 'anonyme' (anonymous) was chosen to make clear that the société was separate from its shareholders. For this reason it was forbidden for the name of the société to be that of a shareholder.

France was a generation ahead of Britain in including in its law provision for businesses to organize themselves as corporations. However the procedure for setting up a société anonyme under the 1807 code was highly complex and in particular the permission of the government was required in every case. For this reason it was little used.

It was not until 60 years later that the law was changed to make it easier to set up a société anonyme. By an act of 1867, the procedure was greatly simplified and the requirement for express permission of the government was abolished. The act also provided that sociétés anonymes should prepare three financial statements which still exist today: an inventory of all assets and liabilities;[3] a balance sheet and a profit and loss account. However the law was completely silent on the accounting principles to be followed in drawing up these statements. Hence the quality of the accounts provided under the terms of the 1867 act was often low; for example it was common for a société anonyme not to provide for depreciation.

The 1867 act may also be considered as marking the start of auditing in France, in that it provided for the shareholders to appoint commissaires to report on the accounts. However since the law did not specify any minimum qualifications for these persons, in general the audits that they performed were quite inadequate.

These shortcomings in the quality both of the financial statements and of auditing were not to be made good until well into the twentieth century. At its origins, French accounting was characterized by three features that have continue to mark it up until very recently: a major role for the state, a considerable emphasis on the recording of transactions by the enterprise and a lack of interest in how the enterprise reported its activities to outsiders.

6.3 THE FRENCH INSTITUTIONAL FRAMEWORK

6.3.1 The state

In France, the state plays a far more active role in the economy than in the Anglo-Saxon countries. Since the days of Colbert, the government considers that its duty is to promote the development of the economy in every way possible. This attitude of the government survived the transition from the absolute monarchy of Louis XIV through the French Revolution to the present day. The French people as a whole agree that it is the responsibility of the state to ensure that the economy is strong and accept state intervention in economic affairs as normal.

However France is a very democratic society and the state does not seek to achieve this end through simple diktat, as in a command economy. Traditionally the state has always sought to gain support for its policies by involving other elements of society in the governmental process. In the field of accountancy, the French state has made use of two particular methods as a way of ensuring that its actions meet with general acceptability:

(a) **Consensus building.** The state generally seeks to achieve wide consensus in society for its policies. To this end, it has created a number of consultative bodies whose function is to advise the government in specified areas. These bodies are composed of representatives of those most affected by the government's actions. The Conseil National de la Comptabilité (dealt with in section 6.4.4) is one such body.

(b) **State institutions.** An alternative approach is for the government to set up state institutions to perform specified public tasks. Although created by the state and ultimately controlled by the state, these institutions often enjoy considerable independence from the government of the day. Examples of such institutions are the Compagnie Nationale des Commissaires aux Comptes and the Ordre des Experts Comptables, which are covered in section 6.3.5.

Hence it is incorrect to regard the French state as a monolithic structure; the reality is far more nuanced. An example of this is that under the present constitution, power is shared between the President, elected every seven years, and the Prime Minister, who is generally the head of the strongest party in the Assemblé National. Furthermore the attitude of French society to state intervention in the economy has not in recent years been uniformly and strongly positive. There have been continual fluctuations in public attitudes. For example, under François Mitterrand, who was president from 1981 to 1995, many important enterprises were nationalized; under his successor Jacques Chirac, many of these were privatized. With the election in 1997 of a Socialist government headed by Prime Minister Jospin, the privatization process has continued.

6.3.2 Law: the Commercial Code

France has a legal system based on a written code. The theory behind a code is that it should set down all the legal rules in a single document; for example, the Code de Commerce, enacted in 1807 as part of the Code Napoléon, should in principle cover every aspect of business life. However for the first 176 years of its existence, the Code de Commerce made only the most general references to financial reporting; it certainly did not define the contents of financial statements or the accounting principles to be followed in their preparation as one might expect to be the case in a code-based legal system. In 1983 the Code de Commerce was amended to incorporate into French law the provisions of the EU's Fourth Directive. This was done through the Accounting Act of 30 April 1983 and the government decree of 29 November of the same year. The contents of these pieces of legislation bear a remarkable resemblance to the British Companies Act of 1981, which is not surprising since both laws had the same purpose: the implementation of the EU's Fourth Directive. Given these facts it is not correct to assert (as certain commentators have done) that the Code de Commerce has had a distinctive impact on French financial reporting. In fact there seems to be little difference in the role that statute law (law made by the legislator and not by the judges) played in the development of financial reporting in Britain (a Common Law country) compared with France (a country with a code-based system).

6.3.3 Taxation

In France corporate income tax is levied on the profits of corporations. There is a basic rule that the taxation is based on the profits as reported in the accounts; if an expense is not included in the accounts, it is not recognized for tax purposes. By a tax decree of 1984, the tax authorities adopted the definitions of revenue and expense contained in the Plan Comptable Général (see section 6.4.3) for the calculation of taxable income. However this does not mean that the tax authorities passively accepted the figures reported in the accounts and that the tax rules have no influence on how the accounts are prepared. The reality is much more complex as the following points make clear:

(a) Certain categories of expenses are disallowed for tax purposes even if included in the accounts, for example expenses not incurred in the interests of the business such as the personal expenses of the owner.

(b) In certain rare cases the tax authorities insist on certain entries in the financial statements. For example, gains on which capital gains tax has been paid must be transferred to a special reserve.

(c) Where the amount of an expense has to be estimated and the tax authorities are prepared to accept rather generous estimates, the tax payer has an incentive to report the maximum acceptable amount. There are two areas in which this is common:

   (i) **Depreciation.** For the calculation of depreciation, the tax authorities accept estimates of the life of assets that are generally rather shorter than their economic lives; for example 20 years for industrial buildings and five years for cars. Furthermore they accept that depreciation may be charged in the earlier years of an asset's life using the reducing balance method at twice the straight line rate. For example a car is assumed to have a life of five years; in the first year, the depreciation is twice the straight line rate, that is 40 per cent. The tax payer may switch from the reducing balance method to the straight line method when this results in a higher depreciation charge; this will generally be the case when the number of remaining years of life is less than the inverse of the reducing balance rate. On occasions the state has allowed very fast accelerated depreciation for certain categories of assets (for example 100 per cent write-off in the first year on equipment to reduce air and water pollution) with the aim of promoting this type of investment. In all cases the fundamental rule applies: to be tax deductible the depreciation must be reported in the financial statements.

   (ii) **Provisions:** The tax regulations permit enterprises to make charges for setting up a number of provisions that are fiscal in nature and which would not be justified under accepted accounting principles. An example is the provision for inventory; where the price of the closing stock has increased over that of the opening stock, the tax payer may create a provision for the amount of any increase over 10 per cent.

In both cases there is no obligation for the enterprise to make use of the advantages offered by the tax authorities, but, if it does, it must record the charge in its financial statements. The normal consequence is that the enterprise willingly adopts the tax rules in its financial reporting, which tends to distort the information contained therein. French scholars refer to the financial statements being 'polluted' by items included purely for tax purposes. The English use the term 'tax-driven'.

(d) The same principle applies to revenue. If an enterprise were to re-value its property and to report the increased value in its balance sheet, it would be liable to pay capital gains tax on the revaluation surplus. For this reason voluntary revaluations are unknown in France, except by loss-making companies, which are, of course, the very ones whose assets are unlikely to have increased in value!

In assessing the degree to which the financial statements of French enterprises are influenced by tax, there are two important points to be born in mind:

(a) **Consolidated accounts:** In France, as in most other countries, the taxable entity is the individual corporation and not the group. The rule that, for an expense to be tax deductible, it must be reported in the accounts, applies only to the accounts of the individual corpora-tion. The tax authorities have no interest in the consolidated accounts. In certain circumstances, the group may be treated as the taxable entity, but in that case the taxable profit is the sum of the profits of the individual enterprises in the group and not the profit reported in the consolidated accounts. Furthermore French law permits a parent enterprise to use different rules in the consolidated accounts from those used in its individual accounts. For these reasons, tax has far less influence on the consolidated accounts than it does on the accounts of the individual enterprise.

(b) **Damage limitation:** French accountants have devised ways of limit-ing the damage caused by 'tax pollution'. For example in the income statement, a distinction is made between the amount of depreciation that should be charged on economic grounds and the extra which is charged solely for fiscal reasons; the former is charged as an expense against operating income, the latter is reported as an extraordinary charge after income from ordinary activities.

6.3.4 The corporate financing system

In France, the capital market is a less important factor in the financing of enterprises compared with the USA and the UK. This is brought out by the statistics in Exhibit 2.4 which show that the market capitalization of domestic corporations is, in relative terms, less than half the figure in the USA and Britain. Two further factors tend to reduce the influence of the stock exchange on financial reporting:

(a) **Closely held shares:** Most listed corporations have a small number of major shareholders who may own as much as 80 per cent of the shares. The management clearly has an incentive to retain the confidence of these major shareholders and to keep them well informed of the enterprise's affairs. However this is done generally by direct communication and not through the financial statements. Hence the incentive to improve their financial reporting is less strong with these enterprises than it is with those whose shares are widely held. Furthermore it is common for French enterprises to own cross-holdings of each others' shares, which further reduces the need to give much attention to the information needs of the small shareholder.

(b) **Debt capital:** Traditionally French enterprises have preferred debt capital to equity. The principal reason is that many enterprises started life as family businesses, and the family has been reluctant to weaken its control by issuing further equity shares. Hence additional capital is provided through bank loans and through debt instruments quoted on the stock exchange. It is not uncommon for a French enterprise to list its debt securities on the Paris stock exchange without listing its ordinary shares.

However times are changing and it would seem that the influence of the stock exchange over financial reporting is increasing. The government has sought to increase the number of small shareholders by offering them special treatment when privatizing nationalized firms such as Air France. The globalization of business and the increasing activity of foreign investors on the Paris stock exchange have had an impact. In 1999 the French financial world was rocked by two major take-over bids: of Total for Elf Aquitaine and of Banque Nationale de Paris for Société Générale and Paribas. Previously it was considered that the typical cosy relationships between French enterprises and their major shareholders rendered such take-over bids virtually impossible. Take-over bids were considered to be a regrettable feature of the Anglo-Saxon capital markets but not of the well ordered Paris Stock Exchange. Now it would seem that 'the market for corporate control' has finally reached Paris. In the future the management of French corporations can no longer rely on the loyalty of their shareholders and will have to give greater attention to their financial reporting.

6.3.5 The accountancy profession

There are two professional accountancy bodies in France: the Compagnie National des Commissaires aux Comptes and the Order des Experts Comptables.

(a) **The Compagnie Nationale des Commissaires aux Comptes** represents the auditors. Its members are recognized by the courts as qualified to audit the financial statements of enterprises.

(b) **The Ordre des Experts Comptables** represents the accountants. Its members are independent professionals who have a legal monopoly of providing accountancy services to enterprises as independents. These services include preparing the accounts (many small French enterprises do not employ a full-time accountant), advising on accounting systems and tax advice.

The need for two distinct professional bodies comes from the rule in French law that the person who audits the accounts should not provide any other services to the enterprise. Hence a French enterprise that hires an expert comptable to prepare its accounts, must hire a different person, a commissaire aux comptes, to perform the audit. However there is no rule that prohibits an individual from being a member of both bodies. In fact joint membership is the rule rather than the exception. Over half of the members of the Compagnie National des Commissaires aux Comptes are Experts Comptables, as the easiest way to qualify as a Commissaire aux Comptes is to qualify first as an Expert Comptable. In fact the largest French professional firms are so organized that they are able to offer all forms of accountancy services to their clients: auditing, preparation of accounts, taxation advice, consultancy and so on. To avoid breaking the professional rules, they make sure that the same person does not provide both auditing and accountancy services to the same client. Hence the division of the French accountancy profession is limited to the professional bodies and does not generally apply to the firms that provide professional services.

The French accountancy profession differs from those of Britain and the USA in two important respects: size and status.

Size

The French profession is much smaller as is apparent from the figures in Exhibit 6.1

Exhibit 6.1 *The size of the French accountancy profession*

	Number of members at 31 December 1993
Compagnie Nationale des Commissaires aux Comptes	14 850
Ordre des Experts Comptables	11 750
Individuals who are members of both bodies (estimated)	(8 200)
Total membership	18 400

In interpreting these figures, it should be borne in mind that, in France, accountants who are employed in industrial and commercial enterprises do not belong to a professional accountancy body.

Status

Both the Compagnie and the Ordre are essentially state institutions.

(a) **Compagnie:** The post of commissaire aux comptes was created in 1867. Its function was to report on the accounts presented to the shareholders. However the first commissaires were notorious for their incompetence and lack of independence. It was not until 1935 that the law sought to remedy this situation when it was decreed that, for listed sociétés anonymes, the commissaire aux comptes had to be chosen from a list of qualified persons maintained by the court. Admission to this list was by an examination supervised by the state. These persons were obliged to belong to a professional association that was responsible for the maintenance of standards. Originally these associations were organized at the regional level but in 1966 the present national body, the Compagnie Nationale des Commissaires aux Comptes, was created. Gradually over time, the number of enterprises that were required to appoint a member of the Compagnie as auditor has increased so that now this is a requirement for all enterprises of almost any legal form except the very smallest. The public status of the commissaire aux comptes is confirmed by the following considerations:

   (i) The Compagnie Nationale is a state agency that comes under the supervision of the Ministry of Justice
   (ii) Membership of the Compagnie is through an examination supervised by the state
   (iii) Discipline of members is the responsibility of a special commission, the majority of whose members are judges

(iv) In certain respects, the commissaire aux comptes acts more as a public official than as an agent of the shareholders; for example the commissaire aux comptes is obliged to report to the public prosecutor any crime discovered in the course of the audit, including fraud and tax evasion by the management.

(b) **Ordre:** The earliest French accountancy association was the Société de Comptabilité de France formed in 1881, which was a wholly private body. However, unlike their British counterparts, the French accountants never succeeded in establishing themselves as a creditable profession. This was achieved only through the intervention of the state, which in 1942 created the Ordre des Experts Comptables. The Ordre's constitution was modified in 1947 and 1968 and at present includes the following features:

   (i) The Ordre is governed by a council elected by the members, but all decisions of the council have to be ratified by a government official appointed by the Minister of Finance

   (ii) Admission to the Ordre is by an examination supervised by the Ministry of Education

   (iii) Members of the Ordre have a legally protected monopoly of the title of 'Expert Comptable' and of the provision of accountancy services on a fee basis

All these points confirm the Ordre's public status.

6.4 THE FRENCH REGULATORY SYSTEM

Exhibit 6.2 presents the principal features of the French system for the regulation of financial reporting, distinguishing between the rules (shown at the foot of the figure) and the rule-makers. The principal rules and rule-makers are analysed in the following paragraphs.

6.4.1 Laws and decrees

Laws enacted by the legislature, the Assemblé Nationale, are the foundation of the French system in two senses: firstly, as rules, they have the greatest authority and, secondly, they provide the authority for the other lesser rules, notably the decrees, which are issued by government bodies using powers given to them by law.

The most important of the current laws are:

(a) The Accounting Law of 30 April 1983 which implemented the provisions of the EU's Fourth Directive in France; this law was backed up by the government decree of 29 November 1983, which set out the detailed rules.

(b) The law of 3 January 1985 and the associated decree of 17 February 1985, which performed the same function for the EU's Seventh Directive.

(c) The law of 6 April 1998 which permits listed enterprises to use internationally accepted rules for their consolidated accounts.

Laws and decrees make up those rules that French enterprises are obliged to follow; if they do not they are in danger of suffering penalties imposed by the courts. With respect to the remaining rules set out in Exhibit 6.2, French enterprises are not formally obliged to obey them but in fact the great majority do, for reasons explained later. The French have a useful term for such rules: 'doctrine comptable'. The lower authority of these rules is an example of the concept of the hierarchy of rules presented in Chapter 3.

6.4.2 The Comité de Réglementation Comptable (CRC)

The Comité de Réglementation Comptable (CRC) plays a central role in the regulatory system. Its twelve members bring together all the persons who are powerful and influential in the regulation of financial reporting, including three government ministers (Justice, Finance and the Economy), two senior judges, and the heads of the CNC, COB, CNCC and OEC (the significance of the first two bodies is explained later). Its principal function is to issue all government decrees relating to accountancy and financial reporting. The aim of concentrating the decree-issuing power in a single body is to achieve better coordination of the government's action. Given the pre-eminence of its members (particularly the ministers and the judges) its decrees carry great authority. The CRC was set up only in 1998 and it is too early to assess its effectiveness.

6.4.3 The Plan Comptable Général (PCG)

The Plan Comptable Général (PCG) is a most important feature of French accounting. Basically it is a set of rules that covers every aspect of the accounting and financial reporting of enterprises, including:

- The title and function of the accounts that the enterprise should maintain in its internal accounting system
- The accounting principles to be followed for the accounts
- The form and content of the financial statements that are to be prepared from these accounts

A feature of the PCG that most impresses foreigners is that each account is allocated a unique code number which is the same for all enterprises. For example, in virtually every French enterprise, expenditure on office

Exhibit 6.2 *The French system for the regulation of financial reporting*

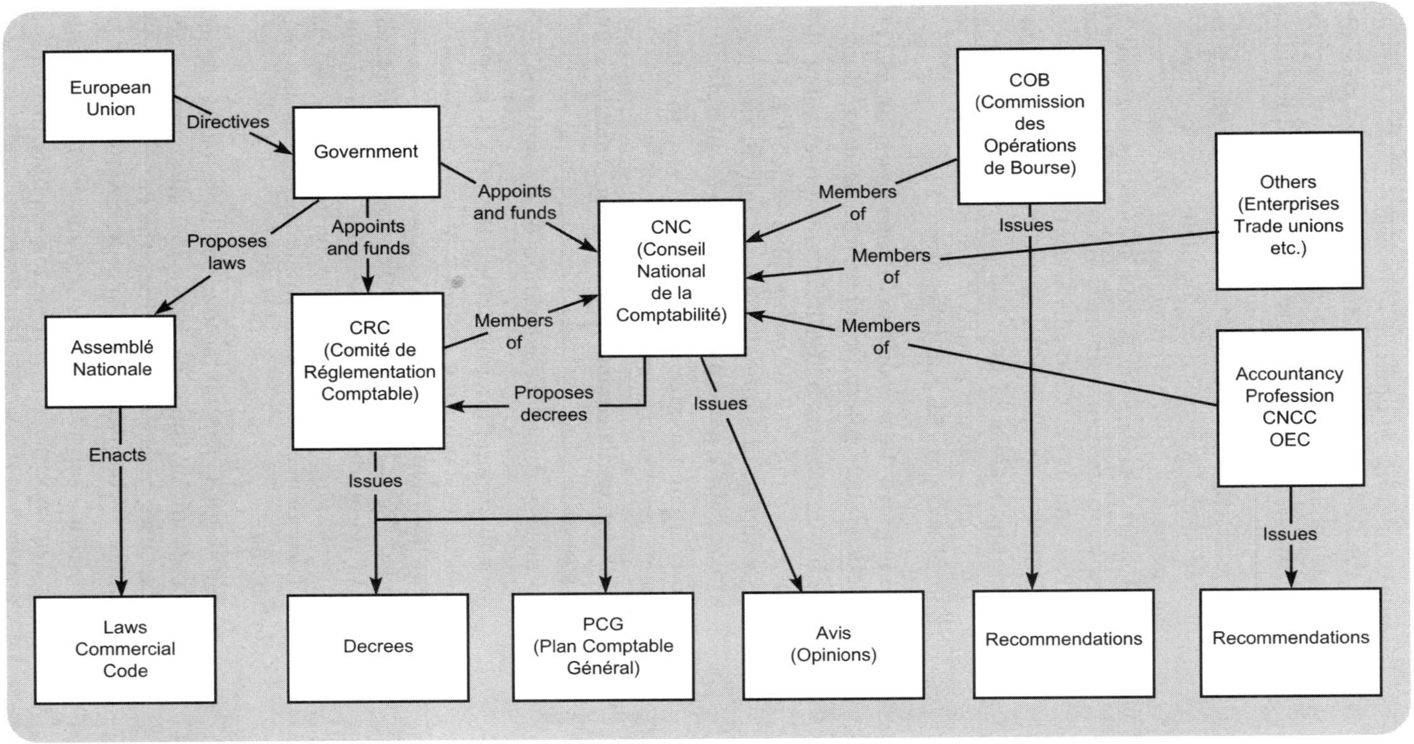

and computing equipment is recorded in account number 2183. However the PCG is very much more than a list of code numbers; it includes the principles and rules to be followed both for the maintenance of the internal accounting system and for the preparation of the financial statements.

The first PCG was drawn up in 1942, during the German occupation of France, and was based on the plan developed by the German accounting academic, Eugen Schmalenbach. However it was never applied. In 1947, after the war, the French government revised the 1942 plan and issued it on its own authority. There were further substantial revisions in 1957 and 1982. Gradually over the years, the PCG developed from being little more than a list of accounts to its present form, a complete accounting manual of over 300 pages.

The French government considered it desirable to issue a national chart of accounts for the following reasons:

- To improve the accounting of enterprises; the PCG represents the best model which enterprises are encouraged to adopt
- To assure comparability; if all enterprises adopt the same plan, then their accounts will be comparable which has advantages both for the government in national planning and for the enterprise management in comparing performance with other enterprises
- To facilitate the raising of taxes and also to assure more equal treatment between tax payers
- To facilitate the compilation of national statistics and to improve their accuracy
- To make possible the education of accountants on a uniform basis

Basically the philosophy behind the PCG is that there is such a thing as the 'best' accounting system and that the whole community would benefit if all enterprises adopted it.

In fact, virtually all French enterprises now base their internal accounting system on the PCG and have done for much of the past half century, notwithstanding that at no time during this period has this been a formal legal obligation. There would appear to be two reasons for this behaviour:

(a) Since 1965, the tax authorities have based the enterprise's annual tax return on the PCG; for the definition and classification of revenue, expenses, assets and liabilities, the PCG's rules apply for tax purposes unless incompatible with specific tax rules.

(b) There are considerable cost advantages in using the same accounting system as other enterprises, for example in training accounting staff and easing the work of auditors.

Recent developments have reduced somewhat the importance of the PCG in French accounting. Lande and Scheid (1999) consider that the turning point was the enactment of the 1983 Accounting Law. They comment, 'The enactment of this legislation has resulted in the fact that the 1982 PCG is no longer in the forefront of French accounting standardisation. Accounting laws and decrees no longer make cross reference to the PCG and its reputation is diminishing. Because it is not (and never was) mandatory, and it has not been updated since 1982, the PCG now plays only a minor role in accounting standardisation.'

Only France of the five countries of the Pentad has a national accounting plan. However a number of other European countries have followed France's example in this field, notably Spain, Portugal, Belgium and Greece. Furthermore a number of developing countries have national accounting plans, including many former French colonies as well as countries not in the French sphere of influence, such as Iraq. Moreover accounting plans are an important feature of accounting in Germany, where they are issued by semi-public bodies such as industrial associations and chambers of commerce. The German state refuses to give official recognition to these plans, because of the association of the concept with the former Nazi regime.

6.4.4 The Conseil National de la Comptabilité (CNC)

The Conseil National de la Comptabilité (CNC) is the official French governmental body responsible for the development and updating of the PCG. It was first set up in 1947 as the Conseil Supérieur de la Comptabilité and is thus the world's oldest established accounting standard-setting body. It is a state agency funded by the government which also nominates all the members and supplies its staff. The CNC at present has 58 members, made up of persons from all branches of French society: government officials, representatives of COB, CNCC and OEC, the trade unions, industrial associations and so on. However accountants make up only a small minority of the CNC's membership; in fact the largest single group (23 members) are representatives of enterprises.

The role of the CNC is to advise government. It was set up with the intention of involving and implicating in the legislative process all parties likely to be affected by laws and decrees in the field of accounting. It is a manifestation of the desire of French society to settle contentious matters through consensus. It has no formal rule-making powers. Its opinions (avis) are not binding in law. It does not even issue the PCG on its own authority. The 1982 PCG was issued by a ministerial order based on a draft prepared by the CNC. However the CNC's prestige is such that, almost invariably, the government accepts its proposals and enterprises accept its opinions. With the decline in importance of the

PCG, it is possible that it will in future play a less important role. However it still has the role of advising the government. Following the establishment of the CRC, it is to give an opinion on all draft decrees put to that body. It is too early to judge how important the CNC will be in its new role.

6.4.5 The Commission des Opérations de Bourse (COB)

The Commission des Opérations de Bourse (COB) is a state agency that was set up in 1967 with the function of regulating the capital market and in particular to protect the interests of investors. It was modelled on the American SEC and has similar functions and powers. In the area of financial reporting, it has the power to issue regulations that are legally binding on listed enterprises but in fact it has made very little use of this power. There are two reasons for this:

- It prefers to work through the CNC of which it is an influential member
- It finds that enterprises invariably follow its recommendations, even though these are not legally binding

6.4.6 Recommendations of the accountancy profession

The position of the accountancy profession is rather similar to that of the COB. The main influence of the CNCC and the OEC on the rule-making process is through their membership of the CNC. However both bodies issue recommendations which are generally followed by their own members, that is the experts comptables in preparing accounts and the commissaires aux comptes in auditing them.

6.5 THE FUTURE OF FRENCH FINANCIAL REPORTING

In recent years, France has been profoundly affected by the globalization of the world economy that was analysed in Chapter 1. In recent years, the larger French enterprises have been lobbying the government for permission to draw up their accounts in accordance with rules accepted by the international capital market, as they found having to prepare two sets of accounts costly and confusing. The government finally agreed to this demand and passed the law of 6 April 1998, by which French-listed enterprises are not obliged to follow French law for the preparation of their consolidated accounts; instead they may use 'internationally recognised rules' that have been adopted by the CRC. The CRC has yet to set out what rules are acceptable. Hence, at present, French-listed enterprises are still required to apply the French rules. In principle the phrase in the law would seem to cover both US GAAP and the IASs. However the law also states that the rules must have been translated into French. This has been done for the IASs but not yet for US GAAP. Furthermore, given the complexity of the latter, it is doubtful whether a French translation will ever be achieved.

SUMMARY

The historical development of financial reporting in France was sketched, starting with Colbert's decree of 1673. The continuing role of the state as the dominant influence over the accounting of French enterprises was analysed, the capital market and the accountancy profession being less influential compared with Britain and the USA. The French regulatory system was examined. Whereas the law was found to play a very similar role in France as in Britain, the distinctive feature of the French system was the central role of the Plan Comptable Général, drawn up by the Conseil National de la Comptabilité. Finally mention was made of the recent changes in the law which permit French MNEs to draw up their consolidated accounts according to internationally accepted standards.

Review questions

1. What aspects of the accounting of enterprises were covered in Colbert's decree of 1673?

2. What role does the state play in determining the financial reporting of French enterprises? What instruments and bodies does it use for this purpose?

3. In what ways does the French accountancy profession differ from those of Britain and the USA?

4. Why, in the past, has the stock exchange been of lesser influence over the financial reporting of enterprises, compared with the position in Britain and the USA? Why may this situation change in the future?

Review questions (cont'd)

5. What is contained in the Plan Comptable Général? What are the advantages of all enterprises adopting the PCG?

6. In what way has the law recently been modified to meet the demands of the French multinational enterprises?

Notes

1. Text of article 10 of the 1673 decree quoted in Mikol (1995).
2. Mikol (1995) points out that the decree provided that the pages of the books of account were to be numbered and initialled by the local magistrate. The penalty for not doing so was death! This requirement still applies (except for computerized records) although, fortunately for the erring accountant, the penalty for non-compliance is not quite so severe as in the seventeenth century.
3. Note that the 'inventaire', which even today the French société anonyme is required to produce, covers all assets and liabilities and not just those which the Americans call inventory.

References

Colasse, B and Standish, P 'De la réforme 1996–1998 du dispositif français de normalisation comptable', *Comptabilité contrôle audit*, **4**(2) (1998), pp. 5–27.

Gélard, G 'France – Individual Accounts', *Transacc: Transnational Accounting*, 2nd edn. D Ordelheide (ed.), Palgrave, Basingstoke (2001).

Horau, C 'A propos de la réforme de la normalisation comptable: adaptation ou rupture?', *Comptabilité contrôle audit*, **4**(2) (1998), pp. 29–30.

Lande, E and Scheid, J-C 'France', *Accounting Regulation in Europe*, S McLeay (ed.), Macmillan – now Palgrave, Basingstoke (1999).

Mikol, L 'The history of financial reporting in France', *European Financial Reporting: a history*, P Walton (ed.), Academic Press, London (1995).

Richard, J 'France: group accounts', *Transacc: Transnational Accounting*, 2nd edn., D Ordelheide (ed.), Palgrave, Basingstoke (2001).

Scheid, J-C and Walton, P *European Financial Reporting: France*, Routledge, London (1992).

Standish, P 'Origins of the Plan Comptable Général: a study in cultural intrusion and reaction', *Accounting and Business Research*, **20**(4) (1990), pp. 337–51.

Standish, P *The French Plan Comptable: explanation and translation*, Expert Comptable Media, Paris (1997).

Further reading

The most comprehensive analysis of French financial reporting is contained in Scheid and Walton (1992); chapters 5, 6 and 7 are particularly recommended. For the historical development, see Mikol (1995). For more recent developments, see Lande and Scheid (1999). For the origins of the Plan Comptable Général, see Standish (1990) and for an a highly detailed exposition of its contents, see Standish (1997). For a French view (in French) of the recent changes, see Colasse (1998) and Horau (1998). For a detailed exposition of the rules of financial reporting, see Gélard (2001) and Richard (2001).

chapter seven

Germany

Chapter objectives

■ To trace the historical development of financial reporting in Germany as the explanation for its predominant characteristic – the protection of creditors through the prudent valuation of assets and liabilities

■ To set out the principal features of the institutional framework: the Commercial Code, the German Accounting Standards Board (DSR), taxation, the corporate financing system and the accountancy profession

■ To explain the elements of the German regulatory system: law, GoB and standards

■ To consider recent developments relating to the financial reporting of German multinational enterprises (MNEs)

7.1 WHY GERMANY IS IMPORTANT FOR THE STUDY OF GLOBAL FINANCIAL REPORTING

The importance of Germany for the study of global financial reporting is very apparent from the statistics presented in Chapter 1. Germany has the third largest economy in the world; it is a major power in world trade, being second only to the USA in the size of its exports and imports; in fact, in certain years its exports even exceeded those of the USA. German enterprises are large investors in other countries in terms both of annual flows and of stock; in both areas Germany is third after the USA and Britain. There are seven German enterprises in the top fifty MNEs: DaimlerChrysler, Volkswagen, Siemens, BMW, Bayer, VIAG and BASF.

However the importance of Germany does not rest exclusively on its size. In the field of financial reporting, three other factors make the study of Germany especially interesting and relevant:

(a) Germany has had a significant influence on the development of financial reporting in a number of other countries in Central Europe and Scandinavia. This influence is still very marked in the law and practice of Austria and Switzerland.

(b) The traditional approach to financial reporting in Germany is fundamentally different from, and in some ways the opposite to, that adopted in the Anglo-Saxon countries that were the subject of Chapters 4 and 5. Hence a study of German accounting provides the material on which to base a critical analysis of the Anglo-Saxon approach. Perhaps the best approach might be a synthesis of the two?

(c) German enterprises are playing a leading role in the globalization of the world economy. A recent striking example was the merger of Daimler Benz with the American Chrysler Corporation to form the world's third largest automobile manufacturer. This development is having a particularly significant impact on German financial reporting: German enterprises are discovering that the traditional German approach to financial reporting is inadequate in dealing with the new problems arising with globalization and they are demanding reform. In response to this demand, German financial reporting is currently undergoing significant changes.

7.2 THE ORIGINS OF GERMAN FINANCIAL REPORTING

Before 1870 Germany was not a united country but was divided among a host of independent states. There were occasional references to accounting in the laws of these states, some of which date back to the sixteenth century. However the accounting requirements of businessmen were first set out in a comprehensive fashion in the Civil Code of the state of Prussia enacted in 1794. This was based closely on French law, notably Colbert's decree of 1673 (see section 6.2). Thus the emphasis was on internal record keeping and not on financial reporting; a balance sheet was required only in the event of bankruptcy.

In 1870 the Aktiengesetz (AktG) was enacted, which made the corporate form of the Aktiengesellschaft (AG) generally available to businesses, by abolishing the previous requirement of a special charter granted by the government. The act required that AGs prepare both a balance sheet and profit and loss account and provided for their disclosure for the benefit of shareholders and creditors. However the act did not lay down strict valuation rules. All assets and liabilities were to be stated at 'attributable value' (beizulegender Wert). To the modern reader this term seems remarkably vague; it seems to imply that the enterprise may report an asset at any value that it attributes to it. In fact it was interpreted to mean, for most assets, current value. Hence at the beginning German financial reporting law was remarkably liberal, one might even describe it as 'modern'. Following this act, there was a flood of formations of AGs; between 1871 and 1873 their number increased fivefold. Many of these newly formed AGs failed with serious losses to shareholders and creditors. The slack financial reporting laws made it easy for promoters to commit frauds. For example they made themselves rich by overvaluing the assets that they contributed to the AG. Also corporations were able to report profits (when in reality they were making losses) by stating their assets at unrealistic values. Dividends were paid out of these fictional profits to the detriment both of shareholders (who were unaware that they were consuming capital) and of creditors (whose security was being reduced by the dissipation of the corporation's funds).

To prevent such frauds, in 1884 the law was amended; henceforth historical cost was the upper limit to the value of fixed assets. Hence, after a false start, the fundamental principle of German financial reporting was established: assets should be valued on a prudent basis so as to prevent the depletion of the corporation's funds through the payment of undue dividends, thus protecting the interests of creditors and contributing to the continued existence of the enterprise.

7.3 THE GERMAN INSTITUTIONAL FRAMEWORK

7.3.1 The state

After the Second World War a particular economic system known as Soziale Marktwirtschaft (social market economy) developed in Germany which aimed to ensure that the economy was managed in the interests of the whole community whilst at the same time circumscribing the role of the state. The social market economy is both 'social' and 'market'. It is 'social', in the sense of being managed for the benefit of society as a whole and not of any privileged group. It is 'market' in that the economy is based on the principles of free enterprise and not on state direction. Of course the great challenge is how to achieve that a market-based economy is run in the interest of the whole of society and not in that of a small group of capitalists.

In Germany this is achieved by a partnership between the state and the rest of society. It is recognized that the state has a vital role to play in achieving a socially just society. In Germany the state has three important economic functions:

(i) To achieve an equitable standard of living for all members of society through a redistributive tax system and, above all, through a very comprehensive and expensive social security system;

(ii) To ensure the smooth running of the market economy through macro-economic measures, such as demand management, and through micro-economic measures, such as taking action against monopolies;

(iii) To aid the economic development of poorer regions through subsidies and income transfers.

However, in deciding important issues of policy, the state will generally seek to achieve a wide level of agreement with the main social groups.

At the level of the enterprise, the social market economy is embodied in the participation of the workers in the management of the business (Mitbestimmung) and in the widely held belief that the enterprise should be managed in the interests of all those connected with it (the 'stakeholders') and not simply those of the shareholders. Although the Mitbestimmung has recently gained further legal support, this view is under attack by the doctrine of 'shareholder value' to which the managers of many German enterprises have been converted.

7.3.2 Law: the Commercial Code

German society is based on the rule of law; economic relationships are governed by law to a greater degree than in many other developed countries. The state is the source of law. However the state shares its law-making power with other groups. Before proposing any change in the law, particularly on economic matters, the government seeks to achieve a wide consensus; to this end it consults not only the legislature (which is composed of democratically elected representatives) but also organizations that represent important elements in society, in particular the trade unions and the employer organizations. An analysis of the process by which the German government seeks to achieve a consensus in framing the laws on financial reporting is given in Ordelheide (1999).

In the field of financial reporting, almost all the important laws are set down in the Commercial Code, known in German as the Handelsgesetzbuch (HGB). In 1985 the HGB's rules were thoroughly revised and expanded when the provisions of the European Union's Fourth and Seventh Directives were incorporated into German law. Following these amendments, the HGB has much in common with the British Companies Act and the French Code de Commerce, which is attributable to the common source of many of their rules – the European Union. The Third Book of the HGB contains the basic provisions on preparation, audit and publication of individual and group financial statements, notes and the management reports. Additional reporting requirements are provided for companies that have a specific legal form (e.g. stock corporations, limited liability companies), size, industry (banks or insurance companies) or listing on a stock exchange.

In 1998, the legalistic tradition of German accounting changed in two ways:

(i) Section 292a HGB allowed parent companies that have listed securities to apply IAS or US GAAP in their consolidated financial statements instead of HGB provisions. This exemption is limited up to the year 2004.

(ii) Section 342 HGB allowed for the foundation of a private German accounting standard setter to develop standards for German consolidated accounts, to advise the Ministry of Justice on accounting law reforms and to represent Germany on international accounting bodies (see section 7.4.3 below).

German legal provisions are quite general and therefore must be interpreted so as to be applied appropriately to individual cases. In practice, solutions for most accounting problems are found in commentaries that are collections of principles, best practices and guidelines supported by reasoning derived from the general provisions.

7.3.3   Grundsätze ordnungsmässiger Buchführung (GoB)

The Grundsätze ordnungsmässiger Buchführung (GoB), literally the principles of orderly book-keeping, are a set of general principles that should be followed by accountants in their work. In fact they cover the whole of accountancy, including both book-keeping and stock-taking, but only those that refer to financial reporting are covered in this chapter. The need for a set of general principles is the inability of the law to cover all possible situations. Hence the HGB, in addition to setting down a host of rules as to formats, valuation rules and so on, includes, in section 243, the general rule that the financial statements must be prepared in accordance with GoB. The position has been described by a leading German author in the following terms:

> GoB is an indefinite legal expression that is made concrete by the decisions of judges, the expertise of practitioners and the exposition of the theory of business economics by academics. The legislator, by referring to GoB, avoids having to lay down a host of detailed specific rules and thus contributes to the greater practicability of the law, but at the same time passing the final responsibility to the courts of law which have to decide on the content of GoB in the individual case. Furthermore, with the help of GoB, the development of financial reporting and its adaptation to new knowledge and practice is not impeded by rigid legal rules.[1]

In addition to the creators of GoB mentioned in the above quotation (judges, practitioners and academics), the HGB may itself be considered to be a source of GoB. It lays down a number of general principles that are generally considered to form part of GoB (although in no sense are they an exhaustive formulation). The following are the more important of the general principles.

(a) Accuracy and objectivity: the financial statements must be based on records that are in accordance with the actual facts.

(b) Clarity: the accounts must be clear and comprehensible. Aspects of this principle are the prohibition of off-setting assets and liabilities and the requirement that assets and liabilities be valued on an item by item basis.

(c) Completeness: the accounts must cover all the transactions, revenues and expenses, assets and liabilities of the enterprise.

(d) Consistency: the principles used for the preparation of the accounts should be applied consistently, both within a period (similar transactions should be accounted for in the same way) and between periods (the same principles should be applied in succeeding periods). Furthermore the opening balance sheet should agree with the closing balance sheet of the previous period.

(e) Timeliness: the accounts must be prepared within a period that accords with orderly business conduct.

(f) Realization principle: profits may only be taken into account if they are realized. The implication of this principle is that assets may not be valued at above historical cost as any increase in an asset's value is unrealized profit.

(g) Imparity principle: all foreseeable risks and losses are to be accounted for even if unrealized. This is known as the 'imparity principle' because losses are treated in a different way from profits, which may only be recognized if they are realized.

(h) The principle of lower value: assets should be valued at the lower of historical cost and actual value, which is generally interpreted as market value for current assets and value in use for fixed assets.

The last three principles are aspects of the prudence principle to which great importance is given. In making the estimates of the future that are an inevitable feature of financial reporting, the accountant should take great care to avoid presenting an over optimistic picture of the enterprise's position and performance. Assets must not be overstated and liabilities must not be understated. As profits are measured as the increase in net assets, this implies that profits must not be overstated. These are fundamental tenets of German financial reporting; to put the matter crudely, it is a far more serious error for a German accountant to be over-optimistic in valuing assets and liabilities, than to be over-pessimistic. The rationale for this approach goes back to the overriding need to maintain the enterprise's capital fund and to prevent it being dissipated by undue distributions of incorrectly measured profits. German accountants do not ignore the accrual principle, which is also part of GoB; this principle is necessary to justify carrying forward the cost of fixed assets so that depreciation may be charged against the income of future periods.

However, while this position appears to be still valid for the level of the individual accounts, globalization of businesses and a higher demand for equity financing have put much more emphasis on comparable investor information in the group accounts. In fact, pressure from capital markets has recently led many groups to report in a way that was unthinkable 10 years ago. Inevitably, these changes are also pressuring the individual company accounts, although the interdependence between accounting and taxation in individual accounts remains in place.

7.3.4 Taxation

(a) The computation of income: the tax balance sheet

Common to all taxes on income (corporation tax and municipal tax) is the computation of the taxable income, which is defined in the Income Tax Act. Enterprises are required to draw up a balance sheet for tax purposes, known as a Steuerbilanz (tax balance sheet) in which the assets and liabilities are valued according to the tax rules. The taxable income is then calculated as:

The net assets at the end of the financial year
less the net assets at the start of the financial year
plus withdrawals of capital by the owner
less capital contributions by the owner
equals profits of the enterprise

(b) The authoritativeness principle (Massgeblichkeitsprinzip)

The big question is how the enterprise's assets are valued in the tax balance sheet. The basic principle is set out in section 5 of the Income Tax Act as follows: 'business assets . . . must be shown according to the commercial principles of proper bookkeeping', that is the Grundsätze ordnungsmässinger Buchführung (GoB) which were explained in section 7.3.3 above. The rule laid down in the above extract from the law is known as the authoritativeness principle (Massgeblichkeitsprinzip). The enterprise's financial statements that have been drawn up in accordance with the principles of regular book-keeping (that is drawn up in accordance with the HGB) form the authoritative basis for the computation of taxable income. In effect the tax balance sheet is to be based on the HGB balance sheet.

The tax authorities do not passively accept the profit of the HGB balance sheet as the taxable income. They have a right to audit it and reject it if fraudulent. This is completely in line with the authoritativeness principle, since such accounts would not comply with GoB. However, in certain limited cases, the tax law does not accept the recognition and valuation of assets and liabilities according to HGB balance sheet; the tax law lays down that the HGB rules do not apply if contradicted by a specific tax rule. For example, the tax law does not allow, for the computation of taxable income, certain provisions for pensions and deferred repairs and also certain assets (such as start-up expenses) that are permitted under the HGB. In general, under the HGB, the reporting of these items is optional so that it is possible to draw up a balance sheet that conforms with both the HGB and the tax laws. However where the enterprise has made use of these options, there will be a difference between the two balance sheets.

(c) The reverse authoritativeness principle (umgekehrte Massgeblichkeitsprinzip)

Under the authoritativeness principle, the tax balance sheet is based on the HGB balance sheet. However on occasions the influence is in the opposite direction: certain items in the HGB balance sheet are based on the amounts in the tax balance sheet. This is known as the reverse authoritativeness principle (die umgekehrte Massgeblichkeit). The basic rule is that the enterprise, if it seeks to claim the benefit of an option provided in the tax law, must also report it in its HGB balance sheet. In crude terms, the HGB balance sheet may be adapted if it is in the interests of the tax authorities, but not if it is in the interests of the tax payer. Hence the tax payer has to ensure that all tax deductible expenses are reported in the HGB accounts. The effect of this rule is most apparent in relation to the depreciation of fixed assets. The tax authorities permit the tax payer to charge against taxable income amounts for depreciation that in most cases are higher than those that would normally be considered appropriate under the HGB rules. In addition, the tax law allows the tax payer to charge an exceptionally large proportion of certain capital expenditures in the first year, for example 60 per cent of the cost of pollution control equipment. Also individual assets costing less than DM 800 need not be capitalized. However all these deductions from taxable income may only be claimed by the tax payer if they are also recorded in the HGB balance sheet. It is lawful to do this, as the HGB contains a special provision that allows the reporting of assets after deductions made according to the tax rules. The effect of the reverse authoritativeness principle is that German enterprises invariably use the maximum rates of depreciation permitted by the tax authorities in their financial statements, which can lead to a considerable understatement of asset values compared with what would be appropriate under GoB. However, in several recent rulings the German fiscal court (Bundesfinanzhof) has emphasized the separation of tax from accounting.

(d) The future of the Massgeblichkeitsprinzip

The ongoing reform of the tax system that the German government initiated in 1998 is having an impact on the Massgeblichkeitsprinzip. Thus the tax authorities are requiring that long-term liabilities be valued on a present value basis in the tax balance sheet which is contrary to the HGB and hence creates a difference between the tax balance sheet and the HGB balance sheet. Many German commentators perceive a long-term trend of increasing separation of the tax balance sheet and the HGB balance sheet.

(e) Tax and the consolidated accounts

In Germany, as in most countries, the entity on which tax is levied is the individual corporation and not the group. Hence the authoritativeness principle (and its reverse) apply only to the financial statements of the individual enterprise and not to the consolidated accounts. It is lawful for a parent enterprise to use different accounting principles in its consolidated accounts from those used in the individual accounts of the separate enterprises that make up the group, provided that they are not contrary to the principles of orderly bookkeeping. Many groups take advantage of this possibility to eliminate tax-driven asset values from their consolidated accounts. This is particularly the case with multinational groups with pressures from capital markets and with many shareholders who otherwise may be misled into believing that the group is doing badly. However, for smaller groups the advantages of reporting a profit that is not distorted by tax-driven values is outweighed by the cost of making the necessary adjustments for the consolidated accounts, in effect maintaining two accounting systems.

7.3.5 The corporate financing system

There are three principal sources of finance for German enterprises: equity, debt and provisions.

(a) Equity

In Germany the equity of enterprises provides about one third of their finance. There are stock exchanges in the principal financial centres but by far the largest is that of Frankfurt. The stock exchange is an important source of finance for the larger enterprises, although not as important as in the Anglo-Saxon countries, as demonstrated by the figures in Exhibit 2.3. In 1999 there were 617 German corporations listed on the German stock exchange, compared with 1826 British companies listed on the London Stock Exchange. In the past,

German investors, both institutions and individuals, have been reluctant to buy ordinary shares preferring less risky fixed-interest securities. There are signs that this attitude is changing. In recent years, the German government has made a big effort to encourage small private investors, for example offering them special terms on the issue of shares in privatized enterprises.

A characteristic of the German economy is the large number of medium-sized enterprises, particularly in the manufacturing and construction industries. They are largely family-owned and obtain their initial capital from close relatives and business contacts. Some in time grow sufficiently large for their shares to be listed although in such cases the family often retains a controlling shareholding. Hence for this significant section of the German economy, the stock exchange is not a significant source of finance.

(b) Debt

Debt is a major element of source of finance of most German enterprises. There are two explanations for the predominance of debt:

(i) Investors have traditionally preferred fixed interest securities to equities;

(ii) Generally the owners of enterprises seek to retain control. Therefore when an enterprise needs additional capital, this is generally raised through incurring more debt and not through an issue of ordinary shares.

Banks are a very important source of finance particularly for medium-sized enterprises. Many enterprises have a long-term relationship with a particular bank with which it places all its banking business. The bank supports the enterprise through loans, which are often long-term, becoming a permanent element of the enterprise's capital structure. An unusual feature is that certain of the larger banks own large blocks of ordinary shares in the major corporations; for example Deutsche Bank owns 12 per cent of DaimlerChrysler and 9 per cent of Allianz Versicherung. In this context it should be noted, however, that many of these shareholdings are in the process of being reduced or eliminated.

(c) Provisions

A remarkable feature of the finance side of the balance sheet of German enterprises is the high proportion of provisions. It seems clear that this does not reflect that the German economy is inherently more risky than that of other countries but rather that German enterprises take a much more careful approach in evaluating future risks. As will be seen in Chapter 23 of this book a recent change in the law, that followed a discussion on corporate governance in Germany, requires companies to report on risks in the management report.

Under the principles of GoB, an enterprise should provide for future losses. The estimation of these losses involves judgement and it appears that in exercising judgement German enterprises tend to be on the side of pessimism. This is in accordance with the principle of prudence to which much weight is given. Setting up large provisions brings two benefits for the enterprise:

(i) It reduces the tax burden, since most provisions are accepted by the tax authorities.
(ii) It retains funds within the enterprise.

Provisions are one aspect of self-financing which is relatively more important for German enterprises than for those of other countries. German managers prefer to finance the expansion of the enterprise out of its own funds rather than risk losing control through an issue of equity or debt. Another aspect of self-financing that does not show up in the statistics is the use of conservative asset valuations. If all assets were valued at their current value, the equity would be increased and the extent to which the enterprise is financed out of retained profits would become clearer.

7.3.6 The accountancy profession

The German accountancy profession is small and of relatively recent origin. Although there are records of audits being performed as early as 1900, it was not until 1931 that the annual audit of a corporation (AG) became a legal obligation and that the accountancy profession was formally organized to provide the skilled persons to undertake these audits. The stimulus to this development was the failure of a number of large insurance companies and banks during the great depression of the early 1930s. In September 1931, all large stock corporations (AGs) were required to appoint an auditor to report on their annual accounts. The auditors had to be persons or firms that were recognized by the authorities as competent and were permitted to use the title 'Wirtschaftsprüfer' (literally business checker). In 1961, the profession was reorganized under its present form, with two bodies:

(i) The Wirtschaftsprüferkammer ('Kammer'), which is a state body under the supervision of the Ministry of Economics charged with the responsibility of representing the profession. All qualified Wirtschaftsprüfer and vereidigte Buchprüfer (see below) are automatically members of this body. The Kammer is self-governing, being managed by a board elected by the members. The Ministry of Economics only intervenes if it perceives that the Kammer is failing to fulfil the functions delegated to it by law. The Kammer's main function is to assure that the profession maintains high standards of competence and integrity, which it does through monitoring the compliance of its members with its rules for professional conduct. The Kammer has only limited disciplinary powers; it may reprimand a member who has broken its rules but, for more severe penalties, it has to refer the case to the courts. It does not control admission to the profession. The entrance examination is administered by the Ministry of Economics with the help of advisers nominated by the Kammer.

(ii) The Institut der Wirtschaftsprüfer (IDW), is a private body, whose function is to promote the interests of the profession. Membership is voluntary but is limited to Wirtschaftsprüfer of whom approximately 85 per cent are members. Its principal functions are to promote the education of both trainees and members, to issue guidance to its members on audit matters and to represent the German profession abroad. The IDW is considerably older than the Kammer, having been founded in 1931.

In 1986 a second tier qualification was established in Germany, that of the vereidigte Buchprüfer (sworn auditors). Their entrance examination is less severe than that of the Wirtschaftsprüfer and they are permitted to undertake the audits of smaller enterprises. One reason for the creation of this qualification was the small numbers of Wirtschaftsprüfer, which can be attributed to the very stiff entrance requirements of a university degree, four years' practical experience and a difficult examination.

A particular feature of the German profession is that a Wirtschaftsprüfer may only work as an independent professional or as an employee of an audit firm. Hence the German profession represents only auditors and not accountants employed in enterprises and administrations. This fact must be taken into account in interpreting the figures for the membership of the profession given in Exhibit 7.1. In effect in Germany, there is no accountancy profession, only an audit profession.

Exhibit 7.1   *The German audit profession*

	Number of members at 31 December 1997
Wirtschaftsprüfer	9 516
Vereidigte Buchprüfer	4 238
Total	13 754

7.4 THE GERMAN REGULATORY SYSTEM

Exhibit 7.2 presents the principal features of the current German system for the regulation of financial reporting, showing both the rules (at the foot of the exhibit) and the bodies that make the rules.

7.4.1 Law

As in other countries, the principal financial reporting rules are laid down in the law. Laws are enacted by the legislature, the Bundestag, which consists of democratically-elected representatives. Generally the government (more specifically the Ministry of Justice) prepares the text of a new law in consultation with interested parties and submits it to the legislature for its approval. Germany, as a member of the European Union, is obliged to incorporate into its national law the provisions of the EU's directives.

Exhibit 7.2 *The German system for the regulation of financial reporting*

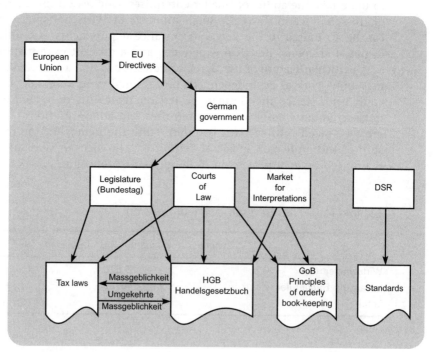

7.4.2 GoB: the market for interpretations

Where the rules set down in the law are insufficient, the German accountant turns for guidance to the principles of orderly book-keeping (GoB). Some of these principles are laid down in the law. However the HGB's principles are expressed in rather vague and general terms and to make them operational they need to be supplemented by more detailed rules. These are provided by the 'market for interpretations'[2] which is an important feature of the German regulatory system and which is unique to that country. This market consists of the writings of experts in financial reporting law and practice, such as lawyers, accountants and, above all, academics, which are presented as interpretations of the law. These writings are published in specialized journals and in very comprehensive commentaries, which seek to set down the rules to be followed in every eventuality. The activity may be characterized as a 'market' because the participants compete with each other in providing relevant and applicable interpretations of the law. There are so many competing interpretations that it is said that someone who wants to account for an item in a particular way can generally find support for the proposed treatment in one of the commentaries. However the market is regulated by the courts of law, which have the last say in whether a particular interpretation is valid; if the courts reject the interpretation of a particular expert this has a considerable impact on that expert's reputation and marketability.

7.4.3 Standards

In September 1998, the Ministry of Justice recognized by contract the German Accounting Standards Board (Deutsche Standardisierungsrat or DSR) as the standard-setting body referred to in section 342 HGB (see section 7.3.2). The Board is staffed by seven independent accounting experts (preparers, auditors, an analyst and an academic). The due process is in many respects similar to that of comparable standard setters: the UK's ASB and the USA's FASB.

The DSR adopts a standard after publishing at least one draft version, discussing the comments received in a public meeting and hearing the consultative council, which comprises about 40 organizations involved in financial accounting. The draft standards are prepared by steering committees and the staff.

Although not formally part of the law, the standards are presumed to be GoB for accounting in consolidated financial statements, once the standards have been published by the Ministry of Justice in the Official Gazette (*Bundesanzeiger*). They are considered to be authoritative interpretations of GoB for the consolidated accounts to which they are addressed.

The DSR comes under the supervision of another private body, which fulfils the same functions as the UK's FRC, in that it provides the funds, appoints the members and protects the DSR from outside pressures, but which does not interfere in the DSR's standard-setting activities.

The principal difference between the ASB's standards and those of the DSR is that the latter apply only to the consolidated financial statements and that the legislative authority remains with the Ministry of Justice. As of July 2001, the DSR has issued fourteen standards, of which six are addressed specifically to banks and insurance companies.

7.5 THE FUTURE OF GERMAN FINANCIAL REPORTING

In the past, the financial reporting of German enterprises has been marked by the following characteristics:

(i) Tax-driven: As a consequence of the authoritativeness principle (Massgeblichkeitsprinzip) and, more importantly, its reverse (die umgekehrte Massgeblichkeit), the tax rules had a considerable influence on the financial statements of all German enterprises.

(ii) Protection of creditors: A major function of accounts has been to regulate the distribution of dividends with the objective of maintaining the value of the corporation's capital. This has been achieved by a prudent valuation of assets, leading to a prudent computation of profit.

(iii) Secrecy: German enterprises have generally been reluctant to disclose much about their financial position to outsiders. For example, few have revealed the value of the hidden reserves that they have built up through the use of prudent valuation of assets and overstatement of provisions.

(iv) Not shareholder friendly: Enterprises in Germany have generally attached little importance to the need to inform shareholders about their financial position and performance, in sharp contrast to the position in the Anglo-Saxon countries.

However, starting in 1993 with the listing of Daimler Benz on the NYSE, the larger German multinational enterprises have discovered that their financial statements drawn up in accordance with the foregoing principles prove to be inadequate when they have to compete with MNEs from other countries on the global capital market, for reasons that are analysed in detail in Chapter 10. As has been mentioned earlier, in response to pressure from these enterprises, the HGB was modified in 1998 to permit listed corporations to draw up their consolidated accounts in accordance with 'internationally recognized accounting principles', i.e. IAS or US GAAP, provided financial reporting remains compatible with EU Directives.

These legal changes are already having a significant effect on German financial reporting. Of the 30 major German enterprises that made up the DAX stock exchange index in October 2000, 14 presented their consolidated accounts according to IAS, 10 according to US GAAP and only 6 according to HGB. In terms of market capitalization, the figures were IAS (38%), US GAAP (54%) and HGB (8%). It seems likely that by 2001 all DAX corporations will apply either IAS or US GAAP. Whether the impact will be limited to the consolidated accounts of listed corporations only time will tell, but it seems likely that the effect will spread even to the individual accounts. However such changes are not to be decided on the national level only, but in accordance with the EU directives as well. The EU's proposal that all EU-listed companies listed should, from 2005, be required to prepare consolidated accounts in accordance with IAS will clearly have a major impact.

SUMMARY

The historical development of financial reporting in Germany was considered and presented as the explanation for its predominant characteristic: the protection of creditors through a prudent valuation of assets and liabilities. The principal features of the institutional framework were examined (the HGB, DSR, taxation, the corporate financing system and the accountancy profession) and their influence on financial reporting analysed. The elements of the German regulatory system were described: the law, GoB (the principles of orderly book-keeping) and standards. The impact of recent changes in the law relating to the consolidated accounts of German multinational enterprises were discussed.

Review questions

1. What was the longer term impact of the large number of business failures following the liberalization of the AG law in 1870?

2. How does German law seek to protect the creditors of corporations?

3. What are the principal characteristics of Soziale Marktwirtschaft (social market economy)?

4. What are GoB? How are they defined?

Review questions (cont'd)

5. How do the tax rules affect the financial reporting of German enterprises? What are the meanings of the terms 'Massgeblichkeitsprinzip'
   (the authoritativeness principle) and 'Umgekehrte Massgeblichkeit' (reverse
   authoritativeness)?

6. In what ways does the German accountancy profession differ from
   those of Britain and the USA?

7. What is meant by the 'market for interpretations'?

8. What have been the recent changes in the law relating to the consolidated accounts of German multinational enterprises?

Notes

1. Coenenberg (1994), p. 26, free translation.
2. The term 'market for interpretations' was invented by Ordelheide. More details of
   this unique German phenomenon can be found in Chapter 6 of Ordelheide and
   Pfaff (1994).

References

Ballwieser, W 'Germany – Individual Accounts', *Transacc: Transnational Accounting*,
   2, D Ordelheide (ed.), Palgrave, Basingstoke (2001).

Busse von Colbe, W 'Relationships between financial accounting research, standards setting and practice in Germany', *European Accounting Review*, 1(1) (1992).

Coenenberg, A *Jahresabschluß und Jahresabschlußanalyse*, Verlag moderne industrie
   (1994).

Ordelheide, D 'Germany', *Accounting Regulation in Europe*, S McLeay (ed.), Macmillan –
   now Palgrave, Basingstoke (1999).

Ordelheide, D and Pfaff, D *European Financial Reporting: Germany*, Routledge, London
   (1994).

Schmalenbach Gesellschaft 'German accounting principles: an institutional framework', *Accounting Horizons*, 9(3) (1995).

Further reading

The most comprehensive explanation of German financial reporting is given in
Ordelheide and Pfaff (1994), in which Chapter 6 is particularly recommended. A
very clear summary of German accounting principles is given by a report of the
Schmalenbach Gesellschaft (1995). For an analysis of the regulatory system, see
Ordelheide (1999). For the role of academics in the regulatory system, see Busse
von Colbe (1992). For a detailed exposition of the rules, see Ballwieser (2001).

chapter eight

Japan

Chapter objectives

■ To explain the present complexity of Japanese financial reporting in terms of its historical development and notably the legacy of the two 'accounting revolutions'

■ To outline the principal features of the Japanese institutional framework, notably the state, the corporate financing system and the accountancy profession

■ To present the three elements of Japanese regulatory system, the Commercial Code, the Securities and Exchange Law and the tax regulations, which together make up the 'triangular system'

■ To set out the role of the Business Accounting Deliberation Council and to consider its achievements

■ To examine certain aspects of the accounts of Japanese MNEs

8.1 THE IMPORTANCE OF JAPAN

Japan is the world's second largest economy. Its gross domestic product (GDP) is almost twice that of Germany, and some three times that of both France and the UK. There are 17 Japanese MNEs in the top 100, more than any country other than the USA. Japanese financial reporting is particularly complicated, more complex than that of any other country of the Pentad. Even the Japanese find it complicated. For Westerners, the complexity is compounded by problems of language and culture. The principal source of this complexity is the recent history of accounting in Japan which will now be considered.

8.2 HISTORY

Kyojiro Someya, a modern Japanese scholar, characterizes the development of accounting in Japan as consisting of two revolutions.

8.2.1 The first accounting revolution, 1853–99

The history of modern Japan starts in 1853 when an American fleet under the command of Commodore Perry arrived in Tokyo Bay, conveying the demand that Japan end its two centuries of self-imposed isolation and enter into commercial relations with the Western world. The Japanese ruling classes were very impressed by the economic power and military might of the West and decided that the only way for Japan to survive as an independent nation was to transform itself into an industrialized country. The government engaged on a deliberate programme of modernization, which consisted principally of studying the practices of the leading industrialized countries, notably the USA, Britain, Germany and France, deciding how they should be adapted for Japan and then imposing them on Japanese society. The transformation covered every aspect of Japanese life: the political system, with the adoption of a new constitution and a system of parliamentary government in 1889; the social system with the abolition of the feudal classes; and the economic system with the creation of new enterprises particularly in heavy industry. The banking system had to be created from scratch. In 1873 the government set up the First National Bank (Japan's first stock corporation) and invited a Scotsman, Alexander Shand, the manager of the Yokohama branch of the Chartered Mercantile Bank of India, London and China, to write a treatise on bank accounting. Shand accepted the invitation and wrote a book entitled 'The Detailed Method of Bank Bookkeeping' that set out the principles of double-entry book-keeping as applied to banks. The First National Bank adopted Shand's methods, basing its financial statements for the year 1873 on them. The practice of double-entry book-keeping spread rapidly; an important factor being that Shand's book was translated into Japanese and was widely read. There was a second book, also published in 1873, that was very influential: a translation of 'Common School Bookkeeping' by the American writers, Bryant and Stratton.

However, although both the Scots and the Americans were in at the beginning, the ultimate character of the first revolution was Germanic. The reason was the decision of the Japanese government to base the modernization of law on a codified system. This was almost inevitable as Common Law does not lend itself to being imposed on a country; it has to develop slowly as judges build up a body of decided cases. The first draft of the Commercial Code was prepared by a German, Hermann Roesler, who (not surprisingly) used the German Commercial Code as his model. Although his draft was subsequently modified by Japanese jurists, the Commercial Code (CC) that was enacted in 1890 (and substantially amended in 1899) had a distinctively Germanic flavour, notably in the emphasis on creditor protection. For example, there was a requirement to prepare a balance sheet listing all assets and liabilities but initially no mention of an income statement. Since 1899, the CC has been modified several times, but has maintained its Germanic character of creditor protection through detailed prescription. Up to 1945, the financial reporting of Japanese enterprises was based solely on the CC. The emphasis was on the maintenance of the enterprise's assets with the objectives of assuring both the financial stability of the enterprise and the protection of creditors. Little consideration was given to the information needs of shareholders. The stock market was undeveloped and there was little trading in the shares of the larger corporations which were closely held by a small number of rich families. The principal sources of corporate capital were the government and the banks; both found that they were able to obtain the information that they needed directly from the corporations and did not rely on the CC's very limited provisions as to financial reporting.

McKinnon (1994) makes an important point about the CC's financial reporting provisions. They were incorporated into Japanese law, not as a response to a financial scandal or to a widespread recognition of the need for better accounting, but because the ruling classes considered that it was necessary for Japan to have a complete code of commercial law. The essential reason was political. In 1858 the USA had pressurized the Japanese government to accept a treaty which opened up the country to external trade; shortly afterwards, similar treaties were signed with the principal European countries. At that time, Japan had no system of civil, commercial and criminal law similar to that of Western countries and therefore these countries insisted on terms in the treaties whereby their own laws had extraterritorial jurisdiction in Japan in cases involving contracts between their subjects and the Japanese. The Japanese considered that these treaties were humiliating and their reversal became an overriding priority of the Japanese government. However the Western countries insisted that a necessary condition for the renegotiation of the treaties was that Japan should have a modern legal system. For the Japanese government, it was important that the CC should be complete (to forestall possible objections from the Western powers) and hence it included provisions on financial reporting. There is no evidence that the Japanese government made any effort to monitor the compliance of corporations with the financial reporting provisions of the CC; for example, initially there was no requirement to deposit accounts with the Ministry of Justice. Similarly there is no evidence that the users (shareholders and creditors) for whom, in principle, the accounts were prepared exerted any pressure on the government to undertake such monitoring. This gives the strong impression that, at least initially, Japanese corporations considered financial reporting as a rather pointless exercise forced on them by a law whose origins were largely foreign. Given the lack of interest on the part of the government and an understandable concern for confidentiality on the part of enterprises, it is not surprising that the financial statements of most corporations were uninformative.

8.2.2 The second accounting revolution, 1945–49

Following Japan's catastrophic defeat in the Second World War, the economy was in ruins. The American occupying forces, under General MacArthur, were determined to effect a thorough reform of the way that the economy was organized. Prior to 1945 the Japanese economy had been dominated by a small number of huge combines, known as zaibatsu, which were owned by a few rich families. The Americans were determined to eliminate this concentration of power and in its place to install a shareholder democracy. Hence the zaibatsu were broken up and their shares sold to the general public. This implied revitalizing the stock market, providing for its proper regulation and assuring that enterprises supplied shareholders with the information that they needed for their investment decisions. The legal framework necessary for the functioning of this new system was provided by the Securities and Exchange Law (SEL), which was enacted in 1948 and was consciously modelled on two American laws: the Securities Act of 1933 and the Securities Exchange Act of 1934. The basic approach of the SEL is that the financial statements of listed corporations should serve the needs of shareholders by providing full information about the enterprise's position and performance. This was in marked contrast to the approach of the Commercial Code (CC) which was based on creditor protection. However the CC was not repealed and corporations are still even today obliged to follow its prescriptions in drawing up their accounts.

Hence the two accounting revolutions were cumulative. Someya (1996) identifies two common factors in these revolutions: that Japan's level of economic development lagged behind the West and that an outside stimulus was involved; he comments, 'the first of these was the major cause of the revolutions; the second served as the trigger.'

8.3 THE JAPANESE INSTITUTIONAL FRAMEWORK

8.3.1 The state

In Japan, there is a long tradition of the state playing a leading role in the economy. The state was both the initiator and the principal actor in the rapid modernization of Japan that occurred in the second half of the nineteenth century. All the major developments of this period were the results of state action: the setting up of a modern banking system, the founding of heavy industry, the creation of a complete legal system based on western principles, and so on. After the Second World War, the American military administration for a short period fulfilled the same function and was the power behind a major reform of the political and economic systems; in the field of financial reporting, its most important achievements were the enactment of the SEL, the revival of the stock exchange and the foundation of the accountancy profession. When the Japanese government took over from the Americans, it further strengthened the state's role; for example it changed the status of the Business Accounting Deliberations Council (the Japanese standard-setting body, see section 8.4.5) from an independent body to an agency of the Ministry of Finance.

The Japanese state is not a single monolithic entity; it consists of a number of sub-entities. In the field of accounting, the most important are:

■ The Ministry of Justice, which is responsible for the CC

■ The Ministry of Finance, which is responsible for the SEL

■ The National Tax Administration Agency, a largely autonomous agency which reports to the Ministry of Finance

The senior permanent officials of these ministries wield very considerable power. Although in principle ultimate authority rests with the legislature, which enacts all laws, in practice the legislature has only on occasions shown a strong interest in financial reporting and generally approves the draft laws presented by the government which have, of course, been drawn up by officials.

8.3.2 Taxation

As in other countries, a major reason for the state's interest in financial reporting is taxation: to ensure the orderly collection of taxes on enterprises. However, in Japan, even greater importance is attached to this aspect, given that 70 per cent of the state's revenue comes from income taxes on enterprises and individuals (Takita and Yumoto, 1995). There are three taxes charged on the profits of corporations:

■ Corporate Income Tax, with a rate of 30 per cent (1999)

■ Enterprise Tax, with a rate 9 per cent (1999)

■ Inhabitant Tax, computed as 17.3 per cent of Corporate Income Tax

The combination of these three taxes represents an effective tax rate of 40.87 per cent (1999), taking into account the deductibility of the enterprise tax. In recent years tax rates have been reduced considerably; in 1997 the effective rate was nearly 50 per cent.

8.3.3　The corporate financing system

In the nineteenth century, stock exchanges were set up in Japan's major commercial centres. However they did not function effectively. Commerce and industry were dominated by the huge financial combines, the zaibatsu; the shares of the zaibatsu enterprises were closely held and rarely changed hands. After the war, the American military administration reorganized the stock exchanges, with the aim that they should play a more important role in the economy. This aim has been largely achieved. The Tokyo stock exchange is one of the largest in the world. In terms of market capitalization it is about equal to NASDAQ and ahead of London, although all three are at present dwarfed by the New York Stock Exchange. In fact for a period in the 1980s the Tokyo stock exchange was the world's largest in terms of market capitalization, but lost this position following the catastrophic fall in share prices in the early 1990s; the Tokyo share index, the Nikkei, fell from an all-time high of 38 916 in December 1990 to a low of 14 390 in August 1992. Since then share prices have never approached the earlier heights. However the high figures for market capitalization should not be taken to indicate that the capital market is as important in Japan as in the USA and Britain. In relative terms, as a proportion of GDP, the Japanese capital market is far smaller. Moreover, the Tokyo stock exchange is far less active than its American and British counterparts; in 1999, the purchases and sales of shares on the Tokyo exchange came to less than one half of the London figure and less than one sixth of the NASDAQ figure.[1] Shares in Japanese corporations change hands much less frequently compared with those of American and British companies. Many shareholdings take the form of long-term investments of one enterprise in another and of cross-holdings; they are not actively traded. Many Japanese enterprises have a close relationship with a bank which supplies much of their capital needs through loans. Sakurai (2001) points out that Japanese enterprises have traditionally relied on borrowings rather than equity issues to finance their activities, with the consequence that debt-equity ratios are generally high. All these factors make the capital market far less important as an influence over financial reporting in Japan than it is in the USA and Britain.

8.3.4　The accountancy profession

The Japanese accountancy profession is of comparatively recent origin. Although the first group of professional accountants is said to have been formed around 1907, it was not until 1927 that the profession received any official recognition, with the enactment of the Accountants Law. After the war, the accountancy profession, like most aspects of Japanese society, was reorganized under the direction of the American occupying forces. In 1948 the Certified Public Accountants Law was enacted which created the qualification of Certified Public Accountant (CPA), provided for the organization of examinations for admission to this qualification and set up the Japanese Institute of Certified Public Accountants (JICPA). The Law provided for the establishment of the CPA Investigation and Examination Board with responsibility for the discipline of CPAs and the supervision of the examination. This board still exists. Its members are appointed by the Ministry of Finance. Hence the Japanese accountancy profession is, like those of France and Germany, an institution created and controlled by the state.

The principal function of CPAs is to audit the financial statements of large corporations. Essentially the profession was recreated in 1948 to back up the reform of financial reporting contained in the Securities and Exchange Law, which required that the financial statements of listed corporations be audited. CPAs may also provide other accountancy services on a fee basis but may not work as an employee except for another CPA or for an audit corporation. Compared with the size of the Japanese economy, the profession is tiny. In 1999, there were some 12 700 Japanese CPAs, that is about 100 qualified accountants per million inhabitants (see Exhibit 2.5). This statistic may be compared with over 3500 in Britain and about 1500 in the USA. One reason for the small number of Japanese CPAs is that the entrance examinations are very difficult. There are two principal examinations: the first is to become a junior CPA for which the pass rate is less than 10 per cent; successful candidates may, after a further three years, including two years' practical experience, take the examination to become a full CPA. Possibly because of its small size, the influence of the accountancy profession over Japanese financial reporting has not been significant. Curiously its influence over international financial reporting has been somewhat greater. The JICPA was a founder member of the IASC and from 1993 to 1995 Eiichi Shiratori, a Japanese CPA, was the IASC's chairman.

8.4 THE JAPANESE REGULATORY SYSTEM: THE TRIANGULAR SYSTEM

In the analysis of the historical development, the two major pillars of Japanese financial reporting were identified as the Commercial Code (CC) and the Securities and Exchange Law (SEL). In fact Japanese writers identify the tax authorities as a third element of the system and for this reason

182

Exhibit 8.1 *The Japanese triangular system*

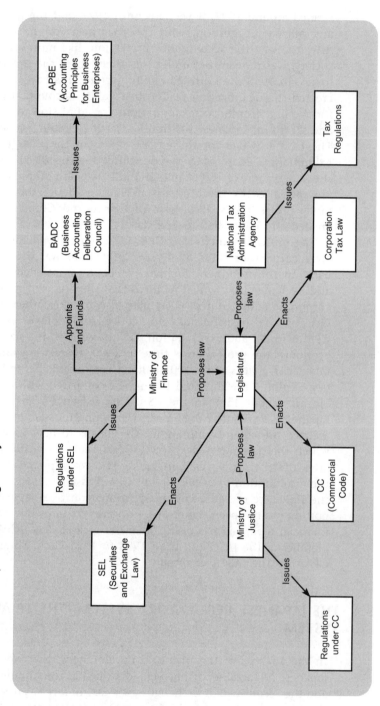

refer to the 'triangular system'. (Arai and Shiratori, 1991). Exhibit 8.1 presents in diagrammatic form the principal elements of the triangular system. Each will now be considered in turn.

8.4.1 The Commercial Code (CC)

The Commercial Code (CC) applies to all forms of business organizations, with special rules relating to the financial reporting of corporations (kabushiki kaisha or KK). These rules distinguish between large, medium-sized and small corporations, but the code makes no distinction between listed and unlisted enterprises. All corporations are required to prepare each year a balance sheet, an income statement and a business report, which is a detailed review of the enterprise's activities. These reports are presented to the shareholders at the annual meeting and subsequently a copy must be kept at the corporation's head office where it may be inspected by shareholders and creditors. Large corporations must publish a summary of the balance sheet in the official gazette or in a newspaper. There is a requirement that the accounts be audited, but only in the case of large corporations must the auditor have a professional qualification (CPA). In many small corporations the auditor is a long-serving employee; this fact must cast doubts on the effectiveness and independence of the audit.

The CC lays down general rules governing the contents of the balance sheet and income statement; the detailed rules are set out in regulations issued by the Ministry of Justice. An important point is that the CC rules apply only to the financial statements of the individual corporation; it makes no reference to consolidated accounts.

8.4.2 The Securities and Exchange Law (SEL)

The SEL's provisions apply only to enterprises that are listed on Japanese stock exchanges. The law's provisions are supplemented by regulations issued by the Ministry of Finance. Together they define in considerable detail the reports that these enterprises have to file with the Ministry of Finance and the stock exchange authorities. These reports include: balance sheet, income statement, statement of appropriations and supporting notes and schedules. Where an enterprise has subsidiaries (as is generally the case with listed enterprises) it has to prepare consolidated accounts as well as those of the individual corporation. In addition there is a securities report, which is similar to the CC's 'business report' but rather more detailed. The SEL's provisions are in addition to those of the CC. Hence listed corporations have to prepare both a CC report and an SEL report, both containing a balance sheet and an income statement.

8.4.3 The tax law

The rules for the computation of the tax are set down in the Corporate Tax Law and the detailed regulations issued by the National Tax Administration Agency. The basic position is rather similar to that in Germany; there is a general rule (with some exceptions) that the computation of tax is based on the figures presented in the financial statements prepared under the CC and approved at the annual shareholders' meeting. There is even a name for this rule, Kakutei Kessan Shugi, (the principle of definitive settlement of accounts), the equivalent of the Massgeblichkeitsprinzip in Germany. An enterprise may not claim an expense as tax deductible if it is not shown in the income statement. The principal exceptions to this rule are the numerous tax incentives offered by the government in pursuit of its economic goals which may be deducted as an expense in the tax computation but which are shown as appropriations of income to tax-free reserves in the CC accounts. Enterprises tend to claim the maximum permitted by the tax authorities for such expenses as depreciation and doubtful debts, even if the amounts are not appropriate from the economic viewpoint. However where the charge allowed for tax purposes is insufficient, most Japanese enterprises make additional provision in their CC accounts. In respect of the provision for doubtful debts, a survey of 499 listed corporations showed that 13 per cent provided only the amount provided for by the tax code, whereas 82 per cent made additional provision based on an evaluation of the individual accounts receivable (JICPA, 1999).

Sakurai (2001) claims the following advantages for linking the tax computation to the published accounts: (a) It regulates the conflict of interest between the shareholders (who seek to minimize the tax burden) and the tax authorities (who have the opposite objective) in an objective fashion; (b) It saves costs for both the corporation and the tax authorities; (c) It avoids the situation (that can arise when the tax computation is not based on the accounts) of an enterprise paying little or no tax despite reporting high profits. This can lead to a loss of confidence in the taxation system on the part of the general public and to demands for an increase in taxes on corporations. Sakurai comments: 'The principle of the definitive settlement of accounts prevents the occurrence of such criticism and the resultant political costs, through consistency between the taxable income assessment and the income determination in the financial statements.'

8.4.4 The functioning of the triangular system

The three different elements of the triangular system are the responsibility of different government departments: the CC comes under the Ministry of Justice; the SEL under the Ministry of Finance and the tax regulations under the National Tax Administrative Agency, a largely autonomous body which reports to the Ministry of Finance. One would expect that the existence of three different sources of rules would lead to confusion and chaos. Certainly it does add considerably to the complexity of the Japanese financial reporting system and on occasions there have been contradictions between the rules. In the past, coordination between these ministries has often been poor and inter-ministerial rivalries have hindered the development of financial reporting. However now the system seems to function quite well. One reason is that all the persons involved in the system, particularly the officials, make great efforts to ensure that there is a large measure of consensus among all interested parties before coming to any decision. To help in the consensus building process, all three ministries have advisory bodies composed of representatives of the major social and economic groups in their field of activity.

Two important points reduce the scope for conflict:

■ The SEL applies only to listed corporations
■ The CC and the tax code do not apply to the consolidated accounts

Hence the area of potential conflict is limited to the accounts of individual corporations that are listed on the stock exchange. A further important point is that both the CC and the SEL are much more specific about disclosure than they are about measurement. They prescribe what should be included in their reports (the SEL in more detail than the CC) but are far less specific about how these items are to be measured. Most commentators agree that Japanese financial reporting is far stronger on disclosure than on measurement; in fact some researchers place Japan in the same category as the USA in terms of disclosure but in a quite different category (either unique or similar to Germany) in terms of measurement. For measurement, Japanese corporations tend to follow the statements of the BADC (see next section) and the tax rules. Research by Hiramatsu (1994) showed that the tax rules were the more important of the two. The influence of the tax rules on the amounts reported for depreciation and doubtful debts has already been mentioned.

Over time the major differences between the CC and the SEL have been eliminated by appropriate amendments to the basic laws and the supporting regulations. The success of this policy can be seen in the fact that, although the CC and the SEL differ considerably as to the rules for the format of financial statements, particularly as to the degree of disclosure which is far higher under the SEL, there is no difference in the amounts reported for total assets and for profits under the two laws. On the relationship between the Ministry of Justice and the Ministry of Finance, Cooke (1991) remarks dryly, 'While conflict was common in the 1950s and 1960s, the two Ministries now enjoy a stable relationship based on mutual mistrust'. In short the Japanese triangular system seems to work far more smoothly than one might expect.

The fact that there is now no difference between the CC and the SEL in the amounts reported for total assets and profit is really rather remarkable, given the fundamentally different objectives of the two laws – creditor protection under the CC and information for investors with the SEL. It is the opinion of one contemporary commentator (Sakurai, 2001) that Japanese corporations, in resolving this conflict of objectives, 'have overwhelmingly emphasized the importance of the protection of creditors'. However, although this may have been the case in the past (notice the word 'have' in the passage just cited) there is clear evidence that the financial reporting of Japanese corporations is becoming increasingly oriented towards the provision of information for investors. It would seem that gradually the SEL is supplanting the CC as the dominant influence over financial reporting, at least as concerns the larger listed enterprises.

8.4.5 The Business Accounting Deliberation Council (BADC)

The Business Accounting Deliberation Council (BADC) may be described as the element in the Japanese system that most closely resembles a standard-setting body as recognized in the West. It functions as an advisory body of the Ministry of Finance which appoints all its members and provides all the funds. In 1999 it had 19 permanent members, including 11 from academia (including the chairman), three from industry and two from the accountancy profession. Hence the professors are in the majority. However almost certainly the most important influence on the BADC are the bureaucrats of the Ministry of Finance. The BADC is a creature of the Ministry of Finance and is in no sense an independent standard-setting body. Financial reporting in Japan is dominated by the government; even the BADC, whose principal function is enable the rest of society to present its opinions, is managed by the government. The BADC never takes a vote; it works through consensus and the views of all its members are taken into account in developing its statements. However in the consensus forming process the bureaucrats of the Ministry of Finance play a central role; among the BADC's other members, there is no doubt that the Keidanren (the powerful employers' organization) is more influential than the tiny accountancy profession. However even the representatives of the Keidanren on occasions feel obliged to modify their position in order to achieve a consensus.

The BADC was set up in 1949 as part of Japan's second accounting revolution and since then has issued a number of statements that have had a considerable influence on financial reporting in Japan; the more important are listed in Exhibit 8.2.

The statements listed in Exhibit 8.2 may be classified into three categories.

Exhibit 8.2 *Important statements of the BADC*

Date	Title	Date of amendments
1949	Accounting principles for business enterprises (APBE)	1954, 1963, 1974, 1982
1951	Opinion on reconciliation between the CC and the APBE	1960
1952	Opinion on reconciliation between the tax laws and APBE	1966
1954	Supplement to APBE	1963, 1974, 1982
1975	Accounting principles for consolidated accounts	1982, 1997
1979	Accounting principles for foreign currency transactions	1983, 1995, 1999
1988	Reporting standards for financial information by segment	
1990	Reporting standards for futures, options and marketable securities	
1993	Accounting principles for lease transactions	
1998	Accounting principles for consolidated cash flow statements	
1998	Accounting principles for research and development costs	
1998	Accounting principles for retirement benefits	
1999	Accounting principles for financial instruments	

Source: adapted from Sakurai (2001)

General statements

These comprise 'Accounting principles for business enterprises'[2] APBE (first issued in 1949 and subsequently updated in every decade) and its supplement (first issued in 1954 and subsequently updated three times). The BADC's objective in issuing these statements may be appreciated from the following quotation from the preface to the 1949 statement:

> APBE is a summary of the accounting conventions which have been generally accepted as fair and proper and should be followed by all business enterprises, even it is has no statutory binding force ... APBE should be highly regarded when the law and ordinances affecting business accounting, such as the Commercial Code or the tax law are enacted, amended or abolished in the future (taken from Hirose, 1987).

In effect the APBE when they were first issued in 1949 were an attempt to create Japanese GAAP (Generally Accepted Accounting Principles). They certainly did not reflect Japanese GAAP at that time as their contents largely reflected American principles, being based on the 1938 report 'A statement of accounting principles' of three American professors, Sanders, Hatfield and Moore. However, since 1949, the APBE (periodically updated) have achieved a considerable degree of recognition, both in law and practice, and in the opinion of some commentators, for example Shiba and Shiba (1997), form the basis of Japanese GAAP.

Reconciliations with other rules

A major part of the BADC's activities has been devoted to achieving a reconciliation between the three elements of the triangular system. In 1974 there was a major reconciliation exercise between the CC and the SEL, partly based on the APBE's principles. As a result there is no difference between net profit and net equity under the two laws. A new article was added to the CC to the effect that 'fair accounting practice should be taken into consideration' when preparing financial statements (Takita and Yumoto, 1995). And, in 1967, the tax law was amended to state that taxable income should be computed in accordance with generally accepted accounting principles (unless there was a specific tax regulation to the contrary). The APBE's claim to represent Japanese GAAP rests largely on these two legislative provisions.

Modernizing standards

In recent years the BADC has issued a number of individual standards with the aim of bringing the financial reporting of Japanese enterprises up to the level of foreign (typically American) enterprises. These include statements on foreign currency translation, leases, segment reporting, cash flow statements, R&D, pensions and financial instruments. They reflect the fact that, in the field of financial reporting over the past fifty years, Japan seems to be engaged in a never-ending struggle to catch up with the most advanced countries. This has been particularly apparent in relation to consolidated accounts.

8.4.6 Reform of the BADC

Early in 2000, the Keidanren (the organization that represents Japanese industry) and the Japanese accountancy profession made a joint proposal to reform the BADC. The basic idea was to convert the BADC into a private body independent of the Ministry of Finance, with a status essentially similar to that of the USA's FASB, the UK's ASB and the newly formed German DSR. The Ministry of Finance seems to support the idea for in April 2000 it agreed to participate in a project team whose task was to prepare a detailed plan for the establishment of the reformed body.

8.5   CONSOLIDATED ACCOUNTS

Before the 1960s very few Japanese corporations, even among the very largest, issued consolidated accounts. The stimuli for this change were both internal and external. In the 1960s there were a number of bankruptcies of large enterprises where losses had been concealed through profit manipulations involving subsidiaries; in 1965 the failure of Sanyo Special Steel provoked considerable public criticism of financial reporting practice and led the legislature to request the Ministry of Finance to improve corporate disclosure (Cooke, 1991). At about the same time, several major Japanese enterprises, including Sony and Toshiba, sought a listing on the New York Stock Exchange. The SEC refused to accept their accounts as they covered only the parent corporation, in this way highlighting the extent to which Japan lagged behind the rest of the world. Hence, in 1976 after a long period of consultation, the Ministry of Finance issued an ordinance making consolidated accounts compulsory for listed enterprises. In the previous year (1975), the BADC had issued its first statement on consolidated accounts.

The Japanese rules are basically similar to those of America and Europe, in that the consolidated accounts include the total assets, liabilities, revenues and expenses of the parent corporation and its subsidiaries, with associates included using the equity method. When the rules were first introduced, many subsidiaries were excluded from the consolidated accounts on the grounds of very lax criteria for materiality, which have now been tightened up.

A more persistent problem is that it is very common for Japanese corporations to maintain a link with another enterprise through owning part of that enterprise's equity. Typically the proportion is small. Where the proportion is between 20 per cent and 50 per cent, the investment is reported in the consolidated accounts using the equity method; but where, as is commonly the case, it is less than 20 per cent, it is reported at historical cost which is very uninformative. Many Japanese enterprises are organized in loose networks known as keiretsu. Most keiretsu consist of a number of enterprises centred around a leading commercial bank or trading company. The cohesion of the keiretsu is maintained through cross-shareholdings and interlocking directorships. Intergroup sales and purchases are often an important unifying element, as well as credit provided by the main bank. According to Kuroda (2001), there were six keiretsu in 1998, known as the 'Big Six': the Mitsui Group, the Mitsubishi Group, the Sumitomo Group, the Fuyo Group, the Sanwa Group and the Daiich-Kangin Group. In each group, the leading companies hold shares in the other members of the keiretsu but typically the proportion is small (rarely above 20 per cent); hence there is no company that is a parent according to the criteria used in western countries and there is

Exhibit 8.3 *Cross shareholdings in the Sumitomo keiretsu*

Investee	Sumitomo Bank	Sumitomo Trust & Banking	Sumitomo Marine & Fire Assurance	Sumitomo Corporation
		Investor		
Sumitomo Bank	X	3.15%	1.77%	1.65%
Sumitomo Trust & Banking	2.28%	X	1.46%	1.81%
Sumitomo Marine & Fire Insurance	4.35%	4.77%	X	2.23%
Sumitomo Corporation	4.84%	5.53%	3.14%	X

Source: Kuroda (2001)

no one who is obliged to prepare consolidated accounts that show the position of the keiretsu as a whole. The Western approach to consolidation, as exemplified in the International Accounting Standards, is clearly not appropriate for the keiretsu. Exhibit 8.3 presents the cross-shareholdings of the leading enterprises in the Sumitomo Group, which in all comprises 20 companies. The important point to note is that the shareholdings are typically small, all less than 10 per cent.

Recently the BADC's standard on consolidated accounts was amended to provide that a subsidiary should be defined on the basis of 'substantial control.'[3] The new rule took effect for the financial year starting 1 April 2000. It remains to be seen whether this will lead to a significant increase in the number of enterprises covered in the consolidated accounts.

8.6 THE FINANCIAL STATEMENTS OF JAPANESE MNEs

Almost all large Japanese MNEs publish English versions of their annual reports. These are known as 'convenience translations' for two reasons:

(a) The Japanese terms are translated into English.

(b) The amounts are presented in both yen and in US dollars. The translation into dollars is done by multiplying all the yen amounts by the same exchange rate (typically the market rate at the balance sheet date). This translation process is quite different from that applied to the translation of foreign transactions and foreign subsidiaries, which is explained in Chapter 21.

These 'convenience translations' may be classified into three categories, according to the accounting principles used in their preparation.

US GAAP

Recently the Ministry of Finance issued a regulation that permits Japanese corporations that are listed in the USA and which therefore are obliged to prepare US GAAP accounts for the American regulatory authorities, to file these US GAAP accounts with the Ministry of Finance instead of the Japanese SEL accounts. About 30 Japanese MNEs are covered by this rule, including most of the larger, internationally renowned enterprises such as Mitsubishi, Toshiba, Sony, Honda, Canon and NEC. Mitsui is one of these enterprises as can be seen from the following note to the 2000 convenience accounts:

> The Company files its consolidated financial statements both with the SEC in the USA and with the Ministry of Finance (MOF) in Japan. Under the Japanese Securities and Exchange Law, approximately 30 Japanese companies, including the Company, that are currently registered with the SEC are permitted by Japanese government authorities to submit consolidated financial statements prepared under US GAAP to the MOF as a special exception to Japanese disclosure regulations.

According to Kuroda (2001) the Ministry of Finance has announced that it will not accept US GAAP financial statements for financial years ending on or after 31 March 2001. In this respect, Japanese policy seems to be the exact opposite of that of France and Germany, which have recently offered their MNEs greater flexibility in preparing their accounts according to internationally accepted norms.

Japanese GAAP accounts, with reconciliation

Some Japanese MNEs present convenience translations of their Japanese accounts with a reconciliation to another GAAP, either US or the IASs. Fujitsu is in this category as may be seen from the following extract from its 2000 annual report:

> The accompanying consolidated financial statements of Fujitsu Limited (the 'Company') and its consolidated subsidiaries (together, the 'Group') have been prepared in accordance with accounting principles and practices generally accepted in Japan and the regulations under the Securities and Exchange Law of Japan. The accounting principles and practices adopted by the consolidated subsidiaries outside Japan in their respective countries basically conform to those adopted by the Company. In presenting the accompanying consolidated financial statements, certain items have been reclassified for the convenience of readers outside Japan.
>
> The differences between the accounting principles and practices adopted by the Group and those prescribed by International Accounting Standards ('IAS') are set forth in Note 2.

Note that Fujitsu has reclassified certain items. This is very common with convenience translations as most foreign readers would be confused by the format prescribed for the SEL accounts. However the amounts reported for important aggregates, such as total assets, equity and profit are not affected.

Exhibit 8.4   *Fujitsu Ltd: Reconciliation between the published accounts (Japanese GAAP) and IAS*

	1999 Yen (millions)	2000 Yen (millions)
Income statement		
Net profit (loss) per Japanese GAAP	(13 638)	42 734
Foreign currency translation	(5927)	see note 1
Recognition of cumulative translation adjustment on sale of subsidiary		
Net profit (loss) per IAS	(19 565)	42 734
Percentage increase in reported loss	43.46%	0.00%
Balance sheet		
Equity per Japanese GAAP	1 165 312	1 291 432
Foreign currency translation		
Recognition of cumulative translation adjustment on sale of subsidiary as an expense (charged to retained earnings under Japanese GAAP)	(5927)	see note 1
Reclassify cumulative translation adjustment (shown under Japanese GAAP as an asset) as an element of equity	(86 660)	(114 904)
Retirement and severance benefits		
Recognition of accrued benefit obligation	(17 149)	see note 2
Scope of consolidation: inclusion of finance subsidiary		see note 3
Increase in assets	306 861	
Increase in liabilities	(306 861)	
Recognition of leased assets see		note 3
Increase in assets	72 830	
Increase in liabilities	(72 830)	
Detachable stock purchase warrants		
Reclassify as equity	8 477	1971
Equity per IAS	1 064 053	1 178 499
Percentage decrease in equity	8.69%	8.74%

Notes

1. The amount is not material
2. Fujtsu was unable to estimate the amount as the pension scheme was being reformed at 31 March 2000
3. Fujitsu has changed its reporting practice in line with the IASs

Note 2 (referred to in the extract) lists nine differences between the Japanese GAAP used in the Fujitsu accounts and the IASs, relating to such matters as foreign currency translation, valuation of marketable securities and inventories, leases and retirement benefits. Exhibit 8.4, adapted from the Fujitsu annual report, presents the impact of the principal differences on the figures for profit and equity. In 1999 there were four significant adjustments to the figure for equity, but the overall effect is not large – a reduction of less than 10 per cent in the reported figure. The impact on income is much greater: an increase of over 40 per cent in the reported loss. In 2000 there were fewer significant adjustments, for two reasons:

(a) The amounts were not material.

(b) Fujitsu changed its reporting practice in line with the IASs. This occurred in two areas: the integration in full of finance subsidiaries in the consolidated accounts and the recognition of leased assets. In both cases, the reporting of these additional items led to equal increases in both assets and liabilities and thus to no change in the reported figure for net equity. However they demonstrate the greater acceptance by Japanese enterprises of the IASC's standards.

Japanese GAAP, with no reconciliation

With these convenience accounts, the amounts reported in the Japanese accounts (normally the SEL accounts) are not altered. However, frequently the sequence of the items is rearranged so as to make them more under-standable to the English reader. Nissho Iwai Corporation is an example of an enterprise that uses this approach. A note to its 2000 accounts states:

> Nissho Iwai Corporation (the 'Company') and its consolidated domestic subsidiaries maintain their accounts and records in accordance with the provisions set forth in the Japanese Commercial Code and the Securities and Exchange Law and in conformity with accounting principles and practices generally accepted in Japan, which are different from the accounting and disclosure requirements of International Accounting Standards. The accounts of overseas consolidated subsidiaries are based on their accounting records maintained in conformity with generally accepted accounting principles and practices prevailing in the respective countries of domicile.
>
> The accompanying consolidated financial statements are a translation of the audited consolidated financial statements of the Company which were prepared in accordance with accounting principles and practice generally accepted in Japan from the accounts and records maintained by the Company and its consolidated subsidiaries and were filed with the Ministry of Finance ('MOF') as required by the Securities

and Exchange Law. In preparing the accompanying consolidated financial statements, certain reclassifications have been made to the consolidated financial statements issued domestically in order to present them in a form which is more familiar to readers outside Japan. . . .

The translation of the Japanese yen amounts to US dollars is included solely for the convenience of readers, using the prevailing exchange rate at 31 March 2000, which was ¥106 to US $1.00. The convenience translations should not be construed as representations that the Japanese yen amounts have been, could have been, or could in the future, be converted into US dollars at this or any other rate of exchange.

There is no reconciliation to US GAAP or IAS included in the published accounts. Notice that, in the convenience translation, Nissho Iwai has reclassified certain items. This is very common as the layout specified in the SEL would confuse most non-Japanese readers.

8.7 CONCLUSIONS

One clear conclusion can be drawn from this short survey: that Japanese financial reporting has failed to keep pace with the country's remarkable economic development. Japan is a major economic power. In terms of absolute GDP, it is second only to the USA. However, in the field of financial reporting, Japan lags behind the Western countries, particularly the USA, and seems to be involved in a continuous struggle to catch up. The situation is well summarized in the following comment that Someya, the leading Japanese accounting historian, made in 1991: 'Since the end of World War II, the Japanese economy has undergone tremendous development, but it is my opinion that the accounting structure in Japan has not kept pace with its own economic growth . . . Although Japan ranks economically among the leading nations of the world, its financial reporting is inadequate' (Someya, 1996).

However considerable progress has been made in recent years. In 1998 and 1999 the BADC made important modifications to its standard on consolidated accounts and issued no less than five statements setting out the accounting principles to be followed in the following important areas: cash flow statements, pensions, tax, R&D and financial instruments. When these statements start to have an impact (generally in the fiscal year 2000/1), many of the significant differences between Japanese GAAP and the IASs will disappear.

SUMMARY

The historical development of financial reporting was outlined with reference to the two 'accounting revolutions' of 1853–99 and 1945–49. The present institutional framework was analysed, covering the state (including taxation), the corporate financing system and the accountancy profession. The three principal elements of the regulatory system were identified as the Commercial Code, the Securities and Exchange Law and the tax regulations, which combine to form the triangular system. The role of the Business Accounting Deliberations Council was analysed. Finally certain aspects of the English language accounts of Japanese MNEs were explained.

Review questions

1. What were the events that triggered Japan's two accounting revolutions and what were the driving forces behind them?

2. What has been the role of the Japanese state in the development of financial reporting?

3. What are the principal differences between the Japanese accountancy profession and those of Britain and the USA?

4. What are the three elements of the triangular system?

5. Why does the triangular system function rather better than one might expect?

6. What is the function of the Business Accounting Deliberations Council? What have been its principal achievements?

7. Outline the different bases on which Japanese multinational enterprises may present their English language accounts.

Notes

1. Figures for equity turnover 1999: Tokyo $1675bn, London £3399bn, NASDAQ $10 467bn (website of the Fédération Internationale des Bourses de Valeurs – www.fibv.com).
2. The Japanese term is Kigyo Kaikei Gensoku, which receives different translations from different writers, for example Financial Accounting Standards for Business (Takita and Yumoto, 1995).
3. The BADC's standard contains detailed rules on how to establish 'substantial control'; these are outlined in Seki (2000).

References

Arai, K and Shiratori, S *Legal and Conceptual Framework of Accounting in Japan*, Japanese Institute of Certified Public Accountants, Tokyo (1991).

Cooke, TE 'The evolution of financial reporting in Japan: a shame culture perspective', *Accounting, Business and Financial History*, **1**(3) (1991), pp. 251–77.

Hiramatsu, K *Kokusai Kakei no Shindoukou (new trends in international accounting)*, Chuo Keizai Sha, Tokyo (1994).

Hirose, Y 'The promulgation and development of financial accounting standards in Japan', *Accounting and Financial Reporting in Japan*, FDS Choi and K Hiramatsu (eds), Van Nostrand Reinhold, London (1987).

JICPA *Corporate Disclosure in Japan*, Japanese Institute of Certified Public Accountants, Tokyo (1999).

Kuroda, M 'Japan – group accounts', *Transacc: Transnational Accounting*, 2nd edn, D Ordelheide (ed.), Palgrave, Basingstoke (2001), pp. 1807–1908.

McKinnon, J 'The historic and social context of the introduction of double entry book-keeping to Japan', *Accounting, Business and Financial History*, **4** (1) (1994), pp. 181–201.

Nobes, C and Parker, R *Comparative International Accounting*, Pearson Education, Harlow (2000).

Roberts, C, Weetman, P and Gordon, P *International Financial Accounting*, Financial Times Management, London (1998).

Sakurai, H 'Japan – individual accounts', *Transacc: Transnational Accounting*, 2nd edn, D Ordelheide (ed.), Palgrave, Basingstoke (2001), pp. 1685–1805.

Seki, M 'Reshaping standards', *Accountancy* (June 2000), p. 166.

Shiba, K and Shiba, L 'Japan', *Financial Reporting in the Pacific Asia Region*, R Ma (ed.), World Scientific, Singapore (1997).

Someya, K *Japanese Accounting: an historical approach*, Clarendon Press, Oxford (1996).

Takita, T and Yumoto, K 'Japan – individual accounts', *Transacc: Transnational Accounting*, D Ordelheide (ed.), Macmillan – now Palgrave, Basingstoke (1995), pp. 1805–1963.

Walton, P, Haller, A and Raffournier, B *International Accounting*, International Thompson Business Press, London (1998).

Further reading

The best comprehensive treatment of Japanese financial reporting available to the English-speaking reader is contained in Sakurai (2001) for the individual accounts and in Kuroda (2001) for the consolidated accounts. The treatment is probably too detailed for most readers. However the opening sections of these chapters give a good summary of the general principles and may be read with profit. One may also refer to the relevant chapters in Nobes and Parker (2000), Walton, Haller and Raffournier (1998) or Roberts, Weetman and Gordon (1998). However these do not deal with the subject in any greater detail than the present chapter. In addition, the publications of the JICPA should be consulted for a presentation of the Japanese viewpoint, notably Arai and Shiratori (1991) and *Corporate Disclosure in Japan* (1999). The Western point of view is given by Cooke (1991) and McKinnon (1994).

chapter nine

The European Union

Chapter objectives

■ To give a brief description of the European Union in general terms: its objectives, its members and its structure

■ To give a more detailed analysis of the EU's activities relating to financial reporting covering:

  ■ the reasons why it aims to achieve harmonization of the accounts of European enterprises

  ■ an analysis of the legal means by which it seeks to achieve its objective (the directives)

  ■ a brief description of the contents of its financial reporting rules

  ■ an analysis of the success of its actions

It is important that the student of financial reporting should know something about the European Union (EU) for two reasons:

■ The EU is a major force in the global economy. As demonstrated by the statistics presented in Chapter 1, the EU countries contribute about half of outward foreign direct investment (FDI), both flows and stocks, and receive about a third of inward FDI. Over half of the hundred largest MNEs are from EU countries.

■ The EU is also a major force in European financial reporting as it has issued a number of important regulations on the accounts of European enterprises.

9.1 THE EUROPEAN UNION: INTRODUCTION

The EU is a union of European countries. Exhibit 9.1 lists EU member states at the end of 2000, together with the dates of their joining the EU and statistics relating to size (population), economic strength (GDP, gross domestic product) and standard of living (GDP per head); they comprise all the countries of Western Europe (except Norway and Switzerland), as well as some countries rather more to the edges, such as Greece and Finland.

The EU member states vary considerably in size. There are four large countries: Germany, France, Italy and the UK. Germany, with a population of over 80 million, is significantly larger than the other three, which each have a population of just under 60 million. At the other end of the scale there is the mini-state of Luxembourg, with a population of only 400 000. In between lie ten countries with populations ranging from Ireland (3.5 million) to Spain (40 million). There are two countries with populations of around 5 million (Denmark and Finland) and five coun-

Exhibit 9.1 *The European Union: basic facts, 1998*

	Date of joining	Population (millions)	GDP (€ billions)*	GDP (€ per head)*
Austria	1995	8.1	181	22 346
Belgium	1958	10.2	230	22 549
Denmark	1973	5.3	128	24 151
Finland	1995	5.1	106	20 784
France	1958	58.7	1205	20 528
Germany	1958	82.1	1788	21 778
Greece	1981	10.5	140	13 333
Ireland	1973	3.7	80	21 622
Italy	1958	57.6	1168	20 278
Luxembourg	1958	0.4	15	35 925
Netherlands	1958	15.7	357	22 739
Portugal	1986	10.0	149	14 900
Spain	1986	39.4	641	16 270
Sweden	1995	8.8	182	20 682
United Kingdom	1973	59.1	1221	20 660
Total		**374.7**	**7591**	**20 259**
USA		268.9	8273	30 766
Japan		126.3	2894	22 914

Note: * in terms of relative purchasing power

Source: European Commission, *Eurostat Yearbook*

tries with populations of around 10 million (Austria, Belgium, Greece, Portugal and Sweden). The Netherlands is significantly larger with 15 million inhabitants. Spain is rather an anomaly. It is hardly a small country, but, with a population that is less than half of that of Germany (and a GDP of only a third), it can hardly be considered a large country. The EU's structure of a few large countries and many smaller countries is generally considered to be a great advantage. No single country dominates the EU, not even Germany, which makes up less than a quarter of the EU's population and GDP.

The last column in Exhibit 9.1 gives an indication of the relative standard of living in each country; it indicates the GDP per head expressed in terms of purchasing power. In all but five countries the standard of living is within 15 per cent of the EU average; the exceptions are Denmark and Luxembourg, which is above the average, and Greece, Spain and Portugal, which are below. However Luxembourg is a statistical freak generated by its small size; in many of the other countries one can find subdivisions of the size of Luxembourg with comparable standards of living. However, in the case of Greece, Spain and Portugal, the standard of living is substantially below the EU average – about three-quarters of the average. The EU aims to secure 'harmonious and balanced development' with no great disparities between member states in terms of living standards. It would seem that in respect of these three countries this objective still remains to be achieved. However it should be remembered that when the EEC was founded in 1957 the standard of living in Italy was very much lower than that of the other five founding member states and that over time this disparity has been almost completely eliminated. This is a measure of the EU's economic success and explains why at the time of writing most of the countries of Eastern Europe are seeking to join.

The last lines of Exhibit 9.1 compare the EU with the USA and Japan. The EU is considerably larger than both these countries in terms of population. In terms of GDP, it is larger than Japan and about equal to the USA. However it lags behind both countries in terms of living standards, a measured by GDP per head.

The EU has always been primarily an economic union. It started life in 1958 as the European Economic Community (EEC) of only six countries, Germany, France, Italy and the Benelux countries. The principal aim of its founders was to establish a common market in which there would be no internal economic frontiers; there would be free circulation of the output of enterprises (goods and services) and of the input factors (materials, labour and capital). The stated objective in establishing a common market was to raise the living standard of European citizens, that is the law of comparative advantage was to be allowed to exercise its benevolent effects without interference from import duties and other barriers to trade. The consumer was to benefit from the availability of goods and services that were produced in the most efficient way, that is in the cheapest location and using the lowest-cost input factors.

In fact the original EEC was spectacularly successful in this aim, as the removal of internal tariffs led to very marked economic growth in the original six members, leading other European countries to join: Britain, Denmark and Ireland in 1973, Greece in 1981, Spain and Portugal in 1986, and Austria, Sweden and Finland in 1995.

9.2 THE EU's INTEREST IN FINANCIAL REPORTING

For more than thirty years the EU has been very active in the field of financial reporting. Its aim has been to 'harmonize' the accounts of enterprises, that is to reduce the differences in this area between the different member states so that any remaining differences do not constitute an impediment to the EU's efficient operation. Harmonization is not the same as uniformity. For the EU to achieve the aim of harmonized accounts, it is not essential that the financial statement of a corporation set up in one member state (say Germany) should be identical as to form and be based on the same principles as those of a corporation from another member state (say France). It is sufficient that the difference should be reduced to the point where they no longer impede significantly the proper functioning of the EU. There are three reasons why the EU aims for harmonization; they relate to the common market, to the protection of shareholders and to competition.

9.2.1 The common market

The accounts of enterprises play an important role in the proper functioning of the common market. Capital is an essential input factor. To achieve the most efficient use of capital, an enterprise should be able to raise its capital in any member state (for example where the capital is cheapest) and put it to work in any other member state (for example where the production opportunities offer the greatest profit). However, if the rules of the various member states on the form and content of accounts are very different, these will act as a severe restraint on the efficient operation of the common capital market. For example, a French investor would be reluctant to buy the shares of a German AG if she finds its accounts strange and mystifying; similarly a German AG will be reluctant to raise capital in France if it has to spend resources on explaining and adapting its accounts for French investors. Hence, for the efficient operation of the capital market, the rules of financial reporting should not differ too much from country to country.

However, the effect of a member state's financial reporting rules is not limited to the capital market. The ultimate aim of the EU is to provide a common environment for business throughout Europe. An enterprise that is based in one member state should not experience major difficulties in carrying on business in another member state either through a branch or through a subsidiary company. The financial reporting requirements of the various member states are a major feature of the business environment and can add considerably to the costs of operating in another member state, particularly if these requirements differ significantly from those of the enterprise's home country. If the requirements of the two member states are inconsistent, or, even worse, contradictory, their effects can be most harmful.

9.2.2 The protection of shareholders

The separation of ownership from control in corporations renders their shareholders particularly vulnerable, since in the event of financial failure the shareholders' claims are limited to the assets of the company; they have no claim against the personal wealth of the company's promoters or managers. For this reason, most countries have enacted laws that are designed to protect the interests of shareholders, notably in relation to the accounts that corporations must render annually to their shareholders. Foreign shareholders are more vulnerable than domestic shareholders. With the creation of the EU it was to be expected that the number of foreign shareholders would increase. Hence when the EU was founded, special attention was given to the need to protect shareholders. Under the terms of article 54.3(g) of the Treaty of Rome, which set up the EEC in 1957, the EU is obliged 'to coordinate the safeguards which, for the protection of the interests of members and others are required by member states of companies[1] with a view to making them equivalent throughout the Community'. The term 'safeguards' in this article is interpreted to include the preparation and publication of financial statements. This is the sole reference to accounts in the treaty and the word is not even mentioned!

9.2.3 'The level playing field'

In order for the common market to operate efficiently, it is necessary that the allocation of resources that results from the interaction of market forces should not be distorted by government action, for example by the government offering subsidies and other benefits to national enterprises. Otherwise one member state would be able to secure for its enterprises a competitive advantage over its foreign rivals. The metaphor of the 'level playing field' is often used to describe the desirable state of the environment in which enterprises should compete with each other within the EU.

The requirement to publish accounts is one of the most important of the obligations imposed by governments on enterprises. In general, enterprises are reluctant to reveal much about their affairs in their published accounts, for fear of aiding their competitors. Hence, if enterprises resident in one member state were to be permitted to get away with publishing uninformative accounts, they would have an unfair advantage over enterprises in other member states. Since, in a common market, there should be no restrictions on where enterprises may establish themselves, there would be a tendency for enterprises to set themselves up in the member state that offered the most favourable financial reporting regime, that is the regime that did not require the publication of any significant information. Since, in general, governments are in favour of enterprises establishing themselves on their territory (they provide employment and pay taxes), they would be reluctant to see enterprises enticed away by incentives offered by other countries. The result would be a form of auction in which governments vied with each other in offering the most favourable financial reporting regime for enterprises; an illustration of 'Gresham's law of accounting': poor financial reporting drives out good financial reporting.

9.2.4 Harmonization before relevance

When the above three reasons are analysed it becomes apparent why the EU places more emphasis on uniformity than on relevance. The effective harmonization of accounts would deal completely with the competition concerns referred to in section 9.2.3; in fact a 'level playing field' could be achieved simply by insisting that member states impose no obligations relating to financial reporting. Harmonization would also go a long way to resolving the problems related to the common market, for, if the accounts of enterprises in all countries were basically similar, both enterprises and shareholders would be less inhibited in investing in other member states. The EU is not uninterested in the quality of financial reporting, for it is concerned to improve both the efficiency of the European capital market and the degree of protection enjoyed by shareholders. However its primary interest is in achieving an acceptable degree of harmonization.

9.3 THE EU's STRUCTURE

The EU comprises, within its organizational structure, institutions that perform the three essential functions of the state: legislative, executive and judicial.

9.3.1 The legislative function

The legislative function is shared between two institutions: the Council and the Parliament.

(a) **The Council** consists of representatives of the governments of the member states, generally government ministers, who meet periodically to discuss and enact laws. During the EU's early years, the Council had a monopoly of the legislative power, which is an indication of the EU's origin as an agreement between sovereign countries. However in recent years, the Council has had to share more and more power with the Parliament.

(b) **The Parliament** is made up of some five hundred members who are elected by the people. Hence the Parliament represents the people, whilst the Council represents the governments. Initially the Parliament had no real legislative power but over the years it has succeeded in wresting some power from the Council. The present position is that neither institution can enact a law against the determined opposition of the other, but the Council is still the more powerful of the two. This means that most EU laws reflect the views of the member states' governments.

9.3.2 The executive function

The executive function is exercised by the European Commission, which consists of some twenty Commissioners (politicians appointed by the governments of the member states for four year terms), supported by a staff of some 10 000 officials. The Commission has three principal functions:

(a) To propose new laws. A strange feature of the EU is that neither the Council nor the Parliament has this right; their powers are limited to enacting and, if necessary, amending laws proposed by the Commission.

(b) Executing these laws, in so far as this requires action at European level. However most EU laws are executed by the governments of the member states.

(c) Monitoring the execution of EU laws by the member states and taking judicial action against any infringing member state.

9.3.3 The judicial function

The judicial function is exercised by the EU's Court of Justice, based in Luxembourg – not to be confused with the European Court of Human Rights based in Strasbourg, which is not an EU body. The EU Court of Justice has two principal functions:

■ To interpret EU law

■ To rule whether the governments of the member states have broken EU law

However the EU has few sanctions that it can impose on a member state that is judged to have broken EU law. The principal reason why member states generally respect the court's judgements is that the alternative would be the collapse of the EU which would be in nobody's interest.

9.4 THE EU's HARMONIZATION PROGRAMME

9.4.1 The role of EU directives

The EU has sought to achieve the harmonization of the accounts of enterprises by enacting directives. A directive is a special type of EU law. It is addressed to the governments of the member states and it requires them to modify their national laws so as to bring into effect the provisions of the directive. The national governments are obliged to comply with the EU's directives under the terms of the treaty that they signed on joining the EU.

In the field of financial reporting, the fact that the EU has taken action through directives has had the following consequences:

(a) The task of incorporating a directive's provisions into the national law is the responsibility of the member states' governments. Leaving this task to national governments has a number of negative effects, including:

    (i) **Delays**: Often many years pass between the enactment of a directive by the EU and its implementation by a member state.

    (ii) **Divergent implementations**: In amending their national laws, member states may differ in their interpretation of particular provisions of a directive with the result that their national laws are not harmonized.

    (iii) **Non-implementation**: a member state may deliberately or through inadvertence fail to implement a particular provision of a directive.

The EU attempts to monitor the implementation of directives by the member states but not with complete success as its powers of enforcement are very limited.

(b) Each member state has retained its own national regulatory system, consisting of laws, standards and so on. Each member state's system consists of elements that are unique to that member state and of common elements resulting from the implementation of the EU's directives.

(c) Citizens and enterprises are obliged to obey national law. For them, the provisions of an EU directive have no effect until they are incorporated into national law.

In the area of financial reporting, the EU has enacted a number of directives of which two are of particular importance:

■ The Fourth Directive of 1978, which deals with the individual accounts

■ The Seventh Directive of 1983, which deals with consolidated accounts

9.4.2 The Fourth Directive: the accounts of the individual enterprise

The principal provisions of the Fourth Directive are:

(a) All corporations should prepare and publish a balance sheet, an income statement and notes to the accounts, with certain exemptions for smaller corporations.

(b) The formats of the balance sheet and the income statement are defined in considerable detail, including such matters as the headings and subheadings to be used.

(c) The matters to be covered in the notes to the accounts are also defined.

(d) The general principles to be followed in preparing the accounts are laid down. They include principles related to going concern, consistency, prudence and accruals.

(e) The basic rule is that assets are to be valued at historical cost less depreciation. However valuation at replacement cost, at revaluation or at an inflation-adjusted figure may be allowed at the discretion of the member state.

(f) Provisions may not exceed the amount that is necessary, thus making it more difficult to maintain secret reserves.

(g) The accounts are to give a true and fair view, if necessary by giving information additional to that required by the directive. In exceptional cases, the directive must be departed from if this is necessary to give a true and fair view.

9.4.3 Options

A feature of the Fourth Directive is the large number of 'options'; these are provisions of the directive that offer a choice of rules. There are two types of options:

(a) **'Member state options'**: These are rules where the choice is left to the government of the member state; it can decide whether or not to incorporate a particular rule into its national law. There is an example of a member state option in the previous list. Although the basic rule for valuation of assets is historical cost, member states have the option of requiring or permitting corporations to use other valuation methods.

(b) **'Company options'**: These are rules where the choice is left up to the preparer of the accounts.

Most of the options in the Fourth Directive are 'member state options'. Once the government has decided which option to incorporate into its law, the enterprise has no choice but to obey the law. However in certain cases the government may adopt the option in a way that also offers a choice to the enterprise.

9.4.4 The Seventh Directive: the consolidated accounts

The principal provisions of the Seventh Directive are:

(a) The parent enterprise of a group above a certain size is required to prepare and publish consolidated accounts, consisting of a consolidated balance sheet, a consolidated income statement and notes, covering the parent enterprise, subsidiaries and associates.

(b) The terms 'parent enterprise', 'subsidiary' and 'associate' are precisely defined, subject to a number of options.

(c) Both the acquisition method and the merger method of capital consolidation are permitted, the latter as an option.

(d) Goodwill is to be capitalized and amortized over five years, with an option for a longer period and another option permitting direct write-off to reserves.

(e) On most other matters, the Fourth Directive's rules apply also to the consolidated accounts, notably formats, valuation methods and the 'true and fair' rule.

9.5　THE IMPACT OF THE FOURTH AND SEVENTH DIRECTIVES

There can be no doubt that these directives have had a considerable impact on financial reporting within the EU. This impact has been most marked in two areas:

(a) **Improved quality.** Previously, many member states had very rudimentary financial reporting laws. Hence the reform of their laws occasioned by the need to implement the directives led to a marked improvement in the quality of financial reporting. This was particularly the case with Italy and Spain and the smaller member states, Belgium, Portugal and Greece.

(b) **Consolidated accounts.** In many member states, before the implementation of the Seventh Directive, there was no legal requirement for consolidated accounts. Now they are prepared by larger groups in all EU member states.

However the extent to which the directives have achieved harmonization is rather limited. In this connection a number of points can be made.

(a) **Matters not covered:** The directives fail to deal with many of the more important issues of financial reporting. For example the following matters are either not covered or dealt with in a very cursory and unsatisfactory manner: foreign currency translation, leasing, pensions, long-term contracts, derivatives, off balance sheet financing and brands.

(b) **Non-implementation:** Certain member states have failed to implement particular provisions of the directives. An example is Germany, which has failed to include in its national law that, in exceptional cases, the directive's rules must be disregarded if this is necessary to give a 'true and fair view'. However it is doubtful whether this particular omission has had a negative impact on harmonization. In fact one may speculate whether in fact the 'true and fair rule' itself is not the source of much disharmony, as it introduces a subjective element into the preparation of accounts. It should be noted that in the decade following the enactment of the Fourth and Seventh Directives, non-implementation was a major problem as many member states were very slow in passing the necessary legislation. However, when the last member state (Italy) enacted the necessary law in 1991, this particular problem was finally resolved.

(c) **Soft transformations:** This is a term invented by Ordelheide (1990) to describe the implementation of a directive's provisions into national law in such a way that, although the letter of the directive is respected, the intention of the EU legislator is thwarted. A notable example is Germany's action in making it a legal requirement for smaller corporations to publish their accounts but fixing no penalty for non-compliance, with the result that these corporations rarely publish their accounts.

(d) **Options:** Both the Fourth and Seventh Directives contain a great number of options, that is provisions that a member state may decide not to implement. When one member state implements an option and another does not, the effect is that the accounts of enterprises in the two countries are no longer harmonized. There are no less than 51 options in the Seventh Directive. Nobes (1990) has estimated that, with all the possible combinations, there are 2 000 000 000 000 000 different ways of preparing the consolidated accounts. Of course this exaggerates the impact of options as only a tiny fraction of the possible combinations are in fact available given the way in which the member states have implemented the directive. Also many options relate to trivial matters. However some relate to important matters. The more significant options (those that have the greatest impact on reported income and values of assets and liabilities) are:

■ **Asset valuation:** the member states have the choice of no less than four methods: historical cost, replacement cost, inflation adjustment and revaluation

■ **Tax-driven asset values:** in principle these are forbidden but member states may opt to retain them

■ **Inventory:** enterprises are permitted a wide range of valuation methods: weighted average, LIFO, FIFO or 'some similar method'

■ **Provisions:** member states may permit the setting up of provisions for charges that are not a liability of the enterprise

■ **Definition of a subsidiary:** member states have the option to define a subsidiary according to the criterion of de facto control

■ **Goodwill:** member states may permit goodwill to be amortized over a period longer than five years or to be written off directly against reserves

■ **Capital consolidation:** the merger method ('pooling of interest') is a member state option

(e) **'Skin-deep harmonization':** The directives are far more detailed and prescriptive on the form of accounts than on the principles to be followed in their preparation. Standard formats of the balance sheet and the income statement are laid down in the Fourth Directive. However the principles to be followed in establishing the figures to be reported in these formats are either expressed in vague terms or are left as options. The result is 'skin-deep harmonization': the accounts are harmonized as to their form but not as to the information that they convey.

Exhibit 9.2 presents the relationship between the EU's financial reporting rules and those of the member states in the form of a Venn diagram. Each circle represents the set of rules of a particular body. There are two circles for the EU: the outer one represents the totality of the rules of the EU's directives (both the mandatory provisions and the options); the inner one the set of the mandatory provisions. In addition there are circles that represent the rules of two hypothetical member states. The diagram shows the various logical possibilities; it is not intended to give an indication of the relative number of rules in each set. In fact theoretically some of the indicated sets should be empty. Thus area A + B represents the EU's mandatory rules that have not been incorporated into the national rules of member state II, and area H + J, the rules of member state I that are in conflict with the EU's rules. In both cases there is a breach of EU law. In reality, rules in areas A, B, C (non-implementation of mandatory EU rules) and H, J, K (conflicts with EU rules) are comparatively rare but they do exist. What are most important are the areas E and G: EU options implemented differently by different member states. Ideally the areas D and F (identical rules in the two member states) should cover most of the rules in both member states, which would indicate a high degree of harmonization. However in reality the areas E and G cover a significant proportion of member states' rules.

Exhibit 9.2 *The relationship between the EU's rules and the member state rules*

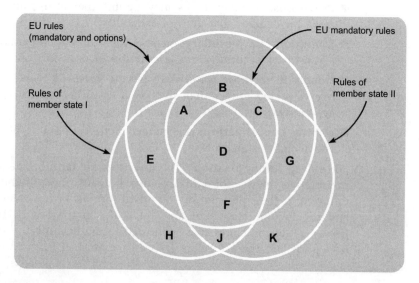

9.6 THE EU's LIMITATIONS AS A RULE MAKER

It is apparent from the foregoing analysis that the EU is *not* a European superstate, the equivalent in Europe of the USA. The EU member states still retain their national identities and most of the powers of government. Only in limited areas have they surrendered powers to the EU institutions.

This is clearly the case with financial reporting. The various countries have all retained their national accounting systems. The impact of the EU's efforts at harmonization through its directives has been very limited. In fact, in financial reporting, the differences within the EU are greater than the differences between certain EU member states and the rest of the world. This is the conclusion of the research discussed in Chapter 2, which is illustrated in Exhibit 2.9; in financial reporting matters, Britain is closer to the USA than it is to France, and Germany is closer to the Japan than it is to the Netherlands. Nevertheless the EU is a major actor in global financial reporting.

Globalization has had a considerable impact on the EU's activities in the field of financial reporting. In particular, the European MNEs have found that the obligation to follow the EU's rules puts them at a disadvantage in their competition with MNEs from other regions. In effect, the EU has discovered that it cannot in isolation set the rules but has to take into account developments on the world stage. The EU is a major actor in global financial reporting because of the importance of the European MNEs and of the authority of its directives, which these enterprises are legally obliged to obey. But there are other major actors. The EU's relationship with these actors and its role in global financial reporting are discussed in detail in Part Three.

SUMMARY

The EU was described in general terms: its objectives, its member states and its institutions.

The EU's programme for the harmonization of the accounts of European enterprises was analysed in detail, covering the following points: why the EU aims at harmonization; the legal means (the directive) by which it seeks to achieve its objective; the contents of the Fourth and Seventh Directives; the significance of options and the overall impact of the EU's programme.

Review questions

1. Name the 15 member states of the European Union. Which is the largest, and what proportion does it have of the EU's population and GDP?

2. What is meant by the term 'harmonization'. Why is the EU interested in the harmonization of the accounts of European enterprises?

3. What is a directive? What is the process by which an enterprise becomes subject to the rules contained in a directive?

4. What is an option? Why do options have a negative impact on harmonization?

5. In what area have the EU's directives had the greatest impact on the financial reporting of European enterprises?

6. What are the principal shortcomings of the EU's directives?

7. Has the EU succeeded in its objective of achieving harmonization?

Note

1. The term 'company' used in the Treaty of Rome and subsequently in all EU acts covers essentially the same field as the authors' preferred term 'corporation'.

References

Flower, J *The Regulation of Financial Reporting in the Nordic Countries*, Fritzes, Stockholm (1994).

Nobes, C 'EC Group Accounting – two zillion ways to do it', *Accountancy*, **106** (December 1990), p. 84.

Ordelheide, D 'Soft transformations of accounting rules of the fourth directive in Germany', *Les Cahiers Internationaux de la Comptabilité (Cahier no. 3)* , Editions Comptables Malesherbes, Paris (1990).

Van Hulle, K 'European Union – Group Accounts', *Transnational Accounting*, D Ordelheide (ed.), Palgrave, Basingstoke (2001).

Van Hulle, K 'European Union – Individual Accounts', *Transnational Accounting*, D Ordelheide (ed.), Palgrave, Basingstoke (2001).

Further reading

For a very brief introduction to the EU's harmonization programme, see Flower (1994) Chapter 1. For a much fuller analysis, see the two references to Van Hulle (2001).

The International Accounting Standards Board

This part deals with the International Accounting Standards Board (IASB), the body that seeks to set standards for the multinational enterprises at the global level.

Chapter 10 deals with two general matters which explain the importance of the IASB and its role:

■ An analysis of the problems that the diversity of national accounting systems causes for the multinational enterprises, leading to a discussion of the advantages of a single set of global rules

■ A discussion on how these global rules may be set. A number of possibilities are considered, including the rules being set by the EU or by two international bodies (the UN and the OECD) but it is concluded that at present there are only two sets of rules that have a realistic probability of becoming the global rules: US GAAP and the standards of the International Accounting Standards Board (IASB)

The remaining four chapters deal specifically with the IASB. They cover certain general points about this organization and are intended to serve as an introduction to the detailed consideration of this body's standards in Parts Four and Five. The IASB is a very new body having been formed as recently as April 2001, when it took over the role of global rule-maker from the International Accounting Standards Committee (IASC). Hence these chapters cover not only the IASB but also its predecessor, the IASC, where this is necessary to gain a fuller understanding of the IASB's activities. There is one chapter on each of the following subjects:

■ The IASB's objectives and organizational structure. This covers both the IASB and its predecessor, the IASC. It is necessary to consider the IASC in some detail, because a study of its activities over the 26 years (1974–2001) of its existence gives an insight into why it was considered necessary to replace the IASC by the IASB and prepares the ground for the examination of the IASB's organization

■ A general introduction to the International Accounting Standards (IASs): what countries and enterprises apply them and why they do so; what constitutes a 'high quality' standard; and how the standard-setting body, through its 'due process', seeks to ensure that its standards are of high quality. In fact all the current IASs were issued by the IASC; the IASB took over these standards when it took office in April 2001. Hence this chapter examines the procedures used by the IASC for the development of these standards. However this serves as a good introduction to the analysis of the IASB's 'due process', because this body has adopted the principal elements of its predecessor's 'due process'

■ The IASB's Framework for the preparation and presentation of financial statements. This is the IASB's 'Conceptual Framework', that is the document that sets out the principles on which the IASB's standards are based. After a general discussion on the role of conceptual frameworks, the provisions of the IASB's Framework are analysed in detail with reference to the text which is included in an annex

■ The detailed analysis of a particular IAS. IAS 1 is examined in detail as a means of explaining the structure and function of the typical IAS

The Global Rule-Makers

- To analyse how the financial reporting problems of the multinational enterprises may be alleviated by a set of global rules
- To discuss the advantages and disadvantages of a set of global rules
- To consider the possible sources of such a set of global rules, including the USA, the EU and three international organizations: the UN, the OECD and the IASB

10.1 THE PROBLEMS FACING THE MULTINATIONAL ENTERPRISES

The diversity of national accounting systems that has been analysed in the previous two parts causes problems for multinational enterprises (MNEs) in two areas:

- Internal management
- External financing

10.1.1 Internal management

The typical structure of a MNE is a group that consists of a parent corporation based in a particular country, which controls a large number of subsidiary enterprises based in countries scattered around the globe. To assure effective management of the group, it is essential that all the corporations use the same principles in drawing up their accounts. The management of an American parent corporation would find it very difficult to assess the true performance of its European subsidiaries if, for example, its German subsidiary valued its assets at historical cost and its British subsidiary reported them at market value. Hence most MNEs have developed standardized accounting principles for all the group enterprises, irrespective of the country in which they were based. The foreign subsidiaries are required to submit reports to the parent enterprise using the group's standardized accounting principles. However the foreign subsidiary is also obliged to draw up a set of financial statements according to the law of the country in which it is located. The need to prepare two sets of accounting reports based on different principles (one for the parent enterprise and another for the local regulatory authority) creates two rather different problems for the group management.

(a) **Consistency.** The two reports may give quite different messages (for example that to the parent indicates a loss, and that according to local law a profit) which can lead to confusion and uncertainty over measuring the performance of the foreign subsidiary. The group management may insist that performance be measured according to its standardized principles. However this does not prevent the local management feeling that it is being treated unfairly in that its performance is being measured according to principles that are not accepted locally.

(b) **Cost.** It is costly to maintain the accounting systems that are required for the preparation of two different financial statements.

Clearly there would be great improvements in economy and consistency if both the internal management accounts and the external financial statements of all enterprises in the group could be based on the same set of accounting principles.

10.1.2 External financing

With the expansion of their activities, the MNEs came to require additional capital. As their capital needs came to exceed the capacity of the capital market in their home country, they turned to other countries. More and more MNEs sought a listing on a stock exchange outside their home country. The motives were not exclusively financial; as Biddle and Saudagaran (1991) have pointed out there are benefits in other areas, such as marketing (publicity for the enterprise's products in the foreign country) and politics (improving relations with the foreign government by demonstrating a commitment to the country). Above all, listing on a foreign stock exchange (or better still several such exchanges) can be a signalling mechanism that the enterprise considers that it is no longer limited to its national base but is truly a 'global player'. It is logical that a world wide corporation should seek its capital on the global capital market.

However when the MNEs sought a listing on certain stock exchanges they discovered that their accounts were not acceptable to the regulatory authorities of the foreign country. In order to obtain a listing, they were obliged to prepare two sets of accounts, one in conformity with their national law and one to satisfy the foreign stock exchange. This was clearly thoroughly unsatisfactory. Not only was it costly but the provision of two sets of accounts, presenting different figures for key items such as profit was confusing to investors and to the public at large.

10.2 THE CASE OF DAIMLER BENZ

These problems are well illustrated by the recent experience of Daimler Benz,[1] the maker of the Mercedes car among other products. Daimler Benz is clearly a global player. Some years ago it evidently decided to convert itself from a basically German enterprise into a worldwide corporation. A major element in this new strategy was for its shares to be listed on the major stock exchanges of the world. The shares had been listed for decades on the Frankfurt stock exchange. But, for a worldwide corporation, this was too limited; it needed access to the international capital market. Hence by 1991, it had sought and been granted listings on five major non-German stock exchanges: Zurich, Tokyo, London, Vienna and Paris. However, in order for Daimler Benz to be truly a worldwide corporation, it was essential that its shares should be listed on Wall Street. The New York Stock Exchange is, by far, the world's largest. In 1999, its market capitalization at $16 604tn exceeded that of the next ten largest non-American stock exchanges combined.

Radebaugh and Gebhardt (1994) have analysed the factors that led Daimler Benz to seek a listing on Wall Street as follows:

(a) **Increased marketability of Daimler Benz shares.** The extent to which Daimler Benz was dependent on the German stock exchanges to provide a market for its shares is demonstrated by two statistics for the year 1992: 90 per cent of all purchases and sales of Daimler Benz shares took place on German stock exchanges, and over 11 per cent of trades on the German stock exchanges were of Daimler Benz shares. Clearly there was a need to develop new markets so as to improve the marketability of Daimler Benz shares.

(b) **Reduced dependence on German bank finance.** Daimler Benz, like many German enterprises, was heavily dependent on German banks for finance. With the increase in German interest rates caused by the enormous growth in government expenditure following German re-unification, the burden of interest costs increased significantly. There were clear economies to be gained by increased equity financing, but this could not easily be achieved on the German capital market.

(c) **Convenience for American shareholders.** Although in 1992 over half of Daimler Benz shares were held by just three shareholders, the remainder were widely held, and of these shareholders over half were resident outside Germany. Clearly Daimler Benz would be a more attractive investment for Americans if its shares were listed on Wall Street.

(d) **Investment in America.** The USA was an important market for Daimler Benz products and the enterprise had decided to increase its physical investment in that country in order to serve this market (an example of foreign direct investment).

However, when Daimler Benz applied for a listing on Wall Street, it found that its financial statements, which were drawn up in accordance with German law, were not acceptable to the Securities and Exchange Commission, the American regulatory authority. In order to be listed, Daimler Benz had to prepare a reconciliation statement, which presented figures for profit and equity according to US GAAP. Not only was this costly but, more seriously, it revealed remarkable differences between the figures for profit and equity under the two sets of accounting rules, as shown in Exhibit 10.1. The different rules applicable in Germany and the USA resulted in different figures reported in respect of a large number of items of which the more important are listed separately in the exhibit. The largest single item concerns provisions and the related taxation. Provisions that Daimler Benz had made in previous years were not recognised under US GAAP. The elimination of these provisions in the US GAAP balance sheet led to a large increase in equity. However in 1993, Daimler Benz had made a transfer from these past provisions to its income statement. Since the original provision was not recognized under US GAAP, similarly the transfer to income in 1993 was not recognized. The elimination of the credit from the income statement led to a large fall in reported net income under US GAAP. Hence for 1993 Daimler Benz reported a net profit of DM 602mn under German accounting rules and a net loss of DM 1839mn under US GAAP. On the other hand, its equity at 31 December 1993 was reported at DM 17 584mn under the German rules and DM 26 281mn under US GAAP. Investors were undoubtedly puzzled by these disclosures and no doubt asked themselves the question as to which set of accounting rules produced the correct figure. They probably concluded that neither figure was to be trusted.

Exhibit 10.1 *Daimler Benz reconciliation statement*

	Net income DM (millions) 1993	Equity DM (millions) 31 December 1993
According to German accounting rules	602	17 584
Adjustments		
Provisions, reserves and valuation differences	(4 262)	5 770
Long-term contracts	78	207
Goodwill	(287)	2 284
Pensions	(624)	(1 821)
Foreign currency translation	(40)	85
Financial instruments	(225)	381
Other valuation differences	292	(698)
Deferred taxes	2 627	2 489
Total adjustments	(2 441)	8 697
According to US GAAP	(1 839)	26 281

Source: Form 20-F submitted to the SEC

10.3 THE NEED FOR A SINGLE SET OF RULES

The problems of Daimler Benz and similar MNEs would have been greatly eased had there been available a single set of financial reporting rules that was accepted by all the regulatory authorities, that is those both of the home country (Germany in the case of Daimler Benz) and of the foreign country (the SEC). Such a single set did not exist in 1993 and does not exist today. In fact to presume that such a set can be developed might seem to be hopelessly optimistic given the need to gain agreement between so many different authorities each with its own private agenda. However, it is a useful exercise to consider what would be the benefits of such a set.

10.3.1 The advantages of uniformity

There are clearly considerable advantages to be gained if the financial statements of all enterprises were to be based on the same rules. Solomons (1983) refers to three arguments in favour of the imposition of uniform rules:

Credibility

Where there exists more than one set of financial reporting rules, it can happen that an enterprise can report quite different results according to the set of rules which it chooses to apply. As illustrated in Exhibit 10.1, this occurred with the Daimler Benz results for 1993 – a profit of DM602mn according to German GAAP and a loss of DM1839mn according to US GAAP. This discrepancy can lead to a loss of confidence by the public in the results reported not just by Daimler Benz but by enterprises in general. The general public only accepts a figure as creditable if there is general agreement among experts as to its magnitude. For example a patient would lose confidence in doctors in general if one told him that his blood pressure was 105 and another that it was 150. The measurement of profit is more complicated than the measurement of blood pressure, but the general public does not appreciate such niceties.

Comparability

The information provided by an enterprise is more valuable if it can easily be compared with that provided by other enterprises. This 'comparison may provide an indication of possible weaknesses or inefficiencies; for example, a certain cost category may be significantly higher than the industry average or inventory turnover may be slower than competitors'. To assure comparability all enterprises should follow the same rules. A by-product of uniform rules (that are also stable over time) is that, for any particular enterprise, the financial statements of the current year are comparable with those of preceding years.

Efficiency of communication

In the absence of an agreed set of rules governing financial reporting in general, it would be very difficult for the user to understand and interpret the financial statements of any particular enterprise. To assist comprehension, the enterprise would have to include with the accounts a lengthy and detailed explanation of the rules that had been followed in their preparation. This procedure imposes costs both on the preparer and on the user, who has to read and understand these explanations, which will be different for every enterprise. These costs may be avoided if a common set of rules (available to and understood by all) were used by all enterprises.

10.3.2 Uniformity versus relevance

It is important to understand that the benefits claimed above for a common set of rules depend entirely on the characteristic of uniformity and on no other characteristic of the rules, such as the value, relevance or quality of the information provided. For example, a rule that required that all fixed assets be depreciated over ten years (regardless of their economic life) would lead to all enterprises reporting comparable information that would be easily understood by users and would avoid the scandal of two identical enterprises reporting different profits. In fact to maximize the benefits, absolute uniformity is necessary; no discretion at all should be given to the preparers of financial statements. This is rather like the rule that all vehicles should drive on the right-hand side of the road. There is no moral or qualitative argument in favour of using the right-hand side rather than the left-hand side, but there are very substantial advantages in all vehicles using the same side. The British drive on the left-hand side, but only in Britain. Outside Britain, it pays them to drive on the right-hand side. This example illustrates perfectly that it is solely the fact of uniformity that counts, not the nature of the rule (that is right or left).

Very considerable benefits would accrue to the MNEs from a single set of rules being accepted in every country and by every stock exchange, irrespective of the relevance of the rules. In particular the MNEs would be relieved of the cost of preparing two sets of accounts and investors would no longer be confused by being presented with competing and conflicting measures of performance.

Certainly a world with a single set of rules would be simpler. But would it be better? To answer that question, it is necessary to consider the quality of the rules. In Chapter 3, the quality of financial reporting was defined in terms of how well it meets the information needs of the users. From the viewpoint of the MNEs, the most important users of their financial statements are the investors. The major reason why they have sought listings on foreign stock exchanges (which action brought to a head the problems connected with the diversity of national accounting systems) was to tap the global capital market. Hence the MNEs consider that high quality information is that which best meets the information needs of investors on the world's stock exchanges. However, given the great variety of users, it seems unlikely that a single set of rules would meet in a satisfactory fashion the needs of all user groups. This would seem to be especially the case with the MNEs, as the users of their accounts are based in such a wide range of countries. Hence any attempt at applying a single set of rules is likely to result in the information needs of particular groups of users being less well served than they were before.

Furthermore it seems improbable that a single set of rules can be developed that would be equally appropriate for all enterprises: for example, that would be equally effective in presenting the financial position and performance both of a multinational oil company (such as ExxonMobil) and of a professional accountancy firm (such as Arthur Andersen). Each enterprise is essentially unique, both in the characteristics of the users for whom it prepares accounts and in the composition of the assets, liabilities, revenues and expenses presented in these accounts. Hence imposing a uniform set of rules on all enterprises inevitably will have the consequence that, for at least some enterprises, the rules will be inappropriate.

This is the conflict between uniformity and relevance. The most that can be expected is a compromise that achieves an acceptable degree of uniformity and meets most of the information needs of the more important users.

10.4 THE POSSIBLE GLOBAL RULE MAKERS

How might a single set of global rules be developed? There are at least three possible ways in which a single set of rules might become adopted for the financial reporting of the MNEs. The global rules may be those of

- A particular country
- A group of countries
- An international organization

Each of these possibilities will now be considered.

10.5 A SINGLE COUNTRY: THE USA

It is not impossible for a particular country to establish itself as the global rule-maker for financial reporting. This would occur if the regulatory authorities of the other countries came to accept the rules set by the other country. They may decide to do this for a number of reasons:

- They may be overwhelmed by the other country's political and economic power
- They may be influenced by lobbying by the MNEs that are based in their country; for example these MNEs may threaten to base themselves elsewhere unless they are permitted to draw up their accounts in conformity with the other country's rules

■ They may be happy to delegate the task of setting rules for the reasons given in Chapter 3 (section 3.7): cost savings, technical complexity, 'passing the buck' and so on

However in general a country's government will not willingly give up the power of setting the rules for the financial reporting of corporations under its jurisdiction, for two reasons:

■ It would consider it to be an impairment of its sovereignty; its national pride would be hurt

■ The government is a prime user of these financial statements and it cannot be sure that the rules set by a body outside its control would serve its purposes

Notwithstanding these considerations, there is one country whose financial reporting rules may well become the global rules of the future. That country is the USA.

The American national accounting system and US GAAP have already been described in Chapter 5. This section covers only US GAAP in so far as it relates to the MNEs. American MNEs are obliged by law to follow US GAAP in drawing up their accounts. However, in the past decade, more and more non-American MNEs have prepared financial statements in conformity with US GAAP. These consist either of a complete set of accounts or of a reconciliation statement included in the notes, similar to that prepared by Daimler Benz (see Exhibit 10.1). Although a reconciliation statement is less voluminous, it costs as much to prepare as a complete set of accounts. Examples of MNEs that prepare accounts according to US GAAP are: Toyota (Japan), DaimlerChrysler (Germany) and BP Amoco (Britain). The principal reason that these enterprises are prepared to incur this expense is to meet the information demands of the global capital market, notably:

(a) The regulatory authorities of the New York Stock Exchange which insist that listed foreign corporations present information on their financial position and performance as measured under the rules of US GAAP in the form either of a full set of accounts or of a reconciliation statement.

(b) Investors in the global corporate bond market, who generally are reluctant to buy the securities of corporations whose accounts do not provide the information that they require.

In both cases, investors (and the regulatory authorities acting on their behalf) have no confidence in accounts drawn up in accordance with the rules of certain countries. There are three different problems:

- The level of disclosure may be inadequate (for example no segmental analysis)

- The use of unacceptable accounting methods (for example excessively prudent valuation methods which make possible the creation of secret reserves)

- The accounting rules and practice of the foreign country may be obscure and investors are not prepared to spend time and money in finding out about them

Hence, the MNEs are driven to publish accounts based on accounting rules in which foreign investors have confidence. The obvious choice is US GAAP, for two reasons:

- Many MNEs already have to prepare US GAAP accounts to meet the listing requirements of the New York Stock Exchange

- It is widely believed among the investing community that accounts based on US GAAP provide the most reliable and relevant information for investment purposes

The number of non-American MNEs that publish accounts based on US GAAP has increased markedly in recent years. They are under no legal obligation to do so but have chosen this course because their management considers it to be in the best interest of the enterprise, in that it facilitates access to the global capital market, offering larger amounts of finance at a lower cost of capital. Essentially the voluntary adoption of US GAAP by non-American MNEs represents a market-driven approach to the problem of devising a global set of rules for financial reporting, as opposed to a solution imposed by a regulator. The MNEs concerned still have to prepare a second set of accounts according to the rules of the country in which they are based. Since they find this costly, many have been lobbying their governments to relieve them of this obligation. This development is considered further in Chapter 12.

Hence there is a real possibility of US GAAP becoming the global standard. However it should be appreciated that US GAAP is the output of a narrowly-based national regulatory system. All the bodies that are involved in the development of US GAAP (Congress, the SEC and the FASB) are composed entirely of American citizens. In setting the rules, they consult with and take into account the needs of American enterprises and investors to the exclusion of non-Americans. As demonstrated in Chapter 5, standard setting in the USA is a highly politicized process from which non-Americans (who have no votes) are largely excluded. In effect, if the rest of the world choses US GAAP as the global standard, it will be accepting the imposition of a set of rules in the formation of which it has no influence.

10.6 A GROUP OF COUNTRIES: THE EUROPEAN UNION

There are a number of organizations in which countries in a particular region seek to promote their common interests through economic cooperation. Examples are the North American Free Trade Area (NAFTA), which consists of the USA, Canada and Mexico; Mercosur (Brazil, Argentina, Chile and Venezuela); and the European Union. Fifteen years ago, one would have added the Communist Bloc (the Soviet Union and its satellites) to this list, but, with the collapse of Communism, there is now no regional organization that covers this part of the world.

It is not impossible that a regional organization might be able to establish itself as the global rule-maker. For this to happen, two conditions are necessary:

- The organization should aim to regulate the financial reporting of its member countries
- The organization should embrace countries which together are of such economic importance in global terms that the rest of the world is prepared to accept its leadership

Of the three regional organizations mentioned above, NAFTA has to be ruled out on the first ground. It has never shown an interest in setting the rules of financial reporting for its members, although no doubt Canada and Mexico would prefer that NAFTA rather than the SEC should set the rules for their enterprises. Mercosur may be ruled out on the second ground, as the countries involved are, in global terms, economic lightweights.

However the European Union (EU) meets both conditions. As demonstrated in Chapter 9, it is a major economic power with a GDP roughly equal to that of the USA and considerably in excess of that of Japan. It includes among its members three countries of the Pentad (Germany, France and Britain). Moreover the EU has sought to regulate financial reporting through the Fourth and Seventh Directives, which set out a number of detailed rules for the accounts of European enterprises. However it is generally agreed that, despite all its efforts, the EU has not succeeded in achieving its stated objective: the harmonization of the accounts of enterprises throughout the EU. For example the financial statements of a British PLC are still significantly different from those of a German AG.

At one time, in the early 1990s, it seemed that the EU had aspirations to become the world's standard setter. It was concerned at the increasing use of US GAAP by multinational enterprises which it perceived as a threat to the authority of its own directives. Hence it sought to establish 'EU GAAP' as an alternative to US GAAP. However in 1995 it announced a fundamental change of policy. It decided to ally itself with the IASC, with the objective that, in the longer run, European MNEs would be permitted to draw up their accounts on the basis of that organization's standards. Essentially the EU renounced all claims to become the world's standard setter.

10.7 INTERNATIONAL ORGANIZATIONS

Logic would suggest that ideally the global rules should be set by a truly international body which represents the whole world and not just one country or a regional grouping. In the field of financial reporting, there are three organizations that have shown an interest in playing the role of global rule-maker: the United Nations, the Organization for Economic Cooperation and Development, and the International Accounting Standards Committee.

10.7.1 The United Nations (UN)

Since its membership covers virtually the whole world, the United Nations (UN) would seem to be the natural choice for the global rule-maker. Moreover, despite all its other concerns, which clearly should have a greater priority, such as preventing wars and the abolition of world poverty, the UN has shown a considerable interest in financial reporting. At one time, in the early 1970s, it seemed possible that the UN would play a leading role as a global rule-maker. It set up a working party to develop rules for the segmental reporting of transnational corporations (the UN's term for multinational enterprises). The impulse was the demand of the developing countries that MNEs disclose more detailed information about their operations in each country in which they operated. The group produced a series of recommendations, which in the words of Walton *et al.* (1998) 'have been politely ignored by the developed countries'.

This incident brings out very clearly why the UN failed to become the world's rule-maker. Given the structure of its membership, the developing countries are in a permanent majority. One of the major concerns of the developing countries is how to control more effectively the activities of the MNEs that operate on their territory. The developing countries hoped that the UN would draw up and impose financial reporting rules that would assist them in this task. However the developed countries considered that, in this matter, their interests were fundamentally opposed to those of the developing countries and therefore gave the UN's actions no support. Instead the developed countries have given far more support to the two other international bodies mentioned above: the OECD and the IASB. Hence, as a rule-maker, the UN has been reduced to a talking-shop which issues non-binding recommendations that have little influence on the actual practice of the MNEs.

The present situation is that the UN has a unit based in Geneva, which specializes in the analysis of the problems of transnational corporations. This unit comes under UNCTAD, the United Nations Conference on Trade and Development, which is a further indication that the UN considers financial reporting largely in terms of the needs of developing countries. The unit is responsible for a number of publications of interest to the student of global financial reporting, notably the World Investment Report (the source of many of the statistics in Chapter 1) and the journal *Transnational Corporations*. It organizes an annual conference, each year on a different theme connected with international accounting; recent themes have been environmental accounting, education for the accountancy profession and the financial reporting of small enterprises. The conference papers which are subsequently published are a useful source of information. Apart from acting as a source of information, the UN's principal value is that it serves as a forum where the developed and developing countries may meet and exchange views. In effect there is no other place where the developing countries can make their concerns heard.

10.7.2 The Organization for Economic Cooperation and Development (OECD)

The Organization for Economic Cooperation and Development (OECD) is an intergovernmental organization that represents the developed countries; its members include the USA, Japan, all the countries of Western Europe, plus a few others such as Canada, Mexico, Australia, New Zealand, Korea and three countries from Eastern Europe (Poland, Hungary and the Czech Republic). It was set up in 1961 to promote economic cooperation among its members and has from time to time displayed an interest in financial reporting, although this has never been its major concern. When in the 1970s the UN proposed developing rules for the segment reporting of transnational corporations, the developed countries working through the OECD preempted the UN by issuing their own set of guidelines, which essentially set out the maximum that they were prepared to concede to the developing countries. These guidelines, which were based on the US standards for segmental reporting, have had some influence over the practice of MNEs. From time to time the OECD promotes research and issues reports on other aspects of financial reporting; subjects that it has tackled recently include environmental accounting and intangible assets. Early in 2000, it decided to revise its guidelines for multinational enterprises. However, in the field of financial reporting, the OECD has never gone further than issuing non-binding recommendations on a number of disconnected subjects. It has never sought to be the global rule-maker for financial reporting.

10.7.3 The International Accounting Standards Board (IASB)

In contrast to the UN and the OECD, the International Accounting Standards Board (IASB) has shown itself to a major contender for the role of global rule-maker.

The IASB is the successor of the International Accounting Standards Committee (IASC), which was set up in 1973 on the initiative of Henry Benson, a British chartered accountant. He persuaded the professional accountancy bodies of the following nine developed countries to join: UK, France, Germany and the Netherlands from Europe; USA, Canada and Mexico from North America; plus Australia and Japan. The IASC's objective, as stated in its constitution, was 'to formulate and publish in the public interest accounting standards to be observed in the presentation of financial statements and to promote their worldwide acceptance and observance'. In effect the IASC sought to replace the great variety of national accounting rules by an international set. This is an extraordinarily ambitious objective and for the first twenty years of its existence the IASC made very little progress towards achieving it. It issued a large number of standards, known as International Accounting Standards (IASs), but these were so vague and permitted so many alternative accounting treatments that they did little to reduce the diversity of financial reporting practice throughout the world. Furthermore the IASC had no means of forcing corporations to follow its standards.

However in the last few years the situation has changed considerably. Two recent developments have increased very significantly the possibility that the IASC's standards would become applied and accepted worldwide. The first development has already been mentioned: the decision of the EU to ally itself with the IASC, with the ultimate aim of permitting European MNEs to use the IASC's standards for their accounts. The second development concerns the acceptability of IAS by the world's stock exchanges. In 1995 the IASC reached an agreement with the International Organization of Securities Commissions (IOSCO), the body that represents the national stock exchange regulatory bodies at the international level, to the effect that if, by 1999, the IASC could develop a set of high quality standards, the IOSCO would recommend that national regulatory bodies would permit foreign multinational corporations to use them.

The impact of both developments has been to enhance to a very significant degree the IASC's status and the potential acceptability of its standards. Recently the IASC underwent a complete reorganization and was reborn as the IASB with the objective of increasing the body's efficiency and effectiveness. However the situation is still developing and it is impossible to judge whether the final result will be the definitive establishment of the IASB as the world's standard setter.

10.8 THE IASB VERSUS THE SEC

At present there is a contest between the IASB's standards and US GAAP for supremacy. Neither set of rules clearly predominates. Some MNEs use IAS; others US GAAP. The present situation is summarized in Exhibit 10.2, which shows the financial reporting rules used by the top 50 MNEs (those listed in Exhibit 1.4). The MNEs are divided into four groups which reflect the groupings established by the research of Doupnik and Salter which was presented in Chapter 2 (section 2.8 and Exhibit 2.9):

USA Group

There are 13 MNEs in this group – 11 from the USA and two from Canada. The US enterprises are obliged by law to use US GAAP. Similarly the two Canadian companies are obliged to use Canadian GAAP; however one of the Canadian companies (Seagram) uses US GAAP, claiming that 'US GAAP applicable to the company conforms, in all material respects, to Canadian GAAP'.

Japan

Of the nine Japanese enterprises, seven use US GAAP for their published consolidated accounts. These are all enterprises that are listed on American stock exchanges which have to prepare accounts according to US

Exhibit 10.2 *The financial reporting rules used by the top 50 MNEs based on the accounts for the year 2000*

	USA Group		UK Group		Japan	Continental Europe			Total
	USA	Others	UK	others		Germany	France	others	
US GAAP	11	1		1	7	1			21
IAS						2		3	5
National GAAP									
Alone		1	1	1	2	2	5	1	13
With reconciliation									
to US GAAP			3	2		2	2	2	11
With reconciliation to IAS									0
Total number of									
enterprises	11	2	4	4	9	7	7	6	50

GAAP to satisfy the SEC. As indicated in Chapter 8 (section 8.6), the Ministry of Finance has given these companies a special dispensation to use US GAAP for the accounts that they have to file under the SEL. The other two Japanese enterprises are not listed in the USA and use Japanese GAAP for their accounts.

UK Group

The four purely British companies in this group are obliged by law to use UK GAAP; in addition three provide a reconciliation to US GAAP. Of the four remaining companies in this group, News Corporation uses Australian GAAP with no reconciliation, and Philips uses Dutch GAAP with a reconciliation to US GAAP. The remaining two MNEs are the Unilever Group and the Royal Dutch/Shell Group. Both consist of an alliance between a British company and a Dutch NV, which creates complications for the preparation of the group accounts. In the case of Unilever, the group accounts are stated to have been prepared in accordance with British law and Dutch law; a reconciliation between these accounts and US GAAP is provided. The situation with the Royal Dutch/Shell Group is rather more complicated. The auditors' report to the group accounts states that they 'present fairly the financial position of the Royal Dutch/Shell Group . . . in accordance with generally accepted accounting principles in the Netherlands and the United States', which seems to imply that the group has achieved the feat of complying simultaneously with both national GAAP and US GAAP. In Exhibit 10.2, the Royal Dutch/Shell Group is classified as using US GAAP.

The Continental European Group

(a) **Germany:** Three of the seven German enterprises make use of the derogation provided in the HGB to draw up their consolidated accounts using internationally accepted rules: one uses US GAAP and two use IAS. The remaining four use German GAAP, with two providing a reconciliation with US GAAP.

(b) **France:** All seven French enterprises use French GAAP, with two providing a reconciliation to US GAAP. This reflects that fact that the French authorities have still to decide how to apply the law that permits French companies to use international rules for their consolidated accounts.

(c) **Other countries:** The three Swiss companies (ABB, Roche and Nestlé) all use IAS for their accounts. The two Italian enterprises use Italian GAAP with a reconciliation to US GAAP. The one Spanish enterprise uses Spanish GAAP with no reconciliation.

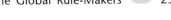

The following tentative conclusions may be drawn from this analysis of the data presented in Exhibit 10.2:

(a) At present, the position of US GAAP is much stronger than that of IAS, with 21 MNEs using US GAAP compared with only five using IAS. There are three principal reasons for US GAAP's leading position:

- It is imposed by law on American corporations
- Certain larger Japanese enterprises are permitted to use it
- Certain European enterprises that are listed in the USA choose it, when they are permitted by their national law

(b) The only enterprises (from the top 50 MNEs) that use IAS are those from Continental Europe, and in fact from only two countries: Germany and Switzerland. No enterprise from France, Italy or Spain uses the IAS or even provides a reconciliation to IAS.

However three possible future developments may cause more MNEs to use IAS and fewer to use US GAAP. These developments (in the order in which they may be expected to occur) are:

- The French authorities put into effect the regulations permitting French listed companies to use IAS (but not US GAAP) for their consolidated accounts
- The Japanese Ministry of Finance withdraws permission to use US GAAP
- The EU begins to accord legal recognition to IAS. Recently the EU proposed that European listed companies should be required to use IAS for their consolidated accounts

The first two points are in fact very likely to occur soon; but it seems rather unlikely that the European Union will be able to keep to its proposed deadline of 2005. However one thing is clear – the contest between US GAAP and IAS is no by means already decided in the Americans' favour.

10.9 FUTURE DEVELOPMENTS

It is unclear how the situation will develop. One can envisage a number of scenarios:

IAS prevail

Under this scenario, the American regulatory authorities agree to accept IAS – initially only for foreign listed corporations – but ultimately also for American listed corporations as the latter, complaining of unfair competition, lobby the politicians. This could occur if the IASB were to develop into a powerful international organization, backed by all countries except the USA, so that its standards gained acceptance worldwide to such an extent that even the American MNEs lobbied their authorities for permission to use them.

US GAAP prevails

The SEC refuses to allow IAS for foreign listed corporations either absolutely or subject to such severe restrictions that make the use of IAS impracticable. Hence all the major MNEs turn to US GAAP – not only those with an American listing but also those with aspirations in that direction. This adds greatly to the prestige of US GAAP to such an extent that most MNEs see no advantage in using IAS.

Neither IAS nor US GAAP prevails

The present stand-off continues for many years, possibly prolonged by the American and European regulatory authorities adopting a stubbornly nationalistic attitude. The SEC could insist that under American law it could not surrender to a foreign body the power to regulate corporations with activities in the USA; whereas the European Union could insist that its law be followed by European corporations.

IAS and US GAAP merge

A gradual merger of IAS and US GAAP occurs as both the IASB and the SEC/FASB issue standards that are increasingly similar. This might occur under two rather different scenarios:

(a) **Market-led:** With increasing globalization, the conditions in capital markets throughout the world become increasingly similar such that the market participants in all countries come to demand the same type of financial information. Thus the financial statements that the SEC consider to be appropriate in the American environment would also meet the needs of investors in London, Frankfurt, Tokyo and Bombay.

(b) **American take-over:** The Americans come to dominate the IASB to such an extent that they can ensure that its standards reflect US GAAP. This could occur if the members of the IASB's standard-setting body, whilst not in the majority American citizens, came to accept the American approach to financial reporting, possibly because they had become convinced of its superiority for intellectual or cultural reasons.

Of the above scenarios, the IAS prevailing seems very unlikely. The SEC shows no signs of being ready to surrender any real powers to the IASB. In 2000, the SEC made a public statement on its views on the acceptability of IAS (SEC, 2000). By and large, they were negative as the SEC was very sceptical about how compliance with the IASB's standards could be assured. However the most significant point was that the SEC made it clear that it had no intention of giving blanket approval to the IASB's standards but would assess each IAS separately as it was issued. Hence the SEC saw itself as having a continuing function as the official endorser of IAS, no doubt rejecting some on the grounds that they assured insufficient protection for American investors and placing severe restrictions on the use of others.

Of the remaining three scenarios, the undisguised triumph of US GAAP also seems rather improbable as the EU can thwart it by insisting on the legal authority of its directives. Thus the scenario where neither prevails is a distinct possibility, but one that is clearly not in the interests of the MNEs or those whose prosperity depends on them, that is a large part of the world's population. In the authors' opinion, the merging-of-both scenario seems the most likely, with an American take-over rather more likely than a market-led merge. Certainly the recent reorganization of the IASB (described in detail in Chapter 11) has greatly increased the USA's influence in this body.

SUMMARY

The diversity of financial reporting practice creates problems for the MNEs in two areas: internal management and external financing. These problems were illustrated by the case of Daimler Benz which was obliged to prepare two sets of financial statements (showing quite different figures for profit and equity) when it listed its shares on the New York stock exchange in 1994. The advantages of a single uniform set of financial reporting rules for all MNEs were analysed under the headings of credibility, comparability and efficiency of communication, but the possibility of a conflict between uniformity and relevance was considered. The possible global rule-makers were analysed under the headings of a single country (the USA), a group of countries (the EU) and an international organization (the UN, the OECD and the IASB). It was concluded that the contest for the position of the global standard setter lay between the USA and the IASB.

Review questions

1. What problems are created for the MNEs by the diversity of financial reporting practice around the world?

2. Why, for 1993, did the German enterprise, Daimler Benz, report its profits and equity according to US GAAP as well as according to the German rules? What did this reveal?

3. What are the advantages of a single uniform set of financial reporting rules for all MNEs? Why is there a possible conflict between uniformity and relevance?

4. Why are many MNEs publishing financial statements based on US GAAP?

5. Why did the United Nations not become the global rule-maker in financial reporting?

6. What are the two recent developments that have greatly enhanced the possibility of the IASB's standards becoming applied and accepted worldwide?

7. What are the various possible outcomes of the current contest between US GAAP and the IASB's standards?

Note

1. In 1998, Daimler Benz merged with the Chrysler Corporation to form DaimlerChrysler.

References

Biddle, GC and Saudagaran, SM 'Foreign stock listings: benefits, costs, and the accounting policy dilemma', *Accounting Horizons*, **5**(3) (1991), pp. 69–80.

Radebaugh, LH, Gebhardt, G *et al.* 'Foreign stock exchange listings: a case study of Daimler Benz', *Journal of International Financial Management and Accounting*, **6**(2) (1995).

SEC *Concept Release on International Accounting Standards*, SEC, Washington (2000).

Solomons, D 'The Political Implications of Accounting and Accounting Standard Setting', *Accounting and Business Research*, **13**(2) (1983), pp. 107–18.

Walton, P, Haller, A and Raffournier, B *International Accounting*, International Thompson Business Press, London (1998).

Further reading

For the problems of the MNEs see Biddle and Saudagaran (1991). For the conflict between uniformity and relevance, see Solomons (1983). The IASC and IASB will be considered in greater detail in the following chapters, so it is not necessary to read further on this subject at this stage.

chapter eleven

The IASB: its Origins and Structure

Chapter objectives

- To present the origins and objectives of the International Accounting Standards Board (IASB), which entails an examination of its predecessor, IASC
- To outline the structure of the IASC and explain why its reform was considered necessary to improve its efficiency and effectiveness as a standard-setting body
- To outline the IASB's organizational structure, comparing it to that of the IASC

The International Accounting Standards Committee (IASB) is the only body that seeks to be the global standard setter which can claim to represent the whole world and not simply a country or a group of countries. This chapter presents a brief introduction to the IASB concentrating on its origins, objectives and structure. The IASB's standards are covered in the subsequent chapters. The IASB was set up in April 2001, but it can trace its origins back a further quarter of a century, for the IASB is essentially the former IASC with a completely reformed structure and revised objectives. Hence the analysis of the IASB's structure and objectives starts by examining those of its predecessor, the IASC.

11.1 THE IASC's ORIGINS AND OBJECTIVES

The IASC was formed in 1973 at the initiative of Henry Benson, a British chartered accountant, who was at that time head of Coopers Brothers, the accountancy firm which through subsequent mergers became Price-waterhouseCoopers. The original members of the IASC were representatives of the accountancy profession of the following nine industrialized countries: Australia, Canada, France, Germany, Japan, Mexico, Netherlands, UK and USA.

The objectives of the IASC as stated in its constitution were:

■ To formulate and publish in the public interest accounting standards to be observed in the presentation of financial statements and to promote their worldwide acceptance and observance

■ To work generally for the improvement and harmonization of regulations, accounting standards and procedures relating to the presentation of financial statements

In effect the IASC's formation represented the response of the professional accountancy bodies of the major western industrialized countries to the developing globalization of the world economy which has already been evoked in Chapter 1. The IASC gave most weight to the first objective; between 1974 and 2000 it issued some forty standards, known as International Accounting Standards.

However right from its formation, the IASC was characterized by two important features which had a major influence on its operations and effectiveness:

(a) The IASC was a private body set up by the professional accountancy bodies of a number of countries. It was not a government body; it had no official status.

(b) Hence the International Accounting Standards (IASs) issued by the IASC had no official status, except in so far as they were endorsed by other bodies. The IASC had no means of enforcing compliance with its standards; it had no authority to impose its standards on enterprises or even on accountants and auditors, who were all primarily obliged to follow national laws and standards. The IASC was quite frank about its limitations, admitting 'neither the IASC nor the accountancy profession has the power ... to require compliance with international accounting standards'.[1]

It would not be an exaggeration to describe the history of the IASC over the quarter century of its existence as a continued struggle to mitigate and overcome the disadvantages that stem from these two characteristics.

11.2 THE IASC's STRUCTURE

In this section the IASC's previous organization is described and analysed. Although this is now past history, as the IASC has been replaced by the IASB, it is still relevant for three reasons:

Exhibit 11.1 *The IASC's structure*

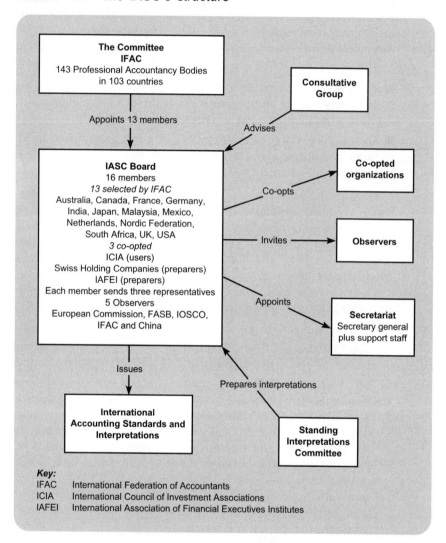

■ It is probable that the IASB under its new constitution will not be very different from the IASC

■ All the current IASs were issued by the IASC, the IASB having adopted them as its own standards shortly after taking office

■ A study of the IASC provides an insight into the reasons why a thorough reform of the organization was considered necessary and helps in assessing whether the IASB will prove more effective

The IASC's organization is set out in diagrammatic form in Exhibit 11.1 which shows the following bodies:

■ The Committee
■ The Board
■ The Standing Interpretations Committee
■ The Secretariat
■ The Consultative Group

11.2.1 The Committee

A curious feature of the IASC is that, although its title included the word 'Committee', in fact the Committee rarely met and had virtually no powers. Formally the members of 'International Accounting Standards Committee' were the professional accountancy associations that were members of the International Federation of Accountants (IFAC) – in December 2000, 143 associations from 104 countries. They included all the major industrialized countries and very many developing countries. In fact, it is easier to specify the countries that are not members of IFAC: these are principally communist and former communist countries, such as Russia, North Korea and Vietnam. The full committee of the IASC met very infrequently (once every $2^{1}/_{2}$ years) and its powers were limited to approving changes to the IASC's constitution. All the IASC's executive powers were delegated to the IASC's Board. Hence the emphasis in this section is on the role of the Board.

11.2.2 The Board's powers

The Board's principal function was to issue International Accounting Standards (IASs). It did this on its own initiative; it did not have to seek the approval of the full committee, which, as already indicated, was largely a symbolic body. Apart from IASs (and the other documents related to the IASs, such as exposure drafts and interpretations), the only other document of real significance issued by the Board was the Framework (which is the subject of Chapter 13).

11.2.3 The Board's composition

Given the central role that the Board played in the issue of standards, it is important to analyse the Board's membership. Exhibit 11.2 presents a diagram showing the composition of the IASC's Board from its creation in 1973 up to its demise in 2001. The Board was composed of representatives from countries, co-opted organizations and observers.

Exhibit 11.2 *The membership of the IASC's Board, 1973 to 2001*

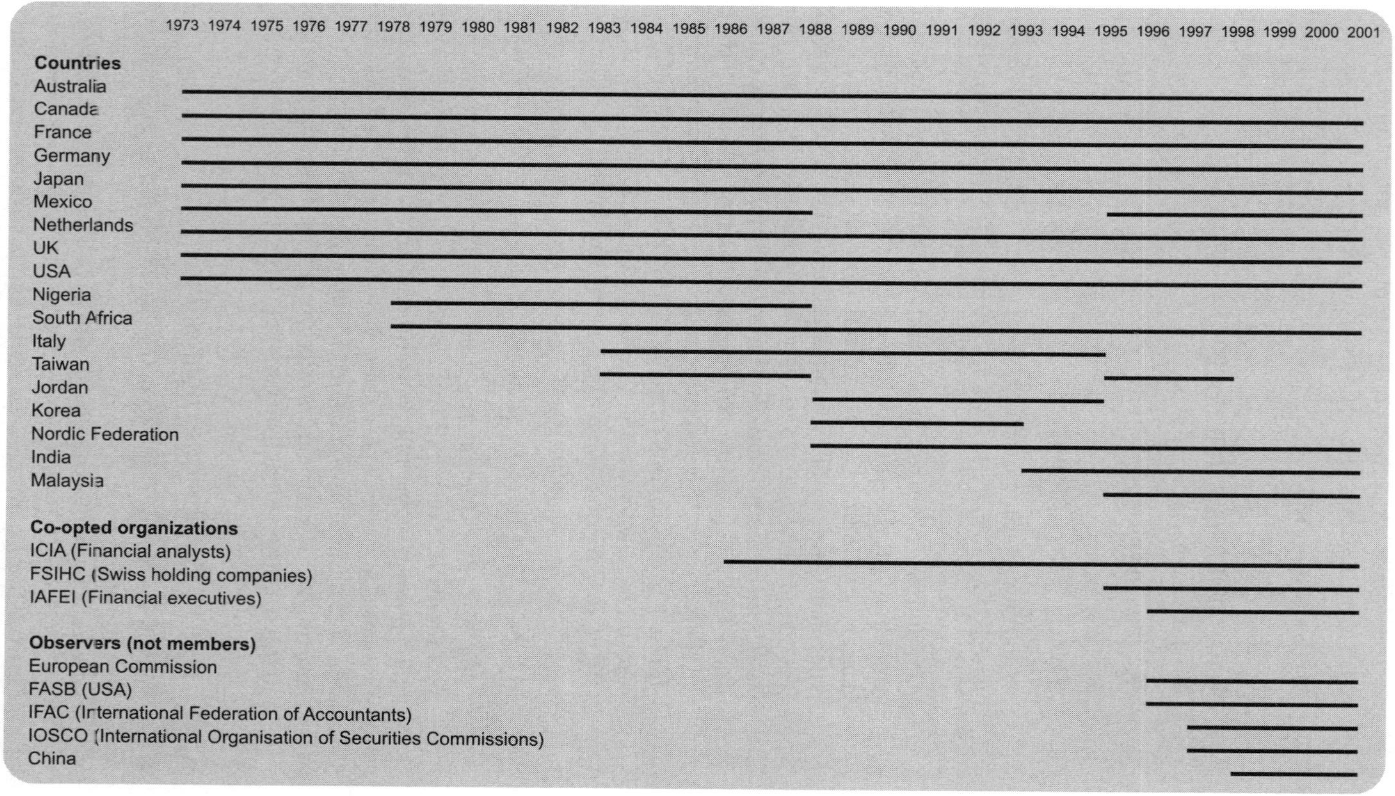

Board members: countries

The countries were nominated by the IFAC Council, but the persons that represented these countries were chosen by the national professional accountancy body or bodies. In December 2000 the country members were: Australia, Canada, France, Germany, India, Japan, Malaysia, Mexico, Netherlands, the Nordic countries (Denmark, Finland, Iceland, Norway and Sweden), South Africa, UK and USA. It was possible for a group of countries to share a country seat, as was the case with the Nordic Federation of Public Accountants. It will be noticed that the nine countries that founded the IASC in 1973 were still on the Board in 2001. In fact the membership of the founding countries was continuous since 1973: they were rather like the permanent members of the UN's Security Council. There was one exception – Mexico was not a member for seven and a half years from 1988 to 1995. It is significant that Mexico was the least industrialized of the nine.

A striking feature of the make-up of the country membership was the dominance of North America (three members: Canada, USA and Mexico) and Europe (five members all from Western Europe: France, Germany, Netherlands, the Nordic Federation and the UK). Asia had three members (India, Japan and Malaysia), but Africa only one (South Africa). There were no members from South America. The developing countries were clearly badly under-represented; of the four countries that might be considered to be developing countries (India, Malaysia, Mexico and South Africa), only India was unambiguously in this category. Former communist countries (Russia and from East Europe) were completely unrepresented, as was China.

In Chapter 2 (section 2.8) the countries of the world were classified according to the characteristics of their national accounting systems, between the 'Anglo-Saxons' and the 'Rest'. This classification scheme may be applied to the countries that were represented on the IASC Board.

(a) **'Anglo-Saxons'**: 9 countries – the UK and countries in the UK subgroup (Australia, Canada, South Africa, India and Malaysia), USA (plus Mexico which is in the USA subgroup), and the Netherlands.

(b) **'Rest'**: 4 countries – France, Germany, the Nordic Federation and Japan.

It is clear that the IASC Board was dominated by countries that follow the Anglo-Saxon approach. This dominance can be traced back to the IASC's origins, for the IASC developed out of the Accountants International Study Group which was set up at the initiative of Henry Benson in 1967 and which consisted of representatives of the professional accountancy bodies of the three principal Anglo-Saxon countries: Britain, USA and Canada.

Board members: co-opted organizations

Co-opted bodies were selected by the IASC Board (not the IFAC). They were full members and had the same voting rights as the country members. The co-opting of outside bodies was clearly an attempt to widen the IASC's base beyond the accountancy profession and thus ensure that its standards achieve greater acceptability. The three co-opted members represented the users (the financial analysts) and the preparers (the financial executives and the Swiss holding companies). The bodies that were conspicuously missing from the IASC's membership were official standard-setting bodies such as France's CNC and the USA's FASB. The reason was that the IASC was a private body. National standard setters did not consider that it was appropriate to be members; these bodies were subject to the authority of their national governments and they could not accept responsibility for the enforcement of the IASC's standards in their own country. However these considerations did not prevent them from attending IASC Board meetings as non-voting observers.

Observers

A number of organizations were entitled to send observers to IASC Board meetings; in 2000 they included the European Commission, the International Organization of Securities Commissions (IOSCO), the USA's FASB and the Chinese Institute of Certified Public Accountants. These observers could speak but had no vote. To a certain extent, the presence of these observers tended to correct certain imbalances in the composition of the IASC Board, for example the exclusion of China and of official standard-setting bodies.

The chairman

The Board members selected one of their number as chairman. Up to June 2000 the chairman had always been a professional accountant from an industrialized country. However the last chairman of the IASC, who took office in June 2000, was Tom Jones of Citicorp, New York, a representative of the International Association of Financial Executives Institutes, one of the co-opted bodies, which represented the preparers.

The IASC Board normally met only about five times a year, each time for about four days. Hence the persons who represented the Board members were from the IASC's viewpoint very much part-timers. They all had important functions outside the IASC: as partners in accountancy firms, company accountants, university professors and so on. They received no remuneration from the IASC for their work.

11.2.4 Other elements of the IASC's organization

Surrounding the IASC Board were a number of other bodies, notably:

The Standing Interpretations Committee (SIC)

The SIC was a very recent addition to the IASC's structure being formed only in 1997. Its function was set out in its terms of reference as: 'to review on a timely basis accounting issues that are likely to receive divergent or unacceptable treatment in the absence of authoritative guidance'. The basic problem was that, where the IASs were ambiguous, imprecise or lacking detail, enterprises were interpreting them in a way that the IASC considered to be incorrect and contrary to the standard's objectives. This arose in two rather different situations:

(a) Where different enterprises applied different interpretations to the provisions of an IAS. This often occurred when the IAS failed to specify clear rules on how to account for a particular transaction or event, possibly because at the time that the IAS was issued these were not significant.

(b) Where an enterprise deliberately applied a strained or perverse interpretation to an IAS's provision as a justification for not reporting in accordance with the IAS's spirit.

The solution was for the IASC to issue interpretations of the IASs. These interpretations were prepared by the SIC. However, in order to give them the same authority as an IAS, they were issued by the Board. Up to 2000, the IASC had issued some twenty Interpretations covering a wide range of issues from consistent application of inventory cost formulas to the reporting of treasury shares.

The Secretariat

The IASC had a small secretariat based in London. It was headed by the Secretary-General, a full-time paid official. The last Secretary-General was Sir Bryan Carsberg, a British chartered accountant (like the IASC's founding father Henry Benson) and a former Professor of Accounting at the London School of Economics. The Secretary-General was supported by a small staff of about 20 professionals who were almost exclusively persons seconded from other organizations (principally accountancy firms) on temporary contracts.

The Consultative Group

The IASC Consultative Group consisted of representatives of a very wide range of organizations, including international associations such as the International Bar Association and the International Chamber of Commerce, and official bodies such as the World Bank, the UN and the OECD. The IASC's motive for establishing this group was 'to ensure that it obtained input to its work from a wide range of users and preparers at the early formative stages of the development of International Accounting Standards' (Cairns, 1997, p. 327).

11.3 EVALUATION OF THE IASC's STRUCTURE

Was the IASC so organized that it could achieve its objective of issuing International Accounting Standards of high quality? Initially the IASC considered that the creation of standards was purely a technical matter which concerned only the experts in the field, that is the accountancy profession. Hence, at first, the IASC Board was made up exclusively of representatives of the national accountancy associations. However, gradually over time, the IASC came to appreciate the need to broaden its organization so as to increase the acceptability of its standards. The process may be traced graphically in Exhibit 11.2. In later years, the IASC Board was expanded to include:

■ Certain preparers and users: the co-opted organizations representing the financial analysts, the financial executives and the Swiss Holding Companies

■ Observers from the users (IOSCO) and other standard setters (the European Commission and the FASB)

However even at the end the IASC Board was still dominated by the accountancy profession – the country members (nominated by the national professional accountancy associations) were in a clear majority with 13 votes against 3 votes for the co-opted organizations, and the observers had no votes. However, it was widely believed that the influence of the observers was much greater than might be expected. The board members probably gave great weight to the views of IOSCO, the European Commission and the FASB, since if any of these bodies were to come out strongly against an IAS, this would have had a markedly negative effect on its acceptability. These remarks would seem to imply that the way in which the IASC operated was not reflected in its formal organization. This is largely a matter of conjecture as it is difficult to establish exactly how the IASC operated. Certainly in the opinion of many people the IASC was still dominated by accountants.

A further criticism of the IASC was that it was dominated by the Western industrialized countries. Two groups of countries were very poorly represented in its organization:

- the developing countries, which had, at the most, three votes on the Board
- the countries in transition from a centrally-planned economy, which were entirely unrepresented on the Board, although China had observer status

It is remarkable that the countries that were among the IASC's most loyal supporters, as measured by the enterprises that applied IAS,[2] were the most poorly represented on the Board. Cynics might comment that, since these countries already applied IAS without Board representation, there was no necessity to grant them this status.

The points made above suggest that the IASC needed to reform its organization in order to improve its effectiveness as the world's standard setter. As emphasized at the beginning of this chapter, the IASC was a private organization set up by the national professional accountancy associations. This characteristic created problems for the IASC in at least three areas:

Co-operation with national standard setters

It was abundantly clear that for the IASC's standards to gain widespread acceptance, they needed to be endorsed by the standard-setting bodies and regulatory authorities of the more important countries. This implied that these bodies should be closely involved in the development of the IASs. However governmental bodies had great difficulties in working with the IASC, because of its lack of official status. In recent years a pragmatic solution was found whereby certain of these bodies sat on the IASC Board as observers (for example, the European Commission, the FASB and the SEC – through IOSCO) or were represented in national delegations (Sir David Tweedie, the chairman of the ASB, was a member of the UK delegation). However this was obviously a stopgap measure and it was clearly desirable that the participation of national standard-setting and regulatory authorities in the IASC's activities be placed on a more permanent and formal basis.

Efficiency of decision making

Over time the IASC, in an attempt to improve the acceptability of its standards, gradually increased the size of the Board, as is graphically demonstrated in Exhibit 11.2. It added members from the developing countries; it co-opted organizations that represented the preparers and the users; it invited influential bodies to attend Board meetings as observers. However the increase in the size of the Board created its own problems. In the end, in 2000, the Board had 16 members, each of whom was entitled to be represented by three persons at Board meetings. When observers and IASC staff are added, the total number of persons attending Board meetings in 2000 regularly exceeded 70. This was far too many for efficient decision-making by a body which under its constitution should consider and approve every IAS, exposure draft and interpretation issued in the name of the IASC. In effect there was a conflict between the need to have a wide representation of interests on the Board and efficient decision-making.

Secretariat

The IASC's secretariat had never been organized on a permanent basis. The only permanent official was the Secretary-General; all the rest were seconded on short-term assignments from other bodies, principally audit firms. This was thoroughly unsatisfactory as it reinforced the impression that the IASC was dominated by the auditors.

11.4 PROPOSALS FOR CHANGE

In 1997, the IASC set up a working party to consider its future structure in the light of the problems outlined in the previous section. In 1998, the working party issued a report 'Shaping IASC for the future' (IASC, 1998) which was a comprehensive analysis of the problems confronting the organization and suggested ways in which it might be reformed. This report is a most useful source of information on the IASC's structure and its perceived weaknesses. One year later, in November 1999, the working party issued its definitive recommendations for the reform of the IASC (IASC, 1999). Early in 2000 the Board and the full committee adopted a revised constitution, based on the working party's recommendations, which came into effect in April 2001, when the IASB replaced the IASC.

11.5 THE IASB's CONSTITUTION

11.5.1 Title

The new body decided to call itself the International Accounting Standards Board (IASB). However the title 'IASC' has survived in certain parts of the new body[3] and in fact the first paragraph of the new body's constitution states: 'The name of the organisation shall be the International Accounting Standards Committee'. This is all very confusing. However the new body is simply carrying on the tradition of the old body in adopting an anomalous title. Whereas the IASC's name included the word 'committee' when in fact the committee had virtually no powers (see section 11.2.1), the IASB has adopted a name that is not sanctioned by its constitution. However, since the title 'International Accounting Standards Board' (IASB) is used in all the new body's publications, including its website (www.iasb.org.uk), this title is used in this book to denote the new body, the title IASC being reserved for the former body that the IASB replaced in April 2001.

11.5.2 The IASB's objectives

The objectives of the IASB are stated in its constitution to be:

(a) to develop, in the public interest, a single set of high quality, understandable and enforceable global accounting standards that require high quality, transparent and comparable information in financial statements and other financial reporting to help participants in the world's capital markets and other users make economic decisions.

(b) to promote the use and rigorous application of these standards.

(c) to bring about convergence of national accounting standards and International Accounting Standards to high quality solutions (sic).

The differences between the former objectives (see section 11.1) and these new objectives may be summarized as follows:

■ There is a greater emphasis on enforceability. Thus in paragraph (a) it is stated that in addition to being 'of high quality' and 'understandable', the IASB's standards should be 'enforceable'. Furthermore, in paragraph (b), the IASB sets itself the objective of promoting the 'rigorous application' of its standards. Undoubtedly these points were included in response to the criticism of the SEC in its comments of the proposed reforms (SEC, 2000) that, under the IASC, compliance with its standards had been unsatisfactory

■ There is specific reference (in paragraph (a)) to the world's capital markets and to users making economic decisions. It is made clear (as was not the case with the IASC) that the IASB adopts the Anglo-Saxon approach to financial reporting (information for decision-making) and not the Germanic approach (protection of creditors and basis for assessment of taxes)

■ There is a specific reference to national standards

■ There are three references to 'high quality'. To a certain extent this is 'puff' as one would hardly expect that the IASB would set as its objective the development of 'low quality' standards. (The question of what is meant by a 'high-quality' standard is discussed in Chapter 12.)

11.5.3 The IASB's structure

The IASB's structure under its new constitution is set out in Exhibit 11.3. It consists of the following bodies:

The trustees

The trustees perform the same function as the USA's Financial Accounting Foundation or Britain's Financial Reporting Council: that is to secure the independence of the standard-setting body, by isolating it from outside pressures. The trustees appoint the members of the standard-setting body and raise the funds necessary for its operations. They also have an overall responsibility for ensuring that the whole organization operates efficiently. However they are excluded from all technical matters relating to accounting standards.

In May 2000 the first board of 19 trustees was appointed. The chairman was Paul Volcker, an American citizen and former chairman of the US Federal Reserve Board. The great majority of the trustees came from North America (six from the USA and one from Canada) and Western Europe (seven); there were two trustees from Japan and one from Australia. Only two trustees were from developing countries (Brazil and Hong Kong).

Exhibit 11.3 *The IASB's structure*

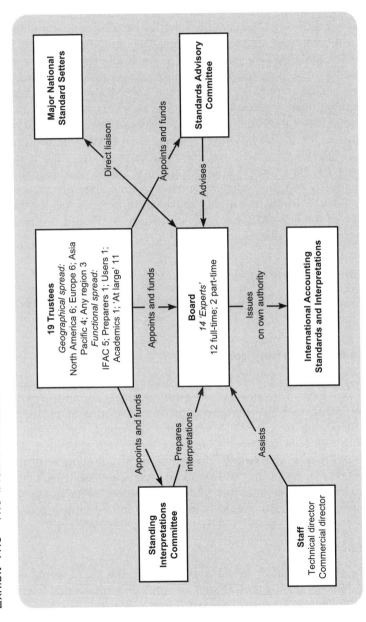

The Board

The Board is the body that issues international accounting standards and interpretations. It does this on its own authority; the trustees have no right to interfere. The Board consists of 14 persons appointed by the trustees, 12 full-time and two part-time. They are selected for their technical knowledge, skills and experience in financial reporting and international business. The Board members are considered to be independent 'experts'; they do not represent any particular constituency, whether geographical or functional. Seven of the full-time members are designated as having formal liaison responsibility with respect to one or more national standard setters. One of the full-time members is designated by the trustees as the chairman of the Board and chief executive of the IASB, that is he combines the functions that under the IASC were performed by the Board Chairman and the Secretary-General. In June 2000 the trustees appointed Sir David Tweedie, the former chairman of Britain's ASB, as the first chairman of the new IASB, followed, in January 2001, with the appointment of the remaining thirteen members.

Standing interpretations committee

This body performs the same functions as its namesake under the former structure. The only difference is that its members are appointed by the trustees.

Standards advisory committee

This body's function is to advise the Board on technical matters relating to standards. It consists of about 30 members appointed by the trustees. The members represent a wide range of constituencies, including those represented on the IASC's Consultative Group, for example the World Bank and IOSCO. However a major element is those national standard setters that do not enjoy a direct liaison with a member of the Board. In fact one suspects that the Standards Advisory Council was created especially to accommodate this group which would otherwise have considered itself to have been excluded from the standard-setting process.

Staff

The working party's report envisaged that the Board would be supported by high-quality technical staff of some 15 professionals, who would be employed on a permanent basis by the IASB.

11.6 THE COMPOSITION OF THE NEW BOARD

Exhibit 11.4 sets out the names of the members of the new Board, together with a limited amount of information about each of them.

The first piece of information is their previous position, before joining the IASB. Five were standard setters, being full-time members of their national standard-setting body. Four were executives in major multinational enterprises, with responsibility for the accounting function. Three were partners in audit firms and two were professors. All will have to resign from their previous jobs, except for Mary Barth and Robert Hertz, who are appointed as part-time members of the Board and, as such, are permitted to continue their outside activities. The authors have made an analysis of the background of the members of the new Board, taking into account not only their position immediately before joining the Board but also positions occupied in the previous twenty years, with the aim of classifying them as standard setter, auditor, preparer, user or academic. Only the last twenty years have been taken into account and more weight has been given to the more recent years, on the grounds that the more remote career experience is less relevant. Certain of the new members present no problems in classification; thus Harry Schmid, who spent his whole career as an accountant with Nestlé, the Swiss multinational, is classified wholly as a preparer. His work as a member of the Swiss standard-setting body is disregarded as it was part-time. However, other members have had much more varied careers. For example, during the past twenty years, Robert Garnett has been a partner with Arthur Andersen (auditor), investment manager with a venture capital group (user) and Executive Vice-President of Anglo-American PLC (preparer). Taking account of the length of time that he spent in each capacity and giving more weight to the more recent past, the authors assess Robert Garnett as being 15 per cent auditor, 50 per cent preparer and 35 per cent user. The full results for all 14 members are presented in Exhibit 11.5. The overall position is shown in the last line of this table. The weightings of the various groups are: standard-setters 25 per cent; auditors 31 per cent, preparers 26 per cent; users 5 per cent and academics 13 per cent.

The second piece of information concerns nationality. Five members are British citizens. This is a remarkably high number, given that, in economic terms (size of GDP), Britain ranks behind the USA, Japan, Germany and France. However the high figure for British citizens is rather misleading, as Robert Garnett is also a citizen of South Africa, where he spends half his time, and both Anthony Cope and Tom Jones have been resident in the USA for at least the last twenty years. The more reliable figure is the number of members from the Anglo-Saxon countries: UK, USA, Canada, Australia and (in its approach to financial reporting) South Africa.

Exhibit 11.4 The members of the IASB

	Previous position	Nationality	Qualified accountant	← – – Connection with – – → National Standard setter	IASC
Sir David Tweedie	Chair ASB (UK)	UK	Yes	Chairman of ASB	Board member
Tom Jones	CFO of Citicorp	UK	Yes	on FASB's EITF	Board member
Mary Barth[a]	Professor	USA	Yes	on FASB's Advisory Council	
Hans-Georg Bruns	Chief accountant, Daimler-Benz	German	No	on DSR's working party	
Anthony Cope	Board member FASB	UK	No	Member of FASB	Observer
Robert Garnett	Vice-President, Anglo-American PLC	UK[b]	Yes	on South Africa's APB	
Gilbert Gélard	Partner KPMG, France	French	Yes	Member of CNC	Board member
Robert Herz[a]	Partner PwC	USA	Yes	on FASB's EITF	
James Leisenring	Board member FASB	USA	Yes	Member of FASB	
Warren McGregor	Director, AARF	Australian	Yes	on staff of AARF	Board member
Tricia O'Malley	Chair ASB (Canada)	Canadian	Yes	Chair of CICA's ASB	
Harry Schmid	Chief accountant, Nestlé	Swiss	No	Member of Swiss FER	Board member
Geoff Whittington	Professor	UK	Yes	Member of ASB	
Tatsumi Yamada	Partner PwC	Japanese	Yes	Member of BADC	Board member

Notes

[a] Part-time member

[b] Robert Garnett is also a South African citizen

The third piece of information concerns the qualifications of the new members. No less than 11 are qualified accountants, being members of their national professional body. Of the three who are not qualified accountants, two, Hans-Georg Bruns and Harry Schmid, are company accountants from countries where the professional accountancy bodies represent only auditors. In effect, the only non-accountant on the new board is Anthony Cope, who is a chartered financial analyst.

Another aspect of the technical expertise of the new members is their experience of standard setting. It is quite remarkable that all 14 members are closely connected with their national standard-setting bodies. Eight were full members of their national standard-setting body: two each from the UK's ASB and the USA's FASB, with one each from the standard-setting bodies of France, Germany, Switzerland and Japan. The others were either staff members (Warren McGregor) or have served on committees or task forces. The four members from the ASB and FASB will probably form a cohesive and therefore effective block.

Half of the new Board sat on the board of the IASC, either as full members or as an observer. In fact Tom Jones was the last chairman of the IASC. This proportion strikes a good balance between assuring continuity and bringing in new blood.

Exhibit 11.5 *The background of the new members*

	Standard-setter	Auditor	Preparer	User	Academic
Sir David Tweedie	70%	30%			
Tom Jones	10%		90%		
Mary Barth		20%			80%
Hans-Georg Bruns			100%		
Anthony Cope	60%			40%	
Robert Garnett		15%	50%	35%	
Gilbert Gélard		80%	20%		
Robert Herz		100%			
James Leisenring	100%				
Warren McGregor	100%				
Tricia O'Malley	10%	90%			
Harry Schmid			100%		
Geoff Whittington					100%
Tatsumi Yamada		100%			
Overall	25%	31%	26%	5%	13%

11.7 COMMENTS ON THE IASB's STRUCTURE

Although it is too early to pass a judgement on the effectiveness of the IASBs structure, it is possible to make some general remarks.

Independence from the accountancy profession

The IASC was much criticized as being dominated by the accountancy profession. The trustees were introduced into the new structure specifically to demonstrate that the Board (the standard-setting body) was independent of the accountancy profession. However this raises the question as to how the trustees are appointed. The IASC took great care to ensure that the first trustees of the IASB were appointed in such a way that no one could doubt their independence. It entrusted the task of selecting the first trustees to a high-powered Nominations Committee of seven persons of whom only one was a professional accountant. Of the rest, four were heads of national regulatory authorities (of the USA, Britain, France and Hong Kong), one was the deputy head of the German standards board and one was the head of the World Bank. Certainly this committee was not dominated by accountants; however equally clearly it was dominated by the developed countries and by persons connected with the capital market.

In selecting trustees the nominating committee followed certain guidelines as to the geographical spread and the functional spread. Thus five of the 19 trustees were to be appointed in consultation with IFAC (the professional accountants). However these trustees would be in a clear minority in the total of 19. In fact the largest element are the 11 'at large' trustees who are selected to represent the public interest. However, as shown in Exhibit 11.4, qualified accountants are in a clear majority on the new Board, providing no less than 11 of the 14 members. At the level of the body that actually sets the standards, the accountants have succeeded in maintaining their dominance.

Dominance of the developed countries and of the Anglo-Saxons

A further criticism of the IASC was its domination by the developed countries. It is clear that this will be the case with the IASB to an even greater extent. This is even more true with respect to the dominance of the Anglo-Saxons which was such a marked feature of the IASC. The two most influential positions in the new structure are occupied by Anglo-Saxons: the chairman of the trustees is the American Paul Volcker and the chairman of the new Board is the Scot, Sir David Tweedie.

With ten of the fourteen members, the Anglo-Saxons will clearly dominate the new Board. In fact given that, under the IASB's constitution, the votes of only eight of the fourteen members are required for the approval of a standard, the Anglo-Saxon members are in a position to secure the passage of any measure on which they are agreed, ignoring the objections of the other members. The *Financial Times*, in its editorial of 26 January 2001, commented that the composition of the new board would inevitably provoke controversy. There are two anomalies:

(a) The relative neglect of Japan and the countries of Continental Europe. Although their combined GDP well exceeds that the Anglo-Saxon countries, they have only four members. The author particularly regrets that there are no members from the Netherlands or from the Scandinavian countries. The trustees (who selected the new members) seem to have taken no heed of the high standing of the Dutch accountancy profession or of the long experience of Scandinavian multinational companies in applying the IASs.

(b) The complete neglect of the less developed countries. The whole of Latin America, Asia (apart from Japan) and Africa (apart from South Africa) are completely unrepresented. The ACCA, the British professional body with the greatest interest in the developing countries, has criticised the new board as having insufficient experience of the developing world, its technical director commenting: 'most of the appointments reinforce the perspective of the larger companies from developed economies . . . the new membership does not go far enough in redressing the perception of exclusion, particularly for developing and transitional economies.'[4] The authors were not surprised at the exclusion of the developing countries. For the last six years (since its agreement with IOSCO in 1995), the IASC spent virtually all its energies in developing standards appropriate for the global capital market. Previously the IASC had considered that one of its prime functions was to develop standards that were appropriate for all countries and ensured that at least three developing countries were represented on the Board. The change in approach was signalled when the IASB adopted a constitution that included the objective 'to help participants in the world's capital markets' and it has been confirmed with not a single person from a developing country on the new Board.

Cooperation with national standard setters

The new structure makes explicit provision for the national standard setters. Seven members of the Board have special responsibility for liaison with one or more national standard setters. In most cases they are former members of the national body, but not current members as they are full-time members of the IASB. These Board members are expected to attend meetings of the national body and there seems to be little doubt that they will act as the IASB's advocate within the national body and the national body's advocate within the IASB. There seems to be no concern on anyone's part that this close relationship would compromise the IASB's independence. Since there are only seven such liaison members, only the standard-setting bodies of certain privileged countries will benefit from this special relationship, notably USA, UK, France, Germany, Japan, Canada and Australia. The smaller countries are excluded. With the IASB, it would seem, to adapt the words of George Orwell, that 'all national standard setters are equal but some are more equal than others'.

The neglect of users

As shown as Exhibit 11.5, the users of financial statements are very poorly represented on the IASB. Only two members have any significant background as users; they are Anthony Cope, who before joining the FASB in 1993 worked for thirty years as a security analyst, and Robert Garnett, who is a member of the Investment Analysts Society of Southern Africa and who, in the course of a very varied career, worked for some ten years for a venture capital group and a merchant bank. However, in neglecting the users, the IASC is following the practice of standard setting bodies throughout the world. Only one of the FASB's seven members has a background as a user, and, on the standard-setting bodies of the European countries, users make up only 14 per cent of the members.[5] Truly the users are the 'Cinderella' of the standard-setting process. According to the IASC's constitution there should be a minimum of three Board members with a background as users of financial statements. Thus, in appointing only two users, the IASC's trustees are not only neglecting an important constituency but also disregarding their own constitution. Paul Volcker has claimed that Geoff Whittington may be considered to be a user, because of his experience with the UK's Monopolies Commission of which he was a member from 1987 to 1996. However this was only a part-time appointment; Geoff Whittington's principal activity throughout his career has been as an academic, as Professor of Accounting, first at the University of Bristol and latterly at the University of Cambridge. Whatever 'spin' the trustees seek to place on their appointments cannot hide the fact that, on the new board, there is only one person, Anthony Cope, whose principal career experience was as a user.

The rise of the professional standard-setters

The members of the new Board, whose previous full-time positions were as a standard setter, may be considered to be the element that balances the conflicting interests of auditors, preparers and users. Persons with their principal background as auditors or preparers make up over half the board; hence auditors and preparers can be confident that their concerns will be fully taken into consideration. However this is not the case with the users. Given the limited presence of members with a background as users, the task of defending the interests of the users will fall on the professional standard setters; that is people like Sir David Tweedie and James Leisenring, whose main activity in the last ten or twenty years has been standard setting. In fact the development of standard setting as a career separate from that of auditor or preparer has been one of the most striking recent developments in financial reporting. The twelve full-time members of the IASB will be a significant addition to this new profession.

Efficiency of operation

The IASB has 14 members, which is significantly more than the FASB (seven) and the ASB (ten). The IASC's working party's report commented: 'While some might believe that a smaller sized Board would be preferable in terms of certain aspects of operating efficiency, the Working Party has come to this number [14] because of the need to have enough people to work closely with national standard setters and the need for involvement of individuals with diverse experience'. Certainly, with respect to its decision-making body, the IASB is significantly smaller than the IASC.

The expert model versus the constituency model

During 1998–9, when the new structure was being developed, the most controversial point was whether the body that had the authority to issue standards should be composed of experts (persons with a technical knowledge of accounting, financial reporting and standard setting) or of representatives (persons representing the different constituencies, of which there was more than one dimension, for example: preparers, users and auditors, developed countries versus developing countries, Europe versus North America, the Anglo-Saxons versus the Rest). The IASC Board consisted of representatives; 13 of the members represented countries and the remainder the preparers and the users. The IASB is based on the expert model. The new constitution specifically states the Board members do not represent constituencies but should act independently in the public interest. The constituencies are represented in the composition of the 19 trustees, but only weakly as the majority of the trustees represent the public 'at large'.

Very many people are unhappy with the 'expert model'. In their opinion, standard setting is essentially a political process. Certainly it involves some technical knowledge, but in the end the ultimate fate of a proposed standard depends on political considerations. This is because financial reporting affects the distribution of wealth between individuals. Society cannot allow such important matters to be settled by the opinions of so-called experts. As was argued in Chapter 3, society considers that the appropriate way of setting the rules that affect the interests of its members is through the political processes of consultation, lobbying, bargaining, debate and in the end voting. Every standard-setting system must include the political element, if only because a standard that is rejected by important parts of society is useless. The importance of the political element was made abundantly clear in the analysis of the American regulatory system in Chapter 5, where the ultimate power lies with the Congress and the SEC. It is evident that the IASB's structure is modelled on the American system: the Board is the equivalent of the FASB and the trustees, the Financial Accounting Foundation. However the IASB has not reproduced within its structure the political elements in the American system: Congress and the SEC. This means that the political element (which is an absolutely essential element of any regulatory system) has to be provided outside the IASB's structure. It will be provided at national level; for example the SEC has already announced (SEC, 2000) that it will vet the IASs to assure itself that they are appropriate for use in the American capital market. The European Union argued strongly but in vain for the new body to be based on the constituency model, as it felt that, only if the EU were represented on the rule-making body, could it ensure that no standards were issued that were contrary to its essential interests. Having failed in this attempt, the EU is now in the process of setting up its own body to check that the IASs conform with EU law and to reject those that do not.

It is perhaps unrealistic to expect that the IASB could have developed within its structure a representative body which would have issued standards that all interested parties would have accepted unconditionally. That would have implied that important actors such as the SEC would have delegated authority to the IASB and, ultimately, the American government would have given up its power to set the rules for enterprises operating in the USA. For the foreseeable future the USA and other countries are unwilling to surrender these important powers to an international body such as the IASB, which implies that there will be an important political element in the rule-making process that is outside the IASB's system. In this case, the expert model can be justified as assuring the efficient operation of the standard-setting process. But it also means that the accountancy profession in a rather surreptitious way retains control of the system since the majority of the new Board are accountants.

11.8 CONCLUSIONS

At the start of the chapter it was remarked that the IASC suffered from two characteristics that severely limited its effectiveness: it was a private organization and its standards had no official status or authority. This is still the case with the IASB. It has made a great effort to improve its status, notably by setting up a prestigious Board of Trustees. But it is still a private organization. Its standards still have no authority. They will only achieve any authority if they are accepted by national authorities. For this reason the IASB places great emphasis on co-operation with national standard setters. It is too early to judge whether this will have the desired result of the IASs being endorsed by the standard setters and regulatory authorities of the major countries.

SUMMARY

The first part of the chapter dealt with the IASC, the body that the IASB replaced in April 2001. The IASC's structure was described and analysed. The functions of the various bodies were explained: the Committee, the Board, the Standing Interpretations Committee, the Consultative group and the Secretariat. The structure of the IASC was evaluated, with the conclusion that certain features tended to have a negative impact on the acceptability of the IASs, which explained why it was found necessary to replace the IASC by the IASB. The IASB's structure was described and analysed in a similar fashion. The question of whether the Board should be based on the expert model or the constituency model was discussed.

Review questions

1. Who were the first members of the IASC?

2. What was the principal function of the IASC's Board?

3. How did the composition of the IASC's Board change between 1974 and 2000? And for what reasons?

4. What is the role of the Standing Interpretations Committee?

5. What features of the IASC's structure had a negative influence over the acceptability of the IASs?

6. What are the principal differences between the IASC and the IASB, with respect to the composition of the decision-making body?

7. What is the difference between the expert model and the constituency model? On which model was the IASC based? Which model has been used for the IASB?

Notes

1. Quote from 'Preface to Statements of International Accounting Standards' (IASC, 2000).
2. This point is explained further in Chapter 12.
3. For example, the trustees' official title is 'Trustees of the IASC Foundation'.
4. Quoted on the ACCA's web-site (http://www.acca.org.uk).
5. For an analysis of the composition of the European standard-setting bodies, see Chapter 13 of Flower and Lefebvre *Comparative Studies in Accounting Regulation in Europe*, Acco, Leuven (1997).

References

Cairns, D 'The future shape of harmonization: a reply', *European Accounting Review*, **6**(2) (1997), pp. 305–48.

Flower, J and Lefebvre, C *Comparative Studies in Accounting Regulation in Europe*, Acco, Leuven (1997).

IASC *Shaping IASC for the Future*, International Accounting Standards Committee, London (1998).

IASC *Recommendations on Shaping IASC for the Future*, International Accounting Standards Committee, London (1999).

IASC *International Accounting Standards 2000*, International Accounting Standards Committee, London (2000).

SEC *Concept Release on International Accounting Standards*, Securities and Exchange Commission, Washington (2000).

Further reading

The best sources of information on the IASC's organization, and that of the IASB, are the two reports of the IASC's working party: 'Shaping IASC for the future' (IASC, 1998) and 'Recommendations on shaping IASC for the future' (IASC, 1999). For the views of the SEC on the IASC's future, see its concept release (SEC, 2000).

chapter twelve

The IASB: Its Standards

Chapter objectives

■ To introduce the International Accounting Standards and to explain why they are followed by many multinational enterprises

■ To discuss what is meant by 'high-quality' standards

■ To outline the 'due process' followed for the preparation and issue of a standard, covering both the IASC and the IASB

12.1 THE INTERNATIONAL ACCOUNTING STANDARDS

Between 1974 and 2000, the IASC issued some forty International Accounting Standards (IASs) of which 34 were still current in 2000. The IASB, on taking office, stated that the IASC's standards continued to be applicable unless and until they were superseded by a standard issued by the IASB. In effect the IASB adopted the IASC's standards as its own standards. A full list of the standards current at 30 June 2001 is presented in Exhibit 12.1, which gives, for each standard, the date of issue and of the last substantial revision. They are all standards of the IASC since, at that date, the IASB had yet to issue its first standard. The IASs cover virtually the whole field of financial reporting; they are very voluminous. The text of the current standards (IASB, 2001) contains over 1000 pages. Readers will be relieved to learn that it is not the authors' intention to cover all these standards in detail. In the chapters in Parts IV and V, which deal with selected issues in financial reporting, only the more important provisions of the relevant IASs are analysed. This chapter deals with two matters relating to the IASs in general: firstly the authority of the IASs (why enterprises should comply with them) and secondly how the IASB seeks to ensure that its standards are of high quality, which involves consideration of the IASB's procedures.

Exhibit 12.1　*The International Accounting Standards at 30 June 2001*

		Date of first issue	Date of last revision
IAS 1	Presentation of financial statements	1974	1997
IAS 2	Inventories	1975	1993
IAS 7	Cash flow statements	1977	1992
IAS 8	Net profit or loss for the period, fundamental errors and changes in accounting policies	1978	1993
IAS 10	Events after the balance sheet date	1978	1999
IAS 11	Construction contracts	1979	1993
IAS 12	Income taxes	1979	1996
IAS 14	Segment reporting	1981	1997
IAS 15	Information reflecting the effect of changing prices	1981	1989
IAS 16	Property, plant and equipment	1982	1993
IAS 17	Leases	1982	1997
IAS 18	Revenue	1982	1993
IAS 19	Employee benefits	1983	1998
IAS 20	Accounting for government grants and disclosure of government assistance	1983	1993
IAS 21	The effects of changes in foreign exchange rates	1983	1993
IAS 22	Business combinations	1983	1993
IAS 23	Borrowing costs	1984	1993
IAS 24	Related party disclosures	1984	
IAS 26	Accounting and reporting by retirement benefit plans	1987	
IAS 27	Consolidated financial statements and accounting for investments in subsidiaries	1989	
IAS 28	Accounting for investments in associates	1989	
IAS 29	Financial reporting in hyperinflationary economies	1989	
IAS 30	Disclosures in the financial statements of banks and similar financial institutions	1990	
IAS 31	Financial reporting of interests in joint ventures	1990	
IAS 32	Financial instruments: disclosure and presentation	1995	
IAS 33	Earnings per share	1997	
IAS 34	Interim financial reporting	1998	
IAS 35	Discontinuing operations	1998	
IAS 36	Impairment of assets	1998	
IAS 37	Provisions, contingent liabilities and contingent assets	1998	
IAS 38	Intangible assets	1998	
IAS 39	Financial instruments: recognition and measurement	1998	
IAS 40	Investment property	2000	
IAS 41	Agriculture	2000	

Notes: All IASs up to IAS 31 were reformatted in 1993; where there was no substantial change, this is not treated as a revision.

12.2 THE AUTHORITY OF IAS

The IASB is a private organization and has no powers to force enterprises to comply with its standards. However it is a fact that very many enterprises in very many countries do comply with IAS – or at least state that their financial statements have been prepared in conformity with IAS. The IASB publishes a list of these companies on its website.[1] At the last count there were over 200 enterprises on the list; they ranged from well-known multinational enterprises such as Deutsche Bank and Nestlé, to lesser known ones such as Agrokor of Croatia and Latvijas Unibanka of Latvia. Why should these enterprises comply with IAS when the IASB has no means of compelling them? There are two main reasons:

National laws and standards

In many countries, the national law and standards require local companies to comply with the IASB's accounting standards. These countries may be classified into two principal groups: countries which do not want to spend resources on creating their own national accounting standards (examples are Kuwait, a very rich country, and Pakistan, a much poorer country) and countries in transition from a centrally-planned economy to a market economy (examples are Poland and China). In 1996 the IASC surveyed 67 countries to discover what use they made of IAS. The results are presented in Exhibit 12.2, which classifies the 67 countries in eight categories from Category A 'IAS used as national standards' through Category G 'National standards developed separately without reference to IAS' to Categories H and I ('No national standards'). Enterprises that are subject to the company law of the countries listed in the categories towards the top of Exhibit 12.2 (particularly Categories A, B, C and D) are obliged to comply with IAS to a greater or lesser extent – greater for Category A where IAS are the national standards and lesser for Category D where the national standards may only be 'similar' to IAS.

Exhibit 12.2 provides a good explanation for why Agrokor of Croatia and the Latvijas Unibanka of Latvia apply IAS, but not for Deutsche Bank and Nestlé. In fact, the home countries of most multinational enterprises are in categories E, F and G towards the bottom of Exhibit 12.2. In fact the USA, Japan, Germany and the UK (the four most important countries in international trade) are all in Category G – the lowest category where national standards are developed without reference to IAS. Hence one has to look for another reason why multinational enterprises should apply IAS.

Exhibit 12.2 *The current status of IAS in 67 countries*

Category	Countries
A	IAS used as national standards Croatia, Cyprus, Kuwait, Latvia, Malta, Oman, Pakistan, Trinidad & Tobago
B	Same as A, but national standards developed for topics not covered by IAS Malaysia, Papua New Guinea
C	IAS are used directly as national standards, but, in some cases may be modified for local conditions or circumstances Albania, Bangladesh, Barbados, Colombia, Jamaica, Jordan, Kenya, Poland, Sudan, Swaziland, Thailand, Uruguay, Zambia, Zimbabwe
D	National accounting standards are separately developed but are based on and similar to relevant IAS. China, Iran, Philippines, Slovenia, Tunisia
E	National accounting standards are separately developed but are based on and similar to relevant IAS in most cases. However, some standards may provide more or less choice than IAS. No reference is made to IAS in the national standards. Brazil, Czech Republic, France, India, Ireland, Lithuania, Mauritius, Mexico, Namibia, Netherlands, Norway, Portugal, Singapore, Slovak Republic, South Africa, Switzerland, Turkey
F	Same as E, but each standard includes a statement that compares the national standard with the relevant IAS Australia, Denmark, Hong Kong, Italy, New Zealand, Sweden, Yugoslavia
G	National standards separately developed Austria, Belgium, Canada, Finland, Germany, Japan, Korea, Luxembourg, Spain, United Kingdom, USA
H & I	No national standards Romania, Botswana, Lesotho

Sources: Status of IASs, *IASC Insight*, October 1997

Capital market pressures

The reason why many of the larger multinational enterprises use IAS for their financial statements is to improve their access to the international capital markets. In Chapter 10 it was explained that, for this reason, many MNEs prepare accounts based on US GAAP. However very many, such as Nestlé and Deutsche Bank, prefer to base their accounts on IAS rather than on US GAAP. There are two reasons:

(a) The stock exchanges in many important financial centres allow foreign listed companies to present their accounts in accordance with IAS.

Exhibit 12.3 *The acceptability of IAS by the leading stock exchanges*

Stock Exchange	Rules
Canada	Only accounts based on Canadian GAAP are permitted
Australia	IAS permitted for non-Australian companies
France	IAS permitted for foreign companies and for the consolidated accounts of French companies
Germany	IAS permitted for foreign companies and for the consolidated accounts of German companies. On the 'Neuer Markt' only IAS or US GAAP is permitted
UK	IAS permitted for foreign companies
Japan	IAS generally permitted for foreign companies
USA	Either full accounts drawn up under US GAAP or a reconciliation between the foreign accounts and US GAAP

The position is summarized in Exhibit 12.3: the stock exchanges of London, Tokyo, Paris and Frankfurt all accept financial statements based on IAS for foreign listed companies. The important exceptions are in North America: companies listed on Canadian stock exchanges must present accounts drawn up according to Canadian GAAP, whilst those listed in the USA must present either accounts using US GAAP or a detailed reconciliation between their accounts and US GAAP.

(b) It is more in keeping with the standing of a 'global player' that its accounts should be based on standards set by an international organization rather than by a national body.

Exhibit 12.4 shows the number of enterprises in each country which report that their accounts comply with IAS. It shows that most enterprises are from countries without strong national standards or are European enterprises whose local capital market is too small to meet their needs. It is remarkable how many enterprises are from relatively small countries such as Switzerland (51), and Denmark (11). Equally remarkable is the absence of enterprises from the USA, Japan and the UK, despite the economic importance of these countries. However the number of German enterprises is rather larger, presumably because of recent developments which are dealt with in section 12.9. Included in Exhibit 12.4 are four international organizations; these include the World Bank, and the European Investment Bank. Their use of IAS adds considerably to the IASB's prestige.

Exhibit 12.4 *The number of enterprises that use IAS*

Enterprise country	Number that use IAS	
The Pentad		
USA	0	
Japan	0	
Britain	0	
Germany	63	
France	2	
		65
Other developed countries		
Switzerland	51	
Denmark	11	
Austria	10	
Others	20	
		92
Eastern Europe		21
Developing countries		
China and Hong Kong	7	
Bahrein	6	
Others	14	
		27
International bodies		
World Bank	1	
European Invetment Bank	1	
African Development Bank	1	
Eutelstat	1	
		4
Total		209

Note: All countries with five or more enterprises are shown separately
Source: IASB (online) (cited July 2001). Available from <http://www.iasb.org.uk>.

12.3 RECENT DEVELOPMENTS

The picture presented in Exhibits 12.2, 12.3 and 12.4 is that the IASs have achieved a reasonable degree of acceptance by countries and enterprises around the world, but that there are some very significant gaps, notably among enterprises from the economically more important countries: the USA, Japan, Britain and other larger EU member states. On the evidence of these tables, the IASB cannot be considered to be the world's standard setter.

However two recent developments have greatly increased the potential authority and acceptability of the IASs. It is too early to assess the full impact of these developments but, in the future, they could lead to the IASB being accepted as the world's standard setter. The two developments are:

- The IASC-IOSCO agreement
- The EU's new accounting strategy

12.3.1 The agreement between the IASC and the IOSCO

The IOSCO (International Organization of Securities Commissions) is the body that represents at the international level the national stock exchange regulatory bodies, including the SEC which has been giving the MNEs so much trouble in insisting on a reconciliation to US GAAP. In 1995, the IASC made an agreement with the IOSCO which had a profound effect on the IASC's activities and may ultimately have an equally important effect on global financial reporting.

The background to the agreement was the difficulties being experienced by the larger multinational corporations in raising capital on stock exchanges outside their home country. The national stock exchange regulatory bodies were acutely aware of the problem. Already in 1986, they had founded the IOSCO as a means of improving co-ordination among themselves at the international level. Right from the start, the IASC sought to establish links with the IOSCO with a view to that body endorsing IAS as the appropriate standards for the MNEs. The IOSCO sympathized with the IASC's aims; for example in 1988 it stated publicly that:

- Different national accounting requirements were an impediment to multinational securities offerings and other foreign listings
- The agreement of mutually acceptable standards of accounting and disclosure was a critical goal

However, although there were many joint meetings between the IOSCO and the IASC, progress was painfully slow. It was not until July 1995, that the two bodies were able to reach an agreement on how to tackle the problem. The essential points of this agreement were that:

■ **If** by 1999 the IASC were to develop a comprehensive set of core standards acceptable to the IOSCO

■ **Then** the IOSCO would recommend to its members that IAS should be accepted for cross-border offerings and other foreign listings

In the agreement, the IOSCO listed 14 IAS as being acceptable and endorsed the IASC's work programme whereby new and modified standards would be developed covering those areas where the present IAS were inadequate. The subjects on which new or improved standards would have to be developed included financial instruments, income taxes, segmental reporting, interim reporting and provisions.

The importance of the agreement was that it set a definite date at which the IOSCO would be obliged to make a decision on endorsing the IASC's standards and thus made much more concrete the possibility that the multinational corporations would be permitted to use IAS for their accounts. The chances of IAS becoming generally accepted around the world received an enormous boost.

In March 1999, with the issue of IAS 39 *Financial Instruments: Recognition and Measurement*, the IASC claimed that it had fulfilled its obligations under its agreement with the IOSCO. In May 2000, the IOSCO announced that it had completed its assessment of 30 IASs and recommended that its members (the national regulatory authorities) allow their use for cross-border listings by multinational enterprises. The endorsement was not unconditional; in its report on IAS, the IOSCO mentioned a number of points where an IAS should be supplemented by additional reconciliations, disclosures or interpretations. It is now up to each national regulatory authority to decide whether to accept the IOSCO's recommendation, which is not binding on them. Given that the IOSCO has already mentioned the need for IAS to be supplemented, it seems improbable that the national authorities will give unconditional endorsement to IAS.

The collaboration with the IOSCO had two major effects on the IASC's activities:

(a) It led to a significant tightening of the rules laid down in IASs. In the first 15 years of its existence the IASC issued some 30 IASs, but they permitted so many alternative accounting treatments that they had little impact on the diversity of financial reporting around the world. Things began to change in 1989 when, under pressure from the IOSCO, the IASC announced that it would examine the existing IASs with a view to reducing the number of permitted alternatives. This has led to the modification of a number of IASs to eliminate previously permitted alternative methods.

(b) It led to the IASC concentrating virtually all its efforts on standards that are relevant to the problems of the larger MNEs, that is the issues identified in the IASC-IOSCO agreement. However, according to its constitution, the IASC should have been concerned with the improvement and harmonization of financial reporting of enterprises throughout the world, regardless of size and of country. In fact, in the past, the developing countries have been among the most loyal supporters of the IASC. Undoubtedly, in allocating virtually all its resources to the completion of the IOSCO project, the IASC neglected a major part of its constituency. In fact in the last decade the IASC has issued only one standard that is of particular relevance to the developing countries – IAS 40 on agriculture.

12.3.2 The EU's new accounting strategy

The IASC-IOSCO agreement must be seen in relation to another very important recent development in the same field – the announcement by the European Commission in November 1995 of a new policy on accounting harmonization (European Commission, 1995). The new policy was the EU's response to the very same problems of the MNEs that led to the IASC-IOSCO agreement. The EU announced that it intended to cooperate with the IASC with the aim of ensuring that European MNEs would in future be able to draw up their consolidated accounts in accordance with IAS. However under EU law, these accounts also had to comply with the Fourth and Seventh Directives. Hence it was necessary to ensure that there were no conflicts between these directives and IAS. To achieve this, the European Commission followed a two-point strategy:

(a) It announced that it was prepared to consider amending any provision in the directives that conflicted with IAS. Thus in May 2001, the EU amended the Fourth and Seventh Directives to permit the reporting of certain financial assets at fair value, as required by IAS 39.

(b) It sought to increase its influence within the IASC's organization to ensure that IAS reflected the EU's requirements and in particular did not contain any provision that was unacceptable to the EU, notably ones that conflicted with essential articles of the directives. The European Commission expected that, by working more closely with the IASC, it would 'allow the Union progressively to gain a position of greater influence on the IASC's work, including the determination of its agenda, so that its output (would) increasingly reflect the EU viewpoint' (European Commission, 1995, paragraph 5.4).

The second point is the most significant aspect of the EU's new policy. The European Commission saw the IASC-IOSCO agreement as a threat to its power to set the accounting rules for European MNEs. The EU could not permit that in future these rules should be set by a body over which it had no influence – hence its bid to increase its influence over the IASC. In effect the EU decided that permitting European MNEs to base their accounts on IAS would be the lesser evil, compared with their choosing US GAAP, for the EU could not expect ever to have any influence over the determination of US GAAP. In effect, the EU gave up any claim to be the global rule-maker for the MNEs. Instead it decided to support the IASC as the best chance of preventing US GAAP becoming the global standard.

In 1996 the European Commission accepted the IASC's invitation to attend Board meetings as an observer. It would seem that it had some success in influencing the IASC's output. The revised version of IAS 1 which was issued in 1997 contains many provisions that bear a remarkable resemblance to those of the EU's directives.

Moreover the European Commission has supported the action taken by a number of member states to permit certain enterprises to present their consolidated accounts in accordance with internationally acceptable standards. In addition to France and Germany which have already been mentioned, five other EU member states (Austria, Belgium, Finland, Italy and Luxembourg) have recently modified their laws in this way. However this was clearly a stop-gap measure which carried with it the danger of reducing the degree of harmonization within the EU for two reasons:

■ Not all member states were covered

■ Both IAS and US GAAP were permitted

Hence in May 2000, the European Commission proposed that, by 2005, listed enterprises in all EU member states should be required to prepare their consolidated accounts in accordance with IAS provided that these had been endorsed by the EU as being in conformity with the directives.

12.3.3 Implications for the acceptability of the IASs

It is too early to judge what the consequences of these recent developments will be for the acceptability of the IASs. Certainly the endorsement by both the IOSCO and the EU should lead to more enterprises adopting IAS. However it should be noted that the endorsement of both bodies was subject to important conditions.

The IOSCO, in recommending that its members should permit foreign MNEs to use IAS, stated that the national regulatory authorities could set further conditions, notably:

(a) **Reconciliations:** MNEs could be required to publish a reconciliation statement which showed the effect of applying a different method from that set out in the IAS.

(b) **Disclosure:** MNEs could be required to disclose additional information.

(c) **Interpretation:** The national regulatory authority could insist that MNEs use a particular interpretation in cases where the IAS was unclear or silent.

(d) **Waiver:** The national regulatory authority could prescribe that a particular aspect of an IAS not be applied, where this is contrary to national rules.

Conditions (a) and (b) present no problems (apart from extra costs for the MNEs) since they concern information that is additional to that provided under IAS. However condition (c) raises the possibility that different national authorities will prescribe different interpretations of particular IASs which would undermine the whole concept of a single set of global standards. But the most alarming condition is (d) – in particular cases, the national regulatory authority may decide to impose a national rule instead of that set out in an IAS.

Furthermore it should be noted that the IOSCO's recommendation is not binding on its members. The SEC has already announced that it has no intention of giving a blanket endorsement to the IASs. It remains to be seen how the SEC will respond to the IOSCO. But it seems very probable that the SEC will only permit the use of IASs subject to important conditions, including that, for certain specific items, US GAAP must be used instead of the IASs.

The EU's attitude seems rather more positive, notably as evidenced by its proposal that, from 2005, all EU listed companies should be required to adopt the IASs. However the EU has already announced that it is setting up a body (known as an endorsement mechanism) to vet the IASs before imposing them on European MNEs. The need for such a procedure arises from two considerations:

(a) **Legal.** The EU cannot insist that European MNEs follow the rules set by a non-EU body. However the EU, by formally endorsing the IASs, transforms them into EU standards.

(b) **Substantial.** The EU, at this stage, is not prepared to run the risk that the IASB will issue a standard that contains a provision that is contrary to its fundamental interests. As explained in Chapter 11, the IASB is based on the expert model. The EU has no direct influence on the standard-setting process and therefore, in the absence of any experience of how the IASB will function, the EU cannot give a blanket endorsement to its standards.

12.4 THE QUALITY OF THE IASs

How does the IASB ensure that the IASs are of high quality? To answer this question, one must first define 'high quality'. This is not a trivial matter and there can be different opinions of what constitutes 'high quality' in an accounting standard.

One can first define certain qualities which should be possessed by a standard, irrespective of the objectives of the body that issues it. The standard's wording should be clear, understandable and unambiguous; the meaning of technical accounting terms (such as assets and equity) should be clearly defined, leaving no room for misunderstanding and misinterpretation; the standard should be internally consistent (one part should not contradict or be in conflict with another part); it should be consistent with other standards issued by the same body.

These points apply to standards issued by all standard-setting bodies. However, in the authors' opinion, for the IASB a high quality International Accounting Standard is one that best achieves that body's objectives. The IASB's objectives are set out in section 11.5.2 of Chapter 11. The first objective starts with the words 'to develop in the public interest a single set of high quality, understandable and enforceable global accounting standards.' Of the three epithets applied to standards, 'understandable' is one of the general qualities referred to in the previous paragraph, 'enforceable' will be considered in the next paragraph, which leaves 'high quality'. What the IASB considers to be a 'high quality' standard can best be judged by the remainder of the first objective: 'standards that require high quality, transparent and comparable information in financial statements and other financial reporting to help participants in the world's capital markets and other users make economic decisions'. Hence, for the IASB, a high quality standard is one that leads to financial statements that are 'transparent', 'comparable' and helpful to users. These points may be developed further:

(a) **'Transparent'**. This presumably means that the financial statements prepared in accordance with the standards should disclose all significant matters about the enterprise. However how is one to decide what is significant? The criterion must be whether it serves the third point – helpful to users.

(b) **'Comparable'**. To a certain extent comparability is achieved through the development of a single set of standards. However this single set may fail to achieve comparability if the standards are unclear, ambiguous, incomplete or permit alternative treatments (as with the EU options).

(c) **Helpful to users.** This is the most fundamental criterion. As already noted, it makes the criterion of 'transparency' operational. The IASB gives prominence to helping participants in the world's capital markets but not exclusively as it also refers to 'other users'.

According to the IASB's first objective, its standards should be 'enforceable'. Furthermore the second objective is that the IASB should 'promote the use and rigorous application' of its standards. This suggests that, for the IASB, a high quality standard is one that is fully complied with by enterprises. To a limited extent a standard's intrinsic qualities such as clarity and consistency have an influence on the way in which it is applied. However much more important is whether its provisions are acceptable to enterprises and to the authorities that govern the financial reporting of enterprises.

The above analysis suggests that two things are necessary for the IASB to develop and issue 'high quality' standards:

(a) The IASB should establish in an authoritative and clear fashion the fundamental principles on which financial reporting is based, including the objectives of financial statements. It has done this in its conceptual framework, *The Framework for the Preparation and Presentation of Financial Statements*, which states that the objective is to provide information for users and, on this basis, establishes the characteristics of financial statements that make the information they contain valuable to users. The IASB's Framework is a most important document, as it sets out the basic principles followed by the IASB in developing standards. For this reason, Chapter 13 is devoted to its analysis. As explained in that chapter, the Framework tends to give greater priority to the information needs of shareholders as compared with other users, such as employees or the general public. In recent years, particularly following the agreement with the IOSCO, the IASC placed ever greater emphasis on the function of accounts to provide information for the capital market (that is to shareholders and potential shareholders in listed enterprises), to the extent that it seems to have accepted this as the overriding objective. In line with this development the IASB's objectives include the words: 'to help participants in the world's capital markets'.

(b) The IASB's organization and working methods should be such that, in developing its standards, it takes fully into account the views and needs of the principal actors in the arena of financial reporting, notably:

- Preparers, for a standard that they reject will not achieve worldwide acceptance
- Regulators, because of their powers to require preparers to observe standards
- Users, because their information needs are central, and lastly
- The accountancy profession – for two reasons: its members are the technical experts and they have some influence over the behaviour of preparers

At the time of writing, the IASB has still to establish its working methods. However the IASB's constitution sets out certain procedures that it should follow in developing its standards. Most of these mirror those employed by the IASC. Hence an analysis of the process used by the IASC to develop its standards (which in fact constitute the entire corpus of currently applicable IASs) offers an insight into how the IASB will probably operate. Furthermore it provides an example of how a standard-setting body may achieve its aim of issuing high-quality standards.

12.5 THE IASC'S 'DUE PROCESS'

In developing a standard, the IASC followed a defined set of procedures known as 'due process', with the aims of ensuring that the resulting standard was of high quality and accepted by the world's financial community.

With 'due process' the emphasis was laid on publicity and consultation. As described by a former Secretary-General (Cairns, 1995, p. 23), the development of a standard involved a number of steps; each step consisted of the preparation within the IASC organization of a document which was then published. Persons outside the IASC were invited to comment. By a process of feedback, the documents were gradually refined and improved, resulting hopefully at the end of the process of an IAS of high quality. Exhibit 12.5 sets out the process in the form of a flow chart.

The principal stages of due process are as follows:

Setting the agenda

How did the IASC decide that it should set in train the process that would lead eventually to the issue of an IAS on a particular topic? This was one the most important steps in the process, for although, at any stage, the IASC might decide to discontinue the process (and give up the idea of issuing an IAS on the topic), it could not issue an IAS without first initiating the process. The decision to add a project to the IASC's agenda was the prerogative of the Board. In fact much of the IASC's agenda in recent years was set by the need to fulfil its agreement with the IOSCO.

Preliminary research: the discussion paper

Commonly the first stage in the process was for the IASC Secretariat (with the approval of the Board) to undertake preliminary research on a particular topic with the aim of clarifying the accounting issues and identifying possible solutions. Frequently this research was carried out

Exhibit 12.5 *The development of an International Accounting Standard*

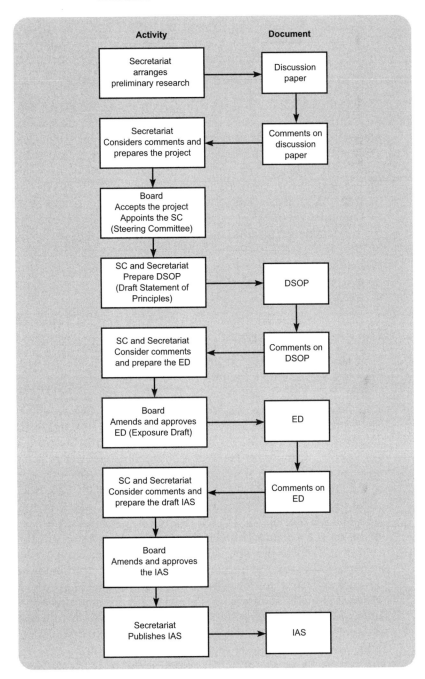

in collaboration with another organization, as the Secretariat's research resources were very limited. In recent years, this research has often been done by the 'G4+1 group' which consists of the standard-setting bodies of Australia, Canada, the UK and the USA ('G4') plus the IASC ('+1'). This research generally took about a year and the results were published in the form of a discussion paper, which, as the title suggests, committed nobody. The discussion paper was circulated widely with an invitation to send comments to the IASC.

In principle, research is very important. In the words of the American Accounting Association: 'Research can be relevant to the standard-setting process when it provides models, theories and/or empirical evidence, which explore the relation between accounting information and various economic metrics (e.g., stock prices, stock returns, bid-ask spreads, cost of capital, market risk, credit risk, insolvency, etc.)' (AAA, 1998). For example, in the USA, 'event studies' have thrown a great deal of light on the fundamental question of whether accounts provide useful information for shareholders. However much of the IASC's recent research has been of indifferent quality; the published discussion papers consist largely of an exposition of the various accounting methods and contain virtually no empirical research. Certainly the IASC is not a patron of research on the scale of the FASB.

The Steering Committee

After having considered the comments received on the discussion paper, the IASC Secretariat normally proposed to the Board that it should add a project on the chosen topic to the work programme, which implied accepting the objective of ultimately issuing an IAS on the subject. If the Board accepted the Secretariat's proposal, the first step was to nominate the members of the Steering Committee for the project. A Steering Committee generally consisted of a Board representative as chairman and up to ten people who were not on the Board. In selecting the members of the Steering Committee, the Board sought to achieve a balanced representation of countries and of parties (preparers, users, auditors) but it did not look outside the IASC's organization (bodies represented on the Board, on the Consultative Group and in IFAC). The task of the Steering Committee was to prepare, with the aid of the Secretariat, all the documents relating to the proposed IAS (exposure draft and so on) for consideration and approval by the Board. The Steering Committee met rather infrequently during the project and its members were all very much part-timers from the IASC's viewpoint. Hence its function was not so much the technical one of preparing the text of the standard but rather the political one of ensuring that its provisions were appropriate and acceptable to the principal actors in the financial community.

The Draft Statement of Principles (DSOP)

The first task of the Steering Committee was to approve for publication a Draft Statement of Principles (DSOP), which was a broad-ranging document that set out the problem, described the possible alternative solutions, and presented reasons for recommending their acceptance or rejection, leading to the Committee's preferred solution. The DSOP was published with an invitation to send comments to the IASC. The IASC Board considered the comments received and often proposed amendments to the DSOP. If the debate at the level of the Board revealed no fundamental objections to the principles set out in the DSOP, the Steering Committee and the Secretariat proceeded with the next stage in the process: the preparation of the Exposure Draft.

The Exposure Draft

An IASC Exposure Draft (ED) consisted of two parts:

■ The text of the proposed IAS; and

■ An invitation to comment, where the IASC asked for comments on the text and set out certain questions on which it was particularly seeking answers.

The text of the proposed IAS was based on the DSOP modified to eliminate the discussion of alternative treatments (which was appropriate in a DSOP but not in an IAS) and to take account of the discussion at Board level. The text of the Exposure Draft was prepared by the Steering Committee in collaboration with the Secretariat. It was then considered by the Board. Under the IASC's constitution a two thirds majority was required for the issue of an Exposure Draft. It was common for the Board to amend the Steering Committee's draft before approving it.

The Secretariat published the Exposure Draft with an invitation to send comments to the IASC. Typically the IASC received comments from a very wide range of organizations and individuals. The Secretariat prepared an analysis of these comments for the benefit of the Steering Committee and the Board. The Board considered the comments and frequently voted on specific issues raised in the comments, leading to amendments to the draft standard. If the Board considered that there was sufficient consensus on the approach outlined in the Exposure Draft, it asked the Secretariat to prepare the final text of the IAS.

The issue of the IAS

The Secretariat prepared the draft text of the IAS. The Board discussed the Secretariat's draft. It often voted on the text of particular paragraphs.

In these votes, a simple majority was sufficient. However, for the issue of an IAS, three quarters of the Board had to vote in favour. It frequently happened that a Board member, who objected to a particular paragraph and had voted against its inclusion, nevertheless voted for the adoption of the IAS as a whole. In effect the Board member was faced with a 'take it or leave it' decision, and would often decide to accept that the IAS be issued with the offending paragraph rather than not at all. After the vote at the Board, the Secretariat prepared the final text for printing and publication.

12.6 THE IMPORTANCE OF DUE PROCESS

The IASC placed great emphasis on the fact that, in developing an International Accounting Standard, it always followed the set procedure that has been described above. The principal features of this procedure were:

(a) All major steps required a vote of the Board:
- To place a project on the work programme (simple majority)
- To appoint the Steering Committee (simple majority)
- To issue an Exposure Draft (two thirds majority)
- To issue an International Accounting Standard (three quarters majority)

The process was not governed by the will of any individual person, no matter how influential (for example the Chairman or the Secretary-General). It depended on achieving a broad consensus at Board level. Furthermore, by bringing the matter before the Board, the organizations that were represented there by observers were fully informed of the project's progress. The most important of these organizations were the IOSCO, the FASB and the European Commission.

(b) At various points in the process, the IASC consulted with other organizations who were not on the Board. It did this through meetings of the Consultative Group and through the public invitation to comment on the DSOP and the Exposure Draft.

(c) The IASC was comparatively open in its procedures. Although the meetings of the Steering Committees were closed, Board meetings were, since March 1999, open to the public. The IASC published all important documents relating to the process, including the comments that it received on the DSOP and ED.

The IASC placed such great emphasis on following due process in order to enhance the acceptability of its standards that the IASC claimed that its standards were not based on the opinion of a few influential people or even of the leading national professional accountancy bodies, but represented the outcome of a formal process during which the views of all persons likely to be affected by the standards were canvassed and considered.

However the possibility must be considered that in developing its standards the IASC might have been unduly influenced by certain important parties, for example by the lobbying of powerful multinational enterprises. Alternatively Board members might have considered solely their own sectional and national interests in voting for standards and not the wider public interest. There have been very little research on how the IASC set standards. One of the few published studies (Kenny and Larson, 1993), which analysed the procedure followed for the issue of IAS 31, found little evidence of undue influence. There was a slight suspicion that the IASC might have been biassed in favour of the Anglo-Saxons. The exposure draft proposed that proportional consolidation should be the required method for accounting for joint ventures. Most of the organizations that responded to the IASC's invitation to comment were opposed to this requirement and preferred that joint ventures should be accounted for using the equity method. Furthermore most of these commentators were from the Anglo-Saxon camp. The IASC Board responded to these criticisms by modifying its proposal to include the equity method as a permitted alternative. This incident can be interpreted either as the IASC Board yielding to pressure from the Anglo-Saxons or alternatively as legitimately taking into account the opinions of the majority of organizations that commented on its exposure draft. What this study does reveal is how difficult it is to establish the real grounds on which the Board's decisions were based.

12.7 'DUE PROCESS' UNDER THE IASB

At the time of writing the IASB has yet to establish its detailed working procedures. However certain procedural matters are covered in the new constitution, which makes specific references to the following points:

- The Board has full discretion over the setting of the agenda
- The Board may outsource research and other work
- The Board should normally form steering committees to give advice on major projects
- The Board is required to publish an exposure draft for all projects and should normally publish a draft statement of principles
- The Board should establish procedures for reviewing comments on documents issued for comment
- The Board should consult the Standards Advisory Council on major projects, agenda decisions and work priorities

The above points mirror features of the IASC's due process as described in section 12.5 above. Certainly one has a strong impression that the IASB's due process will not differ substantially from that of the IASC. The most significant difference is that under the IASB's constitution the majority required for the issue of an exposure draft or a standard is that eight of the 14 members must vote in favour; that is a 57 per cent majority. Under the IASC, the majorities were significantly higher: 67 per cent for an exposure draft and 75 per cent for a standard. The reduced majority surely increases the danger that the IASB may issue a standard that is opposed by a significant part of the financial community.

SUMMARY

The full range of the IASs were presented. The reasons why many enterprises follow IAS in preparing their accounts were analysed as firstly national laws (particularly for the developing countries) and capital market pressures (in which the acceptance of IAS by many stock exchanges is an important factor). The impact of the IASC-IOSCO agreement and the EU's new accounting strategy on the acceptability of IAS was analysed. The criteria for a high-quality standard were discussed with reference to the conflict between uniformity and relevance. The procedure used to develop an IAS ('due process') was described and evaluated.

Review questions

1. What authority do the IASs possess?

2. Why do many enterprises comply with IAS? What are the two categories of enterprises involved?

3. What is the content of the IASC-IOSCO agreement? What impact did it have on the IASC's activities?

4. What recent developments have made it likely that in the future more European enterprises will base their accounts on the IASs?

5. How did the IASC seek to ensure that its standards were of 'high quality'?

6. Why did the IASC place so much stress on due process?

Review questions (cont'd)

7. Outline the procedure used by the IASC to prepare and issue an IAS.

8. What opportunities did bodies that were not represented on the IASC Board have to influence the content of an IAS?

9. Why is it probable that the IASB's due process will not be very different from that of the IASC?

Note

1. The IASB's website (www.iasb.org.uk) is a very useful source of information about the organization.

References

AAA 'Criteria for setting the quality of an accounting standard', *Accounting Horizons*, **12** (June 1998), pp. 161–2.

Cairns, D *A Guide to Applying International Accounting Standards*, Accountancy Books, Milton Keynes (1995).

Cairns, D 'The future shape of harmonization: a reply', *European Accounting Review*, **6**(2) (1997), pp. 305–48.

European Commission *Accounting harmonization: a new strategy vis-à-vis international harmonization*, European Commission, Brussels (1995).

Flower, J 'The future shape of harmonization', *European Accounting Review*, **6**(2) (1997), pp. 281–303.

IASC 'Which countries use IAS?', *IASC Insight* (October 1997), p. 15.

IASC *Annual Review 1997*, International Accounting Standards Committee, London (1998).

IASB *International Accounting Standards 2001*, International Accounting Standards Board, London (2000).

Kenny, S and Larson, R 'Lobbying behaviour and the development of international accounting standards', *European Accounting Review*, **2**(3) (1993), pp. 531–54.

Further reading

For the background to the IASC–IOSCO agreement see Cairns (1997). For the collaboration between the IASC and the European Union, see Flower (1997). For a discussion on the quality of an accounting standard, see the American Accounting Association's report (AAA, 1998). For a rather outdated analysis of the IASC's due process see Kenny and Larson (1993).

chapter thirteen

The IASB's Framework

Chapter objectives

- To discuss the role and function of conceptual frameworks in general
- To analyse the principal provisions of the IASB's Framework, with particular emphasis on the following aspects of financial statements: objectives, qualitative characteristics and elements
- To evaluate the role played by the Framework in the IASB's standard-setting process

13.1 CONCEPTUAL FRAMEWORKS IN GENERAL

13.1.1 Examples of frameworks

The IASB's *Framework for the Preparation and Presentation of Financial Statements* is a very useful document in that it sets out the IASB's approach to financial reporting. The full text of the Framework is presented in the annex. Its very first sentence reads: 'This Framework sets out the concepts that underlie the preparation and presentation of financial statements.' The use of the word 'concept' indicates that the IASB's Framework is an example of a general category of constructs known as conceptual frameworks. Other examples are:

- **USA:** The FASB's conceptual framework, which is set out in seven Statements of Financial Accounting Concepts. The first six statements were issued between 1978 and 1985. However in 2000, after a gap of 15 years, the FASB expanded its framework by issuing a seventh statement, which indicates that conceptual frameworks are now a very topical matter

- **Canada:** The CICA's report *Corporate Reporting: Its Future Evolution* published in 1980 (CICA, 1980)
- **Australia:** The ASRB's three Statements of Accounting Concepts published in 1990
- **UK:** The ASB's *Statement of Principles for Financial Reporting* published in 1999 (ASB, 1999)

The aim of all these documents is to set out the objectives and basic principles of financial statements. The American conceptual framework was developed before that of the IASC which was published in 1989,[1] and undoubtedly had a strong influence on its contents.

13.1.2 Definition and characteristics

A conceptual framework has been defined by Miller, Redding and Bahnson (1998) as 'a collection of broad rules, guidelines, accepted truths and other broad ideas' about the field. However there are two fundamentally different ways in which these broad rules may be developed: deduction and induction.

(a) **Deduction:** When this approach is used, the aim is to set out a logically complete system consisting of a set of axioms and a syntax, whereby the detailed rules of financial reporting may be derived from the axioms by the application of deductive logic, in the same way that the theorems of Euclidian geometry are derived from its axioms.

(b) **Induction:** In this approach, the conceptual framework is based on the existing practice of accountants. However, the inductive approach involves much more than a simple description of what accountants do; it involves an analysis of the great diversity and variety of practice with the aim of discerning the underlying principles which are then presented in the form of a comprehensive and coherent framework.

An alternative way of classifying a conceptual framework is according to whether its objective is normative or positive. A normative framework seeks to prescribe the rules that should be followed for financial reporting. A positive framework limits itself to presenting existing practice, without judging whether it is good or bad. The difference between the two approaches has been neatly summarized as: a normative framework is a prescription for future practice; a positive framework is a description of present practice. In principle, frameworks based on pure deduction cannot be positive, as deduction is based on logical reasoning and not on observation of the real world. Frameworks that use the inductive approach are generally positive but it not impossible for such a framework to include positive elements, particularly if the authors seek to recommend the best features of present practice.

Conceptual frameworks also vary in the degree of detail in which they set out the rules. At least four levels of detail may be envisaged, at least in theory:

(a) The conceptual framework lays down all the necessary rules, or at least the rules that need to be followed in order to establish new rules; this is the objective of a complete logical system based on axioms and the application of deductive logic.

(b) It sets out the basic general principles that should govern financial reporting; the detailed rules are developed by the rule-makers within the limits set by these principles.

(c) It sets out the objectives of financial reporting and leaves it to the rule-makers to construct rules that are in conformity with these objectives.

(d) It limits itself to defining the concepts used by accountants – that is it serves as a form of technical dictionary.

The above approaches are presented in descending order of detail and prescription. They form a hierarchy; the higher levels of the hierarchy incorporate the elements of the lower levels: thus the axiomatic system of paragraph (a) will include the basic principles (b), the objectives (c) and the definitions (d).

The very first conceptual framework to be developed adopted the deductive approach. In 1960, the USA's Accounting Principles Board commissioned two leading academics to research the basic postulates and principles of accounting. The term 'postulate' is generally used by accountants in place of 'axiom' but it has the same meaning: 'something claimed or assumed as a basis for reasoning' (Oxford English Dictionary). The results were published as *The Basic Postulates of Accounting* by Maurice Moonitz (1961) and *A Tentative Set of Accounting Principles for Business Enterprises* by Robert Sprouse and Moonitz (1962). When the second report was published, 'all hell broke loose' – to quote the colourful phrase of a British commentator (Peasnell, 1982). The report contained no less than 24 pages of dissent from the members of the project advisory committee and the APB rejected the report's proposals for reform as 'too radically different from present generally accepted accounting principles to be acceptable at this time'. The trouble was that the report in advocating that assets be reported at their current values was too much at variance with accepted practice. One may also speculate that the axiomatic approach, whilst appropriate for mathematics, is not applicable to accounting which is primarily a social science. This was the opinion of Professor Edward Stamp, the principal author of the Canadian conceptual framework, who considered that 'accounting was not like geometry, with conclusions flowing logically from predetermined axioms and definitions'.

Since 1962 no conceptual framework has adopted the pure axioms/postulates approach or at least none has claimed to; the authors no doubt do not want their work to suffer the same fate as the Moonitz/Sprouse study. However all of the other approaches listed above (or elements of them) may be found in the existing conceptual frameworks.

13.1.3 The benefits of a conceptual framework

The benefits that may be expected from having a conceptual framework have been listed by Solomons (1986) as:

(a) **Economizing of effort:** Once the framework has been put in place, the subsequent development of standards should be made easier. Many financial reporting problems have common elements and they should not have to be thought through afresh each time they are encountered.

(b) **Gain in consistency:** Standards developed on the basis of an agreed framework may be expected to be more consistent with one another than would standards that are developed independently.

(c) **Improved communication:** Improved communication (both within the standard-setting body and between the standard-setting body and the outside world of preparers, auditors and users) should be the result of setting down agreed definitions of concepts such as 'assets'. For example, as Solomons remarks, the term 'materiality' has been widely used by accountants but not always to mean the same thing.

These three benefits are technical in nature and rather modest. There is no suggestion that a conceptual framework should attempt to lay down all the rules. However there is a fourth benefit of rather a different nature:

(d) **Defence against politicization:** Given that accounting standards have an impact on the wealth and welfare of many people, it is be expected that those affected by standards will seek to influence the standard-setting body in its decisions. It is generally agreed that the standard-setting body should take into account the concerns of such persons for, in that way, it is able to develop a standard that is more relevant and practical. That is one of the reasons for the elaborate process of consultation that all standard-setting bodies practise. However there is a danger that outsiders may be able to exert such powerful pressure on the standard-setting body that they are able to secure the inclusion in a proposed standard of particular points on which they place importance. The problem is aggravated by the fact that only those directly affected by a proposed standard are likely to make a serious effort to influence the standard-setting body; the great majority of persons are only slightly affected and do not bother. Such political interference is highly undesirable for a number of reasons:

(i) It leads to inconsistency between standards. This is almost inevitable if each standard is drafted to meet the interests of a different lobby. Inconsistency is not only intellectually and aesthetically unpleasing; it can lead to practical problems – for example which of two mutually inconsistent standards is to be followed. At the very least, inconsistency has a negative impact on the comparability of financial reporting, which is one of the prime objectives of standards.

(ii) At the extreme, it results in standards being based on no principles other than to serve the interests of the most influential and powerful parties.

(iii) The role of the standard-setting body is to apply the principles of financial reporting in an even-handed neutral fashion in the interests of society as a whole. On occasions, it should stand up to particular interests and proclaim that what they are urging is wrong, as being contrary to the fundamental principles of financial reporting.

This analysis suggests that a conceptual framework is a weapon to be used by the 'experts' in financial reporting (typically the auditing and accounting professions) to defend their territory against unwelcome intruders.

The IASB's Framework will now be considered in the light of the above remarks relating to conceptual frameworks in general. Readers should refer to the Framework's text, which is given in the annex.

13.2 THE PURPOSES OF THE IASB's FRAMEWORK

The purposes of the IASB's Framework are set out in its first paragraph as:

■ to assist the IASB in the development of future IASs and in its review of existing IASs; and in reducing the number of permitted treatments in IASs

■ to assist national standard setters in developing national standards

■ to assist preparers in applying IASs and in dealing with topics that have yet to form the subject of an IAS

■ to assist auditors in forming an opinion as to whether financial statements conform with IASs

■ to assist users in interpreting the information contained in financial statements

■ to provide those interested in the work of the IASB with information about its approach to the formulation of IASs

The IASB makes clear that it believes that the Framework will be found helpful by the whole range of persons interested in financial reporting: national standard setters, preparers, auditors, users and even the general public. However the Framework's fundamental purpose is to assist the IASB in developing future IASs and reviewing existing IASs (top of the above list). The Framework therefore gives an indication of the IASB's approach to its task of setting the rules of financial reporting. Note that the Framework only 'assists' the IASB in this task. It does not constrain or bind it. The IASB is free to ignore the principles laid down in the Framework if it so decides. This point is reinforced in paragraph 2[2] which states: 'This Framework is not an International Accounting Standard . . . Nothing in this Framework overrides any specific IAS'. That is the formal position. However in the very next paragraph the IASB states that it 'will be guided by the Framework in the development of future standards'. The text of the Framework will now be examined in order to gain an insight into the IASB's approach to financial reporting and to the principles that it follows in developing standards.

13.3 THE OBJECTIVE OF FINANCIAL STATEMENTS

Paragraph 12 sets out the basic objective: 'The objective of financial statements is to provide information about the financial position, performance and changes in financial position of the enterprise that is useful to a wide range of users in making economic decisions'.

The information needs of users

Users need information to help them make decisions. Information can only be of value if it helps the user to make a better decision than she would have done without the information. This does not mean that the user has to take some action on receiving the information; the appropriate decision may be to do nothing, as, for example, when a shareholder decides neither to sell her shares nor to buy more shares but simply to retain the existing holding. Many decisions concern the future allocation of resources, as, for example, when a customer has to decide whether to enter into a long-term contract with the enterprise. In these cases the user would like to be able to forecast the future and looks to the accounts to help her in this task; for example she examines the accounts and decides that the enterprise is in a sound financial position and unlikely to fail. When information is used to predict the future, it is said to play a predictive role.

However, information also has value when it is used to control or confirm past decisions; this is known as the confirmatory role of information.

Confirmatory information can be used in two rather different ways: to improve the decision-making process so that future decisions are better (past mistakes are not repeated), and to enforce accountability. The latter relates to the stewardship function of accounts, which is referred to in the Framework in the following terms: 'Financial statements also show the results of stewardship of management, or the accountability of management for the resources entrusted to it. Those users who wish to assess the stewardship or accountability of management do so in order to make economic decisions ... for example ... whether to reappoint or replace the management' (paragraph 14). Hence, according to the Framework, the stewardship role of accounts is simply one aspect of the overall objective of financial statements, which is to provide information to assist the users in making decisions.

The diversity of users

The Framework lists users as including 'present and potential investors, employees, lenders, suppliers and other trade creditors, customers, governments and their agencies, and the public' (paragraph 9). The financial statements have to meet the common information needs of a wide range of users and, for this reason are termed 'general purpose' statements. However not all users are considered to be equally important. In effect priority is given to investors as is made very clear in paragraph 10: 'As investors are providers of risk capital to the enterprise, the provision of financial statements that meet their needs will also meet most of the needs of other users.'

The sentence that has just been quoted would hardly score full marks for logic! The IASB presents no arguments to justify its claim that meeting the needs of investors[3] will also meet the needs of other users. This point is covered in the American conceptual framework, notably in Statement of Financial Accounting Concepts No. 1 (FASB, 1978), which, while acknowledging the heterogeneity of external user groups, claims that a common characteristic of all users is their interest in the prediction of the amounts, timing and uncertainties of future cash flows.[4] It should be noted that this argument is based solely on the predictive role of accounts and ignores completely the confirmatory role. There are strong grounds for believing that investors are interested in future cash flows, but, in the opinion of the authors, to claim that this is also the case for other users is, at least, problematic. It is true that the interests of lenders are similar to those of shareholders. Lenders need to assess the probability that the enterprise will be able to make interest payments as they fall due and to repay the loan at the end of its term. Their information needs are not identical with those of shareholders; for example, they have only a limited interest in the absolute level of the enterprise's projected cash flow, provided that there is a comfortable margin above the minimum necessary to service their loan. Lenders may also look to the financial statements to assure themselves that covenants in the loan contract have been respected by the enterprise; for example that the debt/equity ratio has not risen above 1. Thus the information needs of lenders and shareholders are not identical but they are similar.

However, the information needs of the other user groups (for example employees, suppliers and customers) are rather different. Two major differences are firstly that the benefits that investors and lenders derive from the enterprise are delivered solely in money terms and secondly that the benefits are provided by the whole enterprise as a single unit. The shareholder's dividend is paid in cash out of the funds of the whole enterprise (and not from part of the enterprise); the same is true of the lender's annual interest and the final redemption of the loan. However employees, suppliers and customers are generally interested in only a part of the enterprise. Thus an employee is interested in whether the enterprise will continue to offer him secure and stable employment; it is of little solace to him if the enterprise's impressive future cash flow is achieved by closing the factory in which he works or by a massive reduction in the work force through investment in labour-saving machinery. This is not to claim that the employee has no interest in future cash flows – for example, if they are forecast to be negative, this has implications for his job security. But clearly the employee has additional information needs that are different from those of investors.

The heterogeneity of user information needs is presented in diagrammatic form in Exhibit 13.1, which, to avoid making the diagram too complicated, shows only three user groups. The FASB and the IASB maintain that the objective of financial statements is to meet the information needs of investors, which covers a large part of the information needs of lenders but a much smaller part of those of employees.

The Framework's Anglo–American orientation

The emphasis on providing information for shareholders is one example of the Framework's bias towards the Anglo–American approach to financial reporting. A second is that the tax function of accounts (as the basis for the computation of taxes) is not covered. This is not immediately apparent from an examination of paragraph 9, which refers to government as a user and clearly the determination of the amount of tax payable by the enterprise is of great importance to governments. However paragraph 6 states that computations prepared for tax purposes are outside the scope of the Framework. This restriction is based purely on induction; that in the IASB's view general purpose financial statements are not used as the basis for the computation of tax. The implication is that

Exhibit 13.1 *The needs of users*

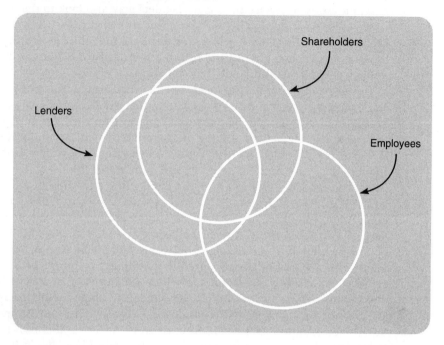

the IASB's Framework and hence the IASs do not refer to that substantial part of financial reporting whose principal function is to facilitate the computation of tax, notably the individual accounts of French, German and Japanese enterprises.

13.4 ASSUMPTIONS

The authors of the Framework set out two explicit assumptions: accrual basis and going concern. Presumably these matters are stated to be assumptions because they cannot be proved by either deductive or inductive reasoning.

Accrual basis

Paragraph 22 states: 'Under this basis, the effects of transactions and other events are recognized when they occur (and not as cash or its equivalent is received or paid) and they are recorded in the accounting records and reported in the financial statements of the periods to which they relate'. Accountants apply the accrual basis every day in their work but seem to have great difficulty in defining it! In the authors' opinion the above definition is incomprehensible or at least incomplete. The one thing that is clear is that it is not cash accounting, which is certainly not universally correct since, even under the accruals basis, many transactions are recorded and reported on the basis of cash payments and receipts (for example a cash sale). The statement that 'transactions ... are recognized when they occur' seems little more than a truism, and the definition depends crucially on the meaning of the word 'relate'. IAS 1, 26 expands the definition by adding: 'Expenses are recognized in the income statement on the basis of a direct association between the costs incurred and the earning of specific items of income (matching).' Hence the accrual basis is deemed to be equivalent to the application of the matching principle.

The authors are doubtful whether treating the accrual basis as an assumption is either necessary or desirable: it is unnecessary to assume it, as the use of the accrual basis can be inferred from the overall objective (there are a number of American studies that demonstrate that accrual accounting provides better information for investors than cash accounting[5]); it is undesirable because the matching principle is inconsistent with the balance sheet approach to valuation and income measurement adopted by the IASB. This point is discussed more fully in Chapter 15.

Going concern

Paragraph 23 states: 'The financial statements are normally prepared on the assumption that the enterprise is a going concern and will continue in operation for the foreseeable future'. This assumption is of a rather different character from that relating to the accrual basis. Whereas the accrual basis assumption applies generally, the going concern assumption is a conditional assumption. It no longer applies when there are serious doubts about the continuity of the enterprise.

13.5 QUALITATIVE CHARACTERISTICS OF FINANCIAL STATEMENTS

Paragraphs 25–42 set out the qualitative characteristics of financial statements, that is they answer the question: 'what makes financial statements valuable to users?' They are not stated to be assumptions (as is the case with the two points mentioned in the previous section); hence they must have been derived from an analysis of users' needs – although this is not clear from the text. The qualitative characteristics are presented in diagrammatic form in Exhibit 13.2, which has been adapted from a similar diagram in the ASB's Framework. The significance of this analysis is that it provides the standard setter with criteria on which to base the choice between alternative accounting rules.

The qualitative characteristics will be discussed in the sequence that they are presented in this figure which differs from that used in the IASB's Framework.

13.5.1 Materiality

Materiality is a type of filter. It filters out information that need not be shown separately in the financial statements (but normally must be included aggregated with other information in order for the balance sheet to balance). Paragraph 30 states that information is material if its omission could influence the economic decisions of users. It also states that materiality depends on the size of the item. In the authors' opinion, this is incorrect since a very small item may be material. However this lapse is corrected in IAS 1 which states: 'Materiality depends on the size and nature of the item judged in the particular circumstances of its omission. . . . Depending on the circumstances, either the nature or the size of the item could be the determining factor' (in deciding materiality). The reference to nature makes it clear that materiality is not simply a question of size. For example a corporation's constitution may specify that each director should be paid an annual fee of €100 for his services. If, in a particular year, the corporation paid a director €150, that item of expense is material, even if it is only .001 per cent of turnover or profits, because one of the prime functions of accounts is to report on the directors' stewardship of the shareholders' funds and in particular whether there has been any breach of trust on the part of a director.

13.5.2 Relevance

Relevance is one of two primary qualities that make financial statements useful. The other is reliability. As indicated in Exhibit 13.2, having more of one of these qualities may mean less of the other – one of the fundamental facts of accounting life, which is discussed in section 13.6.

Paragraph 26 states: 'To be useful information must be relevant to the decision-making needs of users. Information has the quality of relevance when it influences the economic decisions of users by helping them evaluate past, present or future events or by confirming, or correcting, their past evaluations.' The stewardship function of financial reporting is covered principally by the confirmatory role of relevant information. If the accounts reveal that the directors have squandered the shareholders' funds, then presumably the shareholders will decide to dismiss them because their previous faith in the directors' ability has been shown to be incorrect.

However the emphasis is strongly on the predictive role of accounts.

295

Exhibit 13.2 *The qualitative characteristics of financial statements*

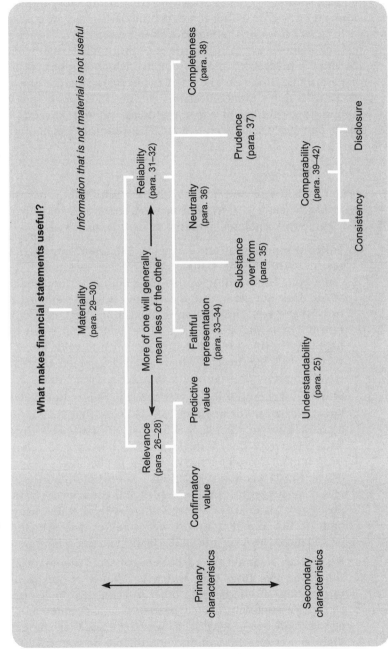

What makes financial statements useful?

Information that is not material is not useful

Primary characteristics

Secondary characteristics

Materiality (para. 29–30)

Relevance (para. 26–28)

Reliability (para. 31–32)

More of one will generally mean less of the other

Confirmatory value

Predictive value

Faithful representation (para. 33–34)

Substance over form (para. 35)

Neutrality (para. 36)

Prudence (para. 37)

Completeness (para. 38)

Understandability (para. 25)

Comparability (para. 39–42)

Consistency

Disclosure

Source: ASB, *Statement of Principles for Financial Reporting* (1999)

This reflects the investor orientation of the IASB's Framework and the modern theory of finance which holds that investors should make decisions on buying or selling shares on the basis of an enterprise's predicted cash flows. However the Framework does not explicitly state that information about future cash flows is relevant. In effect that would represent too great a break with present practice which emphasizes the reporting of past transactions on the basis of accruals and not the reporting of future cash flows. Hence it claims that, to have predictive value, information need not be in the form of an explicit forecast; information about past performance and financial position is frequently useful.

13.5.3　Reliability

Reliability is the second primary quality. 'Information has the quality of reliability when it is free from material error and bias' (paragraph 31). The Framework analyses five aspects of this quality:

(a) **Faithful representation:** Paragraph 33 states: 'information must represent faithfully the transaction or other events it . . . purports to represent'. The wording of this paragraph is tortuous but deliberately so. It does not state that the balance sheet should represent faithfully the assets and liabilities, but rather that it should represent faithfully the transactions and other events that result in assets and liabilities. In this way, the door is left open to value assets at historical cost – a balance sheet in which assets are valued at historical cost is clearly representing faithfully transactions that result in assets; it is much more doubtful that it represents faithfully the assets themselves.

(b) **Substance over form:** Paragraph 35 states that transactions must be accounted for 'in accordance with their substance and economic reality and not merely their legal form'. The reference to economic reality is presumably based on the inclusion in the objective (paragraph 12) of the words 'economic decisions'. The whole question of economic reality versus legal form is complex and controversial, since the legal position is also part of reality – there is legal reality as well as economic reality and it is by no means self-evident which should take precedence. However the IASB clearly favours economic reality.

(c) **Neutrality:** Neutrality is a far easier concept. The financial statements should be free from bias, which is defined as seeking to influence the making of a decision in order to achieve a predetermined result. Neutrality is closely related to a similar but rather more rigorously defined concept – objectivity, which means that the personality of the preparer of the accounts should have no influence on their contents. Financial statements are truly objective if two trained accountants when asked separately to prepare accounts on the basis of the same set of transactions, produce accounts that are not materially different. The IASB Framework does not mention this characteristic, possibly because of the appreciation that, in the present state of accounting practice, it cannot be achieved.

(d) **Prudence:** The need for prudence arises because of the uncertainty that inevitably is associated with the estimates required in drawing up accounts, for example the probability that a debt will prove uncollectible or that the future useful life of a machine will be ten years. Prudence is defined in paragraph 37 as 'the inclusion of a degree of caution in the exercise of the judgements needed in making the estimates required under conditions of uncertainty, such that assets or income are not overstated and liabilities or expenses are not understated'. Prudence is deliberately asymmetric: overstatement of liabilities/expenses is less blameworthy than overstatement of assets/income.

(e) **Completeness:** The financial statements must be complete. They should include all items whose omission would lead to the accounts being false or misleading. The concept seems to be very close to that of materiality; if the omission of an item leads to a different decision on the part of the user, then the accounts are not complete. IAS 1 expands the concept of completeness by prohibiting off-setting. Assets may not be off-set against liabilities; expenses should not be off-set against income.

There are two further qualitative characteristics which are somewhat less fundamental and, for this reason, are denoted in Exhibit 13.2 as secondary characteristics, although the Framework makes no such distinction. They are understandability and comparability.

(f) **Understandability:** This quality is self-evident. The accounts must be understood by the user if they are to have any value. However, it should be noted that the user is assumed to have a reasonable knowledge of business, of economic activities and of accounting, combined with a willingness to study the accounts with reasonable diligence (paragraph 25). In particular, the user is assumed to have a reasonable knowledge of accounting; this implies that it is the user who has to inform himself about accounting and not the accountant who has to adapt her practices to the circumstances of the user. This certainly makes the accountant's task easier. Cynics might comment that this reflects that the Framework was written by accountants, but it is probably inevitable, given the great variety of users.

(g) **Comparability:** Financial information is more useful if it is comparable, both over time (for example last year's profit may be compared with this year's profit) and between two entities at a point of time (for example the profits of enterprise X with those enterprise Y). Comparability is affected by the accounting policies adopted by the enterprise (that is the rules that it follows for the recognition, measurement and presentation of items in the accounts) and particularly by two characteristics of these accounting policies: consistency and disclosure.

(i) **Consistency:** For information to be comparable, it must be measured and presented consistently in three different ways: within the enterprise, over time for the enterprise and between enterprises. However consistency is a necessary but not a sufficient condition for comparability. For example two similar pharmaceutical enterprises may have each spent €100mn on research. With the first enterprise the research is successful – it develops a drug that is expected to be highly profitable. By contrast the second enterprise's research yields nothing of value. Both enterprises charge the entire research costs as an expense. They have applied consistent accounting policies but their accounts do not permit the two enterprises' positions to be compared in a meaningful way. In effect they are shown to be similar when in fact the first enterprise is in the better position. Hence to assure comparability further information is necessary.

(ii) **Disclosure:** In order for users to be able to compare financial statements, they must be informed of the accounting policies used in their preparation and particularly of any changes in these policies. Furthermore these policies should disclose all relevant information about the enterprise. Moreover it is helpful if this year's financial statements present information not only for the current period but also comparable information for previous periods.

13.6 CONSTRAINTS ON THE VALUE OF INFORMATION

There are certain features of the real world which limit the applicability of the qualitative characteristics presented in the previous section. Three are mentioned in the Framework.

Timeliness

In general, the sooner that users are informed about transactions and events, the more useful is the information. This applies to information used for stewardship purposes (if the directors are misappropriating the enterprise's funds, the shareholders would like to informed as quickly as possible so that they can act to limit the loss) and for investment purposes (it is desirable that the price of the enterprise's shares on the stock exchange should reflect the very latest information). However there is a clear relationship between the speed with which information is supplied and its reliability. Thus hasty work can lead to mistakes, as sometimes happen when enterprises cut corners in order to present their annual accounts as soon as possible after the year end. But a more pervasive problem in financial reporting is that many accounting figures are based on estimates of the future. In order to provide timely, relevant information, it may often be necessary to report before all aspects of a transaction are known, requiring that important matters are estimated. Often the degree of uncertainty attached to the estimate is reduced as more information becomes available with the passage of time. For example, when drawing up an enterprise's balance sheet at the end of the financial year, the accountant may be uncertain as to the value to be placed on an account receivable as she has doubts about the debtor's solvency. If she were to wait until the debtor either pays the account in full or is declared bankrupt, she would be able to present a balance sheet (for the year end) that would be highly reliable but not very relevant as it would deal with the position in the rather distant past.

Cost

Financial reporting is an economic activity and, in principle, in deciding how much effort to expend on it, the costs should be compared with the benefits. It is self-evident that financial statements can be made more reliable and more timely by allocating more resources to their preparation, at least within a certain range. The same considerations often apply to making the accounts more relevant; certainly many of the proposals in this area involve significant costs. However there is a major problem in comparing costs and benefits: the costs are incurred by the enterprise and the benefits enjoyed by the users. In theory an enterprise should allocate additional resources to its financial reporting until, at the margin, the extra benefit received by users is equal to the extra cost incurred by the enterprise. However this procedure cannot be applied in practice. Hence the consideration that a proper balance should be struck between costs and benefits is not a matter for preparers and users. Rather it is a matter that has to be considered by the standard setter, acting in the best interests of society as a whole.

Balance between qualitative characteristics

Mention has already been made of the need for a balance between costs and benefits and between the timeliness and the reliability of information. However, this need to balance or trade-off one characteristic against another is much more pervasive; in fact there appears to be a general rule that if excessive weight is given to any one characteristic, this will have a negative impact on others. Further examples are:

(a) **Relevance versus consistency.** In order to produce more relevant financial statements, it may be necessary to change an enterprise's accounting policies which would mean that the accounts are no longer comparable with those of previous years.

(b) **Relevance versus prudence.** One aspect of the conflict between relevance and reliability has already been considered in relation to the timeliness of information. Another aspect is the conflict between relevance and prudence (a constituent quality of reliability). Many commentators claim that the needs of users are best served by providing them with unbiassed information, and not with information that has been preprocessed in the name of prudence so as to report assets at less than their most likely value. According to the modern theory of finance, investors need information on expected (or average) values not on the most pessimistic values.

(c) **Prudence versus consistency.** In many situations, it is impossible to be both consistent and prudent. An example is an enterprise, which in order to be prudent places a relatively low estimate on the expected life of a fixed asset. In the early years of the asset's life, profits tend to be stated prudently, because of the high depreciation charge. However, in the later years of the asset's life, the reverse is the case; there is no depreciation charged in the income statement (because the assets has been fully written off) and hence profits are overstated.

All the qualitative characteristics analysed in this section are desirable and the standard setter would like to ensure that all are fully achieved. However this is impossible because of the fundamental constraint (rather similar to the law of diminishing returns in economics) that securing a higher level of achievement with respect to one qualitative characteristic inevitably leads to a lower level of achievement with respect to another. The conflict between the various qualitative characteristics greatly complicates the task of the standard setter and part of the art of standard setting is to achieve the right balance. The fundamental conflict is between relevance and reliability; accountants would like financial statements to be both highly relevant and absolutely reliable. However the harsh reality of life is, as stated in Exhibit 13.2, 'more of one will generally mean less of the other'.

13.7 THE ELEMENTS OF FINANCIAL STATEMENTS

The basic financial statements are the balance sheet and the income statement. The elements of these statements are (for the balance sheet) assets, liabilities and equity and (for the income statement) income and expenses. In order for an item to be reported in the balance sheet or the income statement, it must meet three conditions:

■ **Definition:** it must meet the definition of one of the above five elements

■ **Recognition:** it must satisfy the recognition criteria

■ **Measurement:** the item must be stated in monetary terms in accordance with an accepted measurement method

Exhibit 13.3 presents these three conditions in the form of a flow chart. An item must pass all three tests before it is reported as an element of the balance sheet or the income statement.

Exhibit 13.3 *The three conditions for reporting an element of the financial statements*

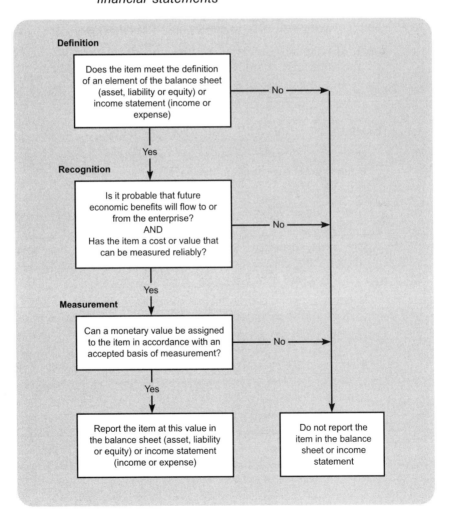

13.7.1 Definition

The Framework's definitions of the five elements are set out in Exhibit 13.4. Almost a third of the Framework's text (35 of the 110 paragraphs) are given over to an exposition of these definitions. To a great extent, the individual IASs are based on these definitions, as will become apparent when certain IASs are considered in later chapters. Hence the discussion here is rather brief as it will be greatly expanded in these later chapters, notably Chapter 15 (assets), Chapter 16 (liabilities and equity) and Chapter 17 (income and expenses).

Assets

The definition given in Exhibit 13.4 sets three conditions for an item to be reported as an asset in the financial statements:

(a) **It should be controlled by the enterprise.** It is not necessary that the enterprise should be the legal owner (see the discussion on 'substance over form' in section 13.2.4). It is not even necessary that the enterprise has a legally recognized right to use the asset; thus an

Exhibit 13.4 *The IASB Framework definitions*

Balance sheet elements (paragraph 49)

■ An asset is a resource controlled by the enterprise as a result of past events and from which future economic benefits are expected to flow to the enterprise

■ A liability is a present obligation of the enterprise arising from past events, the settlement of which is expected to result in an outflow from the enterprise of resources embodying economic benefits

■ Equity is the residual interest in the assets of the enterprise after deducting all its liabilities

Income statement elements (paragraph 70)

■ Income is the increases in economic benefits during the accounting period in the form of inflows or enhancements of assets or decreases of liabilities that result in increases in equity, other than those relating to contributions from equity participants.

■ Expenses are decreases in economic benefits during the accounting period in the form of outflows or depletions of assets or incurrences of liabilities that result in decreases in equity, other than those relating to distributions to equity participants.

unpatented invention may be an asset, particularly when the enterprise keeps the details secret (paragraph 58).

(b) **Future economic benefits should flow to the enterprise.** This is in line with the value of an asset according to economic theory as the present value of future cash flows. However it is important to appreciate that, with its definition, the IASB is not prejudging the question of whether assets should be valued on the basis of future economic benefits. Conceptually, measurement is a separate process from that of meeting the definition.

(c) **There has to be a past event or transaction.** This condition is puzzling as one cannot imagine any 'asset' which accountants would consider recognizing which is not connected in some way with a past event. It has been suggested that this condition is necessary to prevent mere intentions giving rise to assets, for example the intention of an enterprise to buy goods does not of itself make the goods an asset of the enterprise.

Liabilities

The definition of a liability (given in Exhibit 13.4) is exactly analogous to that of an asset; a liability is essentially a negative asset. The above remarks relating to 'economic benefits' and 'past events' apply *mutatis mutandis* also to liabilities. The concept of present obligation replaces that of control.

Equity

'Equity is the residual interest in the assets of the enterprise after deducting all its liabilities' (paragraph 49(c)). The definition of equity reflects the conventional balance sheet equation:

$$\text{Capital} = \text{Assets} - \text{Liabilities}$$

Income

Income is defined as increases in assets or decreases in liabilities. The Framework is clearly adopting a balance sheet approach; the balance sheet, not the income statement, is the fundamental financial statement on which all the others depend.

Expenses

Expenses are defined in an exactly analogous way to income; in effect they are negative income.

13.7.2　Recognition

The concept of recognition relates to the question of whether an item should be included in the financial statements. An item that meets the definition of asset, liability, income or expense should only be reported in the financial statements if it also satisfies the criteria for recognition as set out in paragraph 83, which states:

> An item that meets the definition of an element should be recognized if:
>
> (a) it is probable that future economic benefits will flow to or from the enterprise
> (b) the item has a cost or value that can be measured with reliability.

In effect, this paragraph adds two new hurdles that must be cleared before an item may appear in the financial statements; they are related to the concepts of probability and reliability.

Probability of future economic benefits

The concept of probability relates to the uncertainty surrounding the environment in which the enterprise operates and particularly to the difficulty of forecasting the future. It is a necessary condition for the recognition of assets that the future economic benefits should be probable. In everyday speech, the term probable is often used to mean 'more likely than not' which implies that it is to be applied to any event with a probability of more than 50 per cent, but this interpretation is not confirmed in the Framework which offers no definition of 'probable'. In particular there is no suggestion that a different (higher) level of probability is necessary for the recognition of assets than for liabilities, as the concept of prudence would seem to demand. Thus the Framework can be criticized for a lack of internal consistency; the recognition criteria are not consistent with the qualitative characteristics.

In the case of certain items of income or expense, the inflow or outflow of economic benefits has already occurred and hence the assessment of the probability is trivial; examples are wages paid in cash and cash sales. Generally an item of income and expense is recognized when the increase or decrease in the corresponding asset or liability is recognized.

Reliability of measurement

By including reliability of measurement as a recognition criteria, the Framework is in effect making the qualitative characteristic of reliability a necessary condition for the inclusion of an item in the financial statements. Note that the other recognition test (the probability of future economic benefits) relates to the qualitative characteristic of relevance.

13.7.3 Measurement

Measurement is the process whereby a monetary amount is assigned to an item that meets both the definition of an element and the recognition criteria. The Framework sets out a list of possible measurement bases, including historical cost, current cost, realizable value and present value. This list is not exhaustive as is made clear by the word 'including'. In effect on the crucial question of measurement, the IASB sets on the fence, at least in its Framework if not in its standards. The Framework's treatment of the important subject of measurement is quite inadequate. Only one page of the Framework's 30 pages is devoted to the subject. The analysis is entirely descriptive and no conclusion is reached.

13.7.4 Concepts of capital maintenance

The last nine paragraphs of the Framework set out two alternative models of capital maintenance: financial capital maintenance and physical capital maintenance. The discussion is interesting but the relationship with the rest of the Framework is unclear. No conclusion is reached.

13.8 EVALUATION OF THE IASB's FRAMEWORK

The reader will have noticed that, in the foregoing analysis of the Framework, over nine tenths of the space is taken up with a consideration of the objectives of financial statements, their qualitative characteristics and the definition of their elements. Important subjects such as measurement and concepts of capital maintenance are dealt with much more briefly. This reflects the relative weight given to these topics in the Framework's text. Towards the end of the Framework the treatment of the subject becomes increasingly superficial and sketchy, with no definite conclusions being presented. Less than one eighth of the Framework's text is given over to the important subjects of measurement and capital maintenance, a far lower proportion than in most serious accounting textbooks.

One has the strong impression that the Framework's authors were very happy to deal with a topic in depth and commit themselves to definite statements, as long as the topic was theoretical and had little impact on accounting practice. The structure of the Framework is that first the basic objectives and fundamental principles are established; the Framework deals with these matters in great detail. Subsequently the rules for drawing up financial statements in practice are set. In the later sections, when the Framework's authors come to deal with the topics that have a direct influence on the practical task of preparing financial statements, they back away from committing themselves to anything. This stage was reached with the section on measurement. If the Framework had expressed a definite opinion either for or against a particular measurement base (for example it excluded historical cost on the grounds of its lack of relevance), this would have had immediate practical implications for all accountants. Probably the IASB was unable to reach a consensus on any topic that had a direct impact on practice. Hence the final two sections, on measurement and capital maintenance, are bland and non-committal. The document's final sentences encapsulate the Framework's weak and ineffective conclusions: 'At the present time, it is not the intention of the IASB to prescribe a particular model other than in exceptional circumstances. This intention will, however, be reviewed in the light of world developments'.

A rather similar criticism has been levied at the authors of the FASB's conceptual framework. In this case, the criticism is that the FASB's statement No. 5 on recognition and measurement simply reproduces conventional accounting practice and is not logically derived from the more radical concepts developed in the earlier statements, such as those on objectives and qualitative characteristics (Bromwich, 1992, p. 293). The IASB cannot be criticized on this score. It did not opt for conventional practice in relation to measurement and capital maintenance; it simply made no choice.

This does not mean that the Framework is of no value. In the authors' opinion, it assists the IASB in its task of developing standards in three significant ways:

- In formulating the objectives of financial statements, the Framework gives the IASB an overall objective for its work
- In setting out the desirable qualitative characteristics of financial statements, the Framework provides the IASB with a rational basis for choosing between alternatives
- In defining the elements of financial statements, the Framework greatly facilitates the IASB's task of framing standards that are clear, comprehensible and consistent

SUMMARY

The characteristics and benefits of conceptual frameworks in general were discussed. The IASB's *Framework for the Preparation and Presentation of Financial Statements* was examined with the aim of finding out the principles that the IASB follows in developing its standards. It was noted that this document dealt very fully with the objectives of financial statements, their qualitative characteristics and the definition of the elements, but treated the question of measurement in an inadequate fashion. Nevertheless the Framework was judged to be a useful document.

Review questions

1. Why did the IASB consider it worthwhile to prepare and publish its Framework for the preparation and presentation of financial statements? What functions does this document perform?

2. What category of user did the IASB have principally in mind when it drew up its Framework?

3. According to the Framework, what are the objectives of financial statements?

4. What are the principal qualitative characteristics of financial statements? Give examples of conflicts between these qualitative characteristics?

5. What is meant by the term 'recognition'?

6. Make your own evaluation of the usefulness of the Framework.

Notes

1. The Framework was developed by the IASC but was adopted by the IASB when it took office in April 2001. The IASB's website refers to it as the IASB's Framework [sic] and in quoting from the Framework's text substitutes 'IASB' for 'IASC' which appears in the original. The authors have made a similar modification in the reproduction of the Framework's text that is annexed to this chapter.
2. All paragraph references are to the text of the Framework.
3. The IASC seems to use the term 'investors' as meaning 'shareholders' since, in paragraph 9, it refers to lenders as being different from investors.

4. The IASC's position is similar to that of the FASB. It states 'the economic decisions that are taken by users of financial statements require an evaluation of the ability of the enterprise to generate cash and cash equivalents and of the timing and certainty of their generation' (paragraph 15). However the IASC does not use this as a justification for assuming that the information needs of other users are largely similar to those of investors.
5. This point is discussed further when the cash flow statement is considered in Chapter 18.

References

ASB *Statement of Principles for Financial Reporting*, ASB Publications, Milton Keynes (1999).

Bromwich, M *Financial Reporting, Information and Capital Markets*, Pitman Publishing, London (1992).

CICA *Corporate Reporting: Its Future Evolution*, Canadian Institute of Chartered Accountants, Ontario (1980).

FASB *Statement of Financial Accounting Concepts No. 1: objectives of financial statements.* Financial Accounting Standards Board, Norwalk (1978).

FASB *Statement of Financial Accounting Concepts No. 2: qualitative characteristics of accounting information*, Financial Accounting Standards Board, Norwalk (1980).

FASB *Statement of Financial Accounting Concepts No.5: recognition and measurement in financial statements*, Financial Accounting Standards Board, Norwalk (1984).

FASB *Statement of Financial Accounting Concepts No. 6: elements of financial statements*, Financial Accounting Standards Board, Norwalk (1985).

FASB *Statement of Financial Accounting Concepts No. 7: using cash-flow information in accounting measurements*, Financial Accounting Standards Board, Norwalk (2000).

Gore, P *The FASB Conceptual Framework Project*, Manchester University Press, Manchester (1992).

Macve, RH *The FASB's Conceptual Framework: vision, tool or threat?*, Garland, New York (1997).

Miller, P, Redding, R and Bahnson, P *The FASB: the people, the process and the politics*, Irwin/McGraw-Hill (1998).

Moonitz, M *The Basic Postulates of Accounting*, AICPA (1961).

Peasnell, K 'The function of a conceptual framework for corporate financial reporting', *Accounting and Business Research*, **12** (Autumn 1982), pp. 243–56.

Solomons, D *Making Accounting Policy*, Oxford University Press, Oxford (1986).

Sprouse, RT and Moonitz M *A Tentative Set of Broad Accounting Principles for Business Enterprises*, AICPA (1962).

Further reading

It is strongly recommended to read carefully the text of the Framework as it is always a valuable exercise to study the text of an original document. For conceptual frameworks in general, see Chapter 12 of Bromwich (1992), Macve (1997) and Gore (1992). For an analysis of the FASB's framework, see Miller, Redding and Bahnson (1998). For a fuller discussion of the qualitative characteristics of financial statements, see ASB (1999), which is more succinct and comprehensible than FASB (1980).

The IASB's Framework for the Preparation and Presentation of Financial Statements

This annex sets out the complete text of the Framework with the exception of the preface.

INTRODUCTION

Purpose and status

1. This framework sets out the concepts that underlie the preparation and presentation of financial statements for external users. The purpose of the framework is to:

   (a) assist the IASB in the development of future International Accounting Standards and in its review of existing International Accounting Standards.

   (b) assist the IASB in promoting harmonization of regulations, accounting standards and procedures relating to the presentation of financial statements by providing a basis for reducing the number of alternative accounting treatments permitted by International Accounting Standards.

   (c) assist national standard-setting bodies in developing national standards.

   (d) assist preparers of financial statements in applying International Accounting Standards and in dealing with topics that have yet to form the subject of an International Accounting Standard.

   (e) assist auditors in forming an opinion as to whether financial statements conform with International Accounting Standards.

   (f) assist users of financial statements in interpreting the information contained in financial statements prepared in conformity with International Accounting Standards.

(g) provide those who are interested in the work of IASB with information about its approach to the formulation of International Accounting Standards.

2. This framework is not an International Accounting Standard and hence does not define standards for any particular measurement or disclosure issue. Nothing in this framework overrides any specific International Accounting Standard.

3. The IASB recognizes that in a limited number of cases there may be a conflict between the framework and an International Accounting Standard. In those cases where there is a conflict, the requirements of the International Accounting Standard prevail over those of the framework. As, however, the IASB will be guided by the framework in the development of future Standards and in its review of existing Standards, the number of cases of conflict between the framework and International Accounting Standards will diminish through time.

4. The framework will be revised from time to time on the basis of the IASB's experience of working with it.

Scope

5. The framework deals with:
   (a) the objective of financial statements;
   (b) the qualitative characteristics that determine the usefulness of information in financial statements;
   (c) the definition, recognition and measurement of the elements from which financial statements are constructed; and
   (d) concepts of capital and capital maintenance.

6. The framework is concerned with general purpose financial statements (hereafter referred to as 'financial statements') including consolidated financial statements. Such financial statements are prepared and presented at least annually and are directed toward the common information needs of a wide range of users. Some of these users may require, and have the power to obtain, information in addition to that contained in the financial statements. Many users, however, have to rely on the financial statements as their major source of financial information and such financial statements should, therefore, be prepared and presented with their needs in view. Special purpose financial reports, for example, prospectuses and computations prepared for taxation purposes, are outside the scope of this framework. Nevertheless, the framework may be applied in the preparation of such special purpose reports where their requirements permit.

7. Financial statements form part of the process of financial reporting. A complete set of financial statements normally includes a balance sheet, an income statement, a statement of changes in financial position (which may be presented in a variety of ways, for example, as a statement of cash flows or a statement of funds flow), and those notes and other statements and explanatory material that are an integral part of the financial statements. They may also include supplementary schedules and information based on or derived from, and expected to be read with, such statements. Such schedules and supplementary information may deal, for example, with financial information

about industrial and geographical segments and disclosures about the effects of changing prices. Financial statements do not, however, include such items as reports by directors, statements by the chairman, discussion and analysis by management and similar items that may be included in a financial or annual report.

8. The framework applies to the financial statements of all commercial, industrial and business reporting enterprises, whether in the public or the private sectors. A reporting enterprise is an enterprise for which there are users who rely on the financial statements as their major source of financial information about the enterprise.

USERS AND THEIR INFORMATION NEEDS

9. The users of financial statements include present and potential investors, employees, lenders, suppliers and other trade creditors, customers, governments and their agencies and the public. They use financial statements in order to satisfy some of their different needs for information. These needs include the following:

   (a) **Investors.** The providers of risk capital and their advisers are concerned with the risk inherent in, and return provided by, their investments. They need information to help them determine whether they should buy, hold or sell. Shareholders are also interested in information which enables them to assess the ability of the enterprise to pay dividends.

   (b) **Employees.** Employees and their representative groups are interested in information about the stability and profitability of their employers. They are also interested in information which enables them to assess the ability of the enterprise to provide remuneration, retirement benefits and employment opportunities.

   (c) **Lenders.** Lenders are interested in information that enables them to determine whether their loans, and the interest attaching to them, will be paid when due.

   (d) **Suppliers and other trade creditors.** Suppliers and other creditors are interested in information that enables them to determine whether amounts owing to them will be paid when due. Trade creditors are likely to be interested in an enterprise over a shorter period than lenders unless they are dependent upon the continuation of the enterprise as a major customer.

   (e) **Customers.** Customers have an interest in information about the continuance of an enterprise, especially when they have a long-term involvement with, or are dependent on, the enterprise.

   (f) **Governments and their agencies.** Governments and their agencies are interested in the allocation of resources and, therefore, the activities of enterprises. They also require information in order to regulate the activities of enterprises, determine taxation policies and as the basis for national income and similar statistics.

   (g) **Public.** Enterprises affect members of the public in a variety of ways. For example, enterprises may make a substantial contribution to the local economy in many ways including the number of people they employ and their patronage of local suppliers. Financial statements may assist the public by providing information about the trends and recent developments in the prosperity of the enterprise and the range of its activities.

10. While all of the information needs of these users cannot be met by financial statements, there are needs which are common to all users. As investors are providers of risk capital to the enterprise, the provision of financial statements that meet their needs will also meet most of the needs of other users that financial statements can satisfy.

11. The management of an enterprise has the primary responsibility for the preparation and presentation of the financial statements of the enterprise. Management is also interested in the information contained in the financial statements even though it has access to additional management and financial information that helps it carry out its planning, decision-making and control responsibilities. Management has the ability to determine the form and content of such additional information in order to meet its own needs. The reporting of such information, however, is beyond the scope of this framework. Nevertheless, published financial statements are based on the information used by management about the financial position, performance and changes in financial position of the enterprise.

THE OBJECTIVE OF FINANCIAL STATEMENTS

12. The objective of financial statements is to provide information about the financial position, performance and changes in financial position of an enterprise that is useful to a wide range of users in making economic decisions.

13. Financial statements prepared for this purpose meet the common needs of most users. However, financial statements do not provide all the information that users may need to make economic decisions since they largely portray the financial effects of past events and do not necessarily provide non-financial information.

14. Financial statements also show the results of the stewardship of management, or the accountability of management for the resources entrusted to it. Those users who wish to assess the stewardship or accountability of management do so in order that they may make economic decisions; these decisions may include, for example, whether to hold or sell their investment in the enterprise or whether to reappoint or replace the management.

FINANCIAL POSITION, PERFORMANCE AND CHANGES IN FINANCIAL POSITION

15. The economic decisions that are taken by users of financial statements require an evaluation of the ability of an enterprise to generate cash and cash equivalents and of the timing and certainty of their generation. This ability ultimately determines, for example, the capacity of an enterprise to pay its employees

and suppliers, meet interest payments, repay loans and make distributions to its owners. Users are better able to evaluate this ability to generate cash and cash equivalents if they are provided with information that focuses on the financial position, performance and changes in financial position of an enterprise.

16. The financial position of an enterprise is affected by the economic resources it controls, its financial structure, its liquidity and solvency, and its capacity to adapt to changes in the environment in which it operates. Information about the economic resources controlled by the enterprise and its capacity in the past to modify these resources is useful in predicting the ability of the enterprise to generate cash and cash equivalents in the future. Information about financial structure is useful in predicting future borrowing needs and how future profits and cash flows will be distributed among those with an interest in the enterprise; it is also useful in predicting how successful the enterprise is likely to be in raising further finance. Information about liquidity and solvency is useful in predicting the ability of the enterprise to meet its financial commitments as they fall due. Liquidity refers to the availability of cash in the near future after taking account of financial commitments over this period. Solvency refers to the availability of cash over the longer term to meet financial commitments as they fall due.

17. Information about the performance of an enterprise, in particular its profitability, is required in order to assess potential changes in the economic resources that it is likely to control in the future. Information about variability of performance is important in this respect. Information about performance is useful in predicting the capacity of the enterprise to generate cash flows from its existing resource base. It is also useful in forming judgements about the effectiveness with which the enterprise might employ additional resources.

18. Information concerning changes in the financial position of an enterprise is useful in order to assess its investing, financing and operating activities during the reporting period. This information is useful in providing the user with a basis to assess the ability of the enterprise to generate cash and cash equivalents and the needs of the enterprise to utilize those cash flows. In constructing a statement of changes in financial position, funds can be defined in various ways, such as all financial resources, working capital, liquid assets or cash. No attempt is made in this framework to specify a definition of funds.

19. Information about financial position is primarily provided in a balance sheet. Information about performance is primarily provided in an income statement. Information about changes in financial position is provided in the financial statements by means of a separate statement.

20. The component parts of the financial statements interrelate because they reflect different aspects of the same transactions or other events. Although each statement provides information that is different from the others, none is likely to serve only a single purpose or provide all the information necessary for particular needs of users. For example, an income statement provides an incomplete picture of performance unless it is used in conjunction with the balance sheet and the statement of changes in financial position.

Notes and supplementary schedules

21. The financial statements also contain notes and supplementary schedules and other information. For example, they may contain additional information that is relevant to the needs of users about the items in the balance sheet and income statement. They may include disclosures about the risks and uncertainties affecting the enterprise and any resources and obligations not recognized in the balance sheet (such as mineral reserves). Information about geographical and industry segments and the effect on the enterprise of changing prices may also be provided in the form of supplementary information.

UNDERLYING ASSUMPTIONS

Accrual basis

22. In order to meet their objectives, financial statements are prepared on the accrual basis of accounting. Under this basis, the effects of transactions and other events are recognized when they occur (and not as cash or its equivalent is received or paid) and they are recorded in the accounting records and reported in the financial statements of the periods to which they relate. Financial statements prepared on the accrual basis inform users not only of past transactions involving the payment and receipt of cash but also of obligations to pay cash in the future and of resources that represent cash to be received in the future. Hence, they provide the type of information about past transactions and other events that is most useful to users in making economic decisions.

Going concern

23. The financial statements are normally prepared on the assumption that an enterprise is a going concern and will continue in operation for the foreseeable future. Hence, it is assumed that the enterprise has neither the intention nor the need to liquidate or curtail materially the scale of its operations; if such an intention or need exists, the financial statements may have to be prepared on a different basis and, if so, the basis used is disclosed.

QUALITATIVE CHARACTERISTICS OF FINANCIAL STATEMENTS

24. Qualitative characteristics are the attributes that make the information provided in financial statements useful to users. The four principal qualitative characteristics are understandability, relevance, reliability and comparability.

Understandability

25. An essential quality of the information provided in financial statements is that it is readily understandable by users. For this purpose, users are assumed to have a reasonable knowledge of business and economic activities and accounting and a willingness to study the information with reasonable diligence. However, information about complex matters that should be included in the financial statements because of its relevance to the economic decision-making needs of users should not be excluded merely on the grounds that it may be too difficult for certain users to understand.

Relevance

26. To be useful, information must be relevant to the decision-making needs of users. Information has the quality of relevance when it influences the economic decisions of users by helping them evaluate past, present or future events or confirming, or correcting, their past evaluations.
27. The predictive and confirmatory roles of information are interrelated. For example, information about the current level and structure of asset holdings has value to users when they endeavour to predict the ability of the enterprise to take advantage of opportunities and its ability to react to adverse situations. The same information plays a confirmatory role in respect of past predictions about, for example, the way in which the enterprise would be structured or the outcome of planned operations.
28. Information about financial position and past performance is frequently used as the basis for predicting future financial position and performance and other matters in which users are directly interested, such as dividend and wage payments, security price movements and the ability of the enterprise to meet its commitments as they fall due. To have predictive value, information need not be in the form of an explicit forecast. The ability to make predictions from financial statements is enhanced, however, by the manner in which information on past transactions and events is displayed. For example, the predictive value of the income statement is enhanced if unusual, abnormal and infrequent items of income or expense are separately disclosed.

Materiality

29. The relevance of information is affected by its nature and materiality. In some cases, the nature of information alone is sufficient to determine its relevance. For example, the reporting of a new segment may affect the assessment of the risks and opportunities facing the enterprise irrespective of the materiality of the results achieved by the new segment in the reporting period. In other cases, both the nature and materiality are important, for example, the amounts of inventories held in each of the main categories that are appropriate to the business.
30. Information is material if its omission or misstatement could influence the economic decisions of users taken on the basis of the financial statements. Materiality depends on the size of the item or error judged in the particular

circumstances of its omission or misstatement. Thus, materiality provides a threshold or cut-off point rather than being a primary qualitative characteristic which information must have if it is to be useful.

Reliability

31. To be useful, information must also be reliable. Information has the quality of reliability when it is free from material error and bias and can be depended upon by users to represent faithfully that which it either purports to represent or could reasonably be expected to represent.
32. Information may be relevant but so unreliable in nature or representation that its recognition may be potentially misleading. For example, if the validity and amount of a claim for damages under a legal action are disputed, it may be inappropriate for the enterprise to recognize the full amount of the claim in the balance sheet, although it may be appropriate to disclose the amount and circumstances of the claim.

Faithful representation

33. To be reliable, information must represent faithfully the transactions and other events it either purports to represent or could reasonably be expected to represent. Thus, for example, a balance sheet should represent faithfully the transactions and other events that result in assets, liabilities and equity of the enterprise at the reporting date which meet the recognition criteria.
34. Most financial information is subject to some risk of being less than a faithful representation of that which it purports to portray. This is not due to bias, but rather to inherent difficulties either in identifying the transactions and other events to be measured or in devising and applying measurement and presentation techniques that can convey messages that correspond with those transactions and events. In certain cases, the measurement of the financial effects of items could be so uncertain that enterprises generally would not recognize them in the financial statements; for example, although most enterprises generate goodwill internally over time, it is usually difficult to identify or measure that goodwill reliably. In other cases, however, it may be relevant to recognize items and to disclose the risk of error surrounding their recognition and measurement.

Substance over form

35. If information is to represent faithfully the transactions and other events that it purports to represent, it is necessary that they are accounted for and presented in accordance with their substance and economic reality and not merely their legal form. The substance of transactions or other events is not always consistent with that which is apparent from their legal or contrived form. For example, an enterprise may dispose of an asset to another party in such a way that the documentation purports to pass legal ownership to that party; nevertheless, agreements may exist that ensure that the enterprise

continues to enjoy the future economic benefits embodied in the asset. In such circumstances, the reporting of a sale would not represent faithfully the transaction entered into (if indeed there was a transaction).

Neutrality

36. To be reliable, the information contained in financial statements must be neutral, that is, free from bias. Financial statements are not neutral if, by the selection or presentation of information, they influence the making of a decision or judgement in order to achieve a predetermined result or outcome.

Prudence

37. The preparers of financial statements do, however, have to contend with the uncertainties that inevitably surround many events and circumstances, such as the collectability of doubtful receivables, the probable useful life of plant and equipment and the number of warranty claims that may occur. Such uncertainties are recognized by the disclosure of their nature and extent and by the exercise of prudence in the preparation of the financial statements. Prudence is the inclusion of a degree of caution in the exercise of the judgements needed in making the estimates required under conditions of uncertainty, such that assets or income are not overstated and liabilities or expenses are not understated. However, the exercise of prudence does not allow, for example, the creation of hidden reserves or excessive provisions, the deliberate understatement of assets or income, or the deliberate overstatement of liabilities or expenses, because the financial statements would not be neutral and, therefore, not have the quality of reliability.

Completeness

38. To be reliable, the information in financial statements must be complete within the bounds of materiality and cost. An omission can cause information to be false or misleading and thus unreliable and deficient in terms of its relevance.

Comparability

39. Users must be able to compare the financial statements of an enterprise through time in order to identify trends in its financial position and performance. Users must also be able to compare the financial statements of different enterprises in order to evaluate their relative financial position, performance and changes in financial position. Hence, the measurement and display of the financial effect of like transactions and other events must be carried out in a consistent way throughout an enterprise and over time for that enterprise and in a consistent way for different enterprises.

40. An important implication of the qualitative characteristic of comparability is that users be informed of the accounting policies employed in the preparation of the financial statements, any changes in those policies and the effects of such changes. Users need to be able to identify differences between the accounting policies for like transactions and other events used by the same enterprise from period to period and by different enterprises. Compliance with International Accounting Standards, including the disclosure of the accounting policies used by the enterprise, helps to achieve comparability.

41. The need for comparability should not be confused with mere uniformity and should not be allowed to become an impediment to the introduction of improved accounting standards. It is not appropriate for an enterprise to continue accounting in the same manner for a transaction or other event if the policy adopted is not in keeping with the qualitative characteristics of relevance and reliability. It is also inappropriate for an enterprise to leave its accounting policies unchanged when more relevant and reliable alternatives exist.

42. Because users wish to compare the financial position, performance and changes in financial position of an enterprise over time, it is important that the financial statements show corresponding information for the preceding periods.

CONSTRAINTS ON RELEVANT AND RELIABLE INFORMATION

Timeliness

43. If there is undue delay in the reporting of information it may lose its relevance. Management may need to balance the relative merits of timely reporting and the provision of reliable information. To provide information on a timely basis it may often be necessary to report before all aspects of a transaction or other event are known, thus impairing reliability. Conversely, if reporting is delayed until all aspects are known, the information may be highly reliable but of little use to users who have had to make decisions in the interim. In achieving a balance between relevance and reliability, the overriding consideration is how best to satisfy the economic decision-making needs of users.

Balance between benefit and cost

44. The balance between benefit and cost is a pervasive constraint rather than a qualitative characteristic. The benefits derived from information should exceed the cost of providing it. The evaluation of benefits and costs is, however, substantially a judgmental process. Furthermore, the costs do not necessarily fall on those users who enjoy the benefits. Benefits may also be enjoyed by users other than those for whom the information is prepared; for example, the provision of further information to lenders may reduce the borrowing costs of an enterprise. For these reasons, it is difficult to apply a cost-benefit test in any particular case. Nevertheless, standard-setters in particular, as

well as the preparers and users of financial statements, should be aware of this constraint.

Balance between qualitative characteristics

45. In practice a balancing, or trade-off, between qualitative characteristics is often necessary. Generally the aim is to achieve an appropriate balance among the characteristics in order to meet the objective of financial statements. The relative importance of the characteristics in different cases is a matter of professional judgment.

True and fair view/fair presentation

46. Financial statements are frequently described as showing a true and fair view of, or as presenting fairly, the financial position, performance and changes in financial position of an enterprise. Although this framework does not deal directly with such concepts, the application of the principal qualitative characteristics and of appropriate accounting standards normally results in financial statements that convey what is generally understood as a true and fair view of, or as presenting fairly such information.

THE ELEMENTS OF FINANCIAL STATEMENTS

47. Financial statements portray the financial effects of transactions and other events by grouping them into broad classes according to their economic characteristics. These broad classes are termed the elements of financial statements. The elements directly related to the measurement of financial position in the balance sheet are assets, liabilities and equity. The elements directly related to the measurement of performance in the income statement are income and expenses. The statement of changes in financial position usually reflects income statement elements and changes in balance sheet elements; accordingly, this framework identifies no elements that are unique to this statement.

48. The presentation of these elements in the balance sheet and the income statement involves a process of sub-classification. For example, assets and liabilities may be classified by their nature or function in the business of the enterprise in order to display information in the manner most useful to users for purposes of making economic decisions.

Financial position

49. The elements directly related to the measurement of financial position are assets, liabilities and equity. These are defined as follows:
   (a) An asset is a resource controlled by the enterprise as a result of past events and from which future economic benefits are expected to flow to the enterprise.

(b) A liability is a present obligation of the enterprise arising from past events, the settlement of which is expected to result in an outflow from the enterprise of resources embodying economic benefits.

(c) Equity is the residual interest in the assets of the enterprise after deducting all its liabilities.

50. The definitions of an asset and a liability identify their essential features but do not attempt to specify the criteria that need to be met before they are recognized in the balance sheet. Thus, the definitions embrace items that are not recognized as assets or liabilities in the balance sheet because they do not satisfy the criteria for recognition discussed in paragraphs 82 to 98. In particular, the expectation that future economic benefits will flow to or from an enterprise must be sufficiently certain to meet the probability criterion in paragraph 83 before an asset or liability is recognized.

51. In assessing whether an item meets the definition of an asset, liability or equity, attention needs to be given to its underlying substance and economic reality and not merely its legal form. Thus, for example, in the case of finance leases, the substance and economic reality are that the lessee acquires the economic benefits of the use of the leased asset for the major part of its useful life in return for entering into an obligation to pay for that right an amount approximating to the fair value of the asset and the related finance charge. Hence, the finance lease gives rise to items that satisfy the definition of an asset and a liability and are recognized as such in the lessee's balance sheet.

52. Balance sheets drawn up in accordance with current International Accounting Standards may include items that do not satisfy the definitions of an asset or liability and are not shown as part of equity. The definitions set out in paragraph 49 will, however, underlie future reviews of existing International Accounting Standards and the formulation of further Standards.

Assets

53. The future economic benefit embodied in an asset is the potential to contribute, directly or indirectly, to the flow of cash and cash equivalents to the enterprise. The potential may be a productive one that is part of the operating activities of the enterprise. It may also take the form of convertibility into cash or cash equivalents or a capability to reduce cash outflows, such as when an alternative manufacturing process lowers the costs of production.

54. An enterprise usually employs its assets to produce goods or services capable of satisfying the wants or needs of customers; because these goods or services can satisfy these wants or needs, customers are prepared to pay for them and hence contribute to the cash flow of the enterprise. Cash itself renders a service to the enterprise because of its command over other resources.

55. The future economic benefits embodied in an asset may flow to the enterprise in a number of ways. For example, an asset may be:

(a) Used singly or in combination with other assets in the production of goods or services to be sold by the enterprise.

(b) Exchanged for other assets.

(c) Used to settle a liability.

(d) Distributed to the owners of the enterprise.

56. Many assets, for example, property, plant and equipment, have a physical form. However, physical form is not essential to the existence of an asset; hence patents and copyrights, for example, are assets if future economic benefits are expected to flow from them to the enterprise and if they are controlled by the enterprise.

57. Many assets, for example, receivables and property, are associated with legal rights, including the right of ownership. In determining the existence of an asset, the right of ownership is not essential; thus, for example, property held on a lease is an asset if the enterprise controls the benefits which are expected to flow from the property. Although the capacity of an enterprise to control benefits is usually the result of legal rights, an item may none-theless satisfy the definition of an asset even when there is no legal control. For example, know-how obtained from a development activity may meet the definition of an asset when, by keeping that know-how secret, an enterprise controls the benefits that are expected to flow from it.

58. The assets of an enterprise result from past transactions or other past events. Enterprises normally obtain assets by purchasing or producing them, but other transactions or events may generate assets; examples include property received by an enterprise from government as part of a programme to encourage economic growth in an area and the discovery of mineral deposits. Transactions or events expected to occur in the future do not in themselves give rise to assets; hence, for example, an intention to purchase inventory does not, of itself, meet the definition of an asset.

59. There is a close association between incurring expenditure and generating assets but the two do not necessarily coincide. Hence, when an enterprise incurs expenditure, this may provide evidence that future economic benefits were sought but is not conclusive proof that an item satisfying the definition of an asset has been obtained. Similarly the absence of a related expenditure does not preclude an item from satisfying the definition of an asset and thus becoming a candidate for recognition in the balance sheet; for example, items that have been donated to the enterprise may satisfy the definition of an asset.

Liabilities

60. An essential characteristic of a liability is that the enterprise has a present obligation. An obligation is a duty or responsibility to act or perform in a certain way. Obligations may be legally enforceable as a consequence of a binding contract or statutory requirement. This is normally the case, for example, with amounts payable for goods and services received. Obligations also arise, however, from normal business practice, custom and a desire to maintain good business relations or act in an equitable manner. If, for example, an enterprise decides as a matter of policy to rectify faults in its products even when these become apparent after the warranty period has expired, the amounts that are expected to be expended in respect of goods already sold are liabilities.

61. A distinction needs to be drawn between a present obligation and a future commitment. A decision by the management of an enterprise to acquire assets in the future does not, of itself, give rise to a present obligation. An obligation normally arises only when the asset is delivered or the enterprise enters into an irrevocable agreement to acquire the asset. In the latter case, the irrevocable nature of the agreement means that the economic consequences of failing to honour the obligation, for example, because of the existence of a substantial penalty, leave the enterprise with little, if any, discretion to avoid the outflow of resources to another party.

62. The settlement of a present obligation usually involves the enterprise giving up resources embodying economic benefits in order to satisfy the claim of the other party. Settlement of a present obligation may occur in a number of ways, for example, by:
(a) Payment of cash.
(b) Transfer of other assets.
(c) Provision of services.
(d) Replacement of that obligation with another obligation.
(e) Conversion of the obligation to equity.
   An obligation may also be extinguished by other means, such as a creditor waiving or forfeiting its rights.

63. Liabilities result from past transactions or other past events. Thus, for example, the acquisition of goods and the use of services give rise to trade payables (unless paid for in advance or on delivery) and the receipt of a bank loan results in an obligation to repay the loan. An enterprise may also recognize future rebates based on annual purchases by customers as liabilities; in this case, the sale of the goods in the past is the transaction that gives rise to the liability.

64. Some liabilities can be measured only by using a substantial degree of estimation. Some enterprises describe these liabilities as provisions. In some countries, such provisions are not regarded as liabilities because the concept of a liability is defined narrowly so as to include only amounts that can be established without the need to make estimates. The definition of a liability in paragraph 49 follows a broader approach. Thus, when a provision involves a present obligation and satisfies the rest of the definition, it is a liability even if the amount has to be estimated. Examples include provisions for payments to be made under existing warranties and provisions to cover pension obligations.

Equity

65. Although equity is defined in paragraph 49 as a residual, it may be sub-classified in the balance sheet. For example, in a corporate enterprise, funds contributed by shareholders, retained earnings, reserves representing appropriations of retained earnings and reserves representing capital maintenance adjustments may be shown separately. Such classifications can be relevant to the decision-making needs of the users of financial statements when they indicate legal or other restrictions on the ability of the enterprise to distribute or otherwise apply its equity. They may also reflect the fact that parties

with ownership interests in an enterprise have differing rights in relation to the receipt of dividends or the repayment of capital.

66. The creation of reserves is sometimes required by statute or other law in order to give the enterprise and its creditors an added measure of protection from the effects of losses. Other reserves may be established if national tax law grants exemptions from, or reductions in, taxation liabilities when transfers to such reserves are made. The existence and size of these legal, statutory and tax reserves is information that can be relevant to the decision-making needs of users. Transfers to such reserves are appropriations of retained earnings rather than expenses.

67. The amount at which equity is shown in the balance sheet is dependent on the measurement of assets and liabilities. Normally, the aggregate amount of equity only by coincidence corresponds with the aggregate market value of the shares of the enterprise or the sum that could be raised by disposing of either the net assets on a piecemeal basis or the enterprise as a whole on a going concern basis.

68. Commercial, industrial and business activities are often undertaken by means of enterprises such as sole proprietorships, partnerships and trusts and various types of government business undertakings. The legal and regulatory framework for such enterprises is often different from that applying to corporate enterprises. For example, there may be few, if any, restrictions on the distribution to owners or other beneficiaries of amounts included in equity. Nevertheless, the definition of equity and the other aspects of this framework that deal with equity are appropriate for such enterprises.

Performance

69. Profit is frequently used as a measure of performance or as the basis for other measures, such as return on investment or earnings per share. The elements directly related to the measurement of profit are income and expenses. The recognition and measurement of income and expenses, and hence profit, depends in part on the concepts of capital and capital maintenance used by the enterprise in preparing its financial statements. These concepts are discussed in paragraphs 102 to 110.

70. The elements of income and expenses are defined as follows:
   (a) Income is increases in economic benefits during the accounting period in the form of inflows or enhancements of assets or decreases of liabilities that result in increases in equity, other than those relating to contributions from equity participants.
   (b) Expenses are decreases in economic benefits during the accounting period in the form of outflows or depletions of assets or incurrences of liabilities that result in decreases in equity, other than those relating to distributions to equity participants.

71. The definitions of income and expenses identify their essential features but do not attempt to specify the criteria that would need to be met before they are recognized in the income statement. Criteria for the recognition of income and expenses are discussed in paragraphs 82 to 98.

72. Income and expenses may be presented in the income statement in different ways so as to provide information that is relevant for economic decision-making. For example, it is common practice to distinguish between those items of income and expenses that arise in the course of the ordinary activities of the enterprise and those that do not. This distinction is made on the basis that the source of an item is relevant in evaluating the ability of the enterprise to generate cash and cash equivalents in the future; for example, incidental activities such as the disposal of a long-term investment are unlikely to recur on a regular basis. When distinguishing between items in this way consideration needs to be given to the nature of the enterprise and its operations. Items that arise from the ordinary activities of one enterprise may be unusual in respect of another.

73. Distinguishing between items of income and expense and combining them in different ways also permits several measures of enterprise performance to be displayed. These have differing degrees of inclusiveness. For example, the income statement could display gross margin, profit from ordinary activities before taxation, profit from ordinary activities after taxation, and net profit.

Income

74. The definition of income encompasses both revenue and gains. Revenue arises in the course of the ordinary activities of an enterprise and is referred to by a variety of different names including sales, fees, interest, dividends, royalties and rent.

75. Gains represent other items that meet the definition of income and may, or may not, arise in the course of the ordinary activities of an enterprise. Gains represent increases in economic benefits and as such are no different in nature from revenue. Hence, they are not regarded as constituting a separate element in this framework.

76. Gains include, for example, those arising on the disposal of non-current assets. The definition of income also includes unrealized gains; for example, those arising on the revaluation of marketable securities and those resulting from increases in the carrying amount of long term assets. When gains are recognized in the income statement, they are usually displayed separately because knowledge of them is useful for the purpose of making economic decisions. Gains are often reported net of related expenses.

77. Various kinds of assets may be received or enhanced by income; examples include cash, receivables and goods and services received in exchange for goods and services supplied. Income may also result from the settlement of liabilities. For example, an enterprise may provide goods and services to a lender in settlement of an obligation to repay an outstanding loan.

Expenses

78. The definition of expenses encompasses losses as well as those expenses that arise in the course of the ordinary activities of the enterprise. Expenses that arise in the course of the ordinary activities of the enterprise include,

for example, cost of sales, wages and depreciation. They usually take the form of an outflow or depletion of assets such as cash and cash equivalents, inventory, property, plant and equipment.

79. Losses represent other items that meet the definition of expenses and may, or may not, arise in the course of the ordinary activities of the enterprise. Losses represent decreases in economic benefits and as such they are no different in nature from other expenses. Hence, they are not regarded as a separate element in this framework.

80. Losses include, for example, those resulting from disasters such as fire and flood, as well as those arising on the disposal of non-current assets. The definition of expenses also includes unrealized losses, for example, those arising from the effects of increases in the rate of exchange for a foreign currency in respect of the borrowings of an enterprise in that currency. When losses are recognized in the income statement, they are usually displayed separately because knowledge of them is useful for the purpose of making economic decisions. Losses are often reported net of related income.

Capital maintenance adjustments

81. The revaluation or restatement of assets and liabilities gives rise to increases or decreases in equity. While these increases or decreases meet the definition of income and expenses, they are not included in the income statement under certain concepts of capital maintenance. Instead these items are included in equity as capital maintenance adjustments or revaluation reserves. These concepts of capital maintenance are discussed in paragraphs 102 to 110 of this framework.

RECOGNITION OF THE ELEMENTS OF FINANCIAL STATEMENTS

82. Recognition is the process of incorporating in the balance sheet or income statement an item that meets the definition of an element and satisfies the criteria for recognition set out in paragraph 83. It involves the depiction of the item in words and by a monetary amount and the inclusion of that amount in the balance sheet or income statement totals. Items that satisfy the recognition criteria should be recognized in the balance sheet or income statement. The failure to recognize such items is not rectified by disclosure of the accounting policies used nor by notes or explanatory material.

83. An item that meets the definition of an element should be recognized if:
    (a) It is probable that any future economic benefit associated with the item will flow to or from the enterprise.
    (b) The item has a cost or value that can be measured with reliability.

84. In assessing whether an item meets these criteria and therefore qualifies for recognition in the financial statements, regard needs to be given to the materiality considerations discussed in paragraphs 29 and 30. The interrelationship between the elements means that an item that meets the definition and recognition criteria for a particular element, for example, an asset,

automatically requires the recognition of another element, for example, income or a liability.

The probability of future economic benefit

85. The concept of probability is used in the recognition criteria to refer to the degree of uncertainty that the future economic benefits associated with the item will flow to or from the enterprise. The concept is in keeping with the uncertainty that characterizes the environment in which an enterprise operates. Assessments of the degree of uncertainty attaching to the flow of future economic benefits are made on the basis of the evidence available when the financial statements are prepared. For example, when it is probable that a receivable owed by an enterprise will be paid, it is then justifiable, in the absence of any evidence to the contrary, to recognize the receivable as an asset. For a large population of receivables, however, some degree of non-payment is normally considered probable; hence an expense representing the expected reduction in economic benefits is recognized.

Reliability of measurement

86. The second criterion for the recognition of an item is that it possesses a cost or value that can be measured with reliability as discussed in paragraphs 31 to 38 of this framework. In many cases, cost or value must be estimated; the use of reasonable estimates is an essential part of the preparation of financial statements and does not undermine their reliability. When, however, a reasonable estimate cannot be made the item is not recognized in the balance sheet or income statement. For example, the expected proceeds from a lawsuit may meet the definitions of both an asset and income as well as the probability criterion for recognition; however, if it is not possible for the claim to be measured reliably, it should not be recognized as an asset or as income; the existence of the claim, however, would be disclosed in the notes, explanatory material or supplementary schedules.

87. An item that, at a particular point in time, fails to meet the recognition criteria in paragraph 83 may qualify for recognition at a later date as a result of subsequent circumstances or events.

88. An item that possesses the essential characteristics of an element but fails to meet the criteria for recognition may nonetheless warrant disclosure in the notes, explanatory material or in supplementary schedules. This is appropriate when knowledge of the item is considered to be relevant to the evaluation of the financial position, performance and changes in financial position of an enterprise by the users of financial statements.

Recognition of assets

89. An asset is recognized in the balance sheet when it is probable that the future economic benefits will flow to the enterprise and the asset has a cost or value that can be measured reliably.

90. An asset is not recognized in the balance sheet when expenditure has been incurred for which it is considered improbable that economic benefits will flow to the enterprise beyond the current accounting period. Instead such a transaction results in the recognition of an expense in the income statement. This treatment does not imply either that the intention of management in incurring expenditure was other than to generate future economic benefits for the enterprise or that management was misguided. The only implication is that the degree of certainty that economic benefits will flow to the enterprise beyond the current accounting period is insufficient to warrant the recognition of an asset.

Recognition of liabilities

91. A liability is recognized in the balance sheet when it is probable that an outflow of resources embodying economic benefits will result from the settlement of a present obligation and the amount at which the settlement will take place can be measured reliably. In practice obligations under contracts that are equally proportionately unperformed (for example, liabilities for inventory ordered but not yet received) are generally not recognized as liabilities in the financial statements. However, such obligations may meet the definition of liabilities and, provided the recognition criteria are met in the particular circumstances, may qualify for recognition. In such circumstances, recognition of liabilities entails recognition of related assets or expenses.

Recognition of income

92. Income is recognized in the income statement when an increase in future economic benefits related to an increase in an asset or a decrease of a liability has arisen that can be measured reliably. This means, in effect, that recognition of income occurs simultaneously with the recognition of increases in assets or decreases in liabilities (for example, the net increase in assets arising on a sale of goods or services or the decrease in liabilities arising from the waiver of a debt payable).

93. The procedures normally adopted in practice for recognizing income, for example, the requirement that revenue should be earned, are applications of the recognition criteria in this framework. Such procedures are generally directed at restricting the recognition as income to those items that can be measured reliably and have a sufficient degree of certainty.

Recognition of expenses

94. Expenses are recognized in the income statement when a decrease in future economic benefits related to a decrease in an asset or an increase of a liability has arisen that can be measured reliably. This means, in effect, that recognition of expenses occurs simultaneously with the recognition of an increase in liabilities or a decrease in assets (for example, the accrual of employee entitlements or the depreciation of equipment).

95. Expenses are recognized in the income statement on the basis of a direct association between the costs incurred and the earning of specific items of income. This process, commonly referred to as the matching of costs with revenues, involves the simultaneous or combined recognition of revenues and expenses that result directly and jointly from the same transactions or other events; for example, the various components of expense making up the cost of goods sold are recognized at the same time as the income derived from the sale of the goods. However, the application of the matching concept under this framework does not allow the recognition of items in the balance sheet which do not meet the definition of assets or liabilities.

96. When economic benefits are expected to arise over several accounting periods and the association with income can only be broadly or indirectly determined, expenses are recognized in the income statement on the basis of systematic and rational allocation procedures. This is often necessary in recognizing the expenses associated with the using up of assets such as property, plant, equipment, goodwill, patents and trademarks; in such cases the expense is referred to as depreciation or amortization. These allocation procedures are intended to recognize expenses in the accounting periods in which the economic benefits associated with these items are consumed or expire.

97. An expense is recognized immediately in the income statement when an expenditure produces no future economic benefits or when, and to the extent that, future economic benefits do not qualify, or cease to qualify, for recognition in the balance sheet as an asset.

98. An expense is also recognized in the income statement in those cases when a liability is incurred without the recognition of an asset, as when a liability under a product warranty arises.

MEASUREMENT OF THE ELEMENTS OF FINANCIAL STATEMENTS

99. Measurement is the process of determining the monetary amounts at which the elements of the financial statements are to be recognized and carried in the balance sheet and income statement. This involves the selection of the particular basis of measurement.

100. A number of different measurement bases are employed to different degrees and in varying combinations in financial statements. They include the following:

(a) **Historical cost.** Assets are recorded at the amount of cash or cash equivalents paid or the fair value of the consideration given to acquire them at the time of their acquisition. Liabilities are recorded at the amount of proceeds received in exchange for the obligation, or in some circumstances (for example, income taxes), at the amounts of cash or cash equivalents expected to be paid to satisfy the liability in the normal course of business.

(b) **Current cost.** Assets are carried at the amount of cash or cash equivalents that would have to be paid if the same or an equivalent asset was acquired currently. Liabilities are carried at the undiscounted amount of cash or cash equivalents that would be required to settle the obligation currently.

(c) **Realizable (settlement) value.** Assets are carried at the amount of cash or cash equivalents that could currently be obtained by selling the asset in an orderly disposal. Liabilities are carried at their settlement values; that is, the undiscounted amounts of cash or cash equivalents expected to be paid to satisfy the liabilities in the normal course of business.

(d) **Present value.** Assets are carried at the present discounted value of the future net cash inflows that the item is expected to generate in the normal course of business. Liabilities are carried at the present discounted value of the future net cash outflows that are expected to be required to settle the liabilities in the normal course of business.

101. The measurement basis most commonly adopted by enterprises in preparing their financial statements is historical cost. This is usually combined with other measurement bases. For example, inventories are usually carried at the lower of cost and net realizable value, marketable securities may be carried at market value and pension liabilities are carried at their present value. Furthermore, some enterprises use the current cost basis as a response to the inability of the historical cost accounting model to deal with the effects of changing prices of non-monetary assets.

CONCEPTS OF CAPITAL AND CAPITAL MAINTENANCE

Concepts of capital

102. A financial concept of capital is adopted by most enterprises in preparing their financial statements. Under a financial concept of capital, such as invested money or invested purchasing power, capital is synonymous with the net assets or equity of the enterprise. Under a physical concept of capital, such as operating capability, capital is regarded as the productive capacity of the enterprise based on, for example, units of output per day.

103. The selection of the appropriate concept of capital by an enterprise should be based on the needs of the users of its financial statements. Thus, a financial concept of capital should be adopted if the users of financial statements are primarily concerned with the maintenance of nominal invested capital or the purchasing power of invested capital. If, however, the main concern of users is with the operating capability of the enterprise, a physical concept of capital should be used. The concept chosen indicates the goal to be attained in determining profit, even though there may be some measurement difficulties in making the concept operational.

Concepts of capital maintenance and the determination of profit

104. The concepts of capital in paragraph 102 give rise to the following concepts of capital maintenance:

(a) **Financial capital maintenance.** Under this concept a profit is earned only if the financial (or money) amount of the net assets at the end of the period exceeds the financial (or money) amount of net assets at the beginning of the period, after excluding any distributions to, and contributions from, owners during the period. Financial capital maintenance can be measured in either nominal monetary units or units of constant purchasing power.

(b) **Physical capital maintenance.** Under this concept a profit is earned only if the physical productive capacity (or operating capability) of the enterprise (or the resources or funds needed to achieve that capacity) at the end of the period exceeds the physical productive capacity at the beginning of the period, after excluding any distributions to, and contributions from, owners during the period.

105. The concept of capital maintenance is concerned with how an enterprise defines the capital that it seeks to maintain. It provides the linkage between the concepts of capital and the concepts of profit because it provides the point of reference by which profit is measured; it is a prerequisite for distinguishing between an enterprise's return on capital and its return of capital; only inflows of assets in excess of amounts needed to maintain capital may be regarded as profit and therefore as a return on capital. Hence, profit is the residual amount that remains after expenses (including capital maintenance adjustments, where appropriate) have been deducted from income. If expenses exceed income the residual amount is a net loss.

106. The physical capital maintenance concept requires the adoption of the current cost basis of measurement. The financial capital maintenance concept, however, does not require the use of a particular basis of measurement. Selection of the basis under this concept is dependent on the type of financial capital that the enterprise is seeking to maintain.

107. The principal difference between the two concepts of capital maintenance is the treatment of the effects of changes in the prices of assets and liabilities of the enterprise. In general terms, an enterprise has maintained its capital if it has as much capital at the end of the period as it had at the beginning of the period. Any amount over and above that required to maintain the capital at the beginning of the period is profit.

108. Under the concept of financial capital maintenance where capital is defined in terms of nominal monetary units, profit represents the increase in nominal money capital over the period. Thus, increases in the prices of assets held over the period, conventionally referred to as holding gains, are, conceptually, profits. They may not be recognized as such, however, until the assets are disposed of in an exchange transaction. When the concept of financial capital maintenance is defined in terms of constant purchasing power units, profit represents the increase in invested purchasing power over the period. Thus, only that part of the increase in the prices of assets that exceeds the increase in the general level of prices is regarded as profit. The rest of the increase is treated as a capital maintenance adjustment and, hence, as part of equity.

109. Under the concept of physical capital maintenance when capital is defined in terms of the physical productive capacity, profit represents the increase in that capital over the period. All price changes affecting the assets and liabilities of the enterprise are viewed as changes in the measurement of the

physical productive capacity of the enterprise; hence, they are treated as capital maintenance adjustments that are part of equity and not as profit.

110. The selection of the measurement bases and concept of capital maintenance will determine the accounting model used in the preparation of the financial statements. Different accounting models exhibit different degrees of relevance and reliability and, as in other areas, management must seek a balance between relevance and reliability. This framework is applicable to a range of accounting models and provides guidance on preparing and presenting the financial statements constructed under the chosen model. At the present time, it is not the intention of the IASB to prescribe a particular model other than in exceptional circumstances, such as for those enterprises reporting in the currency of a hyperinflationary economy. This intention will, however, be reviewed in the light of world developments.

chapter fourteen

The Anatomy of an International Accounting Standard: IAS 1

Chapter objectives

■ To gain an understanding of the function and structure of the International Accounting Standards in general through the examination of a specific IAS: IAS 1 *Presentation of Financial Statements*

■ To analyse the specific provisions of IAS 1 relating to:
  ■ the principles to be followed when a matter is not covered by a specific IAS
  ■ compliance with the IASs
  ■ the 'present fairly' rule
  ■ the components of a complete set of financial statements

In this chapter, an international accounting standard (IAS 1) is subjected to a detailed examination. This serves two purposes:

■ It is a means of explaining the structure and functions of the IASs in general

■ To analyse a number of important general points relating to financial reporting that are dealt with in this particular IAS

IAS 1 was IASC's very first standard issued in November 1974. However, it was radically revised in July 1997 and therefore represents the latest approach of the IASB on a number of points. It is a telling commentary on the way that standard setting has developed that, when IAS 1 was first issued in 1974, it consisted of five pages; the revised version of 1997 has 44 pages. The text of IAS 1 may be found in the IASB's volume of current standards (IASB, 2001).

14.1 THE STRUCTURE OF AN INTERNATIONAL ACCOUNTING STANDARD

The typical IAS consists of three parts:

■ The introduction
■ The text of the standard
■ The appendix

In formal terms, only the text of the standard is binding on enterprises, that is an enterprise, when applying the standard, is not obliged to take into account either the introduction or the appendix. Thus the opening sentence of the appendix of IAS 1 reads:

> The appendix is illustrative only and does not form part of the standards. The purpose of the appendix is to illustrate the application of the standards to assist in clarifying their meaning.

However, although they lack formal authority, the introduction and appendix are most useful in helping readers understand the standard. The introduction, which is written in non-technical language, generally gives a brief explanation of the standard's objectives and principal provisions. That of IAS 1 is rather short, but nevertheless quite helpful in listing, in paragraph 2, the four principal elements of IAS 1 and in giving, in paragraph 3, a further commentary on a particularly novel and interesting provision, that relating to the statement of losses and gains (which is discussed later in this chapter in section 14.6.4). The IASB considers that the primary function of the introduction is to assist readers when a standard is first issued. Hence it does not include the introduction to certain of its older standards (for example, IAS 7 and IAS 8) in its volume of current standards. This practice confirms the low importance that the IASB attaches to the introduction.

The appendix of IAS 1 contains illustrative formats of the balance sheet, the income statement and the statement of gains and losses. An enterprise that uses these formats can be sure that it is complying, in this respect, with IAS 1, but, given the non-mandatory nature of the appendix, there is no obligation to use these specific formats; other formats (not set out in the appendix) may also be consistent with the requirements of the standard. There is an important difference between the EU's Fourth Directive (whose formats are mandatory) and IAS 1 in this matter. The appendices attached to other IASs vary considerably in both their length and their usefulness to the reader. Some IASs do not have appendices, for example IAS 2 and IAS 29. For others, the appendix is virtually essential for an understanding of the standard; for example the appendix to IAS 7 'Cash flow statements' shows how to apply the standard's provisions in preparing a cash flow statement. By means of this worked example, the abstract rules of the standard become much more understandable.

14.2 THE TEXT OF THE STANDARD

As stated in the previous section, only the text of the standard is binding on enterprises. This will be illustrated with reference to the text of IAS 1, which consists of 104 numbered paragraphs. In addition there is an opening unnumbered paragraph titled 'Objective', which states that the objective is:

> to prescribe the basis for presentation of general purpose financial statements, in order to ensure comparability both with the enterprises's own financial statements of previous periods and with the financial statements of other enterprises.... The recognition, measurement and disclosure of specific transactions and events is dealt with in other International Accounting Standards.

The IASB's Framework (paragraph 24) listed 'comparability' as one of the four principal qualitative characteristics of financial statements. Hence IAS 1 is solidly based on the Framework, at least in its stated objective.

The text of IAS 1 covers a very wide range and in this chapter it is proposed to deal with only four of its more interesting and important provisions:

- Compliance with IASs
- Matters not covered in an IAS
- The 'present fairly' rule
- The components of a set of financial statements

14.3 COMPLIANCE WITH IAS

As has already been emphasised in Chapter 12, the IASB is a private body and has no means of compelling enterprises to comply with its standards. However this does not mean that it is uninterested in the use that enterprises make of IAS or that it is completely powerless in this matter. The IASB is concerned that certain enterprises may mislead users by claiming that their accounts comply with IAS when this is not the case. The IASB is determined to prevent enterprises from practising 'selective compliance', that is complying with those IASs that they favour and ignoring those that they do not, whilst claiming that their accounts 'comply with International Accounting Standards' or some similar reassuring phrase. The problem is particularly acute with respect to enterprises that do not make all the required disclosures, for example the analysis of the assets and profits of business segments required by IAS 14 (for more information on this IAS, see chapter 17). This matter is dealt with in IAS 1, 11 (that is paragraph 11 of IAS 1) which states:

11. An enterprise whose financial statements comply with International Accounting Standards should disclose the fact. Financial statements should not be described as complying with International Accounting Standards unless they comply with all the requirements of each applicable Standard and each applicable Interpretation of the Standing Interpretations Committee.

Can enterprises be compelled to obey this rule? The IASB has certain sanctions. It could, for example, publish the name of any enterprise whose accounts do not comply with IAS (including IAS 1, 11), even though it claims that they do so. This would be a very effective sanction because it would destroy much of the benefit that the enterprise sought to gain in making the false claim. However, the IASB has not, as yet, made use of this stratagem. Instead, it has relied on others to enforce compliance, for example the control authorities of those stock exchanges that accept accounts based on IAS. The uneven compliance of enterprises around the world with the provisions of the IASB's standards is one of the principal reasons why the USA's SEC has great reservations about permitting foreign enterprises to use IAS on the American capital market. It is generally considered that poor compliance with IAS is the IASB's weak point.

IAS 1, 11 makes clear what is meant by the phrase 'comply with International Accounting Standards' and thus performs the very useful function of removing ambiguity and doubt in what hitherto was a rather confused area. Hence an enterprise which states that its accounts comply with IAS must comply with all the requirements of all relevant IASs. In the rest of this book, when reference is made to a requirement placed by an IAS on an enterprise, this should be construed to refer to an enterprise that states that its financial statements comply with the International Accounting Standards.

14.4 PRINCIPLES TO BE FOLLOWED WHEN THERE IS NO RELEVANT IAS

Enterprises are required to comply with all applicable IASs. But what happens when a matter is not covered by an IAS? The current set of the IASs, as presented in Exhibit 12.1, is certainly very voluminous, but does not at present cover the whole field of financial reporting and probably never will, given the hectic rate of change in the economic and legal environments in which enterprises operate.

This matter is covered in IAS 1, 20–22:

20. Management should select and apply an enterprise's accounting policies so that the financial statements comply with all the requirements of each applicable International Accounting Standard and Interpretation. . . . Where there is no specific requirement, management should develop policies to ensure that the financial statements provide information that is:

(a) relevant to the decision-making needs of users: and

(b) reliable in that they:

    (i) represent faithfully the results and financial position of the enterprise;

    (ii) reflect the economic substance of events and transactions and not merely the legal form;

    (iii) are neutral, that is free from bias;

    (iv) are prudent; and

    (v) are complete in all material respects.

21. Accounting policies are the specific principles, bases, conventions, rules and practices adopted by an enterprise in preparing and presenting its financial statements.

22. In the absence of a specific International Accounting Standard and an Interpretation, management uses its judgement in developing an accounting policy that provides the most useful information to users of the enterprise's financial statements. In making this judgement management considers:

(a) the requirements and guidance in International Accounting Standards dealing with similar and related issues;

(b) the definition, recognition and measurement criteria for assets, liabilities, income and expenses set out in the IASB Framework; and

(c) pronouncements of other standard-setting bodies and accepted industry practices to the extent, but only to the extent, that these are consistent with (a) and (b) of this paragraph.

Note that paragraph 20 is set in **bold italic type**, whereas paragraphs 21 and 22 are set in normal type. The difference is significant and is explained in the opening paragraph of IAS 1 in the following terms:

> The standards, which have been set in bold italic type, should be read in the context of the background material and implementation guidance in this Standard

In the above quote, the word 'standard' is used in two different senses: 'Standard' (capital S and singular) refers to IAS 1; 'standards' (lower case s and plural) refers to those paragraphs of IAS 1 that are set in bold italic type. Hence paragraph 20 is one of the standards, but not paragraphs 21 and 22.

The implication is that only those paragraphs that are set in bold italic type are binding on enterprises; the remaining paragraphs provide only background material and guidance. In fact one can construct a hierarchy of the various parts of a standard according to the authority attached to each; starting with the elements that have the greatest authority, the hierarchy is:

- Paragraphs in the text of the standard that are set in bold italic type
- Other paragraphs in the text of the standard
- The appendix
- The introduction

However this does not mean that the other paragraphs in the text may be ignored by the reader, for the guidance that they provide is often vital. For example, if the reader had to rely solely on the wording of paragraph 20, she would be confronted with many difficult problems of interpretation, such as discerning the precise meaning of the word 'prudent'. The reader turns to paragraph 22 for guidance. Here she learns that she should refer to: (a) other IASs that deal with similar and related issues, (b) the IASB's Framework, and (c) the pronouncements of other standard-setting bodies and accepted industry practice. Point (a) seems very logical. However point (c) is so vague as to place virtually no constraints on the preparer, particularly as no guidance is given as to which standard-setting body should be referred to. Apparently the pronouncements of the USA's FASB may be given the same weight as those of Portugal's Comissão de Normalização Contabilistica. Perhaps this is not very important as the standards of other bodies may only be applied if they are not inconsistent with those of other IASs and the IASB Framework. However the most interesting reference is to the IASB's Framework. In effect the list in paragraph 20 is virtually identical with the qualitative characteristics of information that are set out in the Framework. In this way, certain elements of the Framework (which is definitely not a standard) are given the authority of an IAS, but only when the matter is not covered in a specific IAS.[1] It should be noted that, by including the 'catch-all' rule in IAS 1, 20, the IASB has ensured that IAS cover *all* conceivable transactions and situations.

14.5 THE 'PRESENT FAIRLY' RULE

IAS 1, 10 states:

Financial statements should present fairly the financial position, financial performance and cash flows of an enterprise. The appropriate application of International Accounting Standards, with additional disclosure when necessary, results, in virtually all circumstances, in financial statements that achieve a fair presentation.

IAS 1 does not define further the meaning of 'present fairly'. The term 'present fairly' is of American origin but this is not very helpful in discovering its meaning, for two reasons: firstly there is nothing in IAS 1 to suggest that the American meaning of the term is intended and secondly the American phrase is 'present fairly in accordance with generally accepted accounting principles'. The second point is the more important. The wording of IAS 1 is 'present fairly the financial position'; it is *not* 'present fairly in accordance with international accounting standards the financial position'. The difference is very significant. In the USA the American phrase is interpreted to mean that generally accepted accounting standards must always be followed. It is not permitted to depart from a rule of GAAP in order to achieve fair presentation; hence fair presentation is a concept of operational relevance only in those areas not covered by American GAAP and, as the FASB has been very prolific in issuing statements of financial accounting standards (at the last count they numbered over 130), there is very little that is not so covered. This is emphatically not the case with the IASs as is clear from the second sentence of IAS 1, paragraph 10: 'The appropriate application of International Accounting Standards, with appropriate additional disclosure when necessary, results, in virtually all circumstances, in financial statements that achieve a fair presentation.' The key word is 'virtually'. The IASB admits that it is permissible to depart from the specific provisions of an IAS in order to achieve fair presentation. In fact in this area the IASB's rules are remarkably similar to those of the EU:

(a) Both bodies have set out a general criterion for financial statements.

(b) In both cases the terms ('true and fair view' and 'present fairly') used are ones with which nobody may reasonably disagree (who would claim that the accounts should give 'a false view' or should 'present unfairly'?) but are very vague and notoriously undefined.

(c) In both cases it is stated that, if following the prescribed rules does not achieve the desired result, then additional disclosure is necessary.

(d) Only if, after additional disclosure, the financial statements still do not meet the general criterion, then, in these very rare cases, is departure from the specific rules permitted.

When the specific rules are not followed then the enterprise must disclose this fact and give certain additional information. In fact, in the case of the IASB, the additional disclosure requirements are rather more severe than with the EU. One suspects that they have been made deliberately burdensome in order to deter enterprises from using this excuse to disregard those IASs that they do not like. In addition to the information required by the EU's Fourth Directive (the rule which is disregarded, the reason and the effect on the accounts) the management must state that it has complied with all other IASs, and the reason why complying with the particular IAS would be misleading.

14.6 THE COMPONENTS OF A SET OF FINANCIAL STATEMENTS

IAS 1, 7 defines the components of a set of financial statements in the following terms:

A complete set of financial statements includes the following components:
  (a) balance sheet;
  (b) income statement;
  (c) a statement showing either
    (i) all changes in equity; or
    (ii) changes in equity other than those arising from capital transactions with owners and distributions to owners;
  (d) cash flow statement; and
  (e) accounting policies and explanatory notes.

14.6.1 The balance sheet

IAS 1 does not prescribe a format for the balance sheet but it does list the items that, as a minimum, should appear on the face of the balance sheet and sets out in the appendix an example of a balance sheet drawn up in accordance with the standard. The IASs that deal with specific categories of assets and liabilities (for example, IAS 16 'Plant Property and Equipment') often lay down how they should be presented in the balance sheet. The various elements of the balance sheet are considered further in Chapters 15 (assets) and Chapter 16 (liabilities and equity).

14.6.2　The income statement

The IASB consistently uses the term 'income statement' in its Framework and standards, in contrast to the EU which refers to the 'profit and loss account'. In this conflict between American and British terminology, the authors, for once, prefer the American usage; the profit and loss account is not an 'account' (in the sense of a ledger account) – it is a statement.

As with the balance sheet, IAS 1 does not specify a format for the income statement, but it does list the items that should be shown separately and annexes an illustrative example. The detailed consideration of the income statement is left to Chapter 17.

14.6.3　The cash flow statement

The IASB's detailed rules concerning the 'Cash Flow Statement' are set out, not in IAS 1, but in IAS 7 'Cash Flow Statements', which is covered in Chapter 18.

14.6.4.　The statement of changes in equity

The requirement to present a statement of changes in equity was introduced into IAS 1 when it was revised in 1997. Such a statement serves two purposes:

(a) It demonstrates the integrity of the set of financial statements by proving the link between successive balance sheets. In general, the increase(decrease) in the enterprise's equity between two balance sheets will not be equal to its profit(loss), for two reasons:

  (i) Transactions between the enterprise and its owners (injections of new capital and dividends)

  (ii) Increases(decreases) in the value of assets(liabilities) that do not pass through the income statement

  Hence it is necessary to have a supplementary statement which present these items.

(b) It presents an alternative measure of performance to complement the measure of profit shown in the income statement, by including all increases(decreases) in the value of assets(liabilities) (see point (a)(ii)). An example of such a statement is given in the appendix to IAS 1 where it is described as a statement of total recognized gains and losses.

In both its functions, the statement of changes in equity serves as a complement to the income statement. Hence it is discussed in more detail when the income statement is considered in Chapter 17.

14.6.5 The notes to the accounts

The last element of a complete set of financial statements is the notes. 'Last but not least', because the notes are very important – in two respects: in sheer volume (in the financial statements of the typical publicly listed enterprise, the notes generally make up more than 80 per cent of the pages) and in their information content (in the view of experts, such as financial analysts, the notes contain information that is absolutely vital for a proper understanding of the financial statements).

IAS 1 classifies the information contained in the notes into five categories:

Statement of compliance with International Accounting Standards

The rationale for this statement has already been discussed in section 14.3.

Accounting policies

The enterprise should give details in the notes of the particular accounting policies that have been followed in the preparation of the financial statements. In effect the statement that the financial statements comply with International Accounting Standards is insufficient, for two reasons:

(a) Many IASs allow a choice of accounting method (in much the same way as the EU directives offer options). Thus *IAS 2 Inventories* permits the enterprise to choose between three different methods of valuing stocks of goods: weighted average, FIFO and LIFO. The reader of the accounts must be told which method the enterprise has chosen. Furthermore the reader needs to be informed in detail of how the enterprise has applied the rule set out in an IAS. For example, *IAS 16 Plant, Property and Equipment* requires enterprises to depreciate fixed assets over their useful life. However the choice of depreciation method (straight-line, reducing balance etc.) and the estimate of the useful life have to be made by the enterprise. IAS 16 requires that information on these matters be given in the notes.

(b) The IAS in no way cover all the accounting problems that may be encountered by enterprises. Hence the enterprise's managers have to create their own rule, following the principles set out in paragraph 20 (as already discussed in section 14.2)

IAS 1 sets out a long list of matters for which the accounting policy should be disclosed in the notes. In many cases, it repeats an obligation that is set out in the IAS that deals with the matter. Thus enterprises should disclose their accounting policies in relation to: construction contracts (IAS 11), leases (IAS 17), provisions (IAS 37) and inventories (IAS 2).

Supporting information

Most of the notes consist of additional information relating to specific items in the balance sheet, the income statement and the cash flow statement. The notes expand and supplement the figures given in these statements. The information is placed in the notes and not on the face of the other statements in order to prevent the latter becoming over-loaded with detail. This renders the balance sheet and the other statements more comprehensible at the expense of adding to the length of the notes. A large part of the notes of many enterprises is taken up with two schedules imposed by other IASs: the schedule of fixed assets (required by IAS 16, discussed in Chapter 15) and the segment reports (required by IAS 14 and explained in Chapter 17). The policy of most large enterprises is to make the primary statements (the balance sheet, the income statement and the cash flow statement) very brief and to put all detailed informa-tion in the notes.

Other financial information

It often happens that certain items of a financial nature are not recog-nized as assets or liabilities and therefore are not reported in the balance sheet. An example would be where the enterprise has guaranteed the debt of a third party; if the enterprise considers that there is only a very low probability of it being required to pay up on the guarantee, it will not report the guarantee as a liability. However users should be informed of this potential liability, which is best achieved through the notes.

Non-financial information

IAS 1 requires that the enterprise present a certain amount of non-financial information, which may be set out in the notes if not disclosed else-where. This includes the legal form of the enterprise, its registered office and the number of employees.

SUMMARY

This chapter served as an introduction to the individual international accounting standards which are the subject of the following chapters. The function of the three parts of a typical IAS (the introduction, the text and the appendix) were explained with reference to IAS 1. The text of IAS 1 was examined, notably relating to four matters: (a) the compliance by enterprises with the terms of the individual IASs; (b) the action to be taken by an enterprise in areas not covered by a particular IAS; (c) the 'present fairly' rule; and (d) the components of a complete set of financial statements.

Review questions

1. What is the role and the authority of each of the three parts of a typical IAS (the introduction, the text and the appendix)?

2. In IAS 1, what is the significance of the fact that certain paragraphs are set in bold italic type?

3. How does the IASB seek to ensure that enterprises comply fully with the provisions of its standards?

4. In what way does IAS 1 increase the authority of the Framework for the preparers of financial statements?

5. What are the components of a complete set of financial statements?

6. In what way do the 'present fairly' rule in IAS 1 differ from that in US GAAP? And from the EU's Fourth Directive?

Note

1. In a similar fashion, other paragraphs of IAS 1 give the authority of an IAS to the Framework's principles, notably: going concern (IAS 1, 23), accrual basis (IAS 1, 25), consistency (IAS 1, 27), and materiality (IAS 1, 29).

References

Cairns, D 'Exceptions to the rules', *Accountancy* (November 1999), pp. 84–5.
IASB *International Accounting Standards 2001*, IASB, London (2001).
Pacter, P 'It's all black and white', *IASC Insight* (June 2000), p. 14.

Further reading

It is strongly recommended to refer to the full text of IAS 1 which is contained in the IASB's volume of current standards (IASB, 2001). For an analysis of the problem of enterprises failing to comply fully with all the IASs, see Cairns (1999). For a fuller analysis of the differing authority of the various parts of an IAS, see Pacter (2000).

part four

The Financial Statements

The first four chapters in this part deal with the principal financial statements: the balance sheet, the income statement and the cash flow statement. The rules that govern their form and content are discussed, based principally on an analysis of the IASB's International Accounting Standards but also with reference to the rules and practice in the five countries of the Pentad.

Chapter 15 starts with a discussion on which of the two primary statements (the balance sheet or the income statement) should be considered as the dominant statement. It is noted that the IASB's Framework is based on the primacy of the balance sheet, whereas much of current accounting practice is based on the matching principle which gives priority to the income statement. Thereafter the format of the balance sheet is considered. However the greater part of this chapter is taken up with an exposition of the IASB's rules for the definition, recognition and measurement of the different categories of assets, and for their depreciation and impairment.

Chapter 16 considers the other side of the balance sheet, which presents the liabilities and equity. The IASB's rules relating to the definition, recognition and measurement of liabilities are considered through a detailed examination of IAS 37. The principal components of the equity of corporations are explained in general terms; the specific practice in the countries of the Pentad is illustrated with examples from published accounts. A large part of the chapter is taken up with an analysis of two items (preference shares and convertible debt) which are of particular interest since they lie on the borderline between equity and liabilities.

Chapter 17 deals with the income statement. It covers three principal topics: the recognition of revenue, the presentation of revenue and expenses in the income statement and the measurement of profit. Matters that are covered in detail include the classification of expenses (by nature or by function), extraordinary and exceptional items, segment reporting, prior period adjustments and the alternative concepts of profit: the comprehensive income concept and the current operating performance concept. The chapter includes consideration of alternative measures of performance, including the statement of total recognized gains and losses and the statement of performance proposed by the G4+1 group.

Chapter 18 deals with the cash flow statement. The value of this statement to users is assessed with reference to recent research and to the fundamental qualitative characteristics of reliability and relevance. The IASB's rules for the preparation of the cash flow statement are considered with reference to IAS 7.

Chapter 19, the last chapter in this part, deals with the consolidated accounts. It considers the function of the consolidated accounts, which is compared with the quite different function of the accounts of the individual corporation. The different ways of defining the group (the entity covered in the consolidated accounts) are examined, with reference to the rules of both the IASB and the EU, which entails consideration of the definition of subsidiary. The rules of these bodies for the preparation of the consolidated accounts are considered briefly, with most emphasis on the alternative methods of capital consolidation: the acquisition method and the merger method. Finally the rules for the inclusion in the consolidated accounts of joint ventures and associates are discussed.

chapter fifteen

The Balance Sheet I: Assets

Chapter objectives

- To introduce the balance sheet and the income statement and to discuss whether primacy should be given to the balance sheet (as in the IASB's Framework) or to the income statement (as with the matching principle)

- To consider the principles that govern the reporting of assets under the IASB's rules for the principal categories of assets, with reference to questions of definition, recognition and measurement.

- To set out the principles that govern the depreciation and impairment of assets

- To examine the reporting of assets by the largest MNEs and the asset valuation methods used in the Pentad

15.1 THE BALANCE SHEET VERSUS THE INCOME STATEMENT

15.1.1 The primacy of the balance sheet

The next three chapters consider the two primary financial statements: the balance sheet and the income statement. The balance sheet is considered first. This reflects the primacy given to this statement in the IASB's Framework, as evidenced by the Framework's definitions of the elements of the two statements as presented in Exhibit 13.4. These definitions will be examined in more detail later. For the moment, the important point to note is that the definitions of income and expenses (the elements of the income statement) refer to assets and liabilities, but that the latter (the elements of the balance sheet) are defined independently – they do not refer to income and expenses. Income is defined as

347

increases in the value of assets or decreases in the value of liabilities; expenses are negative income. The elements of the income statement are determined by the elements of the balance sheet; the balance sheet is the dominant statement; the income statement is subordinate to it.

The relationship of the balance sheet and the income statement, as set out in the IASB's Framework, is illustrated in Exhibit 15.1. The values of assets and liabilities are first established. Equity is defined as net assets (assets less liabilities). The total value of equity is broken down into its component parts: contributed capital (increases in net assets resulting from transfers from the owners) and reserves (increases in net assets resulting from other transactions and events). Reserves are broken down into two elements: valuation adjustments (increases in net assets that have not been reported in the income statement) and retained profits (increases in net assets that have been reported in the income statement less dividends). There are two important points to be made about Exhibit 15.1:

(a) The balance sheet and the income statement are interconnected. The figure for the profits for the year 2000 appears both in the income statement and in the balance sheet (as a component of equity). Accountants use the term 'articulation' to describe the interconnection of the balance sheet and the income statement.

(b) The values of assets and liabilities are established independently of the income statement. Hence the figure for profit in the income statement is determined by the values for assets and liabilities reported in the balance sheet, given that the two statements are articulated.

However, there are two exceptions to this articulation:

(a) Transfers to and from the enterprise's owners. The payment of a dividend reduces the assets but the dividend is not considered to be an expense to be reported in the income statement. Instead it is regarded as a distribution of profit and deducted from the balance of retained profits in the balance sheet. Fresh injections of capital are added to contributed capital.

(b) Valuation adjustments. On occasions, increases/decreases in the value of assets/liabilities are not passed through the income statement but are included in the balance sheet as a separate component of equity. An example is given in IAS 16 Plant, Property and Equipment: when plant is valued at fair value, any increase in its value above historical cost is not reported as income in the income statement but is transferred to equity in the balance sheet. In Exhibit 15.1, the relevant equity component is entitled 'Valuation adjustment'. In fact there is no consensus as to the appropriate title: in the Framework, it is termed 'Capital maintenance adjustment'; the term used by IAS 16 is 'Revaluation surplus'.

Exhibit 15.1 *The articulation of the balance sheet and the income statement*

Global Corp Balance sheet at 31 December 2000			
Assets			5253
Less liabilities			−2207
equals Equity (by definition)			3046
Components of equity			
Contributed capital			1300
Reserves			
Valuation adjustments		65	
Retained profits			
Balance at 1 January 2000	1046		
Profit for the year 2000	735		
less dividend paid in year	−100		
Balance at 31 December 2000		1681	
			1746
Total equity			3046
Income statement for the year 2000			
Income			3135
Less expenses			−2400
Profit for the year 2000			735

Both the above exceptions to the articulation raise interesting theoretical questions. Dividends are discussed further in Chapter 16 and valuation adjustments in Chapter 17.

15.1.2 The matching principle

The source of the articulation of the balance sheet and the income statement is the arithmetic of double-entry book-keeping. However simply because the two statements are articulated does not mean that the balance sheet is necessarily the dominant statement that determines the values in the other statement, as is the case with the IASB's Framework. In logic, it is perfectly possible to decide that the income statement should predominate and that the balance sheet should be subordinate. The accountant would first decide what figures she wants to report in the income statement and then adjust the figures in the balance sheet accordingly. This is essentially what happens with the application of the matching principle, which has already been referred to in Chapter 13, section 13.4.

With matching, the accountant first decides what receipts (both past receipts and expected future receipts) should be reported as income in the income statement; this involves difficult decisions relating to the recognition of revenue which are further discussed in Chapter 17. She then decides what payments (both past payments and expected future payments) should be set off against these revenues; these payments are said to be 'matched' against the related revenues and are reported as expenses in the income statement. Past payments that relate to future revenues are carried forward as assets in the balance sheet. Similarly payments that are expected to be incurred in a future period but which should be charged against the income of the current period are brought forward by including a liability in the balance sheet. The principal aim of 'matching' is to assign costs and revenues to the income statement of the appropriate period. With matching, the balance sheet is a means of transferring costs and revenues between periods – it is the link between successive income statements; whereas with the IASB's Framework, the reverse is the case – the income statement is the link between successive balance sheets.

The nature of the balance sheet under the matching principle is presented in Exhibit 15.2. which is based on the work of the Eugen Schmalenbach, the German accounting theorist, whose book 'Dynamic Accounting' published as long ago as 1919 is still the best exposition of the matching principle.[1] It is very clear that the concept of asset under the matching principle is fundamentally different from that set out in

Exhibit 15.2 *The balance sheet under the matching principle*

Assets

1. Past payments carried forward to be reported as expenses in future periods (for example: Plant)
2. Future receipts brought forward; reported as income in the current or past periods (for example, debtor for a sale made in the current period)
3. Past payment that will lead to a receipt in a future period (for example, investments)
4. Cash

Liabilities

1. Past receipts carried forward to be reported as income in a future period (for example, subscriptions received in advance)
2. Future payments brought forward, reported as expenses in the current or past periods (for example, wages owing)
3. Past receipts that will lead to a payment in a future period (for example, amount borrowed by the enterprise)

Equity = Assets less Liabilities

the IASB Framework's definition, 'a resource controlled by the enterprise as a result of past events from which future economic benefits are expected to flow to the enterprise' (see Exhibit 13.4). There is no mention in this definition of payments carried forward or receipts brought forward.

However the IASB's Framework includes the matching principle (see Chapter 13, section 13.4). This means that the IASB's Framework incorporates two fundamentally different concepts of asset. The IASB's position would appear to be that the two concepts are not inconsistent; for example, a payment that is carried forward in the balance sheet may reasonably be treated as an asset, because the enterprise will enjoy a benefit when it can charge the expense in the future income statement without having to pay out cash. As will be demonstrated later, some IASs are based on the matching principle and some on the primacy of the balance sheet. The existence of two different concepts causes problems, particularly when the application of the matching principle leads to the setting up of assets and liabilities that cannot be reconciled with the definitions given in Exhibit 13.4. An example is the 'deferred profit on a sale and lease back transaction' which, under IAS 17, should be reported as a liability, but which does not meet the definition of liability as there is no 'present obligation'. The problems caused by this lack of a consistent concept of asset are discussed when the IASB's rules for the different categories of assets are considered later.

15.2 THE FORMAT OF THE BALANCE SHEET

The IASB (in marked contrast to the EU) does not prescribe a format for the balance sheet. However IAS 1 lists the items that, as a minimum, should appear on the face of the balance sheet, and sets out in an appendix an illustrative balance sheet drawn up in accordance with the standard. An example of a balance sheet drawn up in conformity with IAS 1 is presented in Exhibit 15.3. The most important general points that may be made about the structure of the balance sheet as specified in the IASs are:

(a) The assets are divided between current assets and non-current assets. A current asset is defined in IAS 1 as:

   (i) an asset that is expected to be realised in the normal course of the enterprise's operating cycle;

  (ii) an asset that is held primarily for trading purposes or for the short term, and which is expected to be realized within twelve months of the balance sheet date; or

 (iii) cash or cash equivalent.

Exhibit 15.3 *Global Corp: balance sheet*

	31 December 2000		31 December 1999
ASSETS			
Non-current assets			
Intangible assets*		165	85
Property plant and equipment*		1140	1100
Financial assets*			
Associates*	210		130
Others	440	650	550
Total		1955	1865
Current assets			
Inventories*		1250	1130
Accounts receivable*		1775	1125
Cash*		273	275
Total		3298	2530
Total assets		5253	4395
EQUITY AND LIABILITIES			
Capital and Reserves*			
Issued capital			
Share capital	1200		1000
Share premium	100		0
		1300	1000
Revaluation reserves			
Property revaluation	300		210
Translation	−235		−125
		65	85
Other reserves		130	100
Accumulated profits/losses		1551	946
Total		3046	2131
Minority interest*		100	100
Non-current liabilities			
Interest bearing borrowings*		400	400
Provisions*		160	125
Deferred tax*		175	75
Total		735	600
Current liabilities			
Provisions*		90	90
Interest bearing borrowings*		250	650
Accounts payable*		795	665
Interest owing*		12	9
Tax owing*		225	150
Total		1372	1564
Total equity and liabilities		5253	4395

Note: * marks the items that are required to be shown separately by IAS 1

The division of assets between current assets and non-current assets is useful for assessing the enterprise's liquidity as it gives an indication of the magnitude of the assets that will be converted into cash within the next 12 months or the enterprise's operating cycle, if this is longer.

(b) The other side of the balance sheet has three main headings:

   (i) **Capital and reserves:** This heading is given in IAS 1; it is only appropriate when the enterprise has the legal form of a corporation. The Framework uses the more general term, 'equity'.

   (ii) **Current liabilities:** a current liability is defined as a liability that is expected to be settled within 12 months of the balance sheet date or in the normal course of the enterprise's operating cycle if longer.

   (iii) **Non-current liabilities:** These are all liabilities that are not current liabilities.

The Framework recognizes only three elements of the balance sheet: assets, liabilities and equity. Hence, in Exhibit 15.3, there is no separate heading for provisions, which are included as part of the liabilities. The EU's balance sheet format does have a separate main heading for provisions; this constitutes the principal difference between the EU's and the IASB's format.

Capital and liabilities (including provisions) are dealt with in detail in Chapter 16.

15.3 ASSETS IN THE BALANCE SHEET: THE THREE TESTS

In order for an item to be reported as an asset in the balance sheet, it has to pass three tests:

- **Definition:** it must meet the definition of asset
- **Recognition:** it must satisfy the criteria for recognition
- **Measurement:** its value must be measured in an acceptable way

The three tests are applied in the above order.

15.3.1 Definition

The Framework defines an assets as 'a resource controlled by an enterprise as a result of past events and from which future economic benefits are expected to flow to the enterprise' (paragraph 49(a)).

There are three essential conditions for a 'resource' to be considered to be an asset: control, future economic benefits and a past event.

These three conditions were analysed in Chapter 14; they rarely cause problems when deciding whether specific items meet the definition of asset. Most difficulty arises with the concept of control. The Framework implies that it should be interpreted rather liberally, for it gives, as an example of an item that may be recognized as an asset, know-how obtained from a development activity when, by keeping the know-how secret, the enterprise is able to control the benefits that are expected to flow from it. Know-how (technical knowledge) is an intangible asset and the greatest problems in deciding whether an item meets the definition of an asset arise in this area. Intangible assets are discussed further in Chapter 20.

15.3.2   Recognition

The term 'recognition' refers to the decision to report an item as an asset in the balance sheet. An item that passes the definition test for an asset should be recognized if:

- Its future economic benefits are probable and
- Its cost or value may be measured with reliability

If an item fails the recognition test (on either count), it should not be reported in the balance sheet. However it is possible that its existence should be disclosed in the notes in order that the financial statements as a whole present fairly the enterprise's financial position.

Probability of future benefits

The future economic benefits must be probable. This relates to the qualitative characteristic of relevance. The lower the probability of future benefits, the less relevant the information about the asset is for decision-making. Neither in the Framework nor in the individual IASs does the IASB attempt to give a precise definition of 'probable'; for example it is not defined as a probability of greater than 50 per cent.

Recognition – reliability of measurement

It is an essential condition for the recognition of an asset that the future economic benefits can be measured reliably. The concept of reliable measurement is discussed in the next section which considers how to measure the amount at which the asset is to be reported. Note that, for an item to be recognized as an asset, it must fulfil the two essential qualitative characteristics: relevance and reliability.

The timing of recognition

Problems often arise in deciding the point in time at which an enterprise should recognize an asset, particularly when it is negotiating to acquire an asset controlled by another enterprise or person. For example, *IAS 16 Property, Plant and Equipment* states that an item should be recognized as an asset only when there is sufficient assurance that the enterprise will receive the rewards attaching to the asset and bear the associated risks. Before this occurs the enterprise may generally withdraw from the proposed acquisition and thus the asset may never materialize; hence it should not be recognized. *IAS 18 Revenue* contains a similar provision in the case of sale of goods; an item should continue to be reported as inventory and not as an account receivable until the enterprise has transferred to the buyer the significant risks and rewards of ownership.

15.3.3 Measurement

Measurement is another term for valuation: how to determine the monetary amount at which an asset is reported in the balance sheet. The IASB's Framework mentions four possible measurement bases (historical cost, current cost, realizable value and present value) but does not come down in favour of any particular one. Hence one has to refer to the individual IASs to discover the valuation methods to be used for the various categories of assets.

15.4 THE PRINCIPAL CATEGORIES OF ASSETS

The methods prescribed in the IASs for the valuation of the principal categories of assets are set out in Exhibit 15.4.

15.4.1 Inventories

The valuation of inventories is covered in IAS 2 which defines inventories as assets:

- Held for sale in the ordinary course of business or
- In the process of production for such sale or
- In the form of materials or supplies to be consumed in the production process or in the rendering of services

In the Fourth Directive the EU uses the British term 'stocks' whereas the IASB uses the American term 'inventory'. In this book, 'inventory' is used so as to avoid confusion with the term 'stock' when used by Americans for an element of equity; for similar reasons, the British term 'share' is preferred to the American term 'stock'.

Exhibit 15.4 *Asset valuation methods specified in the IASs*

Asset category	IAS No.	Permitted valuation method
Inventories	2	Lower of cost and realizable value
Plant, property and equipment	16	(a) Historical cost less depreciation, or (b) Fair value
Intangible assets	38	(a) Historical cost less amortization or (b) Fair value
Financial assets		
Investments held for resale	39	Fair value
Derivatives	39	Fair value
Investments held to maturity	39	(a) Historical cost less amortization or
	39	(b) Fair value
Investment property	40	(a) Fair value or (b) Historical cost less depreciation
Biological assets	41	Fair value

According to IAS 2, inventories should be valued at the lower of cost and market. Valuation at the lower of the two possible amounts is a clear example of the prudence principle overriding the need to provide relevant information, for the market value is undoubtedly more relevant than cost for most decisions. It is no surprise that IAS 2 imposes the lower of cost and market rule, which is very well established in accounting practice throughout the world. The main interest is how IAS 2 interprets the concepts of 'cost' and 'market'.

Cost

IAS 2,7 defines the cost of inventories as comprising 'all costs of purchase, costs of conversion and other costs incurred in bringing inventories to their present location and condition.' The definition refers to costs actually incurred (that is to historical costs) and not to hypothetical costs such as replacement cost. IAS 2,10 (an explanatory paragraph) makes clear that costs include a systematic allocation of both fixed and variable overheads. In the matter of fixed overheads, the IASB rule differs markedly from that of the EU which makes their inclusion voluntary. Many European enterprises exclude fixed overheads from the value of inventory, because the lower inventory value leads to lower taxable income.

On cost formulas, IAS 2 allows wide choice, permitting a choice between FIFO, LIFO and weighted average cost for inventories for which the actual cost cannot be specifically identified. The IASB has been widely criticized for allowing the use of LIFO, which frequently results in a balance sheet value of inventory that is unrealistic and out of date. In 1991, the IASC made an attempt to eliminate LIFO as an option when it issued E38. However this proposal met with very widespread opposition, notably from the professional accountancy bodies of Germany, Japan and the USA, where many enterprises use LIFO – mainly because of its tax advantages. The acceptance of LIFO is an extreme example of the matching principle overriding the balance sheet approach to asset valuation.

Market

'Market' is taken as 'net realizable value' which is defined as 'the estimated selling price in the ordinary course of business less the estimated costs of completion and the estimated costs necessary to make the sale' (IAS 2,4). In normal circumstances, net realizable value (as so defined) will be higher than cost, because the enterprise will budget to make a profit over the whole process of producing and marketing the product. In calculating net realizable value, only the future costs of completion and marketing are deducted from the estimated selling price and *not* these costs *plus* the expected profit margin. Hence only when there has been a significant fall in the expected selling price (perhaps provoked by a large decline in the price of raw materials) will the application of the lower market value rule lead to inventories being valued at below cost. Hence the IASB's interpretation of the concept of 'market' is not particularly prudent. If IAS 2 had interpreted 'market' as replacement cost or as the current disposal price, it would have led to inventory being written down below historical cost on many more occasions.

15.4.2 Plant, property and equipment

The IASB's rules for this category of asset are set out in IAS 16 which defines plant, property and equipment as tangible assets that are held by an enterprise for use in the production or supply of goods or services, for rental to others or for administrative purposes and are expected to be used in more than one period (IAS 16, 6). These assets form a major part of the total assets of many enterprises, particularly those in the manufacturing and transport sectors.

IAS 16 allows a choice of valuation methods between cost and fair value.

Cost

Cost is defined as 'the amount of cash or cash equivalents paid or the fair value of the other consideration given to acquire an asset at the time of its acquisition or construction' (IAS 16, 6). This is a straightforward definition of historical cost, extended to cover the situation where the asset was acquired through exchange and not through the outlay of cash.

Fair value

Fair value is defined as 'the amount at which the asset could be exchanged between knowledgeable, willing parties in an arm's length transaction' (IAS 16, 6). When an asset is first acquired, its fair value will normally equal its acquisition cost and hence IAS 16 prescribes that initially these assets should be reported at historical cost and only subsequently may they be revalued at fair value. However this distinction is rather artificial since there is no minimum interval before they may be revalued; in theory this could occur the day after their acquisition. When assets are revalued, they are reported at the fair value at the date of revaluation. Hence, fair value is a measure of current value, although how current depends on when the last revaluation was made. The definition of fair value implies market value. However, for many assets, there is no ready market; IAS 16 states that these assets should be valued at depreciated replacement cost. This is one of the rare references to replacement cost in the IASs. This neglect of this valuation method is regrettable given the importance attached to it by many accounting theorists.

When an asset's value is changed following a revaluation at fair value, the accounting treatment of the value change differs according to whether it is an increase or a decrease. An increase in value should be credited direct to the revaluation reserve (an element of equity); a decrease in value should be charged immediately as an expense in the income statement. This treatment reflects the principle of prudence. When the increase/decrease reverses a previous decrease/increase, it is treated in the same way as the previous accounting entry, an increase is credited to the income statement and a decrease is charged to the revaluation reserve.

When an enterprise avails itself of the option of reporting plant, property and equipment at fair value, there are two basic rules that it must respect:

(a) It must report all assets of the same class at fair value. It cannot pick and choose; it cannot decide to report only certain assets in a class at fair value (for example those which have increased in value since acquisition). However, it is permitted to measure one class of assets (say land) at fair value and another class (say machinery) at cost less depreciation.

(b) Revaluation should be carried out sufficiently frequently to ensure that the carrying amount does not differ materially from the current fair value.

Of the two valuation methods, IAS 16 states that cost is 'the bench-mark treatment' and fair value to be 'the allowed alternative treatment', which gives the impression that the IASB considers that fair value should be the exception rather than the rule. One point must be emphasized: there is absolutely no requirement for enterprises to report plant, property and equipment at fair value. The IASB would never be able to achieve a consensus for a standard that imposed fair value, given that it would be contrary to the law and practice of many countries, including the three largest economies in the world – USA, Japan and Germany.

The measurement basis whereby some fixed assets are reported at historical cost and others at fair value is known as 'modified historical cost'. It is widely used in the UK where many enterprise report land and buildings at fair value and other fixed assets (such as plant and machinery) at historical cost. The advantage of reporting assets at fair value is that it increases the value of equity and therefore improves the debt/equity ratio (at least in the common case where the fair value is greater than cost). The disadvantage is that future depreciation charges are increased. However British enterprises can get the best of both worlds by reporting those assets at fair value which do not have to be depreciated (for example land) or which may be depreciated over a very long period (for example buildings) and by reporting shorter-lived assets (such as machines) at cost. This trick is not available to enterprises in the USA, Japan and Germany, where assets may not generally be reported at above cost.

15.4.3 Intangible assets

An intangible asset is an asset without physical substance. Examples include both specific assets, such as patents, licences and brands, and rather less clearly defined assets such as goodwill and capitalized development expenditure. Largely because they lack physical substance, these assets present difficult problems for accountants. It is widely believed that the reporting of intangible assets offers opportunities for unscrupulous management to manipulate the accounts, for example by reporting intangible assets at inflated values. The IASB's rules for intangible assets are much stricter than those for plant, property and equipment, in respect of both recognition and measurement. An example of this stricter approach is that intangible assets may be valued at fair value only when an active market exists, which is hardly ever the case with intangible assets. Given the specialized nature of intangible assets, they are not considered further in this chapter, but are discussed in detail in Chapter 20.

15.4.4 Prepayments and other accruals

The model balance sheet in IAS 1 includes a heading for prepayments, but otherwise there is virtually no mention of this category of assets in the IASs. This asset is of interest because its inclusion in the balance sheet is based on the matching principle and therefore the question must be considered as to whether it meets the IASB's definition of an asset. In respect of common prepayments, such as prepaid rent, insurance or wages, the IASB's position seems to be that they meet the definition of asset because they bring economic benefits in the future (for example, the service rendered by a rented building). However, the application of the matching principle leads to the reporting of other stranger accruals in the balance sheet whose future economic benefits are far less evident. An accrual which is reported in the balance sheets of many European enterprises is the initial cost of forming the corporation, such as legal fees and registration fees. Under the EU Directives and the law of many Continental European countries, these formation expenses may be capitalized and reported in the balance sheet as an intangible asset, presumably because they do not relate solely to the periods in which they are incurred. However the future economic benefits associated with this 'asset' (the existence of the corporation) are so nebulous that one can state with confidence that they do not meet the IASB's definition. The whole subject of accruals is considered further in Chapter 16, section 16.4 with reference to the liabilities side of the balance sheet.

15.4.5 The dominance of historical cost

For the categories of assets so far considered, the basic valuation method specified in the IASs is historical cost, with fair value as a permitted alternative for plant, property and equipment and also, in rare cases, for intangible assets. This reflects the dominant position of historical cost as the valuation method for assets in accounting law and practice throughout the world. However, the predominance of historical cost has come under threat in recent years, as a result of changes in the environment in which enterprises operate, initially in relation to inflation, and then more recently in connection with financial instruments. The high rates of inflation experienced by many industrialized countries in the mid 1970s brought attention to the inadequacies of historical cost accounting and generated increased interest in alternative methods of asset valuation. The standard-setting bodies of both the USA and the UK developed standards which imposed various forms of inflation accounting on enterprises. In 1981, in line with these developments, the IASC issued its own standard on inflation accounting: *IAS 15 Information Reflecting the Effects of Changing Prices*, which referred to two alternative ways of valuing assets: the current cost approach (assets valued at replacement cost) and the general purchasing power approach (restatement of asset values using a general price index). However, because of the strong attachment both of the accountancy profession and of enterprises to historical cost, IAS 15 does not lay down that the assets in the balance sheet should be valued using one of these alternative methods. Its requirements are very weak, being limited to the provision of certain supplementary information in the notes. In fact, even these very mild requirements proved too much for many enterprises, which declined even to publish this supplementary information. In 1989, following similar developments in the USA and the UK, the IASC decided to make its standard voluntary, stating that 'enterprises need not disclose the information required by IAS 15 in order that their financial statements comply with International Accounting Standards'. Thus historical cost successfully resisted the first attack on its dominance. However the second attack is proving rather more serious. It relates to financial assets which are now considered.

15.4.6 Financial assets

In recent years, there have been considerable changes in the form of the financial assets held by enterprises. Whereas previously these consisted principally of cash, deposit accounts, receivables and investments, now many enterprises hold in addition exotic financial assets such as derivatives. It has become increasingly evident that historical cost is a fundamentally inappropriate basis for the valuation of certain financial assets, in that it results in reporting figures that are most misleading. In fact for certain derivatives, the historical cost is zero, even though they often have a significant current value. With historical cost accounting, these derivatives would not be reported at all in the balance sheet, which is clearly unsatisfactory. The obvious solution is to report these financial assets at current fair value. However the IASB has had great difficulty in reaching agreement on such a solution, as it is so much at variance with its previous approach and with law and practice in many countries. Finally in December 1998, it issued IAS 39 which set out an interim compromise solution in the expectation that agreement would be reached later on a more comprehensive solution. The interim solution provides that certain financial assets and derivatives should be reported at fair value and others at historical cost. Most derivatives and financial assets held for sale would be reported at fair value. The break with the IASB's previous practice is that, for the assets in question, fair value is not presented as an accepted alternative to historical cost but rather as the only acceptable method. This represents a very significant breach of the hegemony of historical cost.

Financial assets include receivables, which are principally amounts owing

by customers in respect of goods sold and services rendered. Receivables are one of the most straightforward of financial assets, but the IASB's rules are convoluted and, in the authors' opinion, wrong. Under IAS 39, receivables are to be reported at cost which is defined as the fair value of the consideration given. In the authors' opinion, the generally accepted accounting practice is to value receivables at the amount that the customer has contracted to pay, subject to possible deductions for discounting the future payment to its present value and for the probability that the customer may default. No doubt the IASB would argue that its measure (the fair value of the consideration given, that is the goods sold) is equal to the contracted amount. However there are two reasons for rejecting this approach:

- It inverts the logic: the fair value of the goods may be estimated as the contracted amount but not vice versa, as the latter is determined by the contract with the customer
- If, for some reason, the contracted amount is not equal to the fair value of the goods (for example, the enterprise made a mistake in pricing the sale) then the contracted amount is the relevant value.

Most financial assets are more complicated than receivables and the IASB's rules relating to them are correspondingly complex. They are considered in detail in Chapter 22.

15.4.7 Investment property

The term investment property is used to denote land and buildings that is held for an investment and not for use (which would be classified as plant, property and equipment) or for sale (which would be the inventory of a property developer). The return on investment property consists of rentals and capital appreciation. Conceptually it is a hybrid of plant, property and equipment on the one hand and financial assets on the other. In fact it gave the IASC great problems. The IASC could not reach an agreement on a standard for many years, mainly because of deep differences among its members. In Britain, the common practice was periodic revaluation, but this was rejected by most other leading countries which were opposed to reporting assets at above historical cost. In the end, the IASC had to accept that it could not bridge the gap between its members and in 2000 it issued IAS 40 which allowed a choice between fair value and historical cost.

15.4.8 Agricultural assets

Recently a further weakening in the dominance of historical cost occurred when in December 2000, the IASC issued IAS 41 Agriculture, which required that the biological assets of an agricultural enterprise should be reported at fair value. The term biological assets refers to crops and livestock. There would appear to be four reasons why the IASC considered that fair value and not historical cost was the appropriate measure for these assets:

- The historical cost of many biological assets is very low or even zero, for example what is the historical cost of a bushel of wheat (the cost of the seed) or of a new-born lamb?

- To attempt to calculate a full historical cost for these assets (for example, by allocating labour and overhead costs) would represent a significant burden for farmers, without providing information of much relevance

- Many agricultural products are traded in open markets and hence a reliable measure of fair value is readily obtainable

- The reporting of these assets at fair value was already the established practice of certain enterprises (notably for plantation crops such as coffee and tea)

15.4.9 Assets not covered by IASs

It is important to note that the IASs that have been issued to date do not cover all possible assets that might be reported by enterprises; for example the costs of exploration and development of oil wells and natural gas fields are not covered (they are specifically exempted from the intangible assets covered in IAS 38). In principle, these assets should be covered by the catch-all rules of IAS 1. However the reference in that standard to the IASB's Framework imposes virtually no restraint on the freedom of preparers, given that the Framework's rules as to the measurement of assets are so vague

15.5 DEPRECIATION AND AMORTIZATION

Tangible and intangible fixed assets should be depreciated. According to the IASB, depreciation is the process whereby the cost or value of an asset is allocated over its useful life. The alternative term 'amortization' is often used for intangible assets; it has exactly the same meaning as 'depreciation'. In the following remarks, the word depreciation is often used to cover both depreciation and amortization. The IASs that deal with tangible and intangible assets define the terms relating to depreciation in a very clear and complete manner:

(a) **Depreciation:** the systematic allocation of the depreciable amount of an asset over its useful life.

(b) **Depreciable amount:** the cost of an asset, or other amount substituted for cost in the financial statements, less its residual value (note that the words 'other amount substituted for cost' refers to the reporting of assets at fair value where this is a permitted alternative).

(c) **Useful life:** either the period of time over which an asset is expected to be used by the enterprise, or the number of production units expected to be obtained from the asset by the enterprise.

(d) **Residual value:** the net amount which the enterprise expects to obtain from an asset at the end of its useful life after deducting expected costs of disposal.

(e) **Carrying amount:** the amount at which an asset is included in the balance sheet after deducting any accumulated depreciation and impairment losses thereon (note that impairment is dealt with in the next section).

To interpret the above definitions one starts with the definition of the first term 'depreciation' and notes that it includes two terms that need to be defined: 'depreciable amount' and 'useful life'. One then turns to the definition of these terms and discovers that the definition of 'depreciable amount' includes the term 'residual value' that needs to be defined. With the definition of this term, the definition of 'depreciation' is complete.

Depreciation according to the IASB should be systematic. At the time that the asset is acquired, the enterprise should decide on a plan for allocating the asset's cost over the accounting periods that are expected to benefit from the asset's availability and use. This involves forecasting two aspects of the future: the asset's useful life and its residual value. The method of depreciation used should reflect the pattern in which the asset's economic benefits are consumed by the enterprise. Note that the annual amount of depreciation does not equal the *value* of these benefits, as depreciation is essentially an allocation of cost. The IASs do not prescribe any particular method: the straight-line, diminishing balance and sum-of-the units methods are all referred to, but the enterprise is free to choose any method provided that the method is applied consistently from period to period and that it results in the depreciation charge in the income statement reflecting the benefits flowing from the asset.

The principal problems relating to depreciation stem from the fact that it is necessary to forecast the future. Hence the IASs contain guidance on how the estimates of useful life and residual value should be made. More importantly they set out the rules to be followed when, inevitably on occasions, these forecasts turn out to be wrong. If economic circumstances change, the depreciation charged to the income statement may no longer reflect the revised estimate of the asset's useful life or the benefits that the enterprise may expect to receive. The estimate of the asset's useful life may be revised upwards if, for example, wear and tear is found to be less than expected, or revised downwards if, for example, it is rendered obsolescent by the invention of a new machine. These examples demonstrate that both technical and economic factors should be taken into account in estimating useful life. When the estimate of the useful life is changed then the depreciation schedule must be revised. The revision is treated as a change in accounting estimates and not as a change in accounting policy. The depreciation charge for the current and future periods may well be modified, but not that reported for past periods. It may be necessary to record that the asset is impaired. This is dealt with in the next section.

The fact that an asset is reported at a revalued amount following a reassessment of its fair value does not exempt it from depreciation. In fact, the amount of the annual charge will be increased when the revalued amount is higher than the previous carrying amount.

When an asset is disposed of or no future economic benefits are expected, it should be eliminated from the balance sheet. The gain or loss on disposal, which is reported in the income statement, is calculated as the difference between the net disposal proceeds and the asset's carrying amount. In the case of assets that are carried at fair value, where the revaluation surplus has been credited to equity, this results in the total charged to the income statement over the asset's life for depreciation and loss on disposal being greater than the asset's net historical cost (original cost less disposal proceeds); the income statement does not report comprehensive income.[2] However when an asset that is carried at fair value is sold or retired, the balance in the revaluation reserve that relates to this asset becomes realized profits. In that case it is appropriate to make a transfer of this amount from revaluation reserve to retained earnings. This transfer does not pass through the income statement. If it were to do so, the income statement would report comprehensive income.

Depreciation, as defined by the IASB, is firmly based on the matching principle. The cost of the asset is to be allocated to the periods in which the enterprise derives benefits from having the asset. The value of the asset reported in the balance sheet is determined by the depreciation charged and to be charged in the income statement – in essence it corresponds to one of the concepts of an asset under the matching principle: a past payment carried forward to be reported as an expense in a future period (see Exhibit 15.2). The income statement determines the balance sheet. This is contrary to the approach set out in the Framework which defines income and expenses in terms of increases and decreases in asset values. Hence it is necessary to include a further concept to reassert the primacy of the balance sheet. This concept is impairment, which will now be considered.

15.6 IMPAIRMENT

15.6.1 The basic rule

The concept of impairment, which is not mentioned in the Framework, is related to the requirement that an asset should not be stated in the balance sheet at an amount that is higher than the value of the future economic benefits that it is expected to generate; if this latter value is lower, the asset's balance sheet value is said to be impaired and should be reduced. The rules relating to impairment are set out in *IAS 36 Impairment of Assets* which includes the following definitions:

- **Carrying amount:** the amount at which an asset is stated in the balance sheet
- **Value in use:** the present value of estimated future cash flows expected to flow from the continuing use of an asset
- **Net selling price:** the amount obtainable from the sale of the asset in an arm's length transaction between knowledgeable, willing parties, less the costs of disposal
- **Recoverable amount:** the higher of an asset's net selling price and its value in use
- **Impairment loss:** the amount by which the carrying amount of an asset is reduced to its recoverable amount

The rules in IAS 36 are based on the well-known principle of economics that the value of an asset to an enterprise is calculated as the present value of future cash flows. If the enterprise keeps the asset, these cash flows will be those arising from its future use (termed value in use); if the enterprise decides to sell the asset, the cash flow will be the net selling price. If the enterprise's management is rational, it will sell the asset if its net selling price is higher than its value in use. Hence the value to the enterprise of an asset is the higher of its net selling price and its value in use; this value is termed 'recoverable amount'. The term 'recoverable amount' is derived from the concept that an enterprise needs to recover the amount invested in an asset if it is not to make a loss. The balance sheet value of an asset (termed 'carrying amount') should not be higher than its recoverable amount; if it is higher, the enterprise should write down the asset's carrying amount to its recoverable amount by charging an impairment loss in the income statement. Where the recoverable amount is higher than the carrying amount, the asset's value is not written up to the recoverable amount.[3] The rule is deliberately prudent and asymmetric: an asset is reported at the lower of the recoverable amount and carrying amount. For assets that are valued at historical cost, the effect of this rule is to report them at the lower of historical

Exhibit 15.5 *The general rule for the reported value of an asset*

```
                          ┌──────────────────────────┐
                          │ Historical cost          │
                          │ (or other allowed        │
                          │ alternative,             │
                          │ such as fair value)      │
                          └──────────────────────────┘
                               ↗
┌────────────────────┐                        ┌──────────────────┐
│ The value of an    │                        │ Net selling price│
│ asset is the lower │                        └──────────────────┘
│ of                 │                             ↗
└────────────────────┘                    
                               ↘          
                          ┌────────────────────────┐
                          │ Recoverable amount,    │
                          │ which is the higher of │
                          └────────────────────────┘
                                                ↘
                                         ┌──────────────────┐
                                         │ Value in use     │
                                         └──────────────────┘
```

cost (less depreciation) and recoverable amount. This rule is demonstrated in Exhibit 15.5.

Various aspects of the impairment rules will now be considered:

15.6.2 How to measure 'value in use'

Value in use is defined as the present value of the future cash flows arising from the continuing use of the asset and from the disposal of the asset at the end of its useful life. Hence for its calculation, one requires two elements: an estimate of future cash flows and an appropriate discount rate.

Future cash flows

Over 20 paragraphs of IAS 36 are given over to the subject of how to estimate future cash flows. The IASB's aim seems to be to make it difficult for management to avoid reporting impairment losses by using unrealistically optimistic estimates of future cash flows. Hence IAS 36 states that cash flow projections should be based on reasonable and supportable assumptions, with greater weight given to external evidence. They should be based on the most recent forecasts which should cover a maximum period of five future years unless a longer period can be justified. If a growth rate is assumed, it should not exceed the long-term average growth rate for the products, industries or countries in which the enterprise operates unless a higher rate can be justified. Cash outflows should include all those necessarily incurred to generate the cash inflows. All these conditions are designed to restrain the optimism of management.

Discount rate

The discount rate should be a market rate that reflects the time value of money and the risks specific to the asset. The basic idea is that the risks associated with the future cash flow are taken into account through the discount rate; the riskier the asset, the higher the discount rate. This implies that the estimated cash flows should be expected or average values and not pessimistic values. However it will rarely be possible to observe on the market an asset-specific interest rate. IAS 36 refers to the possibility of using the cost of capital of a listed enterprise that has a single asset or a portfolio of assets that has a similar risk profile and also to using the enterprise's own cost of capital determined using such techniques as the Capital Asset Pricing Model. Neither suggested method is ideal. It seems rather improbable that another listed enterprise would have a portfolio of assets with a similar risk profile to the asset being valued, whereas to justify the use the enterprise's own cost of capital assumes that the specific asset's risk profile is similar to that of the average asset. However these are the practical problems that are inherent in the use of net present value techniques. Probably the best practical solution is to use the enterprise's average cost of capital for all assets indiscriminately. This will tend to overestimate the present value of the riskier assets and underestimate the value of the less risky assets, but at least the estimates will be unbiassed.

15.6.3 Criticisms of 'value in use'

Some commentators argue that 'value in use' lacks reliability as a measure of an asset's value, since it is based on estimates of future cash flows which are inherently subjective and unverifiable, notwithstanding the IASB's efforts to make them more objective. These critics point out that the subjective nature of value in use provides opportunities for management to manipulate the accounts and to smooth profits, for example by charging large impairment losses in good years and reversing them in poor years. Hence they argue for market value as the sole measure of recoverable amount. Also some argue that to calculate the recoverable amount at the *higher* of value in use and net selling value is contrary to the principle of prudence.

The IASB rejected this approach on the grounds that it would be misleading to report at market value an asset that the enterprise does not intend to sell. To calculate the recoverable amount at the *lower* of value in use and net selling value would, in certain circumstances, result in values that are excessively low. Consider the example of an enterprise that has constructed a plant to manufacture a product (for which it holds the patent) which is expected to yield large future cash flows; the plant is highly specific and, since it cannot be easily adapted for any other purpose, its net selling value is negligible. In this case, to assess the recoverable amount of the plant as zero would be unreasonable. Where it is more profitable for the enterprise to retain and use the asset, the value in use would seem to be most logical measure of its value. In this conflict between reliability and relevance, the IASC opted for relevance.

15.6.4 The 'hotch-potch' of valuation rules

The application of the impairment rule means that, in the same balance sheet, three fundamentally different measurement bases may be used for reporting the same category of asset. Consider the example of an enterprise which owns three factories: A, B and C. Exhibit 15.6 presents the value of each factory under the three measurement bases of historical cost, net selling price and value to owner. Value to owner is calculated, as prescribed in IAS 36, as the present value of the asset's future cash flows discounted at an interest rate that reflects the time value of money and the risks specific to the asset. The amount at which each factory should be reported in the balance sheet is then assessed applying the rule shown in Exhibit 15.5. This leads to the reporting of factory A at historical cost less depreciation, factory B at value in use and factory C at net selling price. At least superficially this seems inconsistent and confused. Certainly the reported figure is a strange patchwork of accounting values (historical cost) and economic values (market values and present values). Some commentators have criticized IAS 36 on the grounds that values based on discounted cash flows are inconsistent with the historical cost basis of accounting, and that such a radical change should not be introduced on a 'piecemeal' basis.

However, although the impairment test may seem to lead to reported figures that are difficult to defend on the basis of theory, it is absolutely necessary as a means of remedying one of the fundamental weaknesses of historical cost accounting. A major problem in historical cost accounting is how to justify the reporting of a non-monetary asset. When an enterprise has made an outlay of resources (say cash), it has to decide whether to report this transaction as an asset or as an expense. To justify reporting

Exhibit 15.6 *Application of the impairment test*

Measurement bases	Factory A €	Factory B €	Factory C €
Historical cost			
Cost	100 000	100 000	100 000
less depreciation	−40 000	−40 000	−40 000
(a) Net value	60 000	60 000	60 000
Net selling price			
Expected sales proceeds	75 000	45 000	52 000
less costs of disposal	−2 500	−1 500	−2 000
(b) Net selling price	72 500	43 500	50 000
Value in use			
Expected future annual cash flow	20 000	15 000	10 000
Number of years	5	5	5
Present value of annual cash flows	72 096	54 072	36 048
Disposal value at end of life	5 000	5 000	5 000
Present value of disposal value	2 837	2 837	2 837
(c) Total present value	74 933	56 909	38 885
Discount rate (reflecting risk of asset)	12%	12%	12%
Recoverable amount			
(d) Higher of (b) and (c)	74 933	56 909	50 000
Carrying amount			
(e) Lower of (a) and (d)	60 000	56 909	50 000

the transaction as an asset, the enterprise must refer to some concept of value other than historical cost; otherwise any outlay of resources could be claimed to be an asset. This is the reason why measurement bases, such as value to owner and net selling price, find their way into the balance sheet, even when the fundamental measurement base is historical cost.

15.6.5 When assets must be tested for impairment

The enterprise should test assets for impairment whenever there is evidence that their recoverable amount may be lower than their carrying amount. This applies to most of the assets listed in Exhibit 15.4. Inventory has its own special impairment test; it should be written down to lower realizable value, which, although not identical to the higher of net selling price and value in use, is similar.

There has been much discussion whether the requirement to carry out a test for impairment is an excessive burden on enterprises. The calculations of net selling price and value in use are certainly not trivial. The IASB's position is that the obligation is not too burdensome for the following reasons:

■ When an asset was tested last year for impairment and its recoverable amount was demonstrated to be significantly higher than its carrying amount, a further test is not necessary this year unless there has been a significant change in circumstances

■ In many cases, it is necessary to measure only one of the two attributes (net selling price and value in use). If this is shown to be higher than carrying amount, the asset is not impaired

However the IASB's rule does mean that, if an asset's value has been written down to recoverable amount in a particular year, one would expect that, in the following year, its (revised) carrying amount would be close to its (revised) recoverable amount and hence a further impairment test will be necessary. In fact for such an asset one would expect that the reporting of impairment losses in the income statement would be a common occurrence.

15.6.6 The IASB compared with the FASB

On impairment, the IASB's approach is fundamentally different from that of the FASB which distinguishes between the 'impairment recognition trigger' (which is the value used to identify whether an asset is impaired) and the 'impaired value' (which is the value that the asset is written down to). Under the IASB's rules these two values are the same: 'recoverable amount'. Under the FASB's rules, the 'impairment recognition trigger' is a relatively high amount (the undiscounted value of future cash flows) and the 'impaired value' a relatively low amount (fair value). With the FASB's rule, impairments losses are recognized less frequently than with the IASB's rule, but when they are recognized they are for larger amounts. One can see advantages and disadvantages in the approaches of both bodies:

(a) the IASB's approach leads to smaller but more frequent impairment losses charged in the income statement, which means that the reported profit is less volatile and reflects more accurately the current situation, but the more frequent impairment tests are costly.

(b) the FASB's approach is to recognize impairment less frequently (thus sparing enterprises some of the costs of impairment tests) with the effect that the reported profit is more volatile, caused by the reporting larger impairment losses at infrequent intervals.

The authors support the IASB's approach. They consider that the FASB's use of undiscounted cash flows cannot be reconciled with the concept of an asset as the embodiment of future economic benefits. This viewpoint has been expressed very clearly by Milburn (1988): 'If the present value principle is a basic economic reality that is incorporated within contracting arrangements and capital market security prices and is widely used by businessmen and investors in making economic decisions as between alternatives involving future cash flows then it would seem reasonable to expect that this principle should be recognized in a rational and consistent way in the measurement of assets and liabilities within GAAP'. However the alternative view is not illogical. It is based on the argument that discounting is incompatible with historical cost accounting; provided that an asset's future cash flows are sufficient to cover its historical cost, the enterprise will not report a loss (before financing charges) and hence the asset's value is not impaired. This viewpoint is well expressed in the Canadian standard (which is similar to that of the FASB): 'Estimated future net cash flow is not discounted in computing net recoverable amount since the purpose of the calculation is to determine recovery and not valuation' (CICA, 1997).

15.7 THE ASSETS OF THE LARGEST MNEs

In order to assess the relative importance of the different categories of assets, the authors have analysed the balance sheets of the world's 50 largest multinational enterprises.[4] The results of this analysis are presented in Exhibit 15.7, which shows the percentage that each of the principal asset categories makes up of total assets. The 50 enterprises are divided into four groups, which reflect the groupings established by the research of Doupnik and Salter (1995) which is described in section 2.8 of Chapter 2 and presented in Exhibit 2.9:

(a) **USA:** this group includes not only the 11 American enterprises listed in Exhibit 1.4, but also two Canadian enterprises, The Seagram Company Ltd and Nortel Networks Corporation, since in Exhibit 2.9 Canada is shown as being part of the USA group. The 13 enterprises in this group make up 42 per cent of the total assets of the 50 enterprises.

(b) **UK:** This group comprises eight enterprises from the UK, the Netherlands and Australia, all members of the UK group in Exhibit 2.9.

(c) **Japan:** This group is made up of nine Japanese enterprises.

(d) **Continental Europe:** This is the largest group in terms of numbers, comprising 20 enterprises from Germany, France, Switzerland, Spain and Italy (but not the Netherlands, which is in the UK group). However in terms of total assets it is smaller than the USA group.

Exhibit 15.7   *The structure of the assets side of the balance sheet: Analysis of the balance sheets of the fifty largest MNEs*

	USA (%)	UK group (%)	Japan (%)	Continental Europe (%)	Overall (%)
Non-current assets					
Intangible assets	6.12%	8.29%	1.63%	8.70%	6.37%
Tangible assets	22.23%	44.72%	21.20%	30.69%	26.90%
Financial and monetary assets	39.51%	14.24%	26.87%	11.78%	26.21%
Not specified	3.20%	0.19%	1.20%	0.29%	1.65%
Total non-current assets	71.06%	67.44%	50.90%	51.47%	61.13%
Current assets					
Receivables	10.06%	18.08%	25.55%	25.77%	18.40%
Inventory	5.89%	7.83%	7.64%	10.33%	7.77%
Accruals	1.85%	0.29%	1.94%	2.14%	1.80%
Cash and investments	10.42%	6.29%	12.35%	9.40%	10.03%
Not specified	0.71%	0.07%	1.63%	0.89%	0.86%
Total current assets	28.94%	32.56%	49.10%	48.53%	38.87%
Total assets	100.00%	100.00%	100.00%	100.00%	100.00%
Group's proportion of total assets	41.86%	9.76%	17.09%	31.29%	100.00%

Notes: All percentages are calculated as weighted averages, taking into account the size of the enterprise. The analysis is based on the 2000 accounts.

Exhibit 15.7 shows that non-current assets make up 61 per cent of total assets for the 50 enterprises overall, with intangible assets (only 6 per cent of total assets) being significantly less important than the other two categories of non-current assets. Tangible non-current assets make up nearly 27 per cent of total assets and are the single largest category of assets. This result is not unexpected. Tangible assets, such as land, buildings, plant, equipment, ships, aircraft and vehicles, are what most people would expect to be the principal assets of firms. However the third category of non-current assets, financial and monetary assets, is almost as large as tangible assets, making up over 26 per cent of total assets. The principal assets in this category are long-term investments in other enterprises. The figures in Exhibit 15.7 do not include investments in most subsidiary companies, because the analysis was performed on the consolidated balance sheets. Hence the investments concerned are principally investments in associates and other long-term investments that do not include any element of control. The percentage for financial assets of Japanese enterprises is significantly higher than that for European and UK firms. The reason is that it is very common for a Japanese enterprises to own less than 50 per cent of the capital of another enterprise. Associated enterprises are much more common in Japan than in Europe, whereas the opposite is the case for subsidiaries. However in addition to long-term investments, the category of financial and monetary assets include long-term receivables (where the customer is not required to settle until more than twelve months after the balance sheet date) and two strange monetary assets that are reported under the financial reporting rules followed by most MNEs: prepaid pension cost and deferred tax assets. Many American MNEs report considerable amounts for these two particular assets which partly accounts for the high percentage for financial and monetary assets reported by American MNEs (nearly 40 per cent of total assets). Another reason is that three mammoth American MNEs (GE, Ford and General Motors) have very large finance subsidiaries whose financial assets are included in their consolidated balance sheets. The finance activities of the non-American MNEs are, by comparison, very much smaller. There are no financial institutions (banks and insurance companies) among the fifty MNEs whose balance sheets were analysed, because they were excluded from the UN's survey (see section 1.5 of Chapter 1).

Current assets make up some 40 per cent of total assets. For the 50 enterprises as a whole, just under 50 per cent are current receivables (debts that are due to be settled within twelve months of the balance sheet date). However there are considerable differences between the groups. Current receivables are very much higher in Continental Europe and Japan (at 25 per cent of total assets) than in the USA and the UK. These percentages reflect genuine differences in the way in which sales are financed in the different countries.

15.8 COMPARATIVE ANALYSIS OF ASSET VALUATION METHODS

This section examines the methods used in the five countries of the Pentad to value two important categories of assets: non-current tangible assets and inventories. The valuation methods used for the remaining asset categories are covered in the specialized chapters: Chapter 20 for intangible assets and Chapter 22 for financial instruments.

15.8.1 Non-current tangible assets

With respect to the reporting of non-current tangible assets, the world may be divided into two broad camps: between those countries where historical cost is the only accepted method of valuation and those countries where alternatives to historical cost are permitted.

The supremacy of historical cost: the USA and Japan

In the USA historical cost is the only permitted valuation method for non-current tangible assets. Certainly historical cost must be reduced by systematic depreciation and by write-offs for impairment as appropriate, but historical cost remains the upper limit at which assets of this category may be reported. The American regulatory authorities take this very firm approach because it is widely believed that a major cause of the Wall Street crash of 1929, which triggered the Great Depression of 1929–34, was the overstatement of profits by many American enterprises through valuing assets at above historical cost. In the USA the supremacy of historical cost has certainly been challenged in recent years. However as yet this has led to a change in the rules only for certain monetary assets, which are to be reported at fair value even when this is higher than historical cost. The position regarding tangible assets remains unchanged.

The position in Japan is similar. When Japan reformed its financial reporting system after the Second World War, it modelled it on the American system and in particular adopted the American practice of insisting on historical cost as the upper limit for the value of non-current tangible assets. Between 1950 and 1973 Japanese enterprises were permitted to revalue depreciable assets at above historical cost, with the surplus being credited to equity; the revaluation led to higher depreciation charges which reduced the distributable profit and thus helped enterprises to maintain the real value of their capital. Recently a new law provides for a very limited degree of revaluation; under the Land Revaluation Law of 1998, large corporations are permitted to restate the book value of the land that they own at market value. The surplus is to be credited to equity.

Diversity: Europe

In contrast to the USA and Japan, where the rules are both clear and uniform, in Europe the position is much more varied. The fundamental reason is that the EU's Directives do not lay down a single method for the valuation of non-current tangible assets. Certainly, article 32 of the Fourth Directive states that assets should be valued at purchase price or production cost (that is historical cost) but the next article (number 33) then gives member states the option of permitting or requiring their companies to use other valuation methods for certain categories of assets. For non-current tangible assets, three alternative methods are offered:

- Valuation at replacement cost
- Valuation at a method that is designed to take into account inflation
- Revaluation

This article is a member state option. The governments of the EU member states are not obliged to incorporate its provisions into their national law and furthermore they can choose how to implement the article; for example to provide for all three alternative methods (or only two or one) and whether to make their adoption by enterprises compulsory or voluntary. The diversity of practice in the EU has its origins in the different ways in which the governments of the various EU member states have implemented article 33 of the Fourth Directive.

Germany

Germany has not incorporated this article into its national law and hence the position in Germany is essentially the same as in the USA. In fact, at the time that the EU was drafting the Fourth Directive, the German government strongly opposed the inclusion of article 33 and insisted that its opposition be recorded in the following declaration which was included in the minutes of the Council meeting that adopted the Fourth Directive: 'for reasons of monetary and economic policy, the Federal Government cannot accept valuation methods designed to take into account inflation as authorized by article 33 of the Fourth Directive by way of derogation from the purchase price principle laid down in article 32. It will therefore not permit such valuation methods in the Federal Republic of Germany'. The reason for this stubborn attitude of the German government is essentially the same as that which causes the American authorities to adopt the same attitude – historical experience. However Germany's bad experience with permitting enterprises to value assets at above historical cost came half a century before that of America, during the 'Gründerjahre' ('promoter years') of the early 1870s when very many newly-formed corporations collapsed with severe losses to shareholders and creditors. The collapses were attributed to slack accounting rules which allowed management to value assets at above historical cost. Hence subsequently in 1884 the law was amended to make historical cost the upper limit for the reported value of assets. Subsequent experience, notably the severe inflation in 1923 and in 1945–6, seems to have strengthened the belief of most Germans that historical cost accounting is a guarantee of economic stability and even one of the major causes of their country's superior economic performance. There is a widespread feeling that to permit inflation-adjusted accounting would weaken the resolve of the government and society in the battle against inflation. The low levels of inflation experienced by Germany since 1949 (significantly lower than in either France or the UK) would seem to indicate that this belief is not groundless.

The UK

The British government incorporated two of the Fourth Directive's three alternative valuation rules into British law when it amended the Companies Act in 1981. British companies are permitted to value tangible fixed assets either at their current cost or at their market value as at the date of the last valuation. There is no compulsion. The British government did not make use of the Fourth Directive's option to *require* corporations to adopt the alternative valuation rules. In fact no EU member state *requires* corporations to value assets at other than historical cost, but all, except Germany, *permit* the use of one or more of the alternative valuation rules. In adopting these rules in the 1981 Companies Act, the British government was giving recognition to the long-standing practice of many British companies (permitted by the law) to report tangible fixed assets using valuation bases other than historical cost. It is estimated that two-thirds of British quoted companies carry some revalued assets in their balance sheets (Company Reporting, 1997). The detailed reporting of tangible assets is regulated not by the Companies Act (which permits valuation at current cost or market value without further defining these terms) but by a standard of the UK's ASB: FRS 15 Tangible Fixed Assets. This permits the reporting of these assets at replacement cost, which is defined as the cost of acquiring an equivalent asset at the balance sheet date. It lays down a number of conditions that are designed to prevent certain abuses which had been very common. Thus valuations should be performed at frequent intervals (not less than every five years) by a valuer external to the entity. This is to ensure that the reported values are not too much out of date and are not too much influenced by the management's wish to paint a rosy picture. More importantly, it is not permitted to revalue some items of a class of assets whilst retaining others at historical cost. This is to prevent 'cherry-picking' – only revaluing those assets whose values have increased. However it is still permitted to report certain categories of tangible assets at revalued amount and other categories at historical cost. When assets are revalued, depreciation is calculated on the new value, which means, although the company reports higher asset value ('good news'), it also reports lower profits which is 'bad news'. For this reason, many British companies revalue land and buildings. The land is not subject to depreciation, whereas the economic life of buildings may be so long that the depreciation charge is trivial. Far fewer British companies revalue machines and other similar assets with shorter lives, as the increased depreciation charges would represent an unacceptable burden. The practice of reporting some assets at historical cost and others at valuation is known as 'modified historical cost'. This mixture of valuation bases is neither consistent nor logical, but it is very popular with British companies. When the ASB issued its current

Exhibit 15.8 *Extract from the 1999 annual report of the Peninsular and Oriental Steam Navigation Company*

'Basis of preparation of the accounts
The accounts are prepared on the historical cost basis modified by the inclusion of the majority of properties at their latest valuation'
Analysis of properties at 31 December 1999

	At valuation (Analysed by date of valuation)			At historical cost less amortization		
	1999 £mn	1998 £mn	1997 £mn	Cost £mn	Amort. £mn	Total £mn
Freehold	705.1	21.4	36.6	58.2	0.0	821.3
Leasehold: over 50 years	163.3	11.1	7.2	2.4	0.0	184.0
Leasehold under 50 years	80.9	3.8	6.8	76.4	(22.9)	145.0
Total	949.3	36.3	50.6	137.0	(22.9)	1150.3

The historical cost of properties net of accumulated amortization is £1088.1mn.

standard, FRS 15, in 1999, it made no attempt to outlaw modified historical cost, which is deeply entrenched in British practice, but contented itself to removing abuses, such as 'cherry-picking'.

The practice of British companies is illustrated in Exhibit 15.8:

Note that, of the total book value of assets (£1150.3mn), the greater part relates to assets reported at valuation but part relates to assets reported at cost less depreciation. The reported value of properties is increased by 6 per cent (from £1088.1mn to £1150.3mn) through the use of modified historical cost. The company does not charge depreciation on its freehold and long leasehold property on the grounds that the amount is not material.

In February 1999, the ASB issued FRS 15 which requires that, for accounting periods ending after 23 March 2000, all assets of the same category should be measured in the same way. However this standard does not apply to investment properties. Hence it is legal for companies to value investment properties at market value and other properties at cost less depreciation.

France

Under French law, as modified in 1984 to implement the EU's Fourth Directive, an enterprise may revalue its non-current tangible assets on condition that, at the same time, it revalues all its non-current tangible and financial assets. In fact, at that time, revalued assets were already a feature of the balance sheets of most French enterprises. In 1976, the French government decreed that all listed enterprises should revalue their tangible assets at 'utility value' subject to the revalued amount not being greater then the historical cost multiplied by a published index. Non-depreciable assets were revalued in 1977 and depreciable assets in the following year. The whole exercise was fiscally neutral; French enterprises were not taxed on the increased asset value and depreciation for tax purposes was calculated on historical cost. Since 1976/7 there have been no further government decreed revaluations, but many French enterprises carry traces of this revaluation in their current balance sheet, as shown in the following extract from the 1999 annual report of Totalfina SA:

> Other property, plant and equipment are carried at cost with the exception of assets that have been acquired before 1976 whose cost has been revalued under French regulations.

Although since 1984, all enterprises are permitted to make further revaluations of their tangible and monetary fixed assets, in fact very few do, probably because they would have to pay tax on the increase in value. This consideration does not apply to the consolidated accounts. However the authors have been unable to find a single major French enterprise that reports any tangible fixed assets at valuation except for those that were revalued in 1977/8.

15.8.2 Inventories

In all five countries of the Pentad, inventories are valued at the lower of historical cost or market value. Although in Britain, the Companies Act permits companies to report inventories at current cost, in fact no major British company does so. The major difference between the five countries in this area relates to the convention used to measure cost. There is general agreement that, where the specific cost of an individual item of inventory can be established without difficulty, this should be used for valuation. However, for inventories of materials and parts that consist of many identical items, there are three widely used alternative methods of establishing cost: FIFO, LIFO and weighted average cost. The major difference between the five countries is in the use of LIFO.

In Europe, the EU's Fourth Directives mentions three permitted methods of inventory valuation (LIFO, FIFO and weighted average cost) but leaves the choice to the member state. The position in the three European countries of the Pentad is as follows:

France

Under French law, the only permitted methods are FIFO and weighted average cost, as the French government did not implement the option of permitting LIFO.

Britain

The Companies Act allows all three methods. However the relevant accounting standard, whilst not actually forbidding the use of LIFO, criticizes its use as leading to a significant misstatement of the value of the asset and suggests that it would not normally give a true and fair view. Furthermore LIFO is not accepted by the tax authorities. For these reasons no major British company uses LIFO.

Germany

German law specifically permits the use of LIFO for the published accounts and, since it is also accepted by the tax authorities, there is a strong incentive for German enterprises to use it. Two of the seven German enterprises in the world's top 50 MNEs state that they use LIFO; most refer to average cost. VIAG is one of the two that uses LIFO, but only for part of its business as is made clear by the following quotation from its 1999 annual report:

> Inventories are carried at acquisition or manufacturing cost. The average-cost method of valuation is ordinarily applied, although for selected similar inventories, particularly in the aluminum business, the LIFO method is used.

The position in the non-European countries is as follows.

USA

US GAAP specifically permits the use of LIFO and in fact many American corporations use this method to value inventory in their balance sheets, notwithstanding that it may lead to a significant understatement of this asset's value. The reason is that the American tax authorities accept LIFO valuations for the assessment of taxable profit on condition that it is also used for the published accounts. Exhibit 15.9 presents a quotation from the 1999 annual report of General Motors that indicates that the firm uses all three methods. This lack of consistency can be attributed partly, but not entirely, to differences in national accounting systems.

Exhibit 15.9 *Extract from the 1999 annual report of General Motors*

Inventories for Automotive, Communications Services and Other Operations	Dollars ($)mn
Productive material, work in progress and supplies	5 505
Finished products, service parts etc.	7 023
Total inventories at FIFO	12 528
Less LIFO allowance	1 890
Total inventories [per the balance sheet]	10 638

Inventories are generally stated at cost, which is not in excess of market. The cost of substantially all US inventories other than the inventories of Saturn Corporation and Hughes is determined by the 'last-in, first-out' (LIFO) method. The cost of non-US, Saturn and Hughes inventories is determined by either the 'first-in, first-out' (FIFO) or average cost methods.

Japan

In Japan, LIFO is specifically mentioned as an acceptable valuation method in the Accounting Principles for Business Enterprises issued by the Business Accounting Deliberation Council. Of the nine Japanese enterprises in the world's top 50 MNEs, two (Toyota and Nissan) state that they use LIFO to value inventories of materials and supplies, which suggests that the method is widely used.

SUMMARY

The concept of assets under the principle of the primacy of the balance sheet was compared with that under the matching principle. The IASB's rules for assets were examined starting with the three tests (definition, recognition and measurement) that an item has to pass before it may be reported in the balance sheet. The valuation methods for the various asset categories were described. The concepts of depreciation and impairment were explained. The asset structure of the largest MNEs was analysed. The five Pentad countries were compared as to the valuation methods that they used for non-current tangible assets and for inventory.

Review questions

1. What is meant by the 'articulation' of the balance sheet and the income statement?

2. With the matching principle, which is the dominant statement, the balance sheet or the income statement?

3. Which is the dominant statement according to the IASB's Framework? Explain.

4. What are the three tests that must be passed before an item may be reported as an asset in the balance sheet?

5. What are the basic rules of IAS 2 for the measurement of inventories? In what ways do these rules incorporate the two desirable qualitative characteristics of relevance and reliability?

6. What is the IASB's definition of 'fair value'? What is the accounting treatment of the gain or loss following the revaluation of plant at 'fair value'?

7. What is the difference between depreciation and impairment?

8. Explain the different valuation bases at which an asset may be reported in the balance sheet when account is taken of the possibility of impairment?

9. What is meant by 'modified historical cost'? In which country is it practised?

10. Outline the practice of the five countries in the Pentad in relation to valuation of non-current tangible assets and to the use of LIFO.

Notes

1. For an analysis of Schmalenbach's contribution to accounting theory see Flower (1996).
2. The term 'comprehensive income' is explained further in Chapter 17. It refers to profit calculated as the increase in value of net assets.
3. Where assets are reported at fair value, the fact that the recoverable amount is higher than the carrying amount is evidence that the asset's valuation may have to be brought up to date. However this is not certain because the defini-

tion of fair value is not identical with the higher of net selling price and value in use. Fair value is essentially market value. IAS 16 permits the use of depreciated replacement cost as a proxy for market value for assets without a ready market but makes no reference to the net present value of future cash flows.

4. The names of the enterprises are given in Exhibit 1.4 of Chapter 1.

References

CICA 'Section 3060: Capital assets', *Handbook*, Canadian Institute of Chartered Accountants, Ontario (1997).

Company Reporting 'Measurement of tangible assets', *Company Reporting* (February 1997), pp. 3–8.

Doupnik, T and Salter, S 'External environment, culture and accounting practice', *International Journal of Accounting*, **30**(3) (1995), pp. 189–207.

Ebbers, G 'Fixed asset revaluation in Europe: interaction between theory, practice and fiscal policies', *Comparative Studies in Accounting Regulation in Europe*, J Flower and C Lefebvre (eds), Acco, Leuven (1997), p. 431.

Flower, J 'Three "Accounting Heroes" of Continental Europe', *Essays in Accounting Thought*, I Lapsley (ed.), ICAS, Edinburgh (1996), p. 201.

Milburn, JA *Incorporating the Time Value of Money within Financial Accounting*, Canadian Institute of Chartered Accountants, Ontario (1988).

Further reading

For further information on the valuation of non-current tangible assets by European enterprises, see Ebbers (1997).

chapter sixteen

The Balance Sheet II: Liabilities and Equity

Chapter objectives

- To analyse the difference between liabilities and equity in the light of the proprietary and enterprise models of the entity
- To explain the principles for the reporting of liabilities, through a detailed analysis of the rules for provisions contained in IAS 37
- To describe the main elements of the equity of corporations
- To consider the reporting of items that combine the characteristics of liabilities and equity, notably preference shares and convertible debt.
- To present an analysis of the equity and liabilities as reported in balance sheets of the major MNEs

16.1 THE FORM OF THE BALANCE SHEET

The previous chapter dealt with the assets side of the balance sheet. The subject of this chapter is the other side of the balance sheet, the side that presents the liabilities and equity. The fact that the total of the assets equals the total of the liabilities and equity – that the balance sheet balances! – is one of the foundations of accounting. It can be presented in the form of the equation:

$$\text{Assets} = \text{Equity} + \text{Liabilities}$$

Traditionally this equality has been demonstrated by presenting the balance sheet as a two-sided document, with the assets on one side and the liabilities and equity on the other. However there is no international consensus on which side to place the assets. In the USA and the countries of Continental Europe, the assets are placed on the left-hand side of the balance sheet (as shown in Exhibit 16.1(1)); in the UK, assets are shown on the right (see Exhibit 16.1(2)). When, in IAS 1, the IASB gave an example of how to present the balance sheet, it cleverly and diplomatically resolved this conflict between its most influential members by placing the assets and liabilities not side by side, but one under the other (as in Exhibit 16.1(3)).

Many large enterprises now present their balance sheet in a vertical form. Frequently the items in the IASB's presentation are rearranged. The liabilities are deducted from the assets to give the amount of net assets, which is followed by the presentation of the figures relating to equity, as shown in Exhibit 16.1(4).

16.2 THE ENTERPRISE MODEL VERSUS THE PROPRIETARY MODEL

There are two different interpretations of the significance of the 'equity + liabilities' side of the balance sheet. They reflect two fundamentally different concepts of the entity, to which the balance sheet refers. Contemporary accounting practice and the IASB's Framework are based on the 'proprietary model' which may be considered to represent conventional wisdom. However there is an alternative concept of the entity that is based on the 'enterprise model', which is championed by a few maverick accounting theorists. It should be emphasized that the differences between the various models of the entity does not affect the assets side of the balance sheet; it affects only the 'equity + liabilities' side and, in particular, the distinction between equity and liabilities.

16.2.1 The proprietary model

With the proprietary model, the emphasis is placed on the rights of the owners[1] of the entity. In effect the accounts are prepared for the benefit of the owners. The accounts present, in the balance sheet, the value of the owners' interest (the equity) and, in the income statement, the amount of the profit, that is the increase in the owners' wealth over the period. The need to report the owners' wealth makes it necessary to measure and report liabilities. A liability is an obligation to transfer wealth to a third person, that is any person who is not an owner. These must be deducted from the entity's assets in order to arrive at a measure of the owners' wealth. However an obligation to transfer wealth to the owners is not a liability; it is part of equity. The emphasis on ownership also

Exhibit 16.1 *Four different ways to present the balance sheet: Global Corp balance sheet at 31 December 2000*

(1) Traditional USA and Continental Europe

Assets	5253	Liabilities	2207
		Equity	3046
Total assets	5253		5253

(2) Traditional UK

Equity	3046	Assets	5253
Liabilities	2207		
	5253		5253

(3) IAS 1

Non-current assets	1955
Current assets	3298
Total assets	5253
Capital and reserves	3046
Non-current liabilities	835
Current liabilities	1372
	5253

(4) Most MNEs

Non-current assets		1955
Current assets	3298	
less current liabilities	−1372	
Net current assets		1926
Total assets less current liabilities		3881
less non-current liabilities		−835
Net assets		3046
Represented by		
Contributed capital	1300	
Reserves	1746	
		3046

governs the definition of 'expense'. A transfer of wealth to a third person should be reported as an expense in the income statement; a transfer of wealth to an owner is not an expense.

The purest example of the proprietary model is that of a business owned by a single individual. However most large businesses are organized in the form of corporations and for them the model has to be adapted. In order to apply the proprietary model to a corporation one must define its owners. In law the corporation's owners are its shareholders. This leads to the definition of a liability as an obligation to transfer wealth to a person who is not a shareholder. Under the proprietary model, the corporation is considered to be an extension of the shareholders. Assets and profits are defined from the viewpoint of the shareholders. In effect, with this model, the basic balance sheet equation is rearranged to emphasize the measurement of equity; it becomes:

$$Equity = Assets - Liabilities$$

In principle, the proprietary model is straightforward. However there are two complications which cause problems for the accountant in applying the model.

In order to apply the proprietary model in practice, a distinction must be drawn between a person as shareholder and the same person in some other capacity, say as debt-holder or employee. For example a shareholder, in addition to subscribing for shares, may have lent money to the corporation; the amount owed by the corporation in respect of this loan is a liability. Similarly, if a shareholder is also employed by the corporation (say as a director), then the amount paid to her as salary is an expense of the corporation. However a dividend (a transfer of wealth to a shareholder in her capacity as shareholder) is not an expense and is not deducted in calculating the enterprise's profit. In fact accountants rarely have difficulty in distinguishing between a person in her capacity as a shareholder and the same person in another capacity, as generally they can rely on the distinctions laid down in law.

A problem arises with the proprietary model when there is a change in the composition of the shareholders. For example, when the corporation acquires a new shareholder, it is possible that the issue of shares to the new shareholder may be so effected that it has an impact on the wealth of the other shareholders. Thus the price at which the new shares are issued may be significantly less than the market price, leading to a fall in value of the other shareholders' shares. Whether or not this fall in the value of the other shareholders' equity interest is to be considered to be an expense depends on how the entity is defined. There are two possible definitions which are both consistent with the proprietary model as broadly defined:

(a) **The 'pre-existing shareholders model'.** With this model the entity is defined as the shareholders prior to the transaction, known as the 'pre-existing shareholders'. Hence the fall in value of their equity interest is an expense of the entity.

(b) **The general body of shareholders.** With this model, no account is taken of changes in the composition of the body of shareholders. Account is taken only of the overall value of the shareholders' interest in the corporation. Hence the fact that, as a result of a transaction, one group of shareholders (the pre-existing shareholders) is worse off and another group (the new shareholder) is better off does not affect the corporation. This model of the corporation is consistent with the legal position that a corporation is a separate person.

The need to distinguish between these two approaches only arises in certain rather unusual transactions involving shareholders, such as the issue of share options. For the great majority of the corporation's transactions, the distinction is not important. Hence the difference between the two versions of the proprietary model is not considered further in this chapter.

16.2.2 The enterprise model

However, the proprietary model is not the only way to view the entity. There is an alternative: the enterprise model. It is a useful exercise to analyse this model for two reasons:

■ It gives some ideas on how contemporary accounting practice may be reformed

■ It throws into relief the particular characteristics of the currently dominant proprietary model

The enterprise model was developed over 70 years ago by the American accounting theorist, William Paton. With this model, the basic balance sheet equation is:

$$\text{Assets} = \text{Equities}$$

The assets side of the balance sheet is essentially the same as with the proprietary model. The essential difference is that the enterprise model does not recognize any fundamental distinction between liabilities and equities. All the items reported on the 'equities' side of the balance sheet are sources of finance which enable the entity to own its assets. In effect the enterprise is viewed as an autonomous economic entity. It is separate from the shareholders, whose interests are not fundamentally different from those of other creditors. Paton rejected the distinction between equity and liabilities for two reasons:

(a) In economic terms there is no fundamental distinction between debt and equity instruments. Both debt and equity involve investors placing wealth at the disposal of the enterprise in the expectation of a higher future return; they involve both the postponement of consumption and the risk that the return will be different from what is expected.

(b) In most large corporations it is unrealistic to treat the shareholders as owners, since they lack the powers that are normally associated with ownership. They have no rights to dispose of the corporation's assets; this is the prerogative of the corporation's managers. The share-holders' principal right is to participate in the election of these managers. However, for the typical small shareholder, this right conveys very little power. Paton concludes that the usual tests of ownership based on control and legal title are unable to distinguish clearly liabilities from equity.

Recently some accounting theorists have taken a fresh look at Paton's ideas in the light of the shareholder values versus stakeholder values controversy. Thus a later extension of Paton's model considers the enter-prise as a social institution that is operated for the benefit of many interested groups: suppliers, customers, employees as well as suppliers of finance (both debt-holders and shareholders).

16.2.3 The dominance of the proprietary model

The IASB's Framework is based on the proprietary model. This is implicit rather than explicit as neither model is mentioned. However the Framework's definition of equity as 'the residual interest in the assets of the enterprise after deducting all its liabilities' is consistent with the proprietary model and the basic equation: Equity = Assets − Liabilities. Also the Framework's definition of expense excludes distributions to eq-uity participants.

Contemporary financial reporting practice is also based on the propri-etary model. This is evidenced by many corporations presenting their balance sheets with equity shown as the difference between assets and liabilities (as in Exhibit 16.1 (4)) and in the emphasis on the figure for net profit in the income statement.

For these reasons, the rest of this chapter (and of the book) is based on the proprietary model. The problems in distinguishing between liabilities and equity that arise with this model are considered in section 16.7, after liabilities and equity have been considered separately. As equity is defined and valued in terms of assets and liabilities, the detailed con-sideration of equity will be left until after liabilities have been dealt with.

16.3 LIABILITIES

The IASB's Framework defines a liability as 'a present obligation of the enterprise arising from past events, the settlement of which is expected to result in an outflow from the enterprise of resources embodying economic benefits' (see the definition in Exhibit 13.4).

A liability is essentially the opposite of an asset: an asset is expected to bring an inflow of future economic benefits; a liability is expected to cause an outflow of future economic benefits. As with assets, for an item to be reported in the balance sheet as a liability, it must pass three tests:

- **Definition:** it must meet the above definition
- **Recognition:** it must fulfill the criteria for recognition
- **Measurement:** the amount of the liability must be measured in an acceptable way

These three matters will be considered through a detailed examination of the rules for provisions as set out in IAS 37 Provisions, Contingent Liabilities and Contingent Assets. Provisions is the category of liability that presents the most difficulties with regards to recognition and measurement. Once the principles that should be applied to the accounting treatment of provisions have been established, it is relatively simple to apply them to other types of liability.

16.4　IAS 37: PROVISIONS

16.4.1　Definition of a provision

IAS 37 repeats the Framework's definition of liability (see above) and then defines provisions as liabilities for which the amount or timing of the expenditure that will be undertaken is uncertain. There are three important points to be made about this definition:

(a) **Provisions are liabilities.** The IASB does not accept the approach of the EU's Fourth Directive which presents provisions under a separate heading in the balance sheet distinct from liabilities. The IASB's approach is conditioned by the fact that its Framework recognizes only three elements of the balance sheet: assets, liabilities and equity. Provisions must be assigned to one of these elements. This means that, according to IAS 37, the term 'provision' should not be used to designate an item that is either equity or part of an asset. In some countries the term 'provision' is used to designate deductions from the value of assets such as depreciation and doubtful debts; this use of the term is not sanctioned by the IASB.

(b) **The essential characteristic of a provision is uncertainty.** Of course almost every item in the financial statements is subject to some degree of uncertainty, but IAS 37 distinguishes provisions from other liabilities, such as accounts payable, where the expected outflow of resources can generally be estimated with considerable confidence, often on the basis of a contractual obligation.

(c) **It is a necessary part of the definition of a liability (and thus also for a provision) that there must be a obligation to transfer resources to a person outside the enterprise.** This obligation must exist at the balance sheet date, although the enterprise may not be obliged to make the transfer until some future date. For example, when an enterprise has purchased goods on credit terms that allow it to defer payment for six months, there is a present obligation, which requires that the debt be reported as an account payable in the balance sheet, even though the supplier cannot insist on immediate settlement.

16.4.2 The recognition of a provision

IAS 37 specifies two conditions for the recognition of a provision:

- an enterprise has a present legal or constructive obligation to transfer economic benefits as a result of past events
- a reasonable estimate of the obligation can be made

According to the Framework, these two conditions apply to liabilities in general. The basic differences between provisions and other liabilities are not ones of principle and definition, but practical ones of implementation and measurement. These practical matters rarely cause difficulties with liabilities other than provisions. Nevertheless the principles set out in IAS 37 for the solution of these problems in relation to provisions apply, in principle, to all liabilities generally.

In respect of many provisions and almost all other liabilities, there will be a legal obligation; the enterprise's obligation arises under a contract or other legal instrument (for example, a statute). However it is not absolutely necessary that the enterprise's obligation is enforceable at law. The Framework states 'obligations also arise however from normal business practice, custom and a desire to maintain good business relations or to act in an equitable manner' (Framework, paragraph 60). Sometimes the past actions or representations of an enterprise have generated such expectations among those outside the enterprise, that the enterprise has no realistic alternative but to undertake certain expenditure. In an appendix, IAS 37 gives a number of examples, including:

(a) Where a retail store habitually refunds purchases by dissatisfied customers even though under no legal obligation, it would not be able to change this policy without incurring unacceptable damage to its reputation.

(b) Where an enterprise, which has a published policy of cleaning up pollution, has identified contamination on land surrounding one of its production sites, it has an obligation to clean up the land, even though under no legal obligation, because its past actions have created a valid expectation by the local community that it would do so.

In both cases, the enterprise's management considers that it is in the enterprise's long-term interest to incur the expenditure. One reason is that the other persons have other sanctions available if it did not; for example the dissatisfied customers may decide to avoid the store in future. IAS 37 considers that, in these cases, the enterprise has no realistic alternative but to incur the expenditure and that therefore it should recognize an obligation even though there is no legal necessity to do so. Such an obligation is termed a 'constructive obligation'.

The test of 'no realistic alternative' which is applied to provisions seems to be rather similar to that of probability of future benefits that is applied to assets. Both relate to the probability that resources will flow out of or into the enterprise in the future. However the impression given by the term 'no realistic alternative' is of a rather more stringent test for provisions than that for assets. It is not sufficient that it should be profitable for the enterprise to incur the future expenditure; it is necessary that it should be so profitable that, if the enterprise did not make the expenditure, it would be severely damaged. It is clearly contrary to the principle of prudence for the rules for the recognition of liabilities to be made more stringent than those for assets. Therefore the IASB's action in this matter is rather puzzling. It can be explained with reference to the manner in which in recent years provisions have been used (or rather abused). The IASB has been particularly concerned about two ways in which enterprises make use of provisions: smoothing of profits and 'big-bath' provisions.

Smoothing of profits

The estimation of the amount at which provisions are to be reported necessitates the exercise of judgement on the part of the enterprise's management in deciding what figure within a wide range should be reported. Hence provisions offer opportunities for management to smooth profits. In a good year, profits can be reduced by increasing the amount at which provisions are stated (choosing a figure from the upper end of the range) and for setting up provisions for even the most unlikely contingency. In a poor year, profits may be boosted by releasing provisions to the income statement, for example in revising the estimate of future expenditures (choosing a figure from the low end of the range) and in being much more discriminating in setting up provisions. The reason why management should want to boost profits in a bad year is obvious; it avoids the danger of the shareholders attempting to dismiss the managers for their bad performance. However it is often in the interests of management to understate the profits in a good year. Certainly the shareholders would be very happy to learn of this year's high profits, but there is a danger that this would lead them to increase their expectations. Unless the enterprise is able to continue to report similar increases in profits in future years, it is very probable that shareholders will become dissatisfied when future years do not display the same rate of profits increase. The higher this year's profits, the more likely shareholders will be dissatisfied in the future. By under-reporting this year's profits, management avoids the situation that the expectations of shareholders are aroused excessively. Moreover, when profits are understated by setting up excessive provisions, the management is provided with the perfect means of boosting reported profits in any poor future year by releasing these excessive provisions to the income statement. In effect these excessive provisions are a form of 'secret reserve'; although they are reported on the face of the balance sheet, they are secret because it is not apparent that the liability has been overstated.

'Big-bath' provisions

This colourful term refers to the practice of corporations making very large excessive provisions for future expenditures on the occasion of some event. For example, when an enterprise's plant has been severely damaged in an earthquake, the management will often find it expedient to over-estimate the future costs to be incurred in repairs. The shareholders are hardly likely to blame the management for the earthquake and future years' profits will be boosted by the release of the excess provision to the income statement. The favourable impact on profits is enhanced if the initial charge is reported as an extraordinary or exceptional item, or, better still, does not pass through the income statement at all. In the latter case, profits from ordinary activities over the period may be reported at an excessively high figure, which does not reflect the underlying profitability. When this happens, 'big-bath' provisions result not only in smoothed profits but also in created profits. A particular example of a 'big-bath' provision is the provision for restructuring costs made when an enterprise is planning to make considerable changes to its operations – for example to close a factory or to sell a major part of its organization. In the takeover boom of the 1980s and early 1990s, many enterprises made very large provisions for restructuring following the takeover of another enterprise; frequently the amounts provided exceeded the costs that were subsequently incurred enabling the enterprise to report enhanced profits in the future through the undisclosed release to the income statement of these excess provisions.

The IASB considers that the two practices described above result in misleading information being reported to shareholders, which is undesirable on a number of counts: it permits management to hide inefficient performance, it may lead to a misallocation of resources and it can cause inequity between successive generations of shareholders. Shareholders should be told the plain truth and not an doctored version of events. Hence, in an attempt to prevent enterprises from setting up excessive provisions, the IASB adopted the rule that a provision may only be recognized when there is a present obligation, which is either a legal obligation or a constructive obligation, where the enterprise has no real alternative but to incur the expenditure. The rules for the recognition of provisions for restructuring were made particularly strict. Such a provision may only be recognized if two additional conditions are fulfilled: firstly that the enterprise has a formal plan, which sets out such details as the factories to be closed and the number of employees to be declared redundant, and secondly that this plan has been communicated to persons outside the enterprise in such a way that the enterprise is committed to the plan in that withdrawal would cause it unacceptable damage. A point that caused the IASC great trouble in the development of IAS 37 was whether it was permitted to recognize a provision for restructuring when the management had decided on a plan before the balance sheet date but not announced it publicly until afterwards. The IASC Board decided in a rather close vote (ten votes to five) not to allow a provision in this case.

16.4.3 The problem of the provision for future expenses

Prior to IAS 37, it was the common practice of enterprises in many countries to create provisions in respect of expenses that they expected to incur in the near future. A common example is the provision for deferred repairs, which is considered in the following example.

The provision for deferred repairs: an example

An enterprise owns a machine, which cost €1000 and has an expected economic life of ten years with zero residual value. The machine requires a major overhaul (costing €100) at the end of every two years. If these overhauls are effected regularly, the services provided by the machine do not deteriorate over time. Since each year benefits equally from the machine's services, it is desirable that the machine's costs (costs of initial acquisition and subsequent overhauls) are charged evenly over the machine's life. This is the aim of the provision for deferred repairs. The figures that would be reported in the balance sheet and the income statement each year with this method are presented in Exhibit 16.2(a). In

Exhibit 16.2 *Accounting for major overhauls*

(a) The provision for deferred repairs

Year	Balance sheet			Income statement			
	Machine	Provision	Net assets	Depreciation	Repairs	Provision	Total costs
0	1000		1000				
1	900	−50	850	100	0	50	150
2	800	0	800	100	100	−50	150
3	700	−50	650	100	0	50	150
4	600	0	600	100	100	−50	150
5	500	−50	450	100	0	50	150
6	400	0	400	100	100	−50	150
7	300	−50	250	100	0	50	150
8	200	0	200	100	100	−50	150
9	100	0	100	100	0	0	100
10	0	0	0	100	0	0	100

(b) The IASC method

Year	Balance sheet			Income statement		
	Machine A	Machine B	Net assets	Depreciation A	Depreciation B	Total costs
0	900	100	1000			
1	810	50	860	90	50	140
2	720	100	820	90	50	140
3	630	50	680	90	50	140
4	540	100	640	90	50	140
5	450	50	500	90	50	140
6	360	100	460	90	50	140
7	270	50	320	90	50	140
8	180	100	280	90	50	140
9	90	50	140	90	50	140
10	0	0	0	90	50	140

year one, the enterprise sets up a provision for one half of the expected cost of the overhaul due at the end of year two. Hence the total costs charged in the income statement for year 1 are €150 (straight-line depreciation of €100 plus increase in provision of €50). At the end of year two, the enterprise incurs overhaul costs of €100, but this cost is partially offset by releasing to the income statement the provision of €50 made in year one. Hence the total costs charged in year two are only €150, equal to that charged in year one. The enterprise has achieved its aim of charging equal costs in each year.

The IASB's approach

The IASB rejects the approach outlined in the previous paragraph because, at the end of year one, the enterprise does not have a present obligation to undertake the overhaul. Instead, the IASB proposes that the overhaul expenditure should be capitalized and spread over the future years that will benefit from this expenditure. In IAS 16,28 it gives an example of a furnace which requires relining at regular intervals and suggests that the lining should be treated as a different asset with a shorter economic life from the rest of the furnace. To apply this approach to the present example, the machine (initial cost €1000) should be divided into two assets: the basic machine (€900) and that part which needs renewing after two years (€100). This has been done in Exhibit 16.2(b), where the different parts of the machine are designated machine A and machine B. Machine A has a life of ten years, so that annual depreciation is €90; machine B has a life of two years, so that annual depreciation is €50. With the overhaul at the end of year two, machine B is in effect replaced; hence the costs of the overhaul are capitalized. With this method, as with the provision for deferred repairs, the costs charged in the income statements of years one and two are equal. However there is a significant difference: in Exhibit 16.2(a) the annual costs are €150; in Exhibit 16.2(b) they are only €140. The source of this difference can be traced to the different figures reported under the two methods in years nine and ten. At the end of year ten, there is no need for an overhaul as the machine is to be scrapped. Hence there is no requirement to make a provision for the overhaul in year nine, and the costs charged in that year in Exhibit 16.2(a) is only the annual depreciation of €100.

Evaluation of the two methods

In the authors' opinion, given that the aim is to spread the total costs of the machine evenly over its life, the IASB's method is to be preferred. The IASB is justified in claiming that the cost of the overhaul is an asset whose costs are to spread out over future years rather than an expense to be provided for in advance. This argument is easiest to grasp in the case where the overhaul creates a new tangible asset such as a furnace lining. However the principle applies even if there is no obvious tangible asset; for example where the overhaul consists solely of dismantling the machine, cleaning all the parts and reassembling them. In this case, the asset that was acquired initially is a machine with clean parts that does not need overhauling for two years. The overhaul restores the parts to their original clean state but does not prevent the gradual deterioration and obsolescence of the machine as a whole which results in it being scrapped at the end of ten years. Hence the idea of dividing the machine into two (conceptual) parts.

Both the provision for deferred repairs and the IASB's method apply the matching principle. The difference between them is that the IASB, in addition, applies a test based on the principle of the primacy of the balance sheet – the provision for deferred repairs is rejected because it does not meet the definition of a liability. The basic principle followed by the IASB is that no provision should be recognized for future costs that need to be incurred in order to operate in the future. Hence an enterprise should not set up a provision for next month's wages. The appendix to IAS 37 gives a number of other examples of future costs that should not be provided for. Thus if an enterprise is required by law to fit smoke filters to its factory next year, the expected cost of installing these filters is an expense of next year and should not be provided for this year. The enterprise could avoid the costs by closing the factory or changing its operating methods. However, the distinction between this future expense (which is not provided for) and that of clearing contaminated land (which is provided for as there is a constructive obligation) is a very fine one, as in both cases the enterprise may have no realistic alternative but to incur the expense.

In outlawing the provision for deferred repairs, the IASB created problems for enterprises in those countries where it was strongly entrenched in law and practice. For example, in Germany, enterprises are required by law to set up a provision for maintenance costs that are expected to be incurred within three months of the balance sheet date. Hence, in Germany, an enterprise is faced with the choice either of obeying IAS 37 or of breaking the law, at least in respect of its individual accounts.

The IASB's approach to the recognition of provisions is marked by the need to give the readers of the accounts an unbiassed picture of the position. A similar approach is followed in respect of the measurement of provisions, which will now be considered.

16.4.4 The measurement of provisions

IAS 37 states that a provision that has passed the recognition test should be reported at the best estimate at the balance sheet date of the expenditure required to settle the present obligation. Generally, given the degree of uncertainty regarding the future, the expectations of management concerning the future expenditure will be represented not by a single amount but by some form of probability distribution. In this case the best estimate is the expected value of the probability distribution.

Two examples of how to calculate the amount of a provision on the basis of a probability distribution are presented in Exhibit 16.3 and 16.4. The first example, in Exhibit 16.3, is very simple; there are only two

Exhibit 16.3 *Example of the calculation of the amount of a provision: simple*

An enterprise is in dispute with a customer over the quality of a batch of goods. Both sides have agreed to submit the case to arbitration and, furthermore, have agreed that, if the arbitrator finds for the customer, the enterprise should pay €1 000 000, but, if the arbitrator finds for the enterprise, the enterprise should pay only €50 000. Hence the only uncertainty concerns whether the arbitrator will rule in favour of the customer or the enterprise.

On the assumption that the enterprise's management estimates that it has a one third chance of winning the case, the amount of the provision may be calculated as follows:

	Probability (%)	Expected value €
Customer wins the case: enterprise pays €1 000 000	66.67	666 666.7
Enterprise wins the case: it pays €50 000	33.33	16 666.6
Amount of the provision		683 333.3

possible outcomes: the enterprise will have to pay either €1 000 000 or only €50 000. If the enterprise's management estimates that there is a one-third chance of having to pay €50 000, the expected value of the obligation may be calculated as €683 333 (2/3 × 1 000 000 plus 1/3 × 50 000). The provision should be reported at its expected value, possibly rounded to €700 000 so as not to give a spurious impression of precision. It is not permitted either to report the provision at the most pessimistic outcome or even the most likely outcome, where these are significantly different from the expected value. In the above case, it would be wrong to report the provision at €1 000 000, which is the most likely value, as this would disregard the not insignificant chances of winning the case. In effect it would be assuming that the probability of losing the case is 100 per cent. In technical terms, the provision should be reported at the value of the mean and not of the median. This has the effect, in this case, that the provision is valued at an amount that it is certain that the enterprise will *not* pay. The enterprise may have to pay €1 000 000 or alternatively €50 000, but never €700 000. It might be claimed that the provision should be reported at €1 000 000 in application of the principle of prudence. IAS 37 does not ignore the prudence principle, but it does circumscribe the way in which it should be applied. Prudence should be exercised in assessing the cash flows and probabilities associated with future events. In the above example, in assessing that the chance of losing is two thirds, the management should carefully consider all the risks and uncertainties that surround the case.

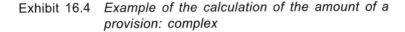
Exhibit 16.4 *Example of the calculation of the amount of a provision: complex*

An automobile manufacturer sells motor cars with a warranty to make good any defects discovered during the following year. The experience of past years indicates that 70 per cent of cars sold give rise to no warranty claims, 20 per cent to small claims (average €50 per car), 9 per cent to moderate claims (average €300 per car) and 1 per cent to large claims (average €2000 per car). In the past year, it sold 100 000 cars.

On the assumption that the enterprise estimates the amount of the provision on the basis of its previous experience, the following calculations are appropriate:

	Probable number of cars	Cost per car €	Expected cost €
No claims	70 000	0	0
Small claims	20 000	50	1 000 000
Moderate claims	9000	300	2 700 000
Large claims	1000	2000	2 000 000
Amount of provision			5 700 000

It would be an acceptable application of the prudence principle for the management to decide that, if it assesses the chances of winning are between one third and a half, it should calculate the provision using the lower probability (one third and not one half). However, once the probabilities have been assessed prudently, they should be used to calculate the expected value.

The second example, in Exhibit 16.4, demonstrates that the calculation of the expected value can be rather complex, particularly when there are a large number of individual items involved and past experience provides a scientific basis for the assessment of probabilities. The provision is estimated on the basis of the expected value of warranty expenditure per car sold, which is calculated using probabilities based on past experience.

These two examples demonstrate that, with IAS 37, statistical analysis has invaded the domain of assessing the amount of a liability in very much the same way that discounting has become part of the way in which the value of an asset is determined. In fact IAS 37 also states that provisions should be stated at the present value of future expenditures, where the effect of discounting is material. The IASB's specification of these two advanced techniques for the valuation of assets and liabilities is very significant in principle but has little impact on practice. Only a small fraction of assets are to be valued at net present value – only those assets for which the recoverable amount is less than historical cost (or fair value) and for which the recoverable amount is measured at net present value. With provisions, the application of statistical analysis is feasible only when data from previous experience is readily available. However the willingness of the IASB to prescribe advanced techniques derived from economics and statistics gives great encouragement to accounting theorists.

16.5 OTHER LIABILITIES: ACCRUALS

The other liabilities of the enterprise include debts, loans, bank overdrafts and accounts payable. In general few problems arise in applying to these other liabilities the principles that have just been analysed concerning the definition, recognition and measurement of provisions. Normally the reporting of these liabilities is simpler because there is less uncertainty involved. However there are three types of liability where problems can arise:

- Financial instruments (this rather specialized subject is covered in Chapter 22)
- Borderline cases, where it is difficult to decide whether an item is a liability or an element of equity or both (this matter is dealt with in section 16.7, after the subject of equity has been analysed)
- Accruals, which will now be considered

Exhibit 15.2 in Chapter 15 gave a three-way classification of the accruals that are reported among the liabilities in the balance sheet. Of the three categories mentioned, the second and third present no real problems, as they refer to the provisions and simpler liabilities that have already been considered. The problems arise with the first category: 'Past receipts carried forward to be reported as income in a future period'. This item is generally reported in the balance sheet as a liability under the heading 'deferred income'. The IASB has issued no general standard on deferred income. Hence normally deferred income is determined using generally accepted accounting principles. Examples of deferred income are:

(a) **Subscriptions received in advance.** A monthly magazine has a price of €10. In June 2000, a reader pays the publisher €120 for the twelve issues from July 2000 to June 2001. According to generally accepted accounting principles, the publisher should report, among the liabilities in its balance sheet at 31 December 2000, an accrual of €60, being the subscription received in advance for the six issues for January to June 2001.

(b) **Royalties received in advance.** The author of a book is entitled according to her contract with the publisher to a royalty of €1 per book sold. Prior to publication, she receives an advance of royalties of €1000, of which half is non-refundable and half is refundable, if the book sells less than 1000 copies. According to generally accepted accounting principles, she must report the refundable part of the advance as a liability (deferred income) and may so report the non-refundable part.

(c) **Deferred profit on a sale and lease back operation.** An enterprise sells for €1500 an asset with a book value of €1000. Normally it should report a profit of €500 on the sale. However, at the same time as the sale, it leases back the asset from the new owner under a finance lease. Under IAS 17, the enterprise should not report the profit in its current income statement but show it in the balance sheet as an accrual (deferred profit) to be allocated to income over the life of the financial lease. This is one of the rare references to deferred income in an IAS.

Do the accruals in the above examples meet the IASB's definition of a liability? A liability is a present obligation arising from past events, the settlement of which is expected to result in an outflow from the enterprise of resources.

In case (a), there would appear to be a present obligation (the obligation to deliver future copies of the magazine without receiving any further payment) and there would appear to be a future outflow of resources (the cost of printing and publishing the magazine). The only doubt is that the liability is not measured at the expected amount of the outflow but as a proportion of the receipt. In the case of provisions, the liability is measured at the amount of the expected expense. Hence there seems to be an inconsistency between the principle used to measure provisions and that used for deferred income.

In case (b), there is a clear future obligation in respect of the refundable advance. However, if the probability that sales will be less than 1000 copies is low (for example, orders have already been received for 5000 copies), it would seem inappropriate to measure the amount of this liability as the whole of the receipt. If the same principles were followed as for provisions, the liability would be measured as the amount of the future repayment multiplied by the associated probability. In the case of the non-refundable advance, there is no obligation and it is absolutely beyond doubt that to report it as deferred income would not meet the IASB's definition of a liability. This is a very clear example of a conflict between the matching principle (royalty income should be matched with the sales of the book) and the balance sheet approach to the definition of liability.

In case (c), there would appear to be a present obligation and future outflows but they relate to the financial lease (which under IAS 17 is reported as a liability) and not to the sale. In relation to the deferred profit, there is neither a present obligation nor any future outflows. Hence the deferred profit does not meet the IASB's definition of a liability.

These three examples demonstrate the difficulties that can arise from the conflict between the principle of the primacy of the balance sheet (on which the definition of a liability is founded) and the matching principle (which is the justification for the reporting of these accruals).

Having concluded the discussion of liabilities, it is appropriate to consider equity.

16.6 THE EQUITY OF CORPORATIONS

Virtually all large enterprises have the legal form of a corporation and therefore the analysis of equity will be made only in respect of corporations. According to the IASB's Framework, equity represents the residual interest in the net assets of the enterprise after deducting all its liabilities (see the definition in Exhibit 13.4). In a corporation, the owners are the shareholders and therefore the equity section of the balance sheet represents the shareholders' interest in the net assets. A corporation is a legal person. It is created by the law and, in most countries, there are specific legal provisions concerning what should be reported in the equity section of the balance sheet. Since each country's law is different, the layout of the equity section of the balance sheet and, in particular, the terms applied to the different elements of equity differ from country to country. This poses a problem for the authors of textbooks on international accounting. The authors of this book have solved the problem by explaining the subject using, for each major component of equity, a general term that is not specific to a particular country and later, in section 16.8, presenting examples from the published balance sheets of enterprises from different countries.

The total of equity is broken down into two major components: (a) contributed capital and (b) reserves.

16.6.1 Contributed capital

The contributed capital represents the amount received by the corporation in the form of cash or other valuable assets from the shareholders when they acquired their shares directly from the corporation either when it was founded or through a subsequent share issue. The contributed capital is split between nominal value and extra over nominal value.

Nominal value

In most countries, it is common for shares to be given a nominal value or par value. For example, each of the 19 484mn ordinary shares of BP Amoco PLC, the parent of the BP Group, has a nominal value of $0.25; the total is reported in the company's balance sheet as 'Equity: ordinary shares $4871mn'. On the formation of a corporation, its shares are generally issued to shareholders in exchange for cash of an amount equal to their nominal value.

Extra over nominal value

This represents the difference between the nominal value of the shares issued and the value of the assets (cash or other assets) received by the corporation. It generally arises when a corporation issues additional shares some time after its formation when the market value of its shares has risen above their nominal value.

The distinction between nominal value and excess over nominal value is of no significance in economic terms, since they both represent amounts contributed by the shareholders, and is rarely of legal significance, since in most countries, the law makes no distinction between the two elements of contributed capital.

In almost all countries, there is a legal requirement that the amount of the contributed capital should be shown separately in the balance sheet. The reason for this requirement is connected with the need to maintain the corporation's capital. Because of limited liability, the creditors of the corporation cannot sue the shareholders if the corporation is unable to pay its debts. The only resources that the creditors can look to for the repayment of their debts are the corporation's assets. These assets form a fund out of which the corporation's creditors can be paid. There is a general principle in the law of most countries that the corporation may not make any payment to shareholders that would have the effect of reducing this fund to less than a certain amount, which is generally the contributed capital. To demonstrate that this has been achieved, the capital contributed by the shareholders has to be shown as a separate item in the equity section. Provided that the total of the other elements of capital (dealt with in the next section) is not negative, the corporation will have maintained its contributed capital.

Hence, in most countries, there is a legal rule that dividends may be paid only out of profits, profits being defined as increases in the value of the corporation's net assets over its contributed capital. This rule serves two purposes: it ensures that the corporation's contributed capital (the minimum fund for the payment of creditors) is not depleted by the payment of dividends and it prevents a fraud that was frequently

perpetuated by unscrupulous managers on shareholders when corporation first became the common business form in the second half of the
nineteenth century. Managers paid dividends out of contributed capital
and in this way the shareholders were motivated to subscribe for more
shares in the belief that the corporation was doing well.

16.6.2 Reserves

The fundamental split in the equity section is between contributed capital and reserves. The reserves represent the increase in the corporation's
net assets other than those arising from contributions from shareholders.
The term 'reserves' is used in IAS 1, in the UK and, in translation, in
Germany and France. The use of the term 'reserves' is criticized by many
commentators who consider that unsophisticated readers may be misled
into believing that the term refers to assets such as cash and investments (that is they may confuse the two sides of the balance sheet).
For this reason, the term 'reserves' is rarely used in the USA; however
American corporations have so far failed to find a single term for the
concept.

The reserves are subdivided between non-distributable reserves and
distributable reserves; the term 'distributable' refers to whether the amounts
in question may be paid out to the shareholders by way of dividend. In
many countries the law places restrictions on the availability of profits
for the payment of dividends, for a number of reasons:

(a) **To increase the minimum capital available for the payment of
    creditors.** In many Continental European countries and in Japan,
    corporations are required to transfer a certain amount (often calcu-
    lated as a stated percentage of each year's profit) to a 'Legal Reserve'
    until the balance of this reserve equals a certain percentage of the
    contributed capital (often 10 per cent). The Legal Reserve is never
    available for the payment of dividends.

(b) **To prevent the distribution of unrealized profits.** In many countries
    the law distinguishes between realized profits and unrealized profits
    and provides that only realized profits are available for the payment
    of dividends. This is the position of the EU's Fourth Directive, which
    provides that, when an enterprise revalues an asset above historical
    cost, the surplus represents unrealized profits, it may not be reported
    as income but should be transferred directly to a 'revaluation reserve'
    which is not available for the payment of dividends.

(c) **To prevent shareholders benefiting unjustly.** Governments often grant
    aid to corporations with the aim of stimulating the economy, gener-
    ating employment, promoting exports or some other generally desirable

purpose. Typically the government would like to ensure that its aid is used for the stated purpose and not to pay a dividend to shareholders. It can achieve this by insisting that an amount equal to the aid received be transferred to a non-distributable reserve. A somewhat similar situation arises when the government decrees that certain profits (say those earned in a particular region) are exempt from tax, provided that they are not distributed to shareholders. It is not illegal to pay a dividend out of these profits but the corporation suffers a tax penalty if it does.

In all the above cases, the aim of ensuring that the surplus or aid is not used to pay a dividend is achieved by reporting it as part of the non-distributable reserves.

A number of IASs require that certain increases (and in some cases decreases) in the value of net assets should not be recognized as gains (or losses) in the income statement but should be reported directly as an element of equity. The gains and losses in question include:

■ Gains on the revaluation of plant, property and equipment (IAS 16)

■ Losses and gains arising from the translation of foreign currency assets and liabilities when the closing rate method of translation is used (IAS 21)

■ Losses and gains arising from valuing certain financial instruments at fair value (IAS 39)

The IASB is not a law-making body and does not specify that the element of equity so created is not available for the payment of dividends. However there is a strong implication that, as the gain has not been recognized as income in the income statement, it should not be distributed to the shareholders. This would be the legal position in many countries. It should be pointed out that, since in certain cases this element of equity may represent unrecognized *losses*, it may be negative. The authors have difficulty in understanding the precise significance of a negative element of equity. In their view, since the total value of equity is established beyond doubt as assets less liabilities, if one element of equity is negative, this must imply that another element of equity is overvalued; in the authors' view, the overvalued element is the balance of retained profits. This point is discussed further when foreign currency translation losses are considered in Chapter 21.

That part of the reserves that is not designated as non-distributable is, by definition, distributable. It will generally represent accumulated past profits (as reported in the income statement) less dividends paid. The fact that this surplus may legally be distributed does not mean that the corporation has the intention of paying a dividend of the full amount of this balance. Some corporations signify that they intend to retain all or part of these reserves by reporting it in the balance sheet under an appropriate heading, such as 'Investment reserve'.

16.6.3　Dividends

An interesting theoretical point is whether a dividend that the enterprise proposes to pay to its shareholders is a liability of the enterprise. The capital contributed by the shareholders is not a liability and it would seem appropriate that a proposed dividend should be treated in the same way. In practice, it is common for American and British enterprises to report the dividend proposed by the management as a current liability, on the grounds that this gives a better view of the cash payments that the enterprise will have to make in the near future and warns shareholders of the strains that the payment of the proposed dividend will place on the enterprise's liquidity. However, under the law of these countries, the enterprise is only permitted to pay the dividend when the management's proposal has been approved by the shareholders. Hence a proposed dividend does not meet the IASB's definition of a liability as there is no present obligation. When IAS 10 was revised in 1999, it was modified to provide that a dividend that is approved after the balance sheet date must not be reported as a liability. Hence with effect from January 2000, American and British corporations have been obliged to change their practice.

16.6.4　Treasury shares

In most countries a corporation is permitted to purchase its own shares. There are several reasons why the management may wish to do this:

(a) To have available an inventory out of which shares may be issued to employees in the context of an incentive plan.

(b) To support the stock exchange price. The management may consider that the stock exchange price of the corporation's shares is too low and it may be justified in feeling that, with its inside knowledge, it has a better understanding of the corporation's long-term prospects than do other market participants. If the current market price is lower than that which the management considers to be appropriate in the longer term, this has two negative consequences: it can cause inequity between successive generations of shareholders (the shareholder who sells her share at the current price does not receive a fair price) and it can encourage a take-over bid. The corporation in buying its own shares increases the demand for the shares which should lead to an increase in the market price.

(c) It may represent the best investment for the corporation's surplus funds. When a corporation buys its own shares, it is essentially making an investment that yields the corporation's cost of capital. If it can find no other investment project with a better return, then the purchase of its own shares is the best one available.

The American term for these shares whilst held by the corporation is 'treasury shares'. These shares do not represent an asset of the corporation, but rather a reduction in its equity. In effect the corporation, in buying the shares from shareholders, is returning to them their original contribution, adjusted for any change in the market price. Hence these shares are treated as a deduction from equity; they are reported as a debit balance (valued at acquisition cost) within the equity section of the balance sheet.

16.7 THE DISTINCTION BETWEEN EQUITY AND LIABILITIES

The distinction between equity and liabilities has already been discussed in connection with the alternative models of the entity: the proprietary model and the enterprise model. However within the prevailing proprietary model of the entity, there are two rather different approaches to drawing the line between equity and liabilities: the legal approach and the economics approach. Both approaches are consistent with the IASB's Framework's definition of equity, in paragraph 49(c), as 'the residual interest in the assets of the enterprise after deducting all its liabilities'. The difference lies in the concept of liabilities. These differences will be discussed for the case where the entity is a corporation, which is the business form adopted by almost all large enterprises.

16.7.1 The legal approach

In the case of corporations, the definition of equity depends on the detailed provisions of the law of the country in which the corporation is registered. However in most major countries the concept of the equity of the corporation is tied up with the legal requirement that the corporation should maintain a minimum level of assets to which creditors may look for payment, the minimum often being set at the contributed capital (see section 16.6.1). The balance sheet demonstrates that the corporation's net assets have not fallen below the minimum level by presenting a figure for its equity. In most countries, if this figure is less than the legal minimum, the corporation may not legally pay a dividend to its shareholders; as already discussed in the previous section, this condition is often demonstrated by the corporation reporting no distributable reserves. Also in some countries, the corporation has to be wound up if its equity falls below half of the legal minimum. This concept of equity implies that liabilities should be measured at the amounts that the corporation is legally obliged to pay out, either in cash or some other valuable asset, to settle the claim against it. If, in respect of a particular claim, the corporation has no legal obligation to make a future payment, then this claim does not represent a valid deduction from the corporation's assets in calculating its equity. To summarize, in most countries, the legal definition of the equity of a corporation is the value of its assets (as measured in a legally acceptable fashion) less the value of its liabilities, as measured by the amount that the corporation will be legally obliged to pay out in order to settle the claim. Hence, with the legal approach, a liability is defined in terms of a legally enforceable obligation of the corporation to transfer assets to an outside party.

16.7.2 The economics approach

In economics, the owners of the equity of a firm are the persons entitled to enjoy the benefits of its profits. Profits play a vital role in economics as the factor which guides the firm's decision-making process and which therefore determines the allocation of resources in the economy. Hence in economics, the suppliers of finance to the firm are divided between

■ The suppliers of debt whose claims are stated at a fixed amount of money, irrespective of whether or not the firm makes a profit

■ The equity which is entitled to receive the surplus after these prior claims have been settled

The equity is entitled to the firm's profits and therefore influences the firm's decisions concerning the allocation of resources. The debtholders are less interested in profits as their rewards are the same whether or not the firm earns a profit. Most of the risks associated with the firm's operations are borne by the equity.

With the economics approach, equity is considered to be the residual interest in the assets and the income of the enterprise after all prior claims have been satisfied. In a corporation, the shareholders represent the equity; their interest, which comes after those of all persons with prior claims, is defined in terms of proportions or shares. The non-equity-holders' claims both in respect of income and of capital is defined in fixed monetary terms and has priority over that of the shareholders. The fundamental difference between the economics approach and the legal approach, is that, in assessing the shareholders' equity, the economics approach deducts, in addition to the legal obligations, certain future claims on the assets of the corporation that are not legal obligations.

In very many cases, the legal approach and the economics approach yield the same answer. This is notably the case of a corporation where

Exhibit 16.5   *The legal approach versus the economics approach*

	Not residual interest	Borderline case	Residual interest
Legal obligation	A: Debts	B:	C:
Borderline case	D: Redeemable preference shares	E: Convertible debt	F:
No legal obligation	G: Preference shares	H: Participating preference shares	I: Ordinary shares

the equity consists entirely of ordinary shares and the liabilities consist entirely of debts. However there are a number of items that do not fit neatly into the straightforward debt and equity dichotomy. The position is illustrated by the matrix presented in Exhibit 16.5. The rows represent the legal approach, with a division between a legal obligation and no legal obligation, with borderline cases in the middle. The columns represent the economics approach, with columns for the residual interest, the non-residual interest and borderline cases in the middle. The various combinations are represented by the cells of the matrix, which are identified by the letters A to I. The most straightforward cases are cells A and I, where the legal approach and the economics approach yield the same logical answer: debts are a legal obligation and are not part of the residual interest; the ordinary shares are the residual interest and are not a legal obligation.

However the remaining cells of the matrix present examples of cases where either the legal approach and the economics approach do not lead to the same answer or the answer is ambiguous, being a borderline case. They refer to two types of financing instrument that pose particular problems in drawing the line between equity and liabilities: preference shares and convertible debt.

16.7.3   Preference shares

Corporations often issue shares which under the terms of its constitution have preferential rights over other shares, that is these shareholders are entitled to be paid the dividend due to them before the other shareholders are paid and similarly with repayments on liquidation. Since these shares carry preferential rights, they are often termed 'preference shares',[2] the other shares being termed 'ordinary shares'. The preferential rights of preference shares are generally defined in fixed money terms; for example the right to receive an annual dividend of €.05 per share and the right to receive €1 on liquidation, in both cases before anything is paid on the ordinary shares. In economic terms, preference shares are not part of the residual interest and therefore are not equity. However in law they are not a liability since the preference shareholders may not sue the corporation for non payment of dividends. The precise rights of preference shareholders are set out either in the corporation's constitution or in a contract between the corporation and the preference shareholders. Commonly, the constitution or contract provides that preference shareholders have no voting rights, except when the corporation has not paid the dividend due on their shares. Hence, as long as the corporation pays the preference dividend, preference shares are, in economic terms, akin to debt, but, if the corporation falls behind in the dividend payments, the preference shares become more like equity.

Moreover, the corporation's constitution or the contract may grant the preference shareholders rights that make their shares even more like equity: for example, that, after payment of the preference dividend of €.05 per share, the preference shareholders may be entitled to a specified proportion (say, one half) of any dividend paid to the ordinary shareholders. Such preference shares participate in the corporation's profits alongside the ordinary shareholders; for this reason, they are often termed 'participating preference shares'. The greater their participating rights, the more that participating preference shares resemble equity. In Exhibit 16.5, participating preference shares are presented in cell H: they are clearly not a legal obligation but for the economist they are a borderline case because they combine features both of a prior claim and of the residual interest.

However, the rights attached to some preference shares may be such that they may be considered to represent a legal obligation. For example, the corporation may be under an obligation to redeem (that is buy back) the shares at a stated price either at a certain future date or at the option of the shareholders.[3] Such shares are termed 'redeemable preference shares'; in Exhibit 16.5, they are shown in cell D. The economist is sure that they are not part of the residual interest, but in law their position is ambiguous.

16.7.4 Convertible loans

A convertible loan is a debt that gives the debt-holder the right to convert the loan into shares. The loan contract between the debt-holder and the corporation sets out the conditions on which this conversion is to take place, notably the dates and the conversion rates. Normally the debt-holder is not obliged to convert and will only do so if the value of the shares that he would receive is greater than the value of the debt. Until the time that the debt is converted into equity, it has the legal character of debt; for example the corporation must pay the contracted rate of interest, whether or not it has made a profit. Clearly after conversion, it is equity, since it cannot be reconverted into debt. Generally it is illegal to convert equity into debt as this would represent a reduction in the corporation's capital that is reserved for the payment of creditors. However, even before conversion, convertible debt may have the economic characteristics of equity. For example the interest rate on the debt may be abnormally low; the debt-holders are prepared to accept this low rate, because they anticipate making a greater gain on the subsequent conversion. If the conditions of issue of convertible debt are such that it is highly probable that conversion will take place, then it is akin to equity or at least potential equity.

16.7.5 The IASB's rules for preference shares and convertible loans

IAS 32 deals with the classification of preference shares and convertible debt in the following terms:

> *18. The issuer of a financial instrument should classify the instrument, or its component parts, as a liability or as equity in accordance with the substance of the contractual arrangement on initial recognition and the definitions of a financial liability and an equity instrument. 19. The substance of a financial instrument rather than its legal form governs its classification in the issuer's balance sheet.*

The reference to 'substance' rather than 'legal form' gives the impression that the IASB adopts the economics approach. However this is misleading; in fact the IASB's approach is largely, if not completely, legalistic. The crucial point is its definition of the term financial liability as 'a contractual obligation to deliver cash or another financial asset to another enterprise' or person. The words 'contractual obligation' make clear that the legal approach predominates.

Preference shares

The holder of a preference share normally has the right to receive from the corporation an annual dividend of a fixed amount. The conditions attached to this right are set down either in the corporation's constitution or in the terms of issue of the shares, both of which may be considered to constitute a contract between the corporation and the shareholder. Generally they make the payment of the dividend conditional on a vote of the general meeting of shareholders and of the availability of sufficient distributable profits. Until these conditions are fulfilled the preference dividend is not a legal obligation of the corporation. Hence, for the IASB, preference shares are not a liability.

However, in the case of redeemable preference shares that are redeemable for cash or another financial asset (other than the enterprise's equity) at a fixed date or at the option of the shareholder, the IASB considers that there is an obligation of the enterprise and hence the preference shares should be classified as a liability. Where it is the enterprise that holds the option to redeem, there is no obligation placed on the enterprise (it is not compelled to redeem) and hence no liability. However IAS 32, 22 refers to situations in which the enterprise may have no realistic alternative but to exercise its redemption option; for example where the shareholders have the contractual right to receive a dividend that increases each year so that in the foreseeable future the dividend will be so high that the enterprise will be compelled (for economic reasons not legal reasons) to redeem the share. In these circumstances the preference share should be classified as a liability because the enterprise has little discretion to avoid redemption.

The IASB's treatment of preference shares is not completely logical and consistent. A normal (unredeemable) preference share is not classified as a liability because the future obligation to pay dividends is not certain, even though in most cases it is highly probable. A redeemable preference share where the shareholder holds an option to redeem is classified as a liability even though it is not certain that it will be redeemed for cash or a financial asset. And this also applies where the enterprise holds the option where circumstances are such that it is highly probable that the enterprise will exercise the option.

Convertible debt

In the view of the IASB, convertible debt is a compound financial instrument consisting of a liability element and an equity element. The liability element is the obligation to pay interest and the possibility of having to redeem the debt for cash. The equity element is the (possible) future conversion into equity. IAS 32 does not prescribe a method for calculating the amounts to be allocated to debt and equity, but it does make some suggestions. Since it is an interesting theoretical problem, a fully worked example is given in Exhibit 16.6, which sets out the two alternative approaches suggested in IAS 32. Both approaches take as a starting point that the value of the convertible bond as a whole is equal to the amount received by the corporation on issue. The two approaches are:

- Estimate the value of the element that is easier to measure (typically the debt part) and allocate the remainder of the value to the other element
- Estimate the value of both elements and adjust their values so that the sum equals the value of the convertible bond

It is comparatively easy to estimate the value of the debt element as the present value of the future cash flows discounted at the market rate of interest for a non-convertible bond (not at the rate of interest on the convertible bond which will generally be lower because of the value of the conversion rights). Hence the first approach is generally the more practicable. However the second approach, which involves evaluating the equity element directly, may be feasible in some cases and always provides a useful check on the figures generated using the first approach. In Exhibit 16.6, the equity element has been estimated using the Black–Scholes formula for the price of a call option. It is not necessary that readers should understand the detailed workings of this formula, but they should note that accountants are beginning to take cognizance of recent developments in the related subject of finance. The second approach gives a slightly higher figure for the value of the equity element, and, for this reason, the values of both elements are reduced *pro rata* to bring the total value of the composite instrument down to its historical cost.

The IASB's division of convertible debt into an equity element and a liability element is consistent with both the legal approach and the economics approach. With the legal approach, the obligation of the corporation

Exhibit 16.6 *An example of the reporting of convertible debt*

A corporation issues a bond with a par value of €1000. The bond pays interest at a rate of 5 per cent per year and is redeemable at par in three years' time. However, at that time, the bond-holder has the right to demand conversion into 100 ordinary shares. The current market price of one share is €9. The market interest rate for similar bonds without conversion rights is 10 per cent, but this bond carries a lower rate because of the value of the conversion rights. The amount of €1000 received on the issue of the bond should be divided between the debt element and the equity element. There are two different approaches to calculating the value of each element:

Approach A
Calculate the value of the element that is easier to measure and allocate the remainder of the €1000 to the other element.

Value of the debt equals the value of the bond without the conversion rights
Present value of the interest payments discounted at
  10 per cent per year: €50 × 2.4865 = €124.34
plus present value of €1000 in three years time: €1000 × .75131 = €751.31
Total present value of the debt element: €875.65
Value of equity is the balance of the total value of €1000:   €124.35

(continued)

Exhibit 16.6 (cont'd)

Approach B

Calculate independently the value of both elements and adjust both values pro rata so that the total of the two values equals €1000.

The equity element may be equated to a call option to buy 100 shares in three years' time at an exercise price of €10. The present market value of a call option (C) may be estimated using the Black–Scholes formula:

$C = N(d_1)S - N(d_2)Ee^{-rT}$, where

$d_1 = (\ln(S/E) + (r + \sigma^2/2)T)/(\sigma \sqrt{T})$

$d_2 = d_1 - \sigma \sqrt{T}$

S is current market price of one share = €9

E is the exercise price of the option = €10

r is the risk free interest rate, say 6 per cent

T is the time to maturity in years = 3

σ is the standard deviation of the share's rate of return, say 18 per cent

ln is the natural logarithm and e is its base (approximately 2.71828)

N(x) is the probability that a random draw from a standard normal distribution is less than x.

Inserting the values given above into the Black–Scholes formula gives a value for C of €1.429

Therefore the option for 100 shares (equals the equity element) has a value of €142.90.

The value of the debt element, as already calculated, is €875.65. Therefore the value of the two elements is €1018.55

Reduce both elements pro rata to give a total value of €1000

Equity element: €142.90 × €1000/€1018.55	=	€140.30
Debt element: €875.65 × €1000/€1018.55	=	€859.70
Total value	=	€1000.00

to make payments must be reported in the balance sheet. However it is acceptable to measure this obligation at the present value of the future payments, which leaves a residue to be reported as equity. For the economist, the interest payments and (possible) cash redemption represent prior claims, but the right to acquire ordinary shares is part of equity.

In the calculation of the amount of the liability element in Exhibit 16.6, it is implicitly assumed that none of the debt-holders will opt for conversion. But a rational debt-holder would choose conversion if the market price of the ordinary shares at the redemption date is greater than €10. If shortly before the conversion date the market price is substantially higher than €10, then it would be reasonable to expect that all the debt-holders will opt for conversion and the whole of the convertible bond should be classified as equity. The logical extension of this line of reasoning is that, as long as the market price of the ordinary shares is below the figure at which debt-holders would be expected to convert, the convertible bond should be classified as a liability, but that, when the market price exceeds that figure, it should be classified as equity. Many commentators reject the IASB's approach of dividing the convertible bond between equity and liability; instead they claim that the bond should be reported as all equity or all debt depending on the circumstances. The authors support the IASB's approach as they consider that with convertible bonds there is an unavoidable uncertainty as to whether they are equity or a liability, which is best expressed in the balance sheet by dividing the bond into two parts. Furthermore the assumption that all debt-holders will choose the cash redemption option is prudent in that it does not understate the amount of the legal liability.

16.8   THE EQUITY AND LIABILITIES OF THE LARGEST MNEs

In order to gain an impression of the relative importance of the various elements of equity and liabilities, the authors have analysed the balance sheets of the world's 50 largest MNEs. The results of their analysis are presented in Exhibit 16.7, which shows the percentage that each element contributes to the financing of total assets.

Relative importance of liabilities and equity

Overall equity makes up a quarter of total finance. However there are remarkable differences between the groups, with the two extremes being the UK (45 per cent) and the USA (20 per cent). Does this disparity represent a genuine difference in financing practice between the various countries or does it only reflect the impact of different reporting practices? It would seem to reflect differences in reality, for three reasons:

(a) It is generally considered that the differences in financial reporting practice between the UK and the USA are not great, and certainly not as great as between these two and the rest of the world.

(b) The lower figure for equity for the USA group can be almost attributed wholly to the higher figures for borrowings (24 per cent for long-term borrowings and 17 per cent for short-term borrowings). The two groupings have basically similar rules for borrowings which leave little discretion as to the figures that have to be reported. Hence one may reasonably conclude that the American enterprises have

Exhibit 16.7 *The structure of the liabilities and equity side of the balance sheet: analysis of the balance sheets of the fifty largest MNEs*

	USA	UK group	Japan	Continental Europe	Overall
Current liabilities					
Payables	8.92%	17.63%	18.77%	16.17%	13.72%
Accruals	7.76%	4.13%	2.45%	4.44%	5.46%
Borrowings	17.36%	6.03%	18.30%	12.97%	15.04%
Unspecified	0.41%	0.23%	3.69%	5.31%	2.49%
Total current liabilities	34.45%	28.02%	43.21%	38.89%	36.71%
Non-current liabilities					
Payables	0.83%	2.28%	0.00%	1.52%	1.05%
Borrowings	23.92%	11.60%	26.62%	13.62%	19.95%
Provisions	16.35%	6.66%	4.73%	16.07%	13.33%
Deferred tax	3.20%	3.11%	1.62%	2.27%	2.63%
Unspecified	0.59%	0.00%	0.74%	0.73%	0.60%
Total non-current liabilities	44.88%	23.65%	33.72%	34.20%	37.56%
Total liabilities	79.33%	51.67%	76.92%	73.10%	74.27%
Minority interest	1.04%	3.04%	0.98%	2.54%	1.69%
Equity					
Contributed capital					
Nominal share capital	3.07%	4.33%	3.44%	3.73%	3.46%
Extra over nominal value	2.88%	3.18%	5.11%	9.69%	5.42%
Non-distributable reserves					
Revaluation reserve	0.31%	0.14%	0.70%	0.51%	0.42%
Translation adjustments (−)	−0.56%	−0.56%	−4.13%	−0.23%	−1.07%
Translation adjustments (+)	0.00%	0.10%	0.00%	0.36%	0.12%
Other	−0.27%	1.66%	0.58%	0.57%	0.33%
Distributable reserves	18.49%	36.69%	16.45%	10.09%	17.29%
Treasury shares	−4.29%	−0.25%	−0.05%	−0.36%	−1.94%
Total equity	19.63%	45.29%	22.10%	24.37%	24.04%
Total assets	100.00%	100.00%	100.00%	100.00%	100.00%

Notes: All percentages are calculated as weighted averages, taking into account the size of the enterprise. The analysis is based on the 2000 accounts

considerably more debt compared with companies in the UK group, at least as far as the largest MNEs are concerned.

(c) The lower figure for the USA is partly attributable to the larger negative amounts reported for treasury shares (see 'The components of equity', paragraph (c)).

Provisions

Overall provisions represent 13 per cent of total equity and liabilities, with considerable differences between the groups, ranging from 5 per cent for Japan to 16 per cent for Continental Europe and the USA. In this case (in contrast to the position with borrowings), the difference can be attributed, at least partially, to differences in financial reporting practice. The higher figure for Continental Europe reflects the greater emphasis on prudence, notably in Germany. The relatively higher figure for the USA reflects principally higher provisions for pensions and, to a lesser degree, for environmental liabilities. It seems probable that American enterprises do in fact have greater obligations in these areas, arising from American law and commercial practice, but it is also the case that they are more likely to report them given the greater strictness of the reporting rules.

The components of equity

(a) Contributed capital makes up a relatively small proportion of total equity, although larger in Continental Europe than elsewhere.

(b) Distributable reserves (which represent accumulated past profits) make up a far larger proportion. This reflects that all the large MNEs were formed many decades ago and have built up their present assets largely through the retention of profits.

(c) Treasury shares are very significant in the USA. In fact American enterprises do acquire their own shares to a far greater extent compared with enterprises in other countries. However the numbers presented in the balance sheet tend to overstate the weight of treasury shares within the figure for total equity. The reason is that treasury shares are valued at acquisition cost, which is generally close to the current stock market price, whereas the rest of equity is based on the book value of assets.

(d) Non-distributable reserves are analysed between revaluation reserves, translation adjustments and other. The low figure for revaluation reserves in the UK is remarkable given the common practice of revaluing property in that country. In fact none of the British companies in the top 50 applied 'modified historical cost'. The higher figure for the USA relates to the revaluation of certain financial assets as required by US GAAP. With respect to translation adjustments, in three groups the net figure is negative; it represents a loss that has not passed through the income statement. The significance of this item is explained further in Chapter 21. Included in 'other' are the legal reserves of the Continental European corporations.

16.9 EXAMPLES

So far in this chapter, the equity section of the balance sheet has been described and analysed using general terms, such as 'contributed capital' and 'distributable reserves'. However, as already explained in section 16.6, each country has its own terms for the components of equity and there is little international agreement on the matter. Hence the application of the general principles discussed in this chapter to the analysis of the balance sheet of any particular MNE is a complex matter. In this section an idea of these complexities is given through an examination of the balance sheet of one typical enterprise from each of the five countries.

16.9.1 USA: General Motors

Using the general terminology employed earlier in this chapter, the extract from the 1999 balance sheet of General Motors given in Exhibit 16.8 may be analysed as follows:

(a) **Contributed capital.** General Motors' contributed capital consists of two classes of ordinary stock, plus the capital surplus of $13 794 million.

Exhibit 16.8 *General Motors 1999*

Stockholders' equity	$ millions
$1-2/3 par value common stock (issued 619 412 233 shares)	1033
Class H common stock (137 115 187 shares)	14
Capital surplus (principally additional paid-in capital)	13 794
Retained earnings	6961
Subtotal	21 802
Accumulated foreign currency translation adjustments	(2033)
Net unrealized gain on securities	996
Minimum pension liability adjustment	(121)
Accumulated other comprehensive loss	(1158)
Total stockholders' equity	20 644

The capital surplus is stated to be *principally* additional paid-in capital, which implies that part may not be contributed capital. Unfortunately the notes do not include any more information on this point.

(b) **Non-distributable reserves.** In the General Motors' balance sheet, there are three items that correspond to this item: the accumulated foreign currency translation adjustment, the unrealized gain on securities and the pension liability adjustment. The last item appears only in the balance sheets of American enterprises and arises from a specific provision in FAS 87, whereby an additional pension liability may be recognized in the balance sheet without a corresponding expense in the income statement. The balance sheet is made to balance by inserting a debit balance in equity. The sum of the three items is termed 'Accumulated other comprehensive loss'. This is a reference to the fact that they relate to reductions in net assets (assets less liabilities) that have not passed through the income statement. They form part of comprehensive income but not of income as reported in the income statement.

(c) **Distributable reserves.** These are represented in the General Motors' balance sheet by the retained earnings of $6961 million

16.9.2 UK: BP Amoco PLC

The consolidated balance sheet of BP Amoco at 31 December 1999 presents the group's assets and liabilities. The net total (assets less liabilities) is described as 'BP Amoco's shareholders' interest', in this way the group indicates in the clearest possible way that it adopts the proprietary model of the entity. At the foot of the balance sheet, there is the analysis of the shareholders' interest that is presented in Exhibit 16.9.

BP Amoco's balance sheet may be analysed as follows:

Contributed capital

BP Amoco's contributed capital consists of both preference shares and ordinary shares. The 8 per cent cumulative preference shares are entitled to an annual dividend of £0.08 per share (8 per cent of the nominal value of £1); the term 'cumulative' indicates that, if the dividend is not paid in one year, the arrears of dividend accumulate and have to be paid in the future before any dividend is paid on the ordinary shares. The two categories of preference share represent only a tiny fraction of the total shareholders' interest – less than 0.05 per cent. Over 99 per cent of the shareholders' interest relates to the 19.4 billion ordinary shares, which each has a nominal value of 25 American cents. Although BP

Exhibit 16.9 *Extract from BP Amoco's balance sheet, 31 December 1999*

	Note	$ millions
BP Amoco's shareholders' interest		43 281
Represented by		
Capital and reserves		
Called up share capital	27	4892
Share premium account		3354
Capital redemption reserve		330
Merger reserve		697
Profit and loss account		34 008
		43 281

Note 27 referred to in the balance sheet outlines the following:

Called up share capital	Shares	$ mn
Non-equity		
8 per cent cumulative first preference shares of £1 each	7 232 838	12
9 per cent cumulative second preference shares of £1 each	5 473 414	9
Equity		
Ordinary shares of $0.25 each	19 484 024 424	4871
		4892

Amoco is a British PLC, it demonstrates its multinational character by denominating its ordinary shares in American currency. The share premium account is the British term for what in section 16.6.1 is referred to as 'excess over nominal value'; it represents the excess of the amount received on the issue of the ordinary shares over their nominal value.

Reserves

BP Amoco's reserves are classified under three headings:

(a) **Capital redemption reserve.** This relates to preference shares that have been redeemed in the past. Under British law, when a company redeems shares, otherwise than through an issue of new shares, it must make a transfer from distributable profits to a non-distributable reserve entitled 'capital redemption reserve'. This reserve is not part of contributed capital, for it reflects the fact that the shareholders' contributions have been repaid. Rather it is an accounting device that aims to ensure that the company does not reduce its net assets (the funds available for the payment of creditors) below its original contributed capital. Hence the requirement that the reserve may not be used for the payment of dividends.

(b) **Merger reserve.** This reserve relates to the merger of the British Petroleum Company PLC and Amoco Corporation in 1998. The merger was effected by the first-named company acquiring all the shares of the second-named corporation and changing its name to BP Amoco PLC. The merger was accounted for using the 'merger method' of consolidation, which leads automatically to the creation of a merger reserve. This matter is explained in detail in Chapter 19.

(c) **Profit and loss account.** This represents the accumulated past profits of the group less dividends paid. It represents almost 80 per cent of the total shareholders' interest. A note to the accounts indicate that, of the balance of $34 008mn, $6276mn is subject to restrictions on distribution. However no details are given. Hence BP Amoco's distributable reserves amount to $27 732mn. Of course it would be impossible for the group to pay a dividend of this amount as virtually the whole balance is invested in illiquid assets.

16.9.3 Japan: Sony

Sony's balance sheet (Exhibit 16.10) bears a very close resemblance to that of General Motors which is analysed in section 16.9.1 above. This can be attributed to the strong American influence on the Japanese SEC law.

(a) **Contributed capital.** Sony's share capital consists of 453 million common stock of ¥50 par value. The balance sheet value does not equal

Exhibit 16.10 *Balance sheet at 30 June 2000*

Stockholders' equity	¥ million	¥ million	$ million
Common stock ¥50 par value:			
shares	453 639 163	451 550	4260
Additional paid-in capital		940 716	8875
Retained earnings		1 223 761	11 545
Accumulated other comprehensive income			
Unrealized gains on securities	61 915		584
Minimum pension liability	(3678)		(35)
Foreign currency translation adjustments	(483 553)		(4562)
		(425 316)	(4013)
Treasury stock at cost		(7805)	(74)
		2 182 906	20 593

the number of shares multiplied by the par value. This is because Japanese law prescribes that, when issuing shares at above nominal value, some part of the excess over nominal value must be credited to capital stock. The balance is credited to additional paid-in capital. The practice in the other countries of the Pentad is to credit the whole excess to additional paid-in capital.

(b) **Non-distributable reserves.** The three items are identical to those in the balance sheet of General Motors and the same term is used for their total – 'accumulated other comprehensive income'.

(c) **Distributable reserves.** These are the retained earnings of ¥1 223 761mn. Again the same term is used as in the General Motors' balance sheet.

(d) **Treasury stock.** The cost of treasury stock is shown as a deduction from total equity. General Motors (unlike most large American enterprises) does not report any treasury stock in its balance sheet. However, in the USA, treasury stock is always shown as a negative item within equity.

16.9.4 France: Alcatel

The Alcatel balance sheet (Exhibit 16.11) presents two alternative calculations of the equity: before and after the payment of the proposed dividend. The management proposes that, out of the 1999 income of €644mn, the corporation pay a dividend of €455mn to the shareholders which would entail an additional tax liability of €64mn. The remaining balance of €125mn is to be transferred to retained earnings. The right-hand column presents the balance sheet as it would appear after the proposed dividend has been approved by the shareholders and has thereby

Exhibit 16.11 *Alcatel: consolidated balance sheet at*
             31 December 1999

	Before appropriation €million	After appropriation €million
Capital stock: 199 895 247 shares of €10 nominal value	1999	1999
Additional paid-in capital	7025	7025
Retained earnings	4190	4315
Cumulative translation adjustments	(570)	(570)
Net income	644	0
Less treasury stock at cost	(1237)	(1237)
Shareholders' equity	12 051	11 532

been transformed into a liability of the corporation. With the revised figure for equity, the balance sheet balances because the reduction in the equity total is offset by an increase in the total of liabilities (dividend €455mn and tax €64mn).

16.9.5 Germany: Volkswagen

An extract from the 1999 balance sheet of the Volkswagen Group is presented in Exhibit 16.12.

(a) **Contributed capital.** The contributed capital of Volkswagen AG consists of both ordinary shares and preferred shares. The balance sheet shows the amounts that have been subscribed and, in addition, the nominal amount of capital that the corporation can issue in the future: 'potential capital' of DM368mn. Note that this last item is not part of the total of the balance sheet. It is rare for corporations to report potential capital on the face of the balance sheet; normally this information is given in the notes.

Exhibit 16.12   *Volkswagen Group: balance sheet at 31 December 1999*

Stockholders' equity	DM million	DM million	DM million
Subscribed capital of Volkswagen AG	2089		
Ordinary shares		1562	
Non-voting preferred shares		527	
Potential capital	368		
Called up capital			2089
Capital reserve			8361
Revenue reserves (note 8)			7708
Net earnings available for distribution			646
Minority interest			385
			19 189

Note 8:	31 December 1999
Legal reserve	60
Reserve for treasury stock	5
Other revenue reserves	7643
	7708

(b) **Capital reserve.** The notes to the balance sheet make clear that this related to the premium on issued shares.

(c) **Revenue reserves.** The breakdown is given in the notes.

(d) **Net earnings available for distribution.** The practice in Germany is to report under this heading the amount that the management proposes to pay out as dividend. The balance of profits that the management proposes to reinvest is reported as part of 'Other revenue reserves'.

(e) **Minority interests.** This item relates to the part of the equity of subsidiary enterprises that is owned by outsiders (that is not by Volkswagen AG). As explained further in Chapter 19, there is no agreement among accountants as to whether this is a liability or part of equity. However German law requires that it be reported as equity.

Volkswagen's equity does not contain a revaluation reserve relating to foreign currency translation, because all translation differences are reported in the income statement.

SUMMARY

The various forms in which the balance sheet can be presented were discussed in terms of the differences between the proprietary model and the enterprise model of the entity. The IASB's rules relating to the definition, recognition and measurement of liabilities were explained with reference to IAS 37 Provisions. The principal components of the equity of corporations were analysed. The distinction between equity and liabilities was discussed with reference to preference shares and convertible debt. An analysis was presented of the equity and liabilities of the largest MNEs. The presentation of equity in the balance sheet was illustrated through extracts from the accounts of five major MNEs.

Review questions

1. What are the fundamental differences between the proprietary model and the enterprise of the entity? Which model has the IASB adopted in its framework?

Review questions (cont'd)

2. What is the definition of a provision in IAS 37?

3. What is meant by a constructive obligation?

4. What were the IASB's reasons for making the rules for the reporting of provisions particularly strict?

5. On what grounds is the provision for deferred repairs as previously practised by many enterprises no longer permitted by IAS 37? What alternative accounting treatment does IAS 37 propose?

6. In what ways is the reporting of deferred income, as currently practised, inconsistent with the IASB's rules for other liabilities?

7. What are the basic sub-divisions of equity?

8. Why does the law in many countries insist that contributed capital be reported separately in the balance sheet?

9. In what circumstances are preference shares more akin to debt and in what circumstances are they more akin to equity?

10. What are the IASB's rules for the reporting of convertible debt?

Notes

1. The term 'proprietary' comes from 'proprietor' which means owner.
2. The term 'preference share' is commonly used in the UK to denote shares with the preferential rights described in this paragraph. This is also the case in the USA (preferred stock), in France (actions préférentielles) and Germany (Vorzugsaktie). However in the Netherlands the term 'preference aandalen' has quite a different meaning. Hence this paragraph describes the situation in the UK, USA, France and Germany.
3. In some countries, the law does not permit corporations to redeem preference shares as this would reduce the capital fund available for the payment of creditors. In those countries that do allow the redemption of preference shares, there is generally a legal requirement for the corporation to maintain its capital fund at the previous level, for example by transferring from distributable reserves to non-distributable reserves an amount equal to the preference shares redeemed.

References

FASB 'Discussion memorandum: distinguishing between liability and equity instruments', FASB, Norwalk (August 1990).

Ma, R and Lambert, C 'In praise of Occam's razor: a critique of the decomposition approach in IAS 32 to accounting for convertible debt', *Accounting and Business Research*, **28**(2) (Spring 1998), pp. 145–53.

Pope, PF and Puxty AG 'What is equity? New financial instruments in the interstices between the law, accounting and economics', *Conflict and Cooperation in the 1990s*, J Freedman and M Power (eds), Paul Chapman, London (1992).

Wahlen, JM *et al.* 'Liability and Equity', *Accounting Horizons*, **13**(3) (September 1999), pp. 305–7.

Further reading

For a fuller analysis of the proprietary model and the enterprise model, see Pope and Puxty (1992). This article is also recommended for its analysis of preference shares and convertible debt. For a criticism of IAS 32's rules on convertible debt, see Ma and Lambert (1998). For a general discussion of the differences between liabilities and equity see Wahlen *et al.* (1999). For a more detailed discussion see FASB (1990).

chapter seventeen

The Income Statement

Chapter objectives

- To set out the principles that govern the recognition of revenue
- To discuss the various ways in which revenues and expenses may be presented, including the classification of expenses, the definition of extraordinary items and the disclosure of discontinued operations
- To consider the presentation of information on the segments of the enterprise
- To examine the various measures of profit, with particular reference to changes in the value of assets that bypass the income statement and to prior period adjustments
- To consider the role of the Statement of Total Recognized Gains and Losses and of the Statement of Changes in Equity
- To discuss the presentation of earnings per share

The elements of the income statement are income and expenses, which, in the balance sheet approach adopted by the IASB, are defined as increases and decreases respectively of net assets. Given that the value of assets and liabilities are determined in the balance sheet, it might be felt that the accountant is faced with no major problems in deciding on the form and content of the income statement. This is very far from being the case. Difficult decisions arise in three broad areas:

- The point of time at which increases in net assets should be reported in the income statement. This is the revenue recognition problem which is discussed in the section 17.1

- The way in which items of income and expense are presented in the income statement. This is the presentation problem, which is discussed in section 17.2

- The extent to which items of income and expense should not be reported in the income statement but directly in the balance sheet. This is the profit calculation problem, which is discussed in sections 17.3, 17.4 and 17.5

17.1 THE RECOGNITION OF REVENUE

The detailed rules relating to revenue are set out in IAS 18 which defines revenue as 'the gross inflow of economic benefits during a period arising in the course of the ordinary activities of an enterprises'. The basic concept of revenue is straightforward – it is the total sales of goods and services arising from the enterprise's ordinary activities.

The major theoretical problem connected with revenue concerns the point of time at which it should be recognized. The importance of this point is connected with the matching principle, under which expenses are matched against income. Until an item of revenue is recognized, expenses related to that revenue are carried forward in the balance sheet as assets, provided that they meet the conditions for the recognition of an asset; hence no profit is recognized on a transaction until the revenue is recognized. According to the IASB's Framework, revenue is subject to the same recognition criteria as the other elements of the financial statements, such as assets and liabilities. Revenue should be recognized when it is probable that future economic benefits will flow to the enterprise and when it has a value that can be measured with reliability. In addition, IAS 18 adds further conditions for the recognition of particular types of revenue: in the sale of goods – when 'the enterprise has transferred to the buyer the significant risks and rewards of ownership' (IAS 18, 14), and in the sale of services – 'when the outcome of a transaction involving the rendering of services can be estimated reliably' (IAS 18, 20). Both are applications of a more general rule formulated by the FASB: '[Revenue] should be identified with the period during which the major economic activities necessary to the creation and disposition of the goods and services has been accomplished' (FASB, 1985).

The question of recognition of revenue will be considered in relation to the sale of manufactured goods; the same general principles apply to other forms of revenue, such as the sale of services. The typical operating cycle of a manufacturing business involves a number of stages: the production of goods, the delivery of goods, the acceptance by the customer of a legal obligation to buy the goods (which may be before, after or on delivery) and payment by the customer. The point of the cycle at which revenue should be recognized is that at which the major activities have been accomplished, which depends critically upon the particular circumstances of each sale. In principle the circumstances may be such that it is appropriate to recognize revenue at any point in the cycle: during production of the goods, on completion of production, on delivery of the goods and on payment. All these relate to economic activities (as mentioned in the FASB's statement quoted above). However, legal acts, such as the signing of a contract or the passing of legal title, are also highly relevant. At some point, the cumulative effect of the latest action plus all the preceding actions is such that one may reasonably conclude that 'the major ... activities ... have been accomplished' and that one should recognize revenue. As always with accounting, the uncertainty attached to the future complicates the matter; the uncertainties that affect the recognition of revenue relate to the ability of the enterprise to produce the goods, to the determination of the cost of producing and delivering the goods, to the date when the goods will be completed and delivered, to the selling price, to whether the customer will accept and pay for the goods. However it is not necessary to wait until the operating cycle is completed before recognizing revenue; that would result in information that is highly reliable but so late as to have very little relevance. Gradually during the operating cycle the uncertainties resolve themselves and, at some point, the remaining uncertain information can be estimated with sufficient precision to enable revenue to be recognized with reasonable accuracy.

With most sales of goods, three significant events (the delivery of the goods, the passing of legal title and the acceptance by the customer of a legal obligation to pay for the goods) occur at the same time, so there is no problem in establishing the point at which to recognize revenue. However it is to interesting to examine the relatively small number of cases where revenue is recognized at other points in the operating cycle. Exhibit 17.1 presents a sample of such cases.

These examples will now be discussed in the light of the IASB's rules.

Exhibit 17.1 *Points of revenue recognition*

The point of recognition	Examples
During production	Long-term construction contracts, using the percentage of completion accounting method
Completion of production	Gold and certain agricultural products
At signing of sales contract (but before delivery)	Certain types of sales contracts (for example, 'bill and hold sales')
On delivery	Most ordinary sales
After delivery	Consignment sales
On payment	Where there is a significant risk of non payment

Long-term construction contracts

Under IAS 11, the revenue and costs of a long-term construction contract (defined as one that spans more than one accounting period) should be recognized with reference to the stage of completion of the contract at the balance sheet date, provided that the total contract revenues and costs can be estimated reliably.

Gold and certain agricultural products

Where there exists a ready market for the commodity, which can absorb the quantity held by the entity without affecting the market price (which should be readily ascertainable), then, according to generally accepted accounting principles, the enterprise may value its closing inventory of the commodity at market price, increasing its revenue by that amount. This is the common practice of producers of gold and of certain plantation crops, such as tea and coffee, which all have the characteristic that there is very little uncertainty regarding the ability of the enterprise to dispose of its inventory at the market price. In December 2000, the IASC issued IAS 41 which required that the inventories of many agricultural products should be valued at market price. Except for agricultural products, the IASB's rules do not refer to the recognition of revenue at the completion of production. In fact the reference in IAS 18, 14 to transferring the significant risks and rewards to the *buyer* would seem to preclude it.

'Bill and hold' sales

Under this form of sales contract, the buyer commits himself to accept delivery and to pay for the goods, but agrees that delivery should not be made until a later date. Under the IASB's rules, the revenue from the sale should be recognized at the time of the contract, provided that another condition specified in IAS 18 is fulfilled, that 'the costs incurred or to be incurred in respect of the transaction can be measured reliably', which implies that the goods should either have been already produced or substantially completed.

'Consignment sales'

Under a consignment sale, the goods are transferred to an agent who undertakes to sell them on behalf of the enterprise to third parties. In this case, there is clearly no sale to the agent; revenue should only be recognized when the agent arranges a sale to a third party, so transferring 'the risks and rewards of ownership'.

Significant risk of non payment

Where there is a significant risk that the customer will not pay the sales price, then revenue should not be recognized until payment has been made. IAS 18, 18 cites an example of a sale in a foreign country where it is uncertain that a governmental authority will grant permission for the remission of the proceeds of the sale. When permission is granted, the uncertainty is removed and revenue is recognized. Cairns (1995) comments that, in practice, an enterprise would be unlikely to deliver the goods if it had significant doubts about the ultimate payment. Uncertainty on this matter normally arises after delivery and is dealt with by adjusting the value of the account receivable.

17.2 THE PRESENTATION OF INCOME AND EXPENSES

17.2.1 The needs of users

In deciding how to present the income and expenses in the income statement, the objective should be to develop the presentation that provides the most useful information for the user. The research on this matter has been well summarized by Todd Johnson (1998), who refers to two types of research:

- Surveys that seek to ascertain the demands of users
- Capital market studies that seek to establish the information content of different elements of the income statement

He presents an interesting list of over 30 'dichotomies' that can be used as a basis for deciding how to classify the elements of income and expense. The list includes:

- Ordinary/Extraordinary
- Recurring/Nonrecurring
- Realized/Unrealized
- Higher/Lower predictive value
- Continuing/Discontinued
- Operating/Holding
- Operating/Nonoperating
- Controllable/Noncontrollable
- Core/Noncore
- Permanent/Temporary

The idea is that users would like the income and the expenses of the enterprise to be classified according to a scheme organized on the basis of one or more of the above 'dichotomies'. Reviewing the list, Todd Johnson discerns three major themes:

(a) **Realization:** Users would like information on the extent to which the elements of income and expenses have been realized.

(b) **Relative predictive value:** Users would like to predict the future earnings and cash flows of the enterprise. To this end, they would like information that has high predictive value to be distinguished from that with low predictive value.

(c) **Functional:** Items associated with the enterprise's ongoing central operations should be should be distinguished from those associated with its more peripheral activities.

In the following sections, which examine the more important of the IASB's rules relating to the presentation of the income statement, the basic principle that the ultimate objective of the income statement is to meet the needs of users should always be kept in mind.

17.2.2   The format of the income statement

In contrast to the EU, the IASB does not prescribe a format for the income statement. However, IAS 1 does list the items that should be shown separately on the face of the income statement and includes rules for the classification of expenses. IAS 1's provisions are demonstrated in Exhibits 17.2(a) and 17.2(b), which are based on the two alternative income statements that are included as illustrative examples in the appendix to the standard. In these tables, the items that have to be shown separately are marked with an asterisk (*). There are very few such items. They may be classified as:

(a) Measures of profit: revenue; profit from operations; profit from ordinary activities; net profit for the year. These represent increasingly refined measures starting with revenue (the gross inflow of resources arising from the enterprise's operations) and ending with the net profit.

(b) Items that need to be reported separately in order for the user to understand the principal sources of the enterprise's net profit. IAS 1 contains a general requirement to report an item separately 'when such presentation is necessary to present fairly the enterprise's financial performance'. In addition four items must always be shown, unless they are not material.

  (i) Finance costs, because the user needs to assess the extent to which the enterprise's profit can be attributed to financial factors (such

Exhibit 17.2   The alternative formats for the income statement

(a) Classification of expenses by nature

Global Corp	2000		1999
	Income statement for the year 2000		*1999*
Revenue*	3000		2925
Other operating income	155		171
Changes in inventories	60		-30
Work performed by the enterprise and capitalized	125	340	0
Raw materials and consumables used	-740		-755
Staff costs	-870		-853
Depreciation and amortization expense	-220		-202
Other operating expenses	-320	-2150	-314
Profit from operations*	1190		943
Interest received	45		23
Interest paid	-38		-36
Finance costs*	7		-14
Income from associates*	90		63
Profit before tax	1287		992
Income tax expense*	-325		-315
Net profit from ordinary activities	962		677
Extraordinary items*	-227		0
Net profit for the period*	735		677

(b) Functional classification of expenses

Global Corp	2000		1999
	Income statement for the year 2000		*1999*
Revenue*	3000		2925
Cost of sales	-1279		-1491
Gross profit	1721		1434
Other operating income	155		171
Distribution costs	-229		-222
Administrative expenses	-137		-126
Other operating expenses	-320	-686	-314
Profit from operations*	1190		943
Interest received	45		23
Interest paid	-38		-36
Finance costs*	7		-14
Income from associates*	90		63
Profit before tax	1287		992
Income tax expense*	-325		-315
Net profit from ordinary activities	962		677
Extraordinary items*	-227		0
Net profit for the period*	735		677

Notes: * marks items that should be shown separately according to IAS 1

as unusually favourable interest rates) rather than operating factors (sales of the product).

(ii) Tax expense, for much the same reason.

(iii) The share of profits of associates and joint ventures, because the method used to calculate these profits (the equity method) is significantly different from that used for the other elements of the income statement; in effect the enterprise's command over this element of profit is shared with other parties.

(iv) Extraordinary items, because users need to know to what extent this year's profits are attributable to unusual factors. These are discussed further in section 17.2.7 below.

17.2.3 Revenue: total sales or total output?

Revenue is the first item in the Exhibit 17.2. In some countries of Continental Europe, notably Germany, the revenue of an enterprise has traditionally been defined, not as total sales (as in IAS 18) but as total output. This approach is presented in article 24 of the Fourth Directive, an option which was clearly included to accommodate practice in Germany. The relevant section of this article is presented in Exhibit 17.3.

The total of the three items presented in Exhibit 17.3 represent the total output of the enterprise. Some of the output is sold to outsiders (that is the net turnover); some is kept within the enterprise (that is the value of own work capitalized, as, for example, when a car manufacturer retains some of the cars that it has produced for the use of its managers); and some goes to swell the inventory of finished goods and work in progress. If there has been a decline in this inventory, this implies that sales have been greater than output, so the amount of the decline must be deducted in calculating total output.

The IASB recognizes that some enterprises prefer this presentation and therefore it includes the figures for changes in inventories and work capitalized in one of its two illustrative income statement (see Exhibit 17.2(a)). However it insists that this presentation should not imply that

Exhibit 17.3 *EU's Fourth Directive, article 24: optional format for the profit and loss account*

B	Income
1	Net turnover
2	Increase in stocks of finished goods and in work in progress
3	Work performed by the undertaking for its own purposes and capitalized

such amounts represent income (IAS 1, 81). The alternative income statement (Exhibit 17.2(b)) presents a single figure for revenue.

The presentation of total output as shown in Exhibit 17.3 was followed by all German enterprises until the Fourth Directive introduced the alternative format into German law in 1985. However most larger German enterprises now use the alternative format (essentially that illustrated in Exhibit 17.2(b)) as it is preferred by investors on the global capital market. However most smaller enterprises and a few larger enterprises (not only in Germany but in other Continental European countries) stick to the traditional approach. One such enterprise is Fiat, the Italian car-maker. The first part of this firm's income statement (up to the calculation of operating profit) is presented in Exhibit 17.4.

One clear advantage of the 'total output' approach is that it provides more information, notably the figure for own work capitalized. However it does suffer from a conceptual weakness: total output is calculated as total sales (valued at selling price) plus work capitalized and change in inventories (valued at cost). This mixture of valuation bases makes the total rather meaningless.

Exhibit 17.4 *Fiat Group: statement of operations, 1999*

	€ millions
Value of production	
Revenues from sales and services	48 402
Change in work in progress, semi-finished and finished products inventories	275
Change in contract work in progress	(279)
Additions to internally produced fixed assets	1107
Other income and revenues	1839
Total value of production	51 344
Costs of production	
Raw materials, supplies and merchandise	25 720
Services	7893
Leases and rentals	299
Personnel	7648
Depreciation and amortization	2603
Changes in raw materials, supplies and merchandise inventory	(64)
Provision for risks and other accruals	862
Other charges	1265
Expenses of financial services companies	694
Insurance claims and other costs	3636
Total costs of production	50 556
Difference between the value and cost of production	788

17.2.4 The classification of expenses

For the presentation of expenses, IAS 1 offers a choice between classification by their nature and classification by their function. The difference between the two income statements in Exhibit 17.2 lies solely in the presentation of revenue and in the classification of expenses. From the line 'profit from operations', the two income statements are identical. This is exactly the same choice as offered by the EU. In fact, the illustrative income statements in Exhibit 17.2 bear a remarkable resemblance to the alternative prescribed formats in articles 23 and 25 of the Fourth Directive, which would seem to imply that the EU is having some success in its stated aim of gaining a position of greater influence over the IASB's work and output (see Chapter 12, section 12.9.2).

Exhibit 17.2(a) presents the classification of expense by nature with separate headings for materials used, staff costs and depreciation. Exhibit 17.2(b) presents the classification of expense by function, with headings for cost of sales, distribution costs and administrative expense. Both approaches have their advantages and disadvantages.

17.2.5 The classification of expenses by nature

The classification of expenses by nature has two undisputed advantages over its rival.

(a) **It is simpler to apply because no allocation of expenses between functions is required.** The figures for materials and wages are generated automatically in the enterprises double-entry system from invoices and payments. On the other hand, to produce figures for cost of sales, distribution costs and administrative expenses, an enterprise has to maintain a fairly complicated costing system. Most large enterprises have set up such a system for internal management purposes and are therefore able to produce the necessary figures for the financial statements at little extra cost. However most small enterprises do not have such a costing system and therefore opt for the classification of costs by nature in their accounts.

(b) **The information that it provides is more reliable.** Where the income statement presents figures for materials, staff costs and depreciation, the user can be reasonably confident that these figures comply with the qualitative characteristic of representational faithfulness – that the information represents faithfully what it purports to represent. This is much more doubtful with expenses classified by function. The calculation of these expenses involves allocations, which 'can be arbitrary and involve considerable judgement' (IAS 1, 82). In the authors' opinion the figures for distribution costs and administrative expense in the accounts of an enterprise represent not facts but interpretations of facts made by the enterprise's accountant. The total of the wages paid by an enterprise is a verifiable fact, part of reality. The total of its administrative expenses is not part of reality; it is created by the accountant in allocating the real payments for wages and so on to the various functional cost headings. Of course classification of costs by nature sometimes involves judgement – for example is food for the staff canteen reported as staff costs, materials or other operating costs? However, with classification by nature, the amount of judgement involved is trivial compared with classification by function.

There is a third advantage of classification by nature that concerns the national accounts. These accounts measure the flows between sectors in the country as a whole, for example the transfers from firms to households in the form of wages. Classification of expenses by nature in the accounts of enterprises is consistent with the classifications used in the national accounts. This eases the preparation of the national accounts relating to the corporate sector. When expenses in the accounts of enterprises are classified by function, certain important statistics (such as wages paid) have to be estimated by other means. This is one of the reasons why the governments of many Continental European countries insist that enterprises use classification by nature.

17.2.6 The classification of expenses by function

Readers will not be surprised to learn that, given the conflict between reliability and relevance that pervades the whole of financial reporting, the great advantage claimed for classification by function is that it provides more relevant information. This applies particularly to the figure for cost of sales (not provided when costs are classified by nature) which enables the user to assess the extent to which the enterprise's profit is affected by variations in sales, as is done with break-even analysis. The further classification between distribution costs and administrative expenses may also prove helpful in this analysis, since it may reasonably be assumed that the former vary more directly with sales than the latter. It is also claimed that comparison between enterprises is facilitated when expenses are classified by function; thus the comparison may show that one enterprise spends a greater proportion of its revenue on administration than its rival. But it is not self-evident that the classification of expenses by nature may not be equally useful; for example, it may show that one enterprise's staff costs are excessive.

IAS 1 seeks to palliate some of the disadvantages of functional classification by requiring that an enterprise that uses it for its income statement

Exhibit 17.5　*Volkswagen Group: statement of earnings for the year ended 31 December 1999*

	DM million
Sales	147 013
Cost of sales	130 347
Gross profit	16 666
Selling and distribution expenses	11 944
General administration expenses	3 334
Other operating income	7 471
Other operating expenses	6 039
Results from participations (positive)	854
Interest results (positive)	1 299
Write-down of financial assets	40
Results from ordinary business activities	4 933

should disclose in the notes the amount of staff costs and deprecation expense.

Almost all large enterprises use the functional classification of expenses. One of the few exceptions is Fiat, as can be seen from this firm's income statement presented in Exhibit 17.4. Fiat's adoption of the natural classification is consistent with its decision to use the total output approach to the reporting of revenue.

Fiat's income statement should be contrasted with that of Volkswagen, the German car manufacturer, presented in Exhibit 17.5. Two points are immediately apparent from even the briefest examination:

■ Volkswagen's statement is much less detailed and therefore much easier to comprehend

■ Volkswagen presents a figure for gross profit which is missing in the Fiat statement

The second point is the more fundamental as the Fiat statement could be made less cluttered by summarizing certain items and providing the detail in the notes; for example the change in inventories could be combined with the cost of raw materials and the two provisions could be combined. However there is no way of calculating gross profit from the information given in the Fiat statement.

17.2.7　Extraordinary items and exceptional items

The last three lines of the illustrative income statements shown in Exhibit 17.2 are:

- Profit from ordinary activities
- Extraordinary items
- Net profit for the period

Extraordinary items are important because it is widely believed that users pay more attention to the amount of profit from ordinary activities than to the final figure of net profit, for two reasons:

- The former figure may provide a better basis for forecasting future profits because the extraordinary items are unlikely to recur in the future
- Often, the management cannot be blamed (or take credit for) losses (or profits) that arise from extraordinary events

The tendency of users to concentrate exclusively on profit from ordinary activities offers an opportunity for management to present the year's results in an unduly favourable light by reporting any unusual losses as 'extraordinary' but reporting unusual gains as part of profit from ordinary activities. There is some evidence of this practice in the 1980s in that overall the total of extraordinary losses exceeded extraordinary gains. The reaction of standard setters was to tighten up the definition of 'extraordinary item'. IAS 8 gives the following definition:

> Extraordinary items are income or expenses that arise from events and transactions that are clearly distinct from the ordinary activities of the enterprise and therefore are not expected to recur frequently or regularly.

This definition implies that any transaction or event that is related to the enterprise's ordinary activities should not be treated as extraordinary. However exceptionally large or unusual items that are related to the enterprise's ordinary activities may well have to be disclosed separately in order that the income statement presents fairly the enterprise's financial performance (IAS 8, 16). In the UK, these items are termed exceptional items; the UK's ASB gives the following definition:

> Exceptional items: Material items which derive from events and transactions that fall within the ordinary activities of the reporting entity and which . . . need to be disclosed by virtue of their size or incidence if the financial statements are to give a true and fair view. (ASB, 1993)

In practice distinguishing between extraordinary items and exceptional items inevitably involves the exercise of judgement. IAS 8, 14 gives two examples of events that generally give rise to extraordinary items for most enterprises:

■ an earthquake or other natural disaster
■ the expropriation of assets

FRS 3 (the UK standard) gives three examples of profits or losses that should be treated as exceptional items (that is not extraordinary), provided that they are material:

■ Profits or losses on the sale or termination of an operation
■ Costs of a fundamental reorganization or restructuring
■ Profits or losses on the disposal of fixed assets

By analysis of the above examples, one can discern a general principle for distinguishing between an extraordinary item and an exceptional item. An event that will occur fairly frequently during the life of a business cannot be considered to be extraordinary. Hence the disposal of a fixed asset is not extraordinary because most fixed assets are disposed of at the end of their life. Similarly, in most enterprises, the disposal of business segments and reorganizations occur with sufficient frequency to disqualify them from being treated as extraordinary. However when an event is statistically very rare (such as an earthquake), it may give rise to an extraordinary loss, at least for an enterprise that is not located in a region prone to earthquakes.

A debatable point is whether it is necessary for an item to be outside the control of the enterprise's management for it to be classified as extraordinary. This is not part of the IASB's definition as given above. However it is part of the standards of at least one country (New Zealand) and controllable/noncontrollable is one of the dichotomies mentioned by Todd Johnson (1998, see section 17.2.4 above). Furthermore there is some evidence that the IASB may consider 'noncontrollable' be part of the characteristics of an extraordinary item. IAS 35 Discontinuing Operations, which was issued five years after IAS 8, contains the following comment: 'The two examples of extraordinary items cited in IAS 8 are expropriations of assets and natural disasters, both of which are types of events that are not within the control of the management of the enterprise.' IAS 35 states that the costs and revenues of a discontinuing operation should not be presented as an extraordinary item, justifying this rule with reference to the criterion of control.

The practice relating to extraordinary items in the major countries is as follows:

(a) **USA.** APB 30 defines extraordinary items as those that are both unusual in nature and infrequent in occurrence. They are required to be shown separately

(b) **UK.** FRS 3 defines extraordinary items as those which arise from events or transactions that fall outside the ordinary activities of the entity; it defines ordinary activities as including the effects on the entity of any event in the various environments in which it operates, including the political, regulatory, economic and geographic environments, irrespective of the frequency or unusual nature of the events. The reference to 'political' and 'geographic' environments would seem to rule out as extraordinary the two examples given in IAS 8, the expropriation of assets and the damage caused by an earthquake. In fact it is hard to think of any item that would qualify as extraordinary under FRS 3 and, following the issue of FRS 3, extraordinary items have virtually disappeared from the accounts of British companies.

(c) **Germany.** German law, following the EU's directives, includes a heading for extraordinary items in the standard format for the income statement. The definition of extraordinary is similar to that used in the USA: the item should be of an unusual character and not regularly recurring. In fact few German MNEs report extraordinary items.

(d) **France.** The French term for extraordinary items ('produits et charges exceptionnels') is apt to mislead British accountants into believing that they are similar to exceptional items in the UK. This is certainly not the case, as the French term covers both extraordinary and exceptional items as defined in Britain, as well as some items peculiar to France, for example, the excess of tax driven depreciation over economic depreciation. In fact, given the wide definition of 'exceptionnel', most French enterprises report some items of this nature in their income statements.

(e) **Japan.** The range of 'special items' under Japanese GAAP is substantially larger than the concept of 'extraordinary items' in IAS 8. They include gains and losses on disposal of fixed assets and prior period adjustments.

However it is by no means certain that users appreciate the subtle distinction between extraordinary and exceptional items. If a particular item of expense is given great prominence in the income statement with the implication that it is unusual and if a figure for profit before this unusual expense is emphasized, it is likely that users will give more attention to this figure than to the final net profit, notwithstanding that the expense is termed exceptional rather than extraordinary. This point is illustrated in Exhibit 17.6, which presents an extract from the annual report of News Corporation, the Australian company with world-wide interests in films, television and newspapers. News Corporation uses the term 'abnormal item' and not 'extraordinary item'. However the way that the 'income statement is presented with equal emphasis on profit before abnormal items and profit after abnormal items gives the strong impression that the abnormal items should be disregarded in assessing the firm's performance. From the rather limited information given in the notes (not all presented in Exhibit 17.6), it would appear that most abnormal items relate to the acquisition or disposal of investments in other entities, which would not qualify as 'extraordinary items' under the IASB's definition, since almost every year News Corporation makes significant acquisitions and disposals. Included in the overall total is an abnormal loss of A$400mn on the transition to digital television, which similarly would not meet the IASB's definition of 'extraordinary' as it relates to the firm's normal operating activities. The UK's ASB seeks to prevent undue attention being given to exceptional items by stating that they should not be shown under a separate heading but that each exceptional item should be reported under the heading to which it relates (for example damage by a fire to inventory would be disclosed separately as part of the cost of materials). There is no such requirement in the IASB's standard.

In its published accounts, News Corporation presents separate figures for abnormal items before tax and the tax thereon. In the extract, in order to simplify the presentation, these figures have been netted.

Exhibit 17.6 *News Corporation Limited: extract from the Profit & Loss Account for the year ended 30 June 1999*

	A$ millions
Operating profit before abnormal items	1471
Abnormal loss (Note 5)	383
Operating profit after abnormal items	1088
Note 5	
Abnormal items (net of tax)	
Abnormal profit (loss)	
Write-down of non-current assets	(206)
Fox Entertainment Group float	948
EchoStar transaction[a]	(612)
Other	(81)
Associated entities[b]	(432)
Abnormal loss	(383)

Notes

[a] In connection with the abnormal loss on the EchoStar transaction, the company recorded a liability of approx. US$800mn related to its requirement to issue redeemable preferred securities

[b] The principal abnormal loss from associated entities relates to the loss incurred by BSkyB on the transition to digital set top boxes

17.2.8 Discontinuing operations

Once an enterprise has decided to discontinue a major part of its business (either through sale or abandonment), it is obliged to report a considerable amount of information about the segment concerned. The rules are set out in IAS 35 Discontinuing Operations. Note that the term is 'discontinuing' and not 'discontinued', because the information about the segment has to be already given whilst it is still in operation and merely in the process of being sold or abandoned. The information that has to be disclosed includes non-financial information such as the identification of the business segment to be discontinued and the date when the transaction is expected to be completed. In the income statement, the following information should be given concerning the business segment that is being discontinued: revenue, expenses, profit/loss from ordinary activities and income tax expense. In effect the elements of income and expense have to be analysed between discontinuing activities and continuing activities.

One problem with the reporting of discontinuing operations is that there is a danger that management may seek to portray the enterprise's performance in an unduly favourable fashion by classifying unprofitable activities as 'discontinuing', merely on the basis of intentions. Hence IAS 35 lays down that, for an activity to be classified as 'discontinuing', the management must have either entered into a binding sales agreement for substantially all the assets or have approved and announced a formal plan; in both cases, the event must take place before the accounts are approved.

Of the major countries, only the USA and Britain have rules that require information relating to discontinued operations to be disclosed separately. In the USA a discontinued operation is one that has been sold, abandoned or is the subject of a formal plan for disposal. In Britain, the definition is stricter in that only operations that have been definitely sold or terminated are included. In both countries the information is often given in an income statement with three adjacent columns: discontinuing activities; continuing activities; and total. In the UK, FRS 3 requires enterprises also to disclose separately the income and expenses of newly acquired operations; but this point is not covered in any IAS or American standard. There is no requirement to present information on discontinuing activities in Germany, France or Japan.

17.2.9 Segment reporting

The analysis between discontinuing and continuing operations is but one facet of a broader subject, which is the analysis of the enterprise's income and expenses between its principal businesses or segments. *IAS*

14 Segment Reporting requires the presentation of a considerable amount of information relating to the different segments of an enterprise, that is information about the different types of products and services that it produces (business segments) and about the geographical areas in which it operates (geographical segments). The rationale for this requirement is that the different segments are subject to different risks and returns, that the risks and returns of the enterprise as a whole are the sum of those of its segments and that, for users to be able to make an informed assessment of the enterprise's risks and returns, they need information about the different segments. Financial analysts consider that an analysis of results and assets by segment is the most valuable supplementary information that an enterprise can offer. Exceptionally, this standard is mandatory only on enterprises whose securities are publicly traded, presumably because, for smaller enterprises, the costs of segmental reporting might often exceed the benefits. The activities of smaller enterprises are often confined to a narrow range of products or geographical areas. Hence a segmental analysis is of less relevance for these enterprises and, for this reason, they often do not prepare such an analysis for internal management purposes. Hence to impose such an obligation would lead smaller enterprises to incur significant costs with little benefit either to the enterprise or to users.

The segmental information required by IAS 14 is essentially a further breakdown of certain figures that are presented in the balance sheet, income statement and cash flow statement for the enterprise as a whole. This detailed analysis is presented in a separate schedule (included in the notes to the accounts). It is not presented on the face of the balance sheet (or income statement), because this would result in the balance sheet becoming cluttered with a mass of detailed information which would make it more difficult to understand.

There are three major problems with segmental reporting:

■ How to define the segments
■ What to report about each segment
■ How to deal with common costs and assets

How to define the segments

In principle segments should be defined in such a way that the value of information for users is maximized. A commonly cited criterion is that activities with similar risk characteristics should be grouped together in the same segment. IAS 14 makes a distinction between business segments and geographical segments.

Business segments

Here the distinction is based on the goods and services that the enterprise produces. There should be one business segment for each principal category of goods and services. All the goods and services within a particular business segment should display basically similar returns and risks. IAS 14 states that an enterprise, in defining business segments for financial reporting purposes, should normally adopt the same definition of segments as it uses for internal management reporting purposes, for two reasons:

(a) It is very likely that information on segments defined in this way is the most relevant for the reader since in this matter the needs of managers and users are essentially the same – both are interested in exceptionally risky or profitable/unprofitable segments.

(b) It saves the enterprise the expense of making a special analysis of revenues and expenses for financial reporting.

IAS 14 suggests that, in defining business segments, one or more of the following criteria should be followed: the nature of the good or service (for example, motor cars and motorcycles); the nature of the production process (for example, mass production versus made to order); the type of customer (for example, the most appropriate segments for a pharmaceutical company may be drugs for humans and drugs for animals); the method of distribution (for example, a brush manufacturer may distinguish between sales to shops and sales by door-to-door salesman); and the nature of the regulatory environment (for example, distinguishing between regulated and non-regulated activities).

Geographical segments

Here the distinction is based on geography. The world should be divided into broad regions. As with business segments, all countries within a particular geographical segment should display similar returns and risks. Analysis by geographical segment can be either by location of the customers or by location of the assets. For example, where an enterprise which manufactures goods in factories located in the UK, Mexico and Russia, sells these goods to many more countries in Europe, America and Asia, it would be possible to analyse results and assets either on the basis of the location of the assets (essentially the source of the sales) or by the location of the customers (the destination of the sales). The countries included in a geographical segment do not have to be contiguous. For example, appropriate geographical segments might be all developed countries and all developing countries. Hence the UK and the USA might reasonably be included in the same segment, as might India and Mexico.

A segment can be as small as a region within a country; for example, Chechnia, which is formally a region of Russia, may be considered to have such peculiar risk characteristics as to justify it being treated as a separate geographical segment.

IAS 14 contains certain rules that are intended to ensure that significant segments are separately identified. Thus, where a particular segment accounts for more than 10 per cent of the enterprise's sales, profit or assets, it should be reported as a separate segment. Furthermore if the segments whose results are reported separately make up less than 75 per cent of the enterprise's overall result, then additional segments must be identified in order to bring the total up to 75 per cent, even if they do not meet the 10 per cent threshold. The clear intention of the IASB is that enterprises should present a breakdown of the overall figures between several segments. It is not permitted to claim that the whole enterprise is a single segment or to identify one or two separate segments, declaring that the remainder of the enterprise is a single amorphous segment.

What information should be given

Three possible ways of defining segments have been described above: by business, by location of customer and by location of assets. IAS 14 requires that enterprises should choose one of the three approaches to define its primary reporting segments; for each primary segment the following information has to be given:

- Revenue from external customers
- Revenue from transactions with other segments
- Segment result
- Segment assets
- Segment liabilities
- Expenditure during the year on fixed assets
- Depreciation and other non-cash expenses

In addition the enterprise should give a limited amount of information for segments defined in a way other than for the primary segments. Thus, if the primary segments are defined as business segments, it has to report sales and assets analysed by geographical segments, which IAS 14 terms secondary segments. Note that the information required for the secondary segments is much less detailed than that for primary segments.

The requirements of IAS 14 may be illustrated using the extract from the 1999 annual report of the Royal Dutch/Shell Group that is presented in Exhibit 17.7. The group's primary segments are business segments;

they are defined by the nature of the process and of the product: exploration and production, downstream gas and power production, oil products and chemicals. Quite a lot of information is given about these primary segments: sales, operating profits, certain other expenses and income (notably relating to interest and foreign currency), total assets, capital expenditure and depreciation. One learns that the group's net income of $8584mn is heavily dependent on the profits earned by two segments: exploration and production, and oil products. Each segment's sales are divided between those to third parties and those to other segments. Thus almost half of the sales of the exploration and production segment are to other segments. Clearly the net income of this segment (a profit of $4519mn) depends on the transfer price at which these intersegment sales are recorded. Reporting the figure for total assets per segment enables the return on assets to be calculated.

The figures in the 'Total Group' column for sales, fixed assets, operating profit, net income and total assets agree with the figures in the group's income statement and balance sheet. Surprisingly IAS 14 does not require that the segment figures should agree with those in the balance sheet and the income statement, presumably because, with some enterprises, the segment figures will be taken from management accounts that are different from the financial accounts. However IAS 14 does require enterprises to provide a reconciliation between its segment information and its financial statements. Many enterprises fail to do this, causing problems for the reader, who often finds that sales or profit according to the segment information do not agree with the figures in the income statement, but has no means of discovering the cause of the discrepancy.

The Royal Dutch/Shell Group's secondary segments are defined by geographical area. Very much less information is given: only the breakdown of sales and of fixed assets. According to IAS 14, sales should be analysed by location of customer and assets by location of assets; however this point is not made clear in the case of Royal Dutch/Shell.

The information given in Example 17.7 meets almost all the requirements of IAS 14 and in some cases exceeds them (for example there is no requirement to show interest expense per segment). The only major item of information required by IAS 14 that is not given is segment liabilities.

How to deal with common costs and assets

A major problem is how to deal with costs and assets that are common to more than one segment. The approach of IAS 14 is to distinguish between:

■ Costs and assets that can be directly attributable to segments;

Exhibit 17.7   *Royal Dutch/Shell Group, 1999 annual report: information by geographical area and industry segment (all figures in $ millions)*

		(a) Geographical area			
	Total Group	*Europe*	*Other Eastern Hemisphere*	*USA*	*Other Western Hemisphere*
Sales	105 366	51 820	21 068	17 306	15 172
Fixed assets	78 529	26 336	23 612	19 815	8 766

		(b) Industry segment				
	Total Group	*Exploration and production*	*Downstream gas and power production*	*Oil products*	*Chemicals*	*Corporate and other*
Sales						
third parties	105 366	9 474	9 729	72 450	12 886	827
intersegment		8 849	295	1 570	748	
Total sales	105 366	18 323	10 024	74 020	13 634	827
Operating						
profit(loss)	15 232	9 526	531	4 265	1 129	−219
Interest income	541	14	172	143	42	170
Interest expense	1 253	240	312	682	284	−265
Currency exchange						
gain	1	−23	−5	9	0	20
Taxation	5 696	4 599	139	952	−13	19
Minority interests	241	159	−6	73	15	0
Net income	8 584	4 519	253	2 710	885	217
Total assets	113 883	36 717	8 743	43 203	17 737	7 483
Capital expenditure	8 433	4 350	840	1 365	1 581	297
Depreciation						
Impairment	147	78	−69	44	75	19
Other	6 373	3 411	155	2 001	682	124

■ Costs and assets that can be attributed to segments on a reasonable basis; and

■ The rest

The first two items are reported as segment costs and assets, whereas the third item is reported as relating to the enterprise as a whole. In allocating indirect costs and assets to segments, the management would generally follow the same procedures as used for the management accounts. Many theorists would probably consider such allocations to be arbitrary and meaningless. However, it does provide valuable information to users, simply because it mirrors the management accounts and thus provides an insight to how the management views the enterprise.

Under IAS 14, the enterprise's liabilities that are sources of finance (that is loans and borrowings, as opposed to liabilities arising from operations, such as trade payables) are not to be allocated to segments. The reason is that they form a pool out of which the assets of the enterprise as a whole are financed. It is incorrect to consider that a particular asset is financed by a particular loan, since the enterprise as a whole is obliged to pay the interest on its loans irrespective of the segment's results. Thus interest on loans should not be allocated to segments.

Royal Dutch/Shell in its segment information presented in Exhibit 17.7 deals with common costs by adding a separate column headed 'Corporate and other'. This shows that sales totalling $827mn have not been allocated to segments. It is also possible to infer that, in addition, operating costs $1046mn have not been allocated since the 'Corporate and other' segment reports an operating loss of $219mn. Royal Dutch/Shell goes further than IAS 14 considers appropriate in allocating interest income and expense to segments. This enables it to divide the group's net income of $8584mn between the segments, which shows that the 'Corporate and other' segment reported a net income of $217mn. This curious result is achieved by crediting this segment with the enormous sum of $435mn for interest income. The group's net interest expense of $712mn is made up of $1147mn expense charged to the operating segments and $435mn income credited to the 'Corporate and other' segment. Presumably this reflects that financing is arranged centrally by the 'Corporate and other' segment which charges the operating divisions a higher rate of interest on funds provided than that paid by the Group.

17.2.10 Conclusions

It is interesting to note how many of the 'dichotomies' identified by Todd Johnson are reflected in the IASB's standards: the most obvious are Ordinary/Extraordinary and Continuing/Discontinued. Of the three 'themes' most weight seems to have been given to 'functional activities'. 'Realization' does not seem to have been considered in the matters so far discussed but it is an important factor in the statement of recognized gains and losses which is dealt with later in section 17.5. That leaves 'relative predictive ability'. Here the action of the IASB in defining extraordinary items more narrowly has probably reduced the predictive value of accounts.

17.3   THE MEASUREMENT OF PROFIT

IAS 8 *Net profit or loss for the period, fundamental errors and changes in accounting policy* deals with how the profit for the period should be measured. It states that all items of income and expense recognized in a period should be included in the determination of the net profit or loss for the period, except when a specific IAS requires or permits otherwise. In principle, the net profit reported for a period in an enterprise's income statement should equal the increase in the enterprise's equity (adjusted for dividends paid and new injections of capital) recorded since the last balance sheet.

However, there are two basic exceptions to this principle:

- Gains and losses taken direct to equity
- Prior period adjustments

17.3.1   Gains and losses taken direct to equity

Several IASs require that certain gains or losses (that is changes in the values of assets and liabilities) should not pass through the income statement but should be reported directly as an element of equity. Three IASs are of particular importance in this respect:

(a) **IAS 16 Property, plant and equipment:** IAS 16 permits enterprises to report property at fair value; the property should be revalued at regular intervals and, if the new value is higher than the previous value, the increase must be credited direct to revaluation surplus (an element of equity). It does not pass through the income statement and therefore is not reported as income.

(b) **IAS 21 The effect of changes in exchange rates:** Similarly IAS 21 provides that, when the closing rate is used, the increase or decrease in the translated value of a foreign subsidiary's assets and liabilities, arising from a change in foreign exchange rates, should be credited or debited direct to equity; it should not pass through the income statement. This provision has a most material effect on the profits reported by most multinational corporations, given their substantial foreign investments. Following a decline in the exchange value of a foreign currency, the losses charged direct to equity can, in some cases, amount to several million dollars. As shown in Exhibit 16.7, for the larger MNEs, negative translation adjustments are equal to about 1 per cent of assets. These represent falls in the value of assets that have not been reported in the income statement. This rather complex issue is discussed further in Chapter 21.

(c) **IAS 39 Financial instruments: recognition and measurement:** In certain circumstances, the losses and gains arising from valuing financial assets and liabilities at fair value should be debited or credited direct to equity.

17.3.2 Prior period adjustments

IAS 8 lays down, as the benchmark treatment, that, when the values of assets and liabilities reported in the last balance sheet need to be re-stated, because accounting policy has been changed or because a fundamental error has been discovered, the correction should be made by adjusting the balance of retained earnings and not by making a debit or credit to the income statement of the current period.

These two cases may be illustrated using the accounts of Global Corp that have already been presented in Exhibit 17.2. It is assumed that, in preparing these statements, Global Corp made decisions relating to two matters reported in the accounts:

Changes in accounting policy

In December 2000, Global Corp decided to change its accounting policy for valuing its inventory of raw materials, from LIFO to FIFO. In prin-ciple, such a change conflicts with the principle of consistency but it is permitted under IAS 8, provided that it leads to the reporting of more relevant information. Under IAS 8, the enterprise should apply this change retrospectively. Thus when drawing up its accounts for the year 2000, Global Corp calculated the cost of materials used on the basis that the inventory at the start of the year was valued at FIFO. In effect it assumed that the change in accounting policy already took effect on 1 January 2000. However in its balance sheet drawn up at the end of the previous year (31 December 1999) inventory is valued at LIFO. If one assumes that the values of inventory at 31 December 1999 according to the different valuation methods were LIFO €980 and FIFO €1130, the enterprise has recognized an increase of €150 in the value of inventory, which is not reported in the income statement of either 1999 or 2000. IAS 8 requires that this amount should be added to the balance of accu-mulated profits at the start of 2000.

Discovery of fundamental errors

In December 2000, Global Corp uncovered a major fraud perpetrated by a director in 1999. A loan which was recorded in its accounts as an asset was found to be entirely fictitious. In effect the financial statements issued by the enterprise in respect of 1999 were incorrect. IAS 8 states that, if the error in a previous year's financial statements is so large that it has effectively destroyed their relevance and reliability, then it should be treated as a fundamental error. IAS 8 states that, when a fundamental error is discovered, it should be treated by correcting the financial statements of all the years affected by the error. In fact it is rarely possible to correct the financial statements of these years; they have already been sent to shareholders and filed with the state's registry. Hence IAS 8 provides that the amount of the correction relating to previous years should be set against the balance of accumulated profits at the start of the current year. In the present example, assume that the recorded value of the fictitious asset in December 1999 is €500, and its book value at 31 December 2000 is €510, then the total loss (decline in value of an asset) is €510, of which €500 is set off against the balance of accumulated profits at 1 January 2000. Only €10 is charged to the income statement of the year 2000.

The IASB makes a distinction between the above items (changes in accounting policy and correction of fundamental errors) and corrections of accounting estimates, for example in assessing whether an account receivable is a bad debt or in estimating the useful life of a fixed asset. Changes in asset values arising from correcting past estimates are always charged as expenses in the current income statement.

With respect to prior period adjustments, the position in the major countries is:

(a) **USA.** Changes in accounting policy are included in income for the current period and not deducted from the balance of retained earnings at the beginning of the period. However information on the effect of the change on the reported income of previous periods has to be given in the notes. On the other hand, the correction of an error in a previously issued financial statement is treated as a prior period adjustment.

(b) **Japan.** In Japan, the restatement of previously issued financial statements is prohibited. The impact of all changes in accounting policy and correction of errors is reported as an extraordinary item in the income statement of the current period.

(c) **Europe.** One of the fundamental valuation rules set out in the EU's Fourth Directive is that 'the opening balance sheet of each financial year must correspond to the closing balance sheet of the preceding financial year'. This would appear to rule out setting off prior year adjustments against the balance of accumulated profits at the start of the current year. All three European members of the Pentad have incorporated this rule into their national law, but the practice in the three countries varies:

(i) **Britain.** Under FRS 3 both changes in accounting policy and correction of fundamental errors in previously issued accounts are treated as prior period adjustments. As explained in Chapter 4, the ASB claims that its standards override the law.

(ii) **France and Germany.** Here the law is applied strictly. The effect of changes in accounting policy and of the correction of past errors are reflected in the current income statement.

17.4 CONCEPTS OF PROFIT

Whether one agrees with the way that the profit of the year 2000 is computed in the example in the previous section depends on which concept of profit one favours. There are two rather different concepts of profit: the comprehensive income concept and the current operating profit concept.

17.4.1 The comprehensive income concept

Under this concept, profit is defined as the increase in the net assets of an enterprise other than that resulting from transactions with the owners (dividends and injections of capital). Over the life-span of an enterprise, its total profit should be calculated as the value of its net assets at the end less their value at the start, adjusted for cash flows between the enterprise and its owners. The calculation of each year's profit should be consistent with the enterprise's total profit over its life-span, that is that the total of the annual profits reported by an enterprise in its income statements over its life-span should be equal to its total life-span profit. To achieve this, all changes in the value of assets and liabilities must be reflected in annually reported profits. The annual profit computed in this way is known as 'comprehensive income'. Note that the term 'income' as used in 'comprehensive income' has a rather different meaning from the term as it is defined in the IASB's Framework. In the Framework 'income' is defined as revenue plus gains; however, the term 'comprehensive income' refers to revenue plus gains less expenses and losses. The concept of comprehensive income can be traced to the FASB's conceptual framework, which presents the following definition: 'Comprehensive income is the change in equity (net assets) of a business enterprise during a period from transactions and other events and circumstances from nonowner sources. It includes all changes in equity during a period except those resulting from investments by owners and distributions to owners.' (FASB Concepts Statement No. 3).

The concept of comprehensive income may be justified with reference to the theory both of economics and of finance.

(a) **Economics:** Comprehensive income is consistent with the well-known definition of income proposed by Sir John Hicks: 'A man's income is

the maximum value he can consume during the week and still expect to be as well off at the end of the week as he was at the beginning.'
(Hicks, 1946). With this definition all changes in wealth are taken
into account; there is no reason to exclude certain changes.

(b) **Finance:** Comprehensive income is at the heart of the modern theory
of finance, which values the firm at the present value of future comprehensive income. This valuation method is known as the 'clean
surplus model' (Walker, 1997). 'Clean surplus' is an alternative American
term for 'comprehensive income' – it refers to the principle that all
increases and decreases in asset values should be summarized in a
single figure at the foot of the income statement.

The proponents of comprehensive profits back up this theoretical
position with the following more practical arguments:

(a) If preparers of accounts were permitted to omit certain changes in
the value of assets and liabilities from the calculation of annual profit,
this would open the door to possible manipulation and smoothing
of profits;

(b) In rather similar vein, standard setters should not be offered the easy
solution of getting rid of awkward gains or losses by transferring
them direct to equity, as happened with foreign currency translation
gains and losses in FAS 52 (see Chapter 21). This is perceived by
many commentators as an illogical compromise or a 'cop-out'.

(c) The function of the income statement is to present the result of all
transactions and events recognized in the period that have affected
the value of assets and liabilities, and should not be limited to certain
selected transactions and events.

(d) Full disclosure of the effect of all transactions and events in the income
statement provides users with the information that they need to make
their own assessment of the enterprise's performance. The processing
of the information so as to make it more suitable for particular purposes
(for example the forecasting of future cash flows) should be done by
the user and not by the preparer.

The comprehensive approach may be summarized very simply by the
observation that a change in value of an asset or liability must be reflected in reported profits. However this approach is challenged by those
who favour the alternative concept.

17.4.2 The current operating performance concept

Under this concept, an enterprise's income statement for a period
should reflect its ordinary, normal recurring operations relating to that

period. Income and expenses that do not relate to these operations should not be reflected in the period's profit. Examples are extraordinary or unusual items and those that relate to previous periods. Thus in the example just given, the income statement for the year 2000 should not be burdened with charges that clearly relate to previous years. The inclusion of such items in the current period's profit might mislead the users, for example into believing that they will be repeated in future periods. The proponents of this approach contend that the persons who are best qualified to assess whether an item of income or expense is unusual or does not really relate to the period being covered, are the enterprise's managers; the most useful information for shareholders is provided by financial statements prepared by the managers and attested by independent auditors, which show the year's normal operating profit shorn of all unusual non-recurring items and items that do not relate to the current year.

17.4.3 Evaluation of the two concepts

It is not possible to state that one concept of profit is inherently better than the other. Each has its particular advantages and disadvantages, and serves a rather different purpose; the comprehensive income approach seems to be more appropriate for monitoring the stewardship of management and the current operating performance approach for forecasting future cash flows. Thus research by O'Hanlon and Pope (1999) has shown that for listed British companies for the period 1972 to 1992, current operating profit was more closely correlated with share returns (and therefore more relevant for investors) than was comprehensive income.

The authors are strongly in favour of the comprehensive income approach, possibly because they attach great importance to the stewardship function of accounts; they are concerned about the possibility that an enterprise can report profits year after year over a period and yet at the end its net assets are worth less than at the start. Furthermore, certain of the advantages of the current operating performance concept can be retained within a calculation of comprehensive income by additional disclosure in the income statement, for example of extraordinary and exceptional items.

The IASB seems to be in agreement with the authors, for in recent years it seems to have moved towards the comprehensive income approach. Thus it has insisted that net profit for the year and, more importantly, earnings per share, be computed after extraordinary items. Perhaps the best signal of the IASB's attitude is that recently it modified IAS 22 to remove the previously permitted option of writing off goodwill directly against equity (see Chapter 20). However, as demonstrated above, there are still a number of situations where IASs do not follow the comprehensive income approach, where changes in values of assets and liabilities that are recognized during a period are not reflected in that period's profits.

17.5 THE STATEMENT OF TOTAL RECOGNIZED GAINS AND LOSSES (STRGL)

17.5.1 The STRGL according to IAS 1

As a means of reporting gains and losses that do not pass through the income statement, IAS 1 includes a supplementary statement, known as a statement of total recognized gains and losses (STRGL); Exhibit 17.8 presents this statement for Global Corp. In view of the previous discussion, one might have expected that the IASB would require a calculation of comprehensive income, consisting of the following elements:

■ Prior year adjustments

■ Gains and losses not recognized in the income statement (principally valuation adjustments)

■ The profit as presented in the income statement

However the IASB does not consider prior year adjustments to be part of the comprehensive profit of the current period. Instead, they are noted at the foot of the table. The arguments for and against including prior year adjustments in the current year's comprehensive profit are:

Exhibit 17.8 *Global Corp: statement of total recognized gains and losses (Year 2000)*

Gains and losses taken direct to equity		
Surplus on revaluation of property	90	
Loss on foreign currency translation	−110	
Net loss not recognized in the income statement		−20
Profit for 2000 (per the income statement)		735
Total recognized gains and losses		715
Note:		
Cumulative effect of prior year adjustments		
Correction of fundamental error	−500	
Change in accounting policy	150	
		−350

(a) **Against.** They do not relate to the current year. This following quotation from the UK ASB's FRS 3 (which was the inspiration of much of IAS 1) makes the point very clearly: 'The correction of fundamental errors and the cumulative adjustments applicable to prior periods have no bearing on the results of the current period and they are therefore not included in arriving at the profit or loss of the period' (ASB, 1993). The correction is made in the financial statements of the prior years, not the current year. Users are informed of the position by means of a note in the current year's financial statements and by the adjustment of the comparative figures included with the current year's accounts. This is the IASB's approach.

(b) **For.** It is a fiction to claim that the correction is made in the financial statements of previous years. The financial statements for these years were prepared and distributed long ago. This is a fact that cannot be undone. If in fact enterprises were to contact all users and ask them to send in the accounts of these years for correction (analogous to the recalls of defective cars by automobile manufacturers), then there might be some merit in the IASB's approach. But this happens only rarely. The consequence is that the profit for these years remains as it was reported at the time, which leads to a violation of the fundamental principle that, over the life of an enterprise, the sum of its reported profits should equal the increase in its assets. In the case of Global Corp, shareholders would receive in January 2000 financial statements reporting profit for 1999 of €1027; in January 2001 they would receive accounts which report profit for 2000 of €735, making reported profits for the two years €1762. However the total profits recognized over the two year period is only €1412, when the prior year adjustments of €350 are taken into account. The figures given in the year 2000 accounts that relate to the previous year (the so-called comparative figures) certainly reveal that the adjusted 1999 profits. Note that in Exhibit 17.2 the 1999 profit is shown as €677, whereas in the original 1999 accounts it was reported as €1027. But this can also mislead shareholders into congratulating the directors in the increase in reported profits in 2000 compared with 1999.

In the authors' opinion, the balance of argument comes down in favour of including prior year adjustments in comprehensive profits, which, however, is not the position of the IASB or of any major standard setter.

17.5.2 The STRGL: a statement of performance?

IAS 1 gives only a very brief explanation of the STRGL; in fact the term 'statement of recognized gains and losses' itself does not appear in the standard's text, but only in the appendix which is not formally part of the standard. There is one important point that remains unresolved: whether the statement of recognized gains and losses is to be considered a statement of performance to be ranked alongside the income statement, or whether its function is to provide additional information that enables the reader better to interpret the income statement. The UK's ASB is an advocate of the first approach which treats the statement of recognized gains and losses as presenting the enterprise's financial performance on the basis of the gains and losses *recognized* in the period, to be contrasted with the income statement which presents the gains and losses *realized* during the period. The ASB seems to consider the two statements to be of equal importance. This approach leads the ASB to the conclusion that, once a gain or loss has been recognized in the statement of recognized gains and losses, it should not be recognized a second time in the income statement. For example, when property is revalued the gain or loss is reported in the statement of recognized gains and losses; when the property is finally sold the gain or loss on disposal should be calculated on the basis of the revalued amount and not on the original cost. The effect of this procedure is that the total profits reported in an enterprise's income statement over a period does not equal its comprehensive profit. However, the total reported in the statement of total recognized gains and losses over a period does equal comprehensive income.

The ASB's prescribed rule has been widely criticized. An interesting example of the difficulties that may arise with this approach is provided by the case of Coillte Teoranta (the Irish Forestry Board Ltd) which is described by McBride (1997). Coillte Teoranta revalued its forests each year, crediting the surplus directly to reserve; however it calculated its annual profits from the sale of timber on the basis of original cost. The ASB issued a statement to the effect that this treatment did not comply with its standard, which required that the annual profit should be calculated on the basis of the revalued amount. Coillte Teoranta could not accept this because it would mean that the increase in the value of its forests would not be reported in its income statement of any year. In order to ensure that this increase in value was ultimately reported as income, it changed its policy for the valuation of its forests, reporting them at historical cost in the balance sheet.

The process whereby a gain that has already been reported in the STRGL is also reported subsequently in the income statement is known as 'recycling': the gain is 'recycled' or reported twice. Recycling is illustrated in the example presented in Exhibit 17.9, which concerns an enterprise which revalues an asset (land) in 1999 and sells it one year later. The enterprise's accounts are presented using three different approaches:

(a) **Historical cost throughout.** This is the most straightforward. No gain is reported in 1999 either in the income statement or in the STRGL. The whole gain of €6000 is taken as profit in the income statement in 2000.

(b) **Revaluation of the land and no recycling.** This is the approach of the UK's ASB. A gain of €5000 is reported in 1999 in the STRGL. In 2000 the profit on the sale of the land is calculated at €1000, being the sales price less the revalued amount of the land. The total gains reported in the STRGL in 2000 is only €1000, but the total for 1999 and 2000 is €6000. In 2000, the balance on the revaluation reserve is transferred to retained earnings; this gain is now realized and is available for distribution as dividend, but it is not part of 2000 income. The total profits reported in the income statements of 1999 and 2000 is only €1000.

(c) **Revaluation of the land, with recycling.** The 1999 accounts are the same as (b). However, for 2000, the profit is reported at €6000, as the gain is calculated on the historical cost of the land. In order to avoid double counting in the STRGL, there has to be an adjustment in respect of the previously reported gain. This adjustment looks awkward, but it has the effect that both the income statement and the STRGL show the correct comprehensive income over the two years.

In the authors' opinion, the ASB's approach is flawed. It is incorrect to consider that the STRGL is as important as the income statement. Users give far more attention to the income statement. The STRGL is not treated by users as an alternative measure of financial performance; for users the fundamental measure of financial performance is the profit reported in the income statement, that is users are interested in realized profit and not recognized profit. The primacy of the income statement is fully backed by the law. In the UK, in Ireland and in the EU, the law requires enterprises to present an income statement; there is no mention in the law of the statement of recognized gains and losses. Furthermore the law makes quite clear that realization and not recognition is the basis for the calculation of profit. In prescribing the statement of recognized gains and losses as an alternative measure of performance, the ASB went beyond what both users and the law were prepared to accept.

It is quite clear that the STRGL was included in IAS 1 at the suggestion of the UK's representatives on the IASC's Board, since in no other country is this statement required. This is the reason why IAS 1 deals with this statement in such a brief manner and, in particular, includes it only in an explanatory appendix and not as part of the mandatory standard.

On the question of recycling the IASB has not followed a consistent line. IAS 16 forbids recycling: the gain on the disposal of an item of plant, property or equipment that has been revalued is calculated on

Exhibit 17.9 *An example of recycling*

An enterprise owns a sole asset, land, which is valued in the balance sheet at its
historical cost of €10 000

At 1 January 1999, the fair value of the land is assessed to be €15 000.
On 31 December 2000, the land is sold for €16 000.
The accounts for 1999 and 2000 are presented on three alternative bases:

■ Historical cost
■ Revaluation without 'recycling'
■ Revaluation with 'recycling'

	Historical cost €	Revaluation without recycling €	Revaluation with recycling €
1999			
Balance sheet			
Assets			
Land	10 000	15 000	15 000
Equity			
Share capital	10 000	10 000	10 000
Revaluation reserve		5000	5000
Total equity	10 000	15 000	15 000
Income statement			
Profit for 1999	0	0	0
Statement of total recognized gains and losses			
Profit for 1999	0	0	0
Revaluation gain	0	5000	5000
Total	0	5000	5000
2000			
Balance sheet			
Assets			
Cash	16 000	16 000	16 000
Equity			
Share capital	10 000	10 000	10 000
Revaluation reserve		0	0
Retained earnings	6000	6000	6000
Total equity	16 000	16 000	16 000
Income statement			
Gain on sale of land	6000	1000	6000
Profit for 2000	6000	1000	6000
Statement of total recognized gains and losses			
Profit for 2000	6000	1000	6000
Recycling adjustment	0	0	−5000
Total	6000	1000	1000

the basis of the revalued amount. However, IAS 21 states that a translation gain or loss that has been transferred directly to reserves should be reported as income in the year that the underlying asset is disposed of.

17.5.3 The statement of changes in equity

IAS 1 does not formally require enterprises to present a statement of total recognized gains and losses; the STRGL is mentioned only in an appendix which is not part of the mandatory standard. The formal requirement, as set out in IAS 1, 86, is for a statement showing:

- The net profit or loss for the period
- Each item of income or expense, gain or loss which, as required by other standards, is recognized directly in equity, and the total of these items
- The cumulative effect of changes in accounting policy and the correction of fundamental errors

These are the basic elements of the STRGL. However IAS 1 adds three further items that should be included either in this statement or in the notes:

- Capital transactions with owners and distributions to owners
- The balance of accumulated profits at the beginning of the period and at the balance sheet date, and the movements for the period
- A reconciliation between the carrying amount of each class of equity capital, share premium and each reserve at the beginning and at the end of the period, separately disclosing each movement

When the last three points are presented in the notes, the statement that presents the first three points may be regarded as an STRGL, according to the form given in Exhibit 17.8. When all six items are presented in the same statement, this statement is termed the statement of changes in equity. Exhibit 17.10 presents this statement for Global Corp.

For the accounting theorist, the statement of changes in equity is far less interesting than the statement of recognized gains and losses which was dealt with in the previous section. However it does fulfil two very worthy, if mundane, functions:

(a) **To report transactions between the corporation and the shareholders.** Notably:
  (i) **Dividends:** In 2000, Global Corp paid a dividend of €100.
  (ii) **New issues of share capital:** In 2000, Global Corp issued 200 new shares of one Euro nominal value at a price of €1.50. The issue of these shares resulted in the increase in the balances of

Exhibit 17.10 *Global Corp: statement of changes in equity for the year 2000*

	Share capital	Share premium	Legal reserve	Revaluation reserve	Translation reserve	Accumulated profits	Total
Balance at 31 December 1999	1000	0	100	210	–125	1296	2481
Prior year adjustments							
Fundamental error						–500	–500
Changes in accounting policy						150	150
Revised balance at 31 December 1999	1000	0	100	210	–125	946	2131
Gains/losses not reported in the income statement							
Translation loss					–110		–110
Revaluation of property				90			90
Profit for year 2000						735	735
Appropriations of profit							
Dividend						–100	–100
Transfer to legal reserve			30			–30	0
Issue of shares	200	100					300
Balance at 31 December 2000	1200	100	130	300	–235	1551	3046

share capital and share premium shown in the first two columns of Exhibit 17.10.

(b) **To report movements of reserves.** Reserves are subdivisions of equity. In corporations, their principal function is to distinguish the part of total equity that may be legally distributed to the shareholders by way of dividend from the part which must be retained by the corporation in order to preserve its capital base. Under the law in many countries a corporation must transfer a certain percentage (often 5 per cent) of each year's profit to a special reserve, known as a 'legal reserve', until the balance of the reserve is equal to a certain percentage (often 10 per cent) of contributed capital. The aim is to increase the corporation's funds that are available for the payment of creditors. For this reason the profits that have been transferred to the legal reserve are not available for distribution to shareholders. In 2000 Global Corp increased its contributed capital by €300; therefore it transferred €30 from profits to legal reserve. This transfer is shown in the third column of Exhibit 17.10.

The function of the statement of changes in equity may be summarized as:

- To present information that is not included in any other element of the financial statements – information that is essential for a proper appreciation of the enterprise's performance.

- To demonstrate the integrity of the financial statements (notably the articulation of the balance sheet and income statement) and to explain how the items reported in the balance sheet and the income statement relate to each other

However, since the statement provides a record of all changes in equity since the last balance sheet, it includes all the elements of comprehensive income. Hence it would seem that this statement can also fulfil the function of the statement of recognized gains and losses (dealt with in the previous section). However this would be a rather unsatisfactory way of reporting comprehensive income since the various elements are scattered around the statement, being mixed up with changes in equity that are not part of comprehensive profit, notably dividends and new share capital. It is far better to have a separate statement as presented in Exhibit 17.8. This point is made very neatly in the following quote: 'the statement of changes in equity mixes apples and oranges in the same statement by including items of financial performance with transactions with owners and transfers between different components of equity' (Todd Johnson, 1998).

Practice throughout the world in relation to the STRGL and the statement of changes in equity is very diverse. Only in the UK are major enterprises required (under FRS 3) to publish both an STRGL and a statement of changes in equity. An example of the practice in the UK is given in Exhibit 17.11 which presents an extract from the annual report of BP Amoco.

In the annual report of BP Amoco, the statement of total recognized gains and losses is placed in a prominent position, alongside the balance sheet, income statement and cash flow statement, giving the impression that it is a measure of performance of equal importance to the other statements. The statement of capital and reserves is hidden among 26 pages of notes. One has the impression that its main function is to provide information on certain matters of a formal legal character.

In other countries there is no obligation to present a separate statement similar to the STRGL. In the USA, the relevant standard, FAS 130, requires that a figure for comprehensive income should be given somewhere in the annual report but there is no obligation that this should be in a separate statement. Most American corporations meet this

Exhibit 17.11 *BP Amoco, annual report 1999*

Statement of total recognized gains and losses (for the year ended 31 December 1999)	$ millions
Profit for the year	5008
Currency translation differences	(921)
Total recognized gains and losses relating to the year	4087
Prior year adjustment – change in accounting policy	715
Total recognized gains and losses	4802

	Share capital	Share premium	Capital redemption reserve	Merger reserve	Profit & loss account	Total
Note 28 Capital and reserves						$ millions
At 1 January 1999	4863	3056	330	697	32 840	41 786
Prior year adjustment					715	715
Restated	4863	3056	330	697	33 555	42 501
Employee share scheme	16	311			(61)	266
Profit for year					5008	5008
Dividends					(3884)	(3884)
Dividends reinvested	13	(13)			311	311
Exchange adjustment					(921)	(921)
At 31 December 1999	4892	3354	330	697	34 008	43 281

requirement by including figures relating to comprehensive income in a statement of changes of equity. Research by Hirst and Hopkins (1998) demonstrated that financial analysts are significantly more likely to take note of the amount of comprehensive income when it is presented in a separate statement connected with the income statement (as is the practice in Britain) than when it is reported in the statement of changes in equity. This finding is puzzling as it seems to imply that financial analysts are not capable of taking into account all the information presented in the financial statements, which contradicts the efficient market hypothesis. However it is generally agreed that the option that permits enterprises to report comprehensive income as part of the statement of changes in equity is one of the weak points of FAS 130.

Exhibit 17.12 presents the statement that appears in the 1999 report of General Motors which may be considered to be typical of American practice. Note that the figures in this statement agree with those in the equity section of General Motors' balance sheet which is presented in section 16.9.2 of Chapter 16. GM's total comprehensive income for 1999 was $10541mn, of which $6002mn was income per the income statement and $4539mn was 'other comprehensive income' which consists principally of the adjustment to the pension liability. The 1999 'other comprehensive income' is deducted from the brought-forward 'other comprehensive loss' resulting in a figure for accumulated other comprehensive loss of $1158mn to be reported in the balance sheet at 31 December 1999. The statement of equity is complicated by the fact that during 1999 GM 'spun-off' a major subsidiary, Delphi, leading to a reduction in equity of $3.3bn effected through adjustments to capital surplus and retained earnings.

The corporations of other countries tend to follow American practice when their shares are listed in Wall Street and they are thus obliged to respect US GAAP. However there is no obligation under the law of Japan, Germany or France to present any figures relating to comprehensive income.

17.6 REPORTING FINANCIAL PERFORMANCE: PROPOSALS FOR CHANGE

In August 1999, the G4+1 group of standard setters issued a position paper entitled 'Reporting financial performance: proposals for change' (G4+1, 1999). The paper sets out certain quite radical proposals for the reform of the principal performance statements, notably the income statement and the STRGL. Although these proposals do not commit any of the standard setters involved (which include the IASB), they are of great

Exhibit 17.12 General Motors: statement of stockholders' equity ($ millions)

	Total capital stock	Capital surplus	Comprehensive income	Retained earnings	Accumulated other comprehensive loss	Total stockholders' equity
Balance at 31 December 1998	1104	12 661		6984	(5697)	15 052
Shares reacquired	(76)	(3794)				(3870)
Shares issued	19	3588				3607
Comprehensive income						
Net income			6002	6002		6002
Other comprehensive income(loss)						
Foreign currency translation adjustments			(944)			
Unrealized gains on securities			515			
Minimum pension liability adjustment			4968			
Total other comprehensive income			4539		4539	4539
Comprehensive income			10 541			
Cash dividends				(1367)		(1367)
Delphi initial public offering		1244			1244	
Delphi spin-off		95		(4658)		(4563)
Balance at 31 December 1999	1047	13 794		6961	(1158)	20 644

interest to students of financial reporting as indicating the future direction in which the reporting of performance is likely to develop, given that in the introduction to the paper it is stated that 'it reflects an agreed approach . . . that each body intends to consider in its own constituency, in most cases aiming towards an accounting standard'.

The position paper proposes that the income statement and the STRGL should be replaced by a single statement of the form shown in Exhibit 17.13. This statement consists of three sections:

- Operating income
- Financing income
- Other gains and losses

Essentially the first two sections comprise most of the items that are currently reported in the income statement. In the proposed statement, there is a subtotal of operating and financing income, which may be considered to be the equivalent of the net profit reported in the income statement. The third section reports gains and losses that currently by-pass the income statement, notably gains on the revaluation of fixed assets and translation gains and losses. However, as proposed by the G4+1, this section also includes some items that are at present included in the income statement, notably gains and losses on the disposal of fixed

Exhibit 17.13 *The statement of financial performance according to the G4+1*

Operating (trading) activities		
Revenues	1000	
Cost of sales	(550)	
Other expenses	(150)	
Operating income		300
Financing and other trading activities		
Interest on debt	(50)	
Gains and losses on financial instruments	35	
Financing income		(15)
Operating and financing income		285
Other gains and losses		
Profit(loss) on disposal of discontinued operations	(110)	
Profit(loss) on sale of fixed assets	20	
Gain on revaluation of fixed assets	60	
Foreign currency translation gain(loss)	(180)	
Total other gains and losses		(210)
Comprehensive income		75

assets. Thus the proposed new statement is essentially the income statement with the STRGL tacked on at the bottom, with a limited amount of rearrangement of the items within the income statement (to separate operating from financing activities) and between the income statement and the STRGL (to put gains and losses on disposal of fixed assets into the STRGL).

There appear to be two principal reasons why the G4+1 group is proposing this reform:

- To make the reporting of the STRGL standard throughout the world; at present it is only required in the UK
- To lessen the emphasis that users put on the figure for net profit in the present income statement

The second reason is the more significant and the more controversial. The G4+1 considered whether it should recommend the continued reporting of financial performance in two statements (the income statement and the STRGL) and came to the conclusion that 'a significant drawback to the two-statement approach is that undue significance may be attached to one statement at the expense of the other (as has been the experience in the UK), and greater significance may be given to the distinction between the two statements than is justified'. This is a convoluted way of saying that, in the UK, users tend to ignore the STRGL and give greater attention to the figure for net profit in the income statement. Essentially the G4+1 group thinks that the users are perverse and it will force the users to stop concentrating on the income statement by abolishing it. In the authors' opinion, such an approach is not only extremely patronizing but also sure to fail, as either the standard setters will fail in their attempt to impose the new statement of performance or, if they succeed, users will simply concentrate on the subtotal for operating and financing profit at the expense of that for comprehensive income.

A major part of the G4+1 paper is given over to a discussion on how to distinguish between items reported as 'other gains and losses' from those reported in 'operating and financing income'. It proposes four major distinguishing characteristics in the form of the matrix presented in Exhibit 17.14.

This matrix should be compared with Todd Johnson's 'dichotomies' (1998, presented in section 17.2.1). There are many common features. In fact all four of the G4+1's 'characteristics' appear in Todd Johnson's list, albeit with slightly different terms; thus Todd Johnson's controllable/noncontrollable dichotomy is essentially similar to the G4+1's internal events/external events characteristic. However there is one very important difference between the G4+1 and Todd Johnson. The G4+1 does not include 'realize/unrealized' as a characteristic that determines how

Exhibit 17.14 *Operating items versus other gains and losses*

Characteristics more typical of operating items	*Characteristics more typical of other gains and losses*
Operating activities	Non-operating activities
Recurring	Non-recurring
Non-holding items	Holding items
Internal events	External events

an item should be reported. It explains its views on this subject in the following terms:

> Realisation may be the critical event in the traditional operating cycle of purchasing, manufacturing, distribution and sale. In the context of many financial exposures today that are affected directly or indirectly by the presence of deep and active markets, the realisation of an item provides information that is of limited value. A realised gain will reflect the same economic event as an unrealised gain; realisation merely represents confirmation of the gain.

The G4+1, in rejecting the concept of realization as a criterion for the reporting of items in the statement of performance, is proposing a revolutionary change in accounting practice. In effect, the total of comprehensive income at the foot of the proposed statement of financial performance (Exhibit 17.13) includes both realized and unrealized income. From the above quotation, one can discern two reasons for the G4+1's attitude:

■ Changes in the business environment have rendered the realized/unrealized dichotomy irrelevant

■ The information on this point is of little value

The G4+1 present no evidence to back up these claims. By contrast Todd Johnson's conclusion that realization was an important characteristic was based on empirical surveys.

It should be noted that the G4+1 position paper makes no change in the reporting of prior period adjustments, which should continue to be reported as adjustments to the balance of accumulated profits at the start of the year. Also it is against recycling within the new statement of performance; once an item has been reported in other gains and losses, it should not be reported later as part of operating and financing income. Hence it goes no way to meeting the criticisms made by the authors in the previous section.

In December 2000, the UK's ASB issued an exposure draft on reporting performance that proposed implementing most of the suggestions contained in the G4+1 paper. This could lead to a revolutionary change in the reporting practice of British companies.

17.7 EARNINGS PER SHARE

Analysts attach great importance to the figure for earnings per share reported by an enterprise as they use it in calculating the price/earnings ratio, which gives an indication of whether an enterprise's shares are over- or underpriced. The IASB was concerned that the practice of enterprises in this matter should be harmonized and, to this end, in 1997 it issued IAS 33 Earnings per share.

Earnings per share is calculated as the total profits of the enterprise divided by the number of ordinary shares. IAS 33 sets out rules on how to calculate both the numerator and the denominator.

Total profits

Total profits should be taken as the net profit after tax as reported in the income statement. This profit is calculated after extraordinary items but does not take into account changes in net asset values taken direct to equity and prior-year adjustments (that is, it is not comprehensive income). The most interesting theoretical problem concerns the treatment of dividends on preference shares. The discussion in Chapter 16 has already brought out the ambiguous nature of preference shares, that they often exhibit the characteristics both of equity and of a liability. Hence, in certain circumstances, preference shares are reported in the balance sheet as liabilities. However, in the income statement, dividends on preference shares are never considered to be expenses; they are always treated as distributions of profit. The reason would appear to be that, in all major countries, this is the legal position, which the IASB has considered that it would be inopportune to contest. However with respect to earnings per share, the IASB has proved rather more daring and requires that earnings be calculated after deducting dividends on preference shares. This is completely logical since what is being calculated is earnings per ordinary share. However clearly earnings in the income statement and earnings in earnings per share are calculated on different bases.

Number of shares

For many enterprises calculating the number of ordinary shares is straightforward. However complications can arise where the enterprise has issued new shares during the period or is committed to issue new shares in the future (as with options granted to directors). IAS 33 sets out very detailed rules on how to calculate the denominator in these cases. They are not dealt with here as they do not concern income which is the principal topic of this chapter. However these rules are valuable in that they bring order into an area where previously practice was very diverse.

The application of IAS 33 is illustrated by DaimlerChrysler's statement which is presented in Exhibit 17.15.

In fact DaimlerChrysler presents four figures for earnings per share, being the four combinations of before and after extraordinary expenses and basic and diluted. IAS 33 states that earnings should be calculated after extraordinary items, but permits the enterprise to present in addition alternative calculations. The diluted figure is calculated on the assumption that all additional shares that could be issued (for example on the conversion of bonds or the exercise of options) are in fact issued.

Exhibit 17.15 *DaimlerChrysler: earnings per share (1999)*

	Euros per share
Basic earnings per share	
Income before extraordinary item	5.09
Extraordinary item	0.64
Net income	5.73
Diluted earnings per share	
Income before extraordinary item	5.06
Extraordinary item	0.63
Net income	5.69

SUMMARY

The three problems connected with the preparation of the income statement were considered in turn:

- The recognition problem: when should revenue be recognized

- The presentation problem: how should income and expenses be presented in the income statement, with particular reference to the classification of expenses (by nature or by function), extraordinary and exceptional items, discontinuing operations and segment reporting

SUMMARY (cont'd)

- The profit measurement problem with reference to the alternative concepts of profit (current operating profit and comprehensive income) and to the treatment of prior year adjustments

The statement of total recognized gains and losses and of the statement of changes in equity were examined and the proposals of the G4+1 group for a new statement of performance was discussed. Finally the presentation of earnings per share was explained.

Review questions

1. Why is the determination of the point in time at which revenue is recognized important for the measurement of profit?

2. What is the difference between the total output and the total sales presentation of the income statement? Which presentation is used by most MNEs?

3. What are the two alternative classifications of expenses permitted by the EU and the IASB? What are their relative advantages and disadvantages?

4. What according to the IASB are the essential characteristics of an extraordinary item?

5. What are the three different ways of defining the segments of an enterprise according to IAS 14?

6. What are the two alternatives concepts of income dealt with in this chapter? What are the fundamental differences between the two concepts?

7. What are the two types of items that, according to IAS 8, should be deducted from the opening balance of retained earnings?

8. What is the function of the statement of total recognized gains and losses?

9. What is the function of the statement of changes in equity?

References

ASB 'FRS 3: reporting financial performance', Accounting Standards Board, London (1993).

Cairns, D *A Guide to Applying International Accounting Standards*, Accountancy Books, Milton Keynes (1995).

FASB *Statement of Financial Accounting Concepts No. 6*, FASB, Norwalk (1985).

G4+1 *Reporting Financial Performance: Proposals for Change*, Accounting Standards Board, London (1999).

Hicks, J *Value and Capital*, Clarendon Press, Oxford (1946).

Hirst, DE and Hopkins, PE 'Comprehensive income reporting and analysts' valuation judgements', *Journal of Accounting Research*, **36** (1998).

McBride, H 'Conflict in financial reporting: the case of Coillte Teorante', *Irish Accounting Review*, **4**(2) (1997), pp. 69–88.

O'Hanlon, J and Pope, P 'The value relevance of UK dirty surplus accounting flows', *British Accounting Review*, **31**(4) (1999), pp. 459–82.

Penman, SM *et al.* 'An Issues Paper on Comprehensive Income', *Accounting Horizons*, **11**(2) (June, 1997), pp. 120–6.

Todd Johnson, L, Reitner, CL and Swieringa, RJ 'Towards reporting comprehensive income', *Accounting Horizons*, **9**(4) (December 1995), pp. 128–37.

Todd Johnson, L *Reporting Financial Performance: current developments and future directions*, FASB, Norwalk (1998).

Walker, M 'Clean surplus accounting models and market-based accounting research', *Accounting and Business Research*, **27**(4) (1997), pp. 341–55.

Further reading

On comprehensive income, the AAA's issues paper (Penman *et al.*, 1997), the G4+1 discussion paper (G4+1, 1999) and the FASB paper (Todd Johnson, 1998) are recommended.

chapter eighteen

The Cash Flow Statement

Chapter objectives

- To analyse the information provided by the cash flow statement in terms of its reliability and relevance
- To set out the IASB's rules for the form and content of the cash flow statement
- To analyse the rules and practice concerning the cash flow statement in the Pentad

18.1 THE CASH FLOW STATEMENT COMPARED WITH THE INCOME STATEMENT

The cash flow statement is one of the components of a complete set of financial statements as specified in IAS 1, alongside the balance sheet and the income statement. As its name implies, it is a flow statement, like the income statement. The relationship between the cash flow statement and the income statement is presented in Exhibit 18.1.[1] In essence the cash flow statement is very straightforward; it is nothing more than the cash account, in which the figures for cash receipts and cash payments are classified and arranged in a particular way. It is the income statement that is complicated, as the amounts of cash receipts and payments have to be adjusted for accruals.

The advocates of the cash flow statement claim that it is a more useful statement than the income statement, because it has advantages with respect to the two qualities that make information valuable: reliability and relevance.

Exhibit 18.1 *The relationship between the cash flow statement and the income statement*

Cash receipts
(Less cash payments)
Net cash inflow (outflow) for the period
Plus (less) increases (decreases) in assets (other than cash)
Less (plus) increases (decreases) in liabilities
Net profit for the period

18.2 THE RELIABILITY OF THE CASH FLOW STATEMENT

The cash flow statement reports cash receipts and cash payments. These are solid verifiable facts. By comparison, the income statement presents cash amounts adjusted for accruals. Accruals are not facts; they are abstractions created by the accountant. The payment of €1000 for a machine is a fact. The depreciation expense of €100 reported in the income statement is not a fact; it is a creation of the accountant. In allocating €100 of the machine's cost to a particular period, the accountant is obliged to exercise judgement on a number of issues: the machine's economic life, the depreciation method to use, and, most crucially, whether to base depreciation on historical cost, replacement cost or some other valuation basis. On all these matters, the accountant's judgement may be questioned. Hence the cash flow statement is more objective than the income statement, which is based on questionable accounting allocations and valuations. Similarly the cash flow statement is less susceptible to manipulation by an unscrupulous management intent on presenting an unduly favourable picture.

However the reliability of the cash flow statement should not be overstated. There are a number of problems connected with the cash flow statement that can affect its reliability:

(a) **Definition of cash.** If cash were to be defined simply as notes and coins, there would be no difficulties in establishing cash inflows and outflows in a completely objective manner. However such a definition of 'cash' is far too narrow for a modern business, and the definition of 'cash' is generally expanded to include bank balances and highly liquid assets, which inevitably creates problems in deciding where to draw the line.

(b) **Allocations.** The term 'allocation' refers to the process in which a single amount (often a receipt or a payment) is divided into two or more sub-elements which are reported differently in the accounts.

The income statement is bedevilled by problems of allocation, as was demonstrated in the above example, in which the cost of a machine was allocated to several periods. However the allocation problem also arises in the preparation of the cash flow statement. As Egginton (1984) points out, in a forceful criticism of the cash flow statement, the preparer of the cash flow statement can only avoid all problems of allocation and classification, if either he presents one global figure for all payments (and a similar one for receipts) or he provides a full description of each individual payment and receipt. Of course this does not happen in practice. As will be shown in section 18.4, the preparation of the cash flow statement as currently prescribed by the IASB involves very considerable problems of allocating receipts and payments to particular categories.

(c) **Foreign currency.** There are a number of difficult problems connected with foreign currency. Are cash flows in foreign currency to be considered as equivalent to those in domestic currency? And, if so, at what exchange rate should they be translated? Is the fall in the translated value of a foreign cash balance, a cash outflow? To these and similar problems, there is no simple answer.

(d) **Manipulation.** The claim that the cash flow statement is immune from manipulation is not completely correct; for example, management can manipulate the reported cash flow by accelerating or delaying payments, especially around the end of the accounting period.

Certainly all these points should be taken into account in assessing the reliability of the cash flow statement. However all of the above considerations apply even more strongly to the income statement – for example, the definitions of 'revenue' and 'expense' cause greater problems than those of 'cash receipt' and 'cash payment', notwithstanding the difficulty in defining 'cash'. In the income statement, the allocation problem goes right to the heart of the calculation of profit; in the cash flow statement, the allocation problem does not affect the figure for net cash flow, only its breakdown. Hence, there is a wide measure of agreement that the information in the cash flow statement is more reliable than that in the income statement.

18.3 THE RELEVANCE OF THE CASH FLOW STATEMENT

Cash may be described as the life blood of the enterprise. Without cash, the enterprise will die, as it will be unable to pay its employees, its suppliers and all the other parties interested in it. Without a positive cash inflow from its activities, it will be unable to satisfy its shareholders' expectations of a satisfactory return on their investment. Hence most users of the enterprise's financial statements are very interested in cash flows. This is the IASB's position as made clear in the following quotation from its Framework: 'The economic decisions that are taken by users of financial statements require an evaluation of the ability of an enterprise to generate cash and cash equivalents and of the timing and certainty of their generation'. More specifically, the cash flow statement provides information that is highly relevant for users in their evaluation of two particular aspects of the enterprise: its value and its solvency.

18.3.1 The value of the enterprise

According to economic theory, the value of an enterprise is equal to the present value of future cash flows. It would seem to be self-evident that information about past cash flows is relevant for the estimation of future cash flows. There is no dispute on this matter concerning the confirmatory role of reported information: the cash flow statement plays a valuable role in assisting the user to assess the accuracy of past forecasts of future cash flows. However there is considerable controversy over the predictive role of the cash flow statement – that is, how useful information on past cash flows is in predicting future cash flows and hence in explaining the value of the enterprise. Many researchers have investigated this matter. Neill *et al.* (1991) classify these studies into three groups:

Market value

In the first group are studies that seek to establish whether there is a relationship between an enterprise's past cash flow and its present market value (as measured by its share price). In general, it is found that there is a correlation between cash flow and share price. However the analysis is complicated, because there is also a correlation between profit and share price, and cash flow is generally highly correlated with profit (since cash flow and earnings have many common elements, such as sales). However two points are clear: firstly the two together (cash flow and profit) provide a better explanation of the share price, than either separately, which demonstrates that cash flows in fact have some relevance for valuation; secondly the explanatory power of profit is significantly greater than that of cash flow, which indicates that the relevance of cash flows for valuation is less than that of profit. This finding provides the empirical justification for the practice of assessing the performance of the enterprise through a measure of profit (involving accruals) rather than through cash flows. One can conclude that the cash flow statement does provide relevant information for valuation, but it is definitely secondary to the income statement.

Information content

In the second group are studies that seek to establish that the cash flow statement provides relevant information in that its publication is associated with an unusual movement in the share price. These studies are subject to a number of methodological problems (such as identifying the date when cash flow information is published) and in general provide only weak evidence that the cash flow statement provides new information.

Predictive value

The third group of studies investigated whether future cash flows may be predicted from past cash flows and whether profits give the better prediction. Although some studies were inconclusive, one study by Greenberg *et al.* (1986) showed that past profits outperformed past cash flows in predicting future cash flows.

All three groups of studies come to the same general conclusion: that cash flow information is less relevant than profit information for the value of the enterprise; however cash flow information has incremental value. Hence the commonsense assumption that cash flow information must be relevant for valuing the enterprise is shown to be justified, but only partially.

18.3.2   The solvency of the enterprise

Solvency refers to the capability of an enterprise to meet its future commitments. If an enterprise is unable to pay its debts as they fall due, it may be made bankrupt. The authorities take possession of the enterprise's assets and sell them in order to pay off the debts. This can happen even if the enterprise is profitable, if the enterprise ties up its funds in illiquid assets (such as machines and inventory), leaving no cash for the payment of creditors. Debts are paid off with cash and not with profits. Hence, for the assessment of solvency, the cash flow statement is more relevant than the income statement. It complements the balance sheet, in that it provides information about flows (essential for assessing the development over a period) whereas the balance sheet presents the position at a point in time.

However the commonsense position presented in the previous paragraph is not confirmed by empirical studies, which show that past cash flow alone is not a good predictor of future bankruptcy.[2] A major reason is that a negative cash flow does not always mean that an enterprise is doing badly. In fact an enterprise may report a negative cash flow in two quite different situations:

(a) The enterprise is suffering operating losses, which if they were to continue would lead to such a loss of cash that ultimately the enterprise would fail.

(b) The enterprise is profitable and is expanding; its negative cash flow is caused by its investment in fixed assets and working capital. It is not impossible for such an enterprise to fail through lack of cash, but, provided that it can demonstrate that it is basically profitable, it will generally be able to cover its cash outflows through borrowing.

Cash flow on its own is not a good predictor of bankruptcy because of the large number of enterprises with poor cash flows that somehow survive. Hence for the assessment of solvency cash flow information has to be supplemented with other information. Cash flow information has incremental value in that, when it is used in combination with other measures, it generally leads to a better prediction.

An interesting finding of these studies is that certain constituent components of overall cash flow (notably dividends and investment flows) provided a better prediction of bankruptcy than overall cash flow. This provides a strong theoretical basis for the classification of the overall cash flow into its component parts.

18.4   IAS 7

The IASB's rules on the cash flow statement are set out in two standards: IAS 1 and IAS 7. IAS 1 includes the cash flow statement as one element of a complete set of financial statements. However the detailed provisions as to its form and content are set out in *IAS 7 Cash Flow Statements*, which the IASC issued in 1992, replacing the previous IAS which was entitled *Statement of Changes in Financial Position*. The change in title reflected a change in content. Previously the idea had been to report the changes in the enterprise's funds over the period. There were two reasons for this shift in emphasis from funds to cash:

(a) The concept of cash is more easily comprehended by users than is the concept of funds. One of the reasons why the IASB made the change is that it could reach no consensus on the definition of funds.

(b) Cash relates much more directly to the needs of users, particularly financial analysts who place so much emphasis on the estimation of future cash flows.

In principle the cash flow statement for a period is little more than a summary of the cash account. Hence in deciding on the form and content of the cash flow statement, there are only two significant points on which choices have to be made: how to define cash and how to analyse cash flows.

18.4.1 The definition of cash

In the theory of economics and finance, cash comprises not only coins and notes (currency) but also financial assets that may be converted into currency quickly and with negligible risk and cost. Hence it is generally agreed that cash includes a current account with a reputable and solvent bank, where the bank is contractually obliged to honour cheques at sight drawn on the account, either by paying out currency or by a transfer to another bank account. Under IAS 7, cash includes cash equivalents which are defined as short-term highly liquid investments which are readily convertible into known amounts of cash and which are subject to negligible changes in value. Examples of a cash equivalent are a deposit account with a bank that may be drawn upon at short notice and a treasury bill that is due to be redeemed in the near future. IAS 7 seems to favour a rather generous definition of cash equivalent as it suggests that an investment that matures in three months' time would qualify. However it is very firm that there should be no uncertainty as to the amount to be received; hence investments in shares, the value of which fluctuates with the market, cannot be cash equivalents.

In defining 'cash', the IASB made a pragmatic decision as to what definition would be most useful to users. Other standard setters have reached different conclusions; for example the UK's ASB defines cash as currency and bank deposits repayable within 24 hours.[3] Thus a transfer of funds to a seven day deposit account would be reported in the cash flow statement as a cash outflow (a financial investment). Under IAS 7, such a transfer would be ignored in the cash flow statement as it represents only a rearrangement of the asset 'cash'. The ASB's definition leads to more reliable information as there is less doubt as to what qualifies as 'cash'. However it can be claimed that the IASB's definition leads to more relevant information.

18.4.2 The classification of cash flows

IAS 7 provides that cash receipts and payments should be reported separately; they may not be offset against each other, except in very restricted circumstances, for example when an agent collects rents for a landlord and pays them over without delay. The cash receipts and payments should be analysed by:

■ Operating activities
■ Investing activities
■ Financing activities

The basic idea behind this three-way classification is that an enterprise acquires resources from suppliers of finance (financing activities), invests these resources in assets (investing activities), which generate future cash inflows (operating activities).

The justification for classifying cash flows in this way is that it provides more information than the figures for overall cash receipts and payments; for example, as noted in section 18.3.2, an enterprise's investment cash flow provides a better basis for assessing its solvency than its overall cash flow. The usefulness of each of the three elements may be assessed as follows:

Cash flows from operating activities

The basic idea of separating cash flows from operating activities from cash flows related to financing and investing activities is that the latter are more irregular in that they relate to transactions that enterprises typically do not undertake at the same scale in each period. Hence cash flows from operations may be considered to be more regular than the other cash flows and provide a more secure basis for estimating the future cash flows of the enterprise. This is certainly the position of financial analysts. When they use cash flows in the analysis of an enterprise's value it is nearly always in the form of operating cash flows (that is cash flows from operations); they exclude the financing and investment cash flows as being too irregular. Financial analysts consider that the quality of profits is measured by the proportion of the reported profits that is covered by operating cash flows: the higher the proportion, the higher the quality of the profits.

Cash flows from investing activities

It is important to disclose separately investment cash flows as they represent expenditures made to generate future cash inflows. For example, if an enterprise reports very low investment cash outflows, this would be grounds for suspecting that it is making insufficient provision for securing the continuation in the future of the present level of operating cash inflows.

Cash flows from financing activities

The basic reason for reporting finance cash flows separately is to ensure that they are not included with operating cash flows. An enterprise should not be able to report a favourable operating cash flow simply by borrowing money with which to cover its operating deficit. In addition, the separate disclosure of finance cash flows is useful in predicting future cash outflows caused by repaying the providers of finance.

18.4.3 Practical problems of classification

The distinction between these three categories of cash flow is largely commonsense and for most cash flows there is little doubt as to the category to which they belong. For example, in the case of an automobile manufacturer, cash received from customers in respect of cars that they have purchased is an operating cash flow, as is cash paid as wages to workers on the production line. Cash paid to an equipment supplier for a new machine is an investment cash flow, as is the cash received when the machine is ultimately sold for scrap. Cash received on the issue of a debenture loan is a finance cash flow as is the cash paid when that loan is finally repaid.

However there are borderline cases; thus is cash paid to acquire raw materials an investment? IAS 7 classifies it as an operating cash flow. The dividing line between investment and operating cash flows seems to be somewhat similar to that between fixed and current assets. Cash payments for the acquisition of fixed assets of any category (intangible, tangible or financial) are always investment cash flows and cash payments for the acquisition of current assets are (almost) always operating cash flows; cash receipts arising from the disposal of these assets are similarly classified. The exception is that cash flows relating to the acquisition and disposal of financial assets that are classified as current assets are treated as investment cash flows, unless the asset is a cash equivalent in which case that cash flow does not figure at all in the cash flow statement. The different treatment of plant, of inventory and of current financial assets, is not justified on theoretical grounds but on the need to have a clear rule that ensures comparability.

On the other side of the balance sheet, all cash inflows relating to the issue of loans and equity are financial cash flows as are cash payments made to redeem these items. However a cash payment made to settle a liability incurred in acquiring a non-cash asset (for example a creditor who has supplied equipment or raw materials) is an investment or operating cash flow that is classified according to the asset acquired.

18.4.4 The classification of interest and dividends

The biggest problem with classifying cash flows is how to treat cash receipts and payments that relate to finance and investments but which are of the nature of income and not of capital. Examples are interest paid on a loan, dividends paid to shareholders and interest received on financial assets (both fixed and current). IAS 7 states that there is no consensus on the classification of these cash flows: interest and dividends paid may be classified as either financial cash flows or as operating cash flows; interest and dividends received as investment cash flows or as operating cash flows. IAS 7 simply demands that enterprises disclose the amounts and treat them consistently from period to period.

The UK's ASB when faced with this problem solved it by adding a fourth category of cash flows: returns on investment and servicing of finance. The ASB's approach has the advantage of clarity and is consistent with IAS 7. Hence it has been used in the examples of cash flow statements that are presented later.

In the authors' opinion, interest and dividends received on financial assets are operating cash flows. No distinction is made between financial assets and tangible assets (such as machines) in classifying their costs as investment cash flows. The return from the investment in machines is reported as an operating cash flow. For consistency, the return on the investment in financial assets (the interest and dividends received) should also be reported as an operating cash flow. Having classified interest and dividends received as operating cash flows, it seems natural to classify interest and dividends paid in a similar fashion, particularly as an increase in interest paid is often coupled with an increase in interest received. The comparison of investment and finance cash flows is more meaningful if they are computed on the same basis, that is excluding those elements that relate to income.

Two other arguments may be advanced in support of reporting interest payments as operating cash flows:

(a) Financial analysts generally deduct interest payments in calculating operating cash flow, as this gives a better indication of the enterprise's continuing cash flows and they often compare operating cash flow with profits (for example in assessing the quality of income). As interest is deducted in the calculation of profit, it should also be deducted in calculating operating cash flow. For the same reason, financial analysts do not deduct dividends paid from operating cash flows.

(b) It increases the usefulness of the cash flow statement if finance cash flows are so defined that, over the life of the enterprise, they sum to zero – at least with respect to the non-equity finance cash flows. In this case, the user would expect that every finance cash inflow would have to be offset by a future cash outflow. This would be very helpful in assessing the future cash obligations of the enterprise. To achieve this, interest payments should not be included in finance cash flows. Also it would be desirable that, among the finance cash flows, equity cash flows are reported separately from non-equity cash flows.

The FASB standard FAS 95 requires that interest payments should be classified as operating cash flows. The principal reason is to enhance the comparability of the cash flow statement with the income statement. As far as practicable, items that are reported in the income statement should be included as operating cash flows in the cash flow statement. The FASB refers to this approach as the 'inclusion concept' and justifies it in the following terms: 'operating cash flow should, insofar as possible, include items whose effects are included in determining net income to facilitate an understanding of the differences between net income and net cash flow from operating activities' (FAS 95, paragraph 90). Nurnberg and Largay (1998) criticize this approach, claiming that interest payments are considered to be financing cash flows in financial management theory. In fact, there seems to be no consensus among financial analysts on this matter, but at least one authority treats interest paid as part of operating cash flows (see Bodie and Merton (1998) pages 67–8). The authors support the FASB for the reasons already given.

18.5 THE FORM OF THE CASH FLOW STATEMENT

IAS 7 offers a choice of two fundamentally different ways of presenting the cash flow statement: the direct method and the indirect method.

The direct method

The cash flow statement of Global Corp according to the direct method is presented in Exhibit 18.2. Essentially it is an analysis of the cash account, defining cash to include cash equivalents. The figures reported in the statement are what they purport to be: cash receipts and payments. They differ from the amounts reported in the income statement. For example, the amount received from customers is not the same as sales, because part of the receipts relate to last year's sales and part of the sales of this year are still owing at the end of the year. The dividend reported in the cash flow statement is that paid during 2000, which is the dividend for 1999 outstanding at the end of the previous year.

The indirect method

The indirect method is illustrated in Exhibit 18.3. Compared with Exhibit 18.2, it is far more complex and hence more difficult to understand. In fact many of the figures that are reported are not in themselves cash flows; in some cases, the cash flow is calculated as the difference or sum of two or more magnitudes that are not cash flows. This is very confusing for the reader. In effect, for the user, Exhibit 18.3 offers no advantages over Exhibit 18.2. However, for enterprises the indirect method is often easier and cheaper to implement than the direct method and it is for this reason that IAS 7 allows it, although it states that enterprises are encouraged to use the direct method.

Exhibit 18.2 *Global Corp: cash flow statement, the direct method*

Cash flow statement for the year 2000		
Cash flows from operating activities		
Receipts from customers	2505	
Payments to suppliers	−1025	
Wages paid	−800	
		680
Returns on investment and servicing of finance		
Interest received	45	
Dividend received from associates	10	
Interest paid	−35	
Dividend paid	−100	
		−80
Tax and extraordinary items		
Extraordinary expense	−227	
Taxation	−150	
		−377
Cash flows from investing activities		
Purchase of plant		−125
Cash flows from financing activities		
Repayment of loan	−400	
Issue of share capital	300	
		−100
Total cash flow		−2
Reconciliation		
Cash balance at 31 December 1999		275
Cash balance at 31 December 2000		273
Decrease in cash balance		−2

The indirect method starts with the figure for profit and makes two types of adjustment relating to items in the income statement that do not represent cash flows and which must be excluded in order to convert the profit flow into a cash flow:

(a) **Adjustments for change in working capital.** In order to convert the amounts stated in the income statement to cash flows, they have to be adjusted for the change in balances relating to working capital items over the period – that is the difference between the amounts reported in the balance sheet at the start of the period and those at

Exhibit 18.3 *Global Corp: cash flow statement, the indirect method*

Cash flow statement for the year 2000		
Operating profit		1190
Adjustments for		
Depreciation	220	
Reduction in provisions	35	
Own work capitalized	−125	
Increase in inventories	−120	
Increase in accounts receivable	−650	
Increase in accounts payable	130	
		−510
Cash flow from operations		680
Returns on investment and servicing of finance		
Interest received	45	
Dividend received from associates	10	
Interest paid	−35	
Dividend paid	−100	
		−80
Extraordinary expense	−227	
Taxation	−150	
		−377
Cash flows from investing activities		
Purchase of plant		−125
Cash flows from financing activities		
Repayment of loan	−400	
Issue of share capital	300	
		−100
Total cash flow		−2
Reconciliation		
Cash balance at 31 December 1999		275
Cash balance at 31 December 2000		273
Decrease in cash balance		−2

the end of the period. The logic behind this curious procedure is that it reverses the accruals that were made in drawing up the income statement. The items of working capital that should be taken into account in this calculation are the current assets (except financial assets) and those current liabilities that relate to operations and not to finance (for example trade creditors).

(b) **Adjustments in respect of other items.** The items in the income statement that represent increases or decreases in the balance sheet value of other items, must also be eliminated from the profit figure in order to convert it to a cash flow figure. The other items involved are those not taken into account in the calculation in (a) above: that is fixed assets, financial assets included in current assets, provisions, long-term liabilities and borrowings included in current liabilities. The most important item in this category is depreciation, which is an expense deducted in the calculation of profit which does not involve a cash flow in the period.

The amounts included in the two types of adjustments are not cash flows. In no sense can the charge for depreciation or a decrease in inventory be considered to be a cash flow. There is only one figure in the top half of Exhibit 18.3 that is a genuine cash flow – that is the final figure for cash flow from operations. Users are understandably perplexed by the inclusion of amounts that are not cash flows, which can lead to such confused and false notions that in order to increase cash flow one should increase the charge for depreciation. Compared with the direct method, the indirect method of presenting the cash flow statement is clearly far less informative and helpful. Regrettably, the indirect method is very widely used in practice. In the UK, it is used by 96 per cent of listed companies (Company Reporting, 1996) and the proportion in other European countries is probably even higher. The reason is that enterprises want to save the cost of analysing cash receipts and payments relating to operations, which in a large enterprise can number several thousands or even millions. There are generally far fewer cash transactions relating to investment and finance activities and, for this reason, IAS 7 requires that, even with the indirect method, the actual cash flows should be reported for these items.

18.6 THE RECONCILIATION WITH THE BALANCE SHEET

The net cash flow over a period as reported in the cash flow statement should equal the change in value of cash and cash equivalents between the opening and closing balance sheets. IAS 7 requires that the enterprise should present a reconciliation between the cash flow statement and the balance sheet and also disclose the principal components of cash and cash equivalents. The need for the cash flow statement to be consistent with the balance sheet determines the way that the cash flows of subsidiaries and other group members are treated in the consolidated cash flow statement.

18.7 CASH FLOWS OF SUBSIDIARIES, JOINT VENTURES AND ASSOCIATED ENTERPRISES

IAS 7's rules relating to reporting the cash flows of group members are rather arbitrary. For subsidiaries, the full cash flows are included in the consolidated cash flow statement, on the grounds that the consolidated accounts should present the group as if it were a single enterprise. However, with respect to associated enterprises, only the cash flows between the parent enterprise and the associated enterprise are included, for example dividends received. For joint ventures, IAS 7 pronounces a judgement of Solomon: for a joint venture that is accounted for by proportional consolidation, the appropriate proportion of the entity's cash flow should be included in the group cash flow statement, but, for a joint venture that is accounted for using the equity method, only the direct cash flows are reported (as for an associated enterprise). The reason for this differential treatment is to ensure that the cash flow statement reconciles with the balance sheet; note that, only with a joint venture accounted for using proportional consolidation, is the entity's cash reported as cash in the consolidated balance sheet.

These rules may be criticized on two grounds:

■ They introduce a discord between the consolidated income statement and the consolidated cash flow statement: the consolidated accounts includes the group's share of the profits of associated enterprises but not the full amount of their cash flows

■ The comparability of financial statements is impaired by permitting two quite different ways of reporting the cash flows of joint ventures

When a parent acquires a subsidiary, it generally disburses cash, which, according to IAS 7, is shown in the group cash flow statement as a cash outflow on investing activities. However, generally the subsidiary's assets (reported in the consolidated balance sheet) include cash. In principle this cash may be deducted from the cash outflow, in that it reduces the amount of cash that has left the group as a result of the acquisition. Hence, according to IAS 7, the amount must be disclosed. The same principles apply, in reverse, to disposals of subsidiaries. IAS 7 is silent on how to account for the acquisition of associates and joint ventures, but, given the need for the cash flow statement to reconcile with the balance sheet, the cash acquired with these entities should not be treated as a reduction in the cash outflow, except where the entity's cash balance is included as cash in the consolidated balance sheet. This will be the case only with joint ventures accounted for using proportional consolidation.

18.8 NON-CASH TRANSACTIONS

It is possible for an enterprise to acquire an asset or to incur a liability without cash being paid or received. Examples of such non-cash transactions are:

- The purchase of a building that is financed by a mortgage loan
- The acquisition of a machine by means of a finance lease (under IAS 17, the machine is reported as a fixed asset and the finance lease as a liability)
- The acquisition of an asset (say shares in another enterprise) in exchange for an issue of equity
- The conversion of a loan into equity
- An oil company exchanges a quantity of crude oil for the right to exploit a certain oil well, with only the difference in values being settled in cash

The first three points consist of a combined finance and investment transaction; in the fourth point the decrease in one source of finance is offset by the increase in another; the fifth is similar to the fourth except that it affects the assets side of the balance sheet.

In theory, there are two possible ways of reporting these non-cash transactions:

(a) **As fictional cash flows.** The transaction is reported in the cash flow statement as if it had involved cash, by reporting a cash inflow and an equal cash outflow. The advantage of this approach is that it enables the cash flow statement to give a realistic picture of the enterprise's finance and investment activities – of the resources that it has acquired through finance activities and that it has disbursed in investment activities.

(b) **As a note.** The transaction is not reported in the body of the cash flow statement. The cash flow statement reports only actual cash flows; however to inform users of the totality of the enterprise's finance and investment activities, details of such transactions are reported in a note.

The justification for treatment (b) is simply that the cash flow statement should report actual cash flows and not fictional cash flows. This is a very persuasive argument which seemingly settled the matter for the IASB, for IAS 7 includes the following rule:

Investing and financing transactions that do not require the use of cash or cash equivalents should be excluded from a cash flow statement. Such transactions should be disclosed elsewhere in the financial statements in a way that provides all the relevant information about investing and financing activities. (IAS 7, 43)

However the authors have a slight preference for treatment (b) for two reasons. Firstly, in many cases, it is a trivial matter whether or not there is a cash receipt and an offsetting cash payment from the viewpoint of the enterprise; for example, when the enterprise purchases a building with the aid of a mortgage loan, in some cases the lender will pay the seller directly and in other cases it will transfer the funds to the enterprise which then pays the seller. Whether or not the enterprise actually handles the cash is not a substantial feature of the transaction and should not govern how it is reported in the cash flow statement.

Secondly, it is desirable that there should be a certain symmetry with finance cash flows so that, in the long run, all non-equity finance inflows are offset by non-equity cash outflows. This will not occur in bullet points one, two and four unless the transaction is reported as a finance cash flow in the cash flow statement. Otherwise in points one and two, the repayment of the liability will be reported in the cash flow statement, but not the initial loan; 'from a cash flow perspective, the enterprise appears to be paying off a phantom loan' (Nurnberg, 1993). And in point four, the redemption of the liability is ignored in the cash flow statement.

18.9 FOREIGN CURRENCY CASH FLOWS

The treatment of foreign currency items in the balance sheet and income statement is covered in Chapter 21. This section deals only with the cash flow statement. The problem of how to deal with foreign currency cash flows and cash balances arises when the enterprise seeks to draw up its cash flow statement that is denominated in its own currency. Consider the example of a British company which owns a subsidiary based in South Africa whose only asset is a bank account of which the details are given in Exhibit 18.4. In deciding how to treat the cash flows of its South African subsidiary in its own consolidated cash flow statement, the British company has to resolve three issues:

■ Should the cash flows in South African rands be reported as if they were in UK pounds?

■ If yes, at what exchange rate should they be translated from rands to pounds?

■ How should the fall in the translated value of the bank balance be reported?

Exhibit 18.4 *The South African subsidiary's bank account*

| Date | Subsidiary's accounts | | Consolidated accounts | |
	Transaction	Amount (rands)	Exchange rate	Amount (£)
1 April 2000	Balance b/f	500 000	10.0 rands = £1	50 000
30 June 2000	Payment for wages	(240 000)	10.0 rands = £1	(24 000)
31 December 2000	Receipt of fees	240 000	11.3 rands = £1	23 239
31 March 2001	Balance	500 000	11.5 rands = £1	43 478

Reporting rands as pounds

The British company draws up its consolidated accounts (including its cash flow statement) in UK pounds. Is it reasonable to report the rand cash flows in the consolidated cash flow statement in terms of UK pounds, when in fact they are not pounds? To answer this conundrum, one must refer to the basic definition of consolidated accounts as presented in IAS 27: consolidated financial statements are the financial statements of a group presented as those of a single enterprise. Clearly, the consolidated accounts must be presented in a single currency – generally that of the parent enterprise, in the present example pounds. In respect of the balance sheet and the income statement, there is general agreement that the South African subsidiary's assets and liabilities, revenues and expenses should be reported in the consolidated accounts in terms of pounds even though they are basically denominated in rands. The only disagreement is on the exchange rate to be used to translate the rand amount. In effect, the consolidated accounts report the group's assets and liabilities, revenues and expenses, on a worldwide basis. Although the consolidated accounts are denominated in pounds, there is no implication that the assets reported there are located solely in the UK, and the same applies, *mutatis mutandis*, to liabilities, revenues and expenses. Following this principle, it is reasonable to report rands as pounds in the consolidated cash flow statement because the user should be aware that there is no implication that all the cash flows are pounds. However there is one situation in which it would not be appropriate to include the South African subsidiary's cash flows in the consolidated cash flow statement: this would occur if the South African government were to place restrictions on the transfer of funds out of the country with the effect that the British parent could not expect to draw any benefit from its subsidiary's cash flows. Under the rule in IAS 27, 13, the South African subsidiary should, in this case, be excluded from the consolidated accounts; hence it should be excluded from the cash flow statement which is part of the accounts. IAS 7, 48 also requires that the enterprise should disclose by way of a note the amount of cash and cash equivalent balances (not flows) that are not available to the group.

The translation rate

In the case of the income statement, there is considerable controversy as to the exchange rate to be used to translate the foreign currency accounts, for example whether depreciation should be translated at the historical rate or the average rate for the period. However, for the cash flow statement, there are no real grounds for differences of opinion; cash flows should be translated at the exchange rate ruling at the date of the cash flow (in the foreign subsidiary). This is the rule set down in IAS 7, 25 which has been followed in Exhibit 18.4. Hence in the consolidated cash flow statement, the payment of 240 000 rands for wages is reported as £24 000 and the receipt of 240 000 rands for fees as £23 239. Although this rule is very logical and conceptually impeccable, it has the unfortunate effect that the translated version of the subsidiary's cash flow statement is not a linear transformation of the original foreign currency version. In rands, the amounts of the payment and of the receipt are equal, but, in pounds, the receipt is less than the payment. Thus one of the aims of translation (that it should preserve the relationships in the foreign currency accounts) is not achieved. On this point, see Chapter 21, section 21.10.2 and Georgiou (1993).

The fall in value of the bank balance

This problem can best be envisaged in the case of a foreign subsidiary that has a bank balance but no receipts or payments in the period. Assume for example that the South African subsidiary in Exhibit 18.4 had no receipts or payments in the period so that its closing bank balance was the same as its opening bank balance of 500 000 rands. The translated value of its opening bank balance is £50 000; the translated value of its closing bank balance is £43 478. There has been a fall in translated value of £6522. Is this to be reported as a cash outflow, even though there was no cash flow in rands? It has to be reported somewhere in the cash flow statement, given that the total of cash inflows and outflows has to be reconciled with the change in the cash balance over the period. According to the IASB, although the fall in the translated value of the bank balance is not a cash flow, it should be reported as a separate item in the cash flow statement in order to reconcile the opening and closing cash balances.

18.10 COMPARATIVE ANALYSIS

18.10.1 Laws and standards

In three of the five countries of the Pentad there is no legal obligation for enterprises to issue a cash flow statement. However, in fact all major multinational enterprises include a cash flow statement in their published accounts – for two reasons:

- They are following the rules set out in standards which in many countries have the force of law
- The enterprises are responding to the demands of investors on the international capital market

The position in each country is as follows:

USA

In the US, a statement of cash flows is required for business enterprises by FAS 95, which replaced the previous requirement for a statement of changes in financial position.

Japan

Under the SEL, listed enterprises are required to prepare a consolidated cash flow statement. Most major MNEs follow the rules laid down in 'Accounting principles for consolidated cash flow statement' which was issued by the BADC in 1998 and which prescribes rules very similar to those of IAS 7.

Germany

Until recently, German companies were not required to present a cash flow statement in the annual report, as the matter was covered only in non-mandatory recommendations – of the accountancy profession and of the academics. However, with the revision of paragraph 297 of the Commercial Code (HGB) in 1998, German listed companies are required to present cash flow statements for the first time for financial years beginning after 31 December 1998. However the law does not specify the detailed rules for the preparation of a cash flow statement. The task of implementing the rules was delegated to the national standard setter. In October 1999, The DSR (the German Accounting Standards Board), published its second standard, DRS 2 *Kapitalflussrechnung*, which lays down the rules for the presentation of cash flow statements. Internationally unique is the publication by the DSR of specific standards for the

presentation of cash flow statements of banks and insurance companies, DRS 2–10 and DRS 2–20, respectively.

France

The PCG includes a funds flow statement as one of the schedules annexed to the accounts, based on movements in working capital. The CNC has recommended that enterprises should prepare such a statement but there is no legal obligation. In 1988 the OEC issued its own recommendation, for a statement based on cash flows, very similar to IAS 7. Thus in France there is no consensus as to whether the statement should be based on the flow of funds or the flow of cash. However Griziaux (1995) comments that 'the CNC model, still very much in use, should gradually be superseded by the OEC type of statement'. Most larger MNEs issue cash flow statements based on the OEC/IAS 7 model.

Britain

In the UK, the first Financial Reporting Standard, FRS 1, of the ASB was on the issue of cash flow statements in 1991. It superseded SSAP 10 *Statements of Source and Application of Funds*, which required the preparation of a funds statement.

18.10.2 The direct method versus the indirect method

As already explained in section 18.5, cash flow statements may be prepared using either the direct method or the indirect method. Under IAS 7, although enterprises should report cash flows from operating activities using either the direct or the indirect method, they are encouraged to use the direct method. Similarly in the USA, while companies are encouraged to report gross operating cash flows by major classes of operating cash receipts and payments (the direct method) presenting the net amount of such items (the indirect method) is also allowed.

By contrast in the UK, preference is given to the indirect method. FRS 1 states that the indirect method should be used in all circumstances but the standard provides an option to provide information by the direct method as well. Where the direct method is used, a reconciliation statement with the indirect method should be shown by way of a note. The ASB explained its position in the following terms: 'The Board noted that it did not believe that in all cases the benefits to users of this information (provided by the direct method) outweighed the costs to the reporting entity of providing it and, therefore, did not require the information to be given. The Board remained of this view, and the FRS continues to encourage the direct method when the potential benefits to users outweigh

Exhibit 18.5 *The direct method versus the indirect method*

Standard states preference for the direct method	Standard states no preference for either method	Standard states preference for the indirect method
IASB: IAS 7 USA: FAS 95	Germany: DRS 2 France: OEC opinion No. 1–22–1988.	UK: FRS 1

the costs of providing it.' This is an interesting example of a standard setting body having to assess the costs and benefits of information.[4]

A more neutral position has been adopted in Germany and France. DRS 2 allows the use of the direct and the indirect method for the presentation of cash flows from operating activities without giving a preference to either of them. The position in the various countries is summarized in Exhibit 18.5.

In all countries under scrutiny the presentation of cash flows resulting from investment and financing activities should be presented in accordance with the direct method only. Because of its ease of application, companies, especially groups, use the indirect method for the presentation of cash flow statements, as is demonstrated in the examples given in section 18.11.

18.10.3 Definition of cash and cash equivalents

Further differences between the national frameworks are the definition of cash and cash equivalents, particularly with regard to overdrafts and short term marketable securities as is summarized in Exhibit 18.6. The ASB's definition of 'cash' includes only deposits repayable within 24 hours; both the FASB and the DSR have a more generous definition, including deposits with a maturity of less than three months. The definition in IAS 7 is less precise but there is a reference to a maturity of three months in an explanatory paragraph. Both the ASB and the OEC deduct bank overdrafts from 'cash' (note the OEC's definition of 'trésorerie'), a point not covered by the FASB or the DSR. The IASB covers this point in IAS 7,8 (an explanatory paragraph): 'in some countries, bank overdrafts which are repayable on demand form an integral part of an enterprise's cash management. In these circumstances, bank overdrafts are included as a component of cash and cash equivalents'.

Exhibit 18.6 *The definition of cash and cash equivalents*

US *FAS 95*	Cash and cash equivalents include currency on hand, demand deposits, and short-term, highly liquid investments (original maturities of three months or less or remaining maturities of three months or less at the time of acquisition).
UK *FRS 1*	Cash in hand and deposits repayable on demand, less overdrafts repayable on demand. Deposits repayable on demand if they can be withdrawn at any time without notice or period of notice of not more than 24 hours.
Germany *DRS 2*	Cash and cash equivalents include cash on hand and other short-term highly liquid readily convertible investments. 'Short term' is defined as a period not exceeding three months.
France *OEC opinion* *(No. 1–22–1988)*	'Trésorerie' is the difference between the liquid assets (cash plus short-term negotiable investments) and the immediately exigible liabilities (for example, bank overdrafts).
IAS 7	Cash comprises cash on hand and demand deposits. Cash equivalents are short-term, highly liquid investments, that are readily convertible to known amounts of cash and which are subject to an insignificant risk of changes in value.

18.10.4 Which enterprises are required to prepare a cash flow statement?

In the USA a statement of cash flow is required by FAS 95 for all business enterprises (except 'not-for-profit' organizations). In the UK, FRS 1 requires that annual accounts and group accounts for all enterprises, including financial institutions, contain a cash flow statement except for small enterprises, as determined by the Companies Act 1985 and subsidiaries included in group accounts with a cash flow statement. FRS 1 provides examples of cash flow statements for a single company, a group, a property investment company, an investment company, a bank and an insurance company. In Germany, DRS 2 requires listed parent companies to present cash flow statements. As mentioned earlier, specific cash flow standards for banks (DRS 2–10) and insurance companies (DRS 2–20) have also been issued by the German standard setter. As these standards are unique, they do not correspond to IAS 7 or FAS 95, which do not refer to specific industries. In Japan, listed corporations are required to prepare a consolidated cash flow statement; a cash flow statement for the individual corporation is also required when its cash flows are not included in a consolidated cash flow statement.

18.10.5 Classification

In most countries, the cash flows from the different activities of a company are classified into operating, investment and financing activities. These are the rules in IAS 7, in France, Germany and the US, but not in the UK. FRS 1's classification of cash flows is different and unique. It requires companies to classify and present receipts and payments into:

- Operating activities
- Return on investments and servicing of finance
- Taxation
- Investing activities
- Financing

18.11 EXAMPLES FROM PUBLISHED ACCOUNTS

18.11.1 USA

The cash flow statement of the General Electric Company, which, according to Exhibit 1.4, is the world's largest multinational enterprise, is presented in Example 18.7 overleaf.

The following comments on GE's statement should be made:

(a) GE's cash balance increased by $4237mn during 1999, despite the fact that the cash outflow relating to investing activities was a massive $42 179mn, representing very considerable investments, including $15bn on new plant, property and equipment and $13bn relating to increases in financial receivables in GE's insurance and finance business. This outflow was more than offset by the inflow from operating activities ($24bn) and from financing activities ($21bn).

(b) The cash flow from operating activities is calculated using the indirect method, as is the case with all major American corporations. The net earnings (per the income statement) are adjusted for those items included in the income statement that do not entail an inflow or outflow of cash. The largest adjustments are for depreciation and for the increase in insurance liabilities.

(c) The cash flow from financing activities includes $48bn from newly issued debt less $27bn for debt repaid. Note that both amounts are shown; it is not permitted to show only the net figure. GE includes as a cash inflow the net increase in borrowings with a maturity of 90 days or less. This would seem to be contrary to FAS 95 in two respects:

    (i) only the net figure is shown;

    (ii) borrowings with a maturity of less than 90 days are considered by FAS 95 to be cash equivalents and therefore should not appear in the cash flow statement.

Exhibit 18.7 *General Electric Company and consolidated affiliates:* *year ended 31 December 1999*

	$ millions
Cash flows (operating activities)	
Net earnings	10 717
Adjustments to reconcile net earnings to cash provided from operating activities	
Depreciation and amortization of property, plant and equipment	4 908
Amortization of goodwill and intangibles	1 783
Deferred income taxes	1 502
Decrease in current receivables	143
Decrease in inventories	266
Increase in accounts receivable	820
Increase in insurance liabilities and reserves	4 584
Provision for losses on financing receivables	1 678
All other operating activities	(1 808)
Cash from operating activities	24 593
Cash flows (investing activities)	
Additions to property, plant and equipment	(15 502)
Dispositions of property, plant and equipment	6 262
Net increase in GECS financing receivables	(13 088)
Payments for principal businesses purchased	(11 654)
All other investing activities	(8 197)
Cash used for investing activities	(42 179)
Cash flows (financing activities)	
Net increase in borrowings (maturities of 90 days or less)	6 171
Newly issued debt (maturities longer than 90 days)	48 158
Repayments and other reductions (maturities longer than 90 days)	(27 539)
Net purchase of GE shares for treasury	(1 002)
Dividends paid to share owners	(4 587)
All other financing activities	622
Cash from financing activities	21 823
Increase in cash and equivalents during year	4 237
Cash and cash equivalents at beginning of year	4 317
Cash and cash equivalents at end of year	8 554

18.11.2   Britain

Practice in Britain is illustrated by the 1999 cash flow statement of the Cadbury Schweppes group presented in Exhibit 18.8.

Exhibit 18.8   *Cadbury Schweppes Group: cash flow statement for the 52 weeks ending 2 January 2000*

	£ million	£ million
Cash flow from operating activities (note 26)		824
Dividends from associates		13
Return on investments and servicing of finance		(80)
Interest paid	(131)	
Interest received	78	
Dividends paid to minority interests	(27)	
Taxation		(161)
Capital expenditure and financial investments		(196)
Purchase of tangible fixed assets	(128)	
Disposal of tangible fixed assets	20	
Purchase of shares by the Employee Trust	(88)	
Acquisitions and disposals		213
Acquisitions of businesses	(350)	
Proceeds from sale of subsidiaries and investments	563	
Dividends paid to ordinary shareholders		(196)
Cash inflow before use of liquid resources and financing		417
Management of liquid resources		13
Net change in commercial paper investments	216	
Net change in bank deposits	(56)	
Net change in bond investments	(81)	
Net change in equity and non-equity investments	(66)	
Financing		(364)
Issue of ordinary shares	17	
Share repurchases	(79)	
Proceeds of new borrowings	111	
Borrowings repaid	(407)	
Capital element of finance leases repaid	(6)	
Increase in cash		66

Comments on Cadbury Schweppes' statement:

(a) The cash flow statement follows the provisions of FRS 1 and exhibits two specific features of this standard which are not found in the standards of other countries:

   (i) Interest and dividends received and paid (other than dividends paid to Cadbury Schweppes' shareholders) are reported in a separate section entitled 'Returns on investments and servicing of finance'. (See the comment on this point in section 18.10.5.)

   (ii) There is a second special section headed 'Management of liquid resources'. This reports movements on financial investments that are current assets. The definition of cash in FRS 1 is much narrower than that in other standards because it excludes all deposits and investments with a maturity of more than 24 hours. Such a narrow definition has certain shortcomings; for example under FRS 1 an enterprise can report a positive cash flow simply by running down its liquid assets. However an enterprise's solvency is measured more realistically by its liquid assets than by its cash balance as narrowly defined. To a certain extent the separate section on liquid resources helps to correct any wrong impression that arises from the narrow definition of cash used in FRS 1.

(b) The detailed calculation of cash flow from operations is not shown on the face of the cash flow statement but in a separate note. This note (not reproduced here) indicates that the indirect method is used, as is the case with over 90 per cent of British companies.

(c) In 1999, Cadbury Schweppes enjoyed a positive cash flow from operations of £417mn, after taking into account finance costs, taxation and investments. It applied most of this cash flow to repay borrowings and repurchase shares; note that there is a finance outflow of £364mn. The net effect was an increase in cash of £66mn. As this increase was partly achieved through a reduction in liquid resources of £13mn, one can calculate that the increase in liquid resources (including cash) was only £53mn.

18.11.3　France

Practice in France is illustrated by the 1999 cash flow statement of the Alcatel group presented in Exhibit 18.9.

Exhibit 18.9 *Alcatel Group: consolidated statement of cash flows, 1999*

	€ millions	€ millions
Cash flows from operating activities		
Net income		644
Minority interests		37
Adjustments to reconcile income before minority interests		
to net cash provided by operating activities		
Depreciation and amortization	1850	
Changes in reserves for pension obligations	(116)	
Changes in other reserves	(125)	
Net gain on the disposal of non-current assets	(862)	
Share in net income of equity affiliates (net of dividends		
received)	(133)	614
Working capital provided by operations		1295
Net change in current assets and liabilities		
Increase in accounts receivable	(453)	
Increase in inventories	(333)	
Increase in accounts payable and accrued expenses	588	
Changes in reserves on current assets	(21)	(219)
Net cash provided by operating activities		1076
Cash flows from investing activities		
Proceeds from the disposal of fixed assets	191	
Capital expenditures	(1224)	
Increase in loans	(20)	
Cash expenditure for the acquisition of consolidated		
companies, net of cash acquired	(2173)	
Cash proceeds from sale of previously consolidated		
companies, net of cash sold	750	
Net cash used by investing activities		(2476)
Cash flows from financing activities		
Decrease in short-term debt	(352)	
Proceeds from issuance of long-term debt	1756	
Proceeds from issuance of shares	110	
Dividends paid	(391)	
Net cash provided by financing activities		1123
Net effect of exchange rate changes		59
Net decrease in cash and cash equivalents		(218)
Cash and cash equivalents at beginning of the year		3813
Cash and cash equivalents at end of year		3595

Comments on Alcatel's cash flow statement:

(a) The statement uses the standard classification of cash flows into operating, investing and financing activities. Dividends paid are shown as a financing cash outflow. Presumably interest paid and received are treated as operating cash flows as they are not disclosed separately as investing or financing cash flows. Note that the cash outlay on acquiring subsidiaries is reported net of the cash acquired with the subsidiary.

(b) The cash flow from operating activities is calculated by the indirect method. The calculation is made in two parts. The first part takes into account the adjustments in respect of non-current assets and liabilities, giving the amount of the increase in working capital (that is current assets less current liabilities); the second part presents the adjustments for current assets and liabilities, resulting in the increase in cash from operations. In these calculations, the term 'reserve' is used in a rather loose fashion to denote what in this book is termed a provision. The calculation of the increase in working capital is presumably a throw back to the time when French enterprises issued funds statements rather than cash flow statements.

(c) The line 'net effect of exchange rate changes' refers to the fall in the translated value of foreign cash balances.

SUMMARY

The value of the information provided by the cash flow statement was assessed with reference to the qualitative characteristics of reliability and relevance. The rules of IAS 7 with respect to the form and content of the cash flow statement were examined and explained, with particular reference to the definition of cash and the classification of cash flows. The specific problems of reporting the cash flows of group members, non-cash transactions and foreign currency flows and balances were analysed. The standards applicable to cash flow statements in the countries of the Pentad were examined and the practice illustrated with extracts from published accounts.

Review questions

1. What is the fundamental difference between the cash flow statement and the income statement?

2. On what grounds is it often claimed that the information provided by the cash flow statement is more reliable than that of the income statement?

3. What evidence is there that the information provided by the income statement is more relevant to the needs of investors than that of the cash flow statement?

4. What is IAS 7's definition of cash? In what way does it differ from that of the UK's FRS 1?

5. What is the rationale for classifying cash flows into those from operating, investing and financing activities?

6. What are the rules for the reporting of the cash flows of subsidiaries, joint ventures and associates in the group cash flow statement?

7. What is the rule in IAS 7 for the reporting of non-cash transactions, such as the purchase of a building through a mortgage loan? On what grounds did the authors criticize this rule?

8. What are the problems connected with the reporting of foreign currency cash flows?

Notes

1. In principle, the relationship between cash flow and profits shown in Exhibit 18.1 only holds if profits are equal to comprehensive income.
2. These studies are described in Neill *et al.* (1991).
3. FRS 1 Cash Flow Statements.
4. See section 13.6 of Chapter 13 for a discussion on this point.

References

Bodie, Z and Merton, RC *Finance,* Prentice Hall, New Jersey (1997).

Cheng, CSA, Liu, C-S *et al.* 'The value relevance of SFAS 95 cash flow from operations as assessed by security market effects', *Accounting Horizons* **11**(3) (September 1997), pp. 1–15.

Company Reporting 'Cash Flow Statements', *Company Reporting* (May 1996), pp. 3–8.

Egginton, DA 'In defence of profit measurement: some limitations of cash flow and value added as performance measures for external reporting', *Accounting and Business Research,* **14**(2) (Spring 1984), pp. 99–111.

Georgiou, G 'Foreign currency translation and FRS 1', *Accounting and Business Research,* **23**(91) (Summer 1993), pp. 228–36.

Greenberg, RG, Johnson, GL and Ramesh, K 'Earnings versus cash flow as a predictor of future cash flow measures', *Journal of Accounting, Auditing and Finance,* (Autumn 1986), pp. 266–77.

Griziaux, J-P 'France – Individual accounts', *Transacc,* D Ordelheide (ed.), Macmillan – now Palgrave, London (1995).

Neill, JD, Schaefer, TF, Bahnson, PR and Bradbury, ME 'The usefulness of cash flow data: a review and synthesis', *Journal of Accounting Literature,* **10** (1991), pp. 117–50.

Nurnberg, H 'Inconsistencies and ambiguities in cash flow statements under SFAS 95', *Accounting Horizons,* 7(2) (1993), pp. 60–75.

Nurnberg, H and Largay, JA 'Interest payments in the cash flow statement', *Accounting Horizons,* **12**(4) (December 1998), pp. 407–18.

Further reading

For an analysis of the limitations of the cash flow statement, see Egginton (1984). For further analysis of the relevance of the cash flow statement see Neill *et al.* (1991) and the articles quoted therein. For a more recent analysis of this matter, see Cheng *et al.* (1997). For comments on certain aspects of the contents of the cash flow statement, see the two articles by Nurnberg (1993) and Nurnberg and Largay (1998).

chapter nineteen

The Consolidated Accounts

Chapter objectives

- To outline the economic importance of groups of enterprises and to introduce the members of the group: the parent enterprise, subsidiaries, joint ventures and associates

- To explain the function of the individual accounts with respect to dividends, tax and liquidation

- To explain the function of the consolidated accounts

- To consider how the group is defined for the purpose of consolidated accounts, with reference to the two different concepts of the group – the parent company concept and the economic entity concept

- To consider the two ways in which a subsidiary may be defined – *de jure* control and *de facto* control

- To explain briefly the methods for preparing the consolidated accounts with reference to the acquisition method, the merger method and the fresh-start method

- To consider the definition of joint ventures and associates and how they are reported in the consolidated accounts

The subject of this chapter is the financial reporting of groups of enterprises. There are two principal reasons for the importance of this subject:

- The organizational form chosen by most large businesses (particularly MNEs) is that of a group of enterprises

505

■ In these circumstances, the financial statements of the individual enterprises within the group are inadequate and need to be supplemented by the consolidated accounts

19.1 THE ECONOMIC IMPORTANCE OF GROUPS

19.1.1 The Renault Group

In today's industrialized world much economic activity is carried out by groups of enterprises. The typical group consists of several enterprises: one enterprise known as the parent enterprise owns one or more other enterprises known as subsidiaries. In fact, virtually all large businesses are organized in the form of groups of enterprises. For example, the French multinational enterprise, Renault, is organized as a group of well over a hundred enterprises. The structure of this group is set out in Exhibit 19.1, which, given the number of enterprises involved, is able to show only a handful of the larger and more interesting enterprises. However the diagram illustrates very well the complexity of the group. The enterprise at the head of the group is the French société anonyme, Renault SA, which owns shares in 147 other enterprises, of which nine are shown separately. The more important are Renault V.I. SA which is the leading enterprise in Renault's commercial vehicle division, Compagnie Financière which is at the head of the financial division and Nissan Motor, the Japanese car manufacturer. The percentage that Renault SA owns of the equity of each enterprise is shown. The enterprises in which Renault SA owns shares, themselves own shares in other enterprises; thus Renault V.I. owns shares in 20 enterprises of which two are shown separately and Compagnie Financière owns shares in 41 other enterprises. Almost all the enterprises in the Renault Group are corporations. The geographical range of the Renault Group's interests is most impressive; there are group enterprises in 26 countries and in all continents, except Australasia.

The enterprises that are shown in Exhibit 19.1 may be classified into four categories:

(a) **The parent enterprise**: Renault SA.

(b) **Subsidiaries**: These are marked (S) in Exhibit 19.1. The precise definition of 'subsidiary' will be considered later. In broad terms, these are enterprises that are controlled by the parent enterprise. In order to control another corporation it is not necessary to own 100 per cent of the shares: a simple majority will do. Thus Dacia (a Romanian corporation) is a subsidiary of Renault SA, which owns only 51 per cent of the shares. Also it is not necessary for the parent enterprise to control a subsidiary directly. Where A controls B (that is B is a subsidiary

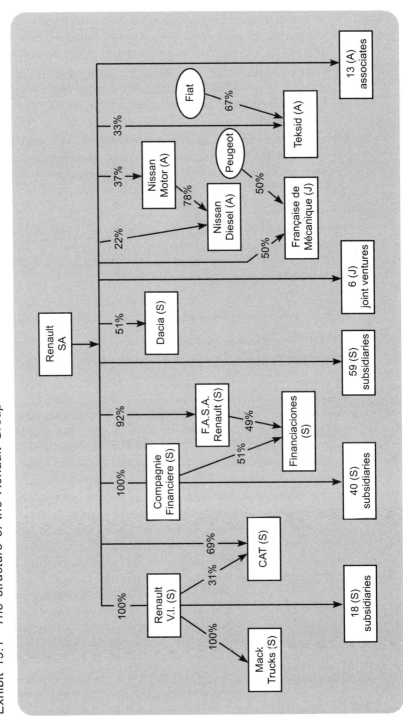

Exhibit 19.1 The structure of the Renault Group

of A) and B controls C (C is a subsidiary of B) then A controls C and C is a subsidiary of A. Thus Financiaciones (owned jointly by two subsidiaries of Renault SA) is a subsidiary of Renault SA.

(c) **Joint ventures:** These are marked (J) in Exhibit 19.1. These are, broadly, enterprises in which Renault shares control with another enterprise. An example is Française de Mécanique which is 50/50 owned by Renault and Peugeot.

(d) **Associated enterprises:** These are marked (A) in Exhibit 19.1. They are enterprises in which Renault has a significant holding but does not control (either fully or jointly). An example is Nissan Motor, in which Renault SA owns 37 per cent of the shares.

The parent enterprise and its subsidiaries may be considered to be full members of the group. Joint ventures and associated enterprises may be considered to be partial members of the group. Initially this chapter concentrates on the full members; only towards the end of the chapter is consideration given to the partial members.

19.1.2 Why large businesses are organized as groups

In total 148 enterprises are referred to in Exhibit 19.1; the sheer number of enterprises in the Renault group is remarkable. There are four principal reasons why large businesses, like Renault, tend to be organized in the form of groups:

(a) **Convenience.** It is often convenient to organize separate sectors of the business in the form of distinct corporate entities, with their own management structure, books of account and so on. Renault seems to have a policy of setting up a separate corporation in each country in which it has significant operations.

(b) **Limited liability.** An enterprise may decide that it is prudent to organize a particular activity as a separate corporation so as to limit its liability if the activity should fail. However, although an enterprise may not be legally liable for the debts of a subsidiary, it may often find that it is in its interests to accept responsibility because to act otherwise would damage its reputation. A good example is the action of Union Carbide Corporation, the American MNE, following the explosion at the plant of its Indian subsidiary which killed and injured some 25 000 people. The American parent paid $470mn to the Indian government in compensation, notwithstanding that in strict law it was not responsible for its subsidiary's debts.

(c) **Mergers and take-overs.** Many of the enterprises in the group started life as completely separate economic units and only later became part of the group through mergers and take-overs. Thus Dacia was an independent car manufacturer until it was taken over Renault but the enterprise has retained its legal identity.

(d) **Cooperation with other businesses.** When a business such as Renault seeks to undertake an activity jointly with another enterprise (such as the second French car manufacturer, Peugeot), this is almost always effected through setting up a separate legal entity (for example, Française de Mécanique, which is owned 50/50 by Renault and Peugeot) as this is the simplest way of defining the responsibilities of the two partners and of isolating this activity from the other activities of both groups.

Almost all the corporations listed on the world's major stock exchanges are parent enterprises. Certainly all the major automobile manufacturers are organized in the form of groups. This is shown in Exhibit 19.2 which presents the number of subsidiaries (Subs.), joint ventures (JVs) and associates (Ass.) in some of the major groups in this economic sector. The record seems to be held by Daimler-Benz AG with no less than 947 subsidiaries, 16 joint ventures and 109 associated enterprises. The enterprises in Exhibit 19.2 include two which, although they are very large corporations owning several subsidiaries, are themselves subsidiaries of the Ford Motor Company Inc. of the USA. This demonstrates how wide-ranging and complex multinational groups can be.

Exhibit 19.2   *The size of groups in the European automobile industry*

Group	Parent corporation	Subs.	JVs	Ass.
Volkswagen	Volkswagen AG	156	31	34
DaimlerChrysler	Daimler-Benz AG	947	16	109
BMW	Bayerische Motoren Werke AG	147	0	14
Fiat	Fiat Auto SpA	73	0	0
Peugeot	Peugeot SA	97	4	42
Renault	Renault SA	124	7	16
Volvo	AB Volvo	21	0	3
Ford (UK)	Ford Motor Company Ltd*	11	0	3
Ford (Germany)	Ford-Werke AG*	10	0	3

Notes: * Subsidiary of the Ford Motor Company Inc. of the USA

19.2 THE INDIVIDUAL ACCOUNTS

Each of the 148 corporations that make up the Renault Group is a separate legal entity which is required by the law of the country in which it is registered to draw up financial statements. These financial statements are referred to in this book as the 'individual accounts' (short for the accounts of the individual corporation) to distinguish them from the consolidated accounts, which cover all the corporations in the group. The individual accounts perform the absolutely vital function of presenting the financial position and performance of the corporation, as a separate legal entity They play an important role in three areas: dividends, tax and liquidation.

19.2.1 Dividends

In general, in most countries, groups are not legal entities and do not have the legal capacity to make contracts. This means that a person (either an individual or a corporation) that has a legal relationship with the group, has a contract, not with the group, but with one of the corporations that make up the group. This applies to employees, suppliers and lenders. When these persons are owed money (for unpaid wages, goods supplied or the amount lent), the debt is payable by the individual corporation with which they have a contract and not by the group as a whole. Similarly a dividend is paid, not by the group as a whole, but by the individual corporation in which the shareholder owns shares. The calculation as to whether the dividend can legally be paid (that the corporation's capital has been maintained) is done at the level of the corporation, not of the group as a whole.

19.2.2 Tax

In general, in most countries, the entity that is subject to tax is the individual corporation and not the group. There are two principal reasons for this:

(a) **Legal certainty.** The corporation, being a legal entity, is clearly defined and it is relatively easy to establish its assets and liabilities. The group, not being a legal entity, is much less clearly defined. As will become clear when the definition of the group is discussed later in section 19.4, the rules that govern whether a particular enterprise is or is not a member of the group are not so clear-cut as to remove all doubt in all cases. This lack of certainty means that, in general, the tax authorities are not prepared to treat the group as the taxable entity.

(b) **History.** when the ground rules for tax were laid down, groups were less important than they are now. However, although the present situation is that, in most countries, the taxable entity is the individual corporation, the situation is changing slowly as the taxation

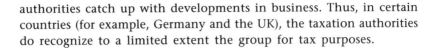

authorities catch up with developments in business. Thus, in certain countries (for example, Germany and the UK), the taxation authorities do recognize to a limited extent the group for tax purposes.

19.2.3 Liquidation

A third situation where the individual accounts are relevant is in the liquidation of a corporation, as is illustrated in the example presented in Exhibit 19.3. In this example, a parent corporation owns all the shares of two subsidiary corporations: A and B. The whole group becomes insolvent and the three corporations are liquidated (dissolved). The balance sheets of the three individual enterprises and the consolidated balance sheet just prior to liquidation are shown in Exhibit 19.3. The amount that the creditors and shareholders of these corporations will receive on liquidation is determined by national law, which varies somewhat from country to country, but generally the following three basic principles apply:

- The legal rights of creditors and shareholders are determined at the level of the individual corporation
- Creditors have priority over shareholders
- Shareholders have limited liability; they are not personally liable for the debts of the corporation whose shares they own

If it is assumed that the intangible and tangible assets prove to be worthless (it is not uncommon for the realized values of these assets in a liquidation to be much less than their book value, which is generally calculated using the 'going concern' assumption), then the amount to be paid to the creditors and shareholders of each corporation is calculated as follows:

(a) **Subsidiary A.** the creditors are paid in full, leaving a cash balance of €10, which is repaid to the shareholder (that is the parent enterprise).

(b) **Parent enterprise.** With its increased cash balance of €30, it is able to pay its creditors (€25) in full and make a small payment to its shareholders. The parent enterprise is not liable to pay the debts of its subsidiary, as it enjoys limited liability.[1]

(c) **Subsidiary B.** With its cash balance of €10, it is able to pay its creditors only 50 per cent of what it owes them.

In a liquidation, the consolidated balance sheet is of no use; in fact the information that it provides is quite misleading. Based on the consolidated balance sheet, one would expect, in a liquidation where the non-cash assets realized nothing, that all creditors would receive

Exhibit 19.3 *An example of the liquidation of a group*

	Parent enterprise €	Subsidiary A €	Subsidiary B €	Group €
Cash	20	30	10	60
Shares in A	50			
Shares in B	40			
Other assets	60	40	50	150
Total assets	170	70	60	210
Creditors	25	20	20	65
Equity	145	50	40	145
Total	170	70	60	210
Cash as % of creditors	80%	150%	50%	93%

93 per cent of the amount owing to them and the shareholders of the parent enterprise nothing. In fact the creditors of the parent enterprise and of subsidiary A are paid in full, whereas those of subsidiary B receive only 50 per cent of the amount due; the shareholders of the parent enterprise receive a small amount.

This example demonstrates very clearly that the balance sheet of the individual corporation provides vital information. Creditors and shareholders need to refer to it to establish their rights. This is particularly true where the corporation in question is a subsidiary. The creditors of the subsidiary cannot normally look to the parent enterprise to pay their debts; the parent enterprise, as a shareholder with limited liability, has no liability, unless it has specifically guaranteed the debt, as is sometimes demanded by prudent and knowledgeable creditors of subsidiaries. Hence creditors should look to the individual accounts and not the consolidated accounts. Similarly the minority shareholders in a subsidiary (that is the shareholders other than the parent enterprise) must look to the individual accounts and not to the consolidated accounts to find out how their investment is faring.

19.3 THE CONSOLIDATED ACCOUNTS

In the last section, it was established that the individual accounts provide vital information for shareholders and creditors. What then is the function of the consolidated accounts? These accounts fulfil two very important functions:

■ They correct many of the deficiencies of the individual accounts in the special case where the corporation is a parent enterprise

■ They provide information about the financial position and performance of the group as a whole

The deficiencies of the individual accounts of a parent enterprise

When a corporation owns subsidiaries, its individual accounts will generally give a completely inadequate picture both of its financial position (its assets and liabilities) and of its financial performance (its income and expenses). This is because, in its balance sheet, its interest in its subsidiaries will be presented as a single figure entitled 'investments' and no information is given about the assets and liabilities of these subsidiaries. These can be very substantial, dwarfing the parent enterprise's own assets and liabilities. Similarly, the parent enterprise's income statement may report nothing about the income and expenses of the subsidiaries. This is because, in the individual accounts, in accordance with generally accepted accounting principles, income from investments is measured on the basis of dividends received. This rule has two consequences: firstly, a subsidiary's income and expenses are never reported as such in the individual accounts of the parent enterprise; secondly, if, in a particular year, a subsidiary pays no dividend, no income at all is reported in respect of that subsidiary.

The individual accounts give shareholders and creditors[2] of the parent enterprise a very imperfect picture of the resources that the latter commands through its ownership of subsidiaries. Hence the need for consolidated accounts which reveal what lies behind the parent enterprise's investment in its subsidiaries. This is not to deny that the individual accounts are not also important for the shareholders and creditors of the parent enterprise (as demonstrated in the example in Exhibit 19.3); but it is very clear that they are quite inadequate and need to be supplemented by the consolidated accounts.

The picture of the whole group

Many people need to be informed about the financial position and performance of the group as a whole rather than of an individual corporation within the group. Such people include:

■ Employees of group enterprises, whose long-term employment prospects may well depend more on the prosperity of the whole group rather than of the individual corporation with which they have an employment contract

■ Suppliers, who may gain a better impression of future sales by looking at the business as a whole

- The government and the general public, who are interested in the whole business and not individual corporations

These two functions of consolidated accounts are very similar and it might be felt that there is no conflict between them. However there is a rather subtle distinction between the two functions. The first function is to expand and supplement the individual accounts of the parent enterprise. When the consolidated accounts fulfil this function, they are addressed to the shareholders and creditors of the parent enterprise. With the second function, all of the members of the group are considered of equal importance; the parent enterprise is no more important than the subsidiaries. This distinction lies behind the two different approaches to the definition of the group which are now considered.

19.4 THE DEFINITION OF THE GROUP

This section addresses the question how to define the group, that is the entity whose financial position and performance are presented in the consolidated accounts. This problem will be tackled from the viewpoint of both theory and practice. In theory, the definition of the group may be based on one of two fundamentally different concepts:

- **The parent company concept.** Under this concept, the group is defined as the parent enterprise plus its subsidiaries; this then leads to a second problem – how to define a subsidiary.
- **The economic entity concept.** Under this concept, the group is defined as those enterprises that form a single economic unit.

Exhibit 19.4 presents the relationship between these concepts in the form of a diagram. It should be emphasized that, in many situations in practice, the application of both concepts lead to the same conclusion, that is that a group defined according to the parent company concept would also frequently be defined as such with the economic entity concept and vice versa.

19.4.1 The parent company concept of the group

With the parent company concept, the group is defined as the parent enterprise plus its subsidiaries. In principle the parent enterprise may be of any legal form; hence a better term would be the parent enterprise concept. However the term 'parent company concept' is used here because it is well established in the literature. The IASB's rules, as set out in *IAS 27 Consolidated Financial Statements and Accounting for Investments*

Exhibit 19.4   *The definition of the group for consolidated accounts*

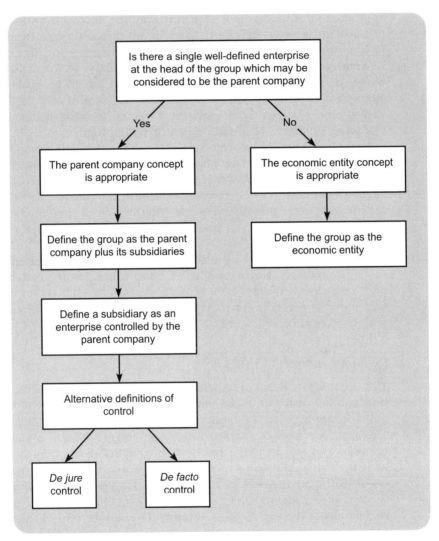

in Subsidiaries, are firmly based on the parent company concept. IAS 27 defines the group as 'a parent plus all its subsidiaries' (IAS 27, 6). The basic problem with this concept is how to define 'subsidiary'. IAS 27 defines a subsidiary as 'an enterprise controlled by another enterprise (known as the parent)'. To make this definition operational, it is necessary to define 'control'. This involves considering two rather different concepts of 'control': *de jure* control and *de facto* control.

De jure *control*

This approach is based on the legal capacity to exercise control over another enterprise. The most common way in which this arises is when one enterprise owns sufficient shares in another enterprise to enable it to command a majority of votes at the shareholders' meeting. By exercizing its votes, it can secure the election of its candidates to the management board. It should be noted that the calculation has to be made on the basis of a majority of voting rights, and not simply of a majority of shares, since, frequently, a enterprise's capital is made up of different categories of shares, each with different voting rights.

However, there are other ways in law by which one enterprise can control another without owning shares that give it a majority of the voting rights. The other shareholders may have entered into a legally binding agreement to vote according to the instructions of the first enterprise. Alternatively, one enterprise may have the right to control another enterprise by virtue of a contract passed with that enterprise or of a clause in that enterprise's constitution.

The essential feature of the *de jure* concept is that one enterprise has the legal power to control another. Where such a power exists, the second enterprise is deemed to a subsidiary of the first. It is not essential under the *de jure* concept that the first enterprise actually exercises its powers of control.

De facto *control*

This approach is based on whether, in fact, one enterprise actually controls another. It is not uncommon for one enterprise to control another, notwithstanding that its legal powers would appear to be inadequate. The most common example is where one enterprise owns a substantial minority (say 45 per cent) of the voting rights in another enterprise, with the remaining shares owned by a large number of small shareholders. In this case, it would be most unusual for the other shareholders to succeed in organizing themselves so as to outvote the large minority shareholder at the shareholders' meeting. Over 80 per cent of them would have to vote (more if some voted with the larger shareholder), a proportion rarely reached in enterprises with many shareholders. So, year after year, the large minority shareholder would be able to secure the election of its candidates to the management board. It will have *de facto* control, even though it has no *de jure* control.

Such *de facto* control can exist even when the percentage of voting rights owned by the first enterprise is relatively small, say 20 per cent. This will often occur when the first enterprise is in a dominant position *vis-à-vis* the second enterprise (for example as the major supplier or customer) and the other shareholders perceive that it is in their long term interest to acquiesce to this dominance. The sign of this dominance will be that the managing board of the second enterprise will be composed of persons who, if not strictly nominees of the first enterprise, will follow its policies in their decisions, so that, in effect, the management of the second enterprise becomes subservient to that of the first enterprise. A *de facto* group can arise in which the two enterprises are managed on a unified basis. This situation can be very stable so long at the other shareholders in the second enterprise are satisfied that it operates to their advantage and that they would not improve their position by attempting to exercize their *de jure* control.

Synthesis

Although in the above paragraphs '*de jure* control' and '*de facto* control' have been presented as alternatives, in the great majority of real cases, both definitions will lead to the same conclusion. There may be a very small minority of enterprises that would be considered as subsidiaries under the *de jure* concept but not under the *de facto* concept. An enterprise that controls a majority of the voting shares in another enterprise may decide not to use these votes, so that the management is appointed on the basis of other shareholders' votes. Apparently it has no *de facto* control over the enterprise. However, one should enquire why the investor enterprise does not seek to exercise its potential control. In many cases, it is because it is satisfied with the subsidiary's results. This is almost certainly a case of control being exercised with a light touch. If the subsidiary's results were to be unsatisfactory, the parent enterprise would not hesitate to assert its control. It is to be expected that the subsidiary's management, aware of the legal situation, would take into account the parent enterprise's interests in its decisions. Hence it is difficult to contest that some degree of *de facto* control must accompany *de jure* control.

The alternative case, *de facto* control without *de jure* control, is probably rather more common. It would arise most frequently where one enterprise owns a substantial minority of shares in another enterprise and the remaining shareholdings are scattered and disorganized.

19.4.2 The economic entity concept

The parent company concept of the group is not the only possible way of defining the group for the purpose of consolidated accounts. An alternative is to define the group as all the enterprises that may be considered to be a single economic entity. For example a group of seemingly unconnected corporations may be managed and operated as a single entity, notwithstanding that the group's assets are owned by several seemingly unconnected legal entities. Such an economic entity often arises in family businesses where there are a number of separate corporations in which the family members own shares. As there is no parent enterprise (in effect the family members replace the parent enterprise), the parent company concept does not apply. However it is not essential for there to be common shareholders for there to be a single economic entity. All that is necessary is that two or more enterprises are managed as a single unit without there being a parent enterprise.

There is much in common between the economic entity concept of the group and the group defined by *de facto* control under the parent company concept. The basic difference is that, with the parent company concept, there must be a single identifiable parent enterprise which controls the subsidiaries, although, with *de facto* control, it is not necessary that it owns any shares in the subsidiaries.

19.4.3 The definition of the group in law and practice

The parent company concept versus the economic entity concept

With very few exceptions, the definition of the group throughout the world is based on the parent company concept. A major reason is that, with this approach, it is very clear who is responsible for preparing the consolidated accounts – the parent enterprise. With the economic entity concept, it may be desirable that consolidated accounts be prepared but it is probable that they are not prepared since no single enterprise is responsible. A rather similar reason is that, with the parent company concept, there is a clearly defined party (the shareholders of the parent enterprise) to whom the consolidated accounts are addressed and which has an interest in ensuring that they are prepared.

The IASB's rules are based exclusively on the parent company concept of the group, since the group is defined as 'a parent and all its subsidiaries' (IAS 27, 6). Similarly the EU's rules are based, almost exclusively, on the parent company concept. However, the EU's Seventh Directive does provide for the economic entity concept as a Member State option. The authors have been able to trace only two groups that are defined in this way: the Unilever Group and the Royal Dutch/Shell Group, both of which consist of a partnership between a British PLC and a Dutch NV. The structure of the Unilever Group is shown in Exhibit 19.5. It consists of two separate groups defined under the parent company concept, one group with the British company, Unilever PLC, as the parent enterprise; the other group with the Dutch corporation, Unilever NV, as the parent enterprise. These two groups are then treated as a single economic entity; the consolidated accounts of the Unilever Group cover both groups.

Exhibit 19.5 *An example of the economic entity concept of the group: the Unilever Group*

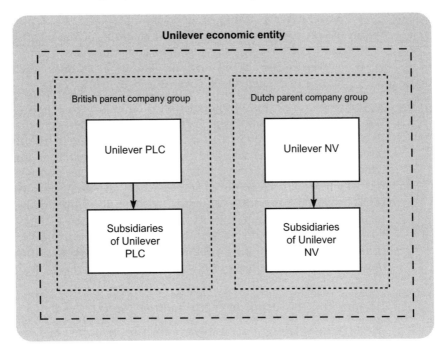

No other major group uses the economic entity concept; throughout the world, the parent company concept dominates.

De jure *control versus* de facto *control: the IASB's rules*

Within the parent company concept, throughout the world more weight is given to *de jure* control than to *de facto* control. In IAS 27,6 the IASB defines a subsidiary as 'an enterprise that is controlled by another enterprise (known as the parent)' and defines 'control' as 'the power to govern the financial and operating policies of an enterprise so as to obtain economic benefits from its activities'. The word 'power' would seem to infer that both *de jure* and *de facto* control are covered. The above definition does not limit 'power' to legal power. The concept of 'power' is expanded in an explanatory paragraph of IAS 27:

> Control is presumed to exist when the parent owns, directly or indirectly through subsidiaries, more than one half of the voting power of an enterprise. . . . Control also exists even when the parent owns one half or less of the voting power of an enterprise when there is:

    (i) power over one half of the voting rights by virtue of an agreement with other investors;

    (ii) power to govern the financial and operating policies of the enterprise under a statute or agreement;

    (iii) power to appoint or remove the majority of the members of the board of directors or equivalent governing body;

    (iv) power to cast the majority of votes at meetings of the board of directors or equivalent governing body. (IAS 27, 12)

The emphasis in the above quotation is on *de jure* control. The principal rule is ownership of more than half the shares. It is accepted that control is possible with less than half the shares. However, of the four cases given, the first two refer to *de jure* control, as there has to be an 'agreement', which presumably must be legally enforceable. That leaves cases (iii) and (iv) which are less clear. For example, where an enterprise owns 40 per cent of the shares of another enterprise and uses the voting rights attached to these shares to ensure that its nominees are elected to the governing board, does this mean that it has 'power' to appoint the board. The authors consider that, in such circumstances, it does have this power and that therefore the other enterprise is a subsidiary under the IASB's rules.

De jure *control versus* de facto *control: the EU*

The EU's rules are set out in its Seventh Directive; they are very similar to those of the IASB. The principal difference is that they are expressed with greater precision, reflecting the fact that the EU's directives are laws. The emphasis is on *de jure* control. Thus a subsidiary is defined as one in respect of which another enterprise (the parent) holds a majority of the voting rights, has the right to appoint a majority of the management board or the right to control through a contract with the enterprise or through an agreement with the shareholders.

However the Seventh Directive does refer to *de facto* control. It is specifically stated that, where a majority of the members of an enterprise's management board are appointed solely as a result of the exercise of a second enterprise's voting rights, then the first enterprise is a subsidiary of the second. This is an example of *de facto* control and not *de jure* control since control depends upon the outcome of the voting process. However the EU's Seventh Directive includes two other cases where an enterprise in which another enterprise holds less than 50 per cent of the shares is held to be a subsidiary on the basis of *de facto* control.

■ Where the parent enterprise exercises a dominant influence over the subsidiary

■ Where the parent enterprise and the subsidiary are managed on a unified basis

These criteria are derived from German law. They are vague, subjective and difficult to verify, when compared with the criteria for *de jure* control. It is much easier to calculate the proportion of voting shares held by the parent enterprise than it is to establish 'dominant influence' or 'unified management'.

All three cases of *de facto* control in the EU's Seventh Directive are Member State options. Exhibit 19.6 indicates which Member States have implemented which options. All Member States, except for Italy and Luxembourg, have implemented at least one option. By contrast the Seventh Directive's rules on *de jure* control are mandatory. The Member States must implement them.

The Seventh Directive's rules on *de facto* control have most influence in France. French law provides that ownership of 40 per cent or more of the votes in another enterprise is presumed to confer control. It is presumed that the other enterprise's management is elected on the basis of these votes (one of the *de facto* control provisions of the EU's Seventh Directive), but this may be rebutted (for example, where the remaining shares are owned by one shareholder). The practical effect of this rule is that many French enterprises substitute 40 per cent for 50 per cent in their definition of subsidiary.

Exhibit 19.6   *Implementation of the* de facto *control provisions of the Seventh Directive*

	Actual votes cast	Dominant influence	Unified management
Belgium	Yes	Yes	Yes
Denmark	No	Yes	No
France	Yes	No	No
Germany	No	No	Yes
Greece	No	Yes	No
Ireland	No	Yes	Yes
Italy	No	No	No
Luxembourg	No	No	No
Netherlands	No	Yes	Yes
Portugal	Yes	No	No
Spain	Yes	No	No
United Kingdom	No	Yes	Yes

De jure *control versus* de facto *control in the USA*

In the past, subsidiaries were always defined in the USA on the basis of *de jure* control, generally on the power to control more than half the voting rights in a corporation. However in 1984 the SEC changed its rules substituting the concept of effective control for the previous concept of legal control. It did this because it was concerned over the growing practice of enterprises setting up corporations in which they held less than 50 per cent of the voting rights but which they effectively controlled through other means. In 1995, the FASB issued an exposure draft that indicated how it proposed to implement the concept of effective control in practice, but has not to date issued a standard.

De facto *versus* de jure *control in Japan*

In Japan, the rules are completely revised in 1998. Under the Ministry of Finance's regulations, a subsidiary is defined as a company that is effectively controlled by a parent company. Unless there is counter-evidence, the parent is presumed to control the subsidiary in the following cases:

(a) The parent owns more than half the voting rights in the subsidiary; or

(b) Ownership of between 40 per cent and 50 per cent of the voting rights, and

 (i) The voting rights owned by the parent company plus those owned by other persons who have agreed to vote in the same sense as the parent or who are presumed to do so because of their close relationship with the parent, amount to more than 50 per cent; or

 (ii) The majority of the members of the management board of the subsidiary are or were directors or employees of the parent; or

 (iii) The parent controls the subsidiary by means of a contract; or

 (iv) The parent provides more than 50 per cent of the fund liabilities of the subsidiary; or

 (v) There exist other facts on the basis of which the company is supposed to control the decision-making organ of the subsidiary.

The most remarkable feature of these rules is long list of situations that are presumed to lead to control under paragraph (b). These include examining the relationship to the parent of the subsidiary's other shareholders and directors, and also considering the amount of the subsidiary's 'fund liabilities' that are provided by the parent. With the revised rules, Japan has moved significantly towards more subsidiaries being recognized as being under *de facto* control.

The effect of the new rules is remarked upon in the extract from Nissan's 1999/2000 annual report that is presented in Exhibit 19.7.

Exhibit 19.7 *Nissan: annual report for the year ended 31 March 2000*

Scope of consolidation

The scope of consolidation has been expanded and the criteria for determining consolidated 'subsidiaries' and 'affiliates' has changed. These changes have led to the inclusion of 45 new consolidated subsidiaries. The rule for consolidating subsidiaries has changed from the 'majority ownership criterion' that included only companies in which the parent had a simple majority of more than 50 per cent, to the 'control criterion'. This rule applies when a parent holds 40 per cent to 50 per cent interest in a subsidiary and has practical or effective control through actions such as a majority vote on the board of directors. . . .

For 'affiliates' the rule has changed from the simple 'ownership criterion' for companies in which the parent holds 20 per cent to 50 per cent, to the 'influence criterion'. This rule applies when a parent holds 15 per cent to 20 per cent or more and has significant influence over the financial and business policy of the affiliate.

The 'affiliates' referred to in the above extract are what in this chapter are called 'associates', which are dealt with in section 19.7.2.

De facto *control in practice*

As emphasized earlier, an enterprise that is considered to be a subsidiary under the *de jure* concept of control would in most cases be found also to be subject to *de facto* control. The interesting question is whether there are a significant number of subsidiaries throughout the world that are so defined under one of the *de facto* criteria, but which are not subject to *de jure* control. Such subsidiaries do exist but one has to look very hard to find them. The vast majority of subsidiaries (over 99 per cent) are so defined on the basis of *de jure* control. The principal reason for the predominance of the *de jure* concept of control is that the rules are more precise, involve less judgement and their implementation is more easily verified.

The predominance of the *de jure* concept is demonstrated by the fact that all of the subsidiaries of the nine European automobile manufacturers that are referred to in Exhibit 19.2 (a total of more than 1500) are defined according to this concept; there is not a single subsidiary in which the parent owns directly or indirectly less than 50 per cent of the shares. The authors had to examine the consolidated accounts of over

100 MNEs before they found a case of a subsidiary in which the parent's shareholding was less than 50 per cent. The consolidated accounts of Inchcape, the British MNE, include the Singaporean company, IRB Finance Berhad, as a subsidiary, even though Inchcape owns only 44 per cent of the shares. The reason is given in a footnote: 'IRB Finance Berhad is consolidated through the Group's control of the Board.' However it is not even certain that this is an example of *de facto* control, since Inchcape's control of the Board could have been achieved through a contract with other shareholders, which is one of the possible means of achieving *de jure* control. It is significant that the authors were unable to find a single example of a Japanese MNE which consolidated a subsidiary in which it owned less than 50 per cent of the shares. This would imply that the change in the rules outlined in '*de facto* versus *de jure* control in Japan' is not at present having a noticeable impact.

19.4.4 Excluded subsidiaries

It frequently happens that a parent enterprise would prefer not to include a particular subsidiary in the consolidated accounts. Where the subsidiary in question has a high level of debt, the consolidated accounts would present a far rosier picture of the group's debt/equity ratio, if the subsidiary's assets and liabilities were not integrated in full but rather reported on the basis of the parent enterprise's investment. In the 1980s, many large British enterprises set up subsidiaries which they effectively controlled but whose share capital was so arranged that it would not be considered a subsidiary under British law, which at that time defined a subsidiary solely on the basis of more than 50 per cent of the equity. Such enterprises were known as 'quasi-subsidiaries'; they were subsidiaries in substance but not in legal form. Various legal devices were used to accomplish this, including options to buy the quasi-subsidiary's shares at very favourable terms, placing voting shares in the hands of trustees and arranging contracts so that all the benefits arising from the quasi-subsidiary's operations and assets accrued to the parent enterprise. Many groups raised the greater part of their finance through debt issued by quasi-subsidiaries. This process was known as 'off balance sheet financing'. The debt was not reported in the consolidated balance sheet because the quasi-subsidiary did not meet the legal definition of a subsidiary.

The UK's standard setter was determined to outlaw the use of quasi-subsidiaries and to reassert the basic principle of substance over form. Initially it was hampered by the British government which insisted that the law must be obeyed and which in 1981 issued a statement that 'any emphasis on substance over form must not be at the expense of compliance with the law', which neatly encapsulates the fundamental dilemma at the heart of the substance over form doctrine. However in 1990 the British standard-setting system was reformed with the formation of the Accounting Standards Board which had the power to issue standards that were recognized as having some legal authority. In 1994 the ASB issued Financial Reporting Standard 5 *Reporting the substance of transactions* which solved the problem by requiring that quasi-subsidiaries should be included in the consolidated accounts as if they were (legal) subsidiaries. A quasi-subsidiary was defined as 'a company, trust, partnership or other vehicle that, though not fulfilling the definition of a subsidiary, is directly or indirectly controlled by the reporting entity and gives rise to economic benefits that are in substance no different from those that would arise were the vehicle a subsidiary.' In this way, the primacy of substance over form was reasserted.

The present rules of the IASB allow for exclusion of subsidiaries on two grounds (IAS 27, 13):

(i) When control is intended to be temporary because the subsidiary is acquired and held exclusively with a view to its subsequent disposal in the near future; or

(ii) When it operates under severe long-term restrictions which significantly impair its ability to transfer funds to the parent.

Both the above grounds are uncontroversial and do not give rise to the problems sketched above in relation to off balance sheet financing. With respect to the first grounds for exclusion, it should be noted that the subsidiary must have been *acquired* with a view to its imminent disposal. Hence a parent cannot exclude an unwanted subsidiary from the consolidated accounts simply by putting it up for sale. The second ground for exclusion refers to subsidiaries in foreign countries, where the law or government actions limit the ability of the parent to draw benefits from the ownership of the subsidiary.

The EU's Seventh Directive includes similar grounds for exclusion but adds a third mandatory ground: where the activities of the subsidiary are so different from those of the rest of the group that, if the subsidiary were to be included, the consolidated accounts would not give a true and fair view. There is no such rule in IAS 27 and this has been identified as the single most important conflict between the IASB's rules and the EU's rules, which makes it difficult for European enterprises to apply the IASB's rules. The European Commission regards the difference as unimportant, remarking that, since the Seventh Directive was issued in 1983, practice has changed and it is now uncommon for groups to exclude subsidiaries on the grounds of dissimilar activities.

Both the IASB and the EU have a general rule that a subsidiary need not be included in the consolidated accounts if it is not material. In principle the test of immateriality should be applied to the total of the excluded subsidiaries. In Japan in the past the materiality threshold was set much higher, as high as 10 per cent of the group assets for the individual subsidiary, resulting in the exclusion of many relatively large subsidiaries, and greatly reducing the usefulness of the consolidated accounts. However the present position is that Japan applies the same materiality criteria as other major countries.

19.5 THE PREPARATION OF CONSOLIDATED ACCOUNTS

19.5.1 The basic principles

Consolidated accounts are prepared by aggregating (or consolidating) the individual accounts of the entities that make up the group. It is assumed that the reader already has a knowledge of the basic procedures and therefore they will be dealt with very briefly. Before the figures in the individual accounts are aggregated, they have to be adjusted for a number of factors. The basic reason for all these adjustments is to ensure that the resulting consolidated accounts present the financial position and performance of the group as if it were a single enterprise. This principle underlies the IASB's rules; IAS 27,16 defines consolidated financial statements as 'the financial statements of a group presented as those of a single enterprise'. The principal adjustments that should be made to the individual accounts are:

■ To eliminate intra-group balances and sales, because a single enterprise cannot owe money or make sales to itself (IAS 27,17)

■ To eliminate intra-group profit included in the value of assets, because a single enterprise cannot earn a profit by selling goods to itself (IAS 27,17)

■ To ensure that all group entities use the same methods for the recognition and measurement of elements in the accounts, because, in accordance with the principle of consistency, an enterprise should account for like transactions in a consistent manner (IAS 27,21)[3]

These adjustments are made only for the purpose of preparing the consolidated accounts; they are not recorded in the individual accounts.

The above three adjustments are made in all cases. However the nature of any further adjustments depends on how the subsidiary whose accounts are being consolidated was acquired by the parent enterprise. There are three possibilities:

(a) The subsidiary was formed by the parent enterprise itself.

(b) The subsidiary was acquired by the parent enterprise some time after its foundation, when it was already a going concern. In that case the acquisition of the subsidiary's shares by the parent enterprise may have been the result of two rather different transactions:

(i) the take-over of the subsidiary by the parent enterprise;
(ii) the merger of the subsidiary and the parent enterprise.

Most subsidiaries fall into category (a) above, particularly smaller subsidiaries formed by the parent for special functions; they rarely cause problems. Generally the parent enterprise owns all the shares so that there is no minority interest to complicate matters. Since the parent enterprise acquired the shares on the formation of the subsidiary, the book value of the subsidiary's shares in the parent's balance sheet will generally be equal to the share capital in the subsidiary's balance sheet, so there is no consolidation difference.

Most problems arise with take-overs and mergers, which now need to be considered.

19.5.2 Take-overs

The basic principle: historical cost to the parent

In a take-over one enterprise acquires the shares of another which becomes its subsidiary. The assets and liabilities of the subsidiary should be incorporated in the consolidated accounts using the acquisition method (known as the purchase method in the USA). With this method, the subsidiary's assets are valued in the consolidated accounts at their historical cost *to the parent*. In the subsidiary's individual accounts they are generally valued at historical cost *to the subsidiary*. This means that for the consolidated accounts the value of the subsidiary's assets has to be restated. The problem is that one knows the historical cost to the parent of the totality of the subsidiary's assets and liabilities. This is the total amount paid to acquire the subsidiary's shares. This total cost has to be divided among the subsidiary's separate assets. In respect of the subsidiary's individual assets, the best measure of the historical cost to the parent is the market value at the date of acquisition. This is essentially the opportunity cost to the parent; if the parent had not gained the assets through the acquisition of the whole subsidiary, it would have had to buy them on the market.

The IASB's rules for the reporting of take-overs are set out in IAS 22 Business Combinations. IAS 22,32 states that the separate assets of the subsidiary should be valued in the consolidated accounts at their fair value (that is their market value) at the date of acquisition. This principle applies even for an asset that is not reported at all in the subsidiary's individual accounts, for example a brand.

Goodwill

However the total amount paid by the parent to acquire the subsidiary is likely to be more than the sum of the fair values of the subsidiary's separate assets; assets in combination are often worth more than when valued separately and, under GAAP, certain 'assets' are not reported in the balance sheet, for example the enterprise's skilled labour force, its organizational structure and its reputation with its customers. The surplus of the cost of the subsidiary as a whole over the sum of the fair values of the individual assets is termed 'goodwill'. Since the parent has expended resources to acquire this 'goodwill' it should be recognized as an asset in the consolidated balance sheet.[4]

Under the rules of IAS 22,44, goodwill should be amortized by periodic charges to income over a useful life that should not exceed 20 years, unless there is strong evidence of a longer life. Prior to 1993, IAS 22 permitted, as an alternative, that goodwill be written off directly against reserves at the time of acquisition. This treatment of goodwill was very popular with British groups, because it eliminated the amortization of goodwill and thus led to the reporting of higher future consolidated profits. However a major criticism of this treatment is that the accounts do not report 'comprehensive income'. This was one of the reasons why this option was removed when IAS 22 was revised in 1993. In 1997, the UK's ASB modified its standard in line with the revised IAS 22 and, for acquisitions made after 1997, British groups are no longer be able to write off goodwill against reserves.

Negative goodwill

It can happen in a take-over that the amount paid by the parent to acquire the subsidiary is less than the sum of the fair values of the subsidiary's separate assets. This deficiency is known as 'negative goodwill'. Two reasons are often given for the existence of negative goodwill:

- The parent made a 'lucky buy' – in fact the fair value of the subsidiary is higher than its acquisition cost
- The parent expects the subsidiary to make losses in the future

The rules of IAS 22, 59–63 relating to negative goodwill are that it should be reported as a deduction from assets in the balance sheet; it should be written off to the income statement (that is credited to profit) as the assets concerned are sold or consumed (in the case of a lucky buy) or as losses are incurred (in the cases of future losses).

Negative goodwill presents a problem for accounting theorists because in principle it should not exist. It is contrary to the principles of historical cost accounting to report an asset at higher than its acquisition cost even when there is evidence that its market value is higher. When the sum of the fair values of the separate assets of the subsidiary is higher than the parent's acquisition cost, then these assets are, in total, being stated at above historical cost. Furthermore, as IAS 37 forbids the setting up of a provision to cover future losses, one cannot justify recognizing negative goodwill with reference to future losses. To a certain extent, the accounting theorists' objections are met by reporting negative goodwill as a deduction from assets. But this still means that the balance sheet includes an item which most users (including the authors) find incomprehensible.

19.5.3 Mergers

In principle the difference between a merger and a take-over is that, in a merger, the two parties involved are approximately equal so that it cannot be said that one has taken over the other. The problem is that most mergers are achieved through one of the parties acquiring the shares of the other in exchange for an issue of its own shares. In this way both parties retain their original corporate form, which generally is desirable for tax reasons. However it means that formally one of the parties ends up by being the subsidiary of the other.

In a merger, the aggregation of the subsidiary's assets with those of the parent is accomplished using the merger method (known in the USA as 'pooling of interests'). With this method all of the balances in the subsidiary's individual accounts are taken unchanged into the consolidated accounts, after having made the three adjustments referred to in section 19.5.1. The parent and the subsidiary are treated as equals and it is not appropriate to substitute the historical cost to the parent for the historical cost to the subsidiary, as happens with the acquisition method. The subsidiary's reserves are incorporated in full in the consolidated balance sheet. In particular, the subsidiary's retained earnings are reported as such in the consolidated balance sheet. This treatment should be contrasted with what happens with the acquisition method, where the subsidiary's reserves that relate to the period before the acquisition are eliminated in the consolidation process and do not appear in the consolidated balance sheet. With the merger method, the only part of the subsidiary's capital and reserves that does not appear in the consolidated balance sheet is its share capital which is offset against the parent's investment in the subsidiary, so that the only share capital reported in the consolidated balance sheet is that held by persons outside the group (the share capital of the parent and not of the subsidiary). Any consolidation difference that arises from this offsetting is reported as part of the consolidated reserves. The inclusion of this curious item means that the figure for the total of reserves reported in the consolidated balance sheet is rather meaningless. The reserves do not perform the traditional function of indicating what is and is not available for distribution as dividend, since the dividend decision is taken at the level of the individual accounts. In fact the principal function of the reserves in the consolidated balance sheet is to ensure that the balance sheet balances!

The theory that underlines the consolidated balance sheet with the merger method is very straightforward. In a take-over one of the parties dominates the other; in the consolidated accounts, it substitutes its values for those of the other party. By contrast, a merger is a marriage of equals; neither party dominates so each retains its own values in the consolidated accounts. The parent and the subsidiary are treated as equals. As far as possible the values reported in the individual accounts of both the parent and subsidiary are retained. The only adjustments that are made are those referred to in section 19.5.1.

IAS 22, 77 requires that the merger method, as described above, should be applied to all 'uniting of interests' which it defines as 'a business combination in which the shareholders of the combining enterprises combine control over the whole, or effectively the whole, of their net assets and operations to achieve a continued mutual sharing in the risks and benefits attaching to the combined entity such that neither party can be identified as the acquirer' (IAS 22, 8). It sets out in an explanatory paragraph (IAS 22, 15) a number of conditions that would normally be necessary to achieve the mutual sharing of risks and benefits, including:

■ The substantial majority of the voting shares of the combining enterprises are combined or pooled

■ The fair value of one enterprise is not significantly different from that of the other

■ The shareholders of each enterprise maintain substantially the same voting rights and interest in the combined entity, relative to each other, after the combination as before

Hence either of the following two factors would rule out the application of the merger method

■ one enterprise being substantially larger than the other

■ one enterprise acquiring the other in any other way than through an exchange of shares (for example for cash) since in that case the former shareholders of the acquired enterprise no longer participate in the risks and benefits of the combined enterprise in the same way as those of the parent

The provisions of IAS 22 as to acquisitions and uniting of interests were the subject of a formal interpretation (SIC 9) issued by the IASB's Standing Interpretations Committee, which states that 'a business combination should be accounted for as an acquisition unless an acquirer cannot be identified; in virtually all business combinations an acquirer can be identified' (SIC 9,4). It elaborates further on the three conditions for a uniting of interest that were mentioned in the previous paragraph:

'an enterprise should classify a business combination as an acquisition, unless all of these three characteristics are present; even if all of the three characteristics are present, an enterprise should classify a business combination as a uniting of interests only if the enterprise can demonstrate that an acquirer cannot be identified' (SIC 9, 6).

These provisions of SIC 9 call for the following comments:

(a) They clearly are intended to make it more difficult for enterprises to use the merger method; SIC 9 adds further hurdles that are not contained in IAS 22, notably the reversal of the burden of proof – the enterprise has to demonstrate that an acquirer cannot be identified.

(b) In IAS 22 the three conditions are contained in an explanatory paragraph which only has the authority of 'background material and implementation guidance'. As already explained in Chapter 13, only the paragraphs of IAS 22 that are set in bold italic type have the authority of a standard. However IAS 1, 11 (which is set in bold italic type) requires enterprises to comply with all applicable International Accounting Standards and Interpretations of the SIC. In effect the SIC's action in including the three conditions in its interpretation elevates them from the lowly status of 'background material and implementation guidance' to a mandatory rule.

IAS 22 requires that the merger method should be applied to the consolidated accounts from the start of the first period covered by the accounts. This means that, except in those cases where the merger occurred at the start of the period, the first consolidated income statement includes the revenues, expenses and profits of both enterprises for that part of the financial year that precedes the merger. This should be contrasted with the position for the acquisition method where the consolidated income statement includes the revenues, expenses and profits of the acquired enterprise, only for the period after the acquisition.

With the merger method, the first consolidated income statement reports figures that are manifestly untrue, when (as normally is the case) the merger did not take place at the beginning of the financial year. The truth would be presented in separate income statements for the two parties for the period before the merger and a merged statement for the period after the merger. The IASB's justifications for reporting figures, which the authors consider to be fiction, would appear to be:

- that it is general practice
- that it would be a waste of resources to prepare the separate statements relating to the period before the merger which is past history
- that the statement of merged income and expenses for a whole period provides useful information to users (for example, in forecasting future results)

19.5.4 The attractions of the merger method

Although in principle the acquisition method and the merger method are not alternatives but are ways of reporting different transactions (the acquisition method for take-overs and the merger method for mergers), in practice the distinction between a take-over and a merger is not always so clear-cut as to remove any doubt on the matter, so that often the management of the group can claim that it may choose between the two methods. In these circumstances it is often alleged that the management prefers the merger method. The reason for this preference is explained in the detailed example that is presented in Exhibit 19.8.

With the acquisition method the assets of the acquired subsidiary (Beta) are reported in the consolidated balance sheet at their market value – taken to be the market value of the shares of Alpha that were issued to effect the acquisition. This is achieved by restating identifiable assets at fair value and inserting a figure for goodwill for any difference. The group profits in the year of the acquisition are taken to be those of the acquirer (Alpha) for the whole year and of the acquiree (Beta) only for the period after the acquisition. Since the acquisition took place on the last day of the year, none of Beta's profits are reported in the consolidated income statement for the year 2000. In future years, the full profits of both Alpha and Beta are included in the consolidated income statement but, in addition, there is a deduction for amortization of goodwill and for the extra depreciation reflecting the higher value of Beta's assets in the consolidated accounts.

With the merger method, the assets in the consolidated balance sheet are reported at their historical cost to the two parties and there is no goodwill. The retained earnings of both parties and the profits for the whole of the year in which the merger took place are reported in the consolidated accounts. There is a 'merger reserve' of €600 (negative) which arises because the book value of the extra share capital of Alpha (€1600) is greater than Beta's share capital (€1000) which is eliminated. The consolidated profits for the year 2000 include the full profits of both Alpha and Beta even though the merger only took place on the last day of the year. This is also the case for future years. There is no deduction for amortization of goodwill or extra depreciation on the difference between book value and fair value of Beta's assets.

The differences between the two methods are summarized in Exhibit 19.9, which brings out very clearly three significant advantages of the merger method:

(a) It enables the management to buy 'instant' profits in the year in which the merger takes place as the acquired enterprise's profits for the whole of that year are reported as group profits; Alpha's profits are boosted from €100 (without the acquisition) to €500 (with the acquisition).

Exhibit 19.8 *Alpha and Beta: the acquisition method compared with the merger method*

On 31 December 2000, Alpha acquired all the shares of Beta in exchange for an issue of 1600 of its own shares. At that date the market value of one share was: Alpha €2.50, Beta €4. Therefore the value of the shares issued (and of the assets acquired in return) was €4000. The balance sheets of Alpha and Beta on 31 December 2000, just before this transaction were:

	Alpha €	Beta €
Net assets at historical cost	4000	2500
Share capital	2000	1000
Retained earnings	1900	1100
Profit for 2000	100	400
Total equity	4000	2500

The consolidated accounts of the Alphabet Group using the two methods are:

	Acquisition method	Merger method
Consolidated balance sheets at 31 December 2000		
Net assets	6500	6500
Excess of the fair value of Beta's assets		
over historical cost	1000	
Goodwill	500	
Total assets	8000	6500
Share capital	3600	3600
Share premium	2400	
Merger reserve		−600
Retained earnings	1900	3000
Profit for 2000	100	500
	8000	6500
Consolidated income statements for 2000		
Combined profits of Alpha and Beta		500
Profits of Alpha	100	
Consolidated income statements for 2001		
Combined profits of Alpha and Beta (assumed)	500	500
Less amortization of excess value and goodwill	300	
Net profit	200	500
The rate of return in 2001 is calculated as		
Net profit	200	500
Assets	8000	6500
Rate of return (%)	2.50	7.69

Exhibit 19.9 *Key figures in the consolidated accounts of the Alphabet Group*

Consolidated accounts	Acquisition method €	Merger method €
Net assets at 31 December 2000	8000	6500
Profit for year 2000	100	500
Profit for year 2001	200	500
Rate of return in year 2001 (%)	2.50	7.69

(b) Future years' profits are reported at a higher figure, as there is no charge for amortization of goodwill or for the extra depreciation on assets restated at fair value, which under the acquisition method constitutes a burden on future earnings; accountants refer to the 'earnings penalty' that arises with the use of the acquisition method.

(c) The reported return on assets is higher.

It must be emphasized that these are all 'cosmetic' effects because there are no differences in the reality behind the reported figures.

19.5.5 The acquisition method and the merger method in practice

In all countries, the acquisition method is the most widely used method for the preparation of consolidated accounts. With respect to the merger method, the world's countries may be divided into three groups:

(a) Those where the merger method is forbidden and all consolidated accounts are prepared using the acquisition method. The principal country in this group is Australia.

(b) Those where the acquisition method is regarded as the normal method and the merger method is permitted only in certain narrowly defined exceptional cases. Most countries fall into this category, including all the European countries. This is also the IASB's position.

(c) Those where the merger method is permitted subject to conditions, which however permit a substantial proportion of business combinations to be accounted for using the merger method. The USA is the principal country in this category. In this country there is no requirement that the two enterprises be of roughly the same size and the merger method is frequently used for business combinations where one enterprise is very much larger than the other (occasionally as much as ten times the size).

Many of the recent mergers between the larger MNEs have been accounted for using the merger method. Examples are DaimlerChrysler, Exxon Mobil, Aventis and BP Amoco. Exhibit 19.10 presents an extract from the BP Amoco 1998 annual report that refers to the merger. It should be noted that the relative sizes of the two enterprises, as measured by the proportion of the shares in BP Amoco held by shareholders of the merging companies, are BP 59.98 per cent and Amoco 40.02 per cent. This give rise to the suspicion that the terms of the merger were so arranged that it would qualify to be reported using the merger method. BP Amoco is a British PLC and therefore subject to the ASB's rules. FRS 6 states that the merger method may not be used where one party dominates the other and that this is presumed where one party is more than 50 per cent larger than the other. If the proportions had been BP 60.01 per cent and Amoco 39.99 per cent then BP would have been 50.06 per cent larger than Amoco and the conditions of FRS 6 for the merger method would not have been fulfilled. However, there is no evidence that the terms of the BP Amoco share exchange were deliberately fixed so as to permit the use of the merger method. The IASB's standard does not include a precise percentage; it simply states that, for the merger method, the fair value of one enterprise should not be significantly different from that of the other. Probably the IASB considered that, if it were to specify a percentage, companies would arrange their mergers so as to qualify for the merger method.

Exhibit 19.10 *BP Amoco annual report 1998*

Merger accounting

The financial statements have been prepared using the merger method of accounting in relation to the merger of BP and Amoco. Under merger accounting, the results and cash flows of BP and Amoco are combined from the beginning of the period in which the merger occurred and their assets and liabilities combined at the amounts at which they are previously recorded after adjusting to achieve consistency of accounting policies.

On 31 December 1998 the company issued 3 797 071 800 ordinary shares with a nominal value of $1 898 535 900 and a fair value of $56 943 166 956 to Amoco shareholders under the terms of the merger agreement between BP and Amoco. Following the merger, former BP shareholders held 5 885 938 223 shares. Assuming conversion of all outstanding BP share options and Amoco stock options on that date and excluding shares held by the respective companies, the ownership interests of former BP and former Amoco shareholders in the combined company were 59.98 percent and 40.02 per cent respectively.

The merger was effected on 31 December 1998 and, in accordance with the general principles of merger accounting, the full profits of both BP and Amoco were included in BP Amoco's income statement for the whole of the year 1998. The group's auditors reported that 'in our opinion the accounts give a true and fair view of the profit of the group for the year [ended 31 December 1998]'. Most non-accountants would find this statement quite extraordinary, given that, for 364 of the 365 days of the year 1998, the group did not exist!

19.5.6 A third possibility: the 'fresh-start' method

In the foregoing sections two alternative methods of preparing the consolidated accounts have been described: the acquisition method and the merger method. However there is a third possibility, the 'fresh-start' method. This is only a theoretical possibility. It is not mentioned in any law or standard and is not used for the preparation of consolidated accounts in any major country. However it is a useful exercise to consider the elements of this third method as it brings out very clearly the characteristics of the two methods that are used.

Under the fresh-start method, it is assumed that a new entity is created that takes over the assets and liabilities of the other two entities. In many take-overs and mergers, this is in fact the formal position. However the validity of the 'fresh-start' method depends on the substance of the transaction that created the new entity not on its legal form.

The basic assumption with the 'fresh-start' method is that a new entity is created. This entity values the assets and liabilities that it acquires from the other entities at their fair value at the time of acquisition. The historical cost of these assets in the accounts of the other entities is irrelevant, since these are separate entities; the acquisition cost to the new entity of these assets is measured by their fair value (market value). The assumption that a new entity has been created also determines the treatment of retained earnings in the consolidated balance sheet (the new entity has no history and therefore no retained earnings) and whether the profits of the other entities for the period prior to the creation of the new entity are reported in the consolidated income statement (the new entity only starts to earn profit from the date of its creation).

The three methods may be compared with a simple example. Assume that enterprise Gamma acquires all the shares of enterprise Delta. The treatment of the assets, retained earnings and profits of Gamma and Delta in the consolidated accounts depends on whether the transaction is treated as a take-over of Delta by Gamma (acquisition method), a merger of Gamma and Delta (merger method), or the creation of a new entity (fresh-start method). The valuation bases are presented in Exhibit 19.11.

Exhibit 19.11   *Comparison of the three methods: Accounting treatment in the consolidated accounts*

	Merger method	Acquisition method	Fresh-start method
Gamma's assets	Historical cost to Gamma	Historical cost to Gamma	Fair value
Delta's assets	Historical cost to Delta	Fair value	Fair value
Gamma's retained earnings	Included	Included	Eliminated
Delta's retained earnings	Included	Eliminated	Eliminated
Gamma's prior profits	Included	Included	Eliminated
Delta's prior profits	Included	Eliminated	Eliminated

Exhibit 19.11 makes clear that the merger method and the fresh-start method are the two extremes, with the acquisition method in the middle, borrowing features from both methods: with the acquisition method, the acquirer is treated in the same way as with the merger method and the acquiree as with the fresh-start method. An important point is that differences between the three methods in the amounts for asset values arise only with historical cost accounting. If assets were always reported at fair values, there would be no differences.

19.5.7   Proposals for change

Many of the world's standard setters are unhappy with the present situation where in practice for many business combinations there is a choice between the acquisition method and the merger method. There are two problems:

(a) The two methods often lead to very different numbers being reported when there is no difference in reality; this is most striking in relation to future earnings, when the two methods report quite different figures although there is no difference in future cash flows.

(b) The suspicion that many business combinations are deliberately set up so as to qualify for the merger method and to avoid the 'earnings penalty' inherent in the aquisition method.

The problem is particularly acute in the USA, where the SEC and the FASB have attempted to restrict the use of the merger method (known there as 'pooling of interests') by setting ever more detailed conditions for its use. Enterprises have responded by taking great care to meet these conditions with the consequence that there has been no reduction in the use of the merger method.

In 1998, the 'G4+1 group' issued a discussion paper on the subject in which it proposed that the use of the merger method be prohibited (G4+1, 1999). It gave two principal reasons:

(a) There are very considerable advantages in having a single method for reporting business combinations. If two methods are permitted there will always be borderline cases, with the result that similar transactions will be reported dissimilarly. The group believed that the advantages of imposing a single method for all business combinations outweighed any possible disadvantages of imposing an inappropriate method on some combinations, particularly as it felt that the situations in which the merger method might properly be used were relatively rare.

(b) It felt that the merger method was not conceptually sound, notably in that it did not respect the basic principles of historical cost accounting.

So far the IASB has not acted on this proposal. However in 1999 the FASB announced that, at some unspecified future date, it intended to ban the merger method. In addition to the reasons given in the G4+1 paper, the FASB mentioned the following criticisms of the merger method:

■ It provides less information than the purchase method, notably the current value of the acquired assets and the total cost of the acquisition

■ The fact that certain companies could use the merger method, and others not, leads to an unlevel playing field and to the misallocation of resources

■ The nature of the consideration (shares or cash) should not determine the method used to value assets

■ The merger method imposes costs on companies, when they take specific actions often of an artificial nature to ensure that the acquisition meets the FASB's conditions for the merger method. There is some evidence that acquiree companies are able to extract a higher price from the acquirer as the reward for permitting the acquisition to be structured as a merger.

Basically the FASB's position is that true mergers of equals are so rare that they can be ignored. The FASB's proposal provoked considerable opposition from companies, which objected to the 'earnings penalty' involved with the acquisition method. In view of this opposition, the

FASB recently modified its proposals: the merger method was still to be banned but the earnings penalty was to be softened by removing the need to depreciate goodwill if it could be shown that it had not fallen in value.

The authors' position is that the merger method is theoretically sound when in fact there is a genuine merger and an acquirer cannot be identified. In these circumstances it is appropriate to carry forward the historical cost of the assets of the two component enterprises into the balance sheet of the merged enterprise. The authors reject the contention of the G4+1 paper that the merger method does not respect the basic principles of historical cost accounting. However the authors appreciate that the FASB was faced with a situation where the merger method was being misused and quite possibly the only practicable solution was to ban it altogether.

19.6 THE MINORITY INTEREST: EQUITY OR LIABILITY?

A minority interest is reported in the consolidated balance sheet where the parent does not own the entire share capital of the subsidiary. This can arise with both the acquisition method and the merger method, although with the latter any minority interest should be relatively small because, for the merger method to be applicable, the parent should have acquired 'the substantial majority' of the shares (IAS 22, 15).

There is a fascinating theoretical point connected with the minority interest – does it represent equity of the group or is it a liability? Are the minority shareholders in partially owned subsidiaries to be considered as partners in the group alongside the shareholders of the parent? Alternatively is the equity of the group solely what relates to the parent's shareholders, so that the minority shareholders are the equivalent of creditors? The answer that one gives to these questions depends on what one considers to be the basic function of the consolidated accounts. If the function is to provide information to the shareholders of the parent, then the minority interest should not be considered to represent equity. If the function is to report on the position and performance of the group as a whole, then the capital contributed by the minority shareholders of subsidiaries fulfils the function of equity in exactly the same way as that contributed by the parent's shareholders. The minority shareholders provide funds which enable the group to hold assets and, as shareholders, they cannot sue for the return of their contribution.

Whether the minority interest is considered to represent equity or a liability influences at least two aspects of the consolidated accounts: presentation and calculation of profit.

Presentation

Most groups sit on the fence. They present the minority interest in the consolidated balance sheet between the equity and the liabilities, without any clear indication to which of these two categories it belongs. However the IASB in the model balance sheet annexed to IAS 1 presents the minority interest as an element of equity, which is at least consistent with the Framework's statement that there are only three elements in the balance sheet: assets, liabilities and equity. Unfortunately the IASB does not maintain this consistency in the model income statement attached to IAS 1 which calculates the net profit for the period after deduction of the minority interest's share, which implies that the minority interest is not equity.

Calculation of profit

If the minority shareholders of subsidiaries are outsiders and not partners then it would be logical for the group to record a profit on sales between the parent and a partially owned subsidiary to the extent that it is not owned by the group. Thus where a sale has been made to a partially owned subsidiary, the proportion of the intra-group profit relating to the minority shareholders would not be eliminated, as to this extent the goods have been sold to persons outside the group. In a similar fashion, when goods have been sold by the subsidiary to the parent, that part of the profit relating to the minority has been earned by and should be credited to the minority interest. In fact IAS 27, 17 requires that the whole of intra-group profit should be eliminated, which implies that the minority interest is an element of equity.

19.7 THE PARTIAL MEMBERS OF THE GROUP

The last section of this chapter considers the partial members of the group: joint ventures and associated enterprises. They are distinguished from the full members of the group in that the parent enterprise does not control them completely. This is clear from the definitions given in the IASs:

■ A joint venture is a contractual arrangement whereby two or more parties undertake an economic activity which is subject to joint control (IAS 31, 2)

■ An associate is an enterprise in which the investor has significant influence but which is neither a subsidiary nor a joint venture of the investor (IAS 28, 3)

19.7.1 Joint ventures

A joint venture is an economic activity that is controlled jointly by the parent enterprise and another party outside the group. According to IAS 31, there must be a contractual arrangement that defines the way in which control is shared. The words 'contractual arrangement' are used because the joint venture may take any form, for example a corporation in which the parties' rights are set out in the constitution, or a partnership in which they are set out in the deed, or a simple contract. Frequently the arrangements set out guidelines for the day-to-day operation of the joint venture (which may be delegated to one of the parties) and provide that the consent of all parties is required for all major decisions.

IAS 31 provides that, in the consolidated accounts, the parent's interest in the assets, liabilities, income and expenses of a joint venture may be reported using proportional consolidation. For example, where the parent has a 50 per cent interest in a joint venture, it would include in the consolidated balance sheet 50 per cent of each category of its assets and 50 per cent of each category of its liabilities. This is a fundamentally different procedure from that used for reporting the assets and liabilities of partially owned subsidiaries, where the assets and liabilities are stated at 100 per cent of their value, which makes it necessary to report a minority interest. With a joint venture, the equivalent of the minority interest (the other party's share) is not reported in the consolidated balance sheet.

The use of proportional consolidation is rather controversial. Thus Professor Nobes asks the pertinent question, 'does 50% of a joint venture's cash balance make any sense?' (Nobes, 1987). In fact the use of the proportional method of consolidation is prohibited in Britain (except for unincorporated joint ventures), and is optional in most other European countries. Where proportional consolidation is not used, joint ventures are accounted for using the equity method, which is an allowed alternative treatment in IAS 31.

The authors support the use of proportional consolidation rather than integration in full for joint ventures They accept the principle that assets that are under the exclusive control of the parent (that is assets of subsidiaries) should be integrated in full in the consolidated accounts. However they consider that, if the assets of joint ventures were incorporated at their full value in the consolidated balance sheets of all the partners, this would lead to two undesirable results:

- In the consolidated balance sheets of the individual partners, the assets might be swollen by including in full assets in which the parent's interest was rather low (for example in a joint venture with three other partners, the parent interest would be only one quarter)
- The same assets would be reported in full in more than one consolidated balance sheet

Since it is highly desirable that the same rule should be applied to all joint ventures, these considerations rule out the use of integration in full. However, if the equity method were used for all joint ventures, this would mean that the assets of joint ventures would not be reported in full in any group's consolidated accounts. When integration in full is used for subsidiaries, proportional consolidation for joint ventures and the equity method for associates, then if one were to sum the amounts reported for tangible and intangible assets in the consolidated accounts of all enterprises, they would equal the total of the underlying assets. This not only helps the preparers of the national accounts but provides a logical basis for using different methods for different group members. It ensures that the same asset is reported in one, but only one, set of consolidated accounts.

19.7.2 Associates

An associate is an enterprise in which the investor has significant influence and which is neither a subsidiary nor a joint venture of the investor (IAS 28, 3). Significant influence is defined as the power to participate in the financial and operating decisions of the investee but is not control over those policies.

Under IAS 28, investments in associates should be reported using the equity method. This is often known as 'one-line-consolidation'. In principle, with the equity method, the same figures are reported for the net assets and the profit as would be reported for a subsidiary, with the difference that, for a subsidiary, the assets, liabilities, income and expenses are integrated in full in the consolidated accounts, whereas for an associate only two net figures are reported: the parent's share of the assets less the liabilities in the balance sheet and the parent's share of the income less the expenses in the income statement.

The justification for the equity method is that the alternative method for reporting the income from the associate is quite inadequate. Under IAS 18 revenue from investments in shares should be recognized on the basis of dividends declared, which would mean that, in a year when the associate declares no dividend, the parent would report no income, irrespective of the profits reported in the associate's accounts. Conversely, in a year that an associate declares a large dividend (perhaps paid out of the profits of several past years), the parent reports high income from the associate. Not only does the process of reporting the income from the associate on the basis of dividends received lead to very misleading figures for income in the parent's accounts, but also offers an opportunity for the manipulation of the parent's profits. By definition, the parent has significant influence over the associate's financial policies. Hence in a good year (for the parent), the parent can put pressure on the associate not to pay a dividend leading to the parent reporting lower profits; whilst in a poor year the parent can do the opposite and induce the associate to pay an unusually high dividend. Since the consolidated accounts incorporate the parent's accounts, they would also be subject to manipulation. To counter the above mentioned problems, IAS 28 states that income from associates should be measured using the equity method as the parent's share of the associate's profit and not on the basis of dividends declared.

The equity method is not uncontroversial. It leads to the parent reporting profits in its consolidated accounts which it has not received in cash but are represented by an increase in the value of the parent's investment in the associate. Are these profits truly realized? Certainly the treatment of the increase in the value of the associate is very different from that prescribed in IAS 16 for the increase in the fair value of plant, property and equipment, which is not considered to be income but is transferred direct to equity as revaluation surplus. There are differences between investments in associates and plant, property and equipment. On the one hand the profit in the associate's own accounts should be measured in accordance with the IASB's rules, that is generally on the basis of historical cost.[5] This is the justification for the parent taking credit for its share of these profits. On the other hand, the parent enjoys a higher level of control over its plant property and equipment than it does over its investment in an associate. The authors' position on this controversial matter is that with associates there is the usual conflict between relevance and reliability. The equity method certainly provides more relevant information on the underlying performance of the associate. However it may lead to reporting as current income, increases in asset values from which the parent may draw benefits only in the distant future, if at all. This would occur where the parent's influence over the associate is not sufficiently significant to ensure that it derives benefits from its shareholding. This analysis suggests that an investment should only be accounted for using the equity method when the parent is reasonably sure that its influence is sufficiently significant.

IAS 28 gives quite detailed guidance on what constitutes 'significant influence'. If the investor holds 20 per cent or more of the voting power of the investee, it is presumed that it does have significant influence. Conversely, where it holds less than 20 per cent, it is presumed that it does not. Both are only presumptions which do not apply when there is other evidence to the contrary.

19.7.3 Synthesis

The IASB's rules relating to subsidiaries, joint ventures and associates make a distinction between measurement and presentation. For the measurement of the equity (equals net assets) and the profit in the consolidated accounts, the same rules apply to all three types of group member. In the consolidated accounts the value of the consolidated equity relating to a group member is taken as the parent enterprise's share of the net assets of that group member, irrespective of whether the parent's interest is 100 per cent (for a wholly owned subsidiary), 51 per cent (for a partially owned subsidiary), 50 per cent (for a joint venture) or 21 per cent (for an associate). The same principle applies to the calculation of the consolidated net profit. This means that, in principle, in preparing the consolidated accounts, the amounts reported in the individual accounts of joint ventures and associates should be adjusted for intra-group transactions and the other factors mentioned in section 19.5.1.

However, with respect to the presentation of the detail of the group members' assets, liabilities, income and expenses in the consolidated accounts, there are different rules for each type of group member:

(a) **Subsidiaries:** assets and liabilities, revenues and expenses are incorporated in full on a line-by-line basis; where the parent does not own 100 per cent of the equity, a minority interest is presented.

(b) **Joint ventures:** only the parent's proportional share of the assets and liabilities, revenues and expenses are incorporated on a line-by-line basis; no minority interest is reported.

(c) **Associates:** only single figures for net equity and net income are disclosed.

In effect the rules provide that the level of disclosure reflects the degree of the parent's control over the group member: high for subsidiaries, low for associates and intermediate for joint ventures.

SUMMARY

The structure of the Renault Group was examined as a means of explaining the nature and importance of groups of enterprises. The function of the individual accounts was analysed with reference to dividends, taxes and liquidation. The function of the consolidated accounts was explained as remedying certain deficiencies in the individual accounts when the entity concerned is a parent enterprise and as providing information about the group as a whole. The question of how to define the group for the consolidated accounts was considered. The parent company concept of

SUMMARY (cont'd)

the group was compared with the economic entity concept, and, within the parent company concept, two concepts of control were examined: *de jure* control and *de facto* control. The procedures for preparing the consolidated accounts were covered briefly, with particular reference to the differences between the acquisition method and the merger method. These two methods were compared with the fresh-start method. The position of the minority interest was considered. Finally there was a discussion on the treatment in the consolidated accounts of the partial members of the group: joint ventures and associated enterprises.

Review questions

1. Why are many large businesses organized in the form of groups?

2. What are the functions performed by the accounts of the individual corporation?

3. What are the two principal functions performed by the consolidated accounts?

4. What is the difference between *de jure* control and *de facto* control? Which of the two concepts is more widely used to define a subsidiary?

5. In preparing the consolidated accounts, what three types of adjustments must always be made to the figures in the individual accounts?

6. What are the essential differences between the acquisition method and the merger method in the figures that are reported in the consolidated accounts?

7. What are the IASB's definitions of subsidiary, joint venture and associate?

8. In what ways do the rules for the reporting of subsidiaries, joint ventures and associates in the consolidated accounts differ in respect of

   ■ measurement?
   ■ presentation?

Notes

1. If the group as a whole were solvent, it is very probable that the management of the parent enterprise would voluntarily pay the creditors of B in order to preserve the group's reputation. However, since the group is going out of business, there is no commercial reason to do this. In fact the liquidator of the parent enterprise is obliged to follow the law, which is that the surplus belongs to the shareholders.
2. It should be noted that where the debt of a creditor of a subsidiary has been guaranteed by the parent enterprise, then in effect this creditor is transformed into a creditor of the parent enterprise with a similar interest in the consolidated accounts.
3. In Japan the practice is not to adjust the accounts of non-Japanese subsidiaries for differences in accounting methods; see the quotation from the annual report of Nissho Awai presented in section 8.6, 'Japanese GAAP, with no reconciliation'.
4. The whole subject of goodwill is considered in more detail in Chapter 20.
5. This means that if the associate revalues its plant property and equipment, the surplus is not treated as income in the associate's accounts.

References

G4+1 'Recommendations for achieving convergence on the methods of accounting for business combinations', IASB, London (1999).

Nobes, C *Some practical and theoretical problems of group accounting*, Certified Accountant Publications, London (1987).

Further reading

For an analysis of the acquisition, merger and fresh-start methods, see the G4+1 discussion paper (G4+1, 1999). Note that the subject of goodwill is considered further in Chapter 20.

Issues

The four chapters in Part Five deal with certain issues which have been selected for special consideration for two reasons:

■ They raise particularly interesting questions of accounting theory

■ They are of considerable practical importance since the way in which enterprises account for these matters has a marked impact on their reported position and performance

All four chapters include an exposition of the relevant accounting theory, an analysis of the IASB's rules and a consideration of present practice.

Chapter 20 deals with intangible assets. This subject is of interest for two reasons: recent economic developments, notably the growth of service industries and of information technology, have increased the amount and the range of intangible assets held by enterprises; and accountants have great problems in reporting these assets in a satisfactory fashion in the financial statements.

The subject of Chapter 21 is foreign currency translation. This topic is of particular concern to multinational enterprises, for whom a greater part of the items in the accounts are denominated in foreign currency. The methods used to translate these items can have a great impact on the figures that they report for income and wealth. In the past, foreign currency translation was a most controversial topic with no consensus on what methods should be used. This chapter explains how the controversy was resolved and analyses the present rules and practice.

Chapter 22 covers financial instruments. This topic has increased considerably in importance in recent years mainly because of developments in financial markets. The IASB has spent much time and effort in the search for the correct solution to the question of how to report the assets and income arising from financial instruments. The IASB's rules are examined with particular attention to those in two areas that present the most problems, both for enterprises and for accounting theory: derivatives and hedging.

Finally, Chapter 23 deals with disclosure. This topic is important, because of the role that the financial statements play in providing information for the capital market and of the weight given to the availability of information about the enterprise according to the 'efficient market hypothesis'. The analysis of recent developments in the disclosures made by enterprises (both the quantity and the nature of information disclosed) leads to the conclusion that more weight is being given to the provision of information for the capital market. Finally, an examination of disclosure practice in the five countries of the Pentad comes to the conclusion that there are still significant differences between the countries in this area.

chapter twenty

Intangible Assets

Chapter objectives

- To discuss the growing importance of intangible assets
- To examine the nature of goodwill and its accounting treatment
- To consider the rules for intangible assets set in IAS 38
- To discuss the limitations of the reporting of various categories of intangible assets: organizational capital (research and development); customer capital (brands) and human resources

20.1 THE GROWTH IN THE IMPORTANCE OF INTANGIBLE ASSETS

There is general agreement that the intangible assets of enterprises have grown enormously in importance in recent years. This is the culmination of a long-term trend. When double-entry book-keeping was first developed in medieval Italy, the first practitioners of the art were bankers and merchants whose principal assets were cash, business debts, stocks of merchandise and other physical objects, such as buildings and ships. The existing asset categories (monetary assets and tangible assets) served the needs of these early book-keepers very well. Later, during the Industrial Revolution of the eighteenth and nineteenth century, there was a great increase in the magnitude and range of assets owned by enterprises but almost all were in the form of tangible assets, such as the locomotives, carriages, bridges, tunnels and tracks of the first railways and the spinning jennies and automatic looms of the early cotton mills. The existing accounting model served the needs of these enterprises quite adequately. However, gradually over the next two centuries, intangible assets became more significant; assets such as the enterprise's reputation with its customers, its skilled and experienced workforce, its organizational structure and its store of technical knowledge. The existing accounting model has difficulty in coping with these intangible assets. Occasionally they are reported as assets in the balance sheet, for example when the cost of patenting a new invention is capitalized. But more frequently they are ignored; they are not reported as assets at all. Tangible assets predominate in manufacturing industry and as, over the last century, the service sector has grown in importance in the developed countries, so the relative importance of tangible assets has declined and that of intangibles increased. In recent years the development of computers and other forms of information technology has further increased the importance of assets that are either not reported in the balance sheet or reported in an inadequate fashion. The result has been a widening gap between the value of the enterprise as reported in the balance sheet and its market value as measured, for example, on the stock exchange. Between 1973 and 1993, the median ratio of market value to book value of American public companies doubled (Lev, 1996). The most dramatic manifestation of this development has been the increase in the market value of information technology firms such as Microsoft Inc, the software developer. At the end of the year 2000, the market price of a single Microsoft share was $43, giving a value for the entire enterprise of $217bn. The book value of the net assets in Microsoft's balance sheet at that date was just $17bn – that is Microsoft's market value was over 12 times higher than its value according to its balance sheet. In fact a year earlier, the share price had been over $100, making the enterprise's market value more than 50 times its book value. As Bill Gates, the founder of Microsoft remarks 'Our primary assets, which are our software and our software-development skills, do not show up on the balance sheet at all' (*The Economist*, 12 June 1999). The failure of the current accounting model to capture the full value of intangibles is demonstrated by the figures for the composition of the assets of the 50 largest MNEs presented in Exhibit 15.7 of Chapter 15: intangibles represent less than 7 per cent of the total assets of these enterprises.

The gap between book values and market values is not attributable entirely to the non-reporting of intangible assets. Logically there may be three reasons for the existence of such a gap:

(a) **Monetary and tangible assets:** These assets may be omitted from the balance sheet. This is not very common as the present accounting model generally captures these assets quite well. However many enterprises continue to hold and operate tangible assets that have been fully depreciated and whose book value is zero. Moreover it is very common, under the historical cost convention, for the book value of tangible assets to be much lower than their market value, particularly with assets, such as land and buildings, for which a ready market exists.

(b) **Intangible assets:** Specific intangible assets may be omitted from the balance sheet or, in the relatively rare cases that they are reported, they are reported at below market value. The consideration of these intangible assets is the principal subject matter of this chapter.

(c) **Goodwill:** The value of the enterprise as a whole may be higher than the sum of the individual assets. This difference is termed 'goodwill' and is considered in section 20.3. However, before doing this, the classification of intangible assets will be considered.

20.2　THE CLASSIFICATION OF INTANGIBLE ASSETS

Intangible assets are dealt with in two International Accounting Standards: IAS 38 Intangible Assets and IAS 22 Business Combinations. Exhibit 20.1 presents a classification scheme which uses concepts contained in these standards. Intangible assets are members of the class of assets and therefore must conform with the definition of 'asset' but otherwise they are defined by what they are not:

- They are not monetary assets
- They are not tangible assets

The distinction from monetary assets creates no problems as the definition of monetary asset is clear cut. IAS 38,7 defines monetary assets as money held and assets to be received in fixed or determinable amounts of money. However the distinction between tangible assets and intangible assets is much more problematical. Almost every asset has some physical object connected with it in some way, even those that accountants typically classify as intangible assets, for example a taxi-cab licence is evidenced by a badge and a patented drug by the patent certificate. However of much more fundamental significance is that the essence of all assets is that they are the source of future benefits. The future benefits that are expected to flow from assets with a strong physical presence, such as machines, are not essentially different from those of assets that are generally classified as intangible; both sets of benefits ultimately resolve themselves into enhanced future cash flows. In effect, in a fundamental sense, all assets are intangible assets. The distinction between tangible and intangible assets is based not on principles but on the traditional practice of accountants. Where there is a substantial physical object which can be identified with the flow of future benefits (such as a building, a machine or even a piece of artwork such as a painting) then it is classified as a tangible asset. When however the physical object

Exhibit 20.1 *The classification of assets*

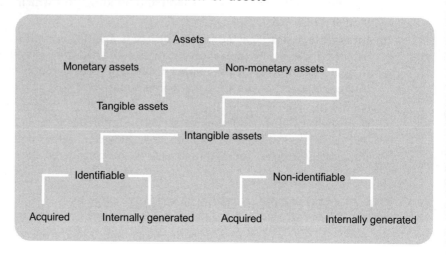

is insubstantial (for example, the CD-Rom on which a computer program is stored) and does not represent the essence of the asset (the computer program can generally be reconstituted if the CD-Rom were to be destroyed), then it is considered to be a intangible asset.

Intangible assets, so defined by negation, are further classified according to two characteristics:

■ Whether they are 'identifiable' or the opposite 'non-identifiable'
■ Whether they are 'acquired' (that is the enterprise acquired the intangible assets in their completed state from outside the enterprise) or they are 'internally generated' (that is the enterprise itself developed the intangible assets)

The second concept is straightforward, but the idea that an asset may be not identifiable seems bizarre. How can one report an asset that one cannot identify? This conundrum is connected with the concept of goodwill which will now be examined in detail.

20.3 GOODWILL

20.3.1 The meaning of the accounting term

The term 'goodwill' as used by accountants has a special technical meaning: the difference between the value of the enterprise as a whole and the sum of the values of the individual assets. For an individual asset to be valued, it must first be identified. Hence the definition of goodwill can

Exhibit 20.2   *The calculation of goodwill*

	€	€
Monetary and tangible assets at book value	500	
Difference between market value and book value	200	
Market value of monetary and tangible assets		700
Identifiable intangible assets at book value	50	
Difference between market value and book value	450	
Market value of identifiable intangible assets		500
Total market value of individual identifiable assets		1200
Value of the enterprise as a whole		2000
Difference (equals 'goodwill')		800

be expanded so that it becomes the difference between the value of the enterprise as a whole and the sum of the values of the identifiable assets. The concept of an unidentified asset now makes sense. It is the residual asset that must be included to ensure that the sum of the values of the individual assets equals the value of the enterprise as a whole.

The concept is illustrated in Exhibit 20.2 with the aid of an example.

Goodwill, as presented in Exhibit 20.2, reflects the fact that the whole is more than the sum of the parts. This is a general phenomenon, not limited to accounting. For example a football team is more than a collection of individual players, particularly when these players combine well having played together many times. Similarly an institution, such as the British Parliament, is much more than the individuals that make it up at any time. In business, assets that are managed in a combination, will generally earn a higher profit than the assets separately. However it requires time and effort to transform a collection of individual assets into an organized combination. Over time the enterprise develops a skilled and experienced workforce backed up by an organizational structure to produce the goods and services which it is able to sell because of the good relations that it has established with its customers through advertising and a record of product quality and reliable service. For these reasons, an established enterprise is generally more valuable than one that has just been formed. Initially, the market value of a new enterprise may be not very different from the market value of its individual assets, and it is only after the problems of operating the assets in combination have been overcome that the value of the enterprise will start to exceed the sum of the values of the individual assets.

Apart from its technical accounting meaning, 'goodwill' has a general meaning of a friendly and positive attitude. In this sense the word is often used by businessmen to denote the enterprise's good name with its customers. The Oxford English Dictionary includes as one definition of 'goodwill': 'the possession of a ready-formed connection with customers considered as a separate element in the saleable value of a business'. It must be emphasized that this is not the meaning attached to the technical accounting term, for two reasons:

■ 'Goodwill' in the accounting sense is made up of much more than the enterprise's reputation with its customers

■ Insofar as 'goodwill' (in the general sense) is 'a *separate* element in the saleable value of a business' (as in the OED's definition), then it is not even part of accountant's 'goodwill', which as demonstrated in Exhibit 20.2 excludes the value of the separately identifiable assets

It must be admitted that the accountant's choice of term is highly unfortunate and is the cause of much misunderstanding on the part of non-accountants. The equivalent German accounting term, Firmenwert (literally firm value), or even the French term, fonds de commerce (literally business funds), is much superior. However the English term 'goodwill' seems to be infiltrating even the foreign language versions of the financial statements of German and French multinationals, which is much to be regretted.

The accounting treatment of 'goodwill' depends crucially on whether it is acquired or generated internally, which explains the further subclassifications of intangible assets in Exhibit 20.1.

20.3.2 Internally generated goodwill

Internally generated goodwill is that which is developed by the enterprise itself. Typically it will arise from a host of seemingly unrelated outlays which have the general effect of improving the enterprise's future prospects, for example the cost of repairing free of charge defective goods returned by customers. The accounting treatment of internally generated goodwill can be described very simply: it is never reported as an asset; the expenditure involved is always charged to the income statement in the period in which it is incurred. The reason is that it is not possible to measure reliably the cost or value of this asset. Consider the previous example of the cost of repairing defective goods; at present there is no reliable method of dividing this cost between that which relates to an asset (the 'goodwill' of customers who are more likely to continue to buy from the enterprise) and that which relates to an expense of the period (putting right mistakes). An even more obvious example is given by the costs of introducing a new process. It is probable that, in the first months after the introduction of a new production process, the productivity of workers will be lower and the wastage of materials will be higher than the levels achieved once the process has become established. Once an enterprise has passed through this introductory phase with its associated 'teething troubles', it is in a better position than before; it has developed an experienced workforce and a smoothly running production system. These advantages could reasonably be reported as 'assets'. However, it is a necessary condition for the recognition of an asset that its cost should be measured reliably. In the case of internally generated goodwill, as there is no reliable way in which the costs of developing this asset may be separated from the costs of everyday operation, all of the relevant costs (wages, materials and so on) are treated as expenses.

The IASB's position is uncompromising and in line with generally accepted practice. It is set out in IAS 38, 36 in the following terms:

Internally generated goodwill should not be recognised as an asset

20.3.3 Acquired goodwill

The nature of acquired goodwill

Acquired goodwill arises when one enterprise acquires the whole of another enterprise or a segment of another enterprise that represents a complete business unit. In these circumstances, accountants are prepared to recognize goodwill because the acquisition is a transaction that establishes reliably both the cost and the value of the enterprise acquired. Goodwill is reported in the consolidated balance sheet as the difference between the value of the acquired enterprise as a whole and the sum of the values of its individual assets. This is the position of the IASB which, in IAS 22, 41, sets out the basic rule:

Any excess of the cost of the acquisition over the acquirer's interest in the fair value of the identifiable assets and liabilities acquired at the date of the exchange transaction should be described as goodwill and recognised as an asset.

The components of acquired goodwill

The amount of goodwill reported in the consolidated balance sheet may be analysed into its component parts using a scheme developed by Todd Johnson and Petrone (1998), as set out in Exhibit 20.3.

Todd Johnson points out that, in principle, points (1), (5) and (6) are aberrations, they arise through not implementing the generally accepted

Exhibit 20.3 *Possible components of acquired goodwill*

(1) **Excess of the fair values over the book values of recognized assets**
The market value of the acquired enterprise's recognized assets may be different from the value reported in the consolidated accounts (€200 in Exhibit 20.2)

(2) **Assets not recognized**
The market value of identifiable intangible assets acquired may not be recognized in the consolidated balance sheet because of the restrictive nature of present accounting rules (€450 in Exhibit 20.2)

(3) **The 'going concern' element of the acquired business**
This reflects the fact that, solely in respect of the acquired enterprise, its assets are worth more in combination than when valued separately (€800 in Exhibit 20.2)

(4) **The value of the synergies**
The acquiring and the acquired enterprises may be worth more in combination than when valued separately; this reflects the fact that the acquirer may be prepared to pay more for the acquired enterprise than its value when considered separately, because it can foresee higher values arising from the combination of the two enterprises; for example, there may be economies of scale permitting cost reductions in both enterprises.

(5) **Overvaluation of consideration**
The consideration paid by the acquirer may be overvalued; this is only likely to occur when the acquisition is effected through an exchange of shares.

(6) **Overpayment by acquirer**
The acquirer in fact paid too much for the acquired enterprise, even when synergies are taken into account, as often happens in the heat of a take-over battle.

rule. Hence in respect of (1) the assets of the acquired enterprise should be reported at market value in the consolidated accounts, in respect of (5) the consideration should be valued at market value and, in respect of (6), if the acquirer paid too high a price, the excess should be charged as an expense at the time of the acquisition. However, undoubtedly in practice goodwill in consolidated accounts does include amounts relating to these points either through inadvertence or, more commonly, through practical difficulties in estimating market values. Furthermore the value referred to in point (2) is not, in principle part of 'goodwill' but arises because, under GAAP, certain of the acquired enterprise's intangible assets are not recognized. This point is explained further in the next section. In effect 'goodwill' is properly restricted to the excess value arising from points (3) and (4) above, of which (3) relates solely to the acquired enterprise and (4) to the combination of the two enterprises. Todd Johnson refers to this as 'core goodwill'. However in practice the goodwill that is reported following an acquisition may relate to any or all of the six reasons listed in Exhibit 20.3.

The accounting treatment of acquired goodwill

There has been much controversy over how acquired goodwill should be reported in the consolidated accounts. In the past, three quite different accounting treatments have been common:

1. Capitalize as an asset and amortize over its estimated life.
2. Capitalize as an asset, but keep the asset at its original value in the balance sheet indefinitely (that is do not amortize) subject to periodic tests for impairment.
3. Write off the goodwill against reserves at the time of the acquisition.

In effect, (1) is the standard accounting treatment for assets and both (2) and (3) represent deviations which need to be explained and justified. A common feature of both treatments is that they seek to deal with the anomaly that acquired goodwill is treated differently from internally generated goodwill, which, under existing practice, is never reported as an asset. In effect the enterprise's expenditure that goes to build up internally generated goodwill (such as advertising, staff training and research costs) is charged to the income statement in the period in which it is incurred. The proponents of treatment (3) argue that, since internally generated goodwill is not reported as an asset, acquired goodwill should also not been treated as an asset in order to assure consistency. The argument in favour of treatment (2) is a little more complex. Commonly, established enterprises seek to maintain the value of their goodwill by regularly incurring costs (on advertising, training, research and so on) that benefit the future, but which are charged as an expense in the current period. Hence the normal situation is that the value of acquired goodwill will not decline over time and it is appropriate to maintain it as an asset in the balance sheet at its original value, subject to periodic impairment tests to guard against the eventuality of the enterprise failing to maintain the original value. If goodwill were to be amortized, there would be a double charge to the income statement: the amortization of the acquired goodwill and the current costs that are incurred in maintaining the value of goodwill. The argument against 'double charging' is also the justification for not writing off goodwill through the income statement under treatment (3).

A further argument used by the proponents of treatment (3) is that, in their view, goodwill is not an asset. This appears to be the view of the UK's ASB which states in the introduction to FRS 10, 'goodwill arising on acquisition is neither an asset like other assets nor an immediate loss in value ... purchased goodwill is not in itself an asset ... [it] is part of a larger asset'. The USA's FASB also considered the matter and came to the conclusion that goodwill is an asset. This is also the IASB's position;[1] see IAS 22's definition of goodwill quoted above. The authors' views on this controversy are:

(a) Goodwill is clearly very different from other assets, certainly in respect of the 'core' goodwill (points (3) and (4) of Exhibit 20.3).

(b) However they consider that goodwill does meet the three conditions set out in the IASB's definition of an asset:

   (i) Future economic benefits (the capability of the enterprise to earn future cash flows that are greater then if the goodwill did not exist);

   (ii) Control (the enterprise can ensure that it receives these cash flows through its ownership of the acquired enterprise);

   (iii) Past event or transaction (the acquisition of the other enterprise).

The arguments in favour of (1) (capitalize and amortize) have been well put by Grinyer et al. (1990). Managers should be held accountable for the resources that they have expended in acquiring other businesses. Accountability is best achieved by initially reporting goodwill as an asset and amortizing it over time. The annual amortization charges to the income statement remind shareholders of the costs of past acquisitions. Neither option (2) nor option (3) involves charges to the income statement at any time: with (2) goodwill is not amortized and with (3) it is charged directly to reserves. With these accounting treatments managers are able to report enhanced incomes and profits without reporting the associated costs. It is accepted that with option (1) there is a double charge to the income statement but this is the inevitable consequence of treating acquired goodwill differently from internally generated goodwill.

IAS 22's rule for acquired goodwill is that it should be capitalized and amortized over its useful life. There is a rebuttable assumption that the useful life may not exceed 20 years. If a longer life is assumed, impairment tests should be carried out annually.

20.4 IDENTIFIABLE INTANGIBLE ASSETS

20.4.1 The general rules of IAS 38

For an item to be reported as an intangible asset in the balance sheet, it must pass three tests:

- It must meet the definition of an intangible asset
- It must satisfy the recognition criteria
- The amount at which it is reported must be calculated in accordance with an acceptable valuation method

Exhibit 20.4 sets out in the form of a flow chart the sequence and content of the various tests. In effect the tests are rather like a hurdle race. If an item fails at any of the hurdles it ends up in the box in the bottom right-hand corner: 'report the outlay as an expense'. One has the impression that very few items will succeed in jumping all the hurdles and end up in the bottom left-hand corner and be reported as an intangible asset.

Definition

IAS 38, 7 gives the following definition:

An intangible asset is an identifiable non-monetary asset without physical substance held for use in the production or supply of goods and services, for rental to others or for administrative purposes.

An asset is a resource:
(a) controlled by an enterprise as a result of past events; and
(b) from which future economic benefits are expected to flow to the enterprise.

Three comments may be made about these definitions:

(a) An intangible asset must be identifiable. According to the IASB's usage of the term, 'goodwill' is not an intangible asset. The authors have not followed the IASB on this point; in Exhibit 20.1, they present goodwill as a subcategory of intangible assets, since to exclude it seems to consign goodwill to limbo.

(b) As defined by the IASB, the term 'intangible asset' does not apply to current assets since the definition does not include assets developed for sale – for example a computer program or a consultancy report being developed for a customer. This restriction is unsatisfactory in principle but not in practice, since these intangible assets are covered quite adequately in other IASs, notably IAS 2 Inventories and IAS 11

Exhibit 20.4 *Intangible assets: their definition, recognition and initial measurement*

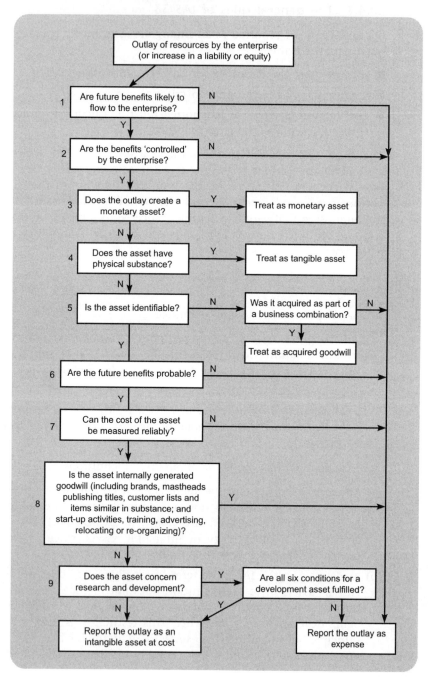

Construction Contracts. In effect, accountants had never had the slightest problems in including intangible elements in the current assets of inventory and work in progress. There would appear to be two reasons why intangible current assets cause no problems:

(i) the prudent rule of 'lower market value' helps to avoid over valuations;

(ii) as they are short-lived, any over valuation soon disappears.[2]

(c) An intangible asset must meet the two conditions that apply to assets in general: control and future economic benefits. Of these the more important is that the asset must be controlled by the enterprise. The concept of control relates to the ability of the enterprise to ensure that it receives the future economic benefits that flow from the asset. Where the enterprise cannot be certain on this point, then it cannot consider that it has an asset. This point is important in a number of fields.

(i) **Training:** When an enterprise incurs costs in recruiting and training its staff, it generally does so in the expectation that this expenditure will lead to an increase in future profits. However it may not report the costs of training as an asset because it does not control the source of these future benefits. The enterprise does not control its employees, in that it cannot ensure that they continue to make their skilled services available to the enterprise in the future. If an employee decides to resign, there is very little, under the law of most democratic countries, that the enterprise can do about it. Only when the employee is bound by a legally enforceable contract to work for the enterprise for a defined period (as is often the case with professional sportsmen and women) does the enterprise have sufficient 'control' to enable it to regard expenditure in acquiring and improving its employees as creating an asset that it may report in its accounts.

(ii) **Advertising and promotional expenditure:** An enterprise may expend considerable resources in building up its relationships with customers through advertising, sponsorship and similar promotional activities. However it does not own its customers; they have the right to take their custom elsewhere. Hence any 'asset' created by such expenditure is not controlled by the enterprise and may not be reported as an asset. The same reasoning applies to a data bank of customer information. Only when the enterprise has some legal right that it can prevent other enterprises from using, such as for example the right to a certain trade mark or brand name, can the enterprise consider that it 'controls' an asset relating to its market position.

(iii) **Research:** When an enterprise incurs expenditure in developing a new product, it can only consider that it has created an asset if it can prevent other enterprises from copying it, at least for a certain time, either by keeping the product secret or by securing legal protection through a patent. In the area of research, there are many other hurdles to be cleared before an asset is recognized. These are explained in section 20.4.2 below.

Recognition

For an item that meets the above definitions, IAS 38, 19 sets out the basic rules for recognition:

An intangible asset should be recognised if, and only if:
(a) it is probable that the future economic benefits that are attributable to the asset will flow to the enterprise; and
(b) the cost of the asset can be measured reliably.

The recognition criteria relate to the two principal problems connected with accounting for intangible assets:

■ Evaluating the future economic benefits
■ Separating the assets' cost from the other outlays of the enterprise

In relation to the first point (evaluating future economic benefits), the basic problem is that the assessment of future benefits is largely subjective. IAS 38, 20 attempts to introduce an objective element into this assessment with the following rule:

An enterprise should assess the probability of future economic benefits using reasonable and supportable assumptions that present management's best estimate of the set of economic conditions that will exist over the useful life of the asset.

The key words are 'reasonable' and 'supportable'. However it is unclear how effective this rule will be in curbing management's habitual optimism in forecasting the future.

The second point (separating the asset's cost from other outlays), is closely tied up with the concept of identifiability. In effect, both the costs and the benefits of an intangible asset must be identifiable. If the costs of the asset cannot be identified reliably, then the asset should not be recognized, even if the benefits can be identified. On this point, there is a significant difference between the recognition criteria in the Framework and those in IAS 38. In the Framework, an item may be recognized as an asset if it has a cost *or value* that can be measured reliably. In IAS 38, for the reliability of measurement, value is not a permitted alternative to cost.

Measurement

IAS 38,22 states:

An intangible asset should be measured initially at cost.

The basic rule for intangible assets is the same as that for tangible assets; they should be valued initially at cost. IAS 38 permits (but does not require) that, after initial measurement, intangible assets may be reported at fair value. There is a similar provision for plant, property and equipment in IAS 16. However the rule in IAS 38 is much more restrictive than that in IAS 16, because, for intangible assets, there is the additional condition that fair value must be determined with reference to the price in an active market. An active market is defined as one that fulfils all of the following conditions: the items traded are homogeneous; willing buyers and sellers can normally be found at any time; prices are publicly available. Hardly any intangible assets meet these conditions. The most restrictive condition is homogeneity since almost all intangibles are to a greater or lesser extent unique. In certain countries an active market exists for taxi licences and similar rights to undertake activities regulated by the government. It would seem that these licences are the only intangible assets that may be reported at fair value. Many other intangibles such as brands, newspaper titles, music and film publishing rights and patent rights are bought and sold, but since each asset has unique properties, they do not meet IAS 38's conditions for reporting at fair value. One may confidently assert that those intangibles that may be reported at fair value are less than 1 per cent of all reported intangibles.

Reliability versus relevance

In setting the rules for the recognition and measurement of intangible assets, the IASB has preferred reliability over relevance, in two respects:

■ It forbids the recognition of intangible assets whose cost cannot be measured reliably; hence many intangibles are excluded from the balance sheet

■ It insists that over 99 per cent of recognized intangible assets be reported at cost and not at fair value.

Clearly a balance sheet that reports all intangibles at their full value provides more relevant information but the IASB rejects it because the information lacks reliability.

Impairment

Curiously there is no rule in IAS 38 that the cost at which an intangible asset is initially measured should not exceed the value of the future benefits. However, intangible assets, like all assets, are subject to regular impairment tests, which assures that this principle is respected.

Amortization

Intangible assets should be amortized over their useful life. The basic rules are essentially similar to those for tangible assets. In addition there is a rebuttable assumption that, for intangible assets, the useful life may not exceed 20 years. If a longer life is assumed, then impairment tests must be carried out annually.

The rules outlined above apply to all identifiable intangible assets. However, as with goodwill so with identifiable intangibles, IAS 38 makes a distinction between acquired and internally generated assets.

20.4.2 Acquired identifiable intangible assets

As with goodwill, identifiable intangible assets may be acquired when a whole enterprise is taken over. In this case, all the identifiable assets of the acquired enterprise should be reported at fair value in the consolidated accounts. This applies to all assets (monetary, tangible and intangible) and, if an intangible asset of the acquired enterprise meets the general rules relating to definition and measurement outlined in the previous section, it must be reported. Note that reporting these assets at fair value at the time of acquisition is equivalent to reporting them at cost (to the parent enterprise).

However, in contrast to goodwill, identifiable intangibles may be acquired separately. An intangible asset is created whenever an enterprise expends resources (typically cash) to acquire the right to future services. Examples of intangibles that may be acquired in their completed state from another enterprise are:

■ A licence to use an industrial process
■ A licence to produce and sell a drug
■ Brand names and franchises
■ Computer software
■ Copyrights, films and television programmes
■ The transfer fee paid for a professional footballer

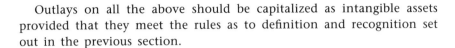

Outlays on all the above should be capitalized as intangible assets provided that they meet the rules as to definition and recognition set out in the previous section.

20.4.3 Internally generated identifiable intangible assets

For internally generated identifiable intangibles, IAS 38 adds a number of further, more restrictive, rules that do not apply to acquired intangible assets. The reason would appear to be that, with acquired assets, because there has been a transaction with an outside party which provides objective evidence, there is less uncertainty both as to the cost of the asset and as to the value of its future economic benefits. With internally generated intangible assets, the assessment of both the cost and the value is much more subjective.

Assets similar to internally generated goodwill

As already mentioned in section 20.3.2, internally generated goodwill may not be recognized as an asset either because it cannot be identified or because its cost cannot be measured reliably. IAS 38 backs up this general rule by listing specifically certain items that may not be reported as intangible assets when they have been generated internally, notably:

- Internally generated brands, mastheads, publishing titles, customer lists and items similar in substance (IAS 38, 51)
- Expenditure on start-up activities, including legal costs in establishing a legal entity and expenditure to open a new facility or business
- Expenditure on training
- Expenditure on advertising and promotional activities
- Expenditure on relocating or re-organizing part or all of an enterprise

The last four points in the above list are set out in IAS 38, 57 which is an explanatory paragraph. The reason for not recognizing these items as intangible assets is the practical difficulty in distinguishing them from internally generated goodwill.

Research and development

IAS 38 breaks down the process of developing an intangible asset into a research phase and a development phase. The research phase precedes the development phase and is characterized by the objective being less well-defined and less certain of achievement. Only when it becomes reasonably certain that the ultimate output of the process will be an identifiable asset does the development phase begin. The distinction between research and development is important because IAS 38 expressly forbids the capitalization of research expenditure in the following terms:

No intangible asset arising from research (or from the research phase of an internal project) should be recognised. Expenditure on research (or on the research phase of an internal project) should be recognised as an expense when it is incurred. (IAS 38, 42)

Expenditure relating to development should be capitalized if all of no less than six strict conditions are met. The enterprise must demonstrate that:

- The completion of the intangible asset is technically feasible
- The enterprise has the technical and financial resources to complete it
- It intends to complete it
- Once completed, it will use or sell it[3]
- The intangible asset will generate future benefits
- It can measure the asset's cost reliably

Of the above conditions, the last two points relate to assets in general. However in respect of the intangible asset the conditions are made more strict because the enterprise has to demonstrate the existence of a market for the output of the intangible asset (or the intangible asset itself) or, if it used internally, the usefulness of the intangible asset. The effect of this condition, plus conditions one to four, is to place obstacles in the path of recognizing internally generated intangible assets. As long as there is reasonable doubt about any of the matters in the above list, the enterprise has to assume that the development phase has not yet been reached and that all expenditure relating to the project should be treated as expenses of the current period.

Of course there are intangible assets whose development involves very little or no research. These are projects where the output is well defined from the outset and where there is never any reasonable doubt about their successful conclusion. An example would be a computer program to be written by the enterprise's own staff to perform a well-defined straightforward task. For such a project, the whole or virtually the whole of the costs are to be capitalized. However, with many, very costly projects, the outcome at the outset of the project is not assured and it is only after much time, effort and money have been expended that the conditions for the recognition of the development phase are reached (if in fact they are ever reached). For such projects the research phase may be long and costly. Examples of such projects are:

■ The development of a new drug by a pharmaceutical enterprise

■ The development of a new model by an automobile manufacturer

■ The design of a new shopping centre by a property company

■ The development of a new operating system by a software house

However there is one very common form of intangible asset that is specifically excluded from IAS 38: mineral rights and expenditure for the exploration and development of natural resources such as oil and natural gas. There is a very clear reason for excluding such assets from IAS 38: the FASB ran into enormous opposition when it attempted to regulate these assets and the IASB does not want to suffer the same experience.

It should be emphasized that the IASB's rules as outlined above are extremely prudent in that in almost all cases they lead to a serious under-statement of the value of intangible assets arising from research and development activities. From the viewpoint of management all research expenditure creates an asset (at least initially) for a rational manager would not decide to embark on a research project unless he estimated that the future benefits exceeded the costs. The IASB's rules ignore this asset completely. Research expenditure is always charged as an expense of the period in which it is incurred. Even if subsequently it can be demonstrated that the research has resulted in a valuable asset, IAS 38 forbids that the research costs that have been written off as expenses be reinstated as an intangible asset. Hence in respect of a successful project, only the development costs are capitalized; furthermore the asset is re-ported at cost and not at the value of the expected benefits.

20.4.4 Comparability of acquired and internally generated intangibles

In general it is desirable that two enterprises should report similar assets in similar ways, as this makes it easier for users to compare the two enterprises. The different rules for the reporting of acquired and inter-nally generated intangible assets makes meaningful comparisons almost impossible where the intangible assets of one enterprise are acquired and of the other are internally generated.

This is very obvious in the case of goodwill. Where an enterprise's assets consist principally of an acquired business, its balance sheet will report its assets at close to their full value, at least initially, if one makes the reasonable assumption that the purchase consideration reflects the acquired enterprise's value. The recognition of acquired goodwill ensures that the whole value of the firm is reported. Where an enterprise's assets include no acquired businesses, it will report no goodwill, so that its balance sheet will not reflect its full value. Over time the acquired goodwill in the first enterprise's balance sheet is amortized. This means that gradually there arises a difference between the reported value of that enterprise and its true value, as internally generated goodwill replaces acquired goodwill. Ultimately there is no difference between the two enterprises.

The same lack of comparability occurs with identifiable intangible assets. Although both acquired and internally generated identifiable intangibles are reported at cost, in general the reported cost of an acquired intangible will be much higher than that of an internally generated intangible. This arises not only because it is much easier to identify reliably the cost of an acquired intangible, but also because of the IASB's very restrictive rules on the capitalization of research costs. For example, if a pharmaceutical enterprise developed a new drug internally, it should report this intangible asset in its balance sheet at its development cost, taking no account of the research costs. If it sold the exclusive right to produce and market the drug to a second enterprise, that enterprise would report this asset at the purchase price, which would normally cover not only the development costs incurred by the first enterprise but also its research costs and its profits on the deal.

20.5 A FUNCTIONAL CLASSIFICATION OF INTANGIBLE ASSETS

An overall classification scheme for intangible assets has already been presented in Exhibit 20.1. However many academic researchers prefer an alternative classification scheme that is based on function. Exhibit 20.5 presents a well known classification scheme applied by Skandia, the Swedish insurance company, and presented in its annual report. It uses the term 'intellectual capital' to denote the totality of the enterprise's intangible assets. Intellectual capital is contrasted with financial capital (which is reported in the financial statements) and is made up of the following elements:

(a) **Organizational capital:** that is the value attached to the enterprise's systems both for the production of the current range of goods and services (Process capital) and for the development of new goods and services (Innovation capital);

(b) **Customer capital:** that is the value attached to the enterprise's relations with its customers; and

(c) **Human capital:** that is the value attached to the enterprise's work force.

The above classification was developed by a non-accountant. It is instructive to consider how well the accountant in preparing financial

Exhibit 20.5 *Skandia's intellectual captial*

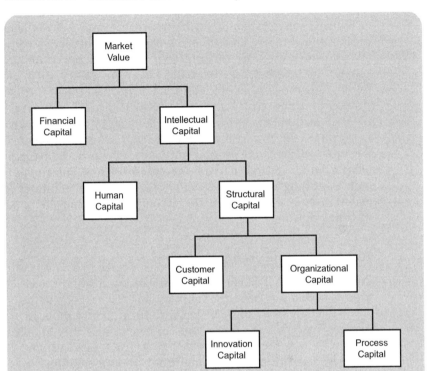

statements under GAAP (as represented by the IASB's rules) reports these three categories of intangible assets. In general accountants are reluctant to report intangible assets. However, the accountant's willingness to report intangible assets, although generally low, varies considerably for the three different elements of value in the above list, as will become apparent when they are examined individually.

20.5.1 Organizational capital

Organizational capital consists of the knowledge and experience embodied in the enterprise's systems and structures both for producing the current range of goods and services and for developing new goods and services. It has been defined as what is left on the enterprise's premises when the employees go home at the weekend. Of course this definition includes many tangible assets but equally clearly the book value of the recognized assets generally fails to capture the full value of the enterprise's organizational structure and systems. The IASB's rules are better at reporting the value of organizational capital than either customer capital or human capital. When intangible assets that form part of the enterprise's organizational capital are acquired separately, the accountant reports them at cost which, at least initially, is a not a bad proxy for value. With respect to internally generated assets, the IASB's rules specifically forbid the recognition of certain categories (see section 20.4.3 'Assets similar to internally generated goodwill'); as to the rest, they are reported at development cost which is likely to be very much less than their value, for two reasons: the research costs are excluded and the measurement basis is cost and not value. However the basic problem is identifiability. A large part of the enterprise's organizational capital is built up through a mass of seemingly unrelated expenditures (on wages, materials and so on) which the accountant is incapable of identifying with any asset.

20.5.2 Customer capital

Customer capital is made up of the relationships that the enterprise has with its customers. These relationships are valuable because the enterprise's future sales are likely to be higher with them than without them. Existing customers are likely to repeat their orders because they are satisfied with the service that they have received in the past; new customers are likely to be attracted through the enterprise's good reputation.

The IASB's rules relating to customer capital are very restrictive. In addition to the need for identifiability (which also applies to organizational capital), another condition set out in IAS 38 bars the recognition of many intangibles relating to customer capital: this is the requirement that, for an item to be reported as an asset, it must be controlled by the enterprise. Control is rarely a problem with intangibles relating to organizational capital but is a major problem with customer capital, for the simple reason that the enterprise does not own its customers – they are not slaves; they are free to take their custom elsewhere. IAS 38, 16 makes the point in the following terms: 'in the absence of legal rights to protect, or other ways to control, the relationships with customers . . . the enterprise usually has insufficient control over the economic benefits from customer relationships . . . to consider that such items (portfolio of customers, market shares, customer relationships, customer loyalty) meet the definition of intangible assets'.

Hence, in the area of customer capital, enterprises may only recognize as intangible assets those items that represent legally protected rights. By far the most common of these rights is the right to use a name or title (and to prevent other persons using it) such as trademark, a brand name, a franchise and the title of a newspaper or journal. It is generally recognized that these names are a valuable asset; the owner of the name (the person with the legal right to use it) sells more goods and services with the name than without it. In fact the value of certain internationally renowned brands is enormous. Exhibit 20.6 presents a list of the twelve most valuable global brands based on estimates made by Interbrand, a consultancy firm. Although Interbrand's estimating techniques have been criticized as involving subjective estimates of future sales, there is sufficient objective evidence of brand values (gained when brands have been purchased either separately or as part of a complete business) to remove any doubts that brands can be extremely valuable.

However this does not mean that enterprises generally recognize the brands that they own as assets in their balance sheet. In fact the whole issue of reporting brands is highly controversial. There are three possible accounting treatments for brands:

(a) No recognition – brands are not reported as an asset.

(b) Recognize only acquired brands.

(c) Recognize both acquired and internally generated brands.

The IASB's position seems to be (b). It clearly rejects (c) since IAS 38, 51 sets out the uncompromising rule:

Internally generated brands, mastheads, publishing titles, customer lists and items similar in substance should not be recognised as intangible assets.

Exhibit 20.6   *The twelve most valuable global brands*

Rank	Brand name	Value ($ billion)
1	Coca-Cola	72.5
2	Microsoft	70.2
3	IBM	53.2
4	Intel	39.0
5	Nokia	38.5
6	General Electric	38.1
7	Ford	36.4
8	Disney	33.6
9	McDonald's	27.9
10	AT&T	25.5
11	Marlboro	27.9
12	Mercedes	21.1

Source: Interbrand, quoted in *The Independent*, 19 July 2000

However there is no similar prohibition for acquired brands and, in fact, provided that these items meet the IASB's conditions relating to definition and recognition, the enterprise is required to report them as assets. In fact, in the case of an acquired brand, it is generally possible to identify both the cost and the value of the asset and it should therefore be reported as an asset. The prohibition on recognizing an internally generated brand is essentially based on the practical difficulties of identifying the costs of developing this asset. IAS 38 refers to the difficulty of distinguishing expenditure on building up a brand from expenditure on developing the business as a whole. Since it is forbidden to recognize internally generated goodwill as an asset, the same prohibition should apply to internally generated brands. This rule in IAS 38 has been criticized for its arbitrary nature; it simply sets out a list of four items that are proscribed plus 'items similar in substance' without any clear indication of what are the characteristics of these items that disqualifies them from being recognized as assets. Hence the phrase 'items similar in substance' is not operational. In effect the IASB has resorted to *ad hoc* prohibitions.

20.5.3 Human capital

The human capital of an enterprise is essentially its workforce. There can be little doubt that, for certain enterprises, their workforce is their most valuable asset. This particularly applies to enterprises whose principal output is knowledge and information, such as consultancy firms, advertizing agencies and software developers; often these firms are little more than a network of highly skilled and productive people.

However, in attempting to report these human assets in the balance sheet, the accountant is faced with the problem of control in an even more acute form than is the case with customer capital. The enterprise does not own its employees, as slavery has been abolished. This means that its employees can literally walk away at any time and there is very little in practice that the enterprise can do to stop them. Hence even when the costs and benefits relating to its employees can be identified with reasonable certainty, as for example with the costs and benefits of a training programme, they are never reported as an intangible asset; the costs are always charged to the period in which they are incurred.

The only occasion on which an enterprise reports an intangible asset in relation to employees is when the enterprise has expended resources in acquiring the legal right to the employee's services which it can enforce both against the employee and against other enterprises. This situation often arises in relation to professional sportsmen, such as professional footballers. A football club pays a fee (known as a transfer fee) to the player's former employer to release the player from his existing contract and a further fee (known as a signing-on fee) to the player to induce him to sign a new contract. As a result of this expenditure, the club acquires the exclusive right to the player's services. Since the new contract is enforceable at law, both against the player and against other enterprises, the club has control over the player and should recognize the costs of acquiring the player's services as an intangible asset.

20.6 REPORTING OF INTANGIBLE ASSETS IN PRACTICE

In this final section, financial reporting practice will be examined for three particular intangible assets, being one asset chosen from each of the major categories identified in the previous section.

20.6.1 Organizational capital: research and development

In principle there is a major difference between the USA and other countries with regard to the reporting of expenditure on research and development (R&D). In the USA all such expenditure must be charged as an expense in the period in which it is incurred. This rule even applies to the R&D acquired as a result of a business combination. The only exception is expenditure incurred in developing computer software, which should be capitalized under the provisions of FAS 86. The position in Germany and Japan is very similar. German law forbids the capitalization of all internally generated intangibles. In Japan, in 1998 the BADC issued a standard that required both research costs and development costs to be charged as expenses when incurred. In most other countries, development expenditure that meets certain conditions should be capitalized. This is also the position with IAS 38; development that passes all of the tests mentioned in section 20.4.3 should be capitalized – it is not a permitted option to write it off as it is incurred. However the difference is more apparent in theory than in practice. The common practice throughout the world is to charge all research and development expenditure against profits in the period in which it is incurred. In effect the provision in IAS 38 that it should be capitalized is largely ignored; most enterprises act as if this expenditure fails the tests set out in IAS 38.

Present practice will be illustrated by using the example of the pharmaceutical industry. Firms in this industry spend enormous sums on R&D and it is generally considered that their success is critically dependent on developing new drugs. Exhibit 20.7 presents certain information relating to firms in the European pharmaceutical industry taken from the annual reports. On average these enterprises spend about one eighth of their turnover on R&D. Clearly the management of these firms undertake

Exhibit 20.7 *The research and development of European pharmaceutical firms*

	R&D expense charged in the income statement (millions)	R&D expense as a % of sales	Intangible assets (other than goodwill) (millions)
AstraZeneca	$2923	15.85	$2651
Bayer	DM 2141	7.84	DM 1508
Novartis	CHF 4246	13.08	CHF 1680
Roche	CHF 3782	13.72	CHF 10 283
SmithKline Beecham	£1018	12.15	£926

research and development activities in the expectation of generating future benefits. However, without exception, these enterprises charge all research and development expenditure against profits in the year in which it is incurred, except when the expenditure results in a tangible asset such as a laboratory. The only intangible assets reported by these enterprises are, apart from goodwill, those that have been acquired from other enterprises.

The following note from the 1999 annual report of Roche is typical of the accounting policies of these firms in relation to R&D:

Research costs are charged against income as incurred with the exception of buildings and major items of equipment, which are capitalised and depreciated. Development costs are also charged against income as incurred since in the opinion of management the criteria for their recognition as an asset are not currently being met.

Many financial analysts regard the capitalization of development costs as a sign of weakness, that an enterprise is searching for any trick that will increase its reported profit. On the other hand, reporting a large R&D *expense* is regarded as a very positive signal as to the enterprise's future profitability. There are a number of American econometric studies that demonstrate that R&D intensity (ratio of R&D expenditure to sales) is positively associated with stock market values.[4] Lev (1999) has estimated that, for the American pharmaceutical industry, $1 of R&D expense leads to increased future profits of $2.63. He also calculated what value should be placed on the asset R&D in the balance sheet on the basis of its contribution to profits; in the case of the American pharmaceutical concern, Merck, the figure came to over $3bn representing a 60 per cent addition to the firm's equity base. These studies would seem to confirm the efficient market hypothesis, that the stock market value of an enterprise's shares is determined by all the information available about the enterprise and not simply the figures for assets and profits in its accounts.

20.6.2 Customer capital: brands

Brand names, such as Coca-Cola and McDonald's, are among the most valuable assets owned by many enterprises as is abundantly clear from the values presented in Exhibit 20.6. The practice with regard to reporting these names as assets varies considerably throughout the world.

USA

In the USA the matter is not covered specifically in any law or standard and, in principle, a brand would qualify for reporting as an intangible asset under the general principles of US GAAP. In practice most American enterprises do not report their brands as assets in their balance sheets. This is the case with the first five enterprises listed in Exhibit 20.6. However Philip Morris, the owner of a number of tobacco and food brands of which the most famous is 'Marlboro' (number 11 in Exhibit 20.6) does capitalize acquired brands. Its balance sheet includes the sub-heading 'Goodwill and other intangible assets $16 879mn' and the notes explain this item in the following terms: 'Goodwill and other intangible assets substantially comprise brand names purchased through acquisitions which are amortised on the straight-line method over 40 years' (Philip Morris, annual report 1999). This is the only information that the enterprise supplies concerning an asset that makes up 27.5 per cent of its total assets.

Japan

No Japanese MNE reports brands as an asset. In fact in the balance sheets of Japanese enterprises, intangibles are rarely significant, as is demonstrated by the statistics presented in Exhibit 15.7: for Japanese enterprises intangibles are less than 3 per cent of total assets, whereas for the other countries of the Pentad, they are over 7 per cent. The only intangible assets reported in the balance sheets of the major Japanese corporations are computer software, goodwill and balances relating to pensions and tax.

UK

The position in the UK is most interesting. It is because of the practice of British companies that, over the last decade, the whole question of reporting brands became a highly controversial issue. In the late 1980s a number of British companies started to report their brand names as intangible assets in their balance sheets. There were two reasons for this development:

(a) It was felt that without this asset the balance sheet would be seriously understating the company's assets. In 1988 the Swiss MNE, Nestlé, made a take-over bid for the British company, Rowntree. It was widely believed that the principal attraction of Rowntree for Nestlé was its brand names, such as Kit-Kat. However these brands were not reported as an asset in Rowntree's balance sheet, leading in the opinion of many that Rowntree's shares were undervalued on the stock exchange. Nestlé won the take-over bid, possibly because Rowntree's shareholders did not fully appreciate the proper value of the company's assets. Other British companies, determined not to be the next take-over victim, resolved to put their brands in their balance sheet.

(b) At that time, British companies were permitted to write off goodwill on acquisition directly against reserves. However, during the take-over boom of the 1980s, the premiums paid over the book values of assets became so large, that in many cases the amount of goodwill to be written off exceeded the reserves available. However, by allocating a considerable part of the premium to the fair value of acquired brands, the value of goodwill could be reduced to a more manageable figure.

The British standard-setting body was perturbed at the growing practice of reporting brands in the balance sheet as it felt that the information lacked reliability. However it was slow to introduce stricter rules and for many years the practice was largely unregulated, which led to some highly controversial reporting practices. For example, one company, Rank Hovis McDougall, reported internally generated brands at a value which was based, *inter alia*, on an estimate of future earnings. In 1997, the ASB restored order when it issued FRS 10, which prescribes rules for the reporting of intangible assets that are essentially the same as those of IAS 38. The principal differences are that an internally generated brand may be recognized if it has a readily ascertainable market value (IAS 38 has an absolute prohibition) and that a brand need not be amortized if it is regarded as having an indefinite useful economic life. In fact, since 1997, no major British company has reported internally generated brands as an asset and relatively few report acquired brands.[5] One of these is Cadbury Schweppes, the well known chocolate and soft drinks manufacturer; which describes its accounting policy in the following terms:

> Intangibles represent significant owned brands acquired since 1985 valued at historical cost. No amortisation is charged as the annual results reflect significant expenditure in support of these brands. For the 1998 financial statements, the Group has adopted FRS 10... As

permitted by FRS 10, the Group will continue its policy of capitalising acquired intangible assets (brands) and reviewing the carrying values on an annual basis for any impairment in value. (Cadbury Schweppes, annual report 1998)

The value of Cadbury Schweppes' brands in its 1999 balance sheet is £1656mn. They are valued at cost, with no deduction for amortization or impairment. Brands make up a substantial proportion (33 per cent) of total assets and are very large in relation to equity (£2240mn). If brands were not included as an intangible asset, the equity would be reduced to 26 per cent of its presently reported magnitude and the group's debt/equity ratio would be reported as 127 per cent instead of 33 per cent. The form 20-F which the group files with the SEC reveals that under US GAAP the brands would have been valued at £1431mn (historical cost of £1660mn less amortization of £229mn). This information confirms that the reporting of brands is permitted by US GAAP but that, by contrast with UK GAAP, amortization is always necessary.

Germany and France

Developments in Britain have had a rather differentiated impact on practice in its two principal EU partners.

(a) **Germany.** Under German GAAP, there is an absolute prohibition in reporting internally generated intangible fixed assets. However this does not apply to acquired brands. The authors have failed to find a single German enterprise that includes brands as an asset in its balance sheet, not even DaimlerChrysler, whose principal brand Mercedes is shown in Exhibit 20.6 to have a value of $21.1bn.

(b) **France.** Following the example of British companies, many French enterprises report brands as intangible assets; examples are LVMH, the producer of brandy and luxury goods, which reports brands of FF8954mn (9 per cent of total assets) and Danone, the food manufacturer with reported brands of FF12 069mn (12 per cent of total assets).

20.6.3 Human capital: professional sportsmen

The only enterprises that include in their balance sheets intangible assets relating to their employees are professional sports clubs. An example is Tottenham Hotspur PLC, the owner of a famous football club of the same name in the English Premier Division. An extract from its 1996 annual report is given in Exhibit 20.8. The reference in this note to the Bosmans Case is to a famous judgement of the European Court of Justice to the effect that an employer could not prevent an employee moving

Exhibit 20.8   *Tottenham Hotspur PLC: annual report, 1996*

Note 1: Accounting policies
Transfer fees: The cost of players' registrations are capitalized and amortized over the period of the respective players' contracts.

Note 12: Intangible fixed assets
Players' registrations

	Cost £ thousand	Amortization £ thousand	Net book value £ thousand
Balance at 1 June 1995	19 028	3212	15 816
Additions	10 407		10 407
Disposals	(7964)	(1190)	(6774)
Amortization charged in period		1944	(1944)
Exceptional item (note 3)		7290	(7290)
Balance at 31 July 1996	21 471	11 256	10 215

Note 3

Following the outcome of the Bosmans Case whereby a player, at the end of his contract, can move to a new club within the European Union without his current club being able to demand a transfer fee, the Board has reduced the player values contained in the balance sheet. This adjustment reflects the Board's assessment of the permanent diminution in value that the ruling potentially causes and is dealt with as a one-off exceptional charge to the Profit and Loss Account. The charge is simply an accounting adjustment and has no effect in cash terms.

to another employer at the end of his contract. Previously football clubs had been able to demand payment of a transfer fee from the new employer, even after the employment contract had expired, and had taken into account the expected amount of the transfer fee in valuing their players. However the judgment in the Bosmans Case essentially reduced the player's residual value to zero. This is a nice example of an asset becoming impaired as a result of a change in the law.

SUMMARY

The growing importance of intangible assets was linked to economic trends such as the relative decline of manufacturing industry and the development of services and information technology. The term 'goodwill' was defined and its components analysed; the rules for the reporting of both

SUMMARY (cont'd)

acquired and internally generated goodwill were explained. The rules for the reporting identifiable intangible assets were considered, again distinguishing between acquired and internally generated assets. With respect to three categories of intangible assets (organizational capital, customer capital and human capital), there was a discussion on the extent that the accountant's rules permitted these assets to be reported at their proper value and an analysis of present practice.

Review questions

1. What are the various sources of the difference between the overall value of a business and the book values of its assets?

2. What are the IASB's rules for the accounting treatment of goodwill?

3. On what grounds is it sometimes claimed that the amortization of goodwill leads to a 'double charge' in the income statement?

4. What are the arguments for the capitalization and amortization of goodwill?

5. Why does the IASB draw a distinction between acquired and internally generated intangible assets?

6. Why does the basic condition that an asset must be controlled by the enterprise have so much influence on the reporting of intangible assets?

7. Under what conditions may research and development be reported as an intangible asset?

8. What are the three categories of intangible assets in the classification scheme adopted by Skandia? How good are accountants at reporting the value of the assets in each of these categories?

Notes

1. For a clear discussion on the issue of whether goodwill is an asset, see appendix 3 of E60, the IASC's exposure draft on intangible assets (IASC, 1997).
2. However there is a category of assets that is conventionally included with the current assets which does meet IAS 38's definition of intangible: that of pre-payments. IAS 38 does not deal with prepayments specifically except to state, in paragraph 58, that it does not preclude the reporting of prepayments as an asset.
3. The reference to 'sell' in IAS 38,45 is an anomaly because an asset that is developed for sale is inventory and is not covered by IAS 38's rules.
4. These studies are referred to in Lev (1999).
5. According to a survey by Company Reporting (1998), only 8 of 448 British companies reported brands in the balance sheet.

References

Aboody, D and Lev, B 'The value relevance of intangibles: the case of software capitalization', *Journal of Accounting Research* **36**(Supplement) (1998), pp. 161–98.

Company Reporting 'Intangible Assets', *Company Reporting* (June 1998), pp. 3–8.

Economist, The 'A price on the priceless', *The Economist,* (June 1999), pp. 72–4.

Edvinsson, L 'Developing intellectual capital at Skandia', *Long Range Planning*, **30** (June 1997), pp. 366–73.

Grinyer, JR, Russel, A and Walker, M 'The Rationale for Accounting for Goodwill', *British Accounting Review*, **22**(3) (1990), pp. 223–35.

IASC *Exposure Draft E60 Intangible Assets*, IASC, London (August 1997).

Lev, B 'The boundaries of financial reporting and how to extend them', Working paper, University of California, Berkeley (August 1996).

Lev, B 'R&D and capital markets', *Journal of Applied Corporate Finance*, **11**(4) (Winter 1999), pp. 21–35.

Todd Johnson, L and Petrone, KR 'Is Goodwill an asset?', *Accounting Horizons*, **12**(3) (September 1998), pp. 293–30.

Further reading

For a very readable discussion of the whole subject of intangibles, see the article in *The Economist* (1999). Johnson (1998) is an excellent discussion of the nature of goodwill. Grinyer *et al.* (1990) make a strong case for the IASB's preferred treatment of goodwill. Lev (1999) and Aboody and Lev (1999) refer to well-researched studies that seek to establish the value of intangible assets. For a description of Skandia's approach to intangibles, see Edvinsson (1997).

chapter twenty-one

Foreign Currency Translation

Chapter objectives

- To define foreign currency translation and to explain its importance
- To explain the difference between the translation of transactions and the translation of financial statements
- For the translation of transactions, to set out the basic principles, analysing the conflict between the accruals principle and the prudence principle in this matter
- For the translation of financial statements, to outline the development of the rules and practice over the last 30 years, with particular emphasis on the conflict between the temporal method and the closing rate method, and to set out the current rules and practice
- To analyse the current practice in the USA, UK, Germany, France and Japan

The subject of this chapter is foreign currency translation, that is how to account for items denominated in a foreign currency. This topic has been selected not only because it provides particularly interesting insights into how the rules that govern financial reporting are developed but also because it is an important topic in its own right. The remarkable growth in foreign trade and investment in recent decades has led to an equivalent increase in the size of items in accounts that are denominated in foreign currency. This is particularly the case with the larger multinational enterprises, for whom the choice of method for the reporting of foreign currency items can have a most significant effect on the numbers that they report for assets, liabilities and profits.

21.1 THE BASIC TRANSLATION PROBLEM

Before examining the detailed rules in this area, the basics of foreign currency translation will be considered. The word 'translation' when used by accountants has a special technical meaning. It refers to the process whereby an item that is denominated in one currency is restated in terms of another currency. This restatement or translation is necessary because all the items in a set of accounts have to be denominated in the same currency. The problem may be illustrated with a simple example.

On 30 September 2000, a British company sold goods to a customer in Germany for DM 10 000. Under the terms of the sale contract, the debt has to be settled in German marks by 31 March 2001. Under the general principles of translation (to be explained in detail later), the sale is recorded in the books of the British company at the pound value of DM 10 000 using the exchange rate ruling at the date of the transaction. At 30 September 2000, this exchange rate was £1 = DM 2.92.[1] Therefore the sale and the debt would be recorded in the books of the British company as £3425, being DM 10 000 × £1/DM 2.92.

On 31 December 2000 the British company draws up its balance sheet. At that date, the exchange rate was £1 = DM 3.15, the market value of the DM having fallen against the pound in the previous three months. This reflects a fact of modern life: that the exchange rates between currencies are not fixed but are determined by market forces, which lead to considerable and generally unpredictable fluctuations in rates.[2]

The fact that exchange rates are not fixed creates two problems for the accountant:

■ What is the appropriate rate to use in translating an asset/liability denominated in a foreign currency?

■ How should one account for the gain or loss that arises when exchange rates change?

These problems may be illustrated using the previous example. When the accountant draws up the British company's balance sheet at 31 December 2000, she has to decide what value, in terms of British pounds, to place on the debt of DM 10 000. Two possible rates suggest themselves:

(a) The exchange rate at the time when the debt was acquired; that is at 30 September 2000 when the sale was made. Using the exchange rate of £1 = DM 2.92, the translated value is £3425, which may be interpreted as the historical cost of the asset in terms of British pounds. The exchange rate at a past date is known as the 'historical rate'.

(b) The exchange rate at the balance sheet date of 31 December 2000. Using the rate of £1 = DM 3.15, the translated value of the debt is £3175, which is, in effect, the current value of the asset at 31 December

2000. The exchange rate at the balance sheet date is known as the 'closing rate'.

When the historical rate is used for translation, the asset's value in terms of pounds is frozen at the time of acquisition. In the above example, the debt would be valued at £3425 on 30 September 2000 when it arose and subsequently this value would remain unaltered. However, when the closing rate is used, the translated value varies over time. On 30 September 2000 the debt is valued at £3425 and on 31 December 2000 it is valued at £3175. This decrease in value of £250 is caused solely by the process of translation since the German mark value of the asset has remained unchanged. Hence it is customarily termed 'gain/loss on translation', or sometimes more neutrally 'translation difference'. This gain or loss has to be reported in some way in the accounts.

To summarize, there are two major problems connected with translation:

(a) Which rate of exchange should be used to translate the foreign currency value of assets and liabilities: the historical rate or the closing rate?

(b) If the closing rate is used, how should the change in the translated value of the asset (the gain/loss on translation) be reported in the accounts? This has been a controversial subject because, in the area of translation, accountants have often been reluctant to follow the general rule that a change in the value of an asset or liability should be reported in the income statement as a gain or loss. Hence, as will be explained later, there has been much discussion on the use of alternative methods of dealing with the translation difference, including reporting it as an element of equity (never reporting the difference in the income statement) and deferring it (reporting it in future income statements)

21.2 THE TRANSLATION OF TRANSACTIONS VERSUS THE TRANSLATION OF FINANCIAL STATEMENTS

The accountant is faced with the problems of translation in two broad areas:

The translation of transactions

This refers to the recording of transactions denominated in foreign currency in the books of account of an individual enterprise, and the subsequent preparation of the financial statements of that enterprise from the books of account. This was the problem encountered in the example in the previous section. In 'translation of transactions' there is only one set of books (and one set of financial statements) which are denominated in the enterprise's reporting currency, hereafter termed 'home' currency. The accountant has to make a decision concerning translation at the moment that she records a transaction denominated in a foreign currency in the books of account. Subsequently she has to review periodically the translated value of assets and liabilities to check that they comply with the basic principles of valuation.

The translation of financial statements

This refers to the preparation of the consolidated financial statements of a group of enterprises, where the financial statements of the parent enterprise and those of one or more of its subsidiaries are not denominated in the same currency. The problem of 'translation of financial statements' arises when a parent enterprise owns an interest in an entity (a subsidiary, joint venture or associate) which maintains its books of account and draws up its financial statements in a foreign currency. The problem of translation arises at the end of the period, when the foreign currency financial statements are translated in order for them to be incorporated into the consolidated accounts which are denominated in the 'home' currency. The problem of translation of financial statements will be considered after that of translation of transactions.

21.3 THE TRANSLATION OF TRANSACTIONS: THE THEORY

21.3.1 Basic principles

For transactions denominated in a foreign currency, the basic rule is that they are initially recorded in the books of account translated at the exchange rate ruling at the date of the transaction. This procedure is consistent with general valuation principles. In the case of an asset acquired through the outlay of foreign currency, the cost to the enterprise in terms of its home currency is the amount spent in acquiring the foreign currency or, where the enterprise already holds the foreign currency, the amount of home currency foregone due to it no longer being able to convert the foreign currency into home currency. In the first case the cost in terms of home currency is the amount of foreign currency translated at the market buying rate; in the second case it is the amount of foreign currency translated at the selling rate. However, since the difference between buying rates and selling rates is rarely material, accountants generally translate all transactions at the average of the market buying and selling rates. The same principles apply to the translation of liabilities, expenses and income. Where an asset is acquired (or an expense incurred) in exchange for a liability denominated in a foreign currency, the liability is valued, at the date that it is incurred, at the amount of home currency that would be spent if it were settled at that time: that is, the foreign currency liability is translated at the market exchange rate ruling at the time of the transaction.[3]

The rule that was set out in the previous paragraph leads to all assets being initially recorded in the books at their historical cost in terms of home currency. For non-monetary assets, all subsequent adjustments to this figure follow the normal rules of accounting, that is systematic depreciation in the case of fixed assets and reduction to lower market value in the case of inventory. In effect the fact that the assets were acquired by an outlay of foreign currency is no longer relevant, once the assets have been recorded in the books of account at their historical cost in terms of home currency.

In the case of monetary assets and liabilities the situation is rather different, because the historical cost in terms of home currency may no longer be the appropriate value to place on these items when a balance sheet is drawn up at a later date. In principle one can conceive of three different ways in which monetary assets and liabilities that are denominated in foreign currency may be translated.

(a) **At the historical rate.** With this method, the home currency amount of these items is left unchanged and no translation gain or loss is reported.

(b) **At the closing rate.** Translation at the balance sheet rate gives the current value of these items in terms of home currency, that is the amount of money that would be received on the balance sheet date if the monetary asset were to be converted into home currency (*mutatis mutandis* for liabilities). When the closing rate is different from the historical rate, a translation difference arises.

(c) **At the lower (higher) of the historical rate and the closing rate for assets (liabilities).** When this method is used, assets are stated at the lower of two possible values and liabilities at the higher. The closing rate is only used if it gives rise to a loss on translation.

Of the three methods, the first method must be rejected because it leads to reporting monetary assets at higher than their current value in terms of home currency when the foreign currency has fallen in value (vice versa for liabilities). Some accountants justify its application on the grounds that, in a period of fluctuating exchange rates, the historical rate is a good guide to the rate at which the debtor or creditor will be settled, possibly as good a guide as the closing rate. Particularly in respect of long-term monetary assets and liabilities, they consider it premature to report a gain or loss arising from a fluctuation in exchange rates, which may be reversed in a future period. In the author's opinion, this argument is invalid. It is contrary to basic accounting principles to report monetary assets at higher than their current values and liabilities at lower than their current values.

However, there are good arguments, well grounded in accounting theory, for both the second method and the third method. The second method is based on the 'accrual principle' and the third on the 'prudence principle'. So in deciding between the second and third methods, a judgement has to be made on the relative weight to be given to these two fundamental principles of accounting.

21.3.2 The accrual principle versus the prudence principle

The accrual principle

When the accrual principle is applied, the accountant should not wait until the foreign monetary asset or liability has been turned into cash (in home currency) before recognizing the change in its value. Provided that she has objective evidence of the current value (provided by the exchange rate quoted on the market), she should recognize the changed value now. The loss or gain that arises from the recognition of the current value relates to the current period since it was caused by the change in exchange rates that occurred during that period. It does not relate to the future period when the monetary asset or liability will be liquidated.

The prudence principle

However some accountants give preference to the prudence principle over the accrual principle. They are not prepared to recognize gains that result from the increased value of a foreign monetary asset (following a rise in the foreign currency) or the reduced value of a foreign liability (following a fall in the foreign currency). They claim that the realization of these monetary assets/liabilities in terms of (home) cash cannot be assessed with reasonable certainty. A future change in exchange rates may well cancel out a gain made in the current period. Hence it would be imprudent to report this gain; since it is unrealized, it may well disappear in the future.

Since both methods are soundly and rationally based on (different) generally accepted accounting principles, it is impossible to choose between them on grounds of logic or theory. The authors' view is that there is something to be said for both methods.

In general, the first method (based on the accrual principle) gives the more relevant information, as may be illustrated with the following

Exhibit 21.1 *The disappearing Brazilian loan*

On 31 December 1993, a German enterprise borrowed 100 million Brazilian Cruzieros

Translated value of the loan at the 1993 exchange rate:
Cr 100 000 000 × DM 1 / Cr 70.60 = DM 1 416 431

Translated value of the loan at the 1997 exchange rate:
Cr 100 000 000 × DM 1 / Cr 2 083 862 = DM 48

example. The calculations are given in Exhibit 21.1. On 31 December 1993, a German company borrowed 100 million Brazilian cruzeiros, when the market exchange rate was one DM equals 70.60 cruzeiros. At 31 December 1997 the loan is still outstanding, but the value of the cruzeiro has fallen to 2 083 862 cruzeiros to the mark after taking into account the introduction of a new Brazilian currency, the real. The loan has to be reported as a liability in the company's balance sheet. Translation at the historical rate gives a value of DM 1 416 431; the translated value at the closing rate is only DM 48, which is the amount that it would cost to pay off the loan in 1997. There can be no doubt that DM 48 is by far the better measure of the burden of the liability in 1997. Given the continuous fall in the exchange value of the Brazilian currency, year after year, there is no reasonable chance that it will ever in the future regain its 1993 value.

However, the prudence principle acts as a necessary check on the optimism of management which is always trying to present the results of its endeavours in the best possible light. This will be illustrated with a counter example; the calculations are given in Exhibit 21.2. On 31 December 1989, a British company borrowed $1000 repayable on 31 December 1992. The liability is initially recorded in its books at £547.95, using the exchange rate at 31 December 1989. A year later, at 31 December 1990, the value of the loan at the closing rate is £519.48. Should the company take credit for a gain of £28.47 arising from the fall in value of the liability? When one considers the subsequent fluctuations in the £:$ exchange rate, it would seem rather premature to report any gain. In the succeeding two years, the pound fell against the dollar, leading to an increase in the value of the liability in terms of pounds. In fact, when the loan was finally repaid on 31 December 1992, the pound had fallen below its 1989 value, so that overall a loss of £111.68 was made on the loan. Hence it is argued that the translation gain calculated for 1990 should not be regarded as realized. If the 1990 'gain' had been

Exhibit 21.2　*Don't count your chickens before they are hatched!*

> On 31 December 1989, a British company borrowed $1000 repayable on
> 31 December 1992
>
> Value of the loan at successive closing rates
> 31 December 1989: $1000 × £1/$1.825 = £547.95
> 31 December 1990: $1000 × £1/$1.925 = £519.48
> 31 December 1991: $1000 × £1/$1.920 = £520.83
> 31 December 1992: $1000 × £1/$1.516 = £659.63

distributed to shareholders, the company would subsequently have been obliged to ask for its money back if it had wanted to maintain its capital.

The proponents of the accrual principle would claim in relation to the above example that the loss caused by the fall of the exchange value of the pound in 1991 and 1992 properly relates to these years and should be reported in the income statements of these years. Similarly the profit resulting from the increase in the pound's exchange value in 1990 relates to that year. Furthermore it may be possible to realize the profit made in the first year by entering into a forward contract on 31 December 1990 to buy $1000 on 31 December 1992 for £519 (plus charges). The proponents of the prudence principle concede that, if the British company had in fact made such a forward contract, there would be a good case for regarding the 1990 profit as realized. However, if there is no contract, the accounts should not be drawn up as though a forward contract had been made. Accounts should be based on facts and not potential facts; otherwise one could justify valuing inventory at selling price on the argument that the goods may easily be sold on the market.

However it is generally accepted that the prudence principle should not be taken to excess. Thus if, at the balance sheet date, an enterprise has both an account receivable and an account payable in the same foreign currency of a similar amount and with similar settlement date, then the enterprise is not exposed to any foreign exchange risk; any loss on the account receivable will be offset by the gain on the account payable, and vice versa. Hence even the most fanatical supporters of the prudence principle accept, in this case, to offset the translation gain against the translation loss, which is the equivalent of crediting the gain to the income statement. However there is considerable controversy over how far offsetting may be extended, for example to items with different maturities.

As already suggested, one cannot decide between the accrual principle and the prudence principle purely on the grounds of logic or of accounting theory. Probably the best solution is a compromise that takes something from both methods; as shown in a later section, it is common to value monetary assets and liabilities at the closing rate, but to defer the transfer of any gain to the profit and loss account until the foreign currency asset/liability is realized.

21.4 THE TRANSLATION OF TRANSACTIONS: THE RULES

In 1983 the IASC issued *IAS 21 Accounting for the effects of changes in exchange rates* which was revised in 1993 and given the revised title *The effects of exchange rate changes*. Most of this standard deals with the translation of financial statements; this part is dealt with later in this chapter. In respect of translation of transactions, IAS 21 specifies that monetary items must be translated using the closing rate and that, with certain exceptions,[4] all translation gains and losses should be recognized in the profit and loss account of the period in which they arise. IAS 21 does not permit that monetary items be valued at the historical rate or that, with certain exceptions, translation gains be deferred.

21.5 THE TRANSLATION OF FINANCIAL STATEMENTS

The 'translation of financial statements' arises when a parent enterprise owns an interest in an entity (a subsidiary, joint venture or associate) that maintains its books of account and draws up its financial statements in a foreign currency. Typically this entity will be located in a foreign country and will carry out its principal activities there. In fact multinational groups are exceedingly common. Virtually all major European and American enterprises have foreign subsidiaries. The special problem of consolidation faced by such multinational groups is that the component financial statements are denominated in different currencies. To prepare the consolidated balance sheet of a group consisting of an American parent enterprise and its German subsidiary, the two balance sheets must be denominated in the same currency. One cannot add together the parent enterprise's assets valued in terms of American dollars and the subsidiary's assets valued in terms of German marks – one of the currencies must be changed. It is normal to denominate consolidated financial statements in the currency of the parent enterprise (that is the 'home currency'), since the main users of the consolidated statements are the shareholders and creditors of the parent enterprise. Therefore it is the financial statements of the subsidiary that are translated from marks to dollars. There are two widely used methods for translating financial statements: the closing rate method and the temporal method. The closing rate method is very simple: all items in the balance sheet are translated at the closing rate. The temporal method is rather more complicated.

21.6 THE TEMPORAL METHOD OF TRANSLATION

21.6.1 Basic principles

The temporal method of translation of financial statements is essentially the application of the principles that govern the translation of transactions that have already been outlined in section 21.4. The numbers produced by this method are identical to those that would be obtained if the subsidiary were to maintain a set of books denominated in the home currency (parallel to those denominated in the foreign currency) and were to enter every transaction in these books as it occurred. Of course the subsidiary prepares accounts only in foreign currency and the equivalent home currency figures have to be produced by translating these foreign currency accounts. To decide which exchange rate should be used in translating each item in the foreign entity's accounts, one has only to consider at what point of time the subsidiary would have to make an entry in its (hypothetical) books of account denominated in the home currency. This procedure leads to the following rules:

(a) Assets that are reported in the foreign entity's balance sheet at historical cost should be translated at the exchange rate ruling at the date that they were acquired. This will result in most fixed assets and inventory being translated at the historical rate. However if a fixed asset has been revalued, the appropriate exchange rate to use is that ruling at the date of revaluation. Similarly, if inventory has been restated at lower market value, this value should be translated at the exchange rate ruling at the balance sheet date, that is the closing rate. This rate would also apply to fixed assets that are reported at their replacement cost or realizable value at the balance sheet date.

(b) Income and expenses are translated at the exchange rate ruling at the date of the transaction, that is the historical rate. In the case of depreciation expense, the appropriate exchange rate is that ruling at the date that the fixed asset was acquired or revalued, which may be several years previously. Cost of goods sold has to be decomposed into its component elements (opening inventory, purchases and closing inventory) and each element translated at the appropriate rate.

(c) Monetary assets and liabilities are always translated at the exchange rate ruling at the balance sheet date, that is the closing rate. The alternative approach of translating these items at the lower or higher of the historical or closing rates (lower for assets and higher for liabilities) is never applied in the translation of financial statements. In effect the rules for the preparation of the individual accounts differ from those that apply to the consolidated accounts, at least in those countries that apply the lower/higher rule (such as Germany). This difference in treatment (which is essentially illogical) is explained by the fact that tax considerations are less important in the consolidated accounts.

21.6.2 The Lorensen study and FAS 8

The theoretical basis of the temporal method of translation was developed by an American researcher, Leonard Lorensen, in a study that he undertook for the American Institute of Certified Public Accountants (Lorensen, 1972). Lorensen coined the term 'temporal method' with reference to the basic principle that the exchange rate to be used to translate each item in the foreign entity's accounts should be that ruling at the time[5] that the item's value was established, for example the historical rate for assets valued at historical cost and the closing rate for monetary assets. The background to the Lorensen study was that, at that time (the early 1970s), the American standard setters were concerned at the diversity of translation methods used by American enterprises, arising from the lack of any generally accepted principles in this area. No less than three quite different methods were in general use: the current/non-current method which used the closing rate for current assets and current liabilities and the historical rate for the rest; the monetary/non-monetary method which used the closing rate for monetary items and the historical rate for the rest; and the closing rate method which used the closing rate for all items. In fact this diversity was a worldwide problem, but the Americans were the first to make a serious effort to tackle it.

The US Financial Accounting Standards Board (FASB) came to the conclusion that Lorensen had discovered the correct principles to be used for the translation of financial statements and in October 1975 it issued FAS 8 (FASB, 1975), which made the use of the temporal method obligatory for consolidated accounts relating to accounting years beginning on or after 1 January 1976. No alternative methods were permitted.

21.6.3 The great debate on translation

FAS 8 caused a furore, particularly from American corporations that found themselves obliged to report substantial losses on translation in their consolidated accounts. For reasons that are explained later, they would not have reported such losses if they had used the closing rate method. These corporations lobbied hard for FAS 8 to be withdrawn. Thus, after 1975, there began a spirited public debate over the temporal method, that started in America and spread to the rest of the world. This is the subject of an excellent article by Nobes (1980), which graphically describes the contest between the temporal method and the closing rate method.

21.7 COMPARISON OF THE TWO METHODS

The two methods will be compared with the aid of a simple example using exchange rates from the period following the issue of FAS 8. It is assumed that in 1976 an American corporation set up a German subsidiary. It purchased a plant for DM 100mn with the aid of a local loan for the same amount; in addition it invested $21mn of its own funds in acquiring current assets (inventory and cash) for DM 50mn. The German subsidiary's balance sheet at 31 December 1976 is shown in Exhibit 21.3. There were no transactions in 1977; hence its balance sheet at 31 December 1977 is identical with that at the end of 1976. This assumption has been made so as to isolate the gain or loss on translation; any gain or loss reported in 1977 by the American corporation in respect of its German subsidiary must arise from translation.

Exhibit 21.3 presents the translated US dollar balance sheets of the German subsidiary at 31 December 1977 using the two alternative methods. With the temporal method the plant and inventory are translated at the historical rate, that is the rate at 31 December 1976; the monetary items (the cash and the loan) are translated at the closing rate. The net worth of the German subsidiary at 31 December 1977 is calculated as $14.6mn. Its net worth at 31 December 1976 (incorporated in the 1976 consolidated accounts) was $21mn. This is calculated by translating all the DM amounts at the rate at 31 December 1976; there can be no dispute over this figure, because, for the 1976 translation, the historic and closing rates are identical since the plant and inventory were acquired at 31 December 1976. Over 1977, the net worth of the German subsidiary in dollar terms has fallen by $6.4mn. This loss must be reported as loss on translation. It is caused solely by the translation process, since the net worth in DM terms did not change.

With the closing rate method, all the items in the DM balance sheet are translated at the closing rate. The net worth of the German subsidiary at 31 December 1977 is calculated as $25mn, which is $4mn higher than the net worth at the end of 1976. Hence the American corporation reports a gain on translation of this amount.

The difference between the two methods in the results reported is

Exhibit 21.3 *Comparison of the temporal method and the closing rate method*

German subsidiary's balance sheet at 31 December 1976 and 31 December 1977 (no transactions in 1977)	*Translated balance sheets at 31 December 1977*						
				Temporal method		*Closing rate method*	
		Translation factor[a]			*Translation factor*[a]		
	DM	*Type*	*Rate*	*$*	*Type*	*Rate*	*$*
	(million)			*(million)*			*(million)*
Fixed assets (plant)	100	HR	0.42	42.0	CR	0.50	50
Current assets							
Inventory	30	HR	0.42	12.6	CR	0.50	15
Debtors	20	CR	0.50	10.0	CR	0.50	10
Total assets	150			64.6			75
Loan	−100	CR	0.50	−50.0	CR	0.50	−50
Net worth at							
31 December 1977	50			14.6			25
Calculation of translation gain(loss) in 1977							
Net worth at							
31 December 1976	50	[c]	0.42	21.0	[c]	0.42	21
Change in $ net worth over 1977 (equals translation gain (loss))				−6.4			4

Notes
[a] HR = historical rate, CR = closing rate
[b] Calculated as assets less liabilities
[c] Translated at the exchange rate at 31 December 1976:
31 December 1976: DM1 = $0.42
31 December 1977: DM1 = $0.50

extraordinary: a translation loss of $6.4mn with the temporal method and a translation gain of $4mn with the closing rate method: a difference of $10.4mn, almost 50 per cent of the American corporation's net investment of $21mn in 1976. The translation loss and gain are analysed further in Exhibit 21.4. When the foreign currency has gained in value, an enterprise will report a gain on every asset denominated in that currency, provided that the change in the asset's value is reflected in the accounts. This gain is most evident when the asset in question is cash; over 1977 the value of one DM increased from $0.42 to $0.50; so the

Exhibit 21.4 *Analysis of the translation gain(loss)*

	Net assets at risk DM *(millions)*	Translation gain $ per DM	Total translation gain $ *(millions)*
Temporal method	(80)	0.08	(6.4)
Closing rate method	50	0.08	4.0

American corporation made a gain of $0.08 on every DM that it held. It will also report a gain of $0.08 on every asset denominated in German marks provided that its US dollar value is calculated using the closing rate. Hence a translation gain arises in respect of those assets that are translated at the closing rate, but no gain arises in respect of items that are translated at the historical rate. It is straightforward to extend the above principles to liabilities (which are negative assets) and to a fall in the value of the foreign currency. Where the foreign currency value of an asset or liability is translated at the closing rate, its translated value will fluctuate with changes in the exchange rate; it is said to be 'at risk'. Where an asset's value is translated at the historical rate, its value remains unchanged when exchange rates fluctuate; there is no risk of reporting a translation loss or gain.

With the temporal method gains and losses are reported only in respect of monetary items, because a translation difference is reported only on those items that are translated at the closing rate. Since, in the present example, their net value is negative (the loan liability is greater than the cash), a translation loss is reported. No translation gain is reported in respect of the plant and the inventory. With the closing rate method, a translation difference is reported on all assets and liabilities. Since the net worth is positive (assets exceed liabilities) a translation gain is reported.

21.8 THE CASE FOR THE TEMPORAL METHOD

In the authors' opinion, only the temporal method can be justified for use with historical cost accounting. The fundamental objection of the accounting theorist to the closing rate method under historical cost accounting can be stated very simply as follows. The closing rate method, when applied to an asset stated in the foreign subsidiary's balance sheet at historical cost, produces a translated figure which has no meaning (for example the value of $50mn for the plant in the 1977 balance sheet in Exhibit 21.3): it is not the historical cost in terms of the home currency;

neither is it the current replacement cost nor the net realizable value. 'The number is in fact nothing except the product of multiplying two unrelated numbers' (Lorensen, 1972, p. 107). The leading German theorist, Busse von Colbe (1993), makes the same point rather more politely: 'translation of historical costs, expressed in foreign currency, at the current rate does not result in a valuation that can be interpreted in any meaningful sense.' This fault of the closing rate method is so fundamental that, in the opinion of most serious accounting theorists, it makes the use of the method quite unacceptable.

A further objection to the closing rate method is that it is inconsistent with the method used to translate transactions (set out in section 21.3). This means that two enterprises with identical foreign assets will report different amounts for the translated values of these assets, where the first enterprise owns the assets through a foreign subsidiary whose accounts are translated using the closing rate method, and the second enterprise owns the assets directly. In the second case, as there is no separate foreign entity, there are no foreign currency accounts to be translated; the assets are recorded in the home enterprise's books of account using the procedure for translation of transactions. This difference between the two enterprises in the values reported for their foreign assets is difficult to justify.

21.9 THE CASE FOR THE CLOSING RATE METHOD

The proponents of the closing rate method claim that, in comparison with the temporal method, it provides a better representation of economic reality in two areas:

■ The parent's investment in the subsidiary
■ The subsidiary's income statement

21.9.1 The parent's investment in the subsidiary

A strong criticism of the temporal method is that the translation gain or loss reported in respect of a foreign subsidiary following a change in exchange rates will often not reflect the real economic position. Consider the example of the German subsidiary of an American corporation that was presented in Exhibit 21.3. During 1977 the German mark appreciated against the US dollar. This would lead one to expect that, as a result, the American corporation's German investment would be worth more in dollar terms. According to economic theory the value of an investment is the present value of future cash flows. If one makes the reasonably conservative assumption of no change in the subsidiary's future cash flows (as denominated in German marks), then there has been no change in the investment's German mark value and therefore an increase in its current US dollar value. However, with the temporal method, a loss is reported. The principal reason for this loss is that a translation loss is reported on foreign currency borrowings but no gain is reported on the assets acquired with the aid of these loans. Hence, following an appreciation of the foreign currency, translation losses will generally be reported in respect of foreign subsidiaries that have negative monetary assets, generally those that are financed through local loans. The very strong opposition of many American corporations to FAS 8 can be explained by the fact that they were obliged to report substantial losses on the foreign investments following the decline of the US dollar in the late 1970s, when they considered that in reality these investments had increased in value.

Hence it is claimed that the temporal method should not be used when the foreign subsidiary is largely independent of the parent and, in particular, when a large proportion of its assets are financed locally. In these circumstances, the parent's interest is limited to its net investment in the foreign subsidiary, that is the assets less the liabilities. This net investment should be translated at the closing rate, which can be achieved by translating all assets and liabilities at the closing rate. When this is done the reported translation gain does seem to reflect economic reality; for example in Exhibit 21.3, an appreciation of 19 per cent ($0.08 on $0.42) in the dollar value of the German mark leads to an equal appreciation of the dollar value of the American corporation's German investment ($4mn on $21mn).

21.9.2 The income statement

With the closing rate method every item in the foreign subsidiary's income statement is translated using the same rate. Generally this is the average rate for the period, although the closing rate is used in certain countries. The reason for using the average rate is that the elements of the income statement refer to the whole period and not just to the end of the period. As the same rate is used for all items, the translated income statement is a linear transformation of the foreign currency income statement so that ratios, such as the gross profit margin, are the same in both statements. More importantly, the translated profit is simply the foreign currency profit multiplied by the relevant exchange rate. Hence the translated income statement reflects faithfully the foreign currency income statement.

With the temporal method, most items of income and expense are translated at around the average rate but two items (depreciation and inventory used) are translated at historical rates (see section 21.6.1). The fact that different rates are used to translate different items means that the translated income statement is not a linear transformation of the foreign currency income statement. Hence ratios such as the gross profit margin can differ between the two statements which certainly can complicate the task of interpreting the foreign subsidiary's performance. A more serious problem concerns the figure for profit which, with the temporal method, is not translated directly but calculated as the difference between the translated revenues and the translated expenses. It is possible with the temporal method for a profit in the foreign currency accounts to be reported as a loss in the translated accounts (and vice versa). This can arise when a higher exchange rate is used to translate the depreciation expense than that used for the other elements of the income statement, as would happen when the foreign currency has fallen in value since the acquisition of the asset that is being depreciated. In this situation the interpretation of the subsidiary's performance is rendered even more problematic, as the two statements give conflicting messages. In fact one of the authors has demonstrated elsewhere (Flower, 2000) that, in this situation, both statements give a true and fair view for the persons to whom they are addressed: the translated figures give the correct picture for the shareholders of the parent enterprise and the foreign currency figures for the minority shareholders of the foreign enterprise. However the argument is complex and most commentators consider that it cannot be right for a profit to be translated as a loss and hence count this as a serious shortcoming of the temporal method.

21.10 THE VICTORY OF THE CLOSING RATE METHOD: FAS 52

The contest between the temporal method and the closing rate method was decided in favour of the closing rate method. In 1981 the FASB finally succumbed to the considerable pressure to which it had been subjected and withdrew FAS 8. In its place it issued FAS 52, which prescribed the closing rate method in most circumstances and the temporal method in other much more restricted circumstances. As the temporal method survived, the closing rate method's triumph was not a 'knockout' but rather a 'victory on points'; however it deserves to be described as a victory because, under the terms of FAS 52, the closing rate method was to be applied to the translation of the accounts of the vast majority of foreign entities.

The saga of FAS 8 is very revealing about the standard-setting process. It demonstrates the difficulties encountered by standard setters when confronted with the determined opposition of the preparers. In the end, the preparers through lobbying (not only of the FASB but also of its political masters) were able to secure the withdrawal of a standard to which they objected. These objections were based not on the principles on which the standard was based but rather on the numbers (for assets and profits) that resulted from the application of the standard. The preparers had no great knowledge of accounting theory but they certainly felt that the losses that they were obliged to report under FAS 8 were painful and irrational. There are two possible approaches to the development of accounting standards: the principles approach and the consensus approach. With the principles approach, the standard is developed by deductive reasoning from basic principles. With the consensus approach, the emphasis is on developing a standard that will be accepted by the financial community; it is of secondary importance whether or not it is based on sound principles. In developing FAS 8, the principles approach pre-dominated. The Lorensen study was essentially an exercise in deductive reasoning and the FASB accepted its conclusions mainly because its members were persuaded by its arguments. However the fate of FAS 8 demonstrates that it is not feasible to develop standards solely through the application of accounting principles; the 'principles approach' must be backed up by the 'consensus approach', otherwise those most affected by the standard will simply reject it.

21.11   IAS 21

Subsequently, in 1983, the IASC issued its own standard on translation, *IAS 21 The Effect of Changes in Foreign Exchange Rates*, which largely followed FAS 52. In effect the rest of the world had been waiting for the Americans to make up their minds. Given that the more general applicability of IASs, the present rules for the translation of financial statements will be outlined with reference to IAS 21 and not to FAS 52.

Foreign entities and integrated operations

IAS 21 specifies that the closing rate method should be used for the translation of the assets and liabilities of a foreign entity, which is defined as a foreign operation, the activities of which are not an integral part of those of the parent. Where the foreign operation is an integral part of the parent's operations, its financial statements are to be translated as if its transactions had been those of the parent, which means that the temporal method is to be used. Hence the translation method to be used depends on whether or not the foreign operation is classified as a foreign entity. IAS 21 gives a number of situations that indicate that a foreign operation is a foreign entity, whose accounts should be translated using the closing rate method:

- The foreign operation has a significant degree of autonomy from the parent
- Transactions with the parent are not a high proportion of the foreign operation's activities
- The foreign operation is mainly financed from its own operations and local borrowings
- Most of the foreign operation's expenses are paid in local currency
- The foreign operation's sales are mainly in currencies other than the parent's currency
- The parent's cash flows are largely insulated from the day-to-day activities of the foreign operation

The reason why IAS 21 prescribes the closing rate method for foreign entities in the above situations is connected with the concept of the parent's net investment in the subsidiary. Where the foreign entity is largely independent and autonomous, the parent's interest is in its net investment and not in the subsidiary's individual assets and liabilities. Translating this net investment at the closing rate gives the measure of its value that best reflects economic reality, as has already been analysed in section 21.9.1.

On the other hand, where the foreign operation is an integral part of the parent's operations, its assets and liabilities should be translated as if they had been acquired by the parent; this requires that they be translated using the temporal method which, as explained in section 21.6.1, is based on the same principles as the translation of transactions in the parent's accounts. The prohibition of the closing method in these circumstances is an appropriate response to the criticism of this method (set out in section 21.8) that it leads to different values being placed on foreign assets dependent on whether they are owned directly by the parent or through a subsidiary.

Hence the retention of two very different translation methods is based on logical reasoning in that each method is prescribed for the circumstances in which it leads to the more appropriate results. Nevertheless it is regrettable that complete uniformity could not be achieved. The two methods can give remarkably different results (as demonstrated in Exhibit 21.4) which can lead to an arbitrary element in reporting the financial performance of a foreign subsidiary that is on the border between the two categories defined in IAS 21.

The gain or loss on translation

IAS 21 took over with virtually no change FAS 52's rules on the accounting treatment of the gain or loss on translation. The loss or gain under the temporal method (used for integrated operations) is reported as an item of income or expense in the income statement. This was the rule in FAS 8 and follows the normal accounting principle that changes in the values of assets and liabilities are treated as elements of income.

However, for the gains and losses arising from the application of the closing rate method, IAS 21 (following FAS 52) prescribes a fundamentally different treatment. They are to be transferred directly to equity and not reported as elements of income. This treatment is similar to that prescribed for increases in the value of plant, property and equipment following a revaluation above cost, with the important difference that it applies to both gains and losses; that is that the amount reported as an element of equity may be negative. The effect is that the income statement does not report 'comprehensive income'; the fall in the value of equity resulting from the lower value of foreign assets is not reflected in current income.[6] This is contrary to the principle of prudence. Income can be overstated by building up debit balances in the balance sheet that do not represent genuine assets.

IAS 21 gives no reasons for not reporting these translation gains and losses in the income statement. FAS 52 gives two (contradictory) reasons:

- 'The translation adjustment reflects an economic effect of exchange rate changes . . . an unrealised component of comprehensive income . . . that should be reported separately from net income'
- The translation gain or loss is 'merely a mechanical by-product of the translation process'

The first reason recognizes that translation gains and losses are elements of income, which are however reported in a most peculiar way; since 1981 standard setters have found better ways to present the elements of comprehensive income that do not pass through the income statement, notably the Statement of Total Recognised Gains and Losses that is dealt with in Chapter 17. The second reason is, in the authors' opinion, completely invalid. Once an enterprise has decided to place certain values on its assets and liabilities (which it has no hesitation in reporting in its balance sheet as the correct values), it cannot deny that the gains and losses that arise automatically from this decision are real. To describe them as 'mechanical by-products' gives the impression that they represent nothing meaningful.

21.12 THE SOURCE OF REGULATION: LAWS, STANDARDS, RECOMMENDATIONS

Translation rules are a particularly good example of the different authoritative sources of accounting regulation to which multinational companies are subject.

In the USA the rules are set exclusively by a standard: FAS 52, which replaced FAS 8 in 1981 and has remained the effective standard since its introduction. FAS 52 was the inspiration for the IASB's standard, IAS 21, which was issued two years later.

In the European countries, there is considerable disparity as to both the source and the content of the rules. This reflects the neglect of the European Union; the only mention of foreign currency translation in the EC Directives is the requirement that a company should disclose the basis of any such translation (Fourth Directive Article 41, paragraph 1(1); Seventh Directive Article 34, paragraph 1). The fact that the issue is not covered in the EU Directives reflects the degree of disagreement over foreign currency reporting rules in Europe.

The UK followed the USA both in content and in time. It also adopted the same regulatory form – a standard issued by the Accounting Standards Committee (ASC). In fact, even though the ASC had issued several exposure drafts on the topic (ED 16, 1975; ED 21, 1977; ED 27, 1980), the definitive accounting standard, SSAP 20, was not issued until 1983, that is two years after FAS 52.

In contrast in France, the *Conseil National de la Comptabilité* (CNC) formulated the relevant regulations in the *Plan Comptable Général* (PCG). Hence, the rules governing foreign currency reporting have been given some authority. The regulations for foreign currency transactions were already established in the first PCG of 1947, re-affirmed in the PCG of 1957 and extended in the PCG of 1982. However it was not until the requirement for consolidation was incorporated in the 1986 amendment of the PCG that rules for the translation of foreign company accounts were introduced in France.

In Germany, the Commercial Law (Handelsgesetzbuch or HGB) regulates neither the reporting of foreign currency transactions nor the translation of foreign financial statements; the only provisions set out in the law are the EU disclosure requirements. Hence accounting for foreign currency transactions has developed solely on the basis of general principles, that is the German Grundsätze ordnungsmäßiger Buchführung (GoB). The main technical committee of the IdW (Instituts der Wirtschaftsprüfer) published a recommendation with respect to foreign currency reporting in 1977 which was revised in 1986. Since 1998, with the implementation of Article 292(a) into the HGB, German companies whose shares are listed on capital markets may under certain conditions apply IAS or US GAAP in their consolidated accounts.

In Japan the rules for the reporting of foreign currency transaction and financial statements are dealt with in the Accounting Principles for Business Enterprises (APBE). In October 1999, the BADC issued a revised standard on foreign currency translation which follows FAS 52 closely in that all translation gains and losses are to be reported as a separate component of equity and that the closing rate is to be used for all monetary items. The previous practice of Japanese enterprises had been to translate long-term monetary items at the historical rate (Takita and Yumoto, 1995).

21.13 COMPARATIVE COUNTRY ANALYSIS

The content and the application of the rules for foreign currency translation in practice in the selected countries will now be considered.

21.13.1 FOREIGN CURRENCY TRANSACTIONS

In all countries, a foreign currency transaction is initially recorded using the exchange rate ruling at the date that the foreign transaction is recognized. Subsequently, at the end of each accounting period, foreign payables and receivables are, in almost all countries, restated at the closing rate, whereupon translation differences will arise. Comparing the relevant regulatory positions across countries, it is clear that, whilst there is relatively little controversy concerning the exchange rate to be used to translate unsettled foreign currency accounts at the balance sheet date, there is considerable disagreement on whether and to what extent unrealized exchange gains and losses arising from such restatements should be included in the income statement. The differences in the accounting treatment of these gains and losses are based to a great extent on principles of accruals and prudence which differ in interpretation across countries. Nonetheless, as the global players increasingly adopt international accounting standards in their consolidated accounts, some change has occurred in recent years. As a result of the globalization of financial reporting, conservatism and prudence are slowly disappearing, even in Germany and Japan.

The exchange rate

As already explained in section 21.3.1, foreign currency payables and receivables at the balance sheet date may be translated at either the closing rate, the historical rate, or a combination of both. The rule of using the closing rate is followed in most countries, but not in Germany as is shown in the Exhibit 21.5.

In Germany, even though the HGB does not regulate the translation of foreign transactions and contains only a disclosure requirement, a generally accepted accounting principle has been established which applies the same valuation rules to foreign currency assets and liabilities as to balances that are denominated in national currency. In particular, the

Exhibit 21.5 *The exchange rate used to translate foreign receivables and payables*

Country	Closing rate	Lower of the historical rate or the closing rate
USA	X	
UK	X	
Germany		X
France	X	
Japan	X	
IAS 21	X	

general principles set out in the HGB (the historical cost principle, the realization principle and the prudence principle) require the accrual of unrealized losses but forbid the recognition of unrealized gains. Hence, assets denominated in a foreign currency are valued at the lower of the historical rate and the closing rate, whilst liabilities are valued at the higher of the two rates.

The accounting policy of prudence which was prevalent in German accounts in the past is illustrated by the following extracts from the 1993 annual reports of Daimler Benz and Henkel:

> Foreign currency receivables are translated in the individual financial statements at the bid price on the day they are recorded or at the spot rate on the balance sheet date if lower. Foreign currency payables are translated at the asked price on the day they are recorded or at the spot rate on the balance sheet date if higher. (Daimler Benz, 1993)

> Accounts receivable and payable in foreign currency are translated in the financial statements of individual companies at the rates of exchange in force when they first originated. If, however, translation of foreign currency items at the rate in force on the balance sheet date produces a lower amount for receivables or a higher amount for liabilities, then foreign currency items are translated at the rates in force on the balance sheet date, unless amounts receivable and payable in a particular currency balance each other out or the amounts involved are covered by forward exchange transactions. (Henkel, 1993)

Nonetheless, as has been described earlier, since 1998 German companies may use either IAS or US GAAP in their consolidated accounts and many in fact did so before that year.

It is interesting to note however, that, although many German multinational companies claim to follow internationally accepted accounting standards in their consolidated accounts, in many cases they do not comply fully with either IAS 21 or FAS 52. In fact, the following example of BASF demonstrates a compromise applying the international rules to short-term foreign currency payables and receivables only. Long-term foreign currency payables and receivables are accounted for in accordance with the original German rules:

> **Translation of foreign currency items:** The cost of assets acquired in foreign currencies as well as revenues from sales in foreign currencies are recorded at the rates on transaction dates. Short-term foreign currency receivables and liabilities are valued at the rate on the balance sheet date. Long-term foreign currency receivables are recorded at the rate prevailing on the acquisition date or at the lower rate on the balance sheet date. Long-term foreign currency liabilities are recorded at the rate prevailing on the acquisition date or at the higher rate on the balance sheet date. (Notes to the accounts, BASF, 1999)

In Japan, the previous rule whereby long term receivables and payables had to be translated at the historical rates has recently been modified. The present rule is that all monetary items are translated at the closing rate. Nissan still uses the old methods as is clear from the following extract from its 2000 annual report, on the translation of foreign currencies:

> **Receivables and payables denominated in foreign currencies:** Current and non-current receivables and payables in foreign currencies are principally translated at historical rates, except for those translated at contracted foreign exchange rates ... When fluctuations in foreign exchange rates are significant, the current exchange rate is applied to translation of both current and non-current receivables and payables denominated in foreign currency. (Nissan, 2000)

Exchange gains and losses

There is consensus in the rules covering all five countries that losses arising from the restatement of foreign debtors and creditors at the balance sheet date should be taken to income. In contrast, unrealized gains are not accounted for in the same way across countries. In fact, as shown in Exhibit 21.6, there are three different regulatory approaches to the recognition of gains on unsettled foreign balances. The recognition of unrealized currency gains as a profit in the income statement is required in the USA, the UK, Japan and in IAS 21. Conversely, the deferral of unrealized translation gains in the balance sheet is required in France. Finally, in Germany, unrealized foreign currency gains are not recognized at all, that is they are not taken into account, as the receivables (payables) continue to be valued at the lower (higher) historical exchange rate.

Exhibit 21.6   *The recognition of the translation gain on unsettled foreign receivables and payables*

Country	Gain taken to income	Gain deferred in the balance sheet	Gain not recognized
USA	X		
UK	X		
Germany			X
France		X	
Japan	X		
IAS 21	X		

Within the above categories, some differences exist with respect to the distinction between short term and long term monetary items. The IASB has changed its position on the issue of distinguishing between short term and long term transactions. Whilst the original IAS 21 (1983, paragraph 28) authorized the optional deferral not only of exchange gains but also of losses on long term transactions, this option was removed when the standard was revised in 1993.

In Japan, the previous rule was that losses on foreign currency loans could under certain circumstances be deferred over the life of the loan. This treatment will change as Japan moves to the IASB's rules, which will force Japanese companies to recognize all unrealized gains and losses in each period.

In the USA and the UK, the requirement to take unrealized gains to income applies to all such exchange gains. In contrast to the above, exchange differences on short term and long term transactions may be treated differently in France, as the PCG (p. II.13) indicates that, for foreign currency transactions covering more than one accounting period (opérations affectant plusieurs exercises), unrealized exchange losses may be deferred and amortized to maturity.

As is evident from the following example of Matra Hachette, French companies have used internationally accepted practice in their consolidated accounts since the early 1990s, although they have been given legal permission to do so only since 1997:

> Receivables and payables in foreign currencies are translated into the local currency of each company on the basis of year-end exchange rates. Unrealised gains and losses are credited or charged to income. However when a transaction in foreign currency is hedged, the contracted rate will be used. (Matra Hachette, 1993)

21.13.2 Foreign financial statements

Generally the rules at national level follow more or less closely those of IAS 21. The position in specific countries is as follows:

USA

IAS 21 was issued in 1983, two years after FAS 52, the current American standard, and in fact largely copied it. There are no major differences between the two standards; the principal differences are of terminology. For example FAS 52 invents the concept of 'functional currency' and requires that, for the consolidated accounts, a foreign subsidiary's accounts should be drawn up using its 'functional currency'. FAS 52 defines the functional currency to be the local (foreign) currency when the subsidiary's operations are relatively self-contained within a particular country; for these entities the use of the closing rate method is prescribed. The functional currency is the parent's currency when a foreign subsidiary is a 'direct and integral component or extension of the parent company's operations' and, in this case, the foreign currency accounts must be 'remeasured'. However, on closer inspection, 'remeasurement' turns out to be identical with the application of the temporal method. Hence, when FAS 52 is stripped of its confusing terminology, its rules turn out to be essentially the same as those of IAS 21. The division of foreign subsidiaries into two categories, with the closing rate method prescribed for one and the temporal method for the other, is common to FAS 52 and IAS 21.

All listed American corporations are required by the SEC to apply the rules of FAS 52. One example is the Ford Motor Company as is made clear from the following extract on foreign currency translation from its 1999 annual report:

> Assets and liabilities of non-US subsidiaries generally are translated to US dollars at end-of-period exchange rates. The effects of this translation for most non-US subsidiaries are reported in other comprehensive income. Remeasurement of assets and liabilities of non-US subsidiaries that use the US dollar as their functional currency are included in income as transaction gains and losses. Income statement elements of all non-US subsidiaries are translated to US dollars at average period exchange rates and are recognised as part of revenues, costs and expenses. (Ford Motor Company, 1999)

The Ford Motor Company uses the closing rate method for most non-US subsidiaries. For these the translation gains and losses are reported as other comprehensive income; that is, they do not pass through the income statement. Some non-US subsidiaries use the US dollar as their functional currency; their assets and liabilities are 'remeasured' – that is the temporal method is used. There is one anomaly in the above extract: the income statements of all non-US subsidiaries are translated at average rates – this is clearly incorrect for the translation of depreciation where the temporal method is used.

UK

The regulatory position in the UK's SSAP 20 is greatly influenced by IAS 21 and thus by FAS 52, as a similar choice is made between the closing rate method for independent subsidiaries and the temporal method for subsidiaries that are integrated into the parent company's operations. UK reporting practice generally follows the regulatory requirements, as is illustrated in this example:

(f) **Foreign currencies:** The results of overseas undertakings are translated into sterling at average rates. The exchange differences arising as a result of re-stating net assets to closing rate are dealt with as movements on reserves. (Notes to the accounts, Cadbury Schweppes, 1999)

The reference in the above note to 'dealt with as movements on reserves' is to the common practice of British companies of charging translation losses directly against retained earnings and not as an expense in the income statement.

France

Similarly, in France, the PCG requires the use of the closing rate method for independent subsidiaries and the 'historical rate method' for subsidiaries which are integrated into the parent operations. The 'historical rate method' is essentially the same as the temporal method. Renault applies these rules, as is evident form the following extract on the translation of the financial statements of foreign subsidiaries from its 1999 accounts:

a) In general, the financial statements of foreign subsidiaries are translated as follows:

Balance sheet items other than shareholders' equity are translated at the year-end rate of exchange;

Income statement items are translated at the average rate of exchange for the year;

The translation adjustment is included in consolidated shareholders' equity and has no impact on net income;

c) For foreign companies whose activities are an extension of the parent company's business, the historical-rate method is applied for non-monetary balance sheet items and the translation adjustment is included in net income. (Renault SA, 1999)

Japan

In Japan, until recently, companies used a variety of practices for translating the accounts of their foreign subsidiaries. This has changed as a result of the BADC's revised statement on foreign currency translation issued in 1999, which adopts the standard international practice using the closing rate (functional currency) approach. The new approach is illustrated in the following example.

All assets and liability accounts of foreign subsidiaries and affiliates are translated into Japanese yen at appropriate year end current rates and all income and expense accounts are translated at rates that approximate those prevailing at the time of the transactions. The resulting translation adjustments are included as a component of accumulated other comprehensive income. (Translation of foreign currencies, Toyota, 2000)

Germany

In Germany, prior to the recent move to international GAAP, there was no regulatory solution with respect to the translation of foreign financial statements and, in contrast to accounting for foreign transactions, there was no accepted convention. The IdW suggested in its revised proposal (1986) the use of the closing rate method and the temporal method, without however linking their use to the degree of integration of the foreign subsidiary into the parent undertaking. Furthermore a variety of 'modified' methods were prominent in practice. In 1995, Ordelheide (p. 1596) commented that 'the variety of methods used in practice impairs fundamentally the comparison between groups on the basis of their annual accounts, notably for quoted undertakings'.

The diversity which in the past existed in German consolidated statements in this area is illustrated by the following examples from the year 1993:

■ The functional currency approach, including a 'modified' temporal method reported by BASF, the modification consisting of inventory being translated at closing rate

■ A version of the temporal method where the translation difference is not recognized in the profit and loss account, as reported by Bayer

■ The use of the current/non-current method by Daimler Benz

In fact, translation methods are individualized by companies. For instance, Daimler Benz transfers translation differences to reserves and translates 'borrowed capital' (presumably long-term loans) at the current rate, which is not consistent with the current/non-current method. BASF translates inventories at the closing rate under the 'modified' temporal method. However the relevant note to the accounts remains silent on the treatment of the translation difference.

BASF

Currency translation was based on the principle of functional currency. Because of the low direct or indirect effect of the German mark on the trading operations of our subsidiaries and affiliates in North America, Japan and Korea, the local currency is to be regarded as the functional currency. The financial statements of these companies are converted to German marks as follows:

- all income and expense and the profit/loss, at quarterly average rates;
- all assets, liabilities and provisions at year-end current rates;
- the equity is carried forward at the rates at the date of payment or accumulation; the adjustment to the values converted at year end current rates is shown separately in the balance sheet as translation adjustment in the equity.

The other companies, whose business operations are more markedly influenced, directly or indirectly, by changes in the parity of the German mark, are converted in accordance with the modified temporal method. This also applies in principle to companies in high inflation countries, or if the financial statements are influenced by national regulations regarding inflation accounting. In these cases, the financial statements are converted to German Mark as follows:

- fixed assets, except loans, at rates in effect at the date of acquisition or production (historical rates);
- all other assets, liabilities and provisions at year end current rates;
- paid in capital at the rate at the date of payment or acquisition; the earned surplus is determined as a remaining balance in the balance sheets converted in accordance with these principles. (BASF, 1993)

Bayer

Foreign consolidated companies financial statements are translated into DM according to a temporal method which does not affect net income. Foreign currency translation is made as follows:

- fixed assets, intangibles, investment in affiliated companies and other securities included in investments at the average DM exchange rate in the year of addition (historical average rate);
- all other balance sheet items and net income at the year-end rate;
- all income and expenses at the weighted average rate for the year.

Bayer's portion of the adjustments resulting from the translation of foreign currency items in the balance sheet is included in capital reserves, while the minority stockholders' portions are included in minority interest. (Bayer, 1993)

Daimler Benz

The accounts of all foreign companies are translated to DM on the basis of historical exchange rates for non-current assets, and at the year end exchange rates for current assets, borrowed capital, and unappropriated profit. Stockholders' equity in DM is the remaining difference between translated assets less translated liabilities and unappropriated profit. The difference resulting from the translation of balance sheet items is recorded in consolidated retained earnings. Expense and income items are essentially translated at average annual exchange rates. To the extent that they relate to fixed assets (fixed asset depreciation, profit or loss from disposal of fixed assets), they are translated at historical cost. Net income, additions to retained earnings, and the unappropriated profit are translated at year end rates. The difference resulting from the translation of annual net income, between annual average rates and the exchange rate at the balance sheet date is reflected in other operating income. (Daimler Benz, 1993)

In recent years many German global players have moved to IAS or US GAAP in their consolidated accounts and the translation of foreign subsidiaries follows either IAS 21 or FAS 52 as is illustrated by the example of BASF in 1999, which makes specific reference to FAS 52.

The translation of foreign currency financial statements conforms with Statement of Financial Accounting Standards (SFAS) No. 52, Foreign Currency Translation.

The local currency is the functional currency of BASF subsidiaries and joint ventures in North America, Japan, Korea and China as well as for BASF's oil and gas operations in Argentina. The balance sheet items are translated into euros at year-end rates, and expenses and income at quarterly average rates. The effects of rate changes are shown as 'currency translation adjustments' and reported as a separate component of equity. This represents the difference between the company's equity calculated at historical rates and at year-end current rates.

The euro is the functional currency for all other consolidated subsidiaries and affiliated companies. The fixed assets, with the exception of loans, and paid-in equity are converted at rates on the date of acquisition at historical rates, and all other assets, liabilities and provisions at year-end current rates; retained earnings is determined as the remaining balance. Expenses and income are converted at quarterly average rates, except when they are derived from balance sheet items converted at historical rates. The changes in assets caused by translation are included in other operating expenses or income. (BASF, 1999)

The above note gives an exceptionally clear explanation of the closing rate and temporal methods. It even gives an intelligent explanation of the meaning of the accumulated translation differences that are reported as a separate item of equity under the closing rate method, as being 'the difference between the [subsidiary] company's [net] equity translated at historical rates and at year-end current rates'. In its 1999 consolidated balance sheet, BASF reports, as part of its equity, an amount of €549.3mn as 'Currency translation adjustments'; the amount is positive (a credit) which reflects the fact that over time the German currency has lost in value relative to other currencies. In 1999 BASF still translates inventory at the closing rate, even with the temporal method.

21.14 CONCLUDING REMARKS

This comparison of the regulations governing foreign currency reporting in France, Germany, Japan, the UK and the USA demonstrates the widespread consensus with respect to the use of the closing rate method to translate foreign financial statements in the consolidated accounts on the one hand and the diversity in accounting for foreign transactions in individual accounts on the other. With respect to the regulations concerning the recognition of unrealized exchange gains, countries could be divided into three groups – those which recognize unrealized exchange gains in income, those which defer them and those which do not recognize such gains. Moreover, at a detailed level, differing regulatory positions were observed with regard to short term and long term monetary items.

A key factor in the regulation of foreign currency reporting has been the harmonizing effect of FAS 52 and IAS 21 which have progressively gained acceptance throughout the world without the force of legislation. Market forces appear to have led to the widespread adoption of these standards by multinational companies. This was made possible by the lack of other international regulatory positions on this issue, particularly by the European Union. However, because of the linkage between accounting and taxation and because of the emphasis on prudence in many member states, the harmonizing influence of IAS 21 has been limited to consolidated accounts.

SUMMARY

The translation of transactions was analysed. The principal problem was found to be the choice between the historical rate and the closing rate for the translation of monetary items, which was traced to the conflict between the prudence principle and the accruals principle.

The translation of financial statements was examined in more detail concentrating on the two generally accepted methods: the temporal method and the closing rate method. The arguments for and against each method were analysed. The present consensus as set out in FAS 52 was described: the closing rate method is used for most subsidiaries and the temporal method only in exceptional circumstances. The rules and practice in the Pentad were examined with the aid of examples from published accounts.

Review questions

1. What is the meaning of the term 'translation' as used by accountants?

2. On 30 September 2000, a British company purchased a machine on credit from an American supplier for $1 000 000. At what exchange rate (historical or closing) should the British company report in its balance sheet at 31 December 2000, the cost of the machine and the amount still owing to the American company?

3. Explain why certain accountants prefer to translate certain monetary balances at the historical rate. Which balances and in which country?

4. Under the temporal method of translation, what rate (historical or closing) is used to translate the following items: plant reported in the foreign subsidiary's balance sheet at historical cost; plant reported in the foreign subsidiary's balance sheet at replacement cost; the depreciation of this plant reported in the subsidiary's income statement?

5. How is it possible with the temporal method that a profit reported in a subsidiary's income statement can be translated as a loss? Why is this not possible with the closing rate method?

6. What are IAS 21's basic rules for the translation of the financial statements of a foreign subsidiary?

Notes

1. In fact normally two rates are quoted on the market, one for selling marks and one for buying marks. However, if the average of the two rates is used, the difference will rarely be material.
2. An exception to the general rule of fluctuating exchange rates is when the countries in question are members of a monetary union, as is the case with the 11 European countries in the Euro zone.
3. It has been argued that accounts receivable and other monetary assets denominated in foreign currency should be translated at the future exchange rate, that is the rate that will apply when the asset is converted into (foreign) cash. However the use of the current rate is justified by two considerations: (a) the current rate is often the best available estimate of the future rate; (b) where a future rate is quoted on the market that is materially different from the current (or spot) rate, the difference between the two rates will normally be offset by differences in interest rates; that is interest rates will be lower for investments in a currency for which the forward rate is higher than the spot rate. In order for interest income and expense to be allocated to the correct period, monetary items should be translated at the current rate; otherwise an enterprise could report instant profits by investing in bills denominated in a currency for which the forward rate is higher than the current rate. This point is discussed in more detail in Flower (2000).
4. The exceptions relate principally to hedging which is dealt with in Chapter 22.
5. The world 'temporal' means 'pertaining to time'.
6. However, it may be reported as income in the long run, since IAS 21 requires that, on the disposal of a foreign entity, the cumulative amount of translation gains and losses relating to that entity should be recognized as income or expense in the same period in which the gain or loss on disposal is recognized.

References

Busse von Colbe, W 'Foreign currency translation', *International Group Accounting*, SJ Gray, AG Coenenberg and PD Gordon (eds), London, Routledge (1993), pp. 315–33.

Ebbers, G 'Foreign currency reporting in Europe: consensus and conflict', *Comparative Studies in Accounting Regulation in Europe*, J Flower and C Lefebvre (eds), Leuven, Acco (1997), pp. 313–42.

FASB 'Statement of Financial Accounting Standards No. 8: accounting for the translation of foreign currency transactions and foreign currency statements', Financial Accounting Standards Board, Stamford (1975).

FASB 'Statement of Financial Accounting Standards No. 52: foreign currency translation', Financial Accounting Standards Board, Stamford (1981).

Flower, J 'Foreign Currency Translation', *Comparative International Accounting*, C Nobes and RH Parker (eds), Pearson Education, Harlow (2000), pp. 338–69.

Gray, S, Coenenberg, A and Gordon, PD *International Group Accounting*, Routledge, London (1988).

ICAEW *Financial Reporting*, Institute of Chartered Accountants in England and Wales, London (1992).

Lorensen, L *Reporting foreign operations of U.S. companies in U.S. dollars*, American Institute of Certified Public Accountants, New York (1972).

Nobes, C 'A review of the translation debate', *Accounting and Business Research*, (Autumn 1980), pp. 421–3.

Ordelheide, D 'Germany – Group Accounts' in *Transnational Accounting*, D Ordelheide and KPMG (eds), London, Macmillan – now Palgrave (1995), pp. 1547–658.

Takita, T and Yumoto, K 'Japan – Individual Accounts', *Transnational Accounting*, 1st edn, Macmillan – now Palgrave, Basingstoke (1995).

Further reading

For a more detailed and theoretical treatment of the whole subject of this chapter see Flower (2000). For the temporal method versus closing rate method controversy, see Nobes (1980). For more detail of the practice in Europe, see Ebbers (1997).

chapter twenty-two

Financial Instruments

Chapter objectives

- To analyse the problems connected with accounting for financial assets and liabilities
- To set out the IASB's rules for the reporting of financial assets and liabilities in the balance sheet and income statement and for the analysis of risk in the notes
- To explain the characteristics of the three principal types of derivative (forward contracts, options and swaps) and to discuss how they should be reported in the accounts
- To explain the function of hedging and how to account for hedging operations
- To analyse the position concerning financial instruments in the five countries of the Pentad

The subject matter of this chapter is financial instruments. The term 'financial instrument' is used by the IASB to denote any contract that creates either a financial asset or a financial liability. Hence this chapter covers the reporting of financial assets and liabilities in the balance sheet, the reporting of income and gains relating to these items in the income statement and the disclosure of relevant information in the notes. Financial instruments have caused the IASB more problems than any other subject. Much of its recent time and effort has been taken up with the preparation of two IASs on financial instruments, which are among the most important, influential and controversial standards that the body has ever issued. This is the justification for devoting an entire chapter to the subject.

22.1 THE FABLE OF THE TWO INVESTMENT TRUSTS

The reporting of financial assets has been a controversial subject for decades. One of the first persons to tackle the subject was the American accountant, Kenneth MacNeal, whose book *Truth in Accounting*, published over half a century ago in 1939, was a fierce attack on the accounting methods of his day.[1] He recounted the fable of the two investment trusts, The American Trust and The National Trust, which both started with an initial capital of $1mn. The managers of both trusts invest their capital on the stock exchange in a wide range of shares and, as the stock market as a whole goes up by 20 per cent, at the end of the first year the market price of the investments of both trusts is $1 200 000. For both trusts, the interest on these investments is reinvested. At this point, the managers of the American Trust decide to realize the profits earned on their investments, which they do by selling them and reinvesting the proceeds in a similar range of shares. On the other hand the managers of the National Trust decide to hold on to their original investments.

Exhibit 22.1 presents the balance sheets and income statements for the two trusts drawn up in accordance with generally accepted accounting principles, notably stating investments at historical cost and reporting profits only when realized. At the end of the first year, the American Trust reports a profit of $230 000; the National Trust a profit of only $30 000. MacNeal points out that these accounts give a completely misleading picture, since in reality the position of the two trusts is identical; both own investments with a market value of $1 230 000.

Exhibit 22.1 *The fable of the two investment trusts*

	American Trust $	National Trust $
Income statement: year 1		
Interest	30 000	30 000
Gain on sale of investments	200 000	
Profit for year 1	230 000	30 000
Balance sheet: end of year 1		
Investments at cost	1 230 000	1 030 000
Income statement: year 2		
Interest	30 000	30 000
Gain on sale of investments		400 000
Profit for year 2	30 000	430 000
Balance sheet: end of year 2		
Investments at cost	1 260 000	1 460 000

MacNeal assumes that following the publication of these accounts, the market price of the American Trust's shares rises and that of the National Trust falls (as shareholders, disappointed with the low reported profits, sell their shares). The managers of these trusts (possessing inside knowledge of the real situation) sell some of their personal shareholdings in the American Trust and buy more shares in the National Trust. In the following year, it is the turn of the National Trust to realize the profits on its investments; it reports a record profit of $430 000, whereas the American Trust reports a disappointing profit of only $30 000. The market reacts to the reported profits in the same way as in the first year, marking up the price of the trust that reported the higher profit. The trust managers sell their shares in the National Trust (which they bought at a low price a year earlier) and buy shares in the American Trust (which are depressed by the reported low profits but which the managers plan to sell in a year's time when the trick will be repeated). The people who lose are the poor investors who buy and sell shares in the two trusts on the basis of financial reports that are completely misleading, or to quote the terms used by MacNeal in his highly polemical book, 'untruthful', 'deceptive', 'fallacious' and 'false'.

22.2 THE THREE BASIC PROBLEMS WITH FINANCIAL ASSETS

MacNeal's fable is of course simplistic and rather unrealistic. It seems unlikely that many investors would be fooled by the published accounts, particularly as, under the American rules of the time, the trusts would have been obliged to disclose the market values of their investments in a footnote. However the fable is a vivid illustration of the three problems that have dogged the reporting of financial assets for decades:

(a) **Historical cost versus market value:** On what valuation basis should financial assets be reported: historical cost or market value?

(b) **Realized versus unrealized profits:** Should reported profits be restricted to realized profits or should unrealized profits be included?

(c) **'Cherry-picking':** Where reported profits are restricted to realized profits, what can be done about 'cherry-picking' – the practice of management manipulating the reported profit by choosing which profits to realize.

The three problem areas will now be considered with an analysis of the IASB's standards.

22.3 THE IASC's SEARCH FOR A SOLUTION

As early as 1989, the IASC appreciated that it needed to overhaul its standards relating to financial instruments. However it has experienced great difficulties in achieving consensus on the subject. This can be attributed to the great diversity throughout the world in the methods used to report financial instruments. When the IASC attempted to impose a single valuation method throughout the world, it inevitably ran into opposition from countries where the IASC's preferred method conflicted with standard practice.

There are two principal valuation methods for financial instruments (fair value and historical cost) and the debate within the IASC has been essentially between the protagonists of the two methods.

The case for fair value

IAS 32 defines fair value as 'the amount for which an asset could be exchanged between knowledgeable willing parties in an arm's length transaction'. Hence, for an asset that is traded in an active market, fair value will generally be equal to market value. Many financial assets have a readily ascertainable fair value, for example, securities that are quoted on the stock exchange, including government securities and the shares of corporations. To pretend that the value of these investments is their historical cost is nonsense. The fair value principle could also be applied to liabilities. For example an enterprise issues €1 000 000 of long term debt, repayable at par in ten years' time, at the market interest rate of 12 per cent. Shortly afterwards, the market interest rate for this type of debt falls to 10 per cent. At the new rate of 10 per cent, the market value of the enterprise's debt is €1 122 891.[2] The proponents of fair value claim that, as the fair value of its liability has increased by €122 891, the enterprise has lost this amount; this is also the present value of the excess interest charge that the enterprise has to bear for the next ten years – it is having to pay €120 000 per year, when at the market rate it would have to pay only €100 000.[3]

The case for historical cost

The proponents of historical cost consider that it is inappropriate to report investments at fair value in cases where the enterprise has no immediate intention of realizing the asset. Where the fair value of an asset is above its historical cost, the profit (the increase in value) is unrealized and it would be imprudent to report it. Where the fair value is below the historical cost, some argue that the loss should be reported in accordance with the prudence principle but others argue that it is unnecessary to do so before the asset is sold or redeemed, because the fall in value may well reverse itself by then. If the enterprise intends to hold the asset until its maturity, it knows with a high degree of certainty how much it will eventually receive; the enterprise is unaffected by temporary fluctuations in value, and, to report the gains and losses that result from such temporary changes in the fair value of financial assets, would lead to large and quite misleading fluctuations in reported profits. Furthermore to apply the fair value principle to liabilities can lead to ridiculous results. For example, when an enterprise is in financial difficulties such that doubts arise as to its ability to repay its debts, the market value of its debt will generally fall. In such a case it is nonsense to claim that the enterprise has made a larger profit or a smaller loss because of the fall in the value of its debt.

In 1991 the IASC issued an exposure draft (E40) which proposed that all financial instruments be reported at fair value. This proposal was rejected by, among others, Japan and Germany because it was too much at variance with national law and practice. At the time Japanese banks were permitted to report loans to a customer at cost even when it was almost certain that the customer would be unable to repay the loan in full. In Germany, it was forbidden as imprudent to report financial assets at market value when this was above cost but it was required to value them at market when this was below cost. In 1994, the IASC issued a revised exposure draft (E48) which however also failed to secure a consensus. Cairns (1995) notes that, whereas the CONSOB, the Italian regulatory authority, opposed the use of fair value for the measurement of any financial asset, the SEC (the American regulatory authority) held that most marketable securities should be valued at fair value.

In view of the manifest lack of consensus on E48, the IASC decided to divide the task of developing appropriate rules into two phases: to start by tackling the issue of the disclosure and presentation and, only after agreement had been reached on these matters, to deal with the questions of recognition and measurement. The first phase was successfully completed in March 1995 with the issue of IAS 32. However, the IASC then ran into difficulties in gaining agreement on its proposals as to recognition and measurement, which was not surprising, given that they had a direct impact on the figures reported for assets and profits, which was not the case with its rules as to disclosure and presentation. In order to meet its immediate obligations to IOSCO, the IASC decided to issue a temporary stop-gap standard on the subject, which it did in 1999 with the issue of IAS 39.

22.4 THE IASB's RULES FOR FINANCIAL INSTRUMENTS

As mentioned in the previous section, the IASC issued two standards on financial instruments: *IAS 32 Financial Instruments: Disclosure and Presentation* in 1994 and *IAS 39 Financial Instruments: Recognition and Measurement* in 1999. When the IASB took office in April 2001, it adopted the IASC's standards as its own standards. Hence in the remainder of the chapter, IAS 32 and IAS 39 are referred to as standards of the IASB.

IAS 32 deals with two principal subjects:

- The classification of an item between equity and liabilities; the IASB's rules in this area have already been considered in section 16.7.3 of Chapter 16

- The disclosure of information relating to financial instruments, which is dealt with in this chapter alongside the rules of IAS 39

IAS 39 deals with the recognition and measurement of financial instruments. It was issued in March 1999 in a frantic last minute rush to meet the demand of the IOSCO for a comprehensive set of core standards. IAS 39 is very long and very detailed. However it is generally acknowledged that it does not represent a satisfactory solution to the problem. Its weaknesses include a number of compromises (obviously included in order to achieve agreement at the IASC Board) and a large number of arbitrary rules that deal with particular situations and transactions. Both shortcomings may be attributed to a lack of agreement on fundamental principles. The IASC accepted these criticisms, as it described IAS 39 as only an interim solution, and set up a high-powered working group to prepare a better standard. The group issued a discussion paper in December 2000, but the final report is not expected before 2001 and, given the difficulties that the IASC experienced in reaching agreement on IAS 39, it would seem possible that it will be many years before the goal of a completely satisfactory standard is achieved.

For the accounting student, IAS 39 is of only limited interest for two reasons:

- It is designed as an interim solution and may well be replaced in the near future

- Many of its provisions are based not on accounting principles, but on the need to reach a consensus

For these reasons, only a brief analysis is given of the standard, concentrating on its general provisions and ignoring completely its many detailed rules relating to particular transactions and situations. However two subjects are analysed in greater detail: derivatives and hedging.

22.4.1 Categories of financial assets and liabilities

The IASB's ultimate aim is for all financial assets and liabilities to be reported at fair value. If it had succeeded in 1999, it could have issued a very short standard that consisted of a single principal clause: 'all financial assets and liabilities are to be measured at fair value'.

With IAS 39, the IASB failed to achieve this aim, which explains the standard's extraordinary length and complexity. Thus much of the standard is taken up with specifying those financial assets that are to be reported at fair value and those to be reported at historical cost. IAS 39 defines five categories of financial asset:

- **Derivatives:** these are dealt with later in section 22.6
- **Financial assets held for trading:** these are assets acquired by the enterprise with the purpose of generating a short-term profit
- **Receivables and loans originated by the enterprise:** these are receivables arising from the enterprise's operations and loans made by enterprise
- **Held-to-maturity investments:** these are financial assets with fixed payments and a fixed maturity (redemption date) which the enterprise intends to hold to maturity
- **Available-for-sale financial assets:** This is a 'catch-all' category for all financial assets not covered by the other categories

However, in addition, the following very common financial assets are specifically excluded from IAS 39's rules, on the grounds that they are covered by other IASs:

- Investments in subsidiaries, joint ventures and associates
- Assets and liabilities arising from leases
- Assets and liabilities relating to pensions

Liabilities are divided into four categories:

- **Derivatives:** which are dealt with later in section 22.6
- **Financial liabilities held-for-trading:** this is a rather strange object as enterprises do not normally trade in liabilities (other then derivatives); IAS 39 gives as an example the liability arising from a short sale
- **All other financial liabilities:** these will generally constitute the greater part of an enterprise's liabilities
- **Non-financial liabilities:** these are not dealt with in IAS 39 but in IAS 37, which has already been covered in Chapter 16

The IASB's classification of financial assets and liabilities may be criticized on two grounds:

(a) **Complexity.** There are two criticisms: the number of different categories greatly complicates the accountant's task as each category has its own special rules; and the definitions themselves are highly detailed. The full definitions are not given above. In the standard they are much longer; for example the definition of a held-for-trading asset takes up ten lines plus a seven-line explanatory paragraph.

(b) **Management intent.** The definitions of two assets involve an assessment of management's intentions: a held-for-trading asset is one acquired for the purpose of trading; and a held-to-maturity asset is one that management intends to hold to maturity. This introduces a considerable element of subjectivity into the classification of assets and more importantly as to how they are measured, because, as will be explained shortly, the measurement rules are different for each category. IAS 39 attempts to counter this subjective element by including yet more rules; for example, 14 paragraphs (taking up four pages) are taken up with rules governing when assets may not be classified as held-to-maturity because management's intentions are rebutted by its actions.[4] This however only adds to the complexity of the standard.

22.4.2 Recognition of financial assets and liabilities

IAS 39's provisions as to recognition are very brief. A financial asset or financial liability should be recognized when the enterprise becomes a party to the contractual provisions of a financial instrument. There is no reference in IAS 39 to the two conditions for recognition set out in the IASB's Framework: reliability of measurement and probability of future economic benefits. The reason for their absence is connected with derivatives, which, as will be explained later, would often fail these tests. The IASB was determined that derivatives should be reported as assets and liabilities on the balance sheet and did not want to give enterprises any grounds for excluding them. In effect IAS 39 deals with both reliability of measurement and probability of future benefits as part of the measurement process.

22.4.3 Measurement of financial assets and liabilities

Initial measurement

On initial acquisition, all financial assets and financial liabilities are to be measured at cost, which is defined as the fair value of the consideration given (in the case of an asset) or received (in the case of a liability), including all transaction costs. This is a very reasonable rule, given that at the time of acquisition, cost and fair value are equal and will generally result in the asset being measured at the value of the outlays incurred to acquire it.

Subsequent measurement

After initial measurement, the amount at which a financial asset is reported in the balance sheet varies according to the category: the following assets are reported at fair value: derivatives, held-for-trading and available-for-sale; the remainder (that is held-to-maturity and receivables and loans originated by the enterprise) are valued at amortized historical cost. Financial liabilities are reported at amortized historical cost, except for derivatives and held-for-trading liabilities, which are reported at fair value. Exhibit 22.2 summarizes IAS 39's rules as to subsequent measurement.

It should be noted that the enterprise has no option: all the assets and liabilities in a particular category must be valued in the specified way. Hence the enterprise is obliged to report certain financial assets at fair value; historical cost is not an acceptable alternative, as is the case with those other assets which may, under certain IASs, be reported at fair value, notably plant, property and equipment and investment property. Thus IAS 39 represents a most significant weakening of the dominance of historical cost.

The IASB gives three reasons for not requiring fair value for two categories of assets:

(a) It would represent a significant change from the present practice in many countries. This refers to the need for achieve a three quarters majority at Board level.

(b) There is often a linkage between assets and liabilities. Under IAS 39 most liabilities are not reported at fair value. Many transactions

Exhibit 22.2 *Subsequent measurement of financial assets and liabilities*

Financial assets	
Derivatives	Fair value
Held-for-trading	Fair value
Receivables and loans originated by the enterprise	Amortized historical cost
Held-to-maturity	Amortized historical cost
Available-for-sale	Fair value
Financial liabilities	
Derivatives	Fair value
Held-for-trading	Fair value
All others	Amortized historical cost

involve combining a liability and a financial asset. If the asset were to be reported at fair value and the liability not, this might give a false picture of the effect of the transaction and of the enterprise's financial position.

(c) Some question the relevance of fair value for investments that the enterprise intends to hold to maturity. They claim that enterprise is unaffected by fluctuations in the fair value of assets that it has no intention to sell. This applies particularly to receivables and loans which the enterprise plans to hold to maturity and which are so designed as to yield a profit over their whole life.

However although, under the IASB's rules, certain categories of financial assets are not to be reported in the balance sheet at fair value, IAS 32 requires that the fair value of *all* financial assets be disclosed in the notes.

It is remarkable that the IASB was able to reach agreement on the disclosure of fair values in the notes but not on the measurement of assets at fair value in the balance sheet. According to the efficient market hypothesis, it should not make any difference to the market price of a corporation's shares where the information about fair values is presented – in the notes or on the face of the balance sheet. But CONSOB, the Italian capital market regulatory authority, is apparently willing to accept that fair values be disclosed in the notes but resists with all its force the IASB's proposal that financial assets be reported at fair value in the balance sheet. This phenomenon suggests that:

■ The efficient market hypothesis is wrong

■ CONSOB is wrong; or

■ An enterprise's consolidated accounts[5] serve other purposes than providing information for the capital market

Almost all financial liabilities are not reported at fair value. The reporting of liabilities is a highly controversial topic. The opponents of fair value use three arguments with which they have so far successfully resisted the proposals of the opposite camp:

■ It is imprudent to report a financial liability at less than the amount that the enterprise is legally obliged to pay

■ However it is misleading to report a liability at more than the legal amount when the enterprise is under no obligation to settle the debt in the immediate future

■ Where the market value of an enterprise's liabilities fall because it is in financial difficulties and doubts have arisen as to its ability to meet its commitments, it is nonsense to report an increase in the value of its equity

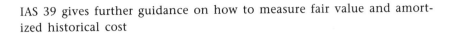

IAS 39 gives further guidance on how to measure fair value and amortized historical cost

Measurement of fair value

Fair value is defined as the amount at which the asset would be exchanged between knowledgeable, willing parties in an arm's length transaction. The best indication of fair value is the quoted market price. Therefore there are few problems in establishing fair value for listed securities and for many derivatives. Where a market price is not available, IAS 39 refers to a number of techniques including the use of a valuation model, such as an option pricing model, and discounted cash flow analysis. As mentioned earlier, IAS 39 does not make reliable measurement a condition for the recognition of a financial asset. It explicitly makes the presumption that fair value may be reliably determined for those financial assets that should be reported at fair value (derivatives, held-for-trading and available-for-sale) and points out that the IASB's Framework accepts the necessity of using estimates in the preparation of financial statements.

However, whether or not it is possible to make a reliable estimate of fair value is essentially a matter of fact, and in IAS 39 it is accepted that, where this is not possible, the asset should be reported at cost. The most common financial asset that would generally be reported at cost under this rule is an investment in the equity of an unquoted company that is not a subsidiary, joint venture or associate which are specifically excluded from the scope of IAS 39.

Amortized historical cost

The amortized historical cost of a financial asset is its acquisition cost adjusted for any repayments of principal, plus or minus the amortization of any difference between the acquisition cost and the amount receivable on maturity and minus any write-downs for impairment. The amortized historical cost of a financial asset should be calculated using the effective interest method, that is using the rate of interest that equates the asset's acquisition cost with the present value of its future cash flows.

Where the amount receivable on maturity is higher than the acquisition cost, the term 'amortized historical cost' is misleading for two reasons:

■ The 'amortization' is negative, in that it increases the asset's reported value

■ Hence the reported figure is higher than historical cost

This phenomenon is illustrated by the example presented in Exhibit 22.3. The investment's reported value at the end of the first, second and third year is increased by the 'amortization' of the redemption premium. The exhibit also illustrates the application of the 'effective interest method'. The amount of each year's amortization is so calculated that the total return on the investment in any year is equal to the internal rate of return of 10 per cent. Note that in the example the income in each year is 10 per cent of the reported value of the asset at the beginning of the year.

Most financial liabilities are also reported at 'amortized historical cost'. Here the term is most misleading, since with a liability there is not a cost but rather a receipt. However, provided that the reader can avoid being confused by the terminology, IAS 39's rules for liabilities that should be reported at 'amortized historical cost' are very straightforward: they are treated as negative held-to-maturity financial assets. For example, Exhibit 22.3 would demonstrate the reporting of a financial liability (with the same terms as the financial asset including an issue price of €825.92) if the debits and credits were reversed.

22.4.4 The income of financial assets

The income of financial assets clearly includes interest and dividends. IAS 18 Revenue provides that interest should be allocated to income on a time proportion basis but that dividends should only be recognized when the shareholders' legal right to the dividend is established. However the more difficult question is whether the increase or decrease in the carrying value of a financial asset should be reported in income or transferred directly to equity. There are four ways in which a financial asset's reported value (carrying value) may be changed:

(a) **Through a repayment of capital or the opposite (an additional outlay)** – these are clearly not income.

(b) **Through impairment.** Financial assets are subject to the same rules as to impairment as other assets (see Chapter 15). If a financial asset's carrying amount exceeds its recoverable amount, its reported value should be reduced to its recoverable amount. The amount of the reduction is always charged as an expense in the income statement. The most common reasons for a financial asset's value to be impaired are that doubts have arisen as to the ability of the other party to meet its commitments or that the economic situation has deteriorated.

(c) **Amortization of assets measured at amortized historical cost.** IAS 39 requires that the amount of the amortization should be reported as an item of income or expense in the income statement. It is universal practice to do this when amortization represents a decline in the asset's value. However when the amortization represents an increase

Exhibit 22.3 *Example of amortized historical cost*

On 1 January 2000, an enterprise buys a government bond with a par value of €1000. The bond pays interest of 3 per cent on the par value on 31 December in each year and is redeemable at par on 31 December 2002. The total costs of acquiring the bond including the transactions cost are €825.92.

The bond's future cash flows are:

31 December 2000	Interest receipt	€30
31 December 2001	Interest receipt	€30
31 December 2002	Interest receipt	€30
31 December 2002	Capital redemption	€1000

The present values of these cash flows at 1 January 2000 at various rates of interest is

8% 871.15
9% 848.12
10% 825.92
11% 804.50
12% 783.84

At the rate of interest of 10 per cent, the present value of the future cash flows is equal to the cost of the bond; therefore this is the effective rate of interest.

The accounts for the investment asset and the investment income over the three years are:

		Asset €	Income €
1 January 2000	Purchase of bond	825.92	
31 December 2000	Interest received		30.00
31 December 2000	Amortization	52.59	52.59
31 December 2000	Total	878.51	82.59
31 December 2001	Interest received		30.00
31 December 2001	Amortization	57.85	57.85
31 December 2001	Total	936.36	87.85
31 December 2002	Interest received		30.00
31 December 2002	Amortization	63.64	63.64
31 December 2002	Cash received on redemption	−1000.00	
31 December 2002	Total	0.00	93.64

(as in the example in Exhibit 22.3) to report it as income would seem to be problematical as it is clearly unrealized.

(d) **Change in the fair value of assets reported at fair value.** This matter is covered in IAS 39. For derivatives and held-for-trading assets, the change in fair value is always reported as an item of income or expense in the income statement. The IASB has no worries about reporting unrealized income, presumably because the fair value of these assets can generally be established with sufficient reliability. For available-for-sale assets, the enterprise has a choice between recognizing gains and losses in the income statement and reporting them as an element of equity. The same rule must be applied to all available-for-sale financial assets; the enterprise cannot 'cherry-pick'. This option is one of the most blatantly unsatisfactory compromises in IAS 39.

IAS 39's rules for the recognition of income and expenses relating to financial liabilities are essentially the same as those for financial assets.

22.4.5　Disclosure of financial assets and liabilities

Under IAS 32, enterprises are required to disclose a considerable amount of information in the notes to the accounts, including for each class of financial asset and liability:

- The fair value
- Significant terms and conditions that affect the amount, timing and certainty of future cash flows
- The accounting policies adopted

22.5　RISK ANALYSIS

Large parts of IAS 32 and IAS 39 are taken up with aspects of risk. There are three reasons why risk is such an important subject in connection with financial instruments:

- Financial assets and liabilities can be very risky. This has been amply demonstrated by the recent experience of many leading enterprises which have suffered very substantial losses connected with financial instruments.
- Certain financial instruments have been specifically developed to assist enterprises in managing risk. This is notably the case with derivatives.
- Some of the actions that enterprises take to mitigate risk give the accountant great problems in deciding how they should be reported in the financial statements. This is notably the case with hedging.

22.5.1 Risk categories

IAS 32 sets out a useful analysis of the risks associated with the enterprise's financial assets and liabilities; it classifies these risks as follows:

(a) **Price risk.** This is the risk that the fair value of a financial asset or liability may be different from what is expected. IAS 39 further divides price risk according to the reason for the change:

   (i) **Foreign currency risk.** This is the risk that fair value in domestic currency will alter as a result of a change in foreign exchange rates.

   (ii) **Interest rate risk.** This is the risk that the fair value of an asset or liability will be affected by a change in market interest rates.

   (iii) **Market risk.** This is a 'catch-all' category covering all other general reasons (that are not specific to the other party to the asset) why there may be a change in fair value, for example an economic recession.

(b) **Cash flow risk.** This is the risk that the future cash flows of the asset will be different from expected. Thus cash flow risk primarily affects the future cash flow statement (and income statement), whereas price risk primarily affects the balance sheet. The future cash flow may be different for the same three reasons as have been mentioned in connection with price risk. For most financial assets and liabilities, price risk and cash flow risk will tend to act in the same direction. If a future event were to have a negative effect on a financial asset's cash flow, it would also normally have a negative effect on its fair value. For example, where an enterprise owns a foreign bond, the translated amount of the bond's fair value and its future cash flows would be reduced by a fall in the exchange rate of the foreign currency in which the bond is denominated. However the analysis between price risk and cash flow risk is important for two reasons:

   (i) Depending on its circumstances, an enterprise may be more concerned about current fair values than future cash flows (or the opposite); for example an enterprise with insignificant current liabilities but with major commitments relating to payments in future years would be more interested in the cash flow risk.

   (ii) For certain financial assets, the effect of the different risks can be materially different; for example a change in market interest rates normally has little effect on the fair value of a floating rate loan but a great impact on its future cash flows. The opposite is the case with a fixed rate loan.

   With both price risk and cash flow risk, the impact of future events can be either favourable or unfavourable; the enterprise runs the risk of making an unexpected profit. With the remaining categories of risk identified in IAS 32, the emphasis is on the possible unfavourable impact of future events.

(c) **Credit risk.** This is the risk that the other party to a financial instrument will not meet his commitments.

(d) **Liquidity risk.** This is the risk that the enterprise may experience difficulty in raising the funds required to meet a future commitment associated with a financial instrument. Liquidity risk is essentially the reverse side of the coin of credit risk: one enterprise's liquidity risk is its counterparty's credit risk.

22.5.2 Disclosure of risks

Under IAS 32, enterprises are required to disclose a considerable amount of information about risks in the notes to the accounts, including:

(a) Its financial risk management objectives. The enterprise should disclose its policy in relation to risk – for example, whether it always takes deliberate action to reduce its exposure to certain specified types of risk, for example by using derivatives and hedging (see later sections), or alternatively its aim is to seek higher profits by actively accepting risks.

(b) Information that enables the reader to assess the enterprise's exposure to:

  (i) **Interest rate risk:** for example in respect of a loan its maturity date and whether the interest payable is a fixed or floating rate.
  (ii) **Credit risk:** the enterprise should disclose the maximum amount of its potential loss in the event that the other parties to financial instruments fail to perform their obligations.

22.6 DERIVATIVES

Derivatives are a class of financial instruments that have gained very considerably in importance in recent years. One function of a derivative is to transfer a specific risk from one party to another. Hence they are often used by enterprises to reduce particular types of risk. But they can also have the effect of increasing the enterprise's risks, either deliberately (the enterprise consciously seeks the possibility of a higher profit with the danger of a possible higher loss) or through their inappropriate use.

Derivatives normally consist of one of the three following types of financial instruments, used either alone or in combination:

■ Forward contracts
■ Options
■ Swaps

22.6.1 Forward contracts

A forward contract is an agreement to buy (or sell) a specified asset at a specified future date at a price fixed in the contract. Enterprises frequently enter into forward contracts to cover their foreign currency requirements. For example a British company may have contracted with an American corporation to buy a machine for $1 000 000, delivery and payment to be made in six months time. The British company is confronted with risk that the exchange rate of the British pound against the American dollar may change unfavourably in the next six months with the result that it may have to pay out more British pounds than originally expected. It can eliminate this risk by making a contract now with its bank to buy $1 000 000 in six months time at a fixed exchange rate, say $1 = £0.60. In this way, the British company gains certainty as to the amount in British pounds that it will have to pay out in six months time, that is £600 000. When, as in the above example, the asset referred to in the forward contract is a financial asset, the contract is a financial instrument and gives rise to a financial asset (or possibly a financial liability) in the balance sheets of the contracting enterprises (the British company and its bank).

However the original contract to buy the machine is not considered to be a financial instrument, even though it creates an obligation to deliver cash in six months' time. The reason is that the present accounting practice does not recognize the rights and obligations under contracts where both parties still have to perform their obligations. Such contracts are known as 'executory contracts'; they are said to be 'equally proportionately unperformed'. Since both the American supplier still has to deliver the machine and the British company still has to pay for the machine, these obligations are not recognized in the accounts of either party. In effect the rule in IAS 39 that a forward contract for a financial asset is itself a financial asset or liability is an exception to this general rule. The reason would seem to be that, where the object of the contract is a financial asset, the obligation can be measured in monetary terms with greater certainty and should be recognized as a financial asset or liability; however, where the contract provides for the future acquisition of a non-monetary item, such as a machine, it should not be recognized as creating assets and liabilities. This distinction cannot be justified on theoretical grounds. In effect the failure of the present financial reporting model to deal adequately with executory contracts is one of its most glaring theoretical weaknesses. With financial instruments, the weakness becomes so obvious that the IASB is obliged to resort to *ad hoc* rules.

Certain institutions, such as the Chicago Board of Trade, offer forward contracts for standard quantities and standard qualities of commodities, such as wheat and oil seeds. Such contracts are known as 'futures'. Although in principal they constitute a contract for the delivery of goods, in practice they are almost always settled in cash by the payment by one party to the other of the difference between the forward price and the current price at the time that the contract is terminated. Such contracts are often used for speculation and, for this reason, the IASB makes an exception to its general rules that an executory contract for goods is not a financial instrument. Forward commodity contracts are to be treated as financial instruments, unless it can be clearly demonstrated that they serve the enterprise's normal operating needs.

22.6.2 Options

An option is a contract that gives one of the parties, in return for a consideration, the right but not the obligation to buy (or alternatively to sell) an asset at a future date at a price fixed in the contract, known as the 'exercise price' or 'strike price'. Where the contract gives the right to buy, it is known as a 'call option'; where it gives the right to sell, it is a 'put option'. The difference between an option and a forward contract is that with an option there is no obligation on the part of the buyer of the option to go through with the purchase or sale. In fact if, at the future date, the market price is such that it would be more favourable to buy or sell the asset on the market rather than at the price fixed in the contract, it would not be rational to exercise the option which therefore lapses. Where the asset referred to in the option contract is a financial asset, the option is a financial instrument which gives rise to financial assets and financial liabilities.

Options are often used to reduce risks. For example the British company in the previous example could cover the risk of having to pay more pounds than expected in six months time by purchasing a call option for $1 000 000 with the exercise price of $1 = £0.60. If, in six months time, the exchange rate is higher than the exercise price (say $1 = £0.70), the British company will exercise the option and buy $1 000 000 for £600 000. If the exchange rate is less than the exercise price, the British company will not exercise the option but will instead buy the necessary dollars at the market rate.

Although both forward contracts and options are used to manage risks, there are two important differences between them:

(a) With a forward contract, all the covered risk is removed – in the example the foreign currency risk. The British company can be sure

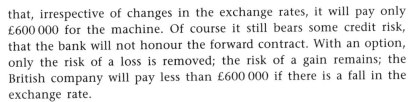

that, irrespective of changes in the exchange rates, it will pay only £600 000 for the machine. Of course it still bears some credit risk, that the bank will not honour the forward contract. With an option, only the risk of a loss is removed; the risk of a gain remains; the British company will pay less than £600 000 if there is a fall in the exchange rate.

(b) An option costs money, whereas typically a forward contract does not involve an outlay by either party at the time the contract is signed. In simple terms, it is not possible to transfer to another party only the risks of a loss, without compensating it for bearing these risks.

22.6.3 Swaps

A swap is a contract whereby two parties exchange certain financial rights and obligations. Swaps are commonly used to exchange patterns of interest rates. Thus an enterprise with an obligation to pay a fixed rate of interest on a loan may use a swap contract to convert it to a variable rate, defined with reference to a published market rate. Under the swap contract, it would receive the fixed rate and pay the market rate; the receipt of the fixed rate interest would offset its own obligation to pay the fixed rate on its loan. In effect, it has converted its debt into a floating rate loan. In principle, there is no difference between a swap and a forward contract. Generally swaps are for a series of cash flows and are therefore the equivalent of a series of forward contracts.

22.6.4 The meaning of the term 'derivative'

In principal forward contracts, options and swaps can relate to any object such as a machine, a building or merchandize. However IAS 39 uses the term 'derivative' for these contracts (and its rules apply) only when:

- The object of the contract is a financial asset (such as foreign currency, a share or a bond), or a rate or index related to financial assets (such as an interest rate or a share index) and/or
- The parties do not intend that there should be delivery of the items specified in the contract but instead that the contract should be settled by a payment in cash from one party to the other

Most derivatives meet both the above conditions, but it is necessary to fulfil only one. Thus a forward contract to purchase foreign currency needed by the enterprise fulfils only the first condition and a commodity future only the second.

The term 'derivative' refers to the characteristic of these contracts that their value depends on the value of the object of the contract. Thus, as will be demonstrated later, the value of a forward contract for the purchase of foreign currency depends on the foreign exchange rate at any particular time. Its value is 'derived' from the foreign exchange rate.

Many derivatives are traded on the market. This is notably the case with the derivative contracts offered by institutions such as brokers and banks which use standard terms and quantities. For these traded derivatives it is very easy to establish the market price. However it is possible to tailor a contract to the specific needs of the parties, for example the forward contract for the trader who requires $1 000 000 on 17 March 2001. It is difficult to sell these contracts once they have been signed as it is necessary to find someone with the same needs. However it is relatively easy to establish a fair value at any time, provided that the object of the contract has an observable market value.

22.6.5 The importance of derivatives

Derivatives have become important because of recent changes in financial markets, in financing techniques and in the practice of enterprises. Market operators now offer a whole range of derivatives (forward contracts, options and so on) which enterprises can use to modify their financial risks, either to reduce their exposure to a particular risk (that is to reduce the probability of making either a large profit or a large loss) or conversely to speculate (so as to increase the expected profit at the cost of increasing any possible loss). Most large multinational enterprises now make considerable use of derivatives, and the profits (and losses) arising from this use are a significant element in their income statement. In many cases they are larger than the profits earned from the enterprise's primary operating activities. In some cases the losses incurred on financial instruments have been so large that they have threatened the very existence of the enterprise. The most well-known example is Barings, the British merchant bank, which collapsed in April 1995 as a result of losses of over £800mn incurred in derivatives trading by its Singapore office.

22.6.6 The inadequacy of present financial reporting techniques

Baring's accounts gave not the slightest hint of the impending disaster, which gave rise to concerns that the rules for reporting financial instruments were inadequate. The position is put very neatly in a recent IASC discussion paper:

Existing accounting practices have been founded on principles developed to meet the needs of a time when the primary focus of accounting was on manufacturing companies that combined inputs (materials, labour, plant and equipment and various types of overheads) to be transformed into outputs (goods or services) that are sold. The accounting for the revenue-generating processes is concerned primarily with principles for recognising and accruing costs to be matched with revenues. . . . The accounting for financial instruments was not a major concern until recent years. When realisation and cost-based matching principles were developed, the financial instruments of normal commercial enterprises consisted of simple receivables, payables and debt. . . . However the world of financial instruments has since undergone fundamental change. The traditional realisation and cost-based measurement concepts considered appropriate accounting for productive revenue-generating activities are no longer appropriate for the recognition and measurement of financial instruments used in active financial risk management (IASC, 1997)

The problems involved in the financial reporting of financial assets and liabilities have never been satisfactorily resolved; thus there is no consensus on whether the valuation of financial investments should be based on historical cost or on future benefits. However this lack of a solid theoretical basis began to cause serious problems only recently with the growth in the use of complex financial instruments, particularly derivatives.

A major problem with the financial reporting of derivatives is that the amount reported in the accounts using traditional accrual accounting methods may give a very false picture of the asset or liability. This is particularly the case with forward contracts and options. Consider the previous example just given of a British company which made a contract with its bank to buy $1 000 000 in six months time. The value of the right and obligation to buy $1 000 000 for £600 000 depends crucially on the market exchange rate. If, at the end of the six months, the exchange rate has risen to $1 = £0.80, then the contractual rights are worth £200 000. The contract holder can acquire $1 000 000 for an outlay of £600 000; without the contract, she would have to pay £800 000. If, on the other hand, the exchange rate had fallen to $1 = £0.50, then the contract has a negative value of £100 000; the contract holder is obliged to purchase $1 000 000 for £600 000 when, without the contract, she need pay only £500 000. Exhibit 22.4 demonstrates how the value of the contract varies with exchange rate. With forward contracts for foreign currency, the rate specified in the contract is commonly very close to the current exchange rate at the time the contract is signed; this will typically be the case when there is no consensus in the market as to whether the exchange rate will rise or fall in the future, so that the current exchange rate is the best estimate of the future exchange rate.[6] In this case, the value of the contract at its inception is zero; this is the value given in Exhibit 22.4 for the case where the contract rate equals the current rate. Since, at the beginning, the value of the contract is zero, nothing is reported in the accounts – the contract is invisible! However over time, as exchange rates fluctuate, the contract will take on a positive or a negative value. For example, if, after three months, the exchange rate has fallen to $1 = £0.55, the company can expect to lose £50 000 on the contract. If the company were to draw up a balance sheet at that date, it would be misleading to value the contract at its initial value of zero. At the very least the reader of the accounts should be informed of the company's obligation to buy in three months time $1 000 000 at above the current rate.

The reporting of options raises very much the same issues as the reporting of forward contracts; the principal difference is that the value of an option can never be negative, as is demonstrated in Exhibit 22.4 which gives the value to the British company of its option to buy $1 000 000 at the exercise price of $1 = £0.60. This is the value of the option if it were to be exercised immediately; this is known as the intrinsic value of the option. However, when there is still some time before the option expires, its value will be higher than its intrinsic value. For example, when the exercise price is equal to the current market price ($1 = £0.60 in Exhibit 22.4), the intrinsic value of the option is zero but the option is not valueless, because it offers the holder the possibility of benefiting

Exhibit 22.4   *Value of the forward foreign exchange contract and of the option*

Current exchange rate ($1 = £)	Value of the forward contract to the British company (£)	Intrinsic value of the option to the British company (£)
0.40	(200 000)	0
0.45	(150 000)	0
0.50	(100 000)	0
0.55	(50 000)	0
0.60	0	0
0.65	50 000	50 000
0.70	100 000	100 000
0.75	150 000	150 000
0.80	200 000	200 000

from future changes in the exchange rate with no possibility of suffering a loss. The difference between the total value of an option and its intrinsic value is known as the time value, because it can only exist if there is still some time for the rate to change before the option expires. In Exhibit 22.4, only the intrinsic value of the option is included. The time value of the option has been ignored.

A second major problem with derivatives is that their value can fluctuate very considerably over time and in particular can vary within a very short period from being positive to negative and even extremely negative. They may also be highly geared; the possibility of a large profit can be obtained for a small outlay, but unfortunately it is coupled with the possibility of a large loss. These problems are illustrated with the example given in Exhibit 22.5. There are three important lessons in this example:

- The final loss is very large. In fact, since there is no limit to the future share price, there is no limit to the potential loss.
- The initial outlay was zero. Even, if in practice there is a small initial cost, it is tiny compared to the loss.
- The value of the derivative fluctuates from positive (when the current share price is below €100) to negative (when the current share price is above €100) in a very short time and the fluctuations in the derivative's value (which varied from €1 000 000 profit to €2 000 000 loss) are much greater than those of the underlying asset (from €90 to €120).

Exhibit 22.5 *How to lose your shirt with a short sale*

A speculator considers that the market price of the shares of the XYZ Corp are overvalued and are sure to fall over the next month. He therefore enters into a forward contract to sell 100 000 shares in one month's time at the current market price of €100 per share. It is generally possible to make such a contract with a broker without making any payment at the outset, provided that one can offer security to cover any losses on the contract. The speculator does not own any shares in the XYZ Corp but hopes to make a profit when the contract terminates in one month when he expects to be able to buy XYZ's shares at less than €100. His expected profit is 100 000 × (100 − expected share price). In fact the speculator is mistaken. Initially the price falls to 90 and the speculator anticipates a profit of €1 000 000. However at the last minute there is an unexpected take-over bid which leads to the price jumping to 120. The expected profit turns out to be a loss of €2 000 000!

22.6.7 The IASB's rules for derivatives

The measurement of derivatives

The rules of IAS 39 for the measurement of derivatives are very simple: they should be reported in the balance sheet at fair value and all changes in fair value are reported as income or expense in the income statement. In this way, the 'invisibility' of derivatives that was remarked on in the previous section is removed. In fact, in IAS 39, there are only two major problems with derivatives:

(a) **No fair value.** For many derivatives the determination of fair value presents no problems; either they are traded on an active market or their value is a function of a market value (as in the case of a forward foreign currency contract). However there is one derivative, whose fair value is often difficult to establish: an option to buy a share in an unquoted corporation.

(b) **Derivatives used for hedging.** The whole subject of hedging is dealt with in the next section.

Disclosure of derivatives

However reporting derivatives at fair value does not solve the problem that derivatives can represent a very large potential loss, even though their current fair value is positive, as was illustrated by the example in Exhibit 22.5. There is no magic solution to this problem. It is not the function of the accountant to tell the enterprise what contracts to enter into but to report faithfully the effect of these contracts. However, when at the balance sheet date the risk of a loss on the derivative lies entirely in the future, it is clear that this risk cannot be reflected in the values reported in the balance sheet. The most that can be done to warn users of the potential risks is to provide further information in the notes. Hence there is a general requirement in IAS 32 that, for each class of financial asset and liability, the enterprise should disclose information about the extent and nature of the financial instruments, including significant terms and conditions that may affect the amount, timing and certainly of future cash flows. This applies even to items that are not recognized in the balance sheet, for example a derivative whose fair value at that date was zero.

22.7 HEDGING

22.7.1 What is 'hedging'

'Hedging' is a term used in business and economics to denote any action of an enterprise that reduces its risk.[7] The term 'hedging' is thought to have originated in the practice of gamblers seeking to preserve a potential gain by erecting a defensive wall or 'hedge' around it by means of a defensive bet, as is illustrated in the following example.

A professional book-maker has taken a number of the bets on the outcome of the Manchester United *versus* Barcelona football match. Just before the match, he calculates that, if Manchester United wins, he will make a profit of €1000 and, if Barcelona wins, he will make a loss of €200. Since he is risk averse (he makes a living by relying on other people being prepared to take risks), he seeks to eliminate the possibility of a loss. He does this by himself making a bet with another bookmaker that Barcelona will win: he pays €500 and will receive €1200 if Barcelona wins and nothing if it loses. In fact he is a Manchester United fan and is sure that his team will win. But he does not let his personal feelings interfere with his business decisions. With this bet, the book-maker has ensured that, whichever team wins, he will make a profit of €500. He has successfully eliminated all risk, except for the credit risk that the other book-maker will not honour his contract.

The following are examples of hedging in business:

Example one

A French corn merchant has a stock of 1000 tonnes of wheat which he purchased some months ago at a price of €500 per ton. The present market price is €600 per ton but the merchant considers that it will probably fall in the future. To guard against this loss, he buys a two-month put option for 1000 tonnes with an exercise price of €600.

Example two

A Japanese airline has placed a firm order for a new aircraft to be delivered next year at a price of $5 000 000. It is concerned that in the interim the $/¥ exchange rate will change unfavourably and therefore makes a forward contract for the purchase of $5 000 000.

Example three

A British airline uses 100 000 litres of aviation fuel a month. Its operating margin is very much affected by changes in the price of fuel. If fuel prices were to rise, it would seek to increase its ticket prices but there would be a delay of three months before the new ticket prices would take effect, leading to a three-month period of reduced operating margins. To guard against this the airline buys three fuel futures contracts of 100 000 litres. If the fuel price goes up, the profit on the future contract will offset the increased cost of the fuel purchased and vice versa for a fall in the price of fuel. In effect the airline fixes the price of fuel over the next three months.

All the above examples have the following common characteristics:

■ The enterprise is concerned about the possible negative consequences of an uncertain future event, which may affect the value either of an existing asset or liability (in Example one) or of a future cash flow (Examples two and three). These items (the asset, liability or cash flows) are exposed to risk.

■ To protect itself against possible loss, the enterprise enters a contract that will yield an offsetting benefit if the outcome of the future event is negative. Using the IASB's terminology, the contract is a 'hedging instrument' and the item whose risk exposure is reduced as a result is the 'hedged item'.

22.7.2 The problems for financial reporting

Hedging causes problems for the accountant because in many cases the standard rules and conventions that she follows do not lead to a realistic presentation of the enterprise's financial position and profits.

This problem may be illustrated with the aid of the example of the French corn merchant. He holds an inventory of 1000 tonnes, purchased some months ago at a price of €500 per ton and is concerned that in the future the price of wheat will fall from its present level of €600 per ton; therefore to counter this risk he buys a two-month put option to sell 1000 tonnes at an exercise price of €600. The hedged item is the inventory of wheat and the option contract is the hedging instrument. Assume that the option was bought on 1 December 2000, the accounts year end is 31 December 2000 and at that date the price of wheat has fallen to €550 per ton and the option has not been exercised. At 31 December 2000 the option has a value of approximately €50 000;[8] the option holder has the right to sell 1000 tonnes of wheat for €600 per ton which he can buy on the market for €550 per ton. In his accounts drawn up on 31 December 2000 the corn merchant would report a profit on the option (which is reported at fair value) but no loss on the wheat, whose reported value (historical cost of €500 per ton) is unaffected by the fall in price from €600 to €550. In effect, he reports a profit on the hedging operation, when in reality he has made neither a profit nor a loss: the profit on the option is offset by the loss on the market value of the wheat. The effect of the fall in the price of wheat in December 2000 is not reported in the accounts until the wheat is finally sold in 2001.

Similar problem arises with the other examples quoted in the previous section.

- **The Japanese airline.** Any change in the $/¥ exchange rate will lead to a profit or loss being reported on the forward contract, but, as the commitment to purchase the aircraft is not recognized in the accounts, there is nothing against which it can be offset until the aircraft is actually purchased.

- **The British airline.** If the price of fuel falls, there will an immediate recognized loss on the futures contract but no offsetting profit until the fuel is consumed in the airline's operations.

In all the above cases, the problem is that the gains and losses on the different sides of a hedging operation (the hedging instrument and the hedged item) are reported in different periods, whereas they should be reported concurrently.

22.7.3   Why conventional accounting gets it wrong

In the above examples, the reason why the profits are not reported concurrently is because there is a mismatch between the accounting rules used for the hedged item and those used for the hedging instrument. The mismatch may relate to the valuation rules or to the recognition rules.

(a) **Mismatch in valuation rules.** This occurs with example one. In example one the asset, the inventory of wheat is valued at historical cost and the hedging instrument (the option) at fair value. A similar problem can occur with liabilities.

(b) **Mismatch in recognition criteria.** This occurs in the other examples. In example two conventional accounting rules do not recognize the commitment to purchase the aircraft as creating an asset or liability; the transaction is only recognized in the accounts when the aircraft is delivered. In Example three, the accountant can think of no way in which she can recognize in this year's accounts, transactions that will take place wholly in the following year.

22.7.4   Possible solutions

It is generally recognized that in at least some of the examples given above, the figures reported by the strict application of the present accounting rules and conventions do not properly represent the results of the hedging operation.

There are three possible ways in which accounting practice may be changed so as to ensure that hedges are reported more realistically:

(a) **Change the valuation rules.** This would solve the problem where the hedged item is an asset or liability. If all assets and liabilities were to be reported at fair value, then the problems identified in Example One would not arise. The French corn merchant's inventory of wheat would be valued at market; during December 2000, he would report a loss on the inventory which would offset the profit on the option.

(b) **Change the recognition criteria.** If the recognition criteria were changed to recognize executory contracts for tangible assets, then in Example Two the change in the liability to the aircraft manufacturer would offset any change in the value of the forward contract. This would not be an enormous change in accounting practice, as recognition would still be based on a transaction: the contract with the aircraft manufacturer. However, with Example Three, the transactions lie entirely in the future and cannot be captured by the present transactions based accounting model.

(c) **Defer the loss or gain.** Any loss or gain that arises from a hedged transaction is not reported as such until the compensating loss or gain is also recognized. Instead it is deferred and carried forward in the balance sheet.

In fact, accounting practice has almost universally adopted method (c) (deferral) as being the lesser of the three evils. Reporting all assets and liabilities at fair value is too big a change for most accountants to accept. The same is true for the general recognition of executory contracts and, as already mentioned, accountants can see no way of recognizing future planned transactions in the current accounts.

However, deferral accounting is by no means an ideal solution to the problem of hedging as it creates new problems, notably:

(a) **How to report the deferral in the balance sheet.** A common practice is to adjust the reported value of the hedged item by the amount of the deferred gain or loss. In Example One the profit on the option is deducted from the cost of the inventory. In the other examples there is no asset or liability whose reported value may be adjusted. Therefore it is necessary to include an item deferred gain/loss in the balance sheet. However both practices creates further problems.

(b) **Is a deferred loss an asset?** Where the deferred loss has to be reported as a separate item, the question arises whether it may properly considered to be an asset. It would certainly not appear to fulfil the IASB's Framework's definition. Exactly the same considerations apply to a deferred gain. There is no present obligation attaching to the liability that represents a deferred gain.

(c) **Proper valuation of assets.** Where the reported value of the asset or liability is adjusted for the amount of the deferred gain or loss, is it being reported according to the general rules; for example is the inventory in Example One being reported at the lower or cost or market? The answer is surely no. Hedge accounting deliberately suspends or bends the rules so as to achieve a desired result. However this only leads to another problem.

(d) **Different valuations for identical assets.** Where an enterprise owns two identical assets, one of which it has hedged and one not, it will report these two assets at different values. For example, if the French corn merchant had bought an option for only 500 tonnes of wheat, he would report one half of his inventory at a different figure from the other half. This does not seem justified.

22.7.5 The IASB's rules for hedges

No less than 45 paragraphs of IAS 39 are taken up with setting out the IASB's rules for hedge accounting, which is a vivid indication of the problems that hedging causes accountants. Since IAS 39 is intended to be an interim standard, only a summary of these rules will be given here. In broad terms, the approach of IAS 39 is to distinguish between value hedges and cash flow hedges.

(a) **Value hedge.** A value hedge is one designed to protect the value of an asset or liability reported in the balance sheet. The gain or loss on the hedging instrument should be offset against the reported value of the hedged asset or liability.

(b) **Cash flow hedge.** In a cash flow hedge, the hedged item can be either an unrecognized future commitment (as in Example Two) or a future transaction without a commitment (as in Example Three) provided that it is highly probable. The loss or gain on the hedging instrument is reported as an element of equity in the balance sheet and in the statement of total recognized gains and losses or the statement of changes in equity (see Chapter 16). It is taken out of equity when the future transaction takes place. In effect the IASB accepts that the deferred gain or loss is not a liability or an asset, but has to resort to the unsatisfactory device of a direct transfer to equity, which has the effect that the income statement does not report comprehensive income.

IAS 39 includes numerous paragraphs that are intended to prevent preparers from abusing hedge accounting, for example by claiming that losses on derivatives may be carried forward as deferred losses. In general the impact of these rules is to complicate the work of the accountant and to restrict the application of hedge accounting. To summarize, IAS 39 is in no sense an adequate solution to the problems that hedging poses for financial reporting and it is to be hoped that it will soon be replaced by a more satisfactory standard.

22.8 COMPARATIVE ANALYSIS

22.8.1 USA

The USA was the first country to appreciate the problems that developments concerning financial instruments posed for financial reporting and to do something effective about it. More than ten years ago, the FASB set up a long-term project to develop comprehensive rules for the reporting of financial instruments based on thorough research covering both theory and practice, in which American academics have played a leading role. In effect the intellectual leadership in accounting for financial instruments lies firmly in America. The fruits of the FASB's project have been a series of standards which today govern the practice of American enterprises in this field, of which the more important are:

(a) **FAS–105** Disclosure of information about financial instruments with off-balance-sheet risk and financial instruments with concentrations of credit risk. As its title implies, this standard tackled the problem that the effect of many financial instruments were not reported in the accounts, by requiring greater disclosure.

(b) **FAS–107** Disclosures about fair values of financial instruments. This standard introduced the principle that enterprises should disclose the fair value of all financial instruments, including those not recognized in the accounts.

(c) **FAS–119** Disclosure about derivative financial instruments. This standard extended the disclosure requirements of FAS–105 to derivatives, including forwards, swaps and options contracts.

These three standards had the common characteristic of seeking to tackle the problem through greater disclosure in the notes. However in 1998, the FASB finally came round to dealing with the recognition and measurement of financial instruments when it issued:

(d) **FAS–133** Accounting for derivative instruments and hedging activities, which, as its title implies, regulates how the two most complicated aspects of financial instruments (derivatives and hedging) are to be reported in the balance sheet and income statement. This standard also updated the rules in FAS–105, FAS–107 and FAS–119, which it superseded. It is effective for financial statements for periods beginning after 15 June 2000.

It is abundantly clear that the FASB's rules were the source of much of the content of IAS 32 and IAS 39, including their most important provisions as follows:

- The requirement to include an analysis of the risks confronting the enterprise, with an estimate of the maximum potential loss arising from its exposure to credit risk (IAS 32, 66)
- The requirement to disclose the fair value of all financial assets and liabilities, even those not recognized in the balance sheet (IAS 32, 77)
- The requirement to report all derivatives at fair value (IAS 39, 93)
- The classification of financial assets into trading, held-to-maturity and available for sale, with different measurement and income recognition rules for each category. The IASB's rules are essentially the same as those set out in FAS–115 Accounting for certain investments in debt and equity securities
- The different income recognition rules for value hedges and cash flow hedges

In observance of the FASB's standards, American enterprises include a vast amount of information about financial instruments in their published accounts. For example, the 1999 annual report of General Motors includes a comprehensive note of over 1500 words on 'Derivative financial instruments and risk management' which includes paragraphs on 'foreign exchange forward contracts and options', 'interest rate swaps and options', 'mortgage contracts' and 'credit risk', plus a further long note on the fair value of financial instruments. This latter note includes a table on derivatives which is presented in an abbreviated form in Exhibit 22.6. The most interesting feature of this table is the discrepancy between the fair values and the values reported in the balance sheet. According to the balance sheet there is a net liability of $345mn; but the fair values give a net liability of $1048mn (assets of $605mn less liabilities of $1653mn). If FAS 135 had been in effect in 1999, General Motors would have had to report all derivatives at fair value in its balance sheet, with changes in fair value reported in the income statement, which would have resulted in a reduction of $703mn in its equity and profits.

Exhibit 22.6 *General Motors: financial instrument derivatives,*
31 December 1999

Automotive and other operations	Fair value Asset position $ millions	Fair value Liability position $ millions	Reported in balance sheet $ millions
Foreign exchange forward contracts	13	83	(32)
Foreign exchange options	17	2	17
Interest rate swaps	2	16	(10)
Interest rate options	0	2	(2)
Financing and insurance operations			
Foreign exchange forward contracts	386	862	(374)
Interest rate swaps	81	586	33
Interest rate options	1	0	
Mortgage contracts	105	102	23
Total	605	1653	(345)

Note: In the GM annual report the information on reported balance sheet values is given in minuscule characters in a footnote

22.8.2 Japan

In 1999, the BADC issued 'Accounting standard for financial instruments' which sets out rules for the disclosure and measurement of financial assets and liabilities, including derivatives which are in all material respects similar to those of IAS 32 and IAS 39. The standard is effective for financial years beginning after 31 March 2000. Prior to this standard, it had been common practice for Japanese enterprises to value most financial assets at cost; hence this standard should in principle have a big impact on practice in Japan.

22.8.3 Britain

In 1998, the ASB issued *FRS 13 Derivatives and other financial instruments: disclosures*, which sets out rules for disclosure very similar to those of IAS 32. However this is the only specific reference to financial instruments in British law or standards. Neither the Companies Act nor the ASB deal with the question of the recognition and measurement of financial instruments. However the Companies Act, under its alternative valuation rules, does permit (but not require) companies to value investments (both fixed and current) at current cost, which is generally interpreted as market value. Hence there is little impediment to British companies to apply IAS 39's rules as to the valuation of financial assets, except possibly for derivatives. In fact most major British MNEs disclose a con-

Exhibit 22.7   *BP Amoco: fair values of financial assets and liabilities, 31 December 1999*

	Net fair value asset (liability) $ millions	Net carrying amount asset (liability) $ millions
Primary financial instruments		
Current assets – Debtors	326	326
Investments	221	220
Cash at bank and in hand	1331	1331
Finance debt (short-term borrowings)	(2433)	(2433)
Long-term borrowings	(9979)	(10 118)
Net obligations under finance leases	(1824)	(1802)
Creditors	(1062)	(1062)
Provisions	(408)	(408)
Derivative financial or commodity instruments		
Risk management (interest rate contracts)	37	
Foreign exchange contracts	(209)	(191)
Natural gas contracts	2	0
Trading (oil price contracts)	(61)	(61)
Total	(14 059)	(14 198)

siderable amount of information about financial instruments. For example the 1999 annual report of BP Amoco contains a lengthy note headed 'Derivatives and other financial instruments', with subheadings for Interest rate risk, Foreign exchange rate risk. Risk management and Trading activities. This note includes no less than ten tables, of which the most interesting is the schedule of fair values presented in Exhibit 22.7. The differences between the fair values and the carrying amounts (that is the balance sheet figures) are not great, being less than 1 per cent in total; they are concentrated in the debts (British law does not permit liabilities to be reported at fair value) and derivatives.

22.8.4 Germany

Under German law, it is expressly forbidden to report assets at more than historical cost and liabilities at less than the amount that the enter-prise would have to pay to redeem the liability. However since 1998, German listed corporations are permitted to draw up their consolidated accounts in accordance with internationally accepted standards, provided that they respect the provisions of the EU's accounting directives. Hence these enterprises are able to follow most of the rules in IAS 32 and IAS 39.

22.8.5 France

The situation in France is rather similar to that in Germany. French law places restrictions on reporting investments at market value where this is above cost, but French law is in the process of being amended to permit listed corporations to draw up their consolidated accounts according to internationally accepted rules, provided that the provisions of the EU's directives are respected.

SUMMARY

The problems with which accountants are confronted in the reporting of financial instruments were analysed with the aid of the fable of the two investment trusts. The rules set out in IAS 32 and IAS 39 for the disclosure and measurement of financial instruments were examined, with detailed consideration being given to two areas: derivatives and hedging. The present position in the five countries of the Pentad was reviewed.

Review questions

1. What are the three problems connected with the reporting of financial assets that the 'fable of the two investment trusts' seeks to demonstrate?

2. What are the five categories of financial assets according to IAS 39? What are the measurement rules for each category?

3. How is the income for each category of financial asset reported in the accounts?

4. What is the meaning of the terms 'amortized historical cost' and 'effective interest rate'?

Review questions (cont'd)

5. Under IAS 39, what liabilities are to be reported at fair value?

6. What are the various categories of risk according to IAS 32?

7. What is the essential difference between a forward contract and an option?

8. Why are the conventional rules inadequate for the reporting of derivatives? How has IAS 39 sought to remedy these defects?

9. What are the basic reasons why conventional accounting fails to report hedging operations in a satisfactory manner?

10. What is the difference between a value hedge and a cash-flow hedge?

Notes

1. Kenneth MacNeal's book was originally published in 1939 by the University of Pennsylvania Press. In 1970 it was reprinted by the Scholars Book Company. The most easily accessible source on MacNeal's work is Zeff (1994).

2. This is the present value at a discount rate of 10 per cent of €120 000 per year for ten years plus €1 000 000 at the end of ten years.

3. The present value of €20 000 per year for ten years at a rate of interest of 10 per cent p.a. is €122 891.

4. Management may have an incentive to classify a financial asset as held-to-maturity and not available for sale, because, according to the IASB's rules, the former is valued at cost and the latter at fair value.

5. It is well known that the individual accounts serve other important purposes; but in practice, the IASB is most interested in the consolidated accounts.

6. This analysis ignores the effect of differential interest rates in the two countries.

7. Certain writers (for example Bodie and Merton; 1997) use the term 'hedging' only for actions that remove all risk, both of a loss and a profit. The authors do not accept this restricted usage of the term, which, in their opinion, is not in accord with the common usage, which is to denote any action taken by the enterprise that is intended to reduce risk.

8. In fact the market value of the option will normally be higher than this figure because of its time value, reflecting that the holder has the possibility of benefiting from any further fall in the price of wheat up to the time that the option lapses. This complication is ignored in the example.

References

Adams, JB and Montesi, CJ *Major issues related to hedge accounting*, Financial Accounting Standards Board (1995).

Bodie, Z and Merton, RC *Finance*, Prentice Hall, New Jersey (1997).

Cairns, D *A Guide to applying International Accounting Standards*, Accountancy Books, Milton Keynes (1995).

IASC *Discussion paper: accounting for financial assets and financial liabilities*, International Accounting Standards Committee, London (1997).

IASC *Draft standard and basis for conclusions: financial instruments and similar items*, International Accounting Standards Committee, London (2000).

MacNeal, K *Truth in accounting*, University of Pennsylvania Press, Philadelphia (1939).

Zeff, S 'Truth in Accounting: the ordeal of Kenneth MacNeal', *Twentieth-century accounting thinkers*, JR Edwards (ed.), London, Routledge (1994).

Further reading

For a comprehensive (but advanced) analysis of hedging, see Adams and Montesi (1995). For the IASB's latest proposals, see the IASC (2000).

chapter twenty-three

Global Disclosure

Chapter objectives

■ To examine the influence of the globalization of accounting on the disclosure of financial information by companies

■ To show that the disclosure requirements of Anglo-Saxon accounting rules are investor oriented whilst the EU disclosure requirements also take account of different users of financial accounts

■ To describe the different instruments for the disclosure of financial information

■ To examine the empirical evidence on whether the information disclosed in financial statements is reflected in the capital market

■ To discuss the national disclosure differences depending on the country of incorporation and the stock market listing

■ To examine the costs and benefits of greater disclosure and to describe the sensitive issue of disclosing information on the risk of a company's finances and transactions

■ To present international disclosure practice

23.1 INTRODUCTION

The internationalization of accounting regulation has had an important impact on the content, form and amount of information published in the annual report of a company and of the instruments used to disclose information. Under the laws in many EU countries, multinational companies are permitted to apply IAS or US GAAP instead of domestic GAAP, for example in Germany with the Law to Facilitate the Raising of Capital (Kapitalaufnahmeerleichterungsgesetz) of 1998 and the implementation of section 292(a) of the Commercial Code (HGB). Before this had become permitted by the law in recent years, many European companies already voluntarily or, if listed on the US capital market, mandatorily published accounts in accordance with international accounting rules, in addition to their domestic accounts, or published a reconciliation. This development is the result of the globalization of capital markets and the demands of investors for internationally comparable information.

With the use of IAS or US GAAP in domestic accounts, additional elements of financial statements such as a cash flow statement, a statement on geographic and business segments and a statement of changes in equity or comprehensive income have become part of the annual reports of many EU companies. The publication of earnings per share, required for listed companies by IAS 33 and FAS 128, and of interim reports, are further signs of the increasingly investor-oriented disclosure practice of Continental European companies. In fact, as has been discussed in Part Three of this book, financial statements in accordance with IAS or US GAAP require disclosure of the following elements of financial statements: a balance sheet, an income statement, a statement of changes in equity or other comprehensive income, a cash flow statement and explanatory notes. IAS 14 and FAS 131 require in addition for listed companies to present information on business and geographic segments. Multinational companies that are listed on the NYSE are required by the SEC to disclose an extraordinary amount of additional information required in the 20-F Report.

In contrast, the EU Directives – that date back to the 1970s – do not require a cash flow statement, a statement showing changes in equity or a segment report, although article 43.1.8 of the Fourth Directive requires disclosure of sales information by operating and geographic segments. The elements of financial statements in accordance with the EU Directives include only the balance sheet, the income statement and the notes.

Today many companies voluntarily publish a reconciliation showing the major differences between the national and international (IAS or US GAAP) accounting principles as a means of improving the comparability of the information for financial analysts and investors. The change in disclosure practices by EU companies is a sign of a change in the purpose of annual accounts towards investor and capital market orientation. This change in disclosure behaviour is clearly observable in Germany and France, where the annual accounts traditionally had the objective of creditor protection. In Continental Europe, capital markets formerly did not play an important role in the financing of companies in comparison to the UK and notably the USA. This change in the purpose of accounting is the result of the globalization of capital markets and the need of German and French and other EU companies to be listed abroad and in particular on the US capital market. The demand for equity capital has created a different objective of disclosure for such companies.

However, it is also true that, in spite of the globalization of capital markets and the internationalization of accounting rules, disclosure practices are still different from country to country and are still influenced by traditional reporting behaviour and by the national socio-political context. On the one hand, there are the companies, that are listed only on the national stock exchange. Research by Gray, Meek and Roberts (1993) has shown that there are significant differences in financial reporting behaviour between internationally listed and domestic-only listed companies. On the other hand there are the companies that are not listed at all. These companies have no incentive to disclose information for investors applying IAS or US GAAP. Instead their accounts are determined by the needs of other users such as creditors and employees and are influenced by tax considerations. But, as will be seen later, even the accounts of global players still present many traditional domestic elements of financial information. For instance, some German companies still disclose a value added statement which is intended to present the composition and distribution of economic added value of the production factors capital and labour. In France the detailed and uniform disclosure of accounting information in the plan comptable has been developed as a result of the interaction between accounting and the state's need for information for taxation and statistical purposes. In the UK disclosure of corporate governance information stems from the separation of ownership from management of a company. Furthermore, national reporting differences can be illustrated by newly emerging disclosure developments. Scandinavian companies have pioneered the disclosure of statements of intellectual capital. Intellectual capital statements can be used by companies managing knowledge of products and services to disclose their scope of intangible assets and knowledge resources. Finally, as will be seen in the next section, German companies are now required to disclose a risk report as part of their management report. In general, the Anglo-Saxon (and hence the UK, IAS and US GAAP) approach to disclosure is investor oriented and emphasizes the provision of information on profitability and cash flow. Signs of this are the presentation of cash flow statements and of earnings per share. Another important difference to be noted is that the EU Directives and, following their implementation, the EU member states prescribe the order and items in detail to be included in the balance sheet and the profit and loss account, while there are no such prescriptions in IAS and US GAAP.

The next section describes instruments that are used to disclose financial information. Instead of listing all the items to be disclosed in the balance sheet, the profit and loss account, the segment report, the cash flow statement, the notes to the accounts and the management report, the following discussion rather focuses on emerging disclosure issues in particular the reporting of risk. This reflects national disclosure differences but also shows the need for advanced, future-oriented disclosure requirements in a business environment that is changing towards increasing globalization and capital market-orientation. The third section presents research that has analysed the relationship between information disclosed in the financial statements and the capital market. Obstacles to disclosure such as higher cost are described next. Finally, the chapter presents international disclosure practices of some globally operating companies.

23.2 DISCLOSURE INSTRUMENTS

Part Three of this book has already described the items to be disclosed in the balance sheet and the income statement. In a segment report a company generally discloses information on the basis of its principal operating and geographic segments, in order to give a better insight into the net worth, financial position and results of the separate segments and therefore into the corresponding risks and returns. Segment information must be disclosed consistently with the accounting policies used in the financial statements. In a cash flow statement a company generally reports cash flows classified by operating, investing and financing activities. In the notes to the financial statements a company should describe the accounting policies used as the basis for determining assets and liabilities, income and expense.

In contrast to IAS and US GAAP, the EU Directives and hence the company laws in member states of the European Union require in addition the presentation of a management report outside the financial statements. In it a company should provide a description of the development of the business and the situation of the company in such a manner as to provide a true and fair view of its affairs. Although under IAS there is no equivalent to the management report, IAS 1.8 encourages enterprises to present, outside the financial statements, a financial review by management which describes and explains the main features of the enterprise's financial position and performance as well as the principal uncertainties it faces. Very little specific guidance is given, however, on the actual contents of such a review. It should be noted however, that the SEC requires registrants to publish an extensive Management's Discussion and Analysis of Financial Condition and Results of Operations (MD&A).

In Germany, the management report has been the focus of attention, where disclosures about risks of a company have recently been proposed in detail as part of the management report by the German Accounting Standards Board (DSR). The DSR takes the view that information about risks should be presented in a self-contained section of the management report. Following the introduction of the Law on Control and Transparency within Businesses (KonTraG) in May 1998, the management boards of public corporations are now required to set up a monitoring system to identify at an early stage developments that constitute a risk to the existence of the company (section 91(2) of the Aktiengesetz (AktG)). At the same time new legislation was introduced expanding the disclosure requirements for the management report, requiring a new provision of information about the risks affecting future developments (sections 315(1) and 289(1) of the HGB). This reporting requirement takes effect for the first time for financial years commencing after 31 December 1998. The legislation and the basis for conclusion of the new legislation did not, however, provide any specific details as to how the disclosures about risks should be reported. Therefore in April 2001 the DSR issued a standard on Risk Reporting (DRS 5) which establishes the rules for the contents and structure of the disclosures required by the new legislation. In addition two industry-specific standards on risk reporting have been published for banks and insurance companies which need to comply with further statutory requirements.

In the standard the DSR takes the view that users of financial statements, in particular users participating in capital markets, need relevant and reliable information about the risks affecting future developments of a company. In setting this objective, the standard is following the concepts set out in the Frameworks of the IASB and the FASB. Both frameworks state that information is useful for users if it is understandable, relevant, reliable and comparable. Information is deemed relevant if it influences the economic decisions of users by assisting them to assess past, present or future events or if it confirms or corrects assessments they have previously made.

The standard adopts rules for risk reporting that have been intentionally formulated in a general and conceptual way. Since business risks are always specific to each enterprise, the individual enterprise should be able to devise the most appropriate form of risk reporting for its own specific needs. Risk is defined as the possibility of a future negative impact on the economic position of the company. The economic position encompasses all factors which affect the group's ability to generate net positive cash flows in the future. This demonstrates a dynamic rather than a static understanding of the term 'risk'. In addition, risks are also relevant if they can have an effect on the enterprise's expectations of anticipated developments as disclosed in the management report.

The main focus of risk reporting should be on the specific business risks facing the enterprise. The information provided should address industry and market risks, but it should in particular cover the individual risks facing an enterprise as specifically as possible and should not be overgeneralized. Risks which threaten the existence of the enterprise should be described as such.

The standard requires enterprises to disclose risks arising from concentrations because of the major effect they can have on the future economic position of a group, for example dependence on patents, contracts, and manufacturing processes. Each enterprise should disclose the risks affecting it categorized on the same basis as that it uses internally for risk management purposes. The standard does not set out any mandatory categorization of risks, since each enterprise will be faced with specific risks and will design its own risk management system. Instead, the proposed standard provides an example of how risks could be categorized.

The DSR requires that risks are quantified where three preconditions are met. Firstly, there must be reliable and recognized methods available to quantify risks. Secondly, it must be possible to provide quantified information in a way that is economically justified. Thirdly, quantification should always be relevant for the decision-making process of the user. Since quantification is usually dependent on the assumptions used, the standard requires that the models and assumptions used are described and explained in a way that can be clearly understood.

The DSR takes the view that the description of the risk management system enables the user to gain a better understanding of the risk situation. In order to avoid an excess of detail in the management report which would impair clarity, the standard therefore requires that the information shown about risk management should be presented in an appropriate manner.

As a general rule, reporting on risks should be based on an appropriate forecast period for each risk. At the same time, the reliability of the information is also an important factor. Due to the nature of the reliability of forecasts, the period over which the risk is being measured cannot be extended arbitrarily. For risks that threaten the existence of an enterprise the forecast must be particularly reliable. A relatively short forecast period of at least one year after the balance sheet date seems adequate. This corresponds to the period applied internationally for the *going concern* assumption. In the case of other significant risks, DSR considered that two years is a manageable period. The use of longer forecast periods means that the reliability of the information is likely to be impaired. Nevertheless, where the legal environment or external factors are in the process of change, or in the case of longer market cycles and complex major projects, the forecast period should be adjusted accordingly. Information should be provided first and foremost about the risks affecting future developments. It may, however, also be appropriate to discuss related opportunities.

In the UK, it is not the standard-setting body (ASB), but the Institute of Chartered Accountants of England and Wales (ICAEW) that has been concerned with disclosure of risk information in the annual financial statements. In 1999 it published a report (*No Surprises*) in which it presented recommendations to provide information to investors on companies' business risk and financial risk exposures. The ICAEW's principal argument for risk disclosure for a company is to reduce its costs of capital as the result of the increased transparency. However, since these proposals are not supported by law, nor by an ASB standard, risk disclosures are not yet common in the annual reports of British companies.

The cost of capital and its relationship to disclosure will be referred to next. In fact, to investors on the capital market a higher risk is also related to opportunities – in the form of higher returns.

23.3 DISCLOSURE AND CAPITAL MARKETS

In the US and to a lesser extent in the UK, there have been extensive empirical investigations on the question of whether the information disclosed in the financial statements is actually valued by the capital market. This body of evidence could only be developed with respect to these capital markets, as their counterparts in many European countries are not large enough to be considered efficient.

Market efficiency is a term that is used in many contexts with many different meanings. When the efficiency of a stock market is discussed in the literature of finance, it usually refers to efficiency with respect to pricing. Pricing efficiency implies that the actual market price of a share on a day approximates to its intrinsic value. This implies that, if the market is efficient, prices at any point in time fully reflect all relevant available information. Only 'insider information' would enable an investor to gain an advantage over other investors on the stock market. By definition, then, any new relevant information is quickly and accurately impounded into share prices. A capital market is termed efficient with respect to an information item if the prices of capital market securities fully impound the return implications of that item. There is an enormous body of evidence analysing whether or not a capital market is efficient (Fama, 1970). For a stock market to be efficient, at any time the share price of a company should reflect the value of that company on the basis of its expected future earnings. Why might capital markets be informationally efficient? The following are the major explanations offered in the academic literature (Foster, 1986):

(a) One explanation for market efficiency is the competitive activities of security analysts. Each analyst is seeking to detect mispriced securities. Although each analyst may examine only part of the available information set, the large number of analysts examining this same set increases the likelihood that significant information items will be rapidly impounded into security prices. An extension of this explanation is the conjecture that market efficiencies are most likely for stocks followed by large numbers of analysts and least likely for stocks with limited coverage by analysts.

(b) A second explanation rests on the law of large numbers. Each individual analyst can make mistakes of judgement or estimation. However, to the extent that these mistakes are independent across analysts, they will be diversified away in the price determination process. Given a large number of analysts and independence in their mistakes, the consensus can impound a broader information set than that possessed by even the most sophisticated analyst. Under this explanation, the larger the number of analysts and the lower the correlation between mistakes of judgement or estimation made by the individual analysts, the more efficient will be the market.

In addition to these two explanations, several factors have been stated as important in explaining the broadness of the information set impounded into security prices. One factor is the information disclosed by firms. Adequate disclosure of information minimizes ignorance in the market and causes the market price to reflect the true value of the security (Singhvi and Desai, 1971). This argument is presented by advocates of increased disclosure by firms. It is also used in studies comparing the relative efficiency of different capital markets. For instance in a survey of market efficiency studies across world stock exchanges, Dawson (1984, p. 153) noted: 'Common explanations for the less frequent findings of market efficiency in the less developed exchanges include less stringent information disclosure requirements, less information released by companies, and less rigorous accounting regulations.'

One approach to analyse whether the value of the information disclosed in the annual financial statements matters, is to measure the impact of disclosure of annual accounts and changes in accounting practice on stock market prices. The relation between accounting numbers and share prices has first been examined in a pioneering study by Ball and Brown (1968). They found that for US companies most of the information contained in the annual report had already been anticipated in the price before its release. The anticipation was very accurate and the drift upwards or downwards in share price had begun 12 months before the report was released. Since the early work of Ball and Brown there have been hundreds of other studies into the relationship between a company earnings and its stock market returns.

Another set of evidence that has been developed in recent years, has analysed whether the information content of IAS-based earning or US GAAP-based earnings on the one hand and EU Directives or national GAAP-based earnings on the other have different reactions on capital markets. For instance, research by Auer (1996) suggests that IAS-based earnings announcements convey a statistically significant higher information content than earnings announcements based on Swiss GAAP.

In general however, the evidence over the past 20 years shows a consistent picture with earnings and earnings-related information explaining between 2 per cent and 5 per cent of the time series variability of share price return over short periods of time, and up to 7 per cent for longer periods of time (Samuels, Brayshaw and Craner, 1995). The apparently minor role of accounting earnings numbers in the security valuation by the capital markets seems to be in contradiction with the aim of accounting standard setters to provide information for investors and does not seem to justify the expense of setting up accounting reporting systems to provide information for decision making. Lev (1989) offers three explanations. The first explanation is that earnings figures might be very useful to investors but that the statistical techniques used by research are not appropriate to detect this fact. A second explanation is that investors are irrational and that stock markets are less efficient than is assumed in theory. The third explanation is that because published earnings are based on many assumptions and strategic management choices as to which accounting policies to adopt, the actual figures published are not the ones used by analysts. In other words the information content of the *actual* reported profit figure is low and not useful in predicting future profits. If analysts carry out their own adjustments to the published figures, it could be that these adjusted figures show a very good relationship with security returns. It has been pointed out that much of the research into the information content of accounting numbers is undertaken by non-accountants with access to large computerized databases. While it is easy to regress one set of numbers on another set, it is not easy to go through a set of accounts considering every footnote and assessing the implications. Accountants know that it is not possible to compare the earnings figures of one company with another without making adjustments. Moreover accounting rules give companies much flexibility and this is the reason why unadjusted figures should not be used in statistical analysis. Finally, already quite small changes in accounting policies can have an enormous influence on reported profits. Studies examining the use made by investment analysts of annual reports show that the annual reports and communications with management are the two most important sources of information for analysts. These are followed in the order of perceived importance by interim reports, offer prospectuses and press releases (Arnold and Moizer, 1984; Vergoosen, 1993). It seems therefore that accounting reports do matter. However, the quality of the adjusted earnings figure is a key factor for useful research and analysis.

23.4 THE COSTS OF DISCLOSURE

One factor that management consistently cites as important in disclosure decisions is the cost associated with those disclosures. These costs include collection and processing costs, litigation costs, political costs, competitive disadvantage costs and additional constraints on management decisions.

Collection and processing costs include the costs borne by both the preparers and the users of financial data. Legal suits against the company or its managers are an ever-present threat in the US. In some cases, this threat can operate to reduce disclosure. For instance, one argument against voluntary disclosure of earnings forecasts is that ex-post they may turn out to be overly optimistic; investors then may use the incorrect forecast as one basis to sue management to obtain compensation for a drop in the price of their equity investment. In other cases, the threat of litigation can promote disclosure. For example if securities analysts would make estimates of a company that management considers as incorrect, it would release a corrective statement to reduce the potential losses to shareholders.

Political cost considerations can also influence the disclosure decisions of firms. Governments and competition agencies have the power to expropriate wealth from corporations and redistribute it to other parties in society. Annual reports represent one source of information that can be used to detect firms or industries with excess profits. Companies may disclose certain information items if they provide evidence that the arguments used by those wishing to appropriate wealth from them are invalid. Companies can also choose to aggregate items in such a way that their political cost exposure is reduced. This is one reason why the developing countries pressed for more detailed geographical analysis of multinationals' sales and profits and why the developed countries resisted this proposal.

A common argument presented against disclosure is the cost incurred when competitors use the disclosure to their own advantage. That is, a company discloses information not only to investors, but also to competitors who have an interest for example in the enterprise's technological progress. Hence, one sensitive area in this connection is information about research and development and new products. On the other hand it has been suggested that by disclosing supplementary information to the capital market the company can reduce its costs of capital. Companies that perceive that they have an advantage over competitors in new technology face difficult decisions when raising new capital. Unless they provide some information pertaining to the R&D or new products, the capital market is less likely to support a new share offering. Yet, if they provide detailed information, they may reduce the lead time before competitors learn about developments within the company. Competitive disadvantage costs can also arise if labour unions and other suppliers are able to use the financial disclosures to improve their bargaining power.

Another aspect in this context is the question of whether it is of importance where information is disclosed in the annual report, that is in the balance sheet or income statements on the one hand or in the explanatory notes to the financial statements on the other. The efficient market hypothesis seems to imply that it is of no importance where a matter is disclosed, formally in the financial statements or elsewhere, such as in a footnote or in the operational and financial review. The stock option debate in the USA is revealing in this respect. The FASB wanted to put the costs of stock options in the income statement. It was however forced to back down in the face of strong opposition. But the opponents were quite happy that the costs should be reported in the notes.

23.5 REPORTING PRACTICES

Although multinational companies apply IAS and US GAAP in their financial statements or disclose a reconciliation of national GAAP to internationally accepted GAAP in their annual reports and hence the accounting methods and measurements should get more and more harmonized internationally, an interesting observation is that the disclosure practice in annual reports still varies across countries. Perhaps these inter-country differences are based on differences in the perceived importance of annual report disclosures and reflect more deeply the fact that the conventions of financial reporting still differ from country to country. An interesting research study in this respect is that by Chang, Most and Brian (1983) who found inter-country differences in the importance attached to some parts of the corporate report.

This section illustrates national disclosure practices of some globally operating companies. A good example of a risk report can be found by DaimlerChrysler in the 1999 annual report presented in Example 23.5.1:

23.5.1 Example: DaimlerChrysler annual report 1999

Early recognition and consistent management of future risks

In view of the global operations of the DaimlerChrysler Group's business units and the increasingly intense competition in all markets, the business units are subject to many risks which are inseparably connected with entrepreneurial activity. For the early recognition and assessment of existing risks and the formulation of an appropriate response, we have developed and used effective monitoring and control systems. Among other things, these systems include the application of Group-wide standard guidelines, the use of reliable software, the selection and training of qualified personnel and constant checks by our internal auditors. With a view to the requirements of the German Business Monitoring and Transparency Act (KonTraG), we have integrated the Group's early warning systems into a risk management system. The operating units continuously monitor existing risks and regularly report on them to the Group's Board of Management in the context of planning and controlling processes, taking into consideration agreed-upon thresholds. This ensures that the Group's management recognizes significant risks at an early stage and can initiate appropriate measures to deal with them.

Risks resulting from interest-rate and exchange-rate developments, including our hedging activities, have been described in this section. Additional uncertainties arise from further economic developments in those countries which are important for our businesses, and can be increased by the strong cyclical nature of demand in some of the markets we serve.

The automotive sector, in particular, is marked by dynamic competition which is likely to become even more intense in the future as a result of world wide excess capacity. The introduction of the Euro as a single currency in eleven member states of the European Union and the growing importance of new distribution channels such as the Internet will reinforce this trend. It will therefore continue to be important for us to maintain our position in our traditional markets while exploiting additional market potential with innovative new products. In this context the market success of the Smart and the addition of new models and versions to the Smart product range is of great significance.

Like all internationally active automobile manufacturers, the DaimlerChrysler Group is affected by intensifying legal regulations in its various markets concerning the exhaust emissions and fuel consumption of its range of cars as well as their safety standards. Furthermore, there are several actions for damages pending against companies of the DaimlerChrysler Group as well as an investigation by the European Commission.

Our financial services business is primarily involved in leasing and financing Group products, mainly vehicles, to our customers and for our dealerships. Refinancing is carried out to a considerable extent through external capital markets. This gives rise, not only to credit risks, but also to residual-value risks for the vehicles, which are given back to us for remarketing at the end of their leasing periods.

Adtranz operates in an extremely competitive environment, characterized by industry overcapacity and pricing pressure resulting from the rationalization needs faced by railroad operators. We are confident, however, that the measures we are taking to restructure Adtranz will improve in its competitive situation.

Using a newly developed country-rating system, CRISK-Explorer, we are striving to monitor not only the risk potential but also the opportunities connected with business activities in emerging markets.

Year 2000 adaptation successfully completed

We successfully completed the process of adapting our information and communications systems for year 2000 compliance. All of our computers, technical equipment and machinery in our plants, offices and spare parts centers continued to function properly after the end of the year, so there were no significant disturbances or failures. The project team that was responsible for Group-wide conversion and adaptation has now concluded its work and has handed over responsibility for further system developments to the appropriate functional departments. When carrying out the necessary system adaptations for a smooth transition to the year 2000, it proved to be a great advantage that we had already introduced the euro as our corporate currency on 1 January 1999.

For the DaimlerChrysler Group the costs of ensuring year 2000 compliance amounted to approximately €240mn. Of this total, about €70mn was incurred in the 1999 financial year.

Events after the end of the 1999 financial year

Since the end of the 1999 financial year there have been no further developments, beyond the ones described above, which are of major significance to DaimlerChrysler and which would lead to a changed assessment of the Group's position. The course of business in the first months of 2000 confirms the statements made in the section Outlook.

It has been mentioned earlier that the amount a company discloses depends not only on the country of incorporation but also on the stock exchange on which it is listed. In particular, the SEC requirements for listing on the NYSE are the most comprehensive in the world. For instance when considering the amount of market risk disclosures in the corresponding 1999 20-F report of DaimlerChrysler it can be seen that the company discloses not only detailed qualitative risk information but also an extraordinary amount of quantitative information on its market risk exposure.

With the listing of Daimler Benz at the NYSE in 1993 the company published for the first time a 20-F report in accordance with SEC requirements. While the company had to disclose an enormous amount of additional information in the 20-F report, the domestic annual report established in accordance with the HGB started to change from that year on. Up until 1996 Daimler Benz did not publish pure US GAAP financial statements in addition to HGB accounts in the annual report, but, instead, provided reconciliations from HGB to US GAAP. However, the amount of information Daimler Benz published from 1993 onwards increased from year to year (Ballwieser, 2000). Starting in 1993, Daimler Benz published in its annual report information on business and geographic segments and a cash flow statement. Before 1999, German companies were not required by law to present either a cash flow statement or a segment report. Daimler Benz has also increased disclosure on quantitative and qualitative information on certain financial instruments in the domestic annual report in recent years. This is an item the company has to report extensively on in its 20-F report.

Since 1998, German multinationally listed companies are exempted from applying HGB rules to the consolidated accounts if they provide consolidated accounts in accordance with IAS or US GAAP instead. Some companies provide not only quantitative, but also verbal reconciliations between international GAAP and national GAAP in their annual reports. This information is very informative as it describes and emphasizes the main differences between national and international accounting policies. The extract of the SAP 1999 annual report presented in the example below illustrates such disclosure. SAP applies US GAAP instead of HGB rules to its consolidated financial statements.

23.5.2 Example: SAP annual report 1999

Major Differences Between German and US Accounting Principles

Introduction

Being a holding corporation that owns the majority of voting rights in other enterprises, SAP AG is generally obliged to prepare consolidated financial statements in accordance with the accounting regulations set out in the German Commercial Code (Handelsgesetzbuch HGB). Section 292(a) HGB offers however an exemption from this obligation, if consolidated financial statements are prepared and published that are in accordance with an internationally accepted accounting principle (US GAAP or IAS). To make use of this exemption, the Company is required to describe the significant differences between the accounting methods applied and German accounting methods.

Fundamental Differences

German HGB accounting rules and US GAAP are based on fundamentally different perspectives. While accounting under the German HGB emphasizes the principle of caution and creditor protection, the availability of relevant information for shareholder decision-making is the chief objective of US GAAP. The comparability of the financial statements (both from year to year and from company to company) and the determination of performance on an accrual basis therefore rank higher under US GAAP than under HGB.

Revenue Recognition

Under German HGB, payment terms generally have no impact on revenue recognition. Under the American Institute of Certified Public Accountants Statement of Position 97–2, (Software Revenue Recognition SOP 97–2) extended payment terms may indicate that license fees are not fixed and determinable and should therefore be recognized as payments become due. Generally, software maintenance agreements are concluded in conjunction with the software license agreement. Maintenance fees are mostly based upon a standard percentage of the related software license fee. Under German HGB, the expected costs of the maintenance service are accrued if a free-of-charge service period is provided. SOP 97–2 regards both maintenance fees below the standard percentage and the provision of free maintenance service as discounts to be considered in recognizing software revenue. Therefore the relative fair market value of non-standard maintenance arrangements including free service periods reduce the related software license revenue and are recognized as maintenance revenue when such services are provided in subsequent periods.

Pension Benefits

Until 1997, reserves for pension obligations in Germany were determined by the ongoing-concern method applying an interest rate of 6 per cent per annum, in accordance with German tax law. In 1998 the Company adopted the Projected Unit Credit Method, which is required under US GAAP and permitted under German tax law. In contrast to the ongoing-concern method, the Projected Unit Credit Method makes allowance for projected compensation and pension increases and is based on actual rates of interest derived from the long-term borrowing rates in the countries concerned.

In-Process Research and Development

Under German GAAP, the in-process research and development costs of companies acquired are not identified separately. Under US GAAP, these costs are separately determined at the time of acquisition and charged to expense.

Deferred Taxes

Under German GAAP, deferred tax assets are not recorded for net operating losses. Under US GAAP, deferred tax assets are recorded for net operating losses and a valuation allowance is established when it is more likely than not that deferred tax assets will not be realized.

Stock Appreciation Rights Program (STAR)

The STAR program rewards selected employees based on the appreciation of SAP's preference share price over a predetermined period of time, the nine month period between May 1999 through February 2000, for the 1999 STAR program. The compensation arising from this measurement period is paid to participants in three instalments. Under German GAAP, the total expense is recognized in 1999 as the STAR program was established as a 1999 compensation program. In addition, the accrual is based on the SAP preference share appreciation through the last date available before the preparation of the financial statements is finished. Under US GAAP, the expense is recognized over a period beginning with the start of the STAR program in May 1999 and ending with the payment of the last instalment in the middle of 2001. In addition, the accrual is based on the SAP preference share appreciation through 31 December 1999. Since the preference share price increased significantly after 31 December 1999, the accrual was larger under German GAAP. Under German GAAP, marketable debt and equity securities are valued at the lower of acquisition cost or market value at the balance sheet date. Under US GAAP, marketable debt and equity securities are categorized as either trading, available-for-sale or held to maturity. The Company's securities are considered to be available-for-sale and, therefore, are valued under US GAAP at fair market value as of the balance sheet date. Unrealized gains and losses are excluded from earnings and reported net of deferred tax in other comprehensive income.

Derivatives

Under German GAAP, most derivatives are not recorded on the balance sheet. Unrealized gains are not recognized, unrealized losses are accrued. Under SFAS 133 (which SAP implemented in 1999), derivatives are recorded on the balance sheet at their fair value. Gains or losses on derivatives qualifying as cash flow hedges are reported in other comprehensive income net of tax and are realized in earnings in conjunction with the gain or loss on the hedged item or transaction.

In the UK, companies listed on the London Stock Exchange have to disclose a considerable amount on information on corporate governance. The Listing Rules of the London Stock Exchange incorporate The Principles of Good Governance and a Code of Best Practice which require the disclosure of information about the individual members of the Board of Directors, including their responsibilities, their biographical details, and their remuneration. In the UK, a typical listed company publishes a chairman's statement, a chief executive's report covering operations, a finance director's report, directors profiles and separate sections on corporate governance and remuneration. In addition there may be environmental and social reports.

The amount of detail British companies have to disclose on their remuneration policy is illustrated by a small extract from the Cadbury Schweppes 1999 annual report in Exhibit 23.1. It is part of a 14-page Report of Corporate Governance of which 10 pages comprise the Report of Directors Remuneration.

Exhibit 23.1 *Cadbury Schweppes annual report, 1999*

	Basic Salary/Fees	Annual Incentive Plan/BSRP	LTIP award in 1999	Allowances and benefits	1999 Total
	£ thousand	£ thousand	£ thousand	£ thousand	£ thousand
Sir Dominic Cadbury	621		575	19	1215
JM Sunderland	535	559	450	19	1563
JF Brock	392	544	344	469	1749
ID Johnston	336	260	295	118	1009
DJ Kappler	356	371	310	20	1057
RJ Stack	254	264	215	219	952
RS Braddock	62				62
IFH Davison	36				36
Sir Peter Davis	19				19
FB Humer	36				36
DAR Thompson	28				28
Sir John Whitehead	28				28
Baroness Wilcox	28				28

Note: BSRP = Bonus share retention plan, LTIP = Long-term incentive plan

23.6 CONCLUSION

This chapter has been concerned with the impact that the globalization of accounting has had on the disclosure of financial information published in annual reports. It has demonstrated that the purpose of disclosure has changed towards investor orientation in Europe. With the use of IAS and US GAAP, additional statements such as cash flow statements, segment reports and statements showing changes in equity have become parts of the annual reports of European global players. Reconciliations and other verbal explanations of the differences between international and national GAAP are very informative for the users of annual reports.

At the same time there are still many signs for differences in disclosure behaviour between countries. Domestic disclosure traditions were demonstrated by emphasis for example on corporate governance in the UK. National emerging reporting developments as a consequence of globalization were illustrated with respect to risk reporting in Germany. The chapter has also been concerned with the empirical evidence that analysed the question whether the information disclosed in annual reports actually matters to the stock market.

In addition to the annual report there are many other means for a company to disclose information. During the year companies publish interim reports and release information in press conferences, through prospectus for listing purposes and *ad hoc* publications. Companies regularly brief analysts with information. It has been suggested that companies usually distribute information strategically. The chapter has aimed to emphasize that there are not only benefits but also costs inherent in greater disclosure and that the motivations behind disclosure and non-disclosure are diverse.

SUMMARY

This chapter discussed the impact of the globalization of capital markets on disclosure in financial reports. As a result of the internationalization of accounting regulation additional elements of financial statements, in particular a cash flow statement, a segment report and a statement showing changes in equity, have become part of the annual reports of EU listed companies. The emphasis on investor-oriented information has also led to new disclosure requirements such as a risk report in Germany. There has been much empirical research on the question whether earnings related information explains share price returns and thus whether accounting disclosure matters.

Review questions

1. Summarize the purpose of the different disclosure instruments in financial statements.

2. What is the difference in the disclosure in financial statements for French and German companies that apply IAS or US GAAP compared with disclosure required under domestic accounting regulations.

3. Outline the advantages and the disadvantages of including a risk report in annual accounts.

4. Is the information disclosed in financial statements actually valued by the capital markets?

5. Give examples of national differences in financial disclosure.

6. What are the benefits and what are the costs of greater disclosure?

References

Arnold, J and Moizer, P 'A survey of the methods used by UK investment analysis to appraise investments in ordinary shares', *Accounting and Business Research* (Summer 1984).

Auer, K 'Capital market reactions to earnings announcement: empirical evidence on the difference in the information content of IAS-based earnings and EC-Directives based earnings', *The European Accounting Review*, 5(4) (1996), pp. 583–6.

Ball, R and Brown, P 'An empirical evaluation of accounting income numbers', *Journal of Accounting Research* (Autumn 1968), pp. 159–78.

Ballwieser, W 'Was bewirkt eine Umstellung der Rechnungslegung vom HGB auf US GAAP?', in *US amerikanische Rechnungslegung*, Ballwieser (ed.), Schäffer Poeschl Verlag (2000).

Chang, LS, Most, KS and Brain, CW 'The utility of annual reports: an international study', *Journal of International Business Studies* (Spring/Summer 1983), pp. 63–84.

Dawson, SM 'The trend toward efficiency for less developed stock exchanges: Hong Kong', *Journal of Business Finance and Accounting* (Summer 1984), pp. 151–61.

Fama, EF 'Efficient capital markets: A review of theory and empirical work', *The Journal of Finance* (May 1970), pp. 383–417.

Foster, G *Financial Statement Analysis*, Prentice Hall (international editions) (1986).

Gray, SJ, Meek, GK and Roberts, CB 'International capital market pressures and voluntary disclosure decisions by US, UK and Continental European multinationals' (1993).

Institute of Chartered Accountants of England and Wales *No surprises*, ICAEW (1999).

Lev, B 'On the usefulness or earnings and earnings research: lessons and directions from two decades of empirical research', *Journal of Accounting Research* (1989).

Samuels, JM, Brayshaw, RE and Craner, JM *Financial Statement Analysis in Europe*, Chapman & Hall (1995).

Singhvi, SS and Desai, HB 'An empirical analysis of the quality of corporate financial disclosure', *The Accounting Review* (January 1971), pp. 129–38.

Vergoosen, RGA 'The use and perceived importance of annual reports by investment analysts in the Netherlands', *The European Accounting Review*, 2(2) (1993), pp. 219–43.

Index of Laws and Standards

Index